GENESIS 1–11

Baylor Handbook on the Hebrew Bible

General Editor

W. Dennis Tucker Jr.

GENESIS 1–11
A Handbook on the Hebrew Text

Barry Bandstra

BAYLOR UNIVERSITY PRESS

Cover Design by Pamela Poll
Cover photograph by Bruce and Kenneth Zuckerman, West Semitic Research, in collaboration with the ancient Biblical Manuscript Center. Courtesy Russina National Library (Saltykov-Shchedrin).

Library of Congress Cataloging-in-Publication Data

Bandstra, Barry L.
Genesis 1-11 : a handbook on the Hebrew text / Barry Bandstra.
p. cm. -- (Baylor Handbook on the Hebrew Bible series)
Includes the Hebrew text of Genesis I-XI with an English translation and grammatical analysis.
Includes bibliographical references and index.
ISBN 978-1-932792-70-6 (pbk.)
1. Bible. O.T. Genesis I-XI--Language, style. 2. Hebrew language--Grammar. 3. Hebrew language--Discourse analysis. I. Bible. O.T. Genesis I-XI. Hebrew. 2007. II. Bible. O.T. Genesis I-XI. English. Bandstra. 2007. III. Title.

BS1235.55.B36 2007
222>.11077--dc22

2007044473

Printed in the United States of America on acid-free paper with a minimum of 30% pcw recycled content.

To my biblical Hebrew students at Hope College
and Western Theological Seminary

TABLE OF CONTENTS

PREFACE

This handbook is going to look a little strange to students of the biblical text. The vocabulary and concepts it uses to explain Genesis 1–11 will be challenging in so far as they represent a non-traditional linguistic framework, an approach called functional grammar. But years of using this approach with my students at both Hope College and Western Theological Seminary have convinced me that it does make sense. I want to take this opportunity to thank them for their patience as I worked it out on them.

How did I come to this functional approach? It was a rather lengthy journey. I was trained in classical Hebrew grammar at Calvin Theological Seminary, where Lambdin was (and still is) used. I had a fine teacher, later mentor and friend, in Dr. David Engelhard. I went on to graduate training in ancient near eastern languages and literatures, eventually earning a doctorate after concentrating on the northwest semitic languages. Among my teachers I am proud I can reckon Prof Franz Rosenthal, who taught me Syriac and comparative grammar. No more rigorous scholar and teacher could ever be had, a master of semitic linguistics.

When it came time to formulate a dissertation topic, I decided to try to make sense out of the syntax of particle כִּי in biblical Hebrew and Ugaritic. This is a word that has been variously translated *if, then, when, although, because,* and increasingly by *indeed.* I had been reading texts and commentaries for years by then, and it seemed to me that the treatment of certain high frequency words, and this one in particular, was often impressionistic and arbitrary. So I decided to see if the linguistic and textual environment of כִּי might bring some controls to how we understand it.

Ever since, I have been interested in linguistic structures at the clause level and higher. The problem though, it seemed to me, was that the conceptual toolbox of traditional grammar lacked the needed instruments to disassemble the text at that level. The traditional formal approach excels at verb and noun paradigms. But it falls short when it comes to explaining how words come together to form coherent texts. Along with others in the field, I have been exploring what has come to be called discourse analysis of the biblical text.

There have been some useful efforts at combining discourse notions with traditional formal grammar. Notable among them is the topical grammar of Christo van der Merwe, et al. *A Biblical Hebrew Reference Grammar* (1999) and the teaching grammar of Bryan M. Rocine, *Learning Biblical Hebrew: A New Approach Using Discourse Analysis* (2000). I have gone in a slightly different direction. For better or worse, I decided to wed myself to a new theoretical underpinning, and use it to work out a text level approach to the biblical text. So, I used the perspective of functional grammar to introduce certain text-based concepts to my Hebrew students. They started learning about such matters even as they learned the forms of the language. It is this approach that also forms the basis of book currently in your hands. You will learn more about the approach when you read the Introduction. And read it you probably should. Only if you work through the Introduction and refer to the Glossary throughout, will any of this make any sense at all.

I chose to dedicate this book to my Hebrew students. Although they did not know it at the time, they were guinea pigs in a trial of the viability of this approach. Thank God they survived, and some have even prospered. I will be ever grateful to them for their efforts, and for giving me the opportunity to work things out in this new way.

I would also like to thank Hope College for its generous support. Much of the work leading up to this handbook came by way of generous summer support administered under the Jacob E. Nyenhuis Faculty Development Grants program. I would like to thank Western Theological Seminary for inviting me to teach a full year's worth of biblical Hebrew in their online distance learning degree program.

I would also like to thank Dr. Dennis Tucker, associate professor of Christian Scriptures at George W. Truett Theological Seminary and general editor of the series, for inviting me to undertake this volume in the Baylor Handbook on the Hebrew Bible series. I am very grateful for his courage is accepting a volume such as this, given its unconventional approach. Dr. Cary C. Newman, director of the Baylor University Press, has also been entirely supportive and helpful. Diane Smith, associate director and production manager of the press, has demonstrated dedication throughout, and performed miracles with a very challenging manuscript. I also thank W. Randall Garr for his sage advice on an early form of this project, some of which I followed. And finally, thanks go to my Debra, who has been indulgent all these years, as she has listened to me go on and on about biblical language and linguistics with never a discouraging word—כִּי אֵשֶׁת חַיִל אָתְּ.

ABBREVIATIONS

!	one form where we might on the basis of grammatical congruency expect a different one
[[ ]]	embedded clause
/	the clause that follows the symbol has a hypotactic relationship with another clause; also used in linguistic commentary to separate metafunctions
//	the following clause has a paratactic relationship with the preceding clause
///	beginning of a new clause complex
<< >>	included clause
>	used in linguistic commentary to separate a metafunctional label from its formal realization in that clause
>>	used in linguistic commentary in descriptions of embedded clauses; separates the constituent function of the embedded clause within the enclosing clause from the linguistic analysis of the embedded clause itself
1	first person
2	second person
3	third person
abs	absolute
adj	adjective
art	article
BDB	Brown, Driver, Briggs. *A Hebrew and English Lexicon of the Old Testament* (1907)
BH	biblical Hebrew
c	common

circum	circumstance, circumstantial
cohort	cohortative
conj	conjunction, conjunctive
const	construct
d	dual
def	definite
f	feminine
HALOT	*The Hebrew and Aramaic Lexicon of the Old Testament* (1994–)
impv	imperative, imperatival
indef	indefinite
inf	infinitive, infinitival
m	masculine
MNK	*A Biblical Hebrew Reference Grammar* (1999)
MT	Masoretic Text
NJPS	*New Jewish Publication Society Tanakh* (1999)
NRSV	*New Revised Standard Version* (1989)
p	plural
prep	preposition, prepositional
ptc	participle, participial
s	singular
TDOT	*Theological Dictionary of the Old Testament* (1974–)
WO	*An Introduction to Biblical Hebrew Syntax* (1990)

INTRODUCTION

Introductory courses in biblical Hebrew (BH) grammar typically focus on teaching the grammatical forms and vocabulary of the language. While they might differ considerably when it comes to pedagogical approach, whether deductive or inductive, or a blend, such courses presume that the most important things to learn are the noun and verb paradigms and the forms of other words. It is common practice for a grammar textbook to have one chapter devoted to the qal perfect of each root type (strong and weak), and the qal imperfect of each root type, then one on the nifal of each root type, and so on. The teacher's expectation is that a responsible student of BH will come to recognize whether a subject noun is singular or plural, masculine or feminine, and the like, and how verbs appropriately match such subjects. By the end of the course, passing students will know how to parse each verb form for root, stem, part of speech, person, number and gender. As an overall strategy, the focus of grammar is on the forms of words in the clause, such that a student of the language can recognize the "well-*formed*ness" of the clause and parse each and every word in it.

This handbook to the first eleven chapters of Genesis is part of a series of volumes that is intended to be of use to students of BH at the intermediate and advanced levels. Naturally, it assumes a knowledge of the forms of the language, as characterized above, and looks to take the student further along in understanding the structure of the language and the biblical text. Each volume in the series will reflect its author's particular linguistic approach. This contribution to the series uses insights gained from an approach to linguistic understanding called functional grammar. While formal grammar is strong on conjugating verbs and parsing nouns, functional grammar provides a conceptual and descriptive framework for understanding why clauses are worded the way they are, and why clauses are strung together into texts the way they are.

One of the starting points of functional grammar is the claim that speakers and writers shape their messages in order to accomplish personal and social objectives. With this in mind, grammatical analysis of a functional variety examines texts to discern these purposes and explain the wordings of the messages of texts accordingly. It begins with the reasonable premise that a speaker or writer chooses how to shape the message before it is uttered or written in order best to accomplish certain ends. Functional grammar is designed to provide, as best it can, an explanation of the choices that have been made. The approach to functional grammar employed in this handbook is called systemic functional grammar, and is based on the work of M. A. K. Halliday. In addition to Halliday (2004), see Thompson (2004) for a basic introduction to functional analysis, and see Butler (2003) for a comprehensive description and comparison of the major functional approaches that can be found within the discipline of linguistics.

Three Kinds of Function in the Clause

There are numerous factors that shape the wording of clauses, and each is related to how and why we use language. The functional approach used here identifies what it claims are three core uses of spoken and written communication. One way we use language is to give expression to our experience of the world. We use words to depict external events and our internal thoughts and feelings. Additionally, we use language in order to interact with other people, including attempts to influence their behavior, or engage in transactions, or maintain relationships. Lastly, we shape messages in such a way that they fit with other meanings in the context of our writing and speaking.

Functional grammar sorts these factors out into three main areas of meaning, called metafunctions, and each metafunction has an effect on the wording of a clause. Think of them as three overlays of meaning, much like multiple transparencies on an overhead projector that project a single image. Each has its own integrity, yet taken together they provide a richer account of the meaning of a text than any single one alone could.

Mood: The Interpersonal View of the Clause

The first metafunction of the clause is the interpersonal one, and it has to do with how the clause is structured in order to negotiate a transaction or exchange between a speaker and a hearer. An interpersonal analysis examines the clause for elements that establish the parameters of the negotiation. Above all, this has to do with the Subject of the clause and the Finite verb form of the clause. The interpersonal structure of a clause belongs to the **Mood** system, though this should not be thought of as having to do with emotions. Rather, the term Mood has to do with modes of interaction, for which Subject and Finite are key concepts. Note that in functional grammar, it is conventional practice to capitalize functions such as Subject and Finite.

In traditional grammar, the subject of a clause is understood to be the item about which something is predicated. An intuitive notion of subject often gets attached, such that the subject of the clause is also considered the subject *matter* of the clause, what the clause is "about." Functional grammar takes the notion of Subject in a somewhat different direction. The Subject in functional grammar is the constituent in a clause about which the speaker makes a claim to the hearer, and the item upon which the validity of the clause hangs. Viewing the clause as an interaction between the speaker and the hearer, the Subject is the element in the clause that is subject to negotiation, or the core of the issue at play in the clause. This redefinition of the notion of Subject is not entirely different from the traditional intuitive notion—in a sense it still identifies what the clause is "about"—but it adds precision given the fundamental claim that messages are used to accomplish interpersonal goals.

We can use the following clause to illustrate the functional notion of Subject.

Genesis 1:7(a) וַיַּעַשׂ אֱלֹהִים אֶת־הָרָקִיעַ. Subject—the interpersonal view.

אֶת־הָרָקִיעַ	אֱלֹהִים	וַיַּעַשׂ	**Constituents**
the barrier	*deity*	*and he made*	**Translation**
Residue	Subject	Finite	**Mood**

In this clause, אֱלֹהִים *deity* is labeled the Subject in the interpersonal Mood view. *Deity* is the one about whom a claim is made; it is *deity* who made אֶת־הָרָקִיעַ *the barrier* and not someone else.

There are two linguistic tests that probe for Subject in a clause. The first test is posing a challenge question. If *deity made the barrier* is the statement, then the challenge question would be *No, he didn't* rather than *No, it didn't*. This demonstrates that in this clause *deity* and not *the barrier* is the concern of the predication. The other approach is to add a tag question to the clause, the Subject of which would be the same as the Subject of the main clause. The tag question of this clause would be *didn't he?* as in, *Deity made the barrier, didn't he?* Both tests reveal the clause is about something that deity did.

When it comes to the Subject, BH is designed differently than English. English requires an explicit Subject word in every independent clause, either a noun or pronoun. In BH the Subject of a clause may be an independent word which is a Participant in the Transitivity structure of the clause, as in this clause, or it may not exist independently but simply be evident in the person, gender, and number form of the verb. As we will see, the presence or absence of an explicit Subject is a function of the Textuality dimension of the text.

The other central component of the interpersonal Mood system is the Finite. The Finite is the main verb of a clause in BH that is congruent with the Subject in person, number, and gender. In Genesis 1:7(a) the Subject is ms and the Finite is 3ms, though there is a slight incongruence with אֱלֹהִים in so far as it is formally, though not operationally, plural. The Finite is the clause constituent that, along with the Subject, makes it possible to challenge the validity of the message of the clause. Using the Finite, the speaker signals whether the proposition was valid in the past or at another time (the present or future). This feature of a verb is typically called its tense. Thus, the Finite expresses its "finitude" in two dimensions: (a) by specifying person, gender, and number, and (b) by specifying the time of the process relative to the temporal reference point of the text. The latter is realized by the tense form of the Finite using the choices wayyiqtol, qatal, yiqtol, weqatal.

Together the Subject and the Finite constitute the Mood structure of a clause. The remainder of the clause, אֶת־הָרָקִיעַ *the barrier*, does not have a role in the Mood structure. Functional grammar terms everything outside the Mood of the clause the Residue, though this should not be understood in a derogatory sense. This way of describing a clause as having a Mood core and a Residue might seem strange, since it is not conceptualized this way in traditional grammars of Hebrew. But after discussing the second metafunction of the clause, this way of describing the clause will appear more useful.

The reason the Subject and the Finite components of a clause are isolated and identified is because this facilitates an examination of the clause as interpersonal interaction. The basic purposes of interpersonal communication in a functional sense are giving and getting. When we think about it, the item given or received may be a material thing, such as groceries, or an immaterial thing, such as information. In the case of material goods and services, language plays a role in the success of the transaction, though the main transaction involves commodities and physical activities. When mapped using a table, these basic purposes (in bold) and their respective speech modes look like this.

Table 1. Basic Speech Functions

commodity exchanged →	**Goods & Services**	**Information**
role in exchange ↓		
Giving	offer	statement
Demanding	command	question

The interactive modes of offering, commanding, making a statement, and asking a question, are all reflected in basic structures and forms of the clause. When we come to analyze the components of individual clauses that carry out the transaction, primarily we will be exposing the **Mood** structure of the clause. The Mood structure will indicate the role that the speaker is playing in relation to the hearer. Here is an illustration of each basic speech function.

Giving goods or services—offer: Gen 9:3(a) כָּל־רֶמֶשׂ אֲשֶׁר הוּא־חַי לָכֶם יִהְיֶה לְאָכְלָה. *All creeperkind which is alive will be for food for you.*

Demanding goods or services—directive: Gen 1:28(c-e) פְּרוּ וּרְבוּ וּמִלְאוּ אֶת־הָאָרֶץ. *Bear fruit. And multiply. And fill the earth.*

Giving information—statement: Gen 2:23(b) זֹאת הַפַּעַם עֶצֶם מֵעֲצָמַי וּבָשָׂר מִבְּשָׂרִי. *This one, this time, is bone from my bones and flesh from my flesh.*

Demanding information—question: Gen 3:11(b) מִי הִגִּיד לְךָ כִּי עֵירֹם אָתָּה. *Who told you that you are naked?*

These basic speech functions are associated with typical grammatical realizations. Statements are typically realized as declarative clauses, commands as imperative clauses, and questions as interrogative clauses. Offers can be realized by various clause structures. The following table summarizes how each of the speech function choices are typically realized in clauses.

Table 2. Basic Speech Functions and Their Mood Realizations

commodity exchanged →	**Goods & Services**	**Information**
role in exchange ↓		
Giving	offer > various	statement > declarative
Demanding	command > directive	question > interrogative

Once we have made the connection between functions and their forms, we can make further observations regarding certain structural regularities. For example, a directive clause typically places the Finite first in its clause and has no explicit Subject. And an interrogative clause places the question word first in its clause.

Clauses can be distinguished at a basic level as independent or dependent. Dependent clauses include embedded clauses of various types, such as relative clauses, and hypotactic clauses such as כִּי clauses. Among independent clauses, the most basic choice is between the indicative clauses, which give something to someone, and directive clauses, which demand something from someone. Directive clauses can be cohortative (first person: Let me... or Let us...), imperative (second person: Do...), or jussive (third person: Let him...). Information clauses can be declarative (those that give a declaration) or interrogative (those that ask for a declaration). And interrogative clauses can be either polar (expecting a yes or no answer) or wh- (which is to say, asking for content in response to the question WHo, WHat, WHere, WHen, or WHy; in BH these would be מ- questions: מִי, מָה, etc.).

The following diagram indicates the basic mood system of independent clauses. All of these choices represent different modes of interaction between a speaker and the hearer, and they are used in the description of the Mood structure of the clauses of Genesis 1–11.

Diagram 1. The Mood System

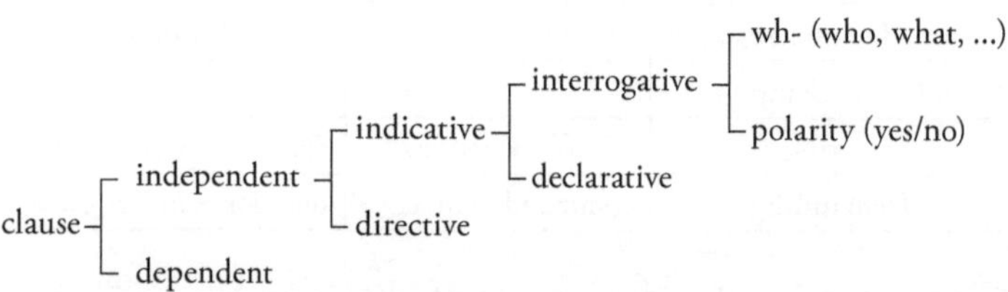

In addition to the Mood structure of Subject plus Finite, the interpersonal view of the clause accounts for other linguistic features that bear upon interpersonal interaction, namely polarity and modality. Polarity is the feature of clauses that makes them positive or negative. Every clause, no matter what the Mood structure, makes some sort of claim about the Subject, and that claim, expressed by the Finite, has either positive or negative validity. The unmarked polarity is positive, which means it is assumed to be positive, and the marked polarity is negative, expressed typically with לֹא. The polarity word is typically in immediate proximity to the Finite because its specific role is to condition the Finite.

Modality has to do with the extent to which a proposition is valid. When it comes to declarative clauses, types of modality include its probability (how likely it is to be true) and its usuality (how often it is true). When it comes to directive clauses, types of modality include the degree of obligation on the other person to carry out the demand. This is reflected, for example, in the difference between לֹא and אַל in negative imperatives. Modality is often expressed by modal adjuncts. These are words that are neither nominals capable of being a Subject nor Finite verb forms. Traditionally they have been called adverbs or particles. In Genesis 1–11 modal adjuncts include words such as מְאֹד and the infinitive absolute.

Transitivity: The Experiential View of the Clause

The second metafunction of clauses is the **experiential**, and it is the system for representing happenings in the physical world or in the mind of the speaker. The experiential analysis of a clause views the clause as a process having participants that perform roles in the process, and optionally, circumstances that establish the setting of the process. The configuration of the Process, Participants, and Circumstance of a clause is called its **Transitivity** structure. In traditional grammar, transitivity typically has to do with whether or not a verbal predicate can take a direct object. Transitivity in functional grammar is more comprehensive.

We will examine Genesis 1:7(a) again, this time adding an analysis of its experiential meaning.

Genesis 1:7 (a) וַיַּעַשׂ אֱלֹהִים אֶת־הָרָקִיעַ. Actor—the experiential view.

אֶת־הָרָקִיעַ	אֱלֹהִים	וַיַּעַשׂ	**Constituents**
the barrier	*deity*	*and he made*	**Translation**
Residue	Subject	Finite	**Mood**
Goal	Actor	Process	**Transitivity**

By adding the functional label Actor to אֱלֹהִים, this indicates that *deity* is the doer of the activity expressed in the Process, in this case the material process of making something. The reason for creating two labels for a single clause constituent will soon become clear. Lastly, by labeling אֶת־הָרָקִיעַ the Goal (traditionally called the direct object), this indicates that *the barrier* is the one affected by the doing of the Process. In this case, it is the thing brought into being by the process of making.

In the majority of cases, the Subject function and the Actor function apply to the same constituent of a clause, as in Genesis 1:7(a); but this is not always the case. Sometimes the interpersonal Subject of a clause is not the same as the Actor of the process. The following clause illustrates that Subject and Actor are separable, and each performs a distinct function.

Genesis 4:18(a) וַיִּוָּלֵד לַחֲנוֹךְ אֶת־עִירָד. Subject ≠ Actor, Subject = Goal.

אֶת־עִירָד	לַחֲנוֹךְ	וַיִּוָּלֵד	**Constituents**
'Irad	*to Chanokh*	*and was born*	**Translation**
Subject		Finite	**Mood**
Goal	Beneficiary	Process	**Transitivity**

In this clause, as typically with passive verbs, the Actor of the Process is not expressed. The Goal of the Process is coded with the goal marker אֶת־. *'Irad* is the Goal or direct object of the process of giving birth. The Beneficiary is the Participant that benefits (though not necessarily in a positive sense) from the doing of the Process, as the one given to or done for, in this case חֲנוֹךְ. Notice how the Subject of the clause (the interpersonal Mood view) is coded by making it grammatically congruent with the verb, matching it in person, number, and gender. Since *'Irad* is the Subject of the clause, the clause presumably makes a claim about *'Irad*. This can be confirmed by adding the appropriate tag question, *wasn't he?*, where the he clearly turns out to be *'Irad* and not *Chanokh*.

This is an especially useful clause because it demonstrates clearly that the Subject is grammatically structured with the Finite in the Mood system, and the Goal, introduced with the goal-marker, works with the Process within the Transitivity system. This illustrates the usefulness of viewing the clause from two perspectives simultaneously. Later, we will see that this two-dimensional way of viewing a finite verb form will help in sorting out how verb tense and verb stem contribute to the meaning of a clause. We will see that the tense meaning of the verb (qatal, yiqtol, wayyiqtol, and weqatal) functions within the Mood system, while the stem meaning of the verb (qal, nifal, piel, pual, hitpael, and the others) functions within the Transitivity system.

The experiential metafunction of language deals with representing the world using words. This view of language expression is the one most concerned with what we ordinarily think of as content, that is, a depiction of happenings in a material or mental world. The Process is considered to be the core of the clause in the experiential view, such that a clause cannot exist, with the exception of certain minor clauses, without a process of some kind and at least one participant, which does not even have to be explicit.

The experiential view describes the relationship of the participants and the process and lays this out by a sequence of labels. In the traditional approach to BH grammar, the labels that apply to participants and processes are rather general, such that they often fail to capture functional relationships adequately enough. Basically, all one has to work with in the traditional approach is subject, direct object, indirect object, and verb. The labels of the functional approach expose more clearly the relationships of the various components of a clause.

A study of the processes that come to expression in BH and the configuration of participant roles that typically accompany these processes results in the following general process categories: material, mental, relational, behavioral, verbal, and existential. What follows is a brief outline of these main process types. We will employ them all in our analysis of the clauses of Genesis 1–11.

Material Processes

A material process typically involves a physical action such as making, walking, killing, or dying. The doer of the activity is the Actor. Material processes can be subdivided into two types: doing and happening. That which only affects the Actor, which is to say, the Actor is the Goal, is called happening. In our linguistic analysis, this type is labeled *material: event.* That which affects a different participant, the one to whom the Process is being done, is called doing. In the analysis, this type is labeled *material: action*. Additionally, a clause that expresses a material process can have a participant that benefits from the action, called the Beneficiary (traditionally called the indirect object), and a Circumstance, which identifies either the temporal or physical location of the action.

Genesis 3:21(a) וַיַּעַשׂ יְהוָה אֱלֹהִים לְאָדָם וּלְאִשְׁתּוֹ כָּתְנוֹת עוֹר. Material process of doing (action): *And YHVH deity made garments of skin for 'Adam and his woman.*

כָּתְנוֹת עוֹר	לְאָדָם וּלְאִשְׁתּוֹ	יְהוָה אֱלֹהִים	וַיַּעַשׂ
garments of skin	*for 'Adam and his woman*	*YHVH deity*	*and he made*
Goal	Beneficiary	Actor	Process

Note that the rendering of such clauses in the analysis tables will translate the person, number and gender of Finite verbs with a pronoun, and a gendered one, even when conventional English would use *it*.

Genesis 11:32(b) וַיָּמָת תֶּרַח בְּחָרָן. Material process of happening (event): *And Terach died in Charan.*

בְּחָרָן	תֶּרַח	וַיָּמָת
in Charan	*Terach*	*and he died*
Circumstance	Actor	Process

In this type of material process, the Actor is also the Goal, the one "happened to."

Mental Processes

A mental process is some sort of goings-on in the world of the mind, such as seeing, hating, or craving. The variety of mental processes can be clustered around processes of perception, emotion, and cognition. The core constituents of clauses that express mental processes are the Senser and the thing sensed, called the Phenomenon. For example,

Genesis 4:23(b) עָדָה וְצִלָּה שְׁמַעַן קוֹלִי. Mental process of perception: *'Adah and Tsilla, hear my voice!*

קוֹלִי	שְׁמַעַן	עָדָה וְצִלָּה
my voice	*hear!*	*'Ada and Tsilla*
Phenomenon	Process	Senser

Relational Processes

As its name might imply, a relational process sets up a relationship between two items. Often no explicit verb is present, as when a clause is constituted by the simple juxtaposition of two components. Other times the verb הָיָה may be used. A third way to realize a relational process is to use a stative verb, such as חיה *be alive*, רבה *be many*, and גדל *be strong*.

There are two main types of relational processes, one which attributes a quality to a participant and another which establishes the identity of something. In a clause with an identifying relational process, there are two components, the Identified and an Identifier. The function of a relational clause of identification is to identify one item in terms of another item. Both terms are typically definite nouns or noun phrases of some kind.

Genesis 2:11(a) שֵׁם הָאֶחָד פִּישׁוֹן. Relational process of identification: *The name of the first is Pishon.*

פִּישׁוֹן	שֵׁם הָאֶחָד
Pishon	*the name of the one*
Identifier	Identified

In this case, the relational process is achieved through the simple juxtaposition of the two components; there is no specific word in the text that expresses the relationship. This is a very common way to structure a relational clause. The thing to be Identified is something that is already known or inferable from prior text. In this case, rivers have already been mentioned, and rivers have names. This clause attaches a proper name to the first head of the primeval river. Terms of this kind of relationship, given the appropriate context, are reversible both in serial order and function.

In a clause with an attributive relational process, there are also two components, the Carrier and the Attribute. This type of relational process applies a description or attribute to an item. The terms of this type of relationship are not functionally reversible. The Carrier is typically a definite nominal and the Attribute is indefinite.

Genesis 1:2(a) וְהָאָרֶץ הָיְתָה תֹהוּ וָבֹהוּ. Relational process of attribution: *And the earth was an emptiness and a void.*

תֹהוּ וָבֹהוּ	הָיְתָה	וְהָאָרֶץ
an emptiness and a void	*she was*	*and the earth*
Attribute	Process	Carrier

Another way to realize an attributive relational process is to employ a stative verb such as כָּבֵד or קָטֹן, though our Genesis 1–11 text sample does not contain any examples.

Verbal Processes

A verbal process is a process of saying, and the thing said can be either a quote or a report of something that was spoken. A clause that expresses a verbal process typically has a Sayer and a Receiver, who are typically persons. The Verbiage is the language content of the verbal event, the spoken message itself, which is spoken by the Sayer to the Receiver.

Genesis 3:2(a) וַתֹּאמֶר הָאִשָּׁה אֶל־הַנָּחָשׁ. Verbal process (followed by a quote): *And the woman said to the snake.*

אֶל־הַנָּחָשׁ	הָאִשָּׁה	וַתֹּאמֶר
to the snake	*the woman*	*and she said*
Receiver	Sayer	Process

Sometimes the verbal process is not directed to a Receiver but instead concerns a Target, in which case there is no quote.

Genesis 1:10(a) וַיִּקְרָא אֱלֹהִים לַיַּבָּשָׁה אֶרֶץ. Verbal process (no quote): *And deity called the dry land earth.*

אֶרֶץ	לַיַּבָּשָׁה	אֱלֹהִים	וַיִּקְרָא
earth	*the dry land*	*deity*	*and he called*
Verbiage	Target	Sayer	Process

The category of verbal process could be thought to reside midway between mental and relational processes. A verbal process is mental in the sense that is the product of mental operations, and it is relational in the sense that it can set up a relation between two elements, as the preceding example illustrates: the dry land is earth.

Behavioral Processes

A behavioral process has to do with human physiological manifestations of mental states. As such it could be considered a blend, like verbal processes, of two more widely used processes; in this case, between material and mental processes. But behavioral processes have distinctive qualities that justify a separate category. The difference between verbal and behavioral processes can be illustrated with the contrastive pair *say* and *speak*. When *say* is used, we expect there to be spoken words present, but when *speak* is found, the act of speaking may be the meaning, as in Genesis 34:3(c) וַיְדַבֵּר עַל־לֵב הַנַּעֲרָ, *and he spoke to the heart of the girl*. Other behavioral verbs are *cry, weep*, and *laugh*. The difference between mental and behavioral processes can be further illustrated with the contrastive pairs *see* and *look, hear* and *listen, feel* and *touch*.

Behavioral processes typically have only one participant, a human Behaver. Some behavioral clauses have what may look like an additional participant, called the Behavior, but it is not truly in the nature of the Goal of a material process, or what traditional grammar calls a direct object, even though it may look that way syntactically. The Behavior is really a further elaboration of the behavioral process itself. In the following example, Esau is the Behaver (mentioned in the prior clause and absent here by ellipsis).

Gen. 27:34(b) וַיִּצְעַק צְעָקָה גְּדֹלָה וּמָרָה. Behavioral process: *And he cried bitterly.*

צְעָקָה גְּדֹלָה וּמָרָה	וַיִּצְעַק
a great and bitter cry	*and he cried*
Behavior	Process

Existential Processes

Existential processes express the existence or non-existence of something. The only "participant" to the process is the Existent. The effect of using an existential process is to deny the Existent the opportunity to be involved in any action; rather, it simply is or is not. A clause with an existential process may have a Circumstance component. Existential processes are closely related to relational processes on the one hand, and they also may have affinities with material processes of happening (in distinction from material processes of doing). An example of a clause with existential processes is

Genesis 1:3(b-c) יְהִי אוֹר וַיְהִי־אוֹר. Existential processes: *Let light be. And light was.*

אוֹר	וַיְהִי־	אוֹר	יְהִי
light	*and he was*	*light*	*let him be*
Existent	Process	Existent	Process

The following table summarizes the basic Process types in the Transitivity system, their core meanings, including sub-types, and Participants to the Process.

Table 3. Process Types, Meanings, and Transitivity Structures

Process type	Core meaning	Sub-types	Participants (opt.)
Material	doing	action	Actor (Goal) (Beneficiary) (Scope)
	happening	event	Actor
Mental	thinking	perception cognition emotion desideration	Senser, Phenomenon
Relational	having	attribution	Carrier, Attribute
	being	identification	Identified, Identifier
Verbal	saying		Sayer (Receiver) (Verbiage) (Target)
Behavioral	behaving		Behaver (Behavior)
Existential	existing		Existent

The participants in parentheses are optional.

Circumstances

In addition to Processes and Participants, Circumstances are a third major component of the transitivity stystem. Circumstances are a representation of the background against which the Participants are involved in the Process. The category of Circumstances includes time, place, manner, and others. These are realized almost always as prepositional phrases. Here is a table of Circumstances that can be identified in BH.

Table 4. Circumstance Types

Circumstance	Sub-categories	Answers this question
Location	time, place	When? Where?
Extent	duration, place	How long or often? How far?
Manner	means, quality, comparison	With what? In what way? Like what?
Cause	reason, purpose	Why? For what purpose?
Contingency	condition, concession	Under what conditions? Despite what?
Accompani-ment	comitative, additive	Who or what with? Who or what else?
Role	guise, product	What as? What into?
Matter		What about?
Angle		Says who? What point of view?

Transitivity Component of the Verb System

In addition to the fund of transitivity structures outlined above, two formal components of the BH verbal system play a direct role in the system of Transitivity, namely the root system and the stem system. The verbal roots provide the basic representational meaning possibilities of clause processes. The stems (qal, nifal, piel, etc.) combine that representational meaning with potential Process + Participant structures. The stems predetermine which Participants may appear with a particular root and in which Participant roles. A verb root in the qal may allow for Actor + Process, in the nifal for Goal (= Subject) + Process, and in the hifil for Actor + Goal + Process. For example, the root ילד has to do with birth; notice how the different stems structure the participant roles differently.

- The qal stem of the root ילד is used of a woman bearing a child. Transitivity > Process + Actor + Goal, where the Goal is the one born. For example, Genesis 4:1(c) וַתֵּלֶד אֶת־קַיִן. *And she bore Qayin.*

• The nifal stem of the root ילד is used of a child being born. Transitivity > Process + Goal (= Subject). The agent is not necessarily specified. If it is, it is as the Beneficiary of the Process, not as the Actor. For example, Genesis 10:1(b) וַיִּוָּלְדוּ לָהֶם בָּנִים אַחַר הַמַּבּוּל. *And sons were born to them after the flood.*

• The piel stem of the root ילד is used of someone helping someone else to bear a child. Transitivity > Process + Actor + Goal, where the Goal is the one giving birth. For example, Exodus 1:16(b) בְּיַלֶּדְכֶן אֶת־הָעִבְרִיּוֹת. *When you assist birthing the female Hebrews . . .*

• The hifil the root ילד is used of causing someone to bear something. Transitivity > Process + Actor (≠ Agent) + Goal, where the Actor causes someone else (the birthing Agent, meaning the woman) to bear. For example, Jeremiah 29:6(a-b) קְחוּ נָשִׁים וְהוֹלִידוּ בָּנִים וּבָנוֹת. *Take wives and father sons and daughters.*

Textuality: The Textual View of the Clause

The third metafunction of the clause is the **textual**, and it has to do with how the clause is structurally related to the larger message. In this view the labels Theme and Rheme are used to identify the internal structure of a clause. The Theme is what the speaker chooses as the starting point of the clause, and the Rheme is everything else. Essentially, the Rheme is what the writer wants to communicate about the Theme. The Theme can consist of multiple elements and can include a conjunction or vocative, but must always include one of the components of the experiential process (either the Process, a Partcipant, or a Circumstance). Later we will see how the internal thematic structure of a clause is a function of the larger message structure of the text. Using our example text, we add the Textuality layer.

Gen. 1:7 (a) וַיַּעַשׂ אֱלֹהִים אֶת־הָרָקִיעַ. Theme—the textual view.

אֶת־הָרָקִיעַ	אֱלֹהִים	וַיַּעַשׂ	**Constituents**
the barrier	*deity*	*and he made*	**Translation**
Rheme		Theme	**Textuality**
Residue	Subject	Finite	**Mood**
Goal	Actor	Process	**Transitivity**

By labeling וַיַּעַשׂ *and he made* as the Theme, the functional approach identifies it as the starting point of the clause and the point of departure for its message. The first constituent of a clause always bears the major weight of responsibility when it comes to connecting a clause to prior text. Its major function is to establish cohesion, which in turn enables the hearer/reader to follow the logic of the discourse. In this case, a wayyiqtol verb is the Theme, which means both that this clause is past tense and that it continues the event sequence being laid out in this part of the text.

The textual view of the clause is the system that accounts for how any one clause fits within the larger message of the text. Focusing on the thematic structures of the clauses reveals, among other things, how the text develops semantically and rhetorically. The reasons for particular Theme choices reveal themselves only upon examination of the set of clauses in which a clause is found.

The scope of the textual view of the clause is the clause complex. A clause complex is the result of combining two or more clauses into a larger unit. Textuality covers the various ways these clauses come to be related. In addition to the Theme–Rheme structure of a clause, there are three categories of relatedness that apply to any particular clause within a text, and each of them gets configured independently of the others. The following table indicates the four main textuality features of a clause that exist as structures within a clause complex. The table will be followed by a brief explanation of each sub-system. All four of these will be specified for each clause in our analysis of the text of Genesis 1–11.

Table 5. Four Components of the Textuality System

Internal clause structure	Theme	First constituent of the clause
	Rheme	Remainder of the clause
Clause combining	Apposition	No explicit conjunctive link with preceding clause
	Conjunction	Linked by conjunction or conjunctive adjunct
Logical-semantic relations	Expansion	Elaborates, extends, or enhances primary clause
	Projection	Locution or idea projected through primary clause
Logical-dependency relations	Paratactic	Linked to a clause of equal status
	Hypotactic	Dependent clause linked to a dominant clause
	Embedded	Clause transformed into a clause constituent

Internal Clause Structure

The Theme is the point of departure of the message, so it is by definition the first constituent of the clause. The Rheme is everything else in the clause. The Theme is instrumental in locating and orienting its clause within the larger context.

Theme choice depends significantly on Mood choice. In narration, which is dominated by declarative clauses which make statements, wayyiqtol is the normal theme choice. In quotes, the constituent selected to be the Theme is more varied and is not typically designed to narrate a sequential story, so wayyiqtols do not dominate. The typical Theme of commands is a directive verb (cohortative, imperative, jussive), and when the directive is not the Theme, then that Theme is marked. The typical Theme of interrogative clauses is the question word (wh- or yes/no), which also fills a constituent slot within the transitivity structure of the clause.

The Theme is calculated to be everything up to and including the first constituent in the Transitivity structure of the clause. The Theme must always include one and only one constituent of the transitivity structure of the clause: the Process, a Participant or a Circumstance. So, every clause must have an experiential Theme. In addition, the clause may include a clause-level conjunction, mostly commonly וְ and and כִּי *if, when, although, that, because*, or a conjunctive adjunct such as אַחֲרֵי־כֵן *afterwards* or וְעַתָּה *and now* at the beginning of the clause. When present, such a word is considered a textual theme. Lastly, an interpersonal adjunct such as הִנֵּה may be present as an interpersonal Theme in a position preceding the experiential Theme.

The Theme of every clause, including embedded clauses, is identified in the analysis tables. The Rheme is everything else in the clause. Ordinarily, that segment of the clause will not be labeled, since it is so easy to figure out, and leaving it out renders the tables easier to scan.

Clause Combining

A clause can be formally related to the preceding clause by conjunction-less juxtaposition. This is termed apposition. Or, a clause can be related to another clause by the use of an explicit conjunctive element such as וְ or כִּי. Within a clause, an embedded clause can be related to the dominant clause either by apposition or by the use of a preposition or by the relative marker אֲשֶׁר *who, which*. Finally, one clause can be related to a preceding clause complex by the use of a conjunctive adjunct such as עַל־כֵּן, כֵּן, or אַחֲרֵי־כֵן. Thus, clauses can be formally combined at three different levels, and with three different word classes.

Table 6. Clause Combining

Combining	Conjoiners*	Class
clause to clause complex	כֵּן,עַל־כֵּן,אַחֲרֵי־כֵן	conjunctive adjunct
clause to clause	וְ,כִּי	conjunction
embedded clause to containing clause	בְּ,לְ,כְּ,אֲשֶׁר	preposition, relative pronoun

**This collection of conjoiners is illustrative, not exhaustive.*

The set of BH verb tense forms is integrally related to the clause combining system in so far as the basic choices in past narration are between wayyiqtol and qatal. The former is the default choice for making the Process the Theme. The latter signals a clause that intentionally breaks the temporally sequential organization in order to insert non-sequential expansion. The relationship of the forms of verbs to the textual and other metafunctions will be addressed systematically below.

A clause complex is a collection of clauses that have an internal structure of relatedness. At the same time, this collection of related clauses exhibits some form of discontinuity with adjacent clause complexes. The opening clause of a new clause complex often has an explicit Subject and a full transitivity structure, including Actor, Goal, and Beneficiary if it has a material Process. It will typically not have pronouns referring to Participants in a prior clause complex. A conjunctive adjunct almost always signals the start of a new clause complex that is logically and semantically related to the prior text. Still, discerning clause complexes is as much art as science, and is subject to interpretation.

Logical-semantic Relations

The clauses that constitute a text cannot be random and unrelated. If they are random, the clauses might make sense individually, but they would not constitute a meaningful text. The dimension of logical meaningfulness in texts is the domain of logical-semantic relations. Considered from the perspective of "making sense," what is termed logical coherence, clauses within clause complexes can be related to each other in ways that can be distinguished. Functional grammar uses the basic notions of **expansion** and **projection** in order to identify a fundamental difference in the way two clauses relate to each other. Expansion is the functional label that applies to a clause that adds meaning to a prior clause in order to build the meaningfulness of the text incrementally.

Here is an example of expansion. The symbol // divides clauses.

Genesis 1:2(a-b). Textuality > expansion.

וְהָאָרֶץ הָיְתָה תֹהוּ וָבֹהוּ // וְחֹשֶׁךְ עַל־פְּנֵי תְהוֹם. *And the earth was an emptiness and a void. // And darkness was on the face of deep-waters.*

Here the second clause adds a new component to the description of the state of the world before the creation of light. *Darkness* and *deep-waters* had not been mentioned before. This sub-type of expansion is called extension. Extension is one of three basic variations on expansion that can be discerned using functional grammar; they are elaboration, extension, and enhancement. Each of these three will be illustrated below. But note that our analysis of the clauses of Genesis 1–11 will not add this level of definition. Use these examples to get a better understanding of the general notion of expansion.

In **elaboration**, one clause elaborates another one by adding specification or further description, but it does not add anything essentially new. Here is an example of elaboration.

Genesis 1:2(b-c). Textuality > expansion: elaboration.

וְחֹשֶׁךְ עַל־פְּנֵי תְהוֹם // וְרוּחַ אֱלֹהִים מְרַחֶפֶת עַל־פְּנֵי הַמָּיִם. *And darkness was on the face of deep-waters. // And a wind of deity hovers on the face of the waters.*

Both clauses talk about the waters, and the second clause adds detail to the first.

In **extension**, one clause adds something new to another clause, as we illustrated above. It can be an addition, or a replacement, or an alternative. Here is another example of extension.

Genesis 2:7. Textuality > expansion: extension.

וַיִּיצֶר יְהוָה אֱלֹהִים אֶת־הָאָדָם עָפָר מִן־הָאֲדָמָה // וַיִּפַּח בְּאַפָּיו נִשְׁמַת חַיִּים. *And YHVH deity formed the human using dust from the ground. // And he breathed in his nostrils a living breath.*

Here, the second clause extends the meaning of the text beyond the prior clause by adding something new, breathing into the newly created form.

In **enhancement**, one clause enhances another clause by enriching the context of the first clause, with reference to time, place, manner, cause, or condition. An enhancement is analogous to the Circumstance component found with many experiential processes.

Genesis 2:1(a)-2:2(a). Textuality > expansion: enhancement.

וַיְכֻלּוּ הַשָּׁמַיִם וְהָאָרֶץ וְכָל־צְבָאָם // וַיְכַל אֱלֹהִים בַּיּוֹם הַשְּׁבִיעִי מְלַאכְתּוֹ אֲשֶׁר עָשָׂה. *And the heavens and the earth and all their host were finished. // And deity finished in the seventh day his work which he did.*

The second clause indicates the temporal situation of the completion of creation. The following table summarizes the main sub-types of expansion.

Table 7. Subcategories of Expansion

Subcategory	Description
elaboration	description, specification
extension	adds something new
enhancement	circumstantial qualification

While expansion is the typical way the narration of happenings develops, it is not the only way two clauses can be related. Expansion can be contrasted with projection. Projection is the way verbal and mental phenomena are inserted into texts. Projection applies to such extra-textual elements as quoted direct speech, reports of speech events, and accounts of thoughts and ideas. These types of elements originally exist outside the text in the sense that they were originally non-written phenomena. They find their way into the text only by a subsequent textual step. Think of such elements as being inserted into the text from an outside "world," hence projected into the text.

The notion of projection might seem unusual at first. Yet the distinction between expansion and projection is an important one to recognize, among other reasons, because the linguistic structure of a projected clause may reflect its original context of occurrence rather than the written text in which it has been placed. Also, a projected clause functions not as a direct textual representation of experience but as someone else's representation of experience. Those different types of linguistic representation may come with different implicit claims to authority and truthfulness. Here is an example of projection.

Genesis 2:16. Textuality > projection.

וַיְצַו יְהוָה אֱלֹהִים עַל־הָאָדָם לֵאמֹר // מִכֹּל עֵץ־הַגָּן אָכֹל תֹּאכֵל.

And YHVH deity set a command on the human by saying // "From all of the trees of the garden you most certainly will eat."

The first clause projects the second clause. The word לֵאמֹר *by saying* marks the following clause as a projection, signaling that its original setting was external to the text, and specifying how it was projected. Projection occurs primarily with verbal and mental processes, and the projected clause can be a quote, a report of a speech event, or an idea.

All of the examples of expansion and projection used in this section happen to exhibit a relationship of parataxis between the two clauses, which is to say, the two clauses are grammatically and logically independent of each other. Extension and projection can also be realized within hypotactic and embedded interclausal relationships. These three types of relationship will be explained in the following section.

Logical-dependency Relations

A clause complex consists of two or more clauses that form a larger sense unit of some kind. Triple forward slashes (///) are used in the analysis of texts to delimit clause complexes. Often the interdependence of clauses that constitute the complex is signaled by a conjunction, but not necessarily so. Apposition at this level also happens in BH. When clauses are conjoined, they can be analyzed and classified by the hierarchy of their relationship. Two clauses can be related to each other in such as way that they are of equal status, or one clause can be dependent on another clause such that the other clause dominates it. This dimension of inter-clausal relations is called logical dependency.

Attention to logical dependence identifies three basic types of clause-to-clause relationship: parataxis, hypotaxis, and embedding. Two clauses exhibit **parataxis** when they have equal status, meaning one is not dependent on the other. Two clauses exhibit **hypotaxis**, traditionally called subordination, when one clause is dependent on another clause. The process of **embedding** transforms a clause such that it can be contained within another clause. The result is that the embedded clause functions as a constituent within the containing clause. Embedding one clause within another does not create a clause complex, because the end result is still just one clause.

An embedded clause is a clause that has been down-ranked from its status as an independent clause, and has been converted so it can be a constituent within another clause. This is to say, it has been changed from being a clause to being a clause constituent. An embedded clause always has a Transitivity structure, which means it consists of a Process with Participants and, optionally, Circumstances. But its transitivity has been restructured in such a way that it can itself be a Participant or Circumstance of the clause that contains it.

The operation of embedding operates within the Textuality structure of the clause, rather than in the Mood or Transitivity structures, for this reason. Embedding is the outcome of choices that writers make regarding the presentation of the message of the text. Some elements of a message are central to the purpose of the communication while other elements are peripheral. Presenting some elements as independent clauses, some as dependent, and some as embedded, give those elements different status in the overall communication. The simple fact is, not everything in a clause or clause complex can carry the same weight or make the same claim on the hearer's attention. And a speaker is always bumping and nudging the listener to attend to this or that in the message.

The following examples illustrate the way a second clause can be related to a prior clause in terms of logical dependency, and now we see how the categories of clause combining, logical-semantics, and logical-dependency are used to characterize the Textuality structure of the clause. The following notation will be used to mark clause divisions and signal the relationship between the clauses. A paratactic relationship will be identified by //, a hypotactic relationship by /, and embedding by double square brackets [[ ]] surrounding the entire embedded clause. Use the following table for reference.

Table 8. Logical-dependency Clause Boundary Markers

Notation	Logical-dependency	Dependency relationship
///	clause complex	begins new clause complex
//	parataxis	clauses have the same status
/	hypotaxis	one clause subordinate to another
[[ ]]	embedding	one clause within another clause

The following examples use these symbols and illustrate the various types of taxis.

Genesis 2:15. Textuality > conjunctive paratactic expansion.

./// וַיִּקַּח יְהוָה אֱלֹהִים אֶת־הָאָדָם // וַיַּנִּחֵהוּ בְגַן־עֵדֶן לְעָבְדָהּ וּלְשָׁמְרָהּ

/// And YHVH deity took the human. // And he rested him in the garden of Eden to work it and to watch it.

Genesis 4:24. Textuality > conjunctive hypotactic expansion. A single forward slash separates a dominant from a dependent clause within a clause complex. In this particular complex, the first clause is dependent on the second clause, which is the dominant one. The direction of dependency can go either way with a hypotactically related pair of clauses.

כִּי שִׁבְעָתַיִם יֻקַּם־קָיִן / וְלֶמֶךְ שִׁבְעִים וְשִׁבְעָה ///. /// *If double-seven Qayin will be avenged / then Lemekh seventy-seven.*

The dependency can also be ordered in the other direction, with the dominant clause first, as in the following verse.

Genesis 3:20. Textuality > conjunctive hypotactic expansion.

וַיִּקְרָא הָאָדָם שֵׁם אִשְׁתּוֹ חַוָּה / כִּי הִוא הָיְתָה אֵם כָּל־חָי ///. /// *And the human called the name of his woman Chavva / because she was mother of all alive.*

Genesis 3:1. Textuality > embedded expansion: relative clause. This embedded clause is a relative clause that adds to the meaning of *all of the animalkind of the field*. Double square brackets enclose the embedded clause.

וְהַנָּחָשׁ הָיָה עָרוּם מִכֹּל חַיַּת הַשָּׂדֶה [[אֲשֶׁר עָשָׂה יְהוָה אֱלֹהִים]] ///. /// *And the snake was more crafty than all of the animalkind of the field [[which YHVH deity made]].*

The second of the two clauses in each of these three examples stands in a logical-semantic relationship of expansion to the first clause. The three logical-dependency relations of parataxis, hypotaxis, and embedding are also found in projection clauses, as the following three examples illustrate.

Genesis 7:1. Textuality > appositive paratactic projection: quote.

וַיֹּאמֶר יְהוָה לְנֹחַ // בֹּא־אַתָּה וְכָל־בֵּיתְךָ אֶל־הַתֵּבָה ///. /// *And YHVH said to Noach. // Go you, and all your house, to the ark.*

Genesis 3:6. Textuality > conjunctive hypotactic projection: report.

וַתֵּרֶא הָאִשָּׁה / כִּי טוֹב הָעֵץ לְמַאֲכָל //. // *And the woman saw / that good was the tree for food.*

Genesis 2:19. Textuality > conjunctive embedded projection. The embedded circumstantial clause לִרְאוֹת מַה־יִּקְרָא־לוֹ contains the embedded projection מַה־יִּקְרָא־לוֹ.

וַיָּבֵא אֶל־הָאָדָם [[לִרְאוֹת [[מַה־יִּקְרָא־לוֹ]]]] //. // *And he brought to the human [[to see [[what he will call him]]]].*

Being able to discern the hierarchic organization of clauses enables us to begin understanding what is more important and what is less important to the writer of a text. We end this section by making two general observations that pertain to these types of clause relationships. If one clause is presented as grammatically **subordinate** to another clause, this reflects the lower functional importance of the message of the subordinate clause. When one clause is grammatically related to another clause, the **order** of clauses matters, and the end position generally reflects greater functional importance. Keeping these principles in mind will help a reader discern how structure creates meaning.

Cohesion in text

The above explained features of theme, conjunction, and dependency, primarily determine how one clause relates structurally to adjacent clauses. Additional devices exist in the language for creating cohesion that extends beyond clause pairs. Cohesion is the quality of a text such that it comes to be recognized as a text and not just a random collection of unrelated words and clauses. Some of the devices that promote this are the use of referencing elements such as the definite article and pronouns, as well as ellipsis and substitution. All of these devices are part of the Textuality system, and if used effectively, tie the text together. Since they are used extensively in Genesis 1–11, a brief explanation of each term should suffice.

A definite article is typically found on a noun in one of two settings. If a noun is part of the general world shared by a speaker and a hearer, then the speaker can assume that the hearer knows it. In such a situation, the noun carries the definite article. For example, in 6:4(a) הַנְּפִלִים *the Nefilim* had not been mentioned previously; the writer assumes everyone knows about whom he is talking. If a noun is new to the message and cannot be assumed, then in its first appearance it is indefinite. In subsequent appearances it is definite. For example, 4:17(d-e) *And he was a builder of **a city**. And he called the name of **the city** like the name of his son Chanokh.* When we hear *the city*, we know it has already been defined.

Ellipsis is the deliberate omission of an element from a clause to avoid needless repetition, because the speaker knows the hearer will insert it from a previous clause. Most often this happens when the Subject is explicit in one clause but omitted in the following clause. It can also happen with Goals; verb ellipsis even happens once in our Genesis 1–11 corpus. Substitution occurs when one word takes the place of wording that needs to be repeated from elsewhere. This happens with the word כֵּן *so* in the clause וַֽיְהִי־כֵֽן *and it was so* in 1:7(c, and frequently elsewhere in chapter 1), where it is used to indicate the performance of divine commands.

Masoretic Apparatus

Lastly, it should be mentioned that the Masoretic annotation of the biblical text is essentially an expression of the Masoretes analysis of textuality. Though perhaps imperfectly actualized by some standards of modern analysis, the versification of the text along with פ and ס function in identifying clause complexes and text hierarchies. The system of conjunctive and disjunctive accents and the maqqef are useful in delimiting multi-word constituents within the transitivity structure of clauses. For the Masoretic sytem, see Scott (1995) and Yeivin (1980).

Focus on the Clause

This is a brief outline of three main ways of analyzing a clause. The important point to remember concerning these three metafunctions is that all three are performed simultaneously. They are the three overlays of meaning which together constitute the overall meaning of the clause, and they are the views whereby we can account for the different types of meaning that are bound up in a clause. We will employ different sets of labels, each applying to its metafunction, to identify these different functional layers. Potentially, each constituent in a clause could be labeled in different ways depending on the function currently under examination.

The following table summarizes the three clause metafunctions, how they each view meaning in the clause, their communication roles, and the terms used in clause analysis.

Table 9. The Three Metafunctions

Metafunction	Clause as ...	Clause Role	Clause Analysis
Textual	message	organizing the message	Textuality
Interpersonal	exchange	interacting and negotiating	Mood
Experiential	representation	representing the world	Transitivity

This framework enables us to discern the internal structure of clauses, the relationships of clauses, and the function roles of clause constituents. Within this framework, no constituent system is richer with possibilities than the BH verb system.

A functional view of verbs

An analysis of BH along functional lines is useful for unpacking the formal components of the verbal system within the systems of the clause. As every student of the language knows, there are multiple variable components of the Hebrew verb. Here are the basic parameters that need to be identified when analyzing any particular form:

- Is it finite (qatal, yiqtol, participle, directive) or non-finite (infinitive)?
- If it is finite, what is its person, number and gender?

- What is its root and what is the core meaning of this root?
- What is its stem, also called its conjugation?

In addition, verb forms can have elements that pre-pose the verb proper, such as the conjunction וְ or a preposition, and elements that post-pose the verb, such as pronoun suffixes designating the Actor, Goal, or Beneficiary of the verb process.

A functional analysis of the BH clause enables a student to make functional sense of the formal complexity of this verbal system. As it turns out, each variable plays a vital role in one of the three functional systems of the clause.

1. Mood system: the interpersonal function of the clause. The choice of which Participant will function as the Subject of the clause, and hence be congruent with the Finite form (person, number gender), is a function of the interpersonal transaction realized by the clause. The choice of indicative versus directive, and declarative versus interrogative, is likewise a choice made by the speaker depending on how the speaker intends to interact with the audience.

2. Transitivity system: the experiential function of the clause. The root is the core semantic value of the form. It gives expression to the type of Process around which the experiential meaning of the clause will be built. The stem (qal, nifal, piel, pual, hifil, hofal, hitpael, etc.), in cooperation with the root meaning, predetermines the framework of possible Participants that can come to expression with this root.

3. Textuality system: the message function of the clause. The w- forms (wayyiqtol and weqatal) versus non-w- forms (yiqtol and qatal) are a function of Theme. Finite forms versus non-finite forms (infinitives) are a function of logical-dependency relationships among clauses, and the hierarchic organization of the message of the clauses.

The discussion of the BH finite verb system in the technical literature can be rather confusing. Some scholars claim that the finite forms indicate the aspect of the verb. Currently, this view tends generally to be in favor. Others view the system as indicating time or tense relative to the time of speaking or writing. The issues are complex and there are other variables under discussion, but all of this has led to a confusing array of terms (perfect and imperfect, suffix tense and prefix tense), made even more confusing because traditional designations also continue to be employed in the field (waw-consecutive and waw-conversive). This has led many analysts of the text to employ designations that are purely formal and claim to be theory neutral: qatal, weqatal, yiqtol, and wayyiqtol. This handbook is not the place to argue a case, yet it can be observed that a tense-based approach aligns with the view of pre-modern Hebrew grammarians, and seems amenable to the functional perspective used here. As we develop an analytic framework, tense turns out to be one of the core parameters of the Finite component of the Mood system. Our analysis distinguishes only past (wayyiqtol and qatal) from non-past (yiqtol and weqatal). Aspect, in so far as it is represented in the verbal system, is viewed here as a component of the Transitivity system, where it is viewed primarily as a feature of lexicon (root and stem), rather than as a feature of the Finite component of the Mood system.

Layout of the analysis

The functional approach employed here views the existing text and its clauses as the end result of a number of choices that the writer has made to bring thoughts to expression. The wording of each and every actual clause has been shaped by decisions, no doubt mostly intuitive and instinctual to the native speaker, about what to make the Theme of the clause, how to communicate authorial perspective, and how to articulate a depiction of the world using words.

The key to analyzing biblical text using a functional approach is identifying and delineating clauses. Once divisions between clauses are recognized, the functional constituents of the clause can be identified. Clause constituents may consist of individual words, groups of words, or suffixes on other constituents. Some constituents may even be missing from a clause and will need to be inferred from a prior clause. This linguistic phenomenon of a constituent having gone "missing" is called ellipsis. Constituents that have been ellided need to be recovered and mentally inserted within the present clause in order to complete that clause's transitivity structure.

Here is an explanation of the layout of the descriptions and analyses that constitute this handbook. Each chapter of Genesis 1–11 is divided into its clause complexes. Each and every clause of each clause complex is then analyzed in the following manner.

1. *Translation.* An English translation of the clause complex is given at the beginning of each clause complex. The clause complex breaks are based on the textuality analysis described above. The translations reflect the linguistic analysis elaborated in the handbook and attempt to communicate the structure and features of the Hebrew text. They do not set out to render the text in smooth and elegant English.

2. *Masoretic text.* The MT form of each verse as a whole is reproduced, including the *te'amim* (the Masoretic accents). The MT is annotated in order to delimit clauses. Three forward slashes (///) mark the beginning of a new clause complex. Two forward slashes (//) mark a paratactic relationship between two clauses within a clause complex. One forward slash (/) marks a hypotactic relationship between two clauses. Note that this handbook attends only to the received text as it stands and tries to make the best linguistic sense out of it. It does not attempt to reconstruct a presumed better text using the versions and manuscript witnesses employed in the discipline of text criticism. Other commentaries are available which adequately attend to such matters, including Wenham and Westermann.

3. *Clause presentation.* The Hebrew text of each clause is then listed separately and labeled sequentially with (a), (b), and so on as needed, and each is described and analyzed individually. If an independent clause contains an embedded clause, the latter is also given full analysis and is labeled with (i), (ii), and so on. Embedded clauses are enclosed in square brackets [[ ]], and sometimes the brackets are nested in cases of embedding within embedding. There are cases where an embedded clause has within itself another embedded clause, and these third-level

clauses are labeled (a'), (b'), and so on. Each clause has one and only one process. That process is realized by a finite verb form, except in cases where the verb is not present because of ellipsis. Relational processes are a special case, because an explicit verb is not needed to establish a meaningful constituent relationship within a clause. Otherwise, only minor clauses, including exclamative clauses, lack a finite verb.

4. *Clause-level analysis.* Each clause is analyzed generally for each metafunction in the order Textuality, Mood, and Transitivity. A wedge is used to separate the functional category from the system choice activated in this particular clause. This level of analysis applies to the clause as a whole. The following diagram indicates the major system choices in this clause-level analysis.

Refer to diagram 2, along with this introduction and the glossary, for explanations of the various functional labels as you study the description of each clause.

5. Constituent-level analysis. The analysis proceeds in the direction from function to form. Each clause constituent is identified and labeled for its function within the three core functional systems. This analysis is presented in the form of a table in order to visualize the structures, and it includes a translation of each component. Every constituent in a clause must have a functional role within at least one of the three metafunctional systems; some constituents have a role in more than one metafunctional system. This is an important feature of functional analysis. There is nothing superfluous in a clause, nothing is meaningless. Absolutely everything has some communicative function.

Regarding the way the Hebrew text is rendered into English in these tables, an explanation is probably in order. You will notice that the constituent translations are intentionally verbose, and they will seem slavishly, even ridiculously, literal at times. For example, verbs are translated to communicate their person, gender (always masculine or feminine, even when in English we would substitute *it*), and number. This is intended as an aid in identifying congruities between Finite and Subject, as well as incongruities, which occur with surpris-

Diagram 2. The Metafunctional Systems and Their Functional Labels

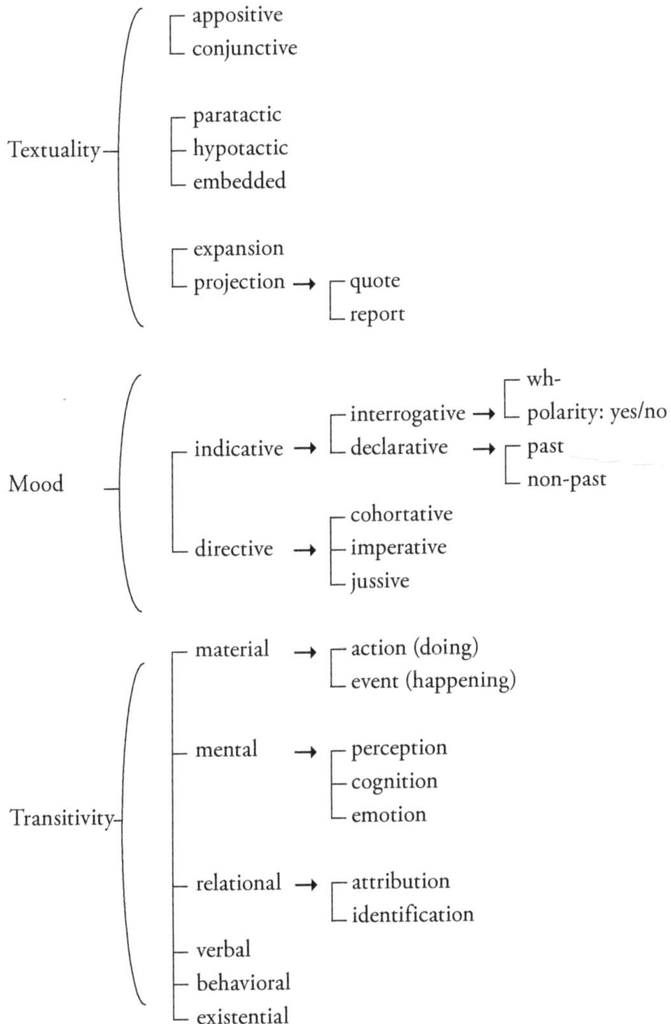

ing frequency. And the translations sometimes employ contrived neologisms to communicate the realities of Hebrew, for example, using words such as *treekind* and *animalkind* to communicate the collective nature of the underlying grammatical and semantic structure. The clause translations, as well as the translations of individual words in the linguistic commentary, are always in italics.

6. Detailed formal analysis. Lastly, following each table, each clause constituent is provided a detailed formal analysis. The functional labels attached to each constituent are followed by formal grammatical descriptions using this format: Function > group form: individual word form. When individual forms are unpacked, individual words, as delineated in the Masoretic text, are separated by a vertical line (|). Individual components of a phrase joined by a *maqqef* (-) are separated by a hyphen. The plus sign (+) separates discernible components of a text word, which is to say, a MT consonant string that has a blank space on either side. There are, of course, many such words in Hebrew given its orthographic practice: nouns with attached prepositions, verbs with attached subjects or objects, and so on. Expanded linguistic commentary is provided throughout the analysis where relevant or deemed helpful.

Keys to analysis

It is my hope that this approach, with its focus on constituents and clauses, will deepen your appreciation of the biblical text. No doubt its approach is different from your introductory course in Hebrew and employs new descriptive vocabulary—not new to functionalism, but certainly new to the field of BH grammar. While it may seem complex and daunting, it all comes down to the following points, which are the keys to a successful linguistic analysis of the biblical text.

1. Discern clause boundaries and identify individual clauses. Embedded clauses can be the trickiest.
2. Discern constituent boundaries within clauses. Constituents are not the same as words. They can be words, but they can

also be phrases and groups, or they can be pronoun suffixes on words. Constituents are clause elements that have a functional role.

3. Attend to the three layers of meaning—the metafunctional systems—of each clause. Every clause constituent has a role in at least one of the three metafunctional systems. Force yourself to account for each and every component of the clause.
4. Resist reading just forms. Rather, train yourself to see the constituent "chunks" of the text: first divide the text into clauses, then into constituent groups and phrases, and lastly into words and morphemes.

Also be aware that functional analysis, or any type of linguistic analysis for that matter, is not a simple mechanical act of applying labels to constituents. Analysis can involve a significant amount of interpretation and discernment, sometimes more and sometimes less, depending on the complexity of the clause. Narration is typically less complex (with conjunctive paratactic clauses in temporal sequence predominating). Quoted speech is more complex (with wide use of appositive hypotactic and embedded clauses) and analysis can often be quite challenging. Uncertainties may sometimes remain, with certain constructions capable of two or more different functional explanations.

For many readers of this handbook, this functional approach will be a new way of organizing the forms of BH and a new way of thinking about their meaning. It is introduced and employed here not out of a desire to be different, and surely not out of a desire to confuse students of the text. Rather, it grew out of a conviction that the traditional grammatical categories are not rich enough to capture systematically the kinds of meanings that are encoded in the biblical text. Traditional BH grammar has a rich and venerable history, but it is showing its age. Many grammatical definitions emerged out of an *ad hoc* reading of biblical texts. It persists in employing opaque latinized descriptions such as *casus pendens*, *nun paragogicum*, and *dativus ethicus* as explanations that do not really explain anything. Many grammatical categories have been applied to the original text on the basis of translations into the target language, and not from categories developed out of sound linguistic practice or out of the logic of the source language itself. Given this situation, a functional analysis may be in a position to make a contribution. It is based on a comprehensive and well-developed theory of language that is employed world wide in such important fields as second language acquisition, which depend on an analysis of how and why language is actually used. It may be a challenge to learn new analytic categories and techniques such as these, yet our understanding of the biblical text just may be enhanced through the process. For more information on the application of functional grammar to biblical Hebrew, visit the author's web site at biblicaltext.org.

Genesis 1:1-5

[1]Initially deity created the heavens and the earth. [2]And the earth was
an emptiness and a void. And darkness is on the surface of deep-water,
and a wind of deity hovers on the surface of the waters. [3]And deity said,
"Let light be." And light was. [4]And deity saw the light that good it is. And
deity made separation between the light and between the darkness. [5]And
deity named the light day, and the darkness he named night. And evening
was. And morning was. Day one!

1:1 /// בְּרֵאשִׁ֖ית בָּרָ֣א אֱלֹהִ֑ים אֵ֥ת הַשָּׁמַ֖יִם וְאֵ֥ת הָאָֽרֶץ׃

בְּרֵאשִׁית בָּרָא אֱלֹהִים אֵת הַשָּׁמַיִם וְאֵת הָאָרֶץ. (a) Textuality > appositive expansion / Mood > declarative: past / Transitivity > material: action.

אֵת הַשָּׁמַיִם וְאֵת הָאָרֶץ	אֱלֹהִים	בָּרָא	בְּרֵאשִׁית	**Constituents**
the heavens and the earth	*deity*	*he created*	*in a first*	**Translation**
			Theme	**Textuality**
	Subject	Finite		**Mood**
Goal	Actor	Process	Circumstance	**Transivity**

The basic Transitivity structure of this clause is for the most part straightforward: the clause is about a deity creating the heavens and the earth. The Mood of the clause is also straightforward: it is declarative, which is to say, it is making a statement, in this case, a statement about the past. It is appositive, meaning that it does not have a conjunction; naturally, since nothing precedes it. It is an expansion, which means it adds to the story; again, naturally, since we had nothing to begin with. The clause is tagged with three slashes (///) because it begins a new clause complex. See the Introduction for further explanation of these terms and symbols.

What is not clear is the relationship of this clause to the following one: is it in a dependent (hypotactic) relationship or is it in an independent (paratactic) relationship? The linguistic interpretation offered in the analysis above indicates it is independent. In this analysis the clause makes a statement that stands on its own, perhaps as the Theme statement of the narrative description that follows it. But there are other viable analyses, and this issue has been much discussed in the history of the interpretation of this text.

Another interpretive option sees the Textuality of this clause as hypotactic expansion rather than as paratactic expansion, rendering it as a temporal circumstantial clause. Interpretations along this line differ on which clause is the dominant clause upon which it depends and the meaning of which it expands: it could be 1:2(a), or 1:2(a-c), or 1:3(a). All three options have found advocates in the history of interpretation. See Wenham.

Part of the difficulty is that this clause is the very first clause of the text, and בְּרֵאשִׁית is the very first word. As such, the בְּרֵאשִׁית prepositional phrase is the Theme of the first clause, and this clause is, linguistically speaking, the Theme of the text. The Theme of a clause typically serves to establish a connection to the context, either the context of speech or the context of situation. In this case, uniquely, there is no obvious context with which to connect, hence no obvious connection to be made. The NRSV reflects the variety of linguistic interpretations that are available and offers three options: (1) in the main text, *In the beginning when God created the heavens and the earth*; and in footnotes (2) *When God began to create...* and (3) *In the beginning God created ...* .

בְּרֵאשִׁית. Theme: textual / Circumstance: location, time > prep phrase: prep + noun common ms. Literally, *in a first*, perhaps meaning *at commencement*, or *initially*. Many translations render the noun רֵאשִׁית as *the beginning* and the prep phrase as *in the beginning*, but the noun is indefinite. The translation *when*, reflected in the NRSV and other versions, comes from analyzing בְּ in a temporal circumstantial sense, which then renders the clause a hypotactic temporal one. Understood this way, the precise meaning of this phrase and its effect on the syntax of the first three verses was famously disputed in the twelfth century when Ibn Ezra viewed verse 1 as a temporal clause subordinate to verse 2 as the main clause, and Rashi viewed verse 1 as a temporal clause subordinate to verse 3 as the main clause.

בָּרָא. Finite > qatal 3ms / Process > qal ברא. The syntactic relationship of בְּרֵאשִׁית and בָּרָא is disputed by some, but should not be. Some interpreters construe בָּרָא as if it were in a construct or bound relationship with רֵאשִׁית, translating *in the beginning of God's creating*. But בָּרָא is a finite verb and not an infinitive; normally both components of a construct phrase must be nominal forms. Furthermore, the disjunctive *tifcha* accent on בְּרֵאשִׁ֖ית argues against it being in construct with the following word.

אֱלֹהִים. Subject > mp / Actor > nominal group: noun common. This is not a name (termed a proper noun). Formally it is mp, but it matches the ms verbal predicate בָּרָא. The plural noun אֱלֹהִים with a singular verb is a convention maintained throughout the Hebrew Bible. The noun is often rendered as if it were a name—*God*. The Hebrew text taken at face value expresses the indefinite term *deity*, which is how we render it here and throughout. Of course, biblical Hebrew does not use initial capital letters to indicate the presence of a personal or divine name (a proper noun) in distinction from a common noun, because it does not have distinctive capital letter forms.

אֵת הַשָּׁמַיִם וְאֵת הָאָרֶץ. Goal > nominal group complex: goal marker | def art + noun common mp | group conj + goal marker | def art + noun common fs. The Goal constitutent of this clause consists of two nominal groups conjoined with the conjunction וְ. An element such as הַשָּׁמַיִם is called a nominal group in our analysis. The term *group* as used here might be confusing at first; note that a nominal group can be a single word such as אֱלֹהִים or a noun along with the elements that define it, such as the definite article, construct nouns, adjectives, and pronouns. A nominal group complex is a collection of two or more nominal groups.

אֵת. The goal marker in BH can be either the independent אֵת carrying its own accent, as here, or the prefixed אֶת־ using the *maqqef* and having no accent. The effect of the independent form may be analogous to the English stressed "the" (pronounced *thee*) when it means "the one and only."

הַשָּׁמַיִם. Goal 1 > def art + noun common mp. It looks formally like a dual because it ends in ־ַיִם, but the form is a plural of שָׁמַי with unaccented ־ִים ending. See TDOT XV: 205. The presence of a definite article presumes that the word to which it is attached has already been defined or is presumably known given a common world view; the latter must be the case here.

וְאֵת. Group conj + goal marker. The BH conjunction וְ can be used in either of two ways, which are distinguished in these analyses. The group conjunction combines nominal groups or prepositional phrases into a functional unit. The unit as a whole plays a role within the clause. In the clause we are examining, the group conjunction combines two nominal groups into one linguistic constituent that functions as the Goal of the clause. In distinction from the group conjunction, the clause conjunction joins a clause to the preceding clause. As such, it has a role in the construction of clause complexes, that is, collections of clauses, within the Textuality metafunction.

הָאָֽרֶץ׃. Goal 2 > def art + noun common fs. The ׃ *sof pasuq* in combination with the אָֽ *meteg* marks the end of a verse. The end of a verse does not necessarily coincide with the end of a clause, and not every verse consists of one and only one clause, as the next verse illustrates.

1:2 // וְהָאָ֗רֶץ הָיְתָ֥ה תֹ֙הוּ֙ וָבֹ֔הוּ // וְחֹ֖שֶׁךְ עַל־פְּנֵ֣י תְה֑וֹם
// וְר֣וּחַ אֱלֹהִ֔ים מְרַחֶ֖פֶת עַל־פְּנֵ֥י הַמָּֽיִם׃

This verse consists of three independent clauses each introduced with the clause conjunction וְ. We are using two slashes (//) to divide a verse into paratactic clauses, though this is not a Masoretic convention. These three are elaborating expansion clauses, adding specification and description to הָאָרֶץ in the first verse. None of these clauses carry the creation narrative forward, nor should they be considered sequential. Rather, in our analysis, each clause makes a statement about a preexisting component in order to characterize the state of the earth before deity's first act of creation.

וְהָאָרֶץ הָיְתָה תֹהוּ וָבֹהוּ. (a) Textuality > conj paratactic expansion / Mood > declarative: past / Transitivity > relational: attribution. This declarative clause contains an attributive relational process of being (*the earth was...*). As a relational clause, it relates its Carrier הָאָרֶץ *the earth* to the attributes תֹהוּ וָבֹהוּ *an emptiness and a void.* The Attribute in an attributive relational clause is typically an indefinite noun or adjective, or a prepositional phrase. The existential verb הָיָה can be present in an attributive relational process clause, but a relational clause can also be constituted by simple juxtaposition, as the next two clauses illustrate.

תֹהוּ וָבֹהוּ	הָיְתָה	וְהָאָרֶץ	**Constituents**
an emptiness and a void	*she was*	*and the earth*	**Translation**
		Theme	**Textuality**
Complement	Finite	Subject	**Mood**
Attribute	Process	Carrier	**Transivity**

וְהָאָרֶץ. Theme: textual > clause conj + Theme: experiential / Subject > fs / Carrier > nominal group: def art + noun common. Here the clause conjunction builds two clauses into a clause complex. This clause also illustrates that the Theme, which is always the first constituent of the clause, can have more than one element. In this case it has an element that functions in the Textuality structure (the conj) and one element that functions in the Transitivity structure (the common noun).

הָיְתָה. Finite > qatal 3fs / Process > qal היה. On this analysis the Process is attributive relational. Alternately, הָיְתָה could be rendered as a material process and be translated as *became*, suggesting that the earth went through a transformation.

תֹהוּ וָבֹהוּ. Complement / Attribute > nominal group: noun common ms | group conj + noun common ms. The *tav* of תֹהוּ does not have a *dagesh lene* because it is preceded by a form ending with a vowel; this indicates it is bound or conjunctive with the preceding word הָיְתָה. The vocalization of the conjunction as וָ with a *qamets* instead of with a *sheva* is typical of idiomatic phrases and has the effect of creating one notion out of two components, called hendiadys, "one through two." Consequently, this is a nominal group: two words in Hebrew forming one group, rather than a group complex, as אֵת הַשָּׁמַיִם וְאֵת הָאָרֶץ in 1:1(a), which consists of two separate nominal groups. There are numerous such hendiadys phrases in BH, including טוֹב וָרָע in 2:9(a).

וְחֹשֶׁךְ עַל־פְּנֵי תְהוֹם. (b) Textuality > conj paratactic expansion / Mood > declarative: non-past / Transitivity > relational: attribution.

עַל־פְּנֵי תְהוֹם	וְחֹשֶׁךְ	**Constituents**
on the face of deep-water	*and darkness*	**Translation**
	Theme	**Textuality**
Complement	Subject	**Mood**
Attribute	Carrier	**Transivity**

וְחֹשֶׁךְ. Theme: textual > clause conj + Theme: experiential / Subject > ms / Carrier > nominal group: noun common.

עַל־פְּנֵי תְהוֹם. Complement / Attribute > prep phrase: prep + noun common mp const ׀ noun common or proper ms. תְהוֹם has no definite article, so it could be an indef common noun. The construct phrase would then be *on deep-water's surface*. Or it could be a proper name, *Tehom* or *Deep*, making the phrase *on Tehom's surface*. Tehom is cognate with Tiamat, the salt-water ocean of the Babylonian Enuma Elish. תְהוֹם has no *dagesh lene* reinforcing that it is bound to פְּנֵי.

וְרוּחַ אֱלֹהִים מְרַחֶפֶת עַל־פְּנֵי הַמָּיִם. (c) Textuality > conj paratactic expansion / Mood > declarative: non-past / Transitivity > material: action.

עַל־פְּנֵי הַמָּיִם	מְרַחֶפֶת	וְרוּחַ אֱלֹהִים	**Constituents**
on the face of the waters	*she hovers*	*and a wind of deity*	**Translation**
		Theme	**Textuality**
	Finite	Subject	**Mood**
Circumstance	Process	Actor	**Transivity**

וְרוּחַ אֱלֹהִים. Theme: textual > clause conj + Theme: experiential / Subject > fs (רוּחַ) / Actor > nominal group: noun common fs const ׀ noun common mp. אֱלֹהִים is either a common noun, *deity*, or, less likely, a noun used attributively, meaning *divine*, making either the bound phrase *a wind of deity* or *a spirit of deity* (depending on how רוּחַ is understood), or a noun plus adjective phrase, *a divine wind*.

מְרַחֶפֶת. Finite > ptc fs / Process > piel רחף. We are interpreting the participle as the main verb of the clause, called a predicative participle. Conventional wisdom had claimed that a participle cannot be the main verb of a clause. More recent research challenges this view. See Smith and Joosten.

עַל־פְּנֵי הַמָּיִם. Circumstance: location, place > prep phrase: prep + noun common mp const ׀ def art + noun common mp. The noun מַיִם (here in pause with stress lengthening of the *patach*), has the appearance of a dual form, but is most likely plural; see *TDOT* VIII: 266, and compare שָׁמַיִם in 1:1(a).

1:3 // וַיֹּאמֶר אֱלֹהִים // יְהִי אוֹר // וַיְהִי־אוֹר׃

וַיֹּאמֶר אֱלֹהִים. (a) Textuality > conj paratactic expansion / Mood > declarative: past / Transitivity > verbal. Typically, a verbal process clause contains both a Sayer and a Receiver, but no Receiver is specified in this clause; to whom is deity speaking? This could be a figure of speech. Or the divine council could be invoked as agents of the creation process.

אֱלֹהִים	וַיֹּאמֶר	**Constituents**
deity	*and he said*	**Translation**
	Theme	**Textuality**
Subject	Finite	**Mood**
Sayer	Process	**Transitivity**

וַיֹּאמֶר. Theme: textual > clause conj + Theme: experiential / Finite > wayyiqtol 3ms / Process > qal אמר.

אֱלֹהִים. Subject > mp / Sayer > nominal group: noun common.

יְהִי אוֹר. (b) Textuality > appositive paratactic projection: quote / Mood > directive: jussive / Transitivity > existential. *Let be light!*

אוֹר	יְהִי	**Constituents**
light	*let him be*	**Translation**
	Theme	**Textuality**
Subject	Finite	**Mood**
Existent	Process	**Transitivity**

יְהִי. Theme: experiential / Finite > jussive 3ms / Process > qal היה.

אוֹר. Subject > ms / Existent > nominal group: noun common.

וַיְהִי־אוֹר. (c) Textuality > conj paratactic expansion / Mood > declarative: past / Transitivity > existential. *And light was.*

אוֹר	וַיְהִי	**Constituents**
light	*and he was*	**Translation**
	Theme	**Textuality**
Subject	Finite	**Mood**
Existent	Process	**Transitivity**

וַיְהִי. Theme: textual > clause conj + Theme: experiential / Finite > wayyiqtol 3ms / Process > qal הָיָה.

אוֹר. Subject > ms / Existent > nominal group: noun common.

1:4 // וַיַּרְא אֱלֹהִים אֶת־הָאוֹר // כִּי־טוֹב // וַיַּבְדֵּל
אֱלֹהִים בֵּין הָאוֹר וּבֵין הַחֹשֶׁךְ׃

וַיַּרְא אֱלֹהִים אֶת־הָאוֹר. (a) Textuality > conj paratactic expansion / Mood > declarative: past / Transitivity > mental: perception.

אֶת־הָאוֹר	אֱלֹהִים	וַיַּרְא	**Constituents**
the light	*deity*	*and he saw*	**Translation**
		Theme	**Textuality**
	Subject	Finite	**Mood**
Phenomenon	Senser	Process	**Transitivity**

וַיַּרְא. Theme: textual > clause conj + Theme: experiential / Finite > wayyiqtol 3ms / Process > qal ראה.

אֱלֹהִים. Subject > mp / Senser > nominal group: noun common.

אֶת־הָאוֹר. Phenomenon > nominal group: goal marker - def art + noun common ms.

כִּי־טוֹב. (b) Textuality > conj hypotactic projection: report / Mood > declarative: non-past / Transitivity > relational: attribution. The

Carrier is הָאוֹר *the light* from the preceding clause, textually absent here by ellipsis. All three metafunctions—the experiential, the interpersonal, and the textual—can at times contribute to the Theme of a clause. For example, when the clause process is expressed by a wayyiqtol or weqatal verb form, this combines a textual Theme (the *way-* or *we-* part of the verb form) with an experiential Theme (the finite component of the form). In the clause here under examination, the Theme is constituted by both כִּי and טוֹב. The first is the textual Theme and the second is the experiential Theme.

טוֹב	כִּי	**Constituents**
good	*that*	**Translation**
Theme		**Textuality**
Attribute		**Transitivity**

כִּי־. Theme: textual > clause conj. This connects the dependent projection clause to the preceding dominant mental process clause.

טוֹב. Theme: experiential / Attribute > adj ms. This is the Attribute of the relational process.

וַיַּבְדֵּל אֱלֹהִים בֵּין הָאוֹר וּבֵין הַחֹשֶׁךְ. (c) Textuality > conj paratactic expansion / Mood > declarative: past / Transitivity > material: action. The Goal of the material process, *separation*, is not expressed by an independent noun, but it is implicit in the hifil verb form.

בֵּין הָאוֹר וּבֵין הַחֹשֶׁךְ	אֱלֹהִים	וַיַּבְדֵּל	**Constituents**
between the light and between the darkness	*deity*	*and made separation*	**Translation**
		Theme	**Textuality**
	Subject	Finite	**Mood**
Circumstance	Actor	Process	**Transitivity**

וַיַּבְדֵּל. Theme: textual > clause conj + Theme: experiential / Finite > wayyiqtol 3ms / Process > hiphil בדל.

אֱלֹהִים. Subject > mp / Actor > nominal group: noun common.

בֵּין הָאוֹר וּבֵין הַחֹשֶׁךְ. Circumstance: location, place > prep phrase complex: prep ו def art + noun common ms ו group conj + prep ו def art + noun common ms. Note that while English would employ only one *between,* BH employs two.

1:5 // וַיִּקְרָ֨א אֱלֹהִ֤ים לָאוֹר֙ י֔וֹם // וְלַחֹ֖שֶׁךְ קָ֣רָא לָ֑יְלָה //
וַֽיְהִי־עֶ֥רֶב // וַֽיְהִי־בֹ֖קֶר // י֥וֹם אֶחָֽד׃ פ

וַיִּקְרָא אֱלֹהִים לָאוֹר יוֹם. (a) Textuality > conj paratactic expansion / Mood > declarative: past / Transitivity > verbal.

יוֹם	לָאוֹר	אֱלֹהִים	וַיִּקְרָא	**Constituents**
day	*the light*	*deity*	*and called*	**Translation**
			Theme	**Textuality**
		Subject	Finite	**Mood**
Verbiage	Target	Sayer	Process	**Transitivity**

וַיִּקְרָא. Theme: textual > clause conj + Theme: experiential / Finite > wayyiqtol 3ms / Process > qal קרא.

אֱלֹהִים. Subject > mp / Sayer > nominal group: noun common.

לָאוֹר. Target > prep phrase: prep + def article + noun common ms. *Light* is the Target of the verbal process, that is, the thing about which something is said; the process of naming light is not actually addressed to the light. The noun is marked definite because it is identifiable to the reader, having been mentioned earlier in the text.

יוֹם. Verbiage > nominal group: noun common ms. *Day* is the label that now attaches to the Target *light* as a result of the naming activity. Less likely, it could be construed as the quote of the verbal process, the actual word that the Sayer said: *Light!*

וְלַחֹשֶׁךְ קָרָא לָיְלָה. (b) Textuality > conj paratactic expansion / Mood > declarative: past / Transitivity > verbal. The Subject / Sayer of the verbal process, אֱלֹהִים *deity*, is presumed from the prior clause, and it is textually absent in this clause by the operation of ellipsis.

לָיְלָה	קָרָא	וְלַחֹשֶׁךְ	**Constituents**
night	*he called*	*and the darkness*	**Translation**
		Theme	**Textuality**
	Finite		**Mood**
Verbiage	Process	Target	**Transitivity**

וְלַחֹשֶׁךְ. Theme: textual > clause conj + Theme: experiential / Target > prep phrase: prep + def art + noun common ms.

קָרָא. Finite > qatal 3ms / Process > qal קרא.

לָיְלָה. Verbiage > nominal group: noun common fs.

וַיְהִי־עֶרֶב. (c) Textuality > conj paratactic expansion / Mood > declarative: past / Transitivity > existential.

עֶרֶב	וַיְהִי	**Constituents**
evening	*and he was*	**Translation**
	Theme	**Textuality**
Subject	Finite	**Mood**
Existent	Process	**Transitivity**

וַיְהִי. Theme: textual > clause conj + Theme: experiential / Finite > wayyiqtol 3ms / Process > qal היה.

עֶרֶב. Subject > ms / Existent > nominal group: noun common.

וַיְהִי־בֹקֶר. (d) Textuality > conj paratactic expansion / Mood > declarative: past / Transitivity > existential.

בֹקֶר	וַיְהִי	**Constituents**
morning	*and he was*	**Translation**
	Theme	**Textuality**
Subject	Finite	**Mood**
Existent	Process	**Transitivity**

וַיְהִי. Theme: textual > clause conj + Theme: experiential / Finite > wayyiqtol 3ms / Process > qal היה.

בֹקֶר. Subject > ms / Existent > nominal group: noun common. A *dagesh lene* is absent from the ב because it is bound to the preceding word, which ends in a vowel. The words *evening* and *morning* in this verse and all analogous verses of Genesis 1 are indefinite, even though they refer to the evenings and mornings of specific days.

יוֹם אֶחָד. (e) Textuality > appositive paratactic expansion / Mood > declarative: non-past / Transitivity > existential. *Day one (it is)!* This is an exclamative existential process. It consists solely of an Existent Subject, with the verbal process assumed; this is not unusual, because a verb expressing the existential process is often not textually explicit in BH. This is an exclamative clause, which is one type of minor clause. A minor clause lacks an explicit transitivity structure, because it does not contain a Process.

יוֹם אֶחָד	**Constituents**
day one	**Translation**
Theme	**Textuality**
Subject	**Mood**
Existent	**Transitivity**

יוֹם אֶחָד. Subject > ms / Existent > nominal group: noun common ms | noun common ms. Even though יוֹם *day* had already been defined (verse 5a), there it specifically labeled *the light*; in this clause it labels the daily cycle of light and darkness. Perhaps since this is a new referent or sense for *day*, it is indefinite. Note that the cardinal number *one* and not the ordinal number *first* is used in this clause.

פ. The *petucha* "open" paragraph marker. See Scott for a description of the Masoretic text divisions.

Genesis 1:6-8

[6]And deity said, "Let a barrier be in the middle of the waters, and let a separator be between waters for the waters." [7]And deity made the barrier. And it made separation between the waters which are below the barrier and the waters which are above the barrier. And such happened. [8]And deity called the barrier heavens. And evening was. And morning was. Second day!

1:6 /// וַיֹּאמֶר אֱלֹהִים // יְהִי רָקִיעַ בְּתוֹךְ הַמָּיִם // וִיהִי
מַבְדִּיל בֵּין מַיִם לָמָיִם׃

וַיֹּאמֶר אֱלֹהִים. (a) Textuality > conj paratactic expansion / Mood > declarative: past / Transitivity > verbal. See 1:3(a).

יְהִי רָקִיעַ בְּתוֹךְ הַמָּיִם. (b) Textuality > appositive paratactic projection: quote / Mood > directive: jussive / Transitivity > existential.

בְּתוֹךְ הַמָּיִם	רָקִיעַ	יְהִי	**Constituents**
in the middle of the waters	*a barrier*	*let him be*	**Translation**
		Theme	**Textuality**
	Subject	Finite	**Mood**
Circumstance	Existent	Process	**Transitivity**

יְהִי. Finite > jussive 3ms / Process > qal היה.

רָקִיעַ. Subject > ms / Existent > nominal group: noun common.

בְּתוֹךְ הַמָּיִם. Circumstance: location, place > prep phrase: prep + noun common ms const | def art + noun common mp.

וִיהִי מַבְדִּיל בֵּין מַיִם לָמָיִם. (c) Textuality > conj paratactic projection: quote / Mood > directive: jussive / Transitivity > existential.

לַמָּיִם	בֵּין מַיִם	מַבְדִּיל	וִיהִי	**Constituents**
for the waters	*between waters*	*a separator*	*and let him be*	**Translation**
			Theme	**Textuality**
		Subject	Finite	**Mood**
Beneficiary	Circumstance	Existent	Process	**Transitivity**

וִיהִי. Theme: textual > clause conj + Theme: experiential / Finite > jussive 3ms / Process > qal היה.

מַבְדִּיל. Subject > ms / Existent > ptc hifil בדל. The participle functions as the Existent in the existential process and can be translated, *a thing separating, a separator*. The participle takes the material process of separating and nominalizes it so that it can become a Participant in the existential process.

בֵּין מַיִם. Circumstance: location, place > prep phrase: prep | noun common mp. Typically this prep is repeated: בֵּין *between* x and בֵּין *between* y (e.g. Gen 1:7b), but a second בֵּין is not found in this clause.

לַמָּיִם. Beneficiary > prep phrase: prep + def art + noun common mp. This phrase specifies the Beneficiary of the existential process. Alternately, this may be the second element of a *between* structure, hence the second of two prepositional phrases forming a prepositional phrase complex. Sometimes ל is used before the second term instead of בֵּין (compare Num 30:17), but if so, why is the second *waters* marked with the definite article, but not the first? Notice also the pausal lengthening of the *a* vowel of מָיִם. *For the waters*, that is, to keep the waters separate.

1:7 // וַיַּעַשׂ אֱלֹהִים֮ אֶת־הָרָקִיעַ֒ // וַיַּבְדֵּל בֵּין הַמַּיִם
אֲשֶׁר֙ מִתַּ֣חַת לָרָקִ֔יעַ וּבֵ֣ין הַמַּ֔יִם אֲשֶׁ֖ר מֵעַ֣ל לָרָקִ֑יעַ
// וַֽיְהִי־כֵֽן׃

וַיַּעַשׂ אֱלֹהִים אֶת־הָרָקִיעַ. (a) Textuality > conj paratactic expansion / Mood > declarative: past / Transitivity > material: action.

אֶת־הָרָקִיעַ	אֱלֹהִים	וַיַּעַשׂ	**Constituents**
the barrier	*deity*	*and he made*	**Translation**
		Theme	**Textuality**
	Subject	Finite	**Mood**
Goal	Actor	Process	**Transitivity**

וַיַּעַשׂ. Theme: textual > clause conj + Theme: experiential / Finite > wayyiqtol 3ms / Process > qal עשׂה.

אֱלֹהִים. Subject > mp / Actor > nominal group: noun common.

אֶת־הָרָקִיעַ. Goal > nominal group: goal marker - def art + noun common ms.

וַיַּבְדֵּל בֵּין הַמַּיִם [[אֲשֶׁר מִתַּחַת לָרָקִיעַ]] וּבֵין הַמַּיִם [[אֲשֶׁר מֵעַל לָרָקִיעַ]]. (b) Textuality > conj paratactic expansion / Mood > declarative: past / Transitivity > material: action. The Subject / Actor of the process is אֱלֹהִים *deity*, textually absent by ellipsis in this clause.

בֵּין הַמַּיִם [[אֲשֶׁר מִתַּחַת לָרָקִיעַ]] וּבֵין הַמַּיִם [[אֲשֶׁר מֵעַל לָרָקִיעַ]]	וַיַּבְדֵּל	**Constituents**
between the waters which are from under the barrier and between the waters which are from above the barrier	*and he made a separation*	**Translation**
	Theme	**Textuality**
	Finite	**Mood**
Circumstance	Process	**Transitivity**

וַיַּבְדֵּל. Theme: textual > clause conj + Theme: experiential / Finite > wayyiqtol 3ms / Process > hifil בדל.

בֵּין הַמַּיִם [[אֲשֶׁר מִתַּחַת לָרָקִיעַ]] וּבֵין הַמַּיִם [[אֲשֶׁר מֵעַל לָרָקִיעַ]]. Circumstance: location, place > prep phrase complex. Both prepositional phrases have an embedded relative clause.

בֵּין הַמַּיִם [[אֲשֶׁר מִתַּחַת לָרָקִיעַ]]. Prep phrase 1 > Head + Post-modifier.

בֵּין הַמַּיִם. Head > prep phrase: prep | def art + noun common mp.

אֲשֶׁר מִתַּחַת לָרָקִיעַ. (i) Post-modifier >> Textuality > embedded expansion: relative clause / Mood > declarative: non-past / Transitivity > relational: attribution. An embedded relative clause is capable of having a fully formed transitivity structure.

מִתַּחַת לָרָקִיעַ	אֲשֶׁר	**Constituents**
from under to the barrier	*which*	**Translation**
	Theme	**Textuality**
Attribute	Carrier	**Transitivity**

אֲשֶׁר. Theme: textual > pronoun relative / Carrier > antecedent הַמַּיִם *the waters.* The relative pronoun is at one and the same time a word that connects the embedded clause to the dominant clause and a word that holds a place in the Transitivity structure of the embedded clause itself.

מִתַּחַת לָרָקִיעַ. Attribute > prep phrase: prep + prep | prep + def art + noun common ms. The three prepositions מִתַּחַת לְ form a preposition group.

וּבֵין הַמַּיִם [[אֲשֶׁר מֵעַל לָרָקִיעַ]]. Group conj + Prep phrase 2 > Head + Post-modifier.

בֵּין הַמַּיִם. Head > prep | def art + noun common ms.

אֲשֶׁר מֵעַל לָרָקִיעַ. (ii) Post-modifier >> Textuality > embedded expansion: relative clause / Mood > declarative: non-past / Transitivity > relational: attribution.

מֵעַל לָרָקִיעַ	אֲשֶׁר	**Constituents**
from on to the barrier	*which*	**Translation**
	Theme	**Textuality**
Attribute	Carrier	**Transitivity**

אֲשֶׁר. Theme: textual > pronoun relative / Carrier > antecedent הַמַּיִם *the waters*.

מֵעַל לָרָקִיעַ. Attribute > prep phrase: prep + prep | prep + def art + noun common ms. These three מֵעַל לְ form another preposition group.

וַיְהִי־כֵן. (c) Textuality > conj paratactic expansion / Mood > declarative: past / Transitivity > existential.

כֵן	וַיְהִי־	**Constituents**
so	*and he was*	**Translation**
	Theme	**Textuality**
Subject	Finite	**Mood**
Existent	Process	**Transitivity**

וַיְהִי. Theme: textual > clause conj + Theme: experiential / Finite > wayyiqtol 3ms / Process > qal היה.

כֵן. Subject > ms / Existent > pronoun textual. כֵּן *such, so* is a pronoun type word that can substitute for a preceding clause complex, in this case referring back to the process of the creation of the barrier. Logically it might be best to consider 1:6(b-c) as the antecedent of the pronoun, but antecedent in a general sense. Within its own clause, כֵּן functions as the Existent of an existential process, *And (it was) so,* or *And such happened.*

// וַיִּקְרָ֨א אֱלֹהִ֛ים לָֽרָקִ֖יעַ שָׁמָ֑יִם // וַֽיְהִי־עֶ֥רֶב // 1:8
וַֽיְהִי־בֹ֖קֶר // י֥וֹם שֵׁנִֽי׃ פ

וַיִּקְרָא אֱלֹהִים לָרָקִיעַ שָׁמָיִם. (a) Textuality > conj paratactic expansion / Mood > declarative: past / Transitivity > verbal.

שָׁמָיִם	לָרָקִיעַ	אֱלֹהִים	וַיִּקְרָא	**Constituents**
heavens	*the barrier*	*deity*	*and he called*	**Translation**
			Theme	**Textuality**
		Subject	Finite	**Mood**
Verbiage	Target	Sayer	Process	**Transitivity**

וַיִּקְרָא. Theme: textual > clause conj + Theme: experiential / Finite > wayyiqtol 3ms / Process > qal קרא.

אֱלֹהִים. Subject > mp / Sayer > nominal group: noun common.

לָרָקִיעַ. Target > prep phrase: prep + def article + noun common ms.

שָׁמָיִם. Verbiage > nominal group: noun common ms. Note that the *patach* of שָׁמַיִם has been stress lengthened by the *atnach* accent and is in pause.

וַיְהִי־עֶרֶב. (b) Textuality > conj paratactic expansion / Mood > declarative: past / Transitivity > existential. See 1:5(c).

וַיְהִי־בֹקֶר. (c) Textuality > conj paratactic expansion / Mood > declarative: past / Transitivity > existential. See 1:5(d).

יוֹם שֵׁנִי. (d) Textuality > conj paratactic expansion / Mood > declarative: non-past / Transitivity > existential. An exclamative existential clause: *A second day (it is)!*

יוֹם שֵׁנִי	**Constituents**
a second day	**Translation**
Theme	**Textuality**
Subject	**Mood**
Existent	**Transitivity**

יוֹם שֵׁנִי. Subject > ms / Existent > noun common ms | numeral ms. שֵׁנִי *second* is an ordinal number. Compare 1:5(e) where the cardinal number *one*, rather than the ordinal number *first*, is used in what is otherwise the same structure.

Genesis 1:9-13

[9]And deity said, "Let be gathered the waters under the heavens to one place, and let the dry ground be seen." And such was. [10]And deity called the dry ground land, and the reservoir of the water he called seas. And

deity saw that (it was) good. [11]*And deity said, "Let the earth produce produce: vegetation seeding seed, treekind of fruit making fruit for its kind, which its seed is in it, on the earth."* [12]*And such happened.* [13]*And the earth brought out produce: vegetation seeding seed for its kinds, and treekind making fruit, which its seed is in it, for its kinds.*

1:9 /// וַיֹּאמֶר אֱלֹהִים // יִקָּווּ הַמַּיִם מִתַּחַת הַשָּׁמַיִם
אֶל־מָקוֹם אֶחָד // וְתֵרָאֶה הַיַּבָּשָׁה / וַיְהִי־כֵן׃

וַיֹּאמֶר אֱלֹהִים. (a) Textuality > conj paratactic expansion / Mood > declarative: past / Transitivity > verbal. See 1:3(a).

יִקָּווּ הַמַּיִם מִתַּחַת הַשָּׁמַיִם אֶל־מָקוֹם אֶחָד. (b) Textuality > appositive paratactic projection: quote / Mood > directive: jussive / Transitivity > material: action.

אֶל־מָקוֹם אֶחָד	הַמַּיִם מִתַּחַת הַשָּׁמַיִם	יִקָּווּ	**Constituents**
to one place	*the waters from under the heavens*	*and let them be gathered*	**Translation**
		Theme	**Textuality**
	Subject	Finite	**Mood**
Circumstance	Goal	Process	**Transitivity**

יִקָּווּ. Theme: textual > clause conj + Theme: experiential / Finite > jussive 3mp / Process > nifal קוה. The nifal stem can be interpreted either as middle voice (*gather themselves*) or passive voice (*be gathered*). It is rendered here as the passive, and if this is correct, then who is the agent? Could it be the divine council, perhaps implied by the *us/our* in 1:26(b)?

הַמַּיִם מִתַּחַת הַשָּׁמַיִם. Subject > mp (הַמַּיִם) / Goal > nominal group: Head + Post-modifier.

הַמַּיִם. Head > def art + noun common mp. Characteristic of passive processes, the Goal of the passive process in the transitivity view is the Subject in the interpersonal view. It is the Head of the Subject that agrees with the verb.

מִתַּחַת הַשָּׁמַיִם. Post-modifier > prep phrase: prep + prep | def art + noun common mp. This prep phrase specifies which waters, i.e. *the waters (which are) from under the heavens*, as if it were a restrictive relative clause. Even though it is a prepositional phrase, it is treated here as a modifier of the noun and hence part of the Goal. Alternately, it could be considered an independent Circumstance indicating the place from which the waters were to be gathered.

אֶל־מָקוֹם אֶחָד. Circumstance: location, place > prep phrase: prep + noun common ms | noun common ms.

וְתֵרָאֶה הַיַּבָּשָׁה. (c) Textuality > conj paratactic projection: quote / Mood > directive: jussive / Transitivity > mental: perception.

הַיַּבָּשָׁה	וְתֵרָאֶה	**Constituents**
the dry land	*and let her be seen*	**Translation**
	Theme	**Textuality**
Subject	Finite	**Mood**
Phenomenon	Process	**Transitivity**

וְתֵרָאֶה. Theme: textual > clause conj + Theme: experiential / Finite > jussive 3fs / Process > nifal ראה. An interesting feature of this mental process is that it really expresses an existential process, with הַיַּבָּשָׁה the dry land as the Existent. So in effect, the mental process is a grammatical metaphor for an existential process. For the notion of grammatical metaphor see Thompson, chapter 9.

הַיַּבָּשָׁה. Subject > 3fs / Phenomenon > nominal group: def art + noun common fs. Again, the object of the process is the Subject of the verb, as is characteristic of passive processes.

וַיְהִי־כֵן. (d) Textuality > conj paratactic expansion / Mood > declarative: past / Transitivity > existential. See 1:7(c).

1:10 // וַיִּקְרָא אֱלֹהִים לַיַּבָּשָׁה אֶרֶץ // וּלְמִקְוֵה הַמַּיִם
קָרָא יַמִּים // וַיַּרְא אֱלֹהִים / כִּי־טוֹב׃

וַיִּקְרָא אֱלֹהִים לַיַּבָּשָׁה אֶרֶץ. (a) Textuality > conj paratactic expansion / Mood > declarative: past / Transitivity > verbal.

אֶרֶץ	לַיַּבָּשָׁה	אֱלֹהִים	וַיִּקְרָא	**Constituents**
earth	*the dry land*	*deity*	*and he called*	**Translation**
			Theme	**Textuality**
		Subject	Finite	**Mood**
Verbiage	Target	Sayer	Process	**Transitivity**

וַיִּקְרָא. Theme: textual > clause conj + Theme: experiential / Finite > wayyiqtol 3ms / Process > qal קרא.

אֱלֹהִים. Subject > mp / Sayer > nominal group: noun common.

לַיַּבָּשָׁה. Target > prep phrase: prep + def art + noun common fs.

אֶרֶץ. Verbiage > nominal group: noun common fs.

וּלְמִקְוֵה הַמַּיִם קָרָא יַמִּים. (b) Textuality > conj paratactic expansion / Mood > declarative: past / Transitivity > verbal. The Subject / Sayer, אֱלֹהִים *deity*, is textually absent by ellipsis and inferable from clause (a).

יַמִּים	קָרָא	וּלְמִקְוֵה הַמַּיִם	**Constituents**
seas	*he called*	*and the reservoir of water*	**Translation**
		Theme	**Textuality**
	Finite		**Mood**
Verbiage	Process	Target	**Transitivity**

וּלְמִקְוֵה הַמַּיִם. Theme: textual > clause conj + Theme: experiential / Target > prep phrase: prep + noun common fs const | def art + noun common mp. We might ask, why was the Target made Theme in this clause, when its Target analog in the prior clause was part of the Rheme? By making the Target the Theme, the verb cannot be the

Theme. The action of this clause is not sequential in relation to the preceding, but simultaneous. If the verb were first, it would necessarily be marked for sequence.

קָרָא. Finite > qatal 3ms / Process > qal **קרא**.

יַמִּים. Verbiage > nominal group: noun common mp.

וַיַּרְא אֱלֹהִים. (c) Textuality > conj paratactic expansion / Mood > declarative: past / Transitivity > mental: perception. There is no explicit Phenomenon to this mental process; what did deity see? Compare 1:4(a-b) where a Phenomenon, *the light*, is specified in an otherwise identical construction to this one and the dependent clause that follows it. Is the Phenomenon here something as specific as the products *earth* and *seas*, or does it refer more abstractly to the processes that transpired on this day?

אֱלֹהִים	וַיַּרְא	**Constituents**
deity	*and he saw*	**Translation**
	Theme	**Textuality**
Subject	Finite	**Mood**
Senser	Process	**Transitivity**

וַיַּרְא. Theme: textual > clause conj + Theme: experiential / Finite > wayyiqtol 3ms / Process > qal **ראה**.

אֱלֹהִים. Subject > mp / Senser > nominal group: noun common.

כִּי־טוֹב. (d) Textuality > conj hypotactic projection: report / Mood > declarative: non-past / Transitivity > relational: attribution. The Carrier is the Phenomenon from the preceding clause where it was textually absent, and it is also absent here. Presumably the Carrier consists of the state of affairs, English *it*, resulting from all the entities that came into existence.

טוֹב	כִּי־	**Constituents**
good	*that*	**Translation**
Theme	Theme	**Textuality**
Attribute		**Transitivity**

כִּי־. Theme: textual > clause conj. It connects the dependent projection clause to the dominant mental process in clause (c).

טוֹב. Theme: experiential / Attribute > adj ms. This is the Attribute of the dependent relational process that constitutes this clause. In a textual sense, it is not clear precisely what is good.

1:11 // וַיֹּ֣אמֶר אֱלֹהִ֗ים // תַּֽדְשֵׁ֤א הָאָ֙רֶץ֙ דֶּ֔שֶׁא עֵ֚שֶׂב
מַזְרִ֣יעַ זֶ֔רַע עֵ֣ץ פְּרִ֞י עֹ֤שֶׂה פְּרִי֙ לְמִינ֔וֹ אֲשֶׁ֥ר זַרְעוֹ־ב֖וֹ
עַל־הָאָ֑רֶץ // וַֽיְהִי־כֵֽן׃

וַיֹּאמֶר אֱלֹהִים. (a) Textuality > conj paratactic expansion / Mood > declarative: past / Transitivity > verbal. See 1:3(a).

תַּדְשֵׁא הָאָרֶץ דֶּשֶׁא עֵשֶׂב [[מַזְרִיעַ זֶרַע]] עֵץ פְּרִי [[עֹשֶׂה פְּרִי לְמִינוֹ [[אֲשֶׁר זַרְעוֹ־בוֹ]]]] עַל־הָאָרֶץ. (b) Textuality > appositive paratactic projection: quote / Mood > directive: jussive / Transitivity > material: action.

עַל־הָאָרֶץ	דֶּשֶׁא עֵשֶׂב [[מַזְרִיעַ זֶרַע]] עֵץ פְּרִי [[עֹשֶׂה פְּרִי לְמִינוֹ [[אֲשֶׁר זַרְעוֹ־בוֹ]]]]	הָאָרֶץ	תַּדְשֵׁא	**Constituents**
on the earth	*produce: vegetation seeding seed, treekind of fruit making fruit for his kind, which his seed is in him*	*the earth*	*let her produce*	**Translation**
			Theme	**Textuality**
		Subject	Finite	**Mood**
Circumstance	Goal	Actor	Process	**Transitivity**

תַּדְשֵׁא. Theme: experiential / Finite > jussive 3fs / Process > hifil דשׁא.

הָאָרֶץ. Subject > fs / Actor > nominal group: def art + noun common.

דֶּשֶׁא עֵשֶׂב [[מַזְרִיעַ זֶרַע]] עֵץ פְּרִי [[עֹשֶׂה פְּרִי לְמִינוֹ [[אֲשֶׁר זַרְעוֹ־בוֹ]]]]. Goal > noun group complex: Head + Post-modifier. This is a rather dense collection of noun groups and embedded clauses, and it is especially challenging to determine the antecedents of the many pronouns. The Head indicates the general category *produce*, and the Post-modifier specifies two sub-categories, though no conjunction separates them. Both sub-categories have embedded clauses, and the second has an embedded clause within it.

דֶּשֶׁא. Head > nominal group: noun common collective ms. This is the most general category, followed by two sub-categories that extend its meaning. This noun is cognate with the verb, meaning they are both derived from the same root.

עֵשֶׂב [[מַזְרִיעַ זֶרַע]] עֵץ פְּרִי [[עֹשֶׂה פְּרִי לְמִינוֹ [[אֲשֶׁר זַרְעוֹ־בוֹ]]]]. Post-modifier > two nominal sub-groups.

עֵשֶׂב [[מַזְרִיעַ זֶרַע]]. Nominal sub-group 1 > Head + Post-modifier. *Vegetation seeding seed.*

עֵשֶׂב. Head > noun common collective ms.

מַזְרִיעַ זֶרַע. (i) Post-modifier >> Textuality > embedded expansion: relative clause / Transitivity > material: action. This type of relative clause does not employ the relative pronoun אֲשֶׁר *which*, and so is called an asyndetic (i.e. without connector) relative clause.

זֶרַע	מַזְרִיעַ	**Constituents**
seed	*seeding*	**Translation**
	Theme	**Textuality**
Goal	Actor / Process	**Transitivity**

מַזְרִיעַ. Theme: experiential / Actor > ptc ms / Process > hifil זרע. This is the material process of the first embedded relative clause. *Seed-producing seeder.*

זֶרַע. Goal > nominal group: noun common ms.

עֵץ פְּרִי [[עֹשֶׂה פְּרִי לְמִינוֹ [[אֲשֶׁר זַרְעוֹ־בוֹ]]]]. Nominal sub-group 2 > Head + Post-modifier. *Trees of fruit making fruit for its* (i.e. *the trees'*) *kind.*

עֵץ פְּרִי. Head > noun common collective ms const | noun common collective ms.

עֹשֶׂה פְּרִי לְמִינוֹ [[אֲשֶׁר זַרְעוֹ־בוֹ]]. (ii) Post-modifier >> Textuality > embedded expansion: relative clause / Transitivity > material: action. The Subject / Actor is עֵץ פְּרִי.

לְמִינוֹ [[אֲשֶׁר זַרְעוֹ־בוֹ]]	פְּרִי	עֹשֶׂה	**Constituents**
for his kind which his seed is in him	*fruit*	*making*	**Translation**
		Theme	**Textuality**
Beneficiary	Goal	Actor / Process	**Transitivity**

עֹשֶׂה. Theme: experiential / Actor > ptc ms / Process > qal עשׂה. This is the material process of the second embedded relative clause.

פְּרִי. Goal > nominal group: noun common collective ms.

לְמִינוֹ [[אֲשֶׁר זַרְעוֹ־בוֹ]]. Beneficiary > Head + Post-modifier.

לְמִינוֹ. Head > prep phrase: prep + noun common ms const + pronoun suffix 3ms, antecedent is עֵץ.

אֲשֶׁר זַרְעוֹ־בוֹ. (a') Post-modifier >> Textuality > embedded expansion / Mood > declarative: non-past / Transitivity > relational: attribution. This relative clause expands the meaning of something in the Head, i.e. *which his seed is in him*, meaning, kinds of trees whose seed is in its fruit.

בוֹ	זַרְעוֹ־	אֲשֶׁר	**Constituents**
in him	*his seed*	*which*	**Translation**
		Theme	**Textuality**
Attribute	Carrier		**Transitivity**

אֲשֶׁר. Theme: textual > pronoun relative. It serves to connect the embedded relative clause to prior text. Determining the specific antecedent is somewhat difficult in this case. Conceivably, it could be עֵץ *tree*, or מִין *kind*, or even פְּרִי *fruit*. All three are masculine in gender, thus, all are able to match the pronoun suffixes. We are interpreting the antecedent as מִין *kind*.

זַרְעוֹ־. Carrier > nominal group: noun common ms const + pronoun suffix 3ms; determining the antecedent is dependent on determining the antecedent of the relative pronoun, either מִין or עֵץ.

בוֹ. Attribute > prep phrase: prep + pronoun suffix 3ms, antecedent is פְּרִי—a different antecedent than that of the previous two pronouns.

עַל־הָאָרֶץ. Circumstance > prep phrase: prep + def art + noun common fs. It is the locational circumstance of the main material process: *let earth produce produce... on the earth*, though NRSV and NJPS attach it to the second nominal group complex of the Goal, and not the main clause.

וַיְהִי־כֵן. (c) Textuality > conj paratactic expansion / Mood > declarative: past / Transitivity > existential. See 1:7(c).

1:12 // וַתּוֹצֵא הָאָרֶץ דֶּשֶׁא עֵשֶׂב מַזְרִיעַ זֶרַע לְמִינֵהוּ
וְעֵץ עֹשֶׂה־פְּרִי אֲשֶׁר זַרְעוֹ־בוֹ לְמִינֵהוּ // וַיַּרְא
אֱלֹהִים / כִּי־טוֹב׃

וַתּוֹצֵא הָאָרֶץ דֶּשֶׁא עֵשֶׂב [[מַזְרִיעַ זֶרַע לְמִינֵהוּ]] וְעֵץ [[עֹשֶׂה־פְּרִי [[אֲשֶׁר זַרְעוֹ־בוֹ לְמִינֵהוּ]]]]. (a) Textuality > conj paratactic expansion / Mood > declarative: past / Transitivity > material: action. This clause is similar to 1:11(b) in its transitivity structure, though not in textuality or mood. And the embedded clauses show differences.

דֶּשֶׁא עֵשֶׂב [[מַזְרִיעַ זֶרַע לְמִינֵהוּ]] וְעֵץ [[עֹשֶׂה־פְּרִי [[אֲשֶׁר זַרְעוֹ־בוֹ]] לְמִינֵהוּ]]	הָאָרֶץ	וַתּוֹצֵא	**Constituents**
produce: vegetation seeding seed for his kinds, and treekind making fruit, which his seed is in him, for his kinds	*the earth*	*and she brought out*	**Translation**
		Theme	**Textuality**
	Subject	Finite	**Mood**
Goal	Actor	Process	**Transitivity**

וַתּוֹצֵא. Theme: textual > clause conj + Theme: experiential / Finite > wayyiqtol 3fs / Process > hifil יצא.

הָאָרֶץ. Subject > fs / Actor > nominal group: def art + noun common.

דֶּשֶׁא עֵשֶׂב [[מַזְרִיעַ זֶרַע לְמִינֵהוּ]] וְעֵץ [[עֹשֶׂה־פְּרִי [[אֲשֶׁר זַרְעוֹ־בוֹ]] לְמִינֵהוּ]]. Goal > nominal group complex: Head + Post-modifier.

דֶּשֶׁא. Head > nominal group: noun common collective ms.

עֵשֶׂב [[מַזְרִיעַ זֶרַע לְמִינֵהוּ]] וְעֵץ [[עֹשֶׂה־פְּרִי [[אֲשֶׁר זַרְעוֹ־בוֹ]] לְמִינֵהוּ]]. Post-modifier > two nominal sub-groups joined by a group conjunction, each with embedded clauses.

עֵשֶׂב [[מַזְרִיעַ זֶרַע לְמִינֵהוּ]]. Nominal sub-group 1 > Head + Post-modifier.

עֵשֶׂב. Head > noun common collective ms.

מַזְרִיעַ זֶרַע לְמִינֵהוּ. (i) Post-modifier >> Textuality > embedded expansion: relative clause / Transitivity > material: action. *Vegetation seeding seed for its* (i.e. *vegetation's*) *kinds.*

לְמִינֵהוּ	זֶרַע	מַזְרִיעַ	**Constituents**
for his kinds	*seed*	*seeding*	**Translation**
		Theme	**Textuality**
Beneficiary	Goal	Actor / Process	**Transitivity**

מַזְרִיעַ. Theme: experiential / Actor > ptc ms / Process > hifil זרע.

זֶרַע. Goal > nominal group: noun common ms.

לְמִינֵהוּ. Beneficiary > prep phrase: prep + noun common mp const + pronoun suffix 3ms, antecedent is עֵשֶׂב. This prep phrase is not present in its analogous clause 1:11(b)(i).

וְעֵץ [[עֹשֶׂה־פְּרִי [[אֲשֶׁר זַרְעוֹ־בוֹ]] לְמִינֵהוּ]]. Group conj + Nominal sub-group 2 > Head + Post-modifier.

עֵץ. Head > noun common collective ms.

עֹשֶׂה־פְּרִי [[אֲשֶׁר זַרְעוֹ־בוֹ]] לְמִינֵהוּ. (ii) Post-modifier >> Textuality > embedded expansion: relative clause / Transitivity > material: action. *Treekind making fruit which his* (i.e. *the treekind's*) *seed is in him* (i.e. *the fruit*) *for his (i.e. the treekind's) kinds.*

לְמִינֵהוּ	פְּרִי [[אֲשֶׁר זַרְעוֹ־בוֹ]]	עֹשֶׂה־	**Constituents**
for his kinds	*fruit, which his seed in him*	*making*	**Translation**
		Theme	**Textuality**
Beneficiary	Goal	Actor/Process	**Transitivity**

עֹשֶׂה. Theme: experiential / Actor > ptc ms / Process > qal עשׂה. This is the material process of the embedded relative clause.

פְּרִי [[אֲשֶׁר זַרְעוֹ־בוֹ]]. Goal > nominal group: Head + Post-modifier.

פְּרִי. Head > noun common collective ms.

אֲשֶׁר זַרְעוֹ־בוֹ. (a') Post-modifier >> Textuality > embedded expansion / Transitivity > relational: attribution. *Which its seed is in it*, meaning, trees whose seed is in their fruit.

בוֹ	זַרְעוֹ־	אֲשֶׁר	**Constituents**
in him	*his seed*	*which*	**Translation**
		Theme	**Textuality**
Attribute	Carrier		**Transitivity**

אֲשֶׁר. Theme: textual > pronoun relative. It serves to connect the embedded relative clause to prior text. Determining the specific antecedent is somewhat difficult in this case. Conceivably it could be עֵץ tree, or פְּרִי fruit, or מִין kind. All three are masculine in gender, so are able to match the following pronouns. We are interpreting the antecedent as עֵץ trees.

זַרְעוֹ־. Carrier > nominal group: noun common ms const + pronoun suffix 3ms, antecedent is עֵץ.

בוֹ. Attribute > prep phrase: prep + pronoun suffix 3ms, antecedent is פְּרִי.

לְמִינֵהוּ. Beneficiary > prep phrase: prep + common noun mp const + pronoun 3ms, antecedent is עֵץ.

וַיַּרְא אֱלֹהִים. (b) Textuality > conj paratactic expansion / Mood > declarative: past / Transitivity > mental: perception. See 1:10(c).

כִּי־טוֹב. (c) Textuality > hypotactic projection: report / Mood > declarative: non-past / Transitivity > relational: attribution. See 1:10(d).

1:13 // וַֽיְהִי־עֶרֶב // וַֽיְהִי־בֹקֶר // יוֹם שְׁלִישִׁי׃ פ

וַיְהִי־עֶרֶב. (b) Textuality > conj paratactic expansion / Mood > declarative: past / Transitivity > existential. See 1:5(c).

וַיְהִי־בֹקֶר. (c) Textuality > conj paratactic expansion / Mood > declarative: past / Transitivity > existential. See 1:5(d).

יוֹם שְׁלִישִׁי. (d) Textuality > conj paratactic expansion / Mood > declarative: past / Transitivity > existential process: Existent. An exclamative existential clause: *A third day (it is)!* Compare 1:5(e).

יוֹם שְׁלִישִׁי	**Constituents**
Third day	**Translation**
Theme	**Textuality**
Subject	**Mood**
Existent	**Transitivity**

יוֹם שְׁלִישִׁי. Subject > ms / Existent > nominal group: noun common ms | noun common ms. **שְׁלִישִׁי** is the ordinal number *third*.

Genesis 1:14-19

[14]And deity said, "Let lights be in the barrier of the heavens to make separation between the day and the night. And they will be for signs and for seasons and for days and years. [15]And they will be for lights in the barrier of the heavens to give light on the earth." And such happened. [16]And deity made the two big lights: the big light for the dominion of the day and the small light for the dominion of the night, and the stars. [17]And them deity put in the barrier of the heavens to give light on the earth [18]to exercise rule in the day and in the night and to make separation between the light and the dark. And deity saw that good it is. [19]And evening was. And morning was. Fourth day!

1:14 /// וַיֹּאמֶר אֱלֹהִים // יְהִי מְאֹרֹת בִּרְקִיעַ הַשָּׁמַיִם
לְהַבְדִּיל בֵּין הַיּוֹם וּבֵין הַלָּיְלָה // וְהָיוּ לְאֹתֹת
וּלְמוֹעֲדִים וּלְיָמִים וְשָׁנִים׃

וַיֹּאמֶר אֱלֹהִים. (a) Textuality > conj paratactic expansion / Mood > declarative: past / Transitivity > verbal. See 1:3(a).

יְהִי מְאֹרֹת בִּרְקִיעַ הַשָּׁמַיִם [[לְהַבְדִּיל בֵּין הַיּוֹם וּבֵין הַלָּיְלָה]]. (b) Textuality > appositive paratactic projection: quote / Mood > directive: jussive / Transitivity > existential.

[[לְהַבְדִּיל בֵּין הַיּוֹם וּבֵין הַלָּיְלָה]]	בִּרְקִיעַ הַשָּׁמַיִם	מְאֹרֹת	יְהִי	**Constituents**
to make separation between the day and between the night	*in the barrier of the heavens*	*lights*	*let him be*	**Translation**
			Theme	**Textuality**
		Subject	Finite	**Mood**
Circumstance	Circumstance	Existent	Process	**Transitivity**

יְהִי. Theme: experiential / Finite > jussive 3ms / Process > qal היה. The Mood structure is incongruent in so far as the Finite is 3ms and the Subject is fp.

מְאֹרֹת. Subject > fp! / Existent > nominal group: noun common.

בִּרְקִיעַ הַשָּׁמַיִם. Circumstance: location, place > prep phrase: prep + noun common ms construct ׀ def art + noun common mp. This specifies the locational setting of the lights.

לְהַבְדִּיל בֵּין הַיּוֹם וּבֵין הַלָּיְלָה. (i) Circumstance: purpose >> Textuality > embedded prep clause / Transitivity > material: action. This embedded dependent clause extends the meaning of the existential process of the dominant clause by specifying the role that the newly created lights would play.

בֵּין הַיּוֹם וּבֵין הַלָּיְלָה	לְהַבְדִּיל	**Constituents**
between the day and between the night	*to make separation*	**Translation**
	Theme	**Textuality**
Circumstance	Process	**Transitivity**

לְהַבְדִּיל. Theme: textual > prep + Theme: experiential / Process > inf const hifil בדל.

בֵּין הַיּוֹם וּבֵין הַלָּיְלָה. Circumstance: location, place > prep phrase complex: prep ׀ def art + noun common ms ׀ group conj + prep ׀ def art + noun common fs.

וְהָיוּ לְאֹתֹת וּלְמוֹעֲדִים וּלְיָמִים וְשָׁנִים. (c) Textuality > conj paratactic projection: quote / Mood > declarative: non-past / Transitivity > relational: attribution. This clause is a paratactic continuation of 1:14(b). The Carrier is מְאֹרֹת *lights* from 1:14(b) and is textually absent by ellipsis. This ellipsis, along with the conjunction, binds clauses 14(b) and 14(c) together.

לְאֹתֹת וּלְמוֹעֲדִים וּלְיָמִים וְשָׁנִים	וְהָיוּ	**Constituents**
for signs and for seasons and for days and years	*and they will be*	**Translation**
	Theme	**Textuality**
	Finite	**Mood**
Attribute	Process	**Transitivity**

וְהָיוּ. Theme: textual > clause conj + Theme: experiential / Finite > weqatal 3cp / Process > qal היה. The verb הָיָה plus לְ can mean *become*, and is here used to relate the Carrier constituent of the attributive relational process, מְאֹרֹת *lights* from 1:14(b), to its Attributes.

לְאֹתֹת וּלְמוֹעֲדִים וּלְיָמִים וְשָׁנִים. Attribute > prep phrase complex. Each of these prepositional phrases appears to articulate a way that the מְאֹרֹת *lights* will function in the newly created world. As is typical of Attributes in attributive relational processes, they are indefinite categories (usually represented as adjectives or indefinite common nouns) that function descriptively, in distinction from identifying relational processes, where the Identifiers are definite nouns.

לְאֹתֹת. Attribute 1 > prep phrase: prep + noun common fp.

וּלְמוֹעֲדִים. Group conj + Attribute 2 > prep phrase: prep + noun common mp.

וּלְיָמִים וְשָׁנִים. Group conj + Attribute 3 > prep phrase: prep + noun common mp | group conj + noun common fp. Notice that there is no ל prep on שָׁנִים. The coordinated nominal group יָמִים וְשָׁנִים together is the object of the preposition on יָמִים.

1:15 // וְהָיוּ לִמְאוֹרֹת בִּרְקִיעַ הַשָּׁמַיִם לְהָאִיר עַל־הָאָרֶץ
// וַיְהִי־כֵן׃

וְהָיוּ לִמְאוֹרֹת בִּרְקִיעַ הַשָּׁמַיִם [[לְהָאִיר עַל־הָאָרֶץ]].
(a) Textuality > conj paratactic projection: quote / Mood > declarative: non-past / Transitivity > relational: attribution. Presumably, the

Carrier is מְאֹרֹת from 1:14(b) and is textually absent by ellipsis. The lights will become lights in the barrier of the heavens. This is another paratactic continuation, along with 1:14(c), of 1:14(b).

[[לְהָאִיר עַל־הָאָרֶץ]]	בִּרְקִיעַ הַשָּׁמַיִם	לִמְאוֹרֹת	וְהָיוּ	**Constituents**
to give light on the earth	*in the barrier of the heavens*	*for lights*	*and they will be*	**Translation**
			Theme	**Textuality**
			Finite	**Mood**
Circumstance	Circumstance	Attribute	Process	**Transitivity**

וְהָיוּ. Theme: textual > clause conj + Theme: experiential / Finite > weqatal 3cp / Process > qal היה. As in 1:14(c), the verb הָיָה plus לְ is interpreted to mean *become.*

לִמְאוֹרֹת. Attribute > prep phrase: prep + noun common fp.

בִּרְקִיעַ הַשָּׁמַיִם. Circumstance: location, place > prep phrase: prep + noun common ms const | noun common mp.

לְהָאִיר עַל־הָאָרֶץ. (i) Circumstance: purpose >> Textuality > embedded prep clause / Transitivity > material: action.

עַל־הָאָרֶץ	לְהָאִיר	**Constituents**
on the earth	*to give light*	**Translation**
	Theme	**Textuality**
Circumstance	Process	**Transitivity**

לְהָאִיר. Theme: textual > prep + Theme: experiential / Process > inf const hifil אור. The hifil form essentially contains within itself both the Process (*give*) and the Goal of the process (*light*).

עַל־הָאָרֶץ. Circumstance: location, place > prep phrase: prep - def art + noun common fs.

וַיְהִי־כֵן. (b) Textuality > conj paratactic expansion / Mood > declarative: past / Transitivity > existential. See 1:7(c).

1:16 // וַיַּ֣עַשׂ אֱלֹהִ֔ים אֶת־שְׁנֵ֥י הַמְּאֹרֹ֖ת הַגְּדֹלִ֑ים אֶת־
הַמָּא֤וֹר הַגָּדֹל֙ לְמֶמְשֶׁ֣לֶת הַיּ֔וֹם וְאֶת־הַמָּא֤וֹר הַקָּטֹן֙
לְמֶמְשֶׁ֣לֶת הַלַּ֔יְלָה וְאֵ֖ת הַכּוֹכָבִֽים׃

וַיַּעַשׂ אֱלֹהִים אֶת־שְׁנֵי הַמְּאֹרֹת הַגְּדֹלִים אֶת־הַמָּאוֹר הַגָּדֹל [[לְמֶמְשֶׁלֶת הַיּוֹם]] וְאֶת־הַמָּאוֹר הַקָּטֹן [[לְמֶמְשֶׁלֶת הַלַּיְלָה]] וְאֵת הַכּוֹכָבִים. (a) Textuality > conj paratactic expansion / Mood > declarative: past / Transitivity > material: action. This clause is much longer than the average clause in biblical Hebrew, and its length is due to its elaborate Goal (or direct object) and its expansions. The Goal consists of two noun groups. The first noun group (*the two big lights*) is extended by two separate noun groups, each of which is then extended by an embedded clause. The second noun group is a single noun (*the stars*). Here is the hierarchic structure of the clause:

And made deity (Process + Actor)
the two big lights: (Goal 1)
the big light for the dominion of the day (Goal 1a)
and the small light for the dominion of the night (Goal 1b)
and the stars. (Goal 2)

אֶת־שְׁנֵי הַמְּאֹרֹת הַגְּדֹלִים אֶת־הַמָּאוֹר הַגָּדֹל [[לְמֶמְשֶׁלֶת הַיּוֹם]] וְאֶת־הַמָּאוֹר הַקָּטֹן [[לְמֶמְשֶׁלֶת הַלַּיְלָה]] וְאֵת הַכּוֹכָבִים	אֱלֹהִים	וַיַּעַשׂ	**Constituents**
the two big lights: the big light for the dominion of the day and the small light for the dominion of the night, and the stars	*deity*	*and he made*	**Translation**
		Theme	**Textuality**
	Subject	Finite	**Mood**
Goal	Actor	Process	**Transitivity**

וַיַּעַשׂ. Theme: textual > clause conj + Theme: experiential / Finite > wayyiqtol 3ms / Process > qal עשׂה.

אֱלֹהִים. Subject > mp / Actor > nominal group: noun common.

אֶת־שְׁנֵי הַמְּאֹרֹת הַגְּדֹלִים אֶת־הַמָּאוֹר הַגָּדֹל לְמֶמְשֶׁלֶת הַיּוֹם וְאֶת־הַמָּאוֹר הַקָּטֹן לְמֶמְשֶׁלֶת הַלַּיְלָה וְאֵת הַכּוֹכָבִים. Goal > nominal group complex. There are two first-level goals: Goal 1 is אֶת־שְׁנֵי הַמְּאֹרֹת הַגְּדֹלִים, *the two big lights*, and Goal 2 is אֵת הַכּוֹכָבִים *the stars*. Goal 1 is expanded when each of the two big lights is given further specification, though it does sound a bit strange when the second "big" light is called the "small" light.

אֶת־שְׁנֵי הַמְּאֹרֹת הַגְּדֹלִים אֶת־הַמָּאוֹר הַגָּדֹל לְמֶמְשֶׁלֶת הַיּוֹם וְאֶת־הַמָּאוֹר הַקָּטֹן לְמֶמְשֶׁלֶת הַלַּיְלָה. Goal 1 > nominal group complex: Head = Goal + Post-modifier (= Goal 1a + Goal 1b). This is Goal 1 as a whole. What follows breaks it down into its components.

אֶת־שְׁנֵי הַמְּאֹרֹת הַגְּדֹלִים. Goal 1 > nominal group: goal marker + noun common mp const | def art + noun common mp | def art + adj mp. *The two big lights.* The following two nominal groups extend the meaning of this Head nominal group. The two sub-groups are joined to each other by a group conjunction, but as a group it is simply juxtaposed to its Head.

אֶת־הַמָּאוֹר הַגָּדֹל לְמֶמְשֶׁלֶת הַיּוֹם. Goal 1a > nominal group: goal marker - def art + noun common ms | def art + adj ms | prep phrase > prep + noun common fs const | def art + noun common ms.

וְאֶת־הַמָּאוֹר הַקָּטֹן לְמֶמְשֶׁלֶת הַלַּיְלָה. Group conj + Goal 1b > nominal group: goal marker - def art + noun common ms | def art + adj ms | prep phrase: prep + noun common fs const | def art + noun common fs.

וְאֵת הַכּוֹכָבִים. Goal 2 > nominal group: group conj + goal marker | def art + noun mp.

1:17-18 // וַיִּתֵּן אֹתָם אֱלֹהִים בִּרְקִיעַ הַשָּׁמָיִם לְהָאִיר
עַל־הָאָרֶץ: וְלִמְשֹׁל בַּיּוֹם וּבַלַּיְלָה וּֽלֲהַבְדִּיל בֵּין הָאוֹר
וּבֵין הַחֹשֶׁךְ // וַיַּרְא אֱלֹהִים / כִּי־טוֹב:

וַיִּתֵּן אֹתָם אֱלֹהִים בִּרְקִיעַ הַשָּׁמָיִם [[לְהָאִיר עַל־הָאָרֶץ
וְלִמְשֹׁל בַּיּוֹם וּבַלַּיְלָה וּלֲהַבְדִּיל בֵּין הָאוֹר וּבֵין הַחֹשֶׁךְ]].

(a) Textuality > conj paratactic expansion / Mood > declarative: past / Transitivity > material: action. This declarative clause is the realization of the directive clause 1:15(a). Clause 1:17(a) extends into 1:18, and serves as an example of how verse divisions do not always align with clause divisions.

[[לְהָאִיר עַל־הָאָרֶץ וְלִמְשֹׁל בַּיּוֹם וּבַלַּיְלָה וּלֲהַבְדִּיל בֵּין הָאוֹר וּבֵין הַחֹשֶׁךְ]]	בִּרְקִיעַ הַשָּׁמָיִם	אֱלֹהִים	אֹתָם	וַיִּתֵּן	**Constituents**
to give light on the earth to rule in the day and in the night and to make separation between the light and between the dark	*in the barrier of the heavens*	*deity*	*them*	*and he put*	**Translation**
				Theme	**Textuality**
		Subject		Finite	**Mood**
Circumstance	Circumstance	Actor	Goal	Process	**Transitivity**

וַיִּתֵּן. Theme: textual > clause conj + Theme: experiential / Finite > wayyiqtol 3ms / Process > qal **נתן**.

אֹתָם. Goal > nominal group: goal marker + pronoun suffix 3mp, antecedent is **מְאֹרֹת** in 1:14(b).

אֱלֹהִים. Subject > mp / Actor > nominal group: noun common.

בִּרְקִיעַ הַשָּׁמָיִם. Circumstance: location, place > prep phrase: prep + noun common ms const | def art + noun common mp.

[[לְהָאִיר עַל־הָאָרֶץ וְלִמְשֹׁל בַּיּוֹם וּבַלַּיְלָה וּֽלֲהַבְדִּיל בֵּין הָאוֹר וּבֵין הַחֹשֶׁךְ]]. Circumstance: cause, purpose > prep phrase complex consisting of three conjoined embedded prepositional purpose clauses.

לְהָאִיר עַל־הָאָרֶץ. (i) Circumstance 1: cause, purpose >> Textuality > embedded prep clause / Transitivity > material: action. This clause expands the meaning of the enclosing clause by explaining why deity put the lights in the barrier. This embedded clause takes what otherwise might be the independent clause (*They provided illumination on the earth*) and, by changing the verb to non-finite, enables it to be embedded within another clause (... *to provide illumination on the earth*) and become a constituent of that clause. This is the first of three expansion clauses embedded within clause 1:17(a).

עַל־הָאָרֶץ	לְהָאִיר	**Constituents**
on the earth	*to give light*	**Translation**
	Theme	**Textuality**
Circumstance	Process	**Transitivity**

לְהָאִיר. Theme: textual > prep + Theme: experiential / Process > inf const hifil אור.

עַל־הָאָרֶץ. Circumstance: location, place > prep - def art + noun common fs.

1:18 וְלִמְשֹׁל֙ בַּיּ֣וֹם וּבַלַּ֔יְלָה וֽ֣לֲהַבְדִּ֔יל בֵּ֥ין הָא֖וֹר וּבֵ֣ין
הַחֹ֑שֶׁךְ // וַיַּ֥רְא אֱלֹהִ֖ים / כִּי־טֽוֹב׃

וְלִמְשֹׁל בַּיּוֹם וּבַלַּיְלָה. (ii) Group conj + Circumstance 2: cause, purpose >> Textuality > embedded prep clause / Transitivity > material: action. This embedded clause and the following one complete clause 1:17(a).

בַּיּוֹם וּבַלַּיְלָה	וְלִמְשֹׁל	**Constituents**
in the day and in the night	*and to exercise rule*	**Translation**
	Theme	**Textuality**
Range	Process	**Transitivity**

וְלִמְשֹׁל. Theme: textual > group conj + prep + Theme: experiential / Process > inf const qal מָשַׁל. This process has been interpreted with preposition בְּ to designate the object ruled as Goal (or direct object). Another possibility, and the one proposed here, is to understand the prepositional phrase as indicating the Range or domain over which rule is exercised. Are day and night entities such that they can be ruled?

בַּיּוֹם וּבַלַּיְלָה. Range > prep phrase complex: prep + def art + noun common ms | group conj + prep + def art + noun common fs.

וּלֲהַבְדִּיל בֵּין הָאוֹר וּבֵין הַחֹשֶׁךְ. (iii) Group conj + Circumstance 3: cause, purpose >> Textuality > embedded prep clause / Transitivity > material: action.

בֵּין הָאוֹר וּבֵין הַחֹשֶׁךְ	וּלֲהַבְדִּיל	**Constituents**
between the light and between the darkness	*and to make separation*	**Translation**
	Theme	**Textuality**
Circumstance	Process	**Transitivity**

וּלֲהַבְדִּיל. Theme: textual > group conj + prep + Theme: experiential / Process > inf const hifil בָּדַל.

בֵּין הָאוֹר וּבֵין הַחֹשֶׁךְ. Circumstance: location, place > prep phrase complex: prep | def art + noun common ms | group conj + prep | def art + noun common ms.

וַיַּרְא אֱלֹהִים. (b) Textuality > conj paratactic expansion / Mood > declarative: past / Transitivity > mental: perception. See 1:10(c).

כִּי־טוֹב. (c) Textuality > conj hypotactic projection: report / Mood > declarative: non-past / Transitivity > relational: attribution. See 1:10(d).

1:19 // וַֽיְהִי־עֶ֥רֶב // וַֽיְהִי־בֹ֖קֶר // י֥וֹם רְבִיעִֽי׃ פ

וַֽיְהִי־עֶרֶב. (a) Textuality > conj paratactic expansion / Mood > declarative: past / Transitivity > existential. See 1:5(c).

וַֽיְהִי־בֹקֶר. (b) Textuality > conj paratactic expansion / Mood > declarative: past / Transitivity > existential. See 1:5(d).

יוֹם רְבִיעִי. (c) Textuality > conj paratactic expansion / Mood > declarative: past / Transitivity > existential. An exclamative existential clause: *A fourth day (it is)!* Compare 1:5(e) and 1:8(d).

יוֹם רְבִיעִי. Subject > ms / Existent > noun common ms | numeral ms. רְבִיעִי is the ordinal number *fourth*.

Genesis 1:20-23

[20]And deity said, "Let the waters swarm with a swarm of living being, and let fowl fly on the earth, on the face of the barrier of the heavens." [21]And deity created the big serpents and all living creeping being with which the waters swarmed for their kinds, and all fowl of wing for his kinds. And deity saw that good it is. [22]And them deity blessed by saying, "Bear fruit. And multiply. And fill the waters in the seas. And the fowl, let it multiply in the earth." [23]And evening was. And morning was. Fifth day!

1:20 /// וַיֹּ֣אמֶר אֱלֹהִ֔ים // יִשְׁרְצ֣וּ הַמַּ֔יִם שֶׁ֖רֶץ נֶ֣פֶשׁ חַיָּ֑ה
// וְעוֹף֙ יְעוֹפֵ֣ף עַל־הָאָ֔רֶץ עַל־פְּנֵ֖י רְקִ֥יעַ הַשָּׁמָֽיִם׃

וַיֹּאמֶר אֱלֹהִים. (a) Textuality > conj paratactic expansion / Mood > declarative: past / Transitivity > verbal. See 1:3(a).

יִשְׁרְצוּ הַמַּיִם שֶׁרֶץ נֶפֶשׁ חַיָּה. (b) Textuality > appositive paratactic projection: quote / Mood > directive: jussive / Transitivity > behavioral.

שֶׁרֶץ נֶפֶשׁ חַיָּה	הַמַּיִם	יִשְׁרְצוּ	**Constituents**
a swarm of living being	*the waters*	*and let them swarm*	**Translation**
		Theme	**Textuality**
	Subject	Finite	**Mood**
Range	Behaver	Process	**Transitivity**

יִשְׁרְצוּ. Theme: experiential / Finite > yiqtol/jussive 3mp / Process > qal שׁרץ. The jussive has the same form as the 3mp yiqtol.

הַמַּיִם. Behaver > nominal group: def art + noun common mp.

שֶׁרֶץ נֶפֶשׁ חַיָּה. Range > nominal group: noun common collective fs const | noun common fs | noun common collective/adjective fs. The relationship of these three nominals is not grammatically clear, in part because חַיָּה can be a noun or an adjective. Also, the term נֶפֶשׁ is provocatively broad and can mean *being* or *life* or many other things. A possible construction, and the one reflected in the translation here, is that the first two words are a construct noun phrase and the third word is an adjective modifying נֶפֶשׁ resulting in the rendition: *a swarm of living being.* The Range of a behavioral process is a nominal clause constituent that does not function as a true participant to the process, but rather adds further specification to the process itself. This is common with behavioral processes, and can be seen in a clause such as *he laughed a hearty laugh.*

וְעוֹף יְעוֹפֵף עַל־הָאָרֶץ עַל־פְּנֵי רְקִיעַ הַשָּׁמָיִם. (c) Textuality > conj paratactic projection: quote / Mood > directive: jussive / Transitivity > behavioral.

עַל־הָאָרֶץ עַל־פְּנֵי רְקִיעַ הַשָּׁמָיִם	יְעוֹפֵף	וְעוֹף	**Constituents**
on the earth on the face of the barrier of the heavens	*let him fly*	*and fowl*	**Translation**
		Theme	**Textuality**
	Finite	Subject	**Mood**
Circumstance	Process	Behaver	**Transitivity**

וְעוֹף. Theme: textual > clause conj + Theme: experiential / Subject > ms / Behaver > nominal group: noun common collective.

יְעוֹפֵף. Finite > yiqtol/jussive 3ms / Process > polel עוף. Note that the Subject and the Finite are cognate.

עַל־הָאָרֶץ עַל־פְּנֵי רְקִיעַ הַשָּׁמָיִם. Circumstance: location, place > prep phrase complex: Head + Post-modifier.

עַל־הָאָרֶץ. Head > prep phrase: prep - def art + noun common ms.

עַל־פְּנֵי רְקִיעַ הַשָּׁמָיִם. Post-modifier > prep phrase: prep - noun common mp const | noun common ms const | def art + noun common mp. This prep phrase adds specification to the preceding one.

1:21 // וַיִּבְרָא אֱלֹהִים אֶת־הַתַּנִּינִם הַגְּדֹלִים וְאֵת כָּל־נֶפֶשׁ
הַחַיָּה הָרֹמֶשֶׂת אֲשֶׁר שָׁרְצוּ הַמַּיִם לְמִינֵהֶם וְאֵת כָּל־
עוֹף כָּנָף לְמִינֵהוּ // וַיַּרְא אֱלֹהִים / כִּי־טוֹב׃

וַיִּבְרָא אֱלֹהִים אֶת־הַתַּנִּינִם הַגְּדֹלִים וְאֵת כָּל־נֶפֶשׁ הַחַיָּה הָרֹמֶשֶׂת [[אֲשֶׁר שָׁרְצוּ הַמַּיִם]] לְמִינֵהֶם וְאֵת כָּל־עוֹף כָּנָף לְמִינֵהוּ. (a) Textuality > conj paratactic expansion / Mood > declarative: past / Transitivity > material: action.

אֶת־הַתַּנִּינִם הַגְּדֹלִים וְאֵת כָּל־נֶפֶשׁ הַחַיָּה הָרֹמֶשֶׂת [[אֲשֶׁר שָׁרְצוּ הַמַּיִם]] לְמִינֵהֶם וְאֵת כָּל־עוֹף כָּנָף לְמִינֵהוּ	אֱלֹהִים	וַיִּבְרָא	**Constituents**
the big serpents and all living creeping being, which the waters swarmed, for their kinds and all fowl of wing for his kinds	*deity*	*and he created*	**Translation**
		Theme	**Textuality**
	Subject	Finite	**Mood**
Goal	Actor	Process	**Transitivity**

וַיִּבְרָא. Theme: textual > clause conj + Theme: experiential / Finite > wayyiqtol 3ms / Process > qal ברא.

אֱלֹהִים. Subject > mp / Actor > nominal group: noun common.

אֶת־הַתַּנִּינִם הַגְּדֹלִים וְאֵת כָּל־נֶפֶשׁ הַחַיָּה הָרֹמֶשֶׂת [[אֲשֶׁר שָׁרְצוּ הַמַּיִם]] לְמִינֵהֶם וְאֵת כָּל־עוֹף כָּנָף לְמִינֵהוּ. Goal > nominal group complex: [Head (Goal 1 + Goal 2) + Post-modifier] + [Head (Goal 3) + Post-modifier]. The Goal consists of three individual goals. The first two goals appear to form a sub-group, both of which are extended by the embedded relative clause אֲשֶׁר שָׁרְצוּ הַמַּיִם and then by the לְמִינֵהֶם prepositional phrase. This is suggested by the 3cp form of שָׁרְצוּ in the relative clause, and the 3mp form of the pronoun in לְמִינֵהֶם. Some translators, however, apply the relative clause and prepositional phrase only to the second Goal.

אֶת־הַתַּנִּינִם הַגְּדֹלִים. Goal 1 > nominal group: goal marker - def art + noun common mp | def art + adj mp. Notice the "defective" form of the noun's mp morpheme: it lacks a *yod*.

וְאֵת כָּל־נֶפֶשׁ הַחַיָּה הָרֹמֶשֶׂת. Group conj + Goal 2 > nominal group: goal marker | noun common collective ms const - noun common collective fs | def art + noun/adj common collective fs | def art + ptc fs qal רָמַשׂ.

אֲשֶׁר שָׁרְצוּ הַמַּיִם. (i) Post-modifier 1 >> Textuality > embedded expansion: relative clause / Mood > declarative: past / Transitivity > behavioral. See 1:20(b) in support of interpreting הַמַּיִם as the Subject / Behaver of the verb in this embedded clause.

הַמַּיִם	שָׁרְצוּ	אֲשֶׁר	**Constituents**
the waters	*they swarmed*	*which*	**Translation**
		Theme	**Textuality**
Subject	Finite		**Mood**
Behaver	Process	Range	**Transitivity**

אֲשֶׁר. Theme: textual > pronoun relative + Theme: experiential / Range > the two Goals of the preceding clause.

שָׁרְצוּ. Finite > qatal 3cp / Process > qal שׁרץ.

הַמַּיִם. Subject > mp / Behaver > nominal group: noun common.

לְמִינֵהֶם. Post-modifier 2 > prep phrase: prep + noun common mp const + pronoun suffix 3mp, antecedent is הַתַּנִּינִם, the Head of Goal 1 and כָּל, the Head of Goal 2.

וְאֵת כָּל־עוֹף כָּנָף. Group conj + Goal 3 > nominal group: goal marker ׀ noun common collective ms const - noun common collective ms const ׀ noun common mp.

לְמִינֵהוּ. Post-modifier > prep phrase: prep + noun common mp const + pronoun suffix 3ms, antecedent is כָּל.

וַיַּרְא אֱלֹהִים. (b) Textuality > conj paratactic expansion / Mood > declarative: past / Transitivity > mental: perception. See 1:10(c).

כִּי־טוֹב. (c) Textuality > hypotactic projection: report / Mood > declarative: past / Transitivity > relational: attribution. See 1:10(d).

1:22 // וַיְבָרֶךְ אֹתָם אֱלֹהִים לֵאמֹר // פְּרוּ // וּרְבוּ //
וּמִלְאוּ אֶת־הַמַּיִם בַּיַּמִּים // וְהָעוֹף יִרֶב בָּאָרֶץ׃

Notice that clauses (b-e) are all directive quotes. The first three contain imperatives (i.e. second person), while clause (e) contains a jussive (i.e. third person). So, the Subject of the imperatives, presumably the serpents and crawling creatures of 1:21, were addressed directly, while the birds were addressed obliquely, using a jussive.

וַיְבָרֶךְ אֹתָם אֱלֹהִים לֵאמֹר. (a) Textuality > conj paratactic expansion / Mood > declarative: past / Transitivity > material: action.

לֵאמֹר	אֱלֹהִים	אֹתָם	וַיְבָרֶךְ	**Constituents**
by saying	*deity*	*them*	*and he blessed*	**Translation**
			Theme	**Textuality**
	Subject		Finite	**Mood**
Circumstance	Sayer	Receiver	Process	**Transitivity**

וַיְבָ֣רֶךְ. Theme: textual > clause conj + Theme: experiential / Finite > wayyiqtol 3ms / Process > piel ברך.

אֹתָ֛ם. Goal > nominal group: goal marker + pronoun suffix 3mp, antecedent is the three Goals in 1:21(a).

אֱלֹהִ֖ים. Subject > mp / Sayer > nominal group: noun common.

לֵאמֹ֑ר. Circumstance: manner, means > prep phrase: prep + inf const qal אמר.

פְּר֣וּ. (b) Textuality > appositive paratactic projection: quote / Mood > directive: imperative / Transitivity > material: action.

פְּר֣וּ	**Constituents**
bear fruit	**Translation**
Theme	**Textuality**
Finite	**Mood**
Process	**Transitivity**

פְּר֣וּ. Theme: experiential / Finite > impv mp / Process > qal פרה.

וּרְב֗וּ. (c) Textuality > conj paratactic projection: quote / Mood > directive: imperative / Transitivity > material: action.

וּרְב֗וּ	**Constituents**
and multiply	**Translation**
Theme	**Textuality**
Finite	**Mood**
Process	**Transitivity**

וּרְב֗וּ. Theme: textual > clause conj + Theme: experiential / Finite > impv mp / Process > qal רבה.

וּמִלְא֤וּ אֶת־הַמַּ֙יִם֙ בַּיַּמִּ֔ים. (d) Textuality > conj paratactic projection: quote / Mood > directive: imperative / Transitivity > material: action.

בַּיַּמִּים	אֶת־הַמַּיִם	וּמִלְאוּ	**Constituents**
in the seas	*the waters*	*and fill*	**Translation**
		Theme	**Textuality**
		Finite	**Mood**
Circumstance	Goal	Process	**Transitivity**

וּמִלְאוּ. Theme: textual > clause conj + Theme: experiential / Finite > impv mp / Process > qal מלא.

אֶת־הַמַּיִם. Goal > nominal group: goal marker - def art + noun common mp.

בַּיַּמִּים. Circumstance: location, place > prep phrase: prep + def art + noun common mp. This prepositional phrase, which brings greater specification to הַמַּיִם *the water*, is needed because there are two great bodies of water (see 1:10).

וְהָעוֹף יִרֶב בָּאָרֶץ. (e) Textuality > conj paratactic projection: quote / Mood > directive: jussive / Transitivity > material: action.

בָּאָרֶץ	יִרֶב	וְהָעוֹף	**Constituents**
in the earth	*let him multiply*	*and the fowl*	**Translation**
		Theme	**Textuality**
	Finite	Subject	**Mood**
Circumstance	Process	Actor	**Transitivity**

וְהָעוֹף. Theme: textual > clause conj + Theme: experiential / Subject > ms / Actor > nominal group: def art + noun common collective.

יִרֶב. Finite > jussive! 3ms / Process > qal רבה. The waters were addressed directly by imperatives, while the fowl are addressed indirectly with the jussive. The sky is not addressed, *bring forth fowl.*

בָּאָרֶץ. Circumstance: location, place > prep phrase: prep + def art + noun common fs.

1:23 // וַיְהִי־עֶרֶב // וַיְהִי־בֹקֶר // יוֹם חֲמִישִׁי׃ פ

וַיְהִי־עֶרֶב. (a) Textuality > conj paratactic expansion / Mood > declarative: past / Transitivity > existential. See 1:5(c).

וַיְהִי־בֹקֶר. (b) Textuality > conj paratactic expansion / Mood > declarative: past / Transitivity > existential. See 1:5(d).

יוֹם חֲמִישִׁי. (c) Textuality > conj paratactic expansion / Mood > declarative: past / Transitivity > existential. An exclamative existential clause: *A fifth day (it is)!* Compare 1:5(e) and 1:8(d).

יוֹם חֲמִישִׁי. Subject > ms / Existent > noun common. | numeral ms. חֲמִישִׁי is the ordinal number *fifth.*

Genesis 1:24-31

[24]And deity said, "Let the earth bring forth living being for her kind: beastkind and creeperkind, and animalkind of earth for her kind." And such happened. [25]And deity made the animalkind of the earth for her kind and the beastkind for her kind and all of the creeperkind of the ground for their kind. And deity saw that good it is. [26]And deity said, "Let us make humankind into our image as our likeness. And they will rule within the fish of the sea and within the fowl of the heavens and within the beastkind and within all of the earth and within all of the creeperkind, the ones creeping on the earth." [27]And deity created the humankind in his image. Into an image of deity he created him. Male and female he created them. [28]And them deity blessed. And to them deity said, "Bear fruit. And multiply. And fill the earth. And subdue her. And rule within the fish of the sea and within the fowl of the heavens and within all livingkind, the ones creeping on the earth." [29]And deity said, "Now I gave to you all plantkind seeding seed which is on the face of all the earth and all treekind which in it is fruit of treekind seeding seed. To you it will be for food. [30]And to all animalkind of the earth and to all fowl of the heavens and to all creeping-on-the-earth-kind, in which is living being, all green plantkind is for food." [31]And deity saw all which he made. And now, very good it is! And evening was. And morning was. Sixth day!

1:24 /// וַיֹּ֣אמֶר אֱלֹהִ֗ים // תּוֹצֵ֨א הָאָ֜רֶץ נֶ֤פֶשׁ חַיָּה֙ לְמִינָ֔הּ
בְּהֵמָ֥ה וָרֶ֛מֶשׂ וְחַֽיְתוֹ־אֶ֖רֶץ לְמִינָ֑הּ // וַֽיְהִי־כֵֽן׃

וַיֹּאמֶר אֱלֹהִים. (a) Textuality > conj paratactic expansion / Mood > declarative: past / Transitivity > verbal. See 1:3(a).

תּוֹצֵא הָאָרֶץ נֶפֶשׁ חַיָּה לְמִינָהּ בְּהֵמָה וָרֶמֶשׂ וְחַיְתוֹ־אֶרֶץ לְמִינָהּ. (b) Textuality > appositive paratactic projection: quote /Mood > directive: jussive / Transitivity > material: action. One grammatical issue of this clause is how to cluster the nominal groups in the Goal such that they are properly related. Based on the placement of the two לְמִינָהּ prepositional phrases and the potential antecedents of their pronoun suffixes, we interpret the בְּהֵמָה וָרֶמֶשׂ nominal group as an appositive expansion of the prior Goal and not of the following one.

נֶפֶשׁ חַיָּה לְמִינָהּ בְּהֵמָה וָרֶמֶשׂ וְחַיְתוֹ־אֶרֶץ לְמִינָהּ	הָאָרֶץ	תּוֹצֵא	**Constituents**
living being for her kind: beastkind and creeperkind, and animal-of-earth-kind for her kind	*the earth*	*let her bring forth*	**Translation**
		Theme	**Textuality**
	Subject	Finite	**Mood**
Goal	Actor	Process	**Transitivity**

תּוֹצֵא. Theme: textual > clause conj + Theme: experiential / Finite > jussive 3fs / Process > hifil **יצא**.

הָאָרֶץ. Subject > fs / Actor > nominal group: def art + noun common.

נֶפֶשׁ חַיָּה לְמִינָהּ בְּהֵמָה וָרֶמֶשׂ וְחַיְתוֹ־אֶרֶץ לְמִינָהּ. Goal > nominal group complex: Goal 1 + Goal 2.

נֶפֶשׁ חַיָּה לְמִינָהּ בְּהֵמָה וָרֶמֶשׂ. Goal 1 > nominal group: Head + Post-modifier 1 (prep phrase) + Post-modifier 2 (nominal group).

נֶפֶשׁ חַיָּה. Head > nominal group: noun common collective fs | noun/adj fs. This is either a construct noun phrase or a noun + adjective phrase.

לְמִינָהּ. Post-modifier 1 > prep phrase: prep + common noun ms const + pronoun suffix 3fs, antecedent is נֶפֶשׁ.

בְּהֵמָה וָרֶמֶשׂ. Post-modifier 2 > nominal group: noun common fs | group conj + noun common ms. Notice the וָ hendiadys form of the conjunction; compare 1:2 תֹהוּ וָבֹהוּ. This noun group is interpreted as an expansion of נֶפֶשׁ חַיָּה, the Head nominal group; it specifies which creatures are meant to be included.

וְחַיְתוֹ־אֶרֶץ לְמִינָהּ. Group conj + Goal 2 > nominal group: Head + Post-modifier.

חַיְתוֹ־אֶרֶץ. Head > nominal group: noun common collective fs const | noun common fs.

לְמִינָהּ. Post-modifier > prep phrase: prep + noun common ms const + pronoun suffix 3fs, antecedent is חַיְתוֹ *animalkind*.

וַיְהִי־כֵן. (c) Textuality > conj paratactic expansion / Mood > declarative: past / Transitivity > existential. See 1:7(c).

1:25 // וַיַּעַשׂ אֱלֹהִים אֶת־חַיַּת הָאָרֶץ לְמִינָהּ וְאֶת־
הַבְּהֵמָה לְמִינָהּ וְאֵת כָּל־רֶמֶשׂ הָאֲדָמָה לְמִינֵהוּ //
וַיַּרְא אֱלֹהִים / כִּי־טוֹב׃

וַיַּעַשׂ אֱלֹהִים אֶת־חַיַּת הָאָרֶץ לְמִינָהּ וְאֶת־הַבְּהֵמָה לְמִינָהּ וְאֵת כָּל־רֶמֶשׂ הָאֲדָמָה לְמִינֵהוּ. (a) Textuality > conj paratactic expansion / Mood > declarative: past / Transitivity > material: action.

וְאֶת־הַבְּהֵמָה לְמִינָהּ וְאֵת כָּל־רֶמֶשׂ הָאֲדָמָה לְמִינֵהוּ	אֱלֹהִים	וַיַּעַשׂ	**Constituents**
the animalkind of the earth for her kind and the beastkind for her kind and all of the creeperkind of the ground for their kind	*deity*	*and he made*	**Translation**
		Theme	**Textuality**
	Subject	Finite	**Mood**
Goal	Actor	Process	**Transitivity**

וַיַּעַשׂ. Theme: textual > clause conj + Theme: experiential / Finite > wayyiqtol 3ms / Process > qal עשׂה.

אֱלֹהִים. Subject > mp / Actor > nominal group: noun common.

אֶת־חַיַּת הָאָרֶץ לְמִינָהּ וְאֶת־הַבְּהֵמָה לְמִינָהּ וְאֵת כָּל־רֶמֶשׂ הָאֲדָמָה לְמִינֵהוּ. Goal > nominal group complex. The Goal consists of three separate goals, each marked with the goal marker and each extended with a prepositional phrase.

אֶת־חַיַּת הָאָרֶץ לְמִינָהּ. Goal 1 > nominal group: Head + Post-modifier.

אֶת־חַיַּת הָאָרֶץ. Head > nominal group: goal marker - noun common collective fs const | def art + noun common fs.

לְמִינָהּ. Post-modifier > prep phrase: prep + common noun ms const + pronoun 3fs, antecedent is חַיַּת.

וְאֶת־הַבְּהֵמָה לְמִינָהּ. Group conj + Goal 2 > nominal group: Head + Post-modifier.

וְאֶת־הַבְּהֵמָה. group conj + Head > nominal group: goal marker - def art + noun common fs.

לְמִינָהּ. Post-modifier > prep phrase: prep + common noun ms const + pronoun 3fs, antecedent הַבְּהֵמָה.

וְאֵת כָּל־רֶמֶשׂ הָאֲדָמָה לְמִינֵהוּ. Group conj + Goal 3 > nominal group: Head + Post-modifier.

וְאֵת כָּל־רֶמֶשׂ הָאֲדָמָה. group conj + Head > nominal group: goal marker | noun common collective ms const - noun common collective ms const | def art + noun common fs.

לְמִינֵהוּ. Post-modifier > prep phrase: prep + common noun mp const + pronoun 3ms, antecedent is כָּל. Notice *his kinds* (plural) in constrast to *her kind* (singular) in the preceding two nominal group complexes.

וַיַּרְא אֱלֹהִים. (b) Textuality > conj paratactic expansion / Mood > declarative: past / Transitivity > mental: perception. See 1:10(c).

כִּי־טוֹב. (c) Textuality > hypotactic projection: report / Transitivity > relational: attribution. The Subject / Carrier is left undefined. Though the Attribute is 3ms!, the Subject is most likely the Goal of 1:25(a): the animalkind, beastkind, and creeperkind. NJPS: *And God saw that this was good.* Compare 1:10(d).

טוֹב	כִּי־	**Constituents**
good	*that*	**Translation**
Theme	Theme	**Textuality**
Attribute		**Transitivity**

כִּי־. Theme: textual > conj.

טוֹב. Theme: experiential / Attribute > adj ms.

1:26 // וַיֹּאמֶר אֱלֹהִים // נַעֲשֶׂה אָדָם בְּצַלְמֵנוּ כִּדְמוּתֵנוּ
// וְיִרְדּוּ בִדְגַת הַיָּם וּבְעוֹף הַשָּׁמַיִם וּבַבְּהֵמָה וּבְכָל־
הָאָרֶץ וּבְכָל־הָרֶמֶשׂ הָרֹמֵשׂ עַל־הָאָרֶץ:

וַיֹּאמֶר אֱלֹהִים. (a) Textuality > conj paratactic expansion / Mood > declarative: past / Transitivity > verbal. See 1:3(a).

נַעֲשֶׂה אָדָם בְּצַלְמֵנוּ כִּדְמוּתֵנוּ. (b) Textuality > appositive paratactic projection: quote / Mood > directive / Transitivity > material: action. This clause is the program statement, as it were, for the creation of people. Apparently deity wanted his divine council to agree on the shape and function of this new entity. So, this particular clause is not articulating the very act of creation—that comes later in 1:27—but the intention of the process.

בְּצַלְמֵנוּ כִּדְמוּתֵנוּ	אָדָם	נַעֲשֶׂה	**Constituents**
into our image as our likeness	*humankind*	*let us make*	**Translation**
		Theme	**Textuality**
		Finite	**Mood**
Circumstance	Goal	Process	**Transitivity**

נַעֲשֶׂה. Theme: experiential / Finite > cohortative 1cp / Process > qal עשׂה. The material process *making* can be thought of as either creative or transformative. In other words, it calls something into being, or it takes something already existing and transforms it in some way. In this case the act is creative.

אָדָם. Goal > nominal group: noun common collective ms. This is the first time אָדָם appears in the biblical text.

בְּצַלְמֵנוּ כִּדְמוּתֵנוּ. Circumstance: role > prep phrase complex: Head + Post-modifier.

בְּצַלְמֵנוּ. Head > prep phrase: prep + noun common ms const + pronoun suffix 1cp, antecedent includes אֱלֹהִים in clause (a) and is often thought also to include the so-called divine council. The prep has been variously interpreted. Here it is interpreted as the Circumstance of the material process expressing the intended role of the element that will be created.

כִּדְמוּתֵנוּ. Post-modifier > prep phrase: prep + noun common fs const + pronoun suffix 1cp; for the antecedent, see the preceding paragraph. Often בְּצַלְמֵנוּ and כִּדְמוּתֵנוּ are translated as if they were stating the same concept using different words. NRSV: *in our image, according to our likeness.* As an appositional Post-modifier, it is here understood to be an expansion of the preceding prepositional phrase, again expressing its functional role.

וְיִרְדּוּ בִדְגַת הַיָּם וּבְעוֹף הַשָּׁמַיִם וּבַבְּהֵמָה וּבְכָל־הָאָרֶץ וּבְכָל־הָרֶמֶשׂ [[הָרֹמֵשׂ עַל־הָאָרֶץ]]. (c) Textuality > conj paratactic projection: quote / Mood > declarative: past / Transitivity > material: action. The Subject / Actor is **אָדָם** *humankind* in the preceding clause, textually absent by ellipsis, and this singular term, understood as collective, is matched to a plural verb.

בִדְגַת הַיָּם וּבְעוֹף הַשָּׁמַיִם וּבַבְּהֵמָה וּבְכָל־הָאָרֶץ וּבְכָל־הָרֶמֶשׂ [[הָרֹמֵשׂ עַל־הָאָרֶץ]]	וְיִרְדּוּ	**Constituents**
in the fish of the sea and in the fowl of the heavens and in the beastkind and in all of the earth and in all of the creeperkind, the ones creeping on the earth	*and they will rule*	**Translation**
	Theme	**Textuality**
	Finite	**Mood**
Scope	Process	**Transitivity**

וְיִרְדּוּ. Theme: textual > clause conj + Theme: experiential / Finite > yiqtol/jussive 3mp / Process > qal **רדה**. The verb form could be rendered as either indicative or directive. The material process of *ruling* does not construe the process of ruling as having a Goal consisting of entities that are ruled, but as a domain, whose territory or Scope is articulated by a set of five coordinated prepositional phrases. Versions typically render this clause as if humankind would rule the fish of the sea, etc. But this does not make logical or conceptual sense. Instead, our analysis suggests that this clause specifies the realm *within* which, more so than *over* which, humanity exercises authority on behalf of deity and the divine council.

בִדְגַת הַיָּם וּבְעוֹף הַשָּׁמַיִם וּבַבְּהֵמָה וּבְכָל־הָאָרֶץ וּבְכָל־הָרֶמֶשׂ הָרֹמֵשׂ עַל־הָאָרֶץ. Scope > prep phrase complex: five prep phrases, the last of which is post-modified by a relative clause.

בִדְגַת הַיָּם. Scope 1 > prep phrase: prep + noun common collective fs const | def art + noun common ms.

וּבְעוֹף הַשָּׁמַיִם. Group conj + Scope 2 > prep phrase: prep + noun common collective fs const | def art + noun common mp.

וּבַבְּהֵמָה. Group conj + Scope 3 > prep phrase: prep + def art + noun common collective fs.

וּבְכָל־הָאָרֶץ. Group conj + Scope 4 > prep phrase: prep + noun common collective ms const - def art + noun common fs.

וּבְכָל־הָרֶמֶשׂ הָרֹמֵשׂ עַל־הָאָרֶץ. Group conj + Scope 5 > prep phrase: Head + Post-modifier.

בְּכָל־הָרֶמֶשׂ. Head > prep phrase: prep + noun common ms const - def art + noun common collective ms.

הָרֹמֵשׂ עַל־הָאָרֶץ. (i) Post-modifier >> Textuality > embedded expansion: relative clause / Transitivity > behavioral. Lacking a relative pronoun, this is an asyndetic relative clause.

עַל־הָאָרֶץ	הָרֹמֵשׂ	**Constituents**
on the earth	*the one crawling*	**Translation**
	Theme	**Textuality**
Circumstance	Behaver/Process	**Transitivity**

הָרֹמֵשׂ. Theme: experiential / Behaver > def art + ptc ms / Process > qal רמשׂ.

עַל־הָאָרֶץ. Circumstance: location, place > prep phrase: prep - def art + noun common fs.

1:27 // וַיִּבְרָא אֱלֹהִים | אֶת־הָאָדָם בְּצַלְמוֹ // בְּצֶלֶם
אֱלֹהִים בָּרָא אֹתוֹ // זָכָר וּנְקֵבָה בָּרָא אֹתָם׃

וַיִּבְרָא אֱלֹהִים אֶת־הָאָדָם בְּצַלְמוֹ. (a) Textuality > conj paratactic expansion / Mood > declarative: past / Transitivity > material: action.

בְּצַלְמוֹ	אֶת־הָאָדָם	אֱלֹהִים	וַיִּבְרָא	**Constituents**
into his image	*the humankind*	*deity*	*and he created*	**Translation**
			Theme	**Textuality**
		Subject	Finite	**Mood**
Circumstance	Goal	Actor	Process	**Transitivity**

וַיִּבְרָא. Theme: textual > clause conj + Theme: experiential / Finite > wayyiqtol 3ms / Process > qal ברא.

אֱלֹהִים. Subject > mp / Actor > nominal group: noun common.

אֶת־הָאָדָם. Goal > nominal group: goal marker - def art + noun common ms. The collective noun אָדָם from 1:26(b) is now definite, since it is known. Has it now also become an individual instead of collective? The pronoun suffix on אֹתָם *them* in clause (c) may suggest it should still be understood as a collective here, if its antecedent is הָאָדָם rather than זָכָר וּנְקֵבָה *male and female.*

בְּצַלְמוֹ. Circumstance: role, product > prep phrase: prep + noun common ms const + pronoun 3ms, antecedent is אֱלֹהִים (consistently till now, this 3mp noun has been treated as a 3ms Subject).

בְּצֶלֶם אֱלֹהִים בָּרָא אֹתוֹ. (b) Textuality > appositive paratactic expansion / Mood > declarative: past / Transitivity > material: action. The Subject / Actor of the process is אֱלֹהִים, textually absent by ellipsis, though it is present in the prep phrase.

אֹתוֹ	בָּרָא	בְּצֶלֶם אֱלֹהִים	**Constituents**
him	*he created*	*into an image of deity*	**Translation**
		Theme	**Textuality**
	Finite		**Mood**
Goal	Process	Circumstance	**Transitivity**

בְּצֶלֶם אֱלֹהִים. Theme: experiential / Circumstance: role, product > prep phrase: prep + noun common ms const ׀ noun common mp. In this case, אֱלֹהִים could be taken in a more general collective sense, or perhaps as an attribute rather than as a noun.

בָּרָא. Finite > qatal 3ms /Process > qal ברא.

אֹתוֹ. Goal > nominal group: goal marker + pronoun suffix 3ms, antecedent is הָאָדָם understood as a collective.

זָכָר וּנְקֵבָה בָּרָא אֹתָם. (c) Textuality > appositive paratactic expansion / Mood > declarative: past / Transitivity > material: action. The Subject / Actor is אֱלֹהִים, textually absent here by ellipsis.

אֹתָם	בָּרָא	זָכָר וּנְקֵבָה	**Constituents**
them	*he created*	*male and female*	**Translation**
		Theme	**Textuality**
	Finite		**Mood**
Goal	Process	Scope	**Transitivity**

זָכָר וּנְקֵבָה. Theme: experiential > nominal group complex / Scope > noun common ms ı group conj + noun common fs.

בָּרָא. Finite > qatal 3ms / Process > qal ברא.

אֹתָם. Goal > nominal group: goal marker + pronoun suffix 3mp, antecedent is הָאָדָם. Notice that now the Goal is plural.

1:28 // וַיְבָ֣רֶךְ אֹתָם֮ אֱלֹהִים֒ // וַיֹּ֨אמֶר לָהֶ֜ם אֱלֹהִ֗ים //
פְּר֥וּ // וּרְב֛וּ // וּמִלְא֥וּ אֶת־הָאָ֖רֶץ // וְכִבְשֻׁ֑הָ //
וּרְד֞וּ בִּדְגַ֤ת הַיָּם֙ וּבְע֣וֹף הַשָּׁמַ֔יִם וּבְכָל־חַיָּ֖ה הָֽרֹמֶ֥שֶׂת
עַל־הָאָֽרֶץ׃

וַיְבָרֶךְ אֹתָם אֱלֹהִים. (a) Textuality > conj paratactic expansion / Mood > declarative: past / Transitivity > material: action.

אֱלֹהִים	אֹתָם	וַיְבָרֶךְ	**Constituents**
deity	*them*	*and he blessed*	**Translation**
		Theme	**Textuality**
Subject		Finite	**Mood**
Actor	Goal	Process	**Transitivity**

וַיְבָרֶךְ. Theme: textual > clause conj + Theme: experiential / Finite > wayyiqtol 3ms / Process > piel ברך. This clause is not followed immediately by a quote clause, as might be expected, but by a verbal clause. For this reason it may be better to understand the process of this clause as material rather than verbal.

אֹתָם. Goal > nominal group: goal marker + pronoun suffix 3mp, antecedent is הָאָדָם.

אֱלֹהִים. Subject > mp / Actor > nominal group: noun common. This clause renominalizes its Subject / Actor. It is the same as in the preceding clauses, but it has not been made explicit since 1:27(a).

וַיֹּאמֶר לָהֶם אֱלֹהִים. (b) Textuality > conj paratactic expansion / Mood > declarative: past / Transitivity > verbal.

אֱלֹהִים	לָהֶם	וַיֹּאמֶר	**Constituents**
deity	*to them*	*and he said*	**Translation**
		Theme	**Textuality**
Subject		Finite	**Mood**
Sayer	Receiver	Process	**Transitivity**

וַיֹּאמֶר. Theme: textual > clause conj + Theme: experiential / Finite > wayyiqtol 3ms / Process > qal אמר.

לָהֶם. Receiver > prep phrase: prep + pronoun suffix 3mp, antecedent is הָאָדָם.

אֱלֹהִים. Subject > mp / Sayer > nominal group: noun common.

פְּרוּ. (c) Textuality > appositive paratactic projection: quote / Mood > directive: imperative / Transitivity > material: action.

פְּרוּ	**Constituents**
bear fruit	**Translation**
Theme	**Textuality**
Finite	**Mood**
Process	**Transitivity**

פְּרוּ. Theme: experiential / Finite > impv mp / Process > qal פרה.

וּרְבוּ. (d) Textuality > conj paratactic projection: quote / Mood > directive: imperative / Transitivity > material: action.

וּרְבוּ	**Constituents**
and multiply	**Translation**
Theme	**Textuality**
Finite	**Mood**
Process	**Transitivity**

וּרְבוּ. Theme: textual > clause conj + Theme: experiential / Finite > impv mp / Process > qal רבה.

וּמִלְאוּ אֶת־הָאָרֶץ. (e) Textuality > conj paratactic projection: quote / Mood > directive: imperative / Transitivity > material: action.

אֶת־הָאָרֶץ	וּמִלְאוּ	**Constituents**
the earth	*and fill*	**Translation**
	Theme	**Textuality**
	Finite	**Mood**
Goal	Process	**Transitivity**

וּמִלְאוּ. Textuality > clause conj + Theme: experiential / Finite > impv mp / Process > qal מלא.

אֶת־הָאָרֶץ. Goal > nominal group: goal marker - def art + noun common fs.

וְכִבְשֻׁהָ. (f) Textuality > conj paratactic projection: quote / Mood > directive: imperative / Transitivity > material: action.

וְכִבְשֻׁהָ	**Constituents**
and subdue her	**Translation**
Theme	**Textuality**
Finite	**Mood**
Process + Goal	**Transitivity**

וְכִבְשֻׁהָ. Theme: textual > clause conj + Theme: experiential / Finite > impv mp / Process > qal כבשׁ + Goal > pronoun suffix 3fs, antecedent is הָאָרֶץ in clause (e). This is the first time we have seen the Goal of a material process expressed as a pronoun attached to the Finite verb form. This has the effect of including it within the Theme of the clause. If it were a separate word—a pronoun suffix attached to the goal marker—it would be the Rheme.

וּרְדוּ בִּדְגַת הַיָּם וּבְעוֹף הַשָּׁמַיִם וּבְכָל־חַיָּה [[הָרֹמֶשֶׂת עַל־הָאָרֶץ]]. (g) Textuality > conj paratactic projection: quote / Mood > directive: imperative / Transitivity > material: action.

בִּדְגַת הַיָּם וּבְעוֹף הַשָּׁמַיִם וּבְכָל־חַיָּה [[הָרֹמֶשֶׂת עַל־הָאָרֶץ]]	וּרְדוּ	**Constituents**
in the fish of the sea and in the fowl of the heavens and in all of the animalkind, the ones creeping on the earth	*and rule*	**Translation**
	Theme	**Textuality**
	Finite	**Mood**
Scope	Process	**Transitivity**

וּרְדוּ. Theme: textual > clause conj + Theme: experiential / Finite > impv mp / Process > qal רדה.

בִּדְגַת הַיָּם וּבְעוֹף הַשָּׁמַיִם וּבְכָל־חַיָּה [[הָרֹמֶשֶׂת עַל־הָאָרֶץ]]. Scope > prep phrase complex: three prepositional phrases, the last one post-modified by a relative clause. By construing this clause constituent as Scope rather than Goal we are motivated by the fact that humans cannot rule fish, fowl, etc. as such, but they may exercise authority over a domain of living creatures. Both syntax, using prep phrases, and semantics would suggest this. See also 1:26(c).

בִּדְגַת הַיָּם. Scope 1 > prep phrase: prep + noun common collective fs const | def art + noun common ms.

וּבְעוֹף הַשָּׁמַיִם. Group conj + Scope 2 > prep phrase: prep + noun common collective ms const | def art + noun common mp.

וּבְכָל־חַיָּה הָרֹמֶשֶׂת עַל־הָאָרֶץ. Group conj + Scope 3 > prep phrase: Head + Post-modifier.

בְּכָל־חַיָּה. Head > prep phrase: prep + noun common ms const - noun common collective fs.

הָרֹמֶשֶׂת עַל־הָאָרֶץ. (i) Post-modifier >> Textuality > embedded expansion: relative clause / Transitivity > behavioral. This clause extends the meaning of חַיָּה, a very general term, by defining it more specifically and limiting its domain.

עַל־הָאָרֶץ	הָרֹמֶשֶׂת	**Constituents**
on the earth	*the one crawling*	**Translation**
	Theme	**Textuality**
Circumstance	Behaver / Process	**Transitivity**

הָרֹמֶשֶׂת. Theme: experiential / Behaver > def art + ptc fs / Process > qal רמשׂ.

עַל־הָאָרֶץ. Circumstance: location, place > prep phrase: prep - noun common fs.

1:29 // וַיֹּ֣אמֶר אֱלֹהִ֗ים // הִנֵּה֩ נָתַ֨תִּי לָכֶ֜ם אֶת־כָּל־עֵ֣שֶׂב
| זֹרֵ֣עַ זֶ֗רַע אֲשֶׁר֙ עַל־פְּנֵ֣י כָל־הָאָ֔רֶץ וְאֶת־כָּל־הָעֵ֛ץ
אֲשֶׁר־בּ֥וֹ פְרִי־עֵ֖ץ זֹרֵ֣עַ זָ֑רַע // לָכֶ֥ם יִֽהְיֶ֖ה לְאָכְלָֽה׃

Clause 1:29(c) is continued in 1:30.

וַיֹּאמֶר אֱלֹהִים. (a) Textuality > conj paratactic expansion / Mood > declarative: past / Transitivity > verbal. See 1:3(a).

הִנֵּה נָתַתִּי לָכֶם אֶת־כָּל־עֵשֶׂב [[זֹרֵעַ זֶרַע]] [[אֲשֶׁר עַל־פְּנֵי כָל־הָאָרֶץ]] וְאֶת־כָּל־הָעֵץ [[אֲשֶׁר־בּוֹ פְרִי־עֵץ]] [[זֹרֵעַ זָרַע]]. (b) Textuality > appositive paratactic projection: quote / Mood > declarative: past / Transitivity > material: action.

אֶת־כָּל־עֵשֶׂב [[זֹרֵעַ זֶרַע]] [[אֲשֶׁר עַל־פְּנֵי כָל־הָאָרֶץ]] וְאֶת־כָּל־הָעֵץ [[אֲשֶׁר־בּוֹ פְרִי־עֵץ]] [[זֹרֵעַ זָרַע]]	לָכֶם	נָתַתִּי	הִנֵּה	**Constituents**
all plantkind seeding seed which is on the face of all the earth and all of the treekind which in him is fruit of a treekind seeding seed	*to you*	*I gave*	*now*	**Translation**
		Theme	Theme	**Textuality**
		Finite		**Mood**
Goal	Beneficiary	Process		**Transitivity**

הִנֵּה. Theme: textual / Adjunct: textual > contra-expectation. The particle הִנֵּה is used more than a thousand times in BH. It has often been translated *behold* or *indeed* out of an intuitive sense that is it associated with something notable or new in the clause. From a functional perspective we can observe that (1) הִנֵּה is always in Theme position within the clause, though it is not always the first component of the clause, (2) it is not a constituent of the experiential transitivity structure of the clause, and (3) it is almost always found in quotes. On this basis it would appear to be an adjunct that marks the constituent that follows it (or is attached to it as a suffix, e.g. Gen 6:17 הִנְנִי—so still follows it) as intentionally thematic. As such it belongs to the

Textuality system and functions to reinforce or call attention to the experiential Theme of the clause, with which it is always associated. Furthermore, it marks the Theme as something unexpected or new or noteworthy in relation to the context of situation or in relation to the prior text. The constituent that follows הִנֵּה typically represents a break with with went before, or is an unexpected consequence of what went before. Such a linguistic resource is useful, even necessary, because the Theme position of a clause is structured to establish continuity with the prior text or the context. Thus, the textual adjunct הִנֵּה is available to signal a break in continuity where otherwise a break would not be expected. In the case of the present clause, הִנֵּה marks נָתַתִּי as the experiential Theme in such as way that it is taken as a significant and new moment in the course of creation. And, indeed, it is a new development, in so far as the product of day three's creative activity is now given over to humans for their use. The question of how to render הִנֵּה remains open. Neither *behold*, *look*, nor *indeed* quite communicate the element of contra-expectation contained within the Theme when it is marked by הִנֵּה. *Now* may not be ideal, though it does suggest the break in continuity signaled by the הִנֵּה textual adjunct. See also MNK 328–30.

נָתַתִּי. Theme: experiential / Finite > qatal 1cs / Process > qal נָתַן.

לָכֶם. Beneficiary > prep phrase: prep + pronoun suffix 2mp, antecedent is הָאָדָם. A second person pronoun rather than a third person one is used here; humanity is being addressed directly.

אֶת־כָּל־עֵשֶׂב [[זֹרֵעַ זֶרַע]] [[אֲשֶׁר עַל־פְּנֵי כָל־הָאָרֶץ]] וְאֶת־כָּל־הָעֵץ [[אֲשֶׁר־בּוֹ פְרִי־עֵץ]] [[זֹרֵעַ זָרַע]]. Goal > nominal group complex: the Goal constituent consists of two conjoined sub-Goals, each a nominal group complex.

אֶת־כָּל־עֵשֶׂב [[זֹרֵעַ ׀ זֶרַע]] [[אֲשֶׁר עַל־פְּנֵי כָל־הָאָרֶץ]]. Goal 1 > nominal group: Head + Post-modifier 1 + Post-modifier 2. The Masoretes inserted the ׀ *paseq* into this group because the two words are very similar, and presumably they did not want anyone to think that this represented a dittographic scribal error.

אֶת־כָּל־עֵשֶׂב. Head > nominal group: goal marker - noun common collective ms const - noun common ms.

זֹרֵעַ זֶרַע. (i) Post-modifier 1 >> Textuality > embedded expansion: relative clause / Transitivity > material: action. This clause extends the meaning of עֵשֶׂב, which is the Subject / Actor of the process.

זֶרַע	זֹרֵעַ	**Constituents**
seed	*seeding*	**Translation**
	Theme	**Textuality**
Goal	Actor/Process	**Transitivity**

זֹרֵעַ. Theme: experiential / Actor > ptc ms / Process > qal זרע.

זֶרַע. Goal > nominal group: noun common ms.

אֲשֶׁר עַל־פְּנֵי כָל־הָאָרֶץ. (ii) Post-modifier 2: Textuality > embedded expansion: relative clause / Mood > declarative: non-past / Transitivity > relational: attribution.

עַל־פְּנֵי כָל־הָאָרֶץ	אֲשֶׁר	**Constituents**
on the face of all of the earth	*which*	**Translation**
	Theme	**Textuality**
Complement	Subject	**Mood**
Attribute	Carrier	**Transitivity**

אֲשֶׁר. Theme: textual and experiential > relative pronoun / Subject > ms (כָּל) / Carrier > antecedent כָּל־עֵשֶׂב.

עַל־פְּנֵי כָל־הָאָרֶץ. Complement / Attribute > prep phrase: prep - noun common mp const | noun common collective mp const - def art + noun common fs.

וְאֶת־כָּל־הָעֵץ [[אֲשֶׁר־בּוֹ פְרִי־עֵץ [[זֹרֵעַ זָרַע]]]]. Group conj + Goal 2 > nominal group: Head + Post-modifier.

וְאֶת־כָּל־הָעֵץ. Head > nominal group: goal marker - noun common collective ms const - def art + noun common ms.

אֲשֶׁר־בּוֹ פְּרִי־עֵץ [[זֹרֵעַ זָרַע]]. (i) Post-modifier >> Textuality > embedded expansion: relative clause / Mood > declarative: non-past / Transitivity > relational: attribution.

פְּרִי־עֵץ [[זֹרֵעַ זָרַע]]	בּוֹ	אֲשֶׁר־	**Constituents**
fruit of treekind seeding seed	*in him*	*which*	**Translation**
		Theme	**Textuality**
Subject	Complement		**Mood**
Carrier	Attribute		**Transitivity**

אֲשֶׁר־. Theme: textual > pronoun relative, antecedent is כָּל־הָעֵץ *all of the treekind.* Within the experiential structure of this embedded clause it functions as the object of the following preposition בְּ.

בּוֹ. Complement / Attribute > prep phrase: prep + pronoun 3ms, antecedent is כָּל־הָעֵץ.

[[זֹרֵעַ זָרַע]] פְּרִי־עֵץ. Subject > ms (פְּרִי) / Carrier > Head + Post-modifier.

פְּרִי־עֵץ. Head > nominal group: noun common collective ms const - noun common ms.

זֹרֵעַ זָרַע. (ii) Post-modifier >> Textuality > embedded expansion: relative clause / Transitivity > material: action. This clause extends the meaning of פְּרִי־עֵץ, which is the Subject / Actor of the process of this embedded clause. This is an asyndetic relative clause.

זָרַע	זֹרֵעַ	**Constituents**
seed	*seeding*	**Translation**
	Theme	**Textuality**
Goal	Actor / Process	**Transitivity**

זֹרֵעַ. Theme: experiential / Actor > ptc ms / Process > qal זרע. *Seeder seeding.*

זָרַע. Goal > nominal group: noun common ms. זֶרַע became זָרַע with a *qamets* here due to stress lengthening of the *atnach.*

לָכֶם יִהְיֶה לְאָכְלָה. (b) Textuality > appositive paratactic projection: quote / Mood > declarative: non-past / Transitivity > relational: attribution. The grammatical 3ms Subject / Carrier is not explicitly identified here; grammatically it would most likely be the collective noun כָּל *all*. The logical Subject / Carrier would then be all the vegetation and trees detailed in 1:29(a).

לְאָכְלָה	יִהְיֶה	לָכֶם	**Constituents**
for food	*he will be*	*to you*	**Translation**
		Theme	**Textuality**
	Finite		**Mood**
Attribute	Process	Beneficiary	**Transitivity**

לָכֶם. Beneficiary > prep phrase: prep + pronoun 2mp, antecedent is הָאָדָם *the humanity*.

יִהְיֶה. Finite > yiqtol 3ms / Process > qal היה.

לְאָכְלָה. Attribute > prep phrase: prep + common noun fs.

1:30 // וּֽלְכָל־חַיַּ֣ת הָ֠אָרֶץ וּלְכָל־ע֨וֹף הַשָּׁמַ֜יִם וּלְכֹ֣ל רוֹמֵ֣שׂ
עַל־הָאָ֗רֶץ אֲשֶׁר־בּוֹ֙ נֶ֣פֶשׁ חַיָּ֔ה אֶת־כָּל־יֶ֥רֶק עֵ֖שֶׂב
לְאָכְלָ֑ה // וַֽיְהִי־כֵֽן׃

וּלְכָל־חַיַּת הָאָרֶץ וּלְכָל־עוֹף הַשָּׁמַיִם וּלְכֹל [[רוֹמֵשׂ עַל־הָאָרֶץ [[אֲשֶׁר־בּוֹ נֶפֶשׁ חַיָּה]]]] אֶת־כָּל־יֶרֶק עֵשֶׂב לְאָכְלָה. (a) Textuality > conj paratactic projection: quote / Mood > declarative: non-past / Transitivity > relational: attribution. This is an interesting clause because it is a major clause, but it does not have a Process. Rather, the Process of the preceding clause, יִהְיֶה *he will be*, is assumed here using the device of ellipsis. It is rare for a verb to be elliptical, though not inconsistent in this case in so far as היה realizes a relational process, and relational processes typically lack an explicit verb. The Subject / Carrier is marked with the so-called goal marker אֶת־.

לְאָכְלָה	אֶת־כָּל־יֶרֶק עֵשֶׂב	וּלְכָל־חַיַּת הָאָרֶץ וּלְכָל־עוֹף הַשָּׁמַיִם וּלְכֹל רוֹמֵשׂ עַל־הָאָרֶץ [[אֲשֶׁר־בּוֹ נֶפֶשׁ חַיָּה]]	**Constituents**
for food	*all green of plant*	*and to all of the animal-kind of the earth and to all of the fowl of the heavens and to all of the crawling-on-the-earth kind, which in him is living being*	**Translation**
		Theme	**Textuality**
Complement	Subject		**Mood**
Attribute	Carrier	Beneficiary	**Transitivity**

וּלְכָל־חַיַּת הָאָרֶץ וּלְכָל־עוֹף הַשָּׁמַיִם וּלְכֹל רוֹמֵשׂ עַל־הָאָרֶץ [[אֲשֶׁר־בּוֹ נֶפֶשׁ חַיָּה]]. Theme: textual > clause conj. + Theme: experiential / Beneficiary > prep phrase complex. The Beneficiary consists of three prepositional phrases. The Head of the last one is constituted using an embedded participial clause, which is itself expanded by an embedded relative clause.

לְכָל־חַיַּת הָאָרֶץ. Beneficiary 1 > prep phrase: prep + noun common collective ms const - noun common collective fs const | def art + noun common fs.

וּלְכָל־עוֹף הַשָּׁמַיִם. Group conj + Beneficiary 2 > prep phrase: prep + common noun collective m s const - common collective noun ms const | def art + common noun mp.

וּלְכֹל רוֹמֵשׂ עַל־הָאָרֶץ [[אֲשֶׁר־בּוֹ נֶפֶשׁ חַיָּה]]. Group conj + Beneficiary 3 > prep phrase: Head + Post-modifier + Post-modifier.

לְכֹל. prep + Head > nominal group: noun common collective ms const.

רוֹמֵשׂ עַל־הָאָרֶץ [[אֲשֶׁר־בּוֹ נֶפֶשׁ חַיָּה]]. (i) Post-modifier >> Textuality > embedded ptc clause / Transitivity > behavioral.

[[אֲשֶׁר־בּוֹ נֶפֶשׁ חַיָּה]]	עַל־הָאָרֶץ	רוֹמֵשׂ	**Constituents**
which in him living being	*on the earth*	*crawler*	**Translation**
		Theme	**Textuality**
Post-modifier	Circumstance	Behaver/Process	**Transitivity**

רוֹמֵשׂ. Theme: experiential / Behaver > ptc ms / Process > qal רמשׂ.

עַל־הָאָרֶץ. Circumstance: location, place > prep phrase: prep - def art + noun common fs.

אֲשֶׁר־בּוֹ נֶפֶשׁ חַיָּה. (a') Post-modifier >> Textuality > embedded expansion: relative clause / Transitivity > relational: attribution. This embedded clause modifies רוֹמֵשׂ *crawler.*

נֶפֶשׁ חַיָּה	בּוֹ	אֲשֶׁר־	**Constituents**
living being	*in him*	*which*	**Translation**
		Theme	**Textuality**
Carrier	Attribute		**Transitivity**

אֲשֶׁר־. Theme: textual > pronoun relative, antecedent is רוֹמֵשׂ *crawler.* Within the experiential structure, this element functions as the object of the following prepositional phrase.

בּוֹ. Carrier > prep phrase: prep + pronoun suffix 3ms, antecedent is רוֹמֵשׂ.

נֶפֶשׁ חַיָּה. Carrier > nominal group: noun common collective fs + adj fs.

אֶת־כָּל־יֶרֶק עֵשֶׂב. Subject > ms (כָּל) / Carrier > nominal group: goal marker - noun common collective ms const - noun common ms const | noun common ms. This constituent is unusual in so far as a goal marker introduces it, when in fact it is the Subject / Carrier of this clause. There is no verbal process for which this constituent can be the Goal or direct object.

לְאָכְלָה. Complement / Attribute > prep phrase: prep + common noun fs.

וַיְהִי־כֵן. (b) Textuality > conj paratactic expansion / Mood > declarative: past / Transitivity > existential. See 1:7(c).

1:31 // וַיַּרְא אֱלֹהִים אֶת־כָּל־אֲשֶׁר עָשָׂה // וְהִנֵּה־טוֹב
מְאֹד // וַיְהִי־עֶרֶב // וַיְהִי־בֹקֶר // יוֹם הַשִּׁשִּׁי׃ פ

וַיַּרְא אֱלֹהִים אֶת־כָּל־אֲשֶׁר עָשָׂה. (a) Textuality > conj paratactic expansion / Mood > declarative: past / Transitivity > mental: perception.

אֶת־כָּל־אֲשֶׁר עָשָׂה	אֱלֹהִים	וַיַּרְא	**Constituents**
all which he made	*deity*	*and he saw*	**Translation**
		Theme	**Textuality**
	Subject	Finite	**Mood**
Phenomenon	Senser	Process	**Transitivity**

וַיַּרְא. Theme: textual > clause conj + Theme: experiential / Finite > wayyiqtol 3ms / Process > qal ראה.

אֱלֹהִים. Subject > mp / Senser > nominal group: noun common.

אֶת־כָּל־אֲשֶׁר עָשָׂה. Phenomenon > nominal group: goal marker + Head + Post-modifier.

כָּל־. Head > noun common ms const.

אֲשֶׁר עָשָׂה. (i) Post-modifier >> Textuality > embedded expansion: relative clause / Mood > declarative: past / Transitivity > material: action. The Subject / Actor is אֱלֹהִים *deity*.

עָשָׂה	אֲשֶׁר	Constituents
he made	*which*	**Translation**
	Theme	**Textuality**
Finite		**Mood**
Process	Goal	**Transitivity**

אֲשֶׁר. Theme: textual > pronoun relative / Goal > antecedent כָּל *all.*

עָשָׂה. Finite > qatal 3ms / Process > qal עשׂה.

וְהִנֵּה־טוֹב מְאֹד. (b) Textuality > conj paratactic expansion / Mood > declarative: past / Transitivity > relational: attribution. *And (all) is very good.* The Subject / Carrier of the Process is כָּל *all* in clause (a), textually absent here by ellipsis.

מְאֹד	טוֹב	וְהִנֵּה־	Constituents
very	*good*	*and now*	**Translation**
	Theme	Theme	**Textuality**
Adjunct			**Mood**
	Attribute		**Transitivity**

וְהִנֵּה־. Theme: textual > clause conj + Adjunct: textual > contra-expectation. Perhaps surprising and notable is how good in fact it turned out to be. For an explanation of הִנֵּה, see 1:29(b).

טוֹב. Theme: experiential / Attribute > adjective group: adj ms.

מְאֹד. Adjunct: interpersonal > modal: extent.

וַיְהִי־עֶרֶב. (c) Textuality > conj paratactic expansion / Mood > declarative: past / Transitivity > existential. See 1:5(c).

וַיְהִי־בֹקֶר. (d) Textuality > conj paratactic expansion / Mood > declarative: past / Transitivity > existential. See 1:5(d).

יוֹם הַשִּׁשִּׁי. (e) Textuality > conj paratactic expansion / Mood > declarative: non-past / Transitivity > existential. An exclamative existential clause: *A sixth day (it is)!* Compare 1:5(e) and 1:8(d). Genesis 2

Genesis 2:1-3

[1]And the heavens and the earth and all their host were finished. [2]And deity finished in the seventh day his work, which he made. And he ceased in the seventh day from all of his work, which he made. [3]And deity blessed the seventh day. And he consecrated it, because in it he ceased from all of his work, which deity created by making.

2:1 /// וַיְכֻלּוּ הַשָּׁמַיִם וְהָאָרֶץ וְכָל־צְבָאָם׃

וַיְכֻלּוּ הַשָּׁמַיִם וְהָאָרֶץ וְכָל־צְבָאָם. (a) Textuality > conj paratactic expansion / Mood > declarative: past / Transitivity > material: action. This clause begins a new clause complex; the Subject is explicit and is new in relation to the preceding clause complex. The Actor of the process is אֱלֹהִים *deity*, though textually absent because the process is passive. The effect of wording this process as a passive is to reintroduce *the heavens and the earth* as the Subject of the text; at issue is not who finished the creation, but that the work was finished and done.

הַשָּׁמַיִם וְהָאָרֶץ וְכָל־צְבָאָם	וַיְכֻלּוּ	**Constituents**
the heavens and the earth and all their host	*and they were finished*	**Translation**
	Theme	**Textuality**
Subject	Finite	**Mood**
Goal	Process	**Transitivity**

וַיְכֻלּוּ. Theme: textual > clause conj + Theme: experiential / Finite > wayyiqtol 3mp / Process > pual כלה.

הַשָּׁמַיִם וְהָאָרֶץ וְכָל־צְבָאָם. Subject > mp / Goal > nominal group complex: three conjoined nominal groups. The interpersonal structure is Finite + Subject, but the interpersonal Subject of passive verbs is the Goal of the experiential structure.

הַשָּׁמַיִם. Nominal group 1 > def art + noun common mp.

וְהָאָרֶץ. Nominal group 2 > group conj + def art + noun common fs.

וְכָל־צְבָאָם. Nominal group 3 > group conj + noun common const + noun common const + pronoun 3mp, antecedent is either הַשָּׁמַיִם the heavens alone, or הַשָּׁמַיִם וְהָאָרֶץ *the heavens and the earth.*

2:2 // וַיְכַל אֱלֹהִים בַּיּוֹם הַשְּׁבִיעִי מְלַאכְתּוֹ אֲשֶׁר עָשָׂה
// וַיִּשְׁבֹּת בַּיּוֹם הַשְּׁבִיעִי מִכָּל־מְלַאכְתּוֹ אֲשֶׁר עָשָׂה׃

(a) **וַיְכַל אֱלֹהִים בַּיּוֹם הַשְּׁבִיעִי מְלַאכְתּוֹ [[אֲשֶׁר עָשָׂה]]**. Textuality > conj paratactic expansion / Mood > declarative: past / Transitivity > material: action. Since the Actor is nominalized in this clause, in distinction from the preceding clause, this may suggest it is the beginning of a new clause complex, though the repetition of the root כלה might suggest otherwise. The Circumstance precedes the Goal, which is atypical. This has the effect of thematizing the Circumstance in relation to the Goal.

מְלַאכְתּוֹ [[אֲשֶׁר עָשָׂה]]	בַּיּוֹם הַשְּׁבִיעִי	אֱלֹהִים	וַיְכַל	**Constituents**
his work which he made	*in the seventh day*	*deity*	*and he finished*	**Translation**
			Theme	**Textuality**
		Subject	Finite	**Mood**
Goal	Circumstance	Actor	Process	**Transitivity**

וַיְכַל. Theme: textual > clause conj + Theme: experiential / Finite > wayyiqtol 3mp / Process > qal כלה.

אֱלֹהִים. Subject > mp / Actor > nominal group: noun common.

בַּיּוֹם הַשְּׁבִיעִי. Circumstance: location, time > prep phrase: prep + def art + noun common ms const | def art + numeral ms. The numeral functions as an adjective.

מְלַאכְתּוֹ [[אֲשֶׁר עָשָׂה]]. Goal > nominal group: Head + Post-modifier.

מְלַאכְתּוֹ. Head > nominal group: noun common fs const + pronoun suffix 3ms, antecedent is אֱלֹהִים *deity*.

אֲשֶׁר עָשָׂה. (i) Post-modifier >> Textuality > embedded expansion: relative clause / Mood > declarative: past / Transitivity > material: action. This embedded relative clause enhances the cohesion of the text by relating the clause in which it is embedded to the preceding story.

עָשָׂה	אֲשֶׁר	**Constituents**
he made	*which*	**Translation**
	Theme	**Textuality**
Finite		**Mood**
Process	Goal	**Transitivity**

אֲשֶׁר. Theme: textual and experiential / Goal > pronoun relative, antecedent is מְלַאכְתּוֹ *his work*.

עָשָׂה. Finite > qatal 3ms / Process > qal עשׂה.

וַיִּשְׁבֹּת בַּיּוֹם הַשְּׁבִיעִי מִכָּל־מְלַאכְתּוֹ [[אֲשֶׁר עָשָׂה]]. (b) Textuality > conj paratactic expansion / Mood > declarative: past / Transitivity > material: action. The Subject / Actor is אֱלֹהִים *deity* in the preceding clause, absent here by ellipsis.

מִכָּל־מְלַאכְתּוֹ [[אֲשֶׁר עָשָׂה]]	בַּיּוֹם הַשְּׁבִיעִי	וַיִּשְׁבֹּת	**Constituents**
from all of his work, which he made	*in the seventh day*	*and he ceased*	**Translation**
		Theme	**Textuality**
		Finite	**Mood**
Scope	Circumstance	Process	**Transitivity**

וַיִּשְׁבֹּת. Theme: textual > clause conj + Theme: experiential / Finite > wayyiqtol 3ms / Process > qal שׁבת.

בַּיּוֹם הַשְּׁבִיעִי. Circumstance: location, time > prep phrase: prep + def art + noun common ms | def art + numeral ms.

מִכָּל־מְלַאכְתּוֹ אֲשֶׁר עָשָׂה. Scope > prep phrase complex: Head + Post-modifier.

מִכָּל־מְלַאכְתּוֹ. Head > prep phrase: prep + noun common ms const - noun common fs const + pronoun suffix 3ms, antecedent is אֱלֹהִים deity in clause (a).

אֲשֶׁר עָשָׂה. (i) Post-modifier >> Textuality > embedded expansion: relative clause / Mood > declarative: past / Transitivity > material: action.

עָשָׂה	אֲשֶׁר	**Constituents**
he made	*which*	**Translation**
	Theme	**Textuality**
Finite		**Mood**
Process	Goal	**Transitivity**

אֲשֶׁר. Theme: textual and experiential / Goal > pronoun relative, antecedent is מְלַאכְתּוֹ *his work.*

עָשָׂה. Finite > qatal 3ms / Process > qal עשׂה.

// וַיְבָרֶךְ אֱלֹהִים אֶת־יוֹם הַשְּׁבִיעִי // וַיְקַדֵּשׁ אֹתוֹ 2:3
/ כִּי בוֹ שָׁבַת מִכָּל־מְלַאכְתּוֹ אֲשֶׁר־בָּרָא אֱלֹהִים
לַעֲשׂוֹת׃ פ

וַיְבָרֶךְ אֱלֹהִים אֶת־יוֹם הַשְּׁבִיעִי. (a) Textuality > conj paratactic expansion / Mood > declarative: past / Transitivity > verbal.

אֶת־יוֹם הַשְּׁבִיעִי	אֱלֹהִים	וַיְבָרֶךְ	**Constituents**
the seventh day	*deity*	*and he blessed*	**Translation**
		Theme	**Textuality**
	Subject	Finite	**Mood**
Target	Sayer	Process	**Transitivity**

וַיְבָרֶךְ. Theme: textual > clause conj + Theme: experiential / Finite > wayyiqtol 3ms / Process > piel ברך.

אֱלֹהִים. Subject > mp / Sayer > nominal group: noun common.

אֶת־יוֹם הַשְּׁבִיעִי. Target > nominal group: goal marker - noun common ms const | def art + numeral ms. Normally an ordinal numeral agrees with its Head in gender and definiteness, but in this case the Head noun lacks the definite article and the nominal group looks more like a constuct noun phrase. Compare 2:2(a-b), and see MNK 270 for the syntax of ordinal numbers.

וַיְקַדֵּשׁ אֹתוֹ. (b) Textuality > conj paratactic expansion / Mood > declarative: past / Transitivity > material: action. The Subject / Actor is absent by ellipsis.

אֹתוֹ	וַיְקַדֵּשׁ	**Constituents**
him	*and he consecrated*	**Translation**
	Theme	**Textuality**
	Finite	**Mood**
Goal	Process	**Transitivity**

וַיְקַדֵּשׁ. Theme: textual > clause conj + Theme: experiential / Finite > wayyiqtol 3ms / Process > piel קדשׁ.

אֹתוֹ. Goal > nominal group: goal marker + pronoun suffix 3ms, antecedent is יוֹם day.

כִּי בוֹ שָׁבַת מִכָּל־מְלַאכְתּוֹ אֲשֶׁר־בָּרָא אֱלֹהִים לַעֲשׂוֹת. (c) Textuality > conj hypotactic expansion / Mood > declarative: past / Transitivity > material: action. The Subject / Actor אֱלֹהִים *deity* is absent by ellipsis from (a). Notice how the use of the embedded clause enables the writer to include three verbal processes within one major clause: שׁבת and ברא and עשׂה; these three verbs together summarize the action of the account.

מִכָּל־מְלַאכְתּוֹ [[אֲשֶׁר־בָּרָא אֱלֹהִים לַעֲשׂוֹת]]	שָׁבַת	בּוֹ	כִּי	**Constituents**
from all of his work which deity created to make	*he ceased*	*in him*	*because*	**Translation**
		Theme	Theme	**Textuality**
	Finite			**Mood**
Scope	Process	Circumstance		**Transitivity**

כִּי. Theme: textual > clause conj.

בּוֹ. Theme: experiential / Circumstance: location, time > prep phrase: prep + pronoun suffix 3ms, antecedent is יוֹם *day*.

שָׁבַת. Finite > qatal 3ms / Process > qal שׁבת.

מִכָּל־מְלַאכְתּוֹ [[אֲשֶׁר־בָּרָא אֱלֹהִים לַעֲשׂוֹת]]. Scope > prep phrase complex: Head + Post-modifier.

מִכָּל־מְלַאכְתּוֹ. Head > prep phrase: prep + noun common ms const - noun common fs const + pronoun suffix 3ms, antecedent is אֱלֹהִים *deity*.

אֲשֶׁר־בָּרָא אֱלֹהִים לַעֲשׂוֹת. (i) Post-modifier >> Textuality > embedded expansion: relative clause / Mood > declarative: past / Transitivity > material: action. This embedded clause adds specification to its antecedent מְלַאכְתּוֹ, and in doing so becomes the occasion to reintroduce the material process בָּרָא *create* with which the entire narrative began in 1:1(a). Notice that this is the third embedded relative clause (see 2:2a-b) that has מְלַאכְתּוֹ as the antecedent and contains the verb עשׂה with אֱלֹהִים as Subject / Actor.

לַעֲשׂוֹת	אֱלֹהִים	בָּרָא	אֲשֶׁר־	Constituents
to make	*deity*	*he created*	*which*	**Translation**
			Theme	**Textuality**
	Subject	Finite		**Mood**
Circumstance	Actor	Process	Goal	**Transitivity**

אֲשֶׁר־. Theme: textual and experiential / Goal > pronoun relative, antecedent is כָּל־מְלַאכְתּוֹ *all of his work*.

בָּרָא. Finite > qatal 3ms / Process > qal ברא.

אֱלֹהִים. Subject > mp / Actor > nominal group: noun common.

לַעֲשׂוֹת. Circumstance: manner, means > prep phrase: prep + inf const qal עשׂה. This is a difficult component to incorporate into the grammatical structure but may mean by making, which is to say, deity created all his work by making it.

Genesis 2:4-7

[4]These are the outcomes of the heavens and the earth when they were created. When in the day YHVH deity made earth and heavens, [5]and before all of the bush of the field will be in the earth, and before all of the plantlife of the field will grow, because YHVH deity caused not rain on the earth, and a humankind is not to work the ground, [6]and (before) a mist will rise from the earth and will water all of the surface of the ground, [7]YHVH deity formed the human using dust from the ground. And he blew in his nostrils a breath of life. And the human became a living being.

2:4 /// אֵלֶּה תוֹלְד֧וֹת הַשָּׁמַ֛יִם וְהָאָ֖רֶץ בְּהִבָּֽרְאָ֑ם ///
בְּי֗וֹם עֲשׂ֛וֹת יְהוָ֥ה אֱלֹהִ֖ים אֶ֥רֶץ וְשָׁמָֽיִם׃

This verse divides into two clauses at the *'atnach*. An interpretative question arises at this point and concerns the cohesion of the text. Does clause (a) attach to the preceding clause complex, or does it introduce a new text segment? Does clause (b) relate to clause (a) or does it begin a new clause complex? NRSV and NJPS interpret clause (a) as the conclusion of the preceding story and clause (b) as the start of a new clause complex. In our analysis, clause (a) is its own clause complex and it functions as the Theme of the entire episode extending as far as 4:26. The primary evidence is the word אֵלֶּה *these.* Elsewhere in Genesis 1–11 it is used in attributive relational clauses joined with תּוֹלְדוֹת outcomes as a cataphoric (forward-looking) pronoun referring to the following clause complex; see 6:9(a), 10:1(a), 11:10(a), 11:27(a).

אֵלֶּה תוֹלְדוֹת הַשָּׁמַיִם וְהָאָרֶץ [[בְּהִבָּרְאָם]]. (a) Textuality > appositive paratactic expansion / Mood > declarative: non-past / Transitivity > relational: identification.

[[בְּהִבָּרְאָם]]	תּוֹלְדוֹת הַשָּׁמַיִם וְהָאָרֶץ	אֵלֶּה	**Constituents**
in their having been created	*outcomes of the heavens and the earth*	*these*	**Translation**
		Theme	**Textuality**
	Complement	Subject	**Mood**
Circumstance	Identifier	Identified	**Transitivity**

אֵלֶּה. Theme: experiential / Subject > 3cp / Identified > pronoun demonstrative. This deictic, or pointing, word is most likely cataphoric, that is, it directs the reader forward to the following clause complex.

תּוֹלְדוֹת הַשָּׁמַיִם וְהָאָרֶץ. Complement > fp / Identifier > nominal group: Head + Post-modifier.

תּוֹלְדוֹת. Head > nominal group: noun common fp const. This word is bound to the following coordinate noun pair, not just to the first word in the pair. While traditionally this word is rendered *generations,* we translate it *outcomes* to indicate more clearly that the following clause complex indicates later developments; in this case, what becomes of the heavens and the earth. תּוֹלְדֹת is also found in 5:1(a),

6:9(a), 10:1(a), 10:32(a), 11:10(a), and 11:27(a). The word is derived from the root ילד, which is used frequently in Genesis 1–11 in the verbal processes of giving birth and fathering.

הַשָּׁמַיִם וְהָאָרֶץ. Post-modifier > nominal group: def art + noun common mp | group conj + def art + noun common fs.

בְּהִבָּרְאָם. (i) Circumstance: location, time >> Textuality > embedded expansion: prep clause / Transitivity > material: action. This prepositional phrase is an embedded clause. It has its own transitivity structure, with a Process > nifal ברא and a Goal > pronoun suffix 3mp. This is a good illustration of the claim of functional grammar that prepositional phrases are contractions of a clause such that they can be included in higher ranked clauses.

בְּהִבָּרְאָם	**Constituents**
in their having been created	**Translation**
Theme	**Textuality**
Process + Goal	**Transitivity**

בְּהִבָּרְאָם. Theme: textual > prep + Theme: experiential / Process > inf const nifal ברא + Goal > pronoun suffix 3mp, antecedent is הַשָּׁמַיִם וְהָאָרֶץ *the heavens and the earth.*

בְּיוֹם עֲשׂוֹת יְהוָה אֱלֹהִים אֶרֶץ וְשָׁמָיִם. (b) Textuality > embedded expansion: prep clause / Transitivity > material: action. This is a material clause that has been rank-shifted to phrase-level, so that it can function as a Circumstance within another clause. The question is, within which clause? If it is the preceding clause, then it functions as an extension of the preceding Circumstance בְּהִבָּרְאָם of that clause. If it is the following clause, then it functions as the temporal Circumstance of the material clause in 2:7(a); but this is a very long span of text over which it would be expected to retain its circumstantial function. Nonetheless, the latter is how it is being analyzed here.

אֶרֶץ וְשָׁמָיִם	יְהוָה אֱלֹהִים	עֲשׂוֹת	בְּיוֹם	**Constituents**
an earth and a heavens	*YHVH deity*	*the making of*	*in the day of*	**Translation**
			Theme	**Textuality**
Goal	Actor	Process	Circumstance	**Transitivity**

בְּיוֹם. Theme: textual > prep + Theme: experiential / Circumstance: location, time > noun common ms const. The object of the preposition is the nominal group (i.e. construct noun phrase) יוֹם עֲשׂוֹת יְהוָה אֱלֹהִים *the day of the making of YHVH deity.*

עֲשׂוֹת. Process > inf const qal עשׂה.

יְהוָה אֱלֹהִים. Actor > nominal group: Head + Post-modifier. This is the first time the compound divine designation occurs in the biblical text. It consists of two nouns, only the first of which is a proper noun. The first is by definition definite (because it is a proper noun), and the second is an indefinite common noun. The first is the Head and the second is a classifying Post-modifier: *YHVH, a deity*, or simply *YHVH deity.*

יְהוָה. Head > noun proper ms.

אֱלֹהִים. Post-modifier > noun common mp.

אֶרֶץ וְשָׁמָיִם. Goal > nominal group: noun common fs | group conj + noun common mp. Notice that these nouns are indefinite, suggesting textually speaking that they have not yet been defined or made known to the hearer. Of course, they had been repeatedly referred to in the preceding text, most recently in 2:4(a). Yet, this suggests that the text is starting over again and going back to beginnings.

2:5 // וְכֹ֣ל ׀ שִׂ֣יחַ הַשָּׂדֶ֗ה טֶ֚רֶם יִֽהְיֶ֣ה בָאָ֔רֶץ // וְכָל־
עֵ֥שֶׂב הַשָּׂדֶ֖ה טֶ֣רֶם יִצְמָ֑ח / כִּי֩ לֹ֨א הִמְטִ֜יר יְהוָ֤ה
אֱלֹהִים֙ עַל־הָאָ֔רֶץ // וְאָדָ֣ם אַ֔יִן לַֽעֲבֹ֖ד אֶת־הָֽאֲדָמָֽה׃

וְכֹל שִׂיחַ הַשָּׂדֶה טֶרֶם יִהְיֶה בָאָרֶץ. (a) Textuality > conj hypotactic expansion / Mood > declarative: non-past / Transitivity > existential. The construction with טֶרֶם + yiqtol in (a) and (b) has a nominal group as textual Theme. This is a way to prepose the clause Theme.

בָאָרֶץ	יִהְיֶה	טֶרֶם	וְכֹל שִׂיחַ הַשָּׂדֶה	**Constituents**
in the earth	*he will be*	*before*	*and all of the bush of the field*	**Translation**
			Theme	**Textuality**
	Finite		Subject	**Mood**
Circumstance	Process	Adjunct	Existent	**Transitivity**

וְכֹל שִׂיחַ הַשָּׂדֶה. Theme: textual > clause conj + Theme: experiential / Subject > ms (כֹּל) / Existent > nominal group: noun common collective ms const ׀ noun common collective ms const ׀ def art + noun common ms. The grammatical Subject, strictly speaking, is the first word of the nominal group. The nominal group as a whole is the Existent and it is a preposed Theme in this clause.

טֶרֶם. Adjunct: experiential > circumstance, time. This טֶרֶם before is almost always followed immediately by a Finite verb, typically a yiqtol, and it is virtually never the first constituent in its clause (see Psalm 119:67 for the exception, and this is in the ט stanza of this acrostic poem). And the clause in which it is found is always subordinate, or hypotactic, in relation to a dominant clause.

יִהְיֶה. Finite > yiqtol 3ms / Process > qal היה.

בָאָרֶץ. Circumstance: location, place > prep phrase: prep + def art + noun common fs.

וְכָל־עֵשֶׂב הַשָּׂדֶה טֶרֶם יִצְמָח. (b) Textuality > conj hypotactic expansion / Mood > declarative: non-past / Transitivity > existential. This clause has essentially the same structure as the preceding clause.

יִצְמָח	טֶרֶם	וְכָל־עֵשֶׂב הַשָּׂדֶה	**Constituents**
he grew	*before*	*and all of the plant of the field*	**Translation**
		Theme	**Textuality**
Finite		Subject	**Mood**
Process	Adjunct	Existent	**Transitivity**

וְכָל־עֵשֶׂב הַשָּׂדֶה. Theme: textual > clause conj + Theme: experiential / Subject > ms (כָל) / Existent > nominal group: noun common collective ms const | noun common collective ms const | def art + noun common ms.

טֶרֶם. Adjunct: experiential > circumstance, time.

יִצְמָח. Finite > yiqtol 3ms / Process > qal צמח.

כִּי לֹא הִמְטִיר יְהוָה אֱלֹהִים עַל־הָאָרֶץ. (c) Textuality > conj hypotactic expansion / Mood > declarative: past / Transitivity > material: action. This clause extends the meaning of clauses (a) and (b) by providing an explanation.

עַל־הָאָרֶץ	יְהוָה אֱלֹהִים	הִמְטִיר	לֹא	כִּי	**Constituents**
on the earth	*YHVH deity*	*he caused rain*	*not*	*because*	**Translation**
		Theme	Theme	Theme	**Textuality**
	Subject	Finite	Adjunct		**Mood**
Circumstance	Actor	Process			**Transitivity**

כִּי. Theme: textual > conj.

לֹא. Theme: interpersonal / Adjunct: interpersonal > polarity: negative. Polarity is a component of the Mood system because it has to do with the positive or negative validity of a proposition.

הִמְטִיר. Theme: experiential / Finite > yiqtol 3ms / Process > hifil מטר.

יְהוָה אֱלֹהִים. Subject > ms / Actor > nominal group: noun proper ms | noun common mp.

עַל־הָאָרֶץ. Circumstance: location, place > prep phrase: prep + def art + noun common fs.

וְאָדָם אַיִן [[לַעֲבֹד אֶת־הָאֲדָמָה]]. (d) Textuality > conj paratactic expansion / Mood > declarative: non-past / Transitivity > existential. This clause is paratactic to the preceding clause, and both 5(c-d) together are hypotactic to 5(b), or to 5(a-b). This clause complex has multiple levels of taxis, and the precise scope of connectedness of each individual clause is subject to interpretation.

[[לַעֲבֹד אֶת־הָאֲדָמָה]]	אַיִן	וְאָדָם	**Constituents**
to work the ground	*is not*	*and a humankind*	**Translation**
		Theme	**Textuality**
	Adjunct	Subject	**Mood**
Circumstance	Process	Existent	**Transitivity**

וְאָדָם. Theme: textual > clause conj + Theme: experiential / Subject > ms / Existent > common collective noun ms. This could also be rendered as a singular noun, a human.

אַיִן. Adjunct: interpersonal > negative / Process > existential.

לַעֲבֹד אֶת־הָאֲדָמָה. (i) Circumstance: cause, purpose >> Textuality > embedded expansion: prep clause / Transitivity > material: action. Prepositional embedded clauses, in distinction from relative embedded clauses, do not have a Mood structure.

אֶת־הָאֲדָמָה	לַעֲבֹד	**Constituents**
the ground	*to work*	**Translation**
	Theme	**Textuality**
Goal	Process	**Transitivity**

לַעֲבֹד. Theme: textual > prep + Theme: experiential / Process > inf const qal עבד.

אֶת־הָאֲדָמָה. Goal > nominal group: goal marker - def art + noun common fs.

2:6 // וְאֵד יַעֲלֶה מִן־הָאָרֶץ // וְהִשְׁקָה אֶת־כָּל־פְּנֵי־
הָאֲדָמָה׃

וְאֵד יַעֲלֶה מִן־הָאָרֶץ. (a) Textuality > conj paratactic expansion / Mood > declarative: non-past / Transitivity > material: action.

מִן־הָאָרֶץ	יַעֲלֶה	וְאֵד	**Constituents**
from the earth	*he will rise*	*and a mist*	**Translation**
		Theme	**Textuality**
	Finite	Subject	**Mood**
Circumstance	Process	Actor	**Transitivity**

וְאֵד. Theme: textual > clause conj + Theme: experiential / Subject > ms / Actor > nominal group: noun common.

יַעֲלֶה. Finite > yiqtol 3ms / Process > qal עלה.

מִן־הָאָרֶץ. Range > prep phrase: prep + def art + noun common fs.

וְהִשְׁקָה אֶת־כָּל־פְּנֵי־הָאֲדָמָה. (b) Textuality > conj paratactic expansion / Mood > declarative: non-past / Transitivity > material: action. The Subject / Actor is אֵד *mist* in the preceding clause, absent here by ellipsis; this creates textual cohesion and binds clause (b) to clause (a). Because 6(a-b) have non-past tense, they may be depicting the pre-creation state referred to in 4(b), and they may be extending the "before" description begun in 5(a-b). With this in mind, we are translating 6(a-b) as if טֶרֶם *before* also applies to them.

אֶת־כָּל־פְּנֵי־הָאֲדָמָה	וְהִשְׁקָה	**Constituents**
all of the face of the ground	*and he will water*	**Translation**
	Theme	**Textuality**
	Finite	**Mood**
Goal	Process	**Transitivity**

וְהִשְׁקָה. Theme: textual > clause conj + Theme: experiential / Finite > weqatal 3ms / Process > hifil שׁקה.

אֶת־כָּל־פְּנֵי־הָאֲדָמָה. Goal > nominal group: goal marker - noun common collective ms const - noun common mp const - def art + noun common fs.

2:7 // וַיִּיצֶר יְהוָה אֱלֹהִים אֶת־הָאָדָם עָפָר מִן־הָאֲדָמָה
// וַיִּפַּח בְּאַפָּיו נִשְׁמַת חַיִּים // וַיְהִי הָאָדָם לְנֶפֶשׁ
חַיָּה׃

וַיִּיצֶר יְהוָה אֱלֹהִים אֶת־הָאָדָם עָפָר מִן־הָאֲדָמָה. (a) Textuality > conj paratactic expansion / Mood > declarative: past / Transitivity > material: action. This is the clause that initiates the narrative event sequence of the clause complex that began with 2:4(b). The preceding clauses established the background conditions within which the event described in this clause took place. Notice that this clause exhibits a full transitivity structure making explicit the Actor, Goal, and Circumstance.

עָפָר מִן־הָאֲדָמָה	אֶת־הָאָדָם	יְהוָה אֱלֹהִים	וַיִּיצֶר	**Constituents**
dust from the ground	*the human*	*YHVH deity*	*and he formed*	**Translation**
			Theme	**Textuality**
		Subject	Finite	**Mood**
Circumstance	Goal	Actor	Process	**Transitivity**

וַיִּיצֶר. Theme: textual > clause conj + Theme: experiential / Finite > wayyiqtol 3ms / Process > qal יצר.

יְהוָה אֱלֹהִים. Subject > ms / Actor > nominal group: noun proper ms | noun common mp.

אֶת־הָאָדָם. Goal > nominal group: goal marker - def art + noun common collective noun ms. This noun can be collective or individual. The ambiguity is presumably intentional. Later, minus the definite article, it becomes a proper noun, that is, a name. NRSV, for example, renders אָדָם as the personal name *'Adam* for the first time in 4:25.

עָפָר מִן־הָאֲדָמָה. Circumstance: material > nominal group: Head + Post-modifier. Specifies the material used in the Process.

עָפָר. Head > nominal group: noun common ms.

מִן־הָאֲדָמָה. Post-modifier > prep phrase: prep - def art + noun common fs. Extends the meaning of עָפָר by specifying the source location of the material.

וַיִּפַּח בְּאַפָּיו נִשְׁמַת חַיִּים. (b) Textuality > conj paratactic expansion / Mood > declarative: past / Transitivity > material: action. The Subject / Actor יְהוָה אֱלֹהִים *YHVH deity* is textually absent by ellipsis, indicating it is part of the clause complex with the preceding clauses.

נִשְׁמַת חַיִּים	בְּאַפָּיו	וַיִּפַּח	**Constituents**
a breath of life	*in his nostrils*	*and he blew*	**Translation**
		Theme	**Textuality**
		Finite	**Mood**
Goal	Circumstance	Process	**Transitivity**

וַיִּפַּח. Theme: textual > clause conj + Theme: experiential / Finite > wayyiqtol 3ms / Process > qal נפח.

בְּאַפָּיו. Circumstance: location, place > prep phrase: prep + noun common md const + pronoun suffix 3ms, antecedent is הָאָדָם *the human* in the preceding clause.

נִשְׁמַת חַיִּים. Goal > nominal group: noun common fs const + noun common mp. A new element, hence indefinite.

וַיְהִי הָאָדָם לְנֶפֶשׁ חַיָּה. (c) Textuality > conj paratactic expansion / Mood > declarative: past / Transitivity > relational: attribution.

לְנֶפֶשׁ חַיָּה	הָֽאָדָם	וַיְהִי	**Constituents**
to a living being	*the human*	*and he was*	**Translation**
		Theme	**Textuality**
	Subject	Finite	**Mood**
Attribute	Carrier	Process	**Transitivity**

וַיְהִי. Theme: textual > clause conj + Theme: experiential / Finite > wayyiqtol 3ms / Process > qal היה. The verb היה followed by לְ has the meaning *become*. The process is thus transformative, even though it is structured as an attributive relational process.

הָֽאָדָם. Carrier > def art + noun common collective ms.

לְנֶפֶשׁ חַיָּה. Attribute > prep phrase: prep + noun common fs | adj fs.

Genesis 2:8-9

[8]And YHVH deity planted a garden in Eden from east. And he put there the human, which he formed. [9]And YHVH deity grew from the ground all treekind pleasant to view and good to consume and the tree of the life in the midst of the garden and the tree of the knowledge of good and bad.

2:8 /// וַיִּטַּ֞ע יְהוָ֧ה אֱלֹהִ֛ים גַּן־בְּעֵ֖דֶן מִקֶּ֑דֶם // וַיָּ֣שֶׂם שָׁ֔ם
אֶת־הָֽאָדָ֖ם אֲשֶׁ֥ר יָצָֽר׃

וַיִּטַּע יְהוָה אֱלֹהִים גַּן־בְּעֵדֶן מִקֶּדֶם. (a) Textuality > conj paratactic expansion / Mood > declarative: past / Transitivity > material: action. This clause, marked by a fully explicit transitivity structure, begins a new clause complex.

בְּעֵדֶן מִקֶּדֶם	גַּן־	יְהוָה אֱלֹהִים	וַיִּטַּע	**Constituents**
in Eden from east	*a garden*	*YHVH deity*	*and he planted*	**Translation**
			Theme	**Textuality**
		Subject	Finite	**Mood**
Circumstance	Goal	Actor	Process	**Transitivity**

וַיִּטַּע. Theme: textual > clause conj + Theme: experiential / Finite > wayyiqtol 3ms / Process > qal נטע.

יְהוָה אֱלֹהִים. Subject > ms / Actor > nominal group: noun proper ms ו noun common mp.

גַּן־. Goal > noun common ms.

בְּעֵדֶן מִקֶּדֶם. Circumstance: location, place > prep phrase complex: Head + Post-modifier.

בְּעֵדֶן. Head > prep phrase: prep + noun proper.

מִקֶּדֶם. Post-modifier > prep phrase: prep + noun common ms. It is not clear what precise meaning is intended. As a post-modifier to the preceding prep phrase, it would appear to be adding further specification. But the point of reference—from east of what?—is not evident. East of the garden? Or east from where the speaker and the audience were positioned?

וַיָּשֶׂם שָׁם אֶת־הָאָדָם [[אֲשֶׁר יָצָר]]. (b) Textuality > conj paratactic expansion / Mood > declarative: past / Transitivity >material: action. The Subject / Actor יְהוָה אֱלֹהִים is absent by ellipsis.

אֶת־הָאָדָם [[אֲשֶׁר יָצָר]]	שָׁם	וַיָּשֶׂם	**Constituents**
the human which he formed	*there*	*and he put*	**Translation**
		Theme	**Textuality**
		Finite	**Mood**
Goal	Circumstance	Process	**Transitivity**

וַיָּשֶׂם. Theme: textual > clause conj + Theme: experiential / Finite > wayyiqtol 3ms / Process > qal שׂים.

שָׁם. Adjunct: experiential > circumstance: place, antecedent is גַּן in clause (a). This kind of back referencing is a feature that contributes to textual cohesion.

אֶת־הָאָדָם אֲשֶׁר יָצָר. Goal > nominal group: Head + Post-modifier.

אֶת־הָאָדָם. Head > goal marker - def art + noun common ms.

אֲשֶׁר יָצָר. (i) Post-modifier >> Textuality > embedded expansion: relative clause / Mood > declarative: past / Transitivity > material: action. This embedded clause expands the meaning of הָאָדָם *the human*. The Subject / Actor of the embedded clause is the Subject/ Actor of the enclosing clause, יְהוָה אֱלֹהִים.

יָצָר	אֲשֶׁר	**Constituents**
he formed	*which*	**Translation**
	Theme	**Textuality**
Finite		**Mood**
Process	Goal	**Transitivity**

אֲשֶׁר. Theme: textual and experiential / Goal > pronoun relative, antecedent is הָאָדָם *the human*.

יָצָר. Finite > qatal 3ms / Process > qal יצר. For the prior instance of formed, see 2:7(a).

2:9 // וַיַּצְמַ֞ח יְהוָ֤ה אֱלֹהִים֙ מִן־הָ֣אֲדָמָ֔ה כָּל־עֵ֛ץ נֶחְמָ֥ד
לְמַרְאֶ֖ה וְט֣וֹב לְמַאֲכָ֑ל וְעֵ֤ץ הַֽחַיִּים֙ בְּת֣וֹךְ הַגָּ֔ן וְעֵ֕ץ
הַדַּ֖עַת ט֥וֹב וָרָֽע׃

וַיַּצְמַח יְהוָה אֱלֹהִים מִן־הָאֲדָמָה כָּל־עֵץ נֶחְמָד לְמַרְאֶה
וְטוֹב לְמַאֲכָל וְעֵץ הַחַיִּים בְּתוֹךְ הַגָּן וְעֵץ הַדַּעַת טוֹב וָרָע.

(a) Textuality > conj paratactic expansion / Mood > declarative: past / Transitivity > material: action. This verse is rather long because the Goal has three parts.

כָּל־עֵץ נֶחְמָד לְמַרְאֶה וְטוֹב לְמַאֲכָל וְעֵץ הַחַיִּים בְּתוֹךְ הַגָּן וְעֵץ הַדַּעַת טוֹב וָרָע	מִן־הָאֲדָמָה	יְהוָה אֱלֹהִים	וַיַּצְמַח	**Constituents**
all treekind pleasant to view and good to consume and the tree of the life in the midst of the garden and the tree of the knowledge of good-and-bad	*from the ground*	*YHVH deity*	*and he grew*	**Translation**
			Theme	**Textuality**
		Subject	Finite	**Mood**
Goal	Circumstance	Actor	Process	**Transitivity**

וַיַּצְמַח. Theme: textual > clause conj + Theme: experiential / Finite > wayyiqtol 3ms / Process > hifil צמח.

יְהוָה אֱלֹהִים. Subject > ms / Actor > nominal group: noun proper ms | noun common mp.

מִן־הָאֲדָמָה. Circumstance: location, place > prep phrase: prep - noun common fs.

כָּל־עֵץ נֶחְמָד לְמַרְאֶה וְטוֹב לְמַאֲכָל וְעֵץ הַחַיִּים בְּתוֹךְ הַגָּן וְעֵץ הַדַּעַת טוֹב וָרָע. Goal > nominal group complex: three nominal groups.

כָּל־עֵץ נֶחְמָד לְמַרְאֶה וְטוֹב לְמַאֲכָל. Goal 1 > nominal group: Head + Post-modifier.

כָּל־עֵץ. Head > noun common collective ms const - noun common ms. This is the head of the two coordinated adjective groups that follow.

נֶחְמָד לְמַרְאֶה וְטוֹב לְמַאֲכָל. Post-modifier > adjective group complex.

נֶחְמָד לְמַרְאֶה. Adj group 1 > Head + Post-modifier.

נֶחְמָד. Head > ptc ms nifal חמד.

לְמַרְאֶה. Post-modifier > prep phrase: prep + noun common fs.

וְטוֹב לְמַאֲכָל. Group conj + Adj group 2 > Head + Post-modifier.

טוֹב. Head > adj ms.

לְמַאֲכָל. Post-modifier > prep phrase: prep + noun common ms.

וְעֵץ הַחַיִּים בְּתוֹךְ הַגָּן. Group conj + Goal 2 > nominal group: Head + Post-modifier.

עֵץ הַחַיִּים. Head > nominal group: noun common ms const | def art + noun common mp.

בְּתוֹךְ הַגָּן. Post-modifier > prep phrase: prep + noun common ms const | def art + noun common ms.

וְעֵץ הַדַּעַת טוֹב וָרָע. Group conj + Goal 3 > nominal group: Head + Post-modifier.

עֵץ הַדַּעַת. Head > nominal group: noun common ms const | def art + noun common fs.

טוֹב וָרָע. Post-modifier > adjective group: adj ms | group conj + adj ms. Note the hendiadys conjunction וָ. This adjective group functions as the Phenomenon of the mental process of cognition *knowing*, which is implicit in the nominal דַּעַת *knowledge*. This nominal is based on the inf const of qal ידע. The phrase הַדַּעַת טוֹב וָרָע *the knowledge of good-and-bad* is a highly compressed form of an embedded expansion clause.

Genesis 2:10-14

10And a river exits from Eden to water the garden. And from there it will divide. And it will become four heads. 11The name of the one is Pishon. It is the one circling all of the land of the Chavila, which there is the gold. [12]And the gold of that land is good. There is the bdellium and the onyx stone. [13]And the name of the second river is Gihon. It is the one circling all of the land of Kush. [14]And the name of the third river is Chideqel. It is the one going east of 'Ashur. And the fourth river, it is Perat.

2:10 /// וְנָהָר֙ יֹצֵ֣א מֵעֵ֔דֶן לְהַשְׁק֖וֹת אֶת־הַגָּ֑ן // וּמִשָּׁם֙ יִפָּרֵ֔ד // וְהָיָ֖ה לְאַרְבָּעָ֥ה רָאשִֽׁים׃

וְנָהָר יֹצֵא מֵעֵדֶן [[לְהַשְׁקוֹת אֶת־הַגָּן]]. (a) Textuality > conj paratactic expansion / Mood > declarative: non-past / Transitivity > material: action.

[[לְהַשְׁקוֹת אֶת־הַגָּן]]	מֵעֵדֶן	יֹצֵא	וְנָהָר	**Constituents**
to water the garden	*from Eden*	*exits*	*and a river*	**Translation**
			Theme	**Textuality**
		Finite	Subject	**Mood**
Circumstance	Circumstance	Process	Actor	**Transitivity**

וְנָהָר. Theme: textual > clause conj + Theme: experiential / Subject > ms / Actor > nominal group: noun common ms.

יֹצֵא. Finite > ptc ms / Process > qal יצא.

מֵעֵדֶן. Circumstance: location, place > prep phrase: prep + noun proper.

לְהַשְׁקוֹת אֶת־הַגָּן. (i) Circumstance: cause, purpose >> Textuality > embedded expansion: prep clause / Transitivity > material: action. This clause extends the meaning of יֹצֵא: *exits from Eden to water the garden.*

אֶת־הַגָּן	לְהַשְׁקוֹת	**Constituents**
the garden	*to water*	**Translation**
	Theme	**Textuality**
Goal	Process	**Transitivity**

לְהַשְׁקוֹת. Theme: textual > prep + Theme: experiential / Process > inf const hifil שׁקה.

אֶת־הַגָּן. Goal > nominal group: goal marker - def art + noun common ms.

וּמִשָּׁם יִפָּרֵד. (b) Textuality > conj paratactic expansion / Mood > declarative: non-past / Transitivity > material: action. Subject / Actor is נָהָר from clause (a), absent here by ellipsis. This clause employs two textual metafunction devices to create cohesion with clause (a): the back referencing circum adjunct שָׁם and the ellipsis of נָהָר.

יִפָּרֵד	וּמִשָּׁם	**Constituents**
he will divide	*and from there*	**Translation**
	Theme	**Textuality**
Finite		**Mood**
Process	Circumstance	**Transitivity**

וּמִשָּׁם. Theme: textual > clause conj + Theme: experiential / Circumstance: location, place > prep phrase: prep + pronoun textual, antecedent is עֵדֶן and הַגָּן.

יִפָּרֵד. Finite > yiqtol 3ms / Process > nifal פרד. The nifal is here construed as middle voice (will divide) rather than as passive voice (will be divided).

וְהָיָה לְאַרְבָּעָה רָאשִׁים. (c) Textuality > conj paratactic expansion / Mood > declarative: non-past / Transitivity > relational: attribution. The Subject / Carrier is נָהָר, absent by ellipsis.

לְאַרְבָּעָה רָאשִׁים	וְהָיָה	**Constituents**
four heads	*and he will be*	**Translation**
	Theme	**Textuality**
	Finite	**Mood**
Attribute	Process	**Transitivity**

וְהָיָה. Theme: textual > clause conj + Theme: experiential / Finite

> weqatal 3ms / Process > qal היה. The verb היה followed by לְ has the meaning *become*.

לְאַרְבָּעָה רָאשִׁים. Attribute > prep phrase: prep + numeral mp + noun common mp.

2:11 // שֵׁ֥ם הָאֶחָ֖ד פִּישׁ֑וֹן // ה֣וּא הַסֹּבֵ֗ב אֵ֚ת כָּל־אֶ֣רֶץ
הַֽחֲוִילָ֔ה | אֲשֶׁר־שָׁ֖ם הַזָּהָֽב׃

שֵׁם הָאֶחָד פִּישׁוֹן. (a) Textuality > appositive paratactic expansion / Mood > declarative: non-past / Transitivity > relational: identification.

פִּישׁוֹן	שֵׁם הָאֶחָד	**Constituents**
Pishon	*the name of the one*	**Translation**
	Theme	**Textuality**
Complement	Subject	**Mood**
Identifier	Identified	**Transitivity**

שֵׁם הָאֶחָד. Theme: experiential / Subject > ms (שֵׁם) / Identified > nominal group: noun common ms const ׀ def art + numeral ms.

פִּישׁוֹן. Complement / Identifier > noun proper.

הוּא הַסֹּבֵב אֵת כָּל־אֶרֶץ הַֽחֲוִילָה [[אֲשֶׁר־שָׁם הַזָּהָב]]. (b) Textuality > appositive paratactic expansion / Mood > declarative: non-past / Transitivity > relational: identification.

הַסֹּבֵב אֵת כָּל־אֶרֶץ הַחֲוִילָה [[אֲשֶׁר־שָׁם הַזָּהָב]]	הוּא	**Constituents**
the one circling all of the land of the Chavila, which there is the gold	*he*	**Translation**
	Theme	**Textuality**
Complement	Subject	**Mood**
Identifier	Identified	**Transitivity**

הוּא. Identified > pronoun suffix 3ms, antecedent is **פִּישׁוֹן** in clause (a).

הַסֹּבֵב אֵת כָּל־אֶרֶץ הַחֲוִילָה אֲשֶׁר־שָׁם הַזָּהָב. (i) Complement / Identifier >> Textuality > embedded ptc clause / Transitivity > material: action.

אֵת כָּל־אֶרֶץ הַחֲוִילָה [[אֲשֶׁר־שָׁם הַזָּהָב]]	הַסֹּבֵב	**Constituents**
all of the land of the Chavila, which there is the gold	*the one circling*	**Translation**
	Theme	**Textuality**
Goal	Actor / Process	**Transitivity**

הַסֹּבֵב. Theme: experiential / Actor > def art + ptc ms / Process > qal **סבב**.

אֵת כָּל־אֶרֶץ הַחֲוִילָה [[אֲשֶׁר־שָׁם הַזָּהָב]]. Goal > nominal group: Head + Post-modifier.

אֵת כָּל־אֶרֶץ הַחֲוִילָה. Head > nominal group: goal marker | noun common collective ms const + noun common fs const | def art + noun proper. For the use of the definite article with proper nouns, compare the Jordan.

אֲשֶׁר־שָׁם הַזָּהָב. (a') Post-modifier >> Textuality > embedded expansion: relative clause / Mood > declarative: non-past / Transitivity > relational: attribution.

הַזָּהָב	שָׁם	אֲשֶׁר־	**Constituents**
the gold	*there*	*which*	**Translation**
		Theme	**Textuality**
Subject	Complement		**Mood**
Carrier	Attribute		**Transitivity**

אֲשֶׁר־. Theme: textual > pronoun relative, antecedent is **כָּל־אֶרֶץ הַחֲוִילָה** or just **הַחֲוִילָה**.

שָׁם. Complement / Attribute > pronoun textual, antecedent is the same as that of **אֲשֶׁר**. The gold is there, in all the land of Chavila.

הַזָּהָב. Subject / Carrier > nominal group: def art + noun common ms. The noun is definite suggesting that this gold is somehow common knowledge, though it has not been mentioned before in the text.

2:12 // וּזֲהַב הָאָרֶץ הַהִוא טוֹב // שָׁם הַבְּדֹלַח וְאֶבֶן הַשֹּׁהַם׃

וּזֲהַב הָאָרֶץ הַהִוא טוֹב. (a) Textuality > conj paratactic expansion / Mood > declarative: non-past / Transitivity > relational: attribution.

טוֹב	וּזֲהַב הָאָרֶץ הַהִוא	**Constituents**
good	*and the gold of that land*	**Translation**
	Theme	**Textuality**
Complement	Subject	**Mood**
Attribute	Carrier	**Transitivity**

וּזֲהַב הָאָרֶץ הַהִוא. Theme: textual > clause conj + Theme: experiential / Subject > ms / Carrier > nominal group: noun common ms const | def art + noun common fs | def art + pronoun demonstrative, antecedent is אֶרֶץ הַחֲוִילָה in 2:11(b).

טוֹב. Complement / Attribute > adj ms.

שָׁם הַבְּדֹלַח וְאֶבֶן הַשֹּׁהַם. (b) Textuality > appositive paratactic expansion / Mood > declarative: past / Transitivity > relational: attribution.

הַבְּדֹלַח וְאֶבֶן הַשֹּׁהַם	שָׁם	**Constituents**
the bdellium and the stone of the onyx	*there*	**Translation**
	Theme	**Textuality**
Subject	Complement	**Mood**
Carrier	Attribute	**Transitivity**

שָׁם. Theme: textual and experiential / Complement / Attribute > circumstance: place; antecedent is אֶרֶץ הַחֲוִילָה.

הַבְּדֹלַח וְאֶבֶן הַשֹּׁהַם. Subject > mp / Carrier > nominal group complex: def art + noun common ms | group conj + noun common fs const | def art + noun common ms.

2:13 // וְשֵֽׁם־הַנָּהָ֥ר הַשֵּׁנִ֖י גִּיח֑וֹן // ה֣וּא הַסּוֹבֵ֔ב אֵ֖ת כָּל־אֶ֥רֶץ כּֽוּשׁ׃

וְשֵׁם־הַנָּהָר הַשֵּׁנִי גִּיחוֹן. (a) Textuality > conj paratactic expansion / Mood > declarative: non-past / Transitivity > relational: identification.

גִּיחוֹן	וְשֵׁם־הַנָּהָר הַשֵּׁנִי	**Constituents**
Gihon	*and the name of the second river*	**Translation**
	Theme	**Textuality**
Complement	Subject	**Mood**
Identifier	Identified	**Transitivity**

וְשֵׁם־הַנָּהָר הַשֵּׁנִי. Theme: textual > clause conj + Theme: experiential / Subject > ms / Identified > nominal group: noun common ms const + def art + noun common ms + def art + adj ms.

גִּיחוֹן. Complement / Identifier > nominal group: noun proper.

הוּא [[הַסֹּבֵב אֵת כָּל־אֶרֶץ כּוּשׁ]]. (b) Textuality > appositive paratactic expansion / Mood > declarative: non-past / Transitivity > relational: identification.

[[הַסֹּבֵב אֵת כָּל־אֶרֶץ כּוּשׁ]]	הוּא	**Constituents**
the one circling all of the land of Kush	*he*	**Translation**
	Theme	**Textuality**
Complement	Subject	**Mood**
Identifier	Identified	**Transitivity**

הוּא. Theme: textual and experiential / Subject > ms / Identified > pronoun personal/demonstrative 3ms.

הַסּוֹבֵב אֵת כָּל־אֶרֶץ כּוּשׁ. (i) Complement / Identifier >> Textuality > embedded ptc clause / Transitivity > material: action.

אֵת כָּל־אֶרֶץ כּוּשׁ	הַסֹּבֵב	**Constituents**
all of the land of Kush	*the one circling*	**Translation**
	Theme	**Textuality**
Goal	Actor / Process	**Transitivity**

הַסֹּבֵב. Theme: textual and experiential / Actor > def art + ptc ms / Process > qal **סבב**.

אֵת כָּל־אֶרֶץ כּוּשׁ. Goal > nominal group: goal marker ׀ noun common collective ms const - noun common fs const ׀ noun proper.

2:14 // וְשֵׁם הַנָּהָר הַשְּׁלִישִׁי חִדֶּקֶל // הוּא הַהֹלֵךְ
קִדְמַת אַשּׁוּר // וְהַנָּהָר הָרְבִיעִי הוּא פְרָת׃

וְשֵׁם הַנָּהָר הַשְּׁלִישִׁי חִדֶּקֶל. (a) Textuality > conj paratactic expansion / Mood > declarative: non-past / Transitivity > relational: identification.

חִדֶּקֶל	וְשֵׁם הַנָּהָר הַשְּׁלִישִׁי	**Constituents**
Chideqel	*and the name of the third river*	**Translation**
	Theme	**Textuality**
Complement	Subject	**Mood**
Identifier	Identified	**Transitivity**

וְשֵׁם הַנָּהָר הַשְּׁלִישִׁי. Theme: textual > clause conj + Theme: experiential / Subject > ms / Identified > nominal group: noun common ms const + def art + noun common ms + def art + adj ms.

חִדֶּקֶל. Complement / Identifier > nominal group: noun proper.

הוּא הַהֹלֵךְ קִדְמַת אַשּׁוּר. (b) Textuality > appositive paratactic expansion / Mood > declarative: non-past / Transitivity > relational: identification.

הַהֹלֵךְ קִדְמַת אַשּׁוּר	הוּא	**Constituents**
the one going east of 'Ashur	*he*	**Translation**
	Theme	**Textuality**
Complement	Subject	**Mood**
Identifier	Identified	**Transitivity**

הוּא. Theme: experiential / Subject > ms / Identified > pronoun personal/demonstrative 3ms, antecedent is חִדֶּקֶל Chideqel.

הַסֹּבֵב אֵת כָּל־אֶרֶץ כּוּשׁ. (i) Complement / Identifier >> Textuality > embedded ptc clause / Transitivity > material: action.

קִדְמַת אַשּׁוּר	הַהֹלֵךְ	**Constituents**
east of 'Ashur	*the one going*	**Translation**
	Theme	**Textuality**
Circumstance	Actor / Process	**Transitivity**

הַהֹלֵךְ. Theme: textual and experiential / Actor > def art + ptc ms / Process > qal הלך.

קִדְמַת אַשּׁוּר. Adjunct / Circumstance: location, place > nominal group: noun common fs const ı noun proper.

וְהַנָּהָר הָרְבִיעִי הוּא פְרָת. (c) Textuality > conj paratactic expansion / Mood > declarative: non-past / Transitivity > relational: attribution.

פְרָת	הוּא	וְהַנָּהָר הָרְבִיעִי	**Constituents**
Perat	*he*	*and the fourth river*	**Translation**
		Theme	**Textuality**
Complement	Subject	Subject	**Mood**
Identifier	Identified	Identified	**Transitivity**

וְהַנָּהָר הָרְבִיעִי. Theme: textual > clause conj + Theme: experiential / Subject > ms / Identified > nominal group: def art + noun common ms | def art + numeral ms. This is a preposed Theme.

הוּא. Subject > ms / Identified > pronoun personal 3ms.

פְרָת. Complement / Identifier > nominal group: noun proper.

Genesis 2:15

[15]And YHVH deity took the human. And he rested him in the garden of Eden to work it and to watch it.

2:15 /// וַיִּקַּח יְהוָה אֱלֹהִים אֶת־הָאָדָם // וַיַּנִּחֵהוּ בְגַן־
עֵדֶן לְעָבְדָהּ וּלְשָׁמְרָהּ׃

וַיִּקַּח יְהוָה אֱלֹהִים אֶת־הָאָדָם. (a) Textuality > conj paratactic expansion / Mood > declarative: past / Transitivity > material: action.

אֶת־הָאָדָם	יְהוָה אֱלֹהִים	וַיִּקַּח	**Constituents**
the human	*YHVH deity*	*and he took*	**Translation**
		Theme	**Textuality**
	Subject	Finite	**Mood**
Goal	Actor	Process	**Transitivity**

וַיִּקַּח. Theme: textual > clause conj + Theme: experiential / Finite > wayyiqtol 3ms / Process > qal לקח.

יְהוָה אֱלֹהִים. Subject > ms / Actor > nominal group: noun proper ms | noun common mp.

אֶת־הָאָדָם. Goal > nominal group: goal marker - def art + noun common ms.

וַיַּנִּחֵהוּ בְגַן־עֵדֶן [[לְעָבְדָהּ וּלְשָׁמְרָהּ]]. (b) Textuality > conj paratactic expansion / Mood > declarative: past / Transitivity > material: action. The Actor is יְהוָה אֱלֹהִים, absent by ellipsis. The pronoun suffix on the verb serves as the Goal. By appending the Goal to the Process, both together become the Theme.

[[לְעָבְדָהּ וּלְשָׁמְרָהּ]]	בְגַן־עֵדֶן	וַיַּנִּחֵהוּ	**Constituents**
to work it and to watch it	*in the garden of Eden*	*and he rested him*	**Translation**
		Theme	**Textuality**
		Finite	**Mood**
Circumstance	Circumstance	Process + Goal	**Transitivity**

וַיַּנִּחֵהוּ. Theme: textual > clause conj + Theme: experiential / Finite > wayyiqtol 3ms / Process > hifil נוח + Goal > pronoun suffix 3ms, antecedent is הָאָדָם the human.

בְגַן־עֵדֶן. Circumstance: location, place > prep phrase: prep + noun common m/fs const - noun proper.

לְעָבְדָהּ וּלְשָׁמְרָהּ. (i) Circumstance: cause, purpose >> embedded prep phrase complex. Each prepositional phrase is an embedded clause. Together they are a single circumstantial constituent of the enclosing clause.

לְעָבְדָהּ. (a') Prep phrase 1 >> Textuality > embedded expansion: prep clause / Transitivity > material: action.

לְעָבְדָהּ	**Constituents**
to work it	**Translation**
Theme	**Textuality**
Process + Goal	**Transitivity**

לְעָבְדָהּ. Theme: textual > prep + Theme: experiential / Process > inf const qal עבד + Goal > pronoun suffix 3fs, antecedent is גַן־עֵדֶן garden of Eden.

וּלְשָׁמְרָהּ. Group conj + (b') Prep phrase 2 >> Textuality > embedded expansion: prep clause / Transitivity > material: action.

וּלְשָׁמְרָהּ	**Constituents**
to watch it	**Translation**
Theme	**Textuality**
Process + Goal	**Transitivity**

וּלְשָׁמְרָהּ. Group conj + Theme: textual > prep + Theme: experiential / Process > inf const qal שׁמר + Goal > pronoun suffix 3fs, antecedent is גַּן־עֵדֶן garden of Eden.

Genesis 2:16-17

[16]And YHVH deity placed a command on the human by saying, "From all of the treekind of the garden you must eat. [17]And from the tree of the knowledge of good and bad, you will not eat from it, because in the day of your eating from it you will certainly die."

2:16 /// וַיְצַו יְהוָה אֱלֹהִים עַל־הָאָדָם לֵאמֹר // מִכֹּל עֵץ־הַגָּן אָכֹל תֹּאכֵל׃

וַיְצַו יְהוָה אֱלֹהִים עַל־הָאָדָם לֵאמֹר. (a) Textuality > conj paratactic expansion / Mood > declarative: past / Transitivity > verbal. The following quote clause indicates that this is a verbal process, but by construing the Receiver almost as a Circumstance, using the prep עַל rather than לְ or אֶל, it has the flavor of a material process. The fully explicit transitivity structure, along with a change in Theme, suggests this is a new clause complex.

לֵאמֹר	עַל־הָאָדָם	יְהוָה אֱלֹהִים	וַיְצַו	**Constituents**
by saying	*on the human*	*YHVH deity*	*and he put a command*	**Translation**
			Theme	**Textuality**
		Subject	Finite	**Mood**
Circumstance	Receiver	Sayer	Process	**Transitivity**

וַיְצַו. Theme: textual > clause conj + Theme: experiential / Finite > wayyiqtol 3ms / Process > piel צוה.

יְהוָה אֱלֹהִים. Subject > ms / Sayer > nominal group: noun proper ms | noun common mp.

עַל־הָאָדָם. Receiver > prep phrase: prep - def art + noun common ms. הָאָדָם is not here a collective noun, as it was in chapter 1; rather, here it refers to the human male.

לֵאמֹר. Circumstance: manner, means > prep + inf const qal אמר. This functions to mark a following quote and could be called the quote marker.

מִכֹּל עֵץ־הַגָּן אָכֹל תֹּאכֵל. (b) Textuality > appositive paratactic projection: quote / Mood > declarative: non-past / Transitivity > material: action. The Subject / Receiver of the quote is הָאָדָם *the human* in the preceding clause.

תֹּאכֵל	אָכֹל	מִכֹּל עֵץ־הַגָּן	**Constituents**
you will eat	*eating*	*from all of the treekind of the garden*	**Translation**
		Theme	**Textuality**
Finite	Adjunct		**Mood**
Process		Range/Goal	**Transitivity**

מִכֹּל עֵץ־הַגָּן. Theme: textual and experiential / Range > prep phrase: prep + noun common collective ms const | noun common ms const - def art + noun common ms. The prep מִן *from* may be construed in its so-called partitive use, meaning a part of the whole, and could be translated *some of*. See MNK 289. Reading it this way, the prepositional phrase would then be a Goal, rather than a Range.

אָכֹל. Adjunct: interpersonal > modal: inf abs qal אכל. This is cognate to the following Finite verb. The inf abs is not a component of the experiential structure of the clause; eliminating it would not detract from the experiential meaning. It is a component of the interpersonal

Mood structure, and adds modality to the Finite verb. In this case, the infinitive absolute indicates a strong degree of obligation: *you must eat. . . .* Comparing this clause with the following one, the אָכֹל here stands essentially in the same position as the לֹא there. This might suggest that the infinitive absolute is akin to an interpersonal adjunct of polarity: a strong *yes* of permission in contrast to the following *no* of prohibition.

תֹּאכֵל. Finite > yiqtol 2ms / Process > qal אכל.

2:17 // וּמֵעֵץ הַדַּעַת טוֹב וָרָע לֹא תֹאכַל מִמֶּנּוּ / כִּי בְּיוֹם אֲכָלְךָ מִמֶּנּוּ מוֹת תָּמוּת׃

וּמֵעֵץ הַדַּעַת טוֹב וָרָע לֹא תֹאכַל מִמֶּנּוּ. (a) Textuality > conj paratactic projection: quote / Mood > declarative: non-past / Transitivity > material: action.

מִמֶּנּוּ	תֹאכַל	לֹא	וּמֵעֵץ הַדַּעַת טוֹב וָרָע	**Constituents**
from him	*you will eat*	*not*	*and from the tree of the knowledge of good-and-bad*	**Translation**
			Theme	**Textuality**
	Finite	Adjunct		**Mood**
Circumstance	Process		Range/Goal	**Transitivity**

וּמֵעֵץ הַדַּעַת טוֹב וָרָע. Theme: textual > clause conj + Range > prep phrase complex: Head + Post-modifier. This is a preposed circumstantial Theme. It is later substituted at the end of the clause. On a possible partitive use of מִן, see the discussion of the preceding clause.

מֵעֵץ הַדַּעַת. Head > prep phrase: prep + noun common ms const | def art + noun common fs.

טוֹב וָרָע. Post-modifier > adjective group: adj ms | group conj + adj ms. See 2:9(a).

לֹא. Adjunct: interpersonal > polarity: negative. לֹא + yiqtol in negative commands is associated with absolute prohibitions, in contrast with אַל + yiqtol.

תֹאכַל. Finite > yiqtol 2ms / Process > qal אכל. Compare 2:16(b) where it is vocalized תֹּאכֵל because it bears pausal stress, being the last word of the verse.

מִמֶּנּוּ. Goal > prep phrase: prep + pronoun suffix 3ms, antecedent is עֵץ. Strictly speaking this reiteration of the Goal from the beginning of the clause is not needed in the experiential structure; both refer to the same thing. Rather, it functions within the textual structure to substitute for the preposed Theme in the place where it would normally be located in the clause structure.

כִּי בְּיוֹם אֲכָלְךָ מִמֶּנּוּ מוֹת תָּמוּת. (b) Textuality > conj hypotactic projection: quote / Mood > declarative: non-past / Transitivity > material: action.

תָּמוּת	מוֹת	בְּיוֹם אֲכָלְךָ מִמֶּנּוּ	כִּי	**Constituents**
you will die	*dying*	*in the day of your eating from it*	*because*	**Translation**
		Theme	Theme	**Textuality**
Finite	Adjunct			**Mood**
Process		Circumstance		**Transitivity**

כִּי. Theme: textual > conj. This signals that the clause is dependent on the preceding clause and expands its meaning.

בְּיוֹם אֲכָלְךָ מִמֶּנּוּ. (i) Theme: experiential / Circumstance: location, time >> Textuality > embedded prep clause / Transitivity > material: action.

מִמֶּנּוּ	אֲכָלְךָ	בְּיוֹם	**Constituents**
from him	*your eating*	*in the day of*	**Translation**
		Theme	**Textuality**
Goal	Process + Actor	Circumstance	**Transitivity**

בְּיוֹם אֲכָלְךָ. Theme: textual > prep + Theme: experiential / Circumstance > noun common ms const + Process > inf const qal אכל + Actor > pronoun suffix 2ms, antecedent is the *you*, that is, the Receiver of the quoted verbal command.

מִמֶּנּוּ. Goal > prep phrase: prep + pronoun suffix 3ms, antecedent is עֵץ־הַגָּן.

מוֹת. Adjunct: interpersonal > modal: inf abs qal מות. This is cognate to the following Finite verb and is not needed for the experiential structure of the clause, but belongs to the Mood system. It expresses modality, in this case, a strong degree of certainty: *must die, will surely die, yes you will die,* or the like.

תָּמוּת. Finite > yiqtol 2ms / Process > qal מות.

Genesis 2:18

[18]*And YHVH deity said, "Not good is the human's being alone. I will make for him a help as his opposite."*

2:18 /// וַיֹּאמֶר יְהוָה אֱלֹהִים // לֹא־טוֹב הֱיוֹת הָאָדָם לְבַדּוֹ // אֶעֱשֶׂה־לּוֹ עֵזֶר כְּנֶגְדּוֹ׃

וַיֹּאמֶר יְהוָה אֱלֹהִים. (a) Textuality > conj paratactic expansion / Mood > declarative: past / Transitivity > verbal. The preceding clause complex was built around a quote addressed to the human. This clause begins a new clause complex. The verbal process does not have a Receiver.

יְהוָה אֱלֹהִים	וַיֹּאמֶר	**Constituents**
YHVH deity	*and he said*	**Translation**
	Theme	**Textuality**
Subject	Finite	**Mood**
Sayer	Process	**Transitivity**

וַיֹּאמֶר. Theme: textual > clause conj + Theme: experiential / Finite > wayyiqtol 3ms / Process > qal אמר.

יְהוָה אֱלֹהִים. Subject > ms / Sayer > nominal group: noun proper + noun common mp.

לֹא־טוֹב [[הֱיוֹת הָאָדָם לְבַדּוֹ]]. (b) Textuality > conj paratactic projection: quote / Mood > declarative: non-past / Transitivity > relational: attribution. This clause consists of one relational attributive clause embedded within another attributive relational clause. In the absence of a Receiver, the words of clauses (b-c) are projected as a record of the deity's thoughts and not as spoken words; notice that לֵאמֹר does not introduce the quote.

[[הֱיוֹת הָאָדָם לְבַדּוֹ]]	טוֹב	לֹא־	**Constituents**
the being of the human to himself	*good*	*not*	**Translation**
	Theme	Theme	**Textuality**
Subject	Complement	Adjunct	**Mood**
Carrier	Attribute		**Transitivity**

לֹא־. Theme: interpersonal / Adjunct: interpersonal > polarity: negative.

טוֹב. Theme: experiential / Complement / Attribute > adj ms. The adjective qualifies the entire embedded infinitive clause that is the Carrier.

הֱיוֹת הָאָדָם לְבַדּוֹ. (i) Subject / Carrier >> Textuality > embedded inf clause / Transitivity > relational: attribution. Before being embedded, this clause would have been, *the human is to himself*, i.e. *the human is alone*.

לְבַדּוֹ	הָאָדָם	הֱיוֹת	**Constituents**
to himself	*the human*	*the being of*	**Translation**
		Theme	**Textuality**
Attribute	Carrier	Process	**Transitivity**

הֱיוֹת. Process > inf const qal הָיָה.

הָאָדָם. Carrier > nominal group: def art + noun common ms.

לְבַדּוֹ. Attribute > prep phrase: prep + noun common ms const + pronoun suffix 3ms, antecedent is הָאָדָם.

אֶעֱשֶׂה־לּוֹ עֵזֶר כְּנֶגְדּוֹ. (c) Textuality > appositive paratactic projection: quote / Mood > declarative: non-past or directive: cohortative / Transitivity > material: action. The Sayer / Actor is יְהוָה אֱלֹהִים *YHVH deity* in clause (a).

עֵזֶר כְּנֶגְדּוֹ	לּוֹ	אֶעֱשֶׂה־	**Constituents**
a help as his opposite	*for him*	*I will make / let me make*	**Translation**
		Theme	**Textuality**
		Finite	**Mood**
Goal	Beneficiary	Process	**Transitivity**

אֶעֱשֶׂה־. Theme: experiential / Finite > yiqtol or cohortative 1cs / Process > qal עשׂה. This form could be either declarative (future) I will make or directive (cohortative) let me make.

לּוֹ. Beneficiary > prep phrase: prep + pronoun suffix 3ms, antecedent is הָאָדָם *the human.* Notice the conj dagesh in the lamed.

עֵזֶר כְּנֶגְדּוֹ. Goal > nominal group: Head + Post-modifier.

עֵזֶר. Head > nominal group: noun common ms.

כְּנֶגְדּוֹ. Post-modifier > prep phrase: prep + prep or noun ms const + pronoun suffix 3ms, antecedent is הָאָדָם *the human.* The force of כְּ and נֶגֶד in combination remains somewhat elusive. Here it is construed as a Circumstance in the the sense of role: a helper as a complement to him.

Genesis 2:19-20

[19]And YHVH deity formed from the ground all of the livingkind of the field and all of the fowl of the heavens. And he brought to the human to

see what he will call it. And all which the human will call a living being, that is its name. [20]*And the human called names to all of the beastkind and to the fowl of the heavens and to all of the livingkind of the field. And for the man, he found not a help as his opposite.*

2:19 /// וַיִּצֶר֩ יְהוָ֨ה אֱלֹהִ֜ים מִן־הָֽאֲדָמָ֗ה כָּל־חַיַּ֤ת הַשָּׂדֶה֙
וְאֵת֙ כָּל־ע֣וֹף הַשָּׁמַ֔יִם // וַיָּבֵא֙ אֶל־הָ֣אָדָ֔ם לִרְא֖וֹת
מַה־יִּקְרָא־ל֑וֹ // וְכֹל֩ אֲשֶׁ֨ר יִקְרָא־ל֧וֹ הָֽאָדָ֛ם נֶ֥פֶשׁ
חַיָּ֖ה ה֥וּא שְׁמֽוֹ׃

וַיִּצֶר יְהוָה אֱלֹהִים מִן־הָאֲדָמָה כָּל־חַיַּת הַשָּׂדֶה וְאֵת כָּל־עוֹף הַשָּׁמַיִם. (a) Textuality > conj paratactic expansion / Mood > declarative: past / Transitivity > material: action.

כָּל־חַיַּת הַשָּׂדֶה וְאֵת כָּל־עוֹף הַשָּׁמַיִם	מִן־הָאֲדָמָה	יְהוָה אֱלֹהִים	וַיִּצֶר	**Constituents**
all of the livingkind of the field and all of the fowl of the heavens	*from the ground*	*YHVH deity*	*and he formed*	**Translation**
			Theme	**Textuality**
		Subject	Finite	**Mood**
Goal	Circumstance	Actor	Process	**Transitivity**

וַיִּצֶר. Theme: textual > clause conj + Theme: experiential / Finite > wayyiqtol 3ms / Process > qal **יצר**.

יְהוָה אֱלֹהִים. Subject > ms / Actor > nominal group: noun proper ms | noun common mp.

מִן־הָאֲדָמָה. Circumstance: material > prep phrase: prep - def art + noun common fs. Compare 2:7(a).

כָּל־חַיַּת הַשָּׂדֶה וְאֵת כָּל־עוֹף הַשָּׁמַיִם. Goal > nominal group complex; only the second is prefixed with the goal marker. Perhaps this was intended to create a disjunction between the two components of the Goal, such that the first one (*all of the livingkind of the field*) were fashioned out of the ground, but not necessarily *all of the birds of the heavens*.

כָּל־חַיַּת הַשָּׂדֶה. Goal 1 > nominal group: noun common collective ms const - noun common collective fs const | def art + noun common ms.

וְאֵת כָּל־עוֹף הַשָּׁמַיִם. Group conj + Goal 2 > nominal group: goal marker | noun common collective ms const + noun common collective ms const | def art + noun common mp.

(b) וַיָּבֵא אֶל־הָאָדָם [[לִרְאוֹת [[מַה־יִּקְרָא־לוֹ]]]]. Textuality > conj paratactic expansion / Mood > declarative: past / Transitivity > material: action. The Subject / Actor and the Goal are absent by ellipsis. The Subject / Actor is יְהוָה אֱלֹהִים in the preceding clause, and the Goal of the material Process is the Goal of the preceding clause, כָּל־חַיַּת הַשָּׂדֶה וְאֵת כָּל־עוֹף הַשָּׁמַיִם; both are textually absent here by ellipsis and must be assumed. This clause is notable in that it contains three verbal processes and two embedded clauses, one embedded in the other.

[[לִרְאוֹת [[מַה־יִּקְרָא־לוֹ]]]]	אֶל־הָאָדָם	וַיָּבֵא	**Constituents**
to see what he will call him	*to the human*	*and he brought*	**Translation**
		Theme	**Textuality**
		Finite	**Mood**
Circumstance	Circumstance	Process	**Transitivity**

וַיָּבֵא. Theme: textual > clause conj + Theme: experiential / Finite > wayyiqtol 3ms / Process > hifil בוא.

אֶל־הָאָדָם. Circumstance: location, place > prep phrase: prep - def art + noun common ms.

לִרְאוֹת [[מַה־יִּקְרָא־לוֹ]]. (i) Circumstance: reason, purpose >> Textuality > embedded extension: prep clause / Transitivity > mental: perception. Notice how the mental process of perception is a metaphor for finding out or coming to know what the man would call them—a mental process of cognition.

[[מַה־יִּקְרָא־לוֹ]]	לִרְאוֹת	**Constituents**
what he will call him	*to see*	**Translation**
	Theme	**Textuality**
Phenomenon	Process	**Transitivity**

לִרְאוֹת. Theme: textual > prep + Theme: experiential / Process > inf const qal ראה.

מַה־יִּקְרָא־לוֹ. (a') Phenomenon >> Textuality > embedded relative clause / Mood > interrogative: non-past / Transitivity > verbal. Before embedding, this clause would be: *What will he call him*? This verbal process clause is the Phenomenon of its enclosing mental process clause.

לוֹ	יִקְרָא־	מַה־	**Constituents**
him	*he will call*	*what*	**Translation**
		Theme	**Textuality**
	Finite		**Mood**
Target	Process	Verbiage	**Transitivity**

מַה־. Verbiage > pronoun interrogative, functioning as a relative pronoun.

יִקְרָא־. Finite > yiqtol 3ms / Process > qal קרא.

לוֹ. Target > prep phrase: prep + pronoun suffix 3ms, antecedent is כָּל־ each, the head noun of the Goals of clause (a). We might have expected this pronoun suffix to be plural. But the singular promotes the notion that he named each member of the collectivities separately.

וְכֹל [[אֲשֶׁר יִקְרָא־לוֹ הָאָדָם נֶפֶשׁ חַיָּה]] הוּא שְׁמוֹ. (c)

Textuality > conj paratactic expansion / Mood > declarative: non-past / Transitivity > relational: identification. The structure of this clause is rather involved; keeping the referents of all the nominal groups straight presented a challenge to the writer and remains a challenge to the reader.

שְׁמוֹ	הוּא	וְכֹל [[אֲשֶׁר יִקְרָא־לוֹ הָאָדָם נֶפֶשׁ חַיָּה]]	**Constituents**
his name	*that*	*and all of which the human will call him a living being*	**Translation**
		Theme	**Textuality**
Subject	Complement	Complement	**Mood**
Identified	Identifier	Identifier	**Transitivity**

וְכֹל [[אֲשֶׁר יִקְרָא־לוֹ הָאָדָם נֶפֶשׁ חַיָּה]]. Theme: textual > clause conj + Theme: experiential / Complement / Identifier > nominal group: Head + Post-modifier. This is a preposed Theme, and a very heavy one.

כֹל. Head > nominal group: noun common collective ms.

אֲשֶׁר יִקְרָא־לוֹ הָאָדָם נֶפֶשׁ חַיָּה. (i) Post-modifier >> Textuality > embedded expansion: relative clause / Mood > declarative: non-past / Transitivity > verbal.

נֶפֶשׁ חַיָּה	הָאָדָם	לוֹ	יִקְרָא־	אֲשֶׁר	**Constituents**
a living being	*the human*	*him*	*he will call*	*which*	**Translation**
				Theme	**Textuality**
	Subject		Finite		**Mood**
Target	Sayer	Target	Process	Verbiage	**Transitivity**

אֲשֶׁר. Theme: textual and experiential > pronoun relative / Verbiage > antecedent כֹל *all.*

יִקְרָא־. Finite > yiqtol 3ms / Process > qal קרא.

לוֹ. Target > prep phrase: prep + pronoun suffix 3ms, the antecedent presumably again is כָּל־ *all*, the head noun of the Goals of clause (a) —also referenced in clause (b). Shortly, the Target will also be glossed with נֶפֶשׁ חַיָּה, lest we forget that to which all the pronouns refer.

הָאָדָם. Subject > ms / Sayer > nominal group: def art + noun common ms.

נֶפֶשׁ חַיָּה. Target > nominal group: noun common fs | adj fs. This nominal group is construed as a a distant post-modifier; it extends the meaning of the pronoun suffix of לוֹ above.

הוּא. Complement / Identifier > pronoun personal 3ms, antecedent is specifically כֹּל, but by extension, it references כֹּל + its embedded relative clause. A pronoun is used here to substitute for a preposed Theme.

שְׁמוֹ. Subject / Identified > nominal group: noun common ms const + pronoun suffix 3 ms, antecedent is הוּא and everything it in turn references.

2:20 וַיִּקְרָא הָאָדָם שֵׁמוֹת לְכָל־הַבְּהֵמָה וּלְעוֹף הַשָּׁמַיִם // וּלְכֹל חַיַּת הַשָּׂדֶה // וּלְאָדָם לֹא־מָצָא עֵזֶר כְּנֶגְדּוֹ׃

וַיִּקְרָא הָאָדָם שֵׁמוֹת לְכָל־הַבְּהֵמָה וּלְעוֹף הַשָּׁמַיִם וּלְכֹל חַיַּת הַשָּׂדֶה. (a) Textuality > conj paratactic expansion / Mood > declarative: past / Transitivity > verbal.

לְכָל־הַבְּהֵמָה וּלְעוֹף הַשָּׁמַיִם וּלְכֹל חַיַּת הַשָּׂדֶה	שֵׁמוֹת	הָאָדָם	וַיִּקְרָא	**Constituents**
to all of the beastkind and to the fowl of the heavens and to all of the livingkind of the field	*names*	*the human*	*and he called*	**Translation**
			Theme	**Textuality**
		Subject	Finite	**Mood**
Target	Verbiage	Sayer	Process	**Transitivity**

וַיִּקְרָא. Theme: textual > clause conj + Theme: experiential / Finite > wayyiqtol 3ms / Process > qal קרא.

הָאָדָם. Subject > ms / Sayer > nominal group: def art + noun common ms.

שֵׁמוֹת. Verbiage > nominal group: noun common fp.

לְכָל־הַבְּהֵמָה וּלְעוֹף הַשָּׁמַיִם וּלְכֹל חַיַּת הַשָּׂדֶה. Target > prep phrase complex.

לְכָל־הַבְּהֵמָה. Target 1 > prep phrase: prep + noun common collective ms const - def art + noun common collective fs.

וּלְעוֹף הַשָּׁמַיִם. Group conj + Target 2 > prep phrase: prep + noun common collective ms const ׀ def art + noun common mp.

וּלְכֹל חַיַּת הַשָּׂדֶה. Group conj + Target 3 > prep phrase: prep + noun common ms const ׀ noun common collective fs const ׀ def art + noun common ms.

וּלְאָדָם לֹא־מָצָא עֵזֶר כְּנֶגְדּוֹ. (b) Textuality > conj paratactic expansion / Mood > declarative: past / Transitivity > mental: cognition. The Subject / Senser is הָאָדָם the human in the preceding clause, absent here by ellipsis. In this clause the Senser is the same as the Beneficiary.

עֵזֶר כְּנֶגְדּוֹ	מָצָא	לֹא־	וּלְאָדָם	**Constituents**
a help as his opposite	*he found*	*not*	*and to a human*	**Translation**
			Theme	**Textuality**
	Finite	Adjunct		**Mood**
Goal	Process		Beneficiary	**Transitivity**

The process could be construed as a material one, taking find in the sense of the activity of searching. Or it could be construed as a mental-cognitive one, as chosen here. In either case, the Actor or Senser is not specified; it is absent by ellipsis, and the antecedent might be either YHVH deity in 2:19(a) or the man in 2:20(a). KJV, NJPS, and the NRSV, avoid the issue by rendering the verb as a passive: *but for the man there was not found a helper as his partner* (2:20a). Friedman construes YHVH as the doer: *But he did not find for the human a strength corresponding to him.* Here is a rendition of the clause as a mental process of cognition having to do with awareness or discovery, with הָאָדָם as the Senser: *But for himself a human, he did not find a helper matching him.*

וּלְאָדָם. Theme: textual > clause conj + Theme: experiential / Beneficiary > prep phrase: prep + noun common ms. Note that there is no definite article on the noun.

לֹא־. Adjunct: interpersonal > polarity: negative.

מָצָא. Finite > qatal 3ms / Process > qal מצא.

עֵזֶר כְּנֶגְדּוֹ. Phenomenon > nominal group: Head + Post-modifier.

עֵזֶר. Head > nominal group: noun common ms.

כְּנֶגְדּוֹ. Post-modifier > prep phrase: prep + prep or noun ms const + pronoun suffix 3ms, antecedent is הָאָדָם the human. See 2:18(c).

Genesis 2:21-23

[21]*And YHVH deity dropped a coma on the human. And he slept. And he took one of his ribs. And he closed flesh under it.* [22]*And YHVH deity built the rib which he took from the man into a woman. And he brought her to the human.* [23]*And the human said, "This one, this time, is bone from my bones and flesh from my flesh. This one will be called woman, because from a man this one was taken."*

2:21 /// וַיַּפֵּל יְהוָה אֱלֹהִים ׀ תַּרְדֵּמָה עַל־הָאָדָם // וַיִּישָׁן
// וַיִּקַּח אַחַת מִצַּלְעֹתָיו // וַיִּסְגֹּר בָּשָׂר תַּחְתֶּנָּה׃

וַיַּפֵּל יְהוָה אֱלֹהִים תַּרְדֵּמָה עַל־הָאָדָם. (a) Textuality > conj paratactic expansion / Mood > declarative: past / Transitivity > material: action. Notice the graphically physical way this material process is worded.

עַל־הָאָדָם	תַּרְדֵּמָה	יְהוָה אֱלֹהִים	וַיַּפֵּל	**Constituents**
on the human	*a coma*	*YHVH deity*	*and he dropped*	**Translation**
			Theme	**Textuality**
		Subject	Finite	**Mood**
Circumstance	Goal	Actor	Process	**Transitivity**

וַיַּפֵּל. Theme: textual > clause conj + Theme: experiential / Finite > wayyiqtol 3ms / Process > hifil נפל.

יְהוָה אֱלֹהִים. Subject > ms / Actor > nominal group: noun proper ms ı noun common mp.

תַּרְדֵּמָה. Goal > nominal group: noun common fs. Traditionally, *a deep sleep*.

עַל־הָאָדָם. Circumstance: location, place > prep phrase: prep - def art + noun common ms.

וַיִּישָׁן. (b) Textuality > conj paratactic expansion / Mood > declarative: past / Transitivity > behavioral. The Subject / Behaver is הָאָדָם *the human* from the preceding clause, absent here by ellipsis.

וַיִּישָׁן	**Constituents**
and he slept	**Translation**
Theme	**Textuality**
Finite	**Mood**
Process	**Transitivity**

וַיִּישָׁן. Theme: textual > clause conj + Theme: experiential / Finite > wayyiqtol 3ms / Process > qal ישׁן.

וַיִּקַּח אַחַת מִצַּלְעֹתָיו. (c) Textuality > conj paratactic expansion / Mood > declarative: past / Transitivity > material: action. Now the Subject / Actor is יְהוָה אֱלֹהִים *YHVH deity* in clause (a), absent here by ellipsis. This represents a switch in Subject from the preceding clause, and neither of them had been explicitly named.

אַחַת מִצַּלְעֹתָיו	וַיִּקַּח	**Constituents**
one from his ribs	*and he took*	**Translation**
	Theme	**Textuality**
	Finite	**Mood**
Goal	Process	**Transitivity**

וַיִּקַּח. Theme: textual > clause conj + Theme: experiential / Finite > wayyiqtol 3ms / Process > qal לקח.

אַחַת מִצַּלְעֹתָיו. Goal > nominal group: Head + Post-modifier.

אַחַת. Head > nominal group: noun common fs.

מִצַּלְעֹתָיו. Post-modifier > prep phrase: prep + noun common fp const + pronoun suffix 3mp, antecedent is הָאָדָם *the human.*

וַיִּסְגֹּר בָּשָׂר תַּחְתֶּנָּה. (d) Textuality > conj paratactic expansion / Mood > declarative: past / Transitivity > material: action. The Subject / Actor is absent by ellipsis and is יְהוָה אֱלֹהִים from clause (a).

תַּחְתֶּנָּה	בָּשָׂר	וַיִּסְגֹּר	**Constituents**
under her	*flesh*	*and he closed*	**Translation**
		Theme	**Textuality**
		Finite	**Mood**
Circumstance	Goal	Process	**Transitivity**

וַיִּסְגֹּר . Theme: textual > clause conj + Theme: experiential / Finite > wayyiqtol 3ms / Process > qal סגר.

בָּשָׂר. Goal > nominal group: noun common ms.

תַּחְתֶּנָּה. Circumstance: location, place > prep phrase: prep + pronoun suffix 3fs, antecedent is אַחַת in clause (c).

2:22 // וַיִּבֶן יְהוָה אֱלֹהִים | אֶת־הַצֵּלָע אֲשֶׁר־לָקַח מִן־
הָאָדָם לְאִשָּׁה // וַיְבִאֶהָ אֶל־הָאָדָם׃

וַיִּבֶן יְהוָה אֱלֹהִים אֶת־הַצֵּלָע [[אֲשֶׁר־לָקַח מִן־הָאָדָם]] לְאִשָּׁה. (a) Textuality > conj paratactic expansion / Mood > declarative: past / Transitivity > material: action.

לְאִשָּׁה	אֶת־הַצֵּלָע [[אֲשֶׁר־לָקַח מִן־הָאָדָם]]	יְהוָה אֱלֹהִים	וַיִּבֶן	**Constituents**
to a woman	*the rib which he took from the human*	*YHVH deity*	*and he built*	**Translation**
			Theme	**Textuality**
		Subject	Finite	**Mood**
Circumstance	Goal	Actor	Process	**Transitivity**

וַיִּבֶן. Theme: textual > clause conj + Theme: experiential / Finite > wayyiqtol 3ms / Process > qal בנה.

יְהוָה אֱלֹהִים. Subject > ms / Actor > nominal group: noun proper ms | noun common mp.

אֶת־הַצֵּלָע [[אֲשֶׁר־לָקַח מִן־הָאָדָם]]. Goal > nominal group: Head + Post-modifier.

אֶת־הַצֵּלָע. Head > nominal group: goal marker - def art + noun common fs.

אֲשֶׁר־לָקַח מִן־הָאָדָם. (i) Post-modifier >> Textuality > embedded extension: relative clause / Mood > declarative: past / Transitivity > material: action.

מִן־הָאָדָם	לָקַח	אֲשֶׁר־	**Constituents**
from the human	*he took*	*which*	**Translation**
		Theme	**Textuality**
	Finite		**Mood**
Circumstance	Process	Goal	**Transitivity**

אֲשֶׁר־. Theme: textual and experiential / Goal > pronoun relative, antecedent is הַצֵּלָע *the rib.*

לָקַח. Finite > qatal 3ms / Process > qal לקח.

מִן־הָאָדָם. Circumstance: location, place > prep phrase: prep - def art + noun common ms.

לְאִשָּׁה. Circumstance: role, product > prep phrase: prep + noun common fs. This is a Circumstance of the main clause, not the embedded relative clause. A product is the result of turning one thing into another, in this case, building the rib into a woman.

וַיְבִאֶהָ אֶל־הָאָדָם. (b) Textuality > conj paratactic expansion / Mood > declarative: past / Transitivity > material: action.

אֶל־הָאָדָם	וַיְבִאֶהָ	**Constituents**
to the human	*and he brought her*	**Translation**
	Theme	**Textuality**
	Finite	**Mood**
Circumstance	Process + Goal	**Transitivity**

וַיְבִאֶהָ. Theme: textual > clause conj + Theme: experiential / Finite > wayyiqtol 3ms / Process > hifil בוא + Goal > pronoun suffix 3fs, antecedent is אִשָּׁה *woman* in the preceding clause. Combining the Process and the Goal into one word enables both to become the Theme.

אֶל־הָאָדָם. Circumstance: location, place > prep phrase: prep - def art + noun common ms.

2:23 // וַיֹּאמֶר הָאָדָם // זֹאת הַפַּעַם עֶצֶם מֵעֲצָמַי וּבָשָׂר
מִבְּשָׂרִי // לְזֹאת יִקָּרֵא אִשָּׁה / כִּי מֵאִישׁ לֻקֳחָה־
זֹּאת׃

וַיֹּאמֶר הָאָדָם. (a) Textuality > conj paratactic expansion / Mood > declarative: past / Transitivity > verbal.

הָאָדָם	וַיֹּאמֶר	**Constituents**
the human	*and he said*	**Translation**
	Theme	**Textuality**
Subject	Finite	**Mood**
Sayer	Process	**Transitivity**

וַיֹּאמֶר. Theme: textual > clause conj + Theme: experiential / Finite > wayyiqtol 3ms / Process > qal **אמר**.

הָאָדָם. Subject > ms / Sayer > nominal group: def art + noun common ms.

זֹאת הַפַּעַם עֶצֶם מֵעֲצָמַי וּבָשָׂר מִבְּשָׂרִי. (b) Textuality > appositive paratactic projection: quote / Mood > declarative: non-past / Transitivity > relational: attribution.

עֶצֶם מֵעֲצָמַי וּבָשָׂר מִבְּשָׂרִי	הַפַּעַם	זֹאת	**Constituents**
bone from my bones and flesh from my flesh	*this time*	*this one*	**Translation**
		Theme	**Textuality**
Complement		Subject	**Mood**
Attribute	Circumstance	Carrier	**Transitivity**

זֹאת. Theme: experiential / Subject > fs / Carrier > pronoun demonstrative, antecedent is אִשָּׁה *woman* in 2:22(a). The demonstrative pronoun might preferably be considered an exophoric referent pointing to the woman in the physical context of the speech event —in effect, pointing right at the woman—rather than referencing prior text.

הַפַּעַם. Circumstance: location, time > nominal group: def art + noun common ms. The def art with nouns of time means *this*; compare הַיּוֹם the day, which means *today*.

עֶצֶם מֵעֲצָמַי וּבָשָׂר מִבְּשָׂרִי. Complement / Attribute > nominal group complex consisting of two conjoined nominal group complexes. Each sub-nominal group complex consists of a Head noun followed by a Post-modifier prepositional phrase.

עֶצֶם מֵעֲצָמַי. Attribute 1 > nominal group: Head + Post-modifier.

עֶצֶם. Head > nominal group: noun common fs.

מֵעֲצָמַי. Post-modifier > prep phrase: prep + noun common fp const + pronoun suffix 1cs.

וּבָשָׂר מִבְּשָׂרִי. Group conj + Attribute 2 > nominal group: Head + Post-modifier.

בָשָׂר. Head > nominal group: noun common ms.

מִבְּשָׂרִי. Post-modifier > prep phrase: prep + noun common ms const + pronoun suffix 1cs.

לְזֹאת יִקָּרֵא אִשָּׁה. (c) Textuality > appositive paratactic projection: quote / Mood > declarative: non-past / Transitivity > verbal.

אִשָּׁה	יִקָּרֵא	לְזֹאת	**Constituents**
woman	*will be called*	*this one*	**Translation**
		Theme	**Textuality**
Subject	Finite		**Mood**
Verbiage	Process	Target	**Transitivity**

לְזֹאת. Theme: textual and experiential / Target > prep phrase: prep + pronoun demonstrative fs, antecedent is the woman who had just been built.

יִקָּרֵא. Finite > yiqtol 3ms / Process > nifal קרא. The verb is passive and there is no apparent grammatical subject of this 3ms form, leaving a peculiar grammatical situation. Most translations render this clause with זאת as subject: e.g. *this one shall be called Woman* (NRSV, NJPS); *This will be called "woman"* (Friedman). The Head of a prep phrase is not typically capable of being the Subject of a verb at the same time. Perhaps the implicit subject is an understood שְׁמָהּ *her name* [compare 2:20(a)], but even this might be somewhat clumsy: *this one, her name will be called "woman."*

אִשָּׁה. Verbiage > nominal group: noun common fs. **אִשָּׁה** is the term applied to **זֹאת**. The Target of a verbal process of naming using **קרא** is typically indicated by preposition **לְ**. Compare 2:19(b.i.a') and (c.i), and 2:20(a).

כִּי מֵאִישׁ לֻקְחָה־זֹּאת. (d) Textuality > conj hypotactic projection: quote / Mood > declarative: past / Transitivity > material: action. As happens with passive processes, the interpersonal Subject is the experiential Goal.

זֹּאת	לֻקְחָה־	מֵאִישׁ	כִּי	**Constituents**
this	*she was taken*	*from a man*	*because*	**Translation**
		Theme	Theme	**Textuality**
Subject	Finite			**Mood**
Goal	Process	Circumstance		**Transitivity**

כִּי. Theme: textual > conj.

מֵאִישׁ. Theme: experiential / Circumstance: location, place > prep phrase: prep + noun common ms.

לֻקְחָה־. Finite > qatal 3fs / Process > qal passive **לקח**.

זֹּאת. Goal > pronoun demonstrative 3fs, antecedent is the newly created woman. Again, the demonstrative pronoun may be "pointing" to the external context rather than to something prior in the text.

Genesis 2:24-25

[24]Therefore, a man will leave his father and his mother. And he will abide in his woman. And they will become one flesh. [25]And the two of them were naked, the human and his woman. And they will not be ashamed.

2:24 עַל־כֵּן֙ יַֽעֲזָב־אִ֔ישׁ אֶת־אָבִ֖יו וְאֶת־אִמּ֑וֹ // וְדָבַ֣ק ///
בְּאִשְׁתּ֔וֹ // וְהָי֖וּ לְבָשָׂ֥ר אֶחָֽד׃

עַל־כֵּן יַעֲזָב־אִישׁ אֶת־אָבִיו וְאֶת־אִמּוֹ. (a) Textuality > conj paratactic expansion / Mood > declarative: non-past / Transitivity > material: action. This clause is not part of the quote, but contains the commentary of the narrator. The fully explicit transitivity structure confirms that this commentary is a new clause complex.

אֶת־אָבִיו וְאֶת־אִמּוֹ	אִישׁ	יַעֲזָב־	עַל־כֵּן	**Constituents**
his father and his mother	*a man*	*he will leave*	*therefore*	**Translation**
		Theme	Theme	**Textuality**
	Subject	Finite		**Mood**
Goal	Actor	Process		**Transitivity**

עַל־כֵּן. Theme: textual > conj adjunct: prep + adjunct. This conjunctive adjunct refers to the preceding clause complex. עַל־כֵּן is often used to refer generally to preceding text as a way to introduce a conclusion based on it. See also 10:9(b) and 11:9(a).

יַעֲזָב־. Theme: experiential / Finite > yiqtol 3ms / Process > qal עזב.

אִישׁ. Subject > ms / Actor > nominal group: noun common ms.

אֶת־אָבִיו וְאֶת־אִמּוֹ. Goal > nominal group complex: two conjoined nominal groups functioning as a compound goal constituent.

אֶת־אָבִיו. Goal 1 > nominal group: goal marker - noun common ms const + pronoun suffix 3ms, antecedent is אִישׁ.

וְאֶת־אִמּוֹ. Group conj + Goal 2 > nominal group: goal marker - noun common fs const + pronoun suffix 3ms, antecedent is אִישׁ.

וְדָבַק בְּאִשְׁתּוֹ. (b) Textuality > conj paratactic expansion / Mood > declarative: non-past / Transitivity > behavioral. The Subject / Behaver is אִישׁ *man* in the preceding clause, absent by ellipsis.

בְּאִשְׁתּוֹ	וְדָבַק	Constituents
in his woman	*and he will abide*	**Translation**
	Theme	**Textuality**
	Finite	**Mood**
Circumstance	Process	**Transitivity**

וְדָבַק. Theme: textual > clause conj + Theme: experiential / Finite > weqatal 3ms / Process > qal דבק. The translation *abide* attempts to convey the positional significance of the preposition בְּ *in* of the following Circumstance.

בְּאִשְׁתּוֹ. Circumstance: location, place > prep phrase: prep + noun common fs const + pronoun suffix 3ms, antecedent is **אִישׁ**.

וְהָיוּ לְבָשָׂר אֶחָד. (c) Textuality > conj paratactic expansion / Mood > declarative: non-past / Transitivity > relational: attribution. The Subject / Carrier is **אִישׁ** and **אִשְׁתּוֹ**, *the man and his woman.*

לְבָשָׂר אֶחָד	וְהָיוּ	Constituents
to one flesh	*and they will be*	**Translation**
	Theme	**Textuality**
	Finite	**Mood**
Attribute	Process	**Transitivity**

וְהָיוּ. Theme: textual > clause conj + Theme: experiential / Finite > weqatal 3cp / Process > qal היה. The verb היה followed by an Attribute with the preposition לְ takes on the meaning *become.*

לְבָשָׂר אֶחָד. Attribute > prep phrase: prep + noun common ms | adj ms.

2:25 // וַיִּהְיוּ שְׁנֵיהֶם עֲרוּמִּים הָאָדָם וְאִשְׁתּוֹ // וְלֹא
יִתְבֹּשָׁשׁוּ׃

וַיִּהְיוּ שְׁנֵיהֶם עֲרוּמִּים הָאָדָם וְאִשְׁתּוֹ. (a) Textuality > conj paratactic expansion / Mood > declarative: past / Transitivity > relational: attribution. While NRSV makes this the last clause of its clause complex, NJPS takes it as the first clause of a new clause complex, continuing through 3:7.

הָאָדָם וְאִשְׁתּוֹ	עֲרוּמִּים	שְׁנֵיהֶם	וַיִּהְיוּ	**Constituents**
the human and his woman	*naked*	*the two of them*	*and they were*	**Translation**
			Theme	**Textuality**
		Subject	Finite	**Mood**
Carrier	Attribute	Carrier	Process	**Transitivity**

וַיִּהְיוּ. Theme: textual > clause conj + Theme: experiential / Finite > wayyiqtol 3mp / Process > qal היה.

שְׁנֵיהֶם. Subject > mp / Carrier > nominal group: noun common mp const + pronoun suffix 3mp, the referent follows at the end of the clause. This is a nicely formed cohesive element: a cataphoric reference anticipating הָאָדָם וְאִשְׁתּוֹ at the end of this clause, as well as an anaphoric reference to 2:24(a-c).

עֲרוּמִּים. Attribute > adj mp.

הָאָדָם וְאִשְׁתּוֹ. Carrier > nominal group complex: def art + noun common ms | group conj + noun common fs const + pronoun suffix 3ms, antecedent is הָאָדָם. This complex is a non-contiguous Post-modifier to שְׁנֵיהֶם.

וְלֹא יִתְבֹּשָׁשׁוּ. (b) Textuality > conj paratactic expansion / Mood > declarative: non-past / Transitivity > mental: emotion. The elliptical Subject / Senser is הָאָדָם וְאִשְׁתּוֹ the human and his woman from the preceding clause.

יִתְבֹּשָׁשׁוּ	וְלֹא	**Constituents**
they will be ashamed	*and not*	**Translation**
	Theme	**Textuality**
Finite	Adjunct	**Mood**
Process		**Transitivity**

וְלֹא. Theme: textual > clause conj + Theme: interpersonal / Adjunct: interpersonal > polarity: negative.

יִתְבֹּשָׁשׁוּ. Theme: experiential / Finite > yiqtol 3mp / Process > hitpolel בּוֹשׁ.

Genesis 3:1-8

[1]And the snake was more clever than all animalkind of the field, which YHVH deity made. And he said to the woman, "Is it true that deity said, 'You will not eat from all of the treekind of the garden.'?" [2]And the woman said to the snake, "From the fruit of the treekind of the garden we will eat. [3]And from the fruit of the tree which is in the middle of the garden—said deity—'you will not eat from it. And you will not touch it, lest you will die.'" [4]And the snake said to the woman, "Certainly you will not die, [5]because deity knows that in the day of your eating from it your eyes will be opened and you will be like deity knowing good and bad." [6]And the woman saw that good is the tree for food and that a delight it is to the eyes, and the tree is desirable for gaining wisdom. And she took from its fruit. And she ate. And she gave also to her man with her. And he ate. [7]And the eyes of the two of them were opened. And they knew that they are naked. And they sewed fig leaf. And they made loincloths for themselves. [8]And they heard the voice of YHVH deity walking in the garden at the wind of the day. And the human and his woman hid from the face of YHVH deity in the midst of the treekind of the garden.

3:1 /// וְהַנָּחָשׁ הָיָה עָרוּם מִכֹּל חַיַּת הַשָּׂדֶה אֲשֶׁר עָשָׂה
יְהוָה אֱלֹהִים // וַיֹּאמֶר אֶל־הָאִשָּׁה // אַף כִּי־אָמַר
אֱלֹהִים // לֹא תֹאכְלוּ מִכֹּל עֵץ הַגָּן׃

וְהַנָּחָשׁ הָיָה עָרוּם מִכֹּל חַיַּת הַשָּׂדֶה [[אֲשֶׁר עָשָׂה יְהוָה אֱלֹהִים]]. (a) Textuality > conj paratactic expansion / Mood > declarative: past / Transitivity > relational: attribution. The fully explicit transitivity structure, along with a nominal Theme instead of wayyiqtol, argues for the beginning of a new clause complex.

עָרוּם מִכֹּל חַיַּת הַשָּׂדֶה [[אֲשֶׁר עָשָׂה יְהוָה אֱלֹהִים]]	הָיָה	וְהַנָּחָשׁ	**Constituents**
clever from all animalkind of the field, which YHVH deity made	*he was*	*and the snake*	**Translation**
		Theme	**Textuality**
	Finite	Subject	**Mood**
Attribute	Process	Carrier	**Transitivity**

וְהַנָּחָשׁ. Theme: textual > clause conj + Theme: experiential / Carrier > nominal group: def art + noun common ms.

הָיָה. Finite > qatal 3ms / Process > qal היה.

עָרוּם מִכֹּל חַיַּת הַשָּׂדֶה [[אֲשֶׁר עָשָׂה יְהוָה אֱלֹהִים]]. Attribute > adjective group: Head + Post-modifier.

עָרוּם. Head > adjective group: adj ms.

מִכֹּל חַיַּת הַשָּׂדֶה [[אֲשֶׁר עָשָׂה יְהוָה אֱלֹהִים]]. Post-modifier > prep phrase: Head + Post-modifier.

מִכֹּל חַיַּת הַשָּׂדֶה. Head > prep phrase: prep + noun common ms const | noun common collective fs const | def art + noun common ms. The Hebrew syntax of comparison is x מִן y. See MNK 235.

אֲשֶׁר עָשָׂה יְהוָה אֱלֹהִים. (i) Post-modifier >> embedded expansion: relative clause / Mood > declarative: past / Transitivity > material: action.

יְהוָה אֱלֹהִים	עָשָׂה	אֲשֶׁר	**Constituents**
YHVH deity	*he made*	*which*	**Translation**
		Theme	**Textuality**
Subject	Finite		**Mood**
Actor	Process	Goal	**Transitivity**

אֲשֶׁר. Theme: textual and experiential / Goal > pronoun relative, antecedent is כֹּל *all.*

עָשָׂה. Finite > qatal 3ms / Process > qal עשׂה.

יְהוָה אֱלֹהִים. Subject > ms / Actor > nominal group: noun proper ms + noun common mp.

וַיֹּאמֶר אֶל־הָאִשָּׁה. (b) Textuality > conj paratactic expansion / Mood > declarative: past / Transitivity > verbal. The Subject / Sayer הַנָּחָשׁ *the serpent* is absent by ellipsis.

אֶל־הָאִשָּׁה	וַיֹּאמֶר	**Constituents**
to the woman	*and he said*	**Translation**
	Theme	**Textuality**
	Finite	**Mood**
Receiver	Process	**Transitivity**

וַיֹּאמֶר. Theme: textual > clause conj + Theme: experiential / Finite > wayyiqtol 3ms / Process > qal אמר.

אֶל־הָאִשָּׁה. Receiver > prep phrase: prep - def art + noun common fs.

Using the concepts of functional grammar, quoted speech is a form of projection. In projection, one clause projects another clause from one setting into another. In this case, the quote frame is clause (b). It projects the quote clause, that is clause (c), into the text. Clause (c) is thus projected as the actual words spoken in the encounter between the snake and the woman. In the case of quotation, as here, projection signals that words spoken elsewhere are taken into the text using the actual wording of the original setting. In this case, think of projection as reported speech. In English, this type of projection is indicated with quotation marks.

אַף כִּי־אָמַר אֱלֹהִים. (c) Textuality > appositive paratactic projection: quote / Mood > interrogative / Transitivity > relational: attribution. This clause is very concise, which is typical of conversational style. We are interpreting it as a relational clause framed as a question, and the question may be read as rhetorical (Is it so that deity said . . . ?!).

כִּי־אָמַר אֱלֹהִים	אַף	**Constituents**
that deity said	*(is it) so*	**Translation**
	Theme	**Textuality**
Complement		**Mood**
Attribute	Carrier	**Transitivity**

אַף. Theme: textual > conj adjunct / Carrier > the referent implied by *so*. A core meaning of **אַף** is *so*, *also*, and thus it plays a role in the textual system, presumably referring to something prior in the conversation or situation. Read as a question, it also plays a role in the interpersonal system, framing the statement as a question, and intending to provoke a response.

כִּי־אָמַר אֱלֹהִים. (i) Complement / Attribute >> Textuality > embedded projection clause: report / Mood > declarative: past / Transitivity > verbal.

אֱלֹהִים	אָמַר	כִּי־	**Constituents**
deity	*he said*	*that*	**Translation**
	Theme	Theme	**Textuality**
Subject	Finite		**Mood**
Sayer	Process		**Transitivity**

כִּי־. Theme: textual > conj. Introduces the embedded report clause.

אָמַר. Theme: experiential / Finite > qatal 3ms / Process > qal אמר.

אֱלֹהִים. Subject > mp / Sayer > nominal group: noun common.

לֹא תֹאכְלוּ מִכֹּל עֵץ הַגָּן. (a') Textuality > embedded projection: quote / Mood > directive: imperative / Transitivity > material: action.

מִכֹּל עֵץ הַגָּן	תֹאכְלוּ	לֹא	**Constituents**
from all of the treekind of the garden	*you will eat*	*not*	**Translation**
	Theme	Theme	**Textuality**
	Finite	Adjunct	**Mood**
Range/Goal	Process		**Transitivity**

לֹא. Theme: interpersonal / Adjunct: interpersonal > polarity: negative.

תֹאכְלוּ. Theme: experiential / Finite > yiqtol 2mp / Process > qal אכל. The verb is masculine plural, so presumes a setting where both the human and the woman were addressed. When there is mixed gender, the masculine form rules.

מִכֹּל עֵץ הַגָּן. Range > prep phrase: prep + noun common ms const | noun common collective ms const | def art + noun common ms. This could also be read as a Goal with the partitive use of the preposition מִין some of.

3:2 // וַתֹּאמֶר הָאִשָּׁה אֶל־הַנָּחָשׁ // מִפְּרִי עֵץ־הַגָּן נֹאכֵל׃

וַתֹּאמֶר הָאִשָּׁה אֶל־הַנָּחָשׁ. (a) Textuality > conj paratactic expansion / Mood > declarative: past / Transitivity > verbal.

אֶל־הַנָּחָשׁ	הָאִשָּׁה	וַתֹּאמֶר	**Constituents**
to the snake	*the woman*	*and she said*	**Translation**
		Theme	**Textuality**
	Subject	Finite	**Mood**
Receiver	Sayer	Process	**Transitivity**

וַתֹּאמֶר. Theme: textual > clause conj + Theme: experiential / Finite > wayyiqtol 3fs / Process > qal **אמר**.

הָאִשָּׁה. Subject > fs / Sayer > nominal group: def art + noun common fs.

אֶל־הַנָּחָשׁ. Receiver > prep phrase: prep - def art + noun common ms.

מִפְּרִי עֵץ־הַגָּן נֹאכֵל. (b) Textuality > appositive paratactic projection: quote / Mood > declarative: non-past / Transitivity > material: action.

נֹאכֵל	מִפְּרִי עֵץ־הַגָּן	**Constituents**
we will eat	*from the fruit of the treekind of the garden*	**Translation**
	Theme	**Textuality**
	Finite	**Mood**
Process	Range/Goal	**Transitivity**

מִפְּרִי עֵץ־הַגָּן. Theme: experiential / Range > prep phrase: prep + noun common collective ms const | noun common collective ms const - def art + noun common ms. The Range is the Theme, which indicates it is the connection to the prior quoted clause, 3:1(d), and it is the point of contention.

נֹאכֵל. Finite > yiqtol 1cp / Process > qal **אכל**.

3:3 // וּמִפְּרִ֣י הָעֵץ֮ אֲשֶׁ֣ר בְּתוֹךְ־הַגָּן֒ אָמַ֣ר אֱלֹהִ֗ים לֹ֤א
תֹֽאכְלוּ֙ מִמֶּ֔נּוּ // וְלֹ֥א תִגְּע֖וּ בּ֑וֹ // פֶּן־תְּמֻתֽוּן׃

וּמִפְּרִי הָעֵץ [[אֲשֶׁר בְּתוֹךְ־הַגָּן]] << אָמַר אֱלֹהִים >> לֹא תֹאכְלוּ מִמֶּנּוּ. (a) Textuality > conj paratactic projection: quote / Mood > directive: imperative / Transitivity > material: action. The words אָמַר אֱלֹהִים are being viewed as an included clause (indicated by wedge brackets), which is to say, it is a clause that interrupts the clause in which it was inserted without being embedded in it. If it were embedded in the surrounding clause, it would have to have a role in the Transitivity structure of the surrounding clause, which it does not.

מִמֶּנּוּ	תֹאכְלוּ	לֹא	<< אָמַר אֱלֹהִים >>	וּמִפְּרִי הָעֵץ [[אֲשֶׁר בְּתוֹךְ־הַגָּן]]	**Constituents**
from him	*you will eat*	*not*	*said deity*	*and from the fruit of the tree which is in the middle of the garden*	**Translation**
				Theme	**Textuality**
	Finite	Adjunct			**Mood**
Range	Process			Range/Goal	**Transitivity**

This is a notable structure, whereby the Range of the quote within the quote is made the Theme to maintain cohesion with the prior quoted clause 3:2(b), and specifically with מִפְּרִי עֵץ־הַגָּן.

וּמִפְּרִי הָעֵץ [[אֲשֶׁר בְּתוֹךְ־הַגָּן]]. Theme: textual > clause conj + Theme: experiential / Range > Head + Post-modifier. This structure is called a preposed Theme. It is referenced later in the clause by a pronoun suffix.

מִפְּרִי הָעֵץ. Head > prep phrase: prep + noun common collective ms const | def art + noun common ms.

אֲשֶׁר בְּתוֹךְ־הַגָּן. (i) Post-modifier >> embedded expansion: relative clause / Mood > declarative: non-past / Transitivity > relational: attribution.

בְּתוֹךְ־הַגָּן	אֲשֶׁר	**Constituents**
in the middle of the garden	*which*	**Translation**
	Theme	**Textuality**
Complement	Subject	**Mood**
Attribute	Carrier	**Transitivity**

אֲשֶׁר. Theme: textual and experiential / Subject > ms / Carrier > pronoun relative, antecedent is הָעֵץ.

בְּתוֹךְ־הַגָּן. Complement > prep phrase / Attribute > prep phrase: prep + noun common ms const - def art + noun common ms.

אָמַר אֱלֹהִים. (b) Textuality > appositive paratactic projection: quote / Mood > declarative: past / Transitivity > verbal. This is an included clause, stated by the woman in order to provide attribution for the words she is quoting. It is positioned in the middle of another quote, but has no role in any of that quote's structures. This included clause projects the remainder of the woman's quote as the quote of deity.

אֱלֹהִים	אָמַר	**Constituents**
deity	*he said*	**Translation**
	Theme	**Textuality**
Subject	Finite	**Mood**
Sayer	Process	**Transitivity**

אָמַר. Finite > qatal 3ms / Process > qal אמר.

אֱלֹהִים. Subject > mp / Sayer > nominal group: noun common.

The main quote resumes, but it is now presented as the quote of deity, no longer the words of the woman.

לֹא. Adjunct: interpersonal > polarity: negative.

תֹאכְלוּ. Finite > yiqtol 2mp / Process > qal אכל. The Subject / Actor of this projection is the human and his woman.

מִמֶּנּוּ. Goal > prep phase: prep + pronoun suffix 3ms, antecedent is פְּרִי הָעֵץ, the preposed Theme of 3:3(a).

וְלֹא תִגְּעוּ בּוֹ. (c) Textuality > conj paratactic projection: quote / Mood > directive: imperative / Transitivity > material: action. This quote continues the speech of **אֱלֹהִים** *deity* from the preceding clause, which was quoted by **הָאִשָּׁה** *the woman.*

בּוֹ	תִגְּעוּ	וְלֹא	Constituents
him	*you will touch*	*and not*	**Translation**
	Theme	Theme	**Textuality**
	Finite	Adjunct	**Mood**
Goal	Process		**Transitivity**

וְלֹא. Theme: textual > clause conj + Theme: interpersonal / Adjunct: interpersonal > polarity: negative.

תִגְּעוּ. Theme: experiential / Finite > yiqtol 2mp / Process > qal **נגע**.

בּוֹ. Goal > prep phrase: prep + pronoun suffix 3ms, antecedent is **פְּרִי הָעֵץ**.

פֶּן־תְּמֻתוּן. (d) Textuality > conj paratactic projection: quote / Mood > declarative: non-past / Transitivity > material: action.

תְּמֻתוּן	פֶּן־	Constituents
you will die	*lest*	**Translation**
Theme	Theme	**Textuality**
Finite		**Mood**
Process		**Transitivity**

פֶּן־. Theme: textual > conj adjunct. It has an anaphoric role in the textual system by connecting this process to the preceding quoted clauses. It also has a conditional effect: if you do this (eat or even touch the fruit of the tree), you will die, ... and you don't want to do that!

תְּמֻתוּן. Theme: experiential / Finite > yiqtol 2mp / Process > qal **מות**. The final nun may have a role in the interpersonal Mood system. It has been interpreted as affirming the certainty of the process. It has been labeled the nun paragogicum and the energic nun; see WO 514–17.

3:4 // וַיֹּאמֶר הַנָּחָשׁ אֶל־הָאִשָּׁה // לֹא־מוֹת תְּמֻתוּן׃

וַיֹּאמֶר הַנָּחָשׁ אֶל־הָאִשָּׁה. (a) Textuality > conj paratactic expansion / Mood > declarative: past / Transitivity > verbal.

אֶל־הָאִשָּׁה	הַנָּחָשׁ	וַיֹּאמֶר	**Constituents**
to the woman	*the snake*	*and he said*	**Translation**
		Theme	**Textuality**
	Subject	Finite	**Mood**
Receiver	Sayer	Process	**Transitivity**

וַיֹּאמֶר. Theme: textual > clause conj + Theme: experiential / Finite > wayyiqtol 3ms / Process > qal אמר.

הַנָּחָשׁ. Subject > ms / Sayer > def art + noun common ms.

אֶל־הָאִשָּׁה. Receiver > prep phrase: prep - def art + noun common fs.

לֹא־מוֹת תְּמֻתוּן. (b) Textuality > appositive paratactic projection: quote / Mood > declarative: non-past / Transitivity > material: action.

תְּמֻתוּן	מוֹת	לֹא־	**Constituents**
you will die	*dying*	*not*	**Translation**
Theme	Theme	Theme	**Textuality**
Finite	Adjunct	Adjunct	**Mood**
Process			**Transitivity**

לֹא־. Theme: interpersonal / Adjunct > polarity: negative.

מוֹת. Theme: interpersonal / Adjunct > modal: inf abs qal מות. The infinitive absolute is a component of the interpersonal mood system; it expresses the speaker's certainty that a material process will, or in this case, will not happen.

תְּמֻתוּן. Theme: experiential / Finite > yiqtol 2mp / Process > qal מות. The final nun on תְּמֻתוּן may be yet another interpersonal Mood component indicating certainty. See 3:3(d). This clause is heavy with modality.

3:5 / כִּי יֹדֵעַ אֱלֹהִים / כִּי בְּיוֹם אֲכָלְכֶם מִמֶּנּוּ וְנִפְקְחוּ
עֵינֵיכֶם // וִהְיִיתֶם כֵּאלֹהִים יֹדְעֵי טוֹב וָרָע׃

כִּי יֹדֵעַ אֱלֹהִים. (a) Textuality > conj hypotactic projection: quote / Mood > declarative: non-past / Transitivity > mental: cognition. This clause is a continuation of the preceding quote and is subordinate to it.

אֱלֹהִים	יֹדֵעַ	כִּי	**Constituents**
deity	*knows*	*because*	**Translation**
	Theme	Theme	**Textuality**
Subject	Finite		**Mood**
Sayer	Process		**Transitivity**

כִּי. Theme: textual > conj.

יֹדֵעַ. Theme: experiential / Finite > ptc ms / Process > qal **ידע**.

אֱלֹהִים. Subject > mp / Senser > nominal group: noun common. Note that it is not YHVH deity here.

כִּי [[בְּיוֹם אֲכָלְכֶם מִמֶּנּוּ]] וְנִפְקְחוּ עֵינֵיכֶם. (b) Textuality > conj paratactic projection: idea / Mood > declarative: non-past / Transitivity > material: action. This is a projection of **יֹדֵעַ** in 3:5(a).

עֵינֵיכֶם	וְנִפְקְחוּ	[[בְּיוֹם אֲכָלְכֶם מִמֶּנּוּ]]	כִּי	**Constituents**
your eyes	*and they will be opened*	*in the day of your eating from him*	*that*	**Translation**
		Theme	Theme	**Textuality**
Subject	Finite			**Mood**
Goal	Process	Circumstance		**Transitivity**

כִּי. Theme: textual > conj. It introduces the projection clause.

בְּיוֹם אֲכָלְכֶם מִמֶּנּוּ. (i) Circumstance: location, time >> Textuality > embedded expansion: prep clause / Transitivity > material: action. This entire embedded clause is the Circumstance of the material process of the clause that contains it: *in the day of your eating from it*. This is the time when your eyes will be opened.

מִמֶּנּוּ	אֲכָלְכֶם	בְּיוֹם	**Constituents**
from him	*of your eating*	*in the day*	**Translation**
		Theme	**Textuality**
Range/Goal	Process + Actor	Circumstance	**Transitivity**

בְּיוֹם. Theme: textual > prep / Circumstance: location, time > noun common ms const.

אֲכָלְכֶם. Process > inf const qal אכל + Actor > pronoun suffix 2mp, antecedent is הָאָדָם וְאִשְׁתּוֹ. See 2:25(a).

מִמֶּנּוּ. Range > prep phrase: prep + pronoun suffix 3ms, antecedent is פְּרִי הָעֵץ.

וְנִפְקְחוּ. Finite > weqatal 3cp / Process > nifal פקח. Eyes will be opened is the wording of a material process, but it is a metaphor for a mental process of cognition, their coming to awareness. The nifal form of the Process could be interpreted either as passive voice (*your eyes will be opened*, as rendered here) or as middle voice (*your eyes will open*). Passive voice implies there is an Actor or Agent involved, though not expressed, while middle voice implies that there is no outside Agent, with the effect that the Goal is the same as the Actor.

עֵינֵיכֶם. Goal > nominal group: noun common fd const + pronoun suffix 2mp, antecedent is הָאָדָם וְאִשְׁתּוֹ *the human and his woman*. The Goal of the material process, a passive verb, is also the Subject of the interpersonal mood system: *your eyes will be opened*. So, while the eyes are acted upon in the process of being opened, and in that sense are the direct object (traditionally so-called) of the activity of the verb, *your eyes* are the grammatical Subject of the verb form.

וְהְיִיתֶם כֵּאלֹהִים יֹדְעֵי טוֹב וָרָע. (c) Textuality > conj paratactic projection: idea / Mood > declarative: non-past / Transitivity > relational: attribution. This projection is a continuation of 3:5(b). The Subject / Carrier of the relational process is the human and his woman, absent here by ellipsis.

כֵּאלֹהִים יֹדְעֵי טוֹב וָרָע	וִהְיִיתֶם	**Constituents**
like deity knowing good-and-bad	*and you will be*	**Translation**
	Theme	**Textuality**
	Finite	**Mood**
Attribute	Process	**Transitivity**

וִהְיִיתֶם. Theme: textual > clause conj + Theme: experiential / Finite > weqatal 2mp / Process > qal היה.

כֵּאלֹהִים יֹדְעֵי טוֹב וָרָע. Attribute > prep phrase: Head + Post-modifier.

כֵּאלֹהִים. Head > prep phrase: prep + noun common mp.

יֹדְעֵי טוֹב וָרָע. (i) Post-modifier >> Textuality > embedded extension: relative clause / Transitivity > mental: perception. The embedded clause extends the meaning of כֵּאלֹהִים by specifying the term of comparison: in what regard would they be like gods.

טוֹב וָרָע	יֹדְעֵי	**Constituents**
good-and-bad	*ones knowing*	**Translation**
	Theme	**Textuality**
Phenomenon	Process + Actor	**Transitivity**

יֹדְעֵי. Theme: experiential / Process + Actor > ptc mp const (qal יָדַע).

טוֹב וָרָע. Phenomenon > adjective group: adj ms + group conj + adj ms. The adjectives could be interpretaed as nominal concepts: goodness and badness. Note also the hendiadys form of the conjunction וָ. See 2:9(a).

3:6 // וַתֵּ֣רֶא הָֽאִשָּׁ֡ה / כִּ֣י טוֹב֩ הָעֵ֨ץ לְמַאֲכָ֜ל // וְכִ֧י
תַֽאֲוָה־ה֣וּא לָעֵינַ֗יִם וְנֶחְמָ֤ד הָעֵץ֙ לְהַשְׂכִּ֔יל // וַתִּקַּ֥ח
מִפִּרְי֖וֹ // וַתֹּאכַ֑ל // וַתִּתֵּ֧ן גַּם־לְאִישָׁ֛הּ עִמָּ֖הּ //
וַיֹּאכַֽל׃

A rather long verse that contains eight clauses.

וַתֵּרֶא הָאִשָּׁה. (a) Textuality > conj paratactic expansion / Mood > declarative: past / Transitivity > mental: perception.

הָאִשָּׁה	וַתֵּרֶא	Constituents
the woman	*and she saw*	**Translation**
	Theme	**Textuality**
Subject	Finite	**Mood**
Senser	Process	**Transitivity**

וַתֵּרֶא. Theme: textual > clause conj + Theme: experiential / Finite > wayyiqtol 3fs / Process > qal ראה.

הָאִשָּׁה. Subject > fs / Senser > def art + noun common fs.

כִּי טוֹב הָעֵץ לְמַאֲכָל. (b) Textuality > conj hypotactic projection: report / Mood > declarative: non-past / Transitivity > relational: attribution. This clause is dependent on clause (a).

לְמַאֲכָל	הָעֵץ	טוֹב	כִּי	Constituents
for food	*the tree*	*good*	*that*	**Translation**
		Theme	Theme	**Textuality**
	Subject	Complement		**Mood**
Circumstance	Carrier	Attribute		**Transitivity**

כִּי. Theme: textual > conj. This introduces the content clause that indicates what she saw. What she saw is more an idea than a visual perception.

טוֹב. Theme: experiential / Complement > ms / Attribute > adj group: adj.

הָעֵץ. Carrier > nominal group: def art + noun common ms.

לְמַאֲכָל. Circumstance: role, product > prep phrase: prep + noun common ms. This extends the Attribute **טוֹב** by specifying that for which הָעֵץ *the tree* is good.

וְכִי תַאֲוָה־הוּא לָעֵינַיִם. (c) Textuality > conj hypotactic projection: report / Mood > declarative: non-past / Transitivity > relational: attribution. This clause is a continuation of clause (b) and is dependent on clause (a).

לָעֵינַיִם	הוּא	תַאֲוָה־	וְכִי	**Constituents**
to the eyes	*he*	*a delight*	*and that*	**Translation**
		Theme	Theme	**Textuality**
	Subject	Complement		**Mood**
Circumstance	Carrier	Attribute		**Transitivity**

וְכִי. Theme: textual > conj group: paratactic clause conj + hypotactic conj. Again, this introduces what she saw. Notice that conjunction groups exist in Hebrew. The וְ conjunction joins this subordinate clause to the preceding one into a hypotactic clause complex.

תַאֲוָה־. Complement > fs / Attribute > adjective group: noun common.

הוּא. Subject > ms / Carrier: pronoun independent ms, antecedent is הָעֵץ in clause (b).

לָעֵינַיִם. Circumstance: role > prep phrase: prep + def art + noun common fd.

וְנֶחְמָד הָעֵץ לְהַשְׂכִּיל. (d) Textuality > conj hypotactic projection: report / Mood > declarative: non-past / Transitivity > relational: attribution. This clause is interpreted as the third clause dependent on the mental process in clause (a), with the כִּי conj adjunct absent in clause (d) by ellipsis.

לְהַשְׂכִּיל	הָעֵץ	וְנֶחְמָד	**Constituents**
for gaining wisdom	*the tree*	*and desirable*	**Translation**
		Theme	**Textuality**
	Subject	Complement	**Mood**
Circumstance	Carrier	Attribute	**Transitivity**

וְנֶחְמָד. Theme: textual > clause conj + Theme: experiential / Complement > ms / Attribute > ptc ms nifal חמד.

הָעֵץ. Subject > ms / Carrier > def art + noun common ms.

לְהַשְׂכִּיל. Circumstance: role > prep phrase: prep + inf const hifil שׂכל.

וַתִּקַּח מִפִּרְיוֹ. (e) Textuality > conj paratactic expansion / Mood > declarative: past / Transitivity > material: action. The Actor is הָאִשָּׁה from clause (a), absent here and also in the following two clauses by ellipsis.

מִפִּרְיוֹ	וַתִּקַּח	**Constituents**
from his fruit	*and she took*	**Translation**
	Theme	**Textuality**
	Finite	**Mood**
Range/Goal	Process	**Transitivity**

וַתִּקַּח. Theme: textual > clause conj + Theme: experiential / Finite > wayyiqtol 3fs / Process > qal לקח.

מִפִּרְיוֹ. Range > prep phrase: prep + common noun ms const + pronoun suffix 3ms, antecedent is הָעֵץ. Or, as previously, it could be construed as a Goal using the partitive מִין: *from his fruit* meaning *some of his fruit*.

וַתֹּאכַל. (f) Textuality > conj paratactic expansion / Mood > declarative: past / Transitivity > material: action. Both the Subject / Actor and the Goal are absent from the text by ellipsis.

וַתֹּאכַל	**Constituents**
and she ate	**Translation**
Theme	**Textuality**
Finite	**Mood**
Process	**Transitivity**

וַתֹּאכַל. Theme: textual > clause conj + Theme: experiential / Finite > wayyiqtol 3fs / Process > qal אכל.

וַתִּתֵּן גַּם־לְאִישָׁהּ עִמָּהּ. (g) Textuality > conj paratactic expansion / Mood > declarative: past / Transitivity > material: action.

לְאִישָׁהּ עִמָּהּ	גַּם־	וַתִּתֵּן	**Constituents**
to her man with her	*also*	*and she gave*	**Translation**
	Adjunct	Theme	**Textuality**
		Finite	**Mood**
Beneficiary		Process	**Transitivity**

וַתִּתֵּן. Theme: textual > clause conj + Theme: experiential / Finite > wayyiqtol 3fs / Process > qal נתן.

גַּם־. Adjunct: textual > additive. This word is hardly needed to fill out the material process, and so does not play a role in the experiential structure of the clause. Rather, it is a component of the textual structure. It references an earlier text notion, in this case the taking of the fruit, and indicates that it is happening again.

לְאִישָׁהּ עִמָּהּ. Beneficiary > prep phrase complex: Head + Post-modifier.

לְאִישָׁהּ. Head > prep phrase: prep + noun common ms const + pronoun suffix 3fs, antecedent is הָאִשָּׁה *the woman*.

עִמָּהּ. Post-modifier > prep phrase: prep + pronoun suffix 3fs, antecedent is הָאִשָּׁה the woman. The phrase is essentially the shortened relative clause *(who was) with her*.

וַיֹּאכַל. (h) Textuality > conj paratactic expansion / Mood >

declarative: past / Transitivity > material: action. Both the Subject / Actor אִישָׁהּ *her man* in the preceding clause and the Goal מִפִּרְיוֹ *some of its fruit* from clause (e) are absent from this clause by ellipsis.

וַיֹּאכַל	**Constituents**
and he ate	**Translation**
Theme	**Textuality**
Finite	**Mood**
Process	**Transitivity**

וַיֹּאכַל. Finite > wayyiqtol 3fs / Process > qal אכל.

3:7 // וַתִּפָּקַ֙חְנָה֙ עֵינֵ֣י שְׁנֵיהֶ֔ם // וַיֵּ֣דְע֔וּ / כִּ֥י עֵירֻמִּ֖ם הֵ֑ם
// וַֽיִּתְפְּרוּ֙ עֲלֵ֣ה תְאֵנָ֔ה // וַיַּעֲשׂ֥וּ לָהֶ֖ם חֲגֹרֹֽת׃

וַתִּפָּקַחְנָה עֵינֵי שְׁנֵיהֶם. (a) Textuality > conj paratactic expansion / Mood > declarative: past / Transitivity > material: action. Compare 3:5(b) and the comments regarding the experiential Goal functioning as the interpersonal Subject of a passive process.

עֵינֵי שְׁנֵיהֶם	וַתִּפָּקַחְנָה	**Constituents**
the eyes of the two of them	*and they were opened*	**Translation**
	Theme	**Textuality**
Subject	Finite	**Mood**
Goal	Process	**Transitivity**

וַתִּפָּקַחְנָה. Theme: textual > clause conj + Theme: experiential / Finite > wayyiqtol 3fp / Process > nifal פקח. See the comments on 3:5(b) regarding the option that this process is middle voice rather than passive voice.

עֵינֵי שְׁנֵיהֶם. Subject > fd / Goal > nominal group: noun common fd const ı noun common mp const + pronoun suffix 3mp, antecedent is הָאָדָם וְאִשְׁתּוֹ *the man and his woman*.

וַיֵּדְעוּ. (b) Textuality > conj paratactic expansion / Mood > declarative: past / Transitivity > mental: cognition. The Subject / Senser of the mental process, *the man and the woman*, is absent by ellipsis.

וַיֵּדְעוּ	**Constituents**
and they knew	**Translation**
Theme	**Textuality**
Finite	**Mood**
Process	**Transitivity**

וַיֵּדְעוּ. Theme: textual > clause conj + Theme: experiential / Finite > wayyiqtol 3mp / Process > qal ידע.

כִּי עֵירֻמִּם הֵם. (c) Textuality > conj hypotactic projection: idea / Mood > declarative: non-past / Transitivity > relational: attribution.

הֵם	עֵירֻמִּם	כִּי	**Constituents**
they	*naked*	*that*	**Translation**
	Theme	Theme	**Textuality**
Subject	Complement		**Mood**
Carrier	Attribute		**Transitivity**

כִּי. Theme: textual > conj. This introduces the idea clause.

עֵירֻמִּם. Complement > mp / Attribute > adj mp.

הֵם. Subject > mp / Carrier > pronoun personal 3mp.

וַיִּתְפְּרוּ עֲלֵה תְאֵנָה. (d) Textuality > conj paratactic expansion / Mood > declarative: past / Transitivity > material: action. The Subject / Actor is absent by ellipsis.

עֲלֵה תְאֵנָה	וַיִּתְפְּרוּ	**Constituents**
leaf of fig	*and they sewed*	**Translation**
	Theme	**Textuality**
	Finite	**Mood**
Goal	Process	**Transitivity**

וַיִּתְפְּרוּ. Theme: textual > clause conj + Theme: experiential / Finite > wayyiqtol 3mp / Process > qal תפר.

עֲלֵה תְאֵנָה. Goal > nominal group: noun common ms const | noun common fs. Note the singular: *leaf of fig, fig leaf,* whereas English might use the plural: *fig leaves.*

וַיַּעֲשׂוּ לָהֶם חֲגֹרֹת. (e) Textuality > conj paratactic expansion / Mood > declarative: past / Transitivity > material: action.

חֲגֹרֹת	לָהֶם	וַיַּעֲשׂוּ	**Constituents**
loincloths	*for themselves*	*and they made*	**Translation**
		Theme	**Textuality**
		Finite	**Mood**
Goal	Beneficiary	Process	**Transitivity**

וַיַּעֲשׂוּ. Theme: textual > clause conj + Theme: experiential / Finite > wayyiqtol 3mp / Process > qal עשׂה.

לָהֶם. Beneficiary > prep phrase: prep + pronoun suffix 3mp, antecedent is הָאָדָם וְאִשְׁתּוֹ *the man and his woman.*

חֲגֹרֹת. Goal > noun common fp.

3:8 // וַיִּשְׁמְעוּ אֶת־קוֹל יְהוָה אֱלֹהִים מִתְהַלֵּךְ בַּגָּן
לְרוּחַ הַיּוֹם // וַיִּתְחַבֵּא הָאָדָם וְאִשְׁתּוֹ מִפְּנֵי יְהוָה
אֱלֹהִים בְּתוֹךְ עֵץ הַגָּן׃

וַיִּשְׁמְעוּ אֶת־קוֹל יְהוָה אֱלֹהִים [[מִתְהַלֵּךְ בַּגָּן לְרוּחַ הַיּוֹם]]. (a) Textuality > conj paratactic expansion / Mood > declarative: past / Transitivity > mental: perception. The Subject / Senser הָאָדָם וְאִשְׁתּוֹ *the human and his woman* is absent by ellipsis.

אֶת־קוֹל יְהוָה אֱלֹהִים [[מִתְהַלֵּךְ בַּגָּן לְרוּחַ הַיּוֹם]]	וַיִּשְׁמְעוּ	**Constituents**
the voice of YHVH deity walking in the garden at the wind of the day	*and they heard*	**Translation**
	Theme	**Textuality**
	Finite	**Mood**
Phenomenon	Process	**Transitivity**

וַיִּשְׁמְעוּ. Theme: textual > clause conj + Theme: experiential / Finite > wayyiqtol 3mp / Process > qal שׁמע.

אֶת־קוֹל יְהוָה אֱלֹהִים [[מִתְהַלֵּךְ בַּגָּן לְרוּחַ הַיּוֹם]]. Goal > nominal group complex: Head + Post-modifier.

אֶת־קוֹל יְהוָה אֱלֹהִים. Head > nominal group: goal marker - noun common ms const | noun proper ms | noun common mp.

מִתְהַלֵּךְ בַּגָּן לְרוּחַ הַיּוֹם. (i) Post-modifier >> Textuality > embedded expansion: relative clause / Transitivity > behavioral. This is an asyndetic relative clause, meaning it lacks אֲשֶׁר.

לְרוּחַ הַיּוֹם	בַּגָּן	מִתְהַלֵּךְ	**Constituents**
at the wind of the day	*in the garden*	*walking*	**Translation**
		Theme	**Textuality**
Circumstance	Circumstance	Behaver / Process	**Transitivity**

מִתְהַלֵּךְ. Theme: experiential / Behaver > ptc ms / Process > hitpael הלך. The antecedent of the relative clause is the Behaver יְהוָה אֱלֹהִים.

בַּגָּן. Circumstance: location, place > prep phrase: prep + noun common ms.

לְרוּחַ הַיּוֹם. Circumstance: location, time > prep phrase: prep + noun common fs const | def art + common noun ms. At the time of the wind? Or perhaps לְ suggests purpose: because of the breeze.

וַיִּתְחַבֵּא הָאָדָם וְאִשְׁתּוֹ מִפְּנֵי יְהוָה אֱלֹהִים בְּתוֹךְ עֵץ הַגָּן.

(b) Textuality > conj paratactic expansion / Mood > declarative: past / Transitivity > behavioral.

בְּתוֹךְ עֵץ הַגָּן	מִפְּנֵי יְהוָה אֱלֹהִים	הָאָדָם וְאִשְׁתּוֹ	וַיִּתְחַבֵּא	**Constituents**
in the midst of the treekind of the garden	*from the face of YHVH deity*	*the human and his woman*	*and he hid*	**Translation**
			Theme	**Textuality**
		Subject	Finite	**Mood**
Circumstance	Circumstance	Behaver	Process	**Transitivity**

וַיִּתְחַבֵּא. Theme: textual > clause conj + Theme: experiential / Finite > wayyiqtol 3ms / Process > hitpael חבא. Note that the Finite is now singular. Compare clause (a) where the Finite is plural. The singular might be considered incongruent because a coordinate, hence plural, Subject / Behaver follows it. However, the singular Finite reveals the overall centrality of the man in the narrative, even though the woman has been the dominant Actor in the preceding clause complex.

הָאָדָם וְאִשְׁתּוֹ. Behaver > nominal group complex: def art + noun common ms | group conj + noun common fs const + pronoun suffix 3ms, antecedent is הָאָדָם *the man.*

מִפְּנֵי יְהוָה אֱלֹהִים. Circumstance: location, place > prep phrase: prep + noun common mp const | noun proper ms | noun common mp.

בְּתוֹךְ עֵץ הַגָּן. Circumstance: location, place > prep phrase: prep + noun common ms const | noun common ms const | def art + noun common ms.

Genesis 3:9-13

[9]And YHVH deity called to the human. And he said to him, "Where are you?" [10]And he said, "Your voice I heard in the garden. And I was afraid, because I am naked. And I hid." [11]And he said, "Who told you

that you are naked? Did you eat from the tree from which I commanded you to not eat?" [12]*And the human said, "The woman, which you put with me, she gave me from the tree. And I ate."* [13]*And YHVH deity said to the woman, "What is this you did?" And the woman said, "The snake deceived me. And I ate."*

3:9 /// וַיִּקְרָ֛א יְהוָ֥ה אֱלֹהִ֖ים אֶל־הָֽאָדָ֑ם // וַיֹּ֥אמֶר ל֖וֹ //
אַיֶּֽכָּה׃

וַיִּקְרָא יְהוָה אֱלֹהִים אֶל־הָאָדָם. (a) Textuality > conj paratactic expansion / Mood > declarative: past / Transitivity > behavioral.

אֶל־הָאָדָם	יְהוָה אֱלֹהִים	וַיִּקְרָא	**Constituents**
to the human	*YHVH deity*	*and he called*	**Translation**
		Theme	**Textuality**
	Subject	Finite	**Mood**
Range	Behaver	Process	**Transitivity**

וַיִּקְרָא. Theme: textual > clause conj + Theme: experiential / Finite > wayyiqtol 3ms / Process > qal קרא. The process is interpreted as a behavior rather than a verbal act. A verbal process follows in clause (b). The distinction is analogous to English *speak* (a behavior) and *say* (a verbal process).

יְהוָה אֱלֹהִים. Behaver > nominal group: noun proper ms + noun common mp.

אֶל־הָאָדָם. Range > prep phrase: prep - def art + noun common ms.

וַיֹּאמֶר לוֹ. (b) Textuality > conj paratactic expansion / Mood > declarative: past / Transitivity > verbal. The Subject / Sayer is יְהוָה אֱלֹהִים YHVH deity from clause (a), absent here by ellipsis.

לוֹ	וַיֹּאמֶר	**Constituents**
to him	*and he said*	**Translation**
	Theme	**Textuality**
	Finite	**Mood**
Receiver	Process	**Transitivity**

וַיֹּאמֶר. Theme: textual > clause conj + Theme: experiential / Finite > wayyiqtol 3ms / Process > qal אמר.

לוֹ. Receiver > prep phrase: prep + pronoun suffix 3ms, antecedent is הָאָדָם *the human.*

אַיֶּכָּה. (c) Textuality > appositive paratactic projection: quote / Mood > interrogative / Transitivity > relational: attribution.

אַיֶּכָּה	**Constituents**
where are you	**Translation**
Theme	**Textuality**
Complement + Subject	**Mood**
Attribute + Carrier	**Transitivity**

אַיֶּכָּה. Theme: experiential / Complement > pronoun interrogative / Attribute > pronoun interrogative + Subject > 2ms / Carrier > pronoun suffix 2ms, antecedent is the Receiver, הָאָדָם *the human.* The interrogative here is a component of the interpersonal mood system of this clause in so far as it shapes the encounter as an exchange of information.

3:10 // וַיֹּאמֶר // אֶת־קֹלְךָ שָׁמַעְתִּי בַּגָּן // וָאִירָא / כִּי־
עֵירֹם אָנֹכִי // וָאֵחָבֵא׃

וַיֹּאמֶר. (a) Textuality > conj paratactic expansion / Mood > declarative: past / Transitivity > verbal. Subject / Sayer and Receiver are inferred from the preceding verse and are absent here by ellipsis.

וַיֹּאמֶר	**Constituents**
and he said	**Translation**
Theme	**Textuality**
Finite	**Mood**
Process	**Transitivity**

וַיֹּאמֶר. Theme: textual > clause conj + Theme: experiential / Finite > wayyiqtol 3ms / Process > qal **אמר**.

אֶת־קֹלְךָ שָׁמַעְתִּי בַּגָּן. (b) Textuality > appositive paratactic projection: quote / Mood > declarative: past / Transitivity > mental: perception.

בַּגָּן	שָׁמַעְתִּי	אֶת־קֹלְךָ	**Constituents**
in the garden	*I heard*	*your voice*	**Translation**
		Theme	**Textuality**
	Finite		**Mood**
Circumstance	Process	Phenomenon	**Transitivity**

אֶת־קֹלְךָ. Theme: experiential / Phenomenon > nominal group: goal marker - noun common ms const + pronoun suffix 2ms, antecedent is יְהוָה אֱלֹהִים *YHVH deity,* the Sayer of the quote in 3:9(a).

שָׁמַעְתִּי. Finite > wayyiqtol 1cs / Process > qal **שמע**.

בַּגָּן. Circumstance: location, place > prep phrase: prep + def art + noun common ms.

וָאִירָא. (c) Textuality > conj paratactic projection: quote / Mood > declarative: past / Transitivity > mental: emotion.

וָאִירָא	**Constituents**
and I was afraid	**Translation**
Theme	**Textuality**
Finite	**Mood**
Process	**Transitivity**

וָאִירָא. Theme: textual > clause conj + Theme: experiential / Finite > wayyiqtol 1cs / Process > qal ירא. The wayyiqtol form is typically used in narration, and only sparingly in dialogue and poetry. Here is one example of the latter.

כִּי־עֵירֹם אָנֹכִי. (d) Textuality > conj hypotactic projection: quote / Mood > declarative: non-past / Transitivity > relational: attribution. This clause extends the meaning of clause (c) by providing a reason for the fear.

אָנֹכִי	עֵירֹם	כִּי־	**Constituents**
I	*naked*	*because*	**Translation**
	Theme	Theme	**Textuality**
Subject	Complement		**Mood**
Carrier	Attribute		**Transitivity**

כִּי־. Theme: textual > conj.

עֵירֹם. Theme: experiential / Complement > ms / Attribute > adj group: adj.

אָנֹכִי. Subject > 1cs / Carrier > pronoun personal 1cs.

וָאֵחָבֵא. (e) Textuality > conj paratactic projection: quote / Mood > declarative: past / Transitivity > behavioral.

וָאֵחָבֵא	**Constituents**
and I hid	**Translation**
Theme	**Textuality**
Finite	**Mood**
Process	**Transitivity**

וָאֵחָבֵא. Theme: textual > clause conj + Theme: experiential / Finite > wayyiqtol 1cs / Process > nifal חבא. The nifal stem is used here in the middle voice rather than passive voice. Nobody hid him. He hid himself.

3:11 // וַיֹּ֕אמֶר // מִ֚י הִגִּ֣יד לְךָ֔ / כִּ֥י עֵירֹ֖ם אָ֑תָּה // הֲמִן־
הָעֵ֗ץ אֲשֶׁ֧ר צִוִּיתִ֛יךָ לְבִלְתִּ֥י אֲכָל־מִמֶּ֖נּוּ אָכָֽלְתָּ׃

וַיֹּ֕אמֶר. (a) Textuality > conj paratactic expansion / Mood > declarative: past / Transitivity > verbal.

וַיֹּאמֶר	Constituents
and he said	**Translation**
Theme	**Textuality**
Finite	**Mood**
Process	**Transitivity**

וַיֹּ֕אמֶר. Theme: textual > clause conj + Theme: experiential / Finite > wayyiqtol 3ms / Process > qal אמר.

מִ֚י הִגִּ֣יד לְךָ֔. (b) Textuality > appositive paratactic projection: quote / Mood > interrogative / Transitivity > verbal.

לְךָ	הִגִּיד	מִי	Constituents
to you	*he told*	*who*	**Translation**
		Theme	**Textuality**
	Finite	Subject	**Mood**
Receiver	Process	Sayer	**Transitivity**

מִ֚י. Subject > ms / Sayer > pronoun interrogative.

הִגִּ֣יד. Finite > qatal 3ms / Process > hifil נגד.

לְךָ֔. Receiver > prep phrase: prep + pronoun suffix 2ms, antecedent is הָאָדָם *the human*.

כִּ֥י עֵירֹ֖ם אָ֑תָּה. (c) Textuality > conj hypotactic projection: quote / Mood > declarative: non-past / Transitivity > relational: attribution. This is a projection clause that is dependent on clause (b). The clause is both a quote (deity's words) and a report (what was told by the who).

אַתָּה	עֵירֹם	כִּי	**Constituents**
you	*naked*	*that*	**Translation**
	Theme	Theme	**Textuality**
Subject	Complement		**Mood**
Carrier	Attribute		**Transitivity**

כִּי. Theme: textual > conj.

עֵירֹם. Theme: experiential / Complement > ms / Attribute > adj group: adj.

אַתָּה. Subject > 2ms / Carrier > pronoun personal 2ms.

הֲמִן־הָעֵץ [[אֲשֶׁר צִוִּיתִיךָ [[לְבִלְתִּי אֲכָל־מִמֶּנּוּ]]]] אָכָלְתָּ. (d) Textuality > appositive paratactic projection: quote / Mood > interrogative / Transitivity > material: action. The structure of this clause is rather complex in so far as it actually consists of three clauses: (1) the main clause with (2) an embedded relative clause, which itself has (3) an embedded projection clause.

אָכָלְתָּ	מִן־הָעֵץ [[אֲשֶׁר צִוִּיתִיךָ [[לְבִלְתִּי אֲכָל־מִמֶּנּוּ]]]]	הֲ	**Constituents**
you ate	*from the tree which I commanded you to not eat from him*	*?*	**Translation**
	Theme	Theme	**Textuality**
Finite		Adjunct	**Mood**
Process	Goal		**Transitivity**

הֲ. Theme: interpersonal / Adjunct: interpersonal > polarity: yes/no.

מִן־הָעֵץ [[אֲשֶׁר צִוִּיתִיךָ [[לְבִלְתִּי אֲכָל־מִמֶּנּוּ]]]]. Theme: experiential / Goal > prep phrase complex: Head + Post-modifier.

מִן־הָעֵץ. Head > prep phrase: prep - def art + noun common ms.

אֲשֶׁר צִוִּיתִיךָ [[לְבִלְתִּי אֲכָל־מִמֶּנּוּ]]. (i) Post-modifier >> embedded expansion: relative clause / Mood > declarative: past / Transitivity > verbal.

[[לְבִלְתִּי אֲכָל־מִמֶּנּוּ]]	צִוִּיתִיךָ	אֲשֶׁר	**Constituents**
to not eat from him	*I commanded you*	*which*	**Translation**
		Theme	**Textuality**
	Finite		**Mood**
Verbiage	Process + Receiver	Target	**Transitivity**

אֲשֶׁר. Theme: textual > pronoun relative + Theme: experiential / Target > antecedent הָעֵץ *the tree.* It is also the referent of the pronoun suffix of מִמֶּנּוּ, which is the Range of the material process אֲכָל of the following embedded extension clause.

צִוִּיתִיךָ. Finite > qatal 1cs / Process > piel צוה + Receiver > pronoun suffix 2ms, antecedent is the Receiver of the command.

לְבִלְתִּי אֲכָל־מִמֶּנּוּ. (i) Verbiage >> Textuality > embedded report clause / Transitivity > material: action. This embedded clause is the reported speech of the צִוִּיתִי verbal process.

מִמֶּנּוּ	אֲכָל־	לְבִלְתִּי	**Constituents**
from him	*eat*	*to not*	**Translation**
	Theme	Theme	**Textuality**
Range	Process		**Transitivity**

לְבִלְתִּי. Theme: textual / Adjunct: interpersonal > polarity: negative. This word always negates an infinite construct.

אֲכָל־. Theme: experiential / Process > inf const qal אכל. This is the process of the clause embedded within the relative clause.

מִמֶּנּוּ. Range > prep phrase: prep + pronoun suffix 3ms, antecedent is הָעֵץ *the tree.*

אָכָלְתָּ. Finite > qatal 2ms / Process > qal אכל. This is the main process of clause (d).

3:12 // וַיֹּאמֶר הָאָדָם // הָאִשָּׁה אֲשֶׁר נָתַתָּה עִמָּדִי הִוא
נָתְנָה־לִּי מִן־הָעֵץ // וָאֹכֵל׃

וַיֹּאמֶר הָאָדָם. (a) Textuality > conj paratactic expansion / Mood > declarative: past / Transitivity > verbal.

הָאָדָם	וַיֹּאמֶר	Constituents
the human	*and he said*	**Translation**
	Theme	**Textuality**
Subject	Finite	**Mood**
Sayer	Process	**Transitivity**

וַיֹּאמֶר. Theme: textual > clause conj + Theme: experiential / Finite > wayyiqtol 3ms / Process > qal אמר.

הָאָדָם. Subject > ms / Sayer > nominal group: def art + noun common ms.

הָאִשָּׁה [[אֲשֶׁר נָתַתָּה עִמָּדִי]] הִוא נָתְנָה־לִּי מִן־הָעֵץ. (b) Textuality > appositive paratactic projection: quote / Mood > declarative: past / Transitivity > material: action.

מִן־ הָעֵץ	לִּי־	נָתְנָה־	הִוא	הָאִשָּׁה [[אֲשֶׁר נָתַתָּה עִמָּדִי]]	Constituents
from the tree	*to me*	*gave*	*she*	*the woman which you put with me*	**Translation**
				Theme	**Textuality**
		Finite	Subject	Subject	**Mood**
Range	Beneficiary	Process	Actor	Actor	**Transitivity**

הָאִשָּׁה [[אֲשֶׁר נָתַתָּה עִמָּדִי]]. Theme: experiential / Subject > fs / Actor > nominal group complex: Head + Post-Modifier. This constituent is a preposed Theme. It is substituted later by הִוא *she*.

הָאִשָּׁה. Head > nominal group: def art + noun common fs.

אֲשֶׁר נָתַתָּה עִמָּדִי. (i) Post-modifier >> Textuality > embedded expansion: relative clause / Transitivity > material: action.

עִמָּדִי	נָתַתָּה	אֲשֶׁר	**Constituents**
with me	*you put*	*which*	**Translation**
		Theme	**Textuality**
	Finite		**Mood**
Range	Process	Goal	**Transitivity**

אֲשֶׁר. Theme: textual and experiential > pronoun relative / Goal > antecedent הָאִשָּׁה *the woman.*

נָתַתָּה. Finite > qatal 2ms / Process > qal נתן. Notice the full spelling final ה that marks the long a vowel.

עִמָּדִי. Range > prep phrase: prep + pronoun suffix 1cs, antecedent is the Sayer of the quote, הָאָדָם *the human.*

הִוא. Subject > fs / Actor > pronoun personal 3fs. This is the so-called perpetual *ketiv-qere.* This 3fs personal pronoun is written consonantally as if it were 3ms, but it is vocalized as if it were הִיא. The MT does not otherwise call attention to this in its notes, as it does with other *ketiv-qere* (*written but read*) instances. This is called a perpetual *ketiv-qere* because of its pervasive nature. This particular הִוא form is found throughout the Pentateuch.

נָתְנָה־. Finite > qatal 3fs / Process > qal נתן.

לִּי. Beneficiary > prep phrase: prep + pronoun suffix 1cs, antecedent is the Sayer הָאָדָם *the human.*

מִן־הָעֵץ. Range > prep phrase: prep - def art + noun common ms. This is referencing specifically the tree of the knowing.

וָאֹכֵל. (c) Textuality > conj paratactic projection: quote / Mood > declarative: past / Transitivity > material: action. Both the Subject / Actor and the Goal of the process are absent by ellipsis.

וָאֹכֵל	Constituents
and I ate	**Translation**
Theme	**Textuality**
Finite	**Mood**
Process	**Transitivity**

וָאֹכֵל. Theme: textual > clause conj + Theme: experiential / Finite > wayyiqtol 1cs / Process > qal **אכל**. Note the quiescence and then disappearance of the alef: **אאֹכֵל** becomes **אֹכֵל**.

3:13 וַיֹּאמֶר יְהוָה אֱלֹהִים לָאִשָּׁה // מַה־זֹּאת עָשִׂית //
// וַתֹּאמֶר הָאִשָּׁה // הַנָּחָשׁ הִשִּׁיאַנִי // וָאֹכֵל׃

וַיֹּאמֶר יְהוָה אֱלֹהִים לָאִשָּׁה. (a) Textuality > conj paratactic expansion / Mood > declarative: past / Transitivity > verbal.

לָאִשָּׁה	יְהוָה אֱלֹהִים	וַיֹּאמֶר	Constituents
to the woman	*YHVH deity*	*and he said*	**Translation**
		Theme	**Textuality**
	Subject	Finite	**Mood**
Receiver	Sayer	Process	**Transitivity**

וַיֹּאמֶר. Theme: textual > clause conj + Theme: experiential / Finite > wayyiqtol 3ms / Process > qal **אמר**.

יְהוָה אֱלֹהִים. Subject > ms / Sayer > nominal group: noun proper ms + noun common mp.

לָאִשָּׁה. Receiver > prep phrase: prep + def art + noun common fs.

מַה־זֹּאת עָשִׂית. (b) Textuality > appositive paratactic projection: quote / Mood > interrogative / Transitivity > relational: identification. The order of Identifier followed by Identified is characteristic of relational clauses of identification in the interrogative mood, whereas clauses in the declarative mood typically have the reverse order.

זֹאת [[עָשִׂית]]	מַה־	**Constituents**
this you did	*what*	**Translation**
	Theme	**Textuality**
Complement	Subject	**Mood**
Identified	Identifier	**Transitivity**

מַה־. Theme: textual and experiential / Subject / Identifier > pronoun interrogative. This interrogative could also be interpreted as an exclamative particle: *what* can be used in both senses in BH as in English. If מַה is exclamative, then the clause would be declarative rather than genuinely interrogative.

זֹאת [[עָשִׂית]]. Complement / Identified > Head + Post-modifier.

זֹאת. Identified > pronoun demonstrative fs, referent is the woman's act of eating some of the fruit. There is no specific fs text constituent that is the referent of the pronoun. זֹאת *this* functions also as the Goal of the embedded clause that follows.

עָשִׂית. (i) Post-modifier >> Textuality > embedded expansion: relative clause / Transitivity > material: action. This is a relative clause without the relative pronoun. *This (which) you did.*

עָשִׂית	**Constituents**
you did	**Translation**
Theme	**Textuality**
Finite	**Mood**
Process	**Transitivity**

עָשִׂית. Finite > qatal 2fs / Process > qal עשׂה. The Goal of the process is זֹאת.

וַתֹּאמֶר הָאִשָּׁה. (c) Textuality > conj paratactic expansion / Mood > declarative: past / Transitivity > verbal.

הָאִשָּׁה	וַתֹּאמֶר	**Constituents**
the woman	*and she said*	**Translation**
	Theme	**Textuality**
Subject	Finite	**Mood**
Sayer	Process	**Transitivity**

וַתֹּאמֶר. Theme: textual > clause conj + Theme: experiential / Finite > wayyiqtol 3fs / Process > qal **אמר**.

הָאִשָּׁה. Subject > fs / Sayer > nominal group: def art + noun common fs.

הַנָּחָשׁ הִשִּׁיאַנִי. (d) Textuality > appositive paratactic projection: quote / Mood > declarative: past / Transitivity > material: action.

הִשִּׁיאַנִי	הַנָּחָשׁ	**Constituents**
deceived me	*the snake*	**Translation**
	Theme	**Textuality**
Finite	Subject	**Mood**
Process + Goal	Actor	**Transitivity**

הַנָּחָשׁ. Theme: experiential / Subject > ms / Actor > nominal group: def art + noun common ms.

הִשִּׁיאַנִי. Finite > qatal 3ms / Process > hifil **נשא** + Goal > pronoun suffix 1cs, antecedent is the Sayer, **הָאִשָּׁה** *the woman*.

וָאֹכֵל. (e) Textuality > conj paratactic projection: quote / Mood > declarative: past / Transitivity > material: action.

וָאֹכֵל	**Constituents**
and I ate	**Translation**
Theme	**Textuality**
Finite	**Mood**
Process	**Transitivity**

וָאֹכֵל. Finite > wayyiqtol 1cs / Process > qal אכל. Note again the quiescence and disappearance of the alef in this form.

Genesis 3:14-19

[14]And YHVH deity said to the snake, "Because you did this, cursed are you from all of the beastkind and from all of the animalkind of the field. You will go on your belly. And dust you will eat all the days of your life. [15]And enmity I made between you and the woman and between your seedkind and her seedkind. They will strike you head-wise. And you will strike them heel-wise." [16]To the woman he said, "Certainly I will increase your pain and your conceiving. In pain you will bear sons. And to your man is your desire. And he will exercise rule over you." [17]And to Adam he said, "Because you listened to the voice of your woman, and you ate from the tree, which I commanded you by saying, 'You will not eat from it,' cursed is the ground on account of you. In pain you will eat it all the days of your life. [18]And thorn and thistle it will grow for you. And you will eat the plantkind of the field. [19]By the sweat of your nostrils you will eat bread until your return to the ground, because from it you were taken. Because dust you are, and to dust you will return."

3:14 /// וַיֹּאמֶר֩ יְהוָ֨ה אֱלֹהִ֥ים ׀ אֶֽל־הַנָּחָשׁ֮ // כִּ֣י עָשִׂ֣יתָ
זֹּאת֒ // אָר֤וּר אַתָּה֙ מִכָּל־הַבְּהֵמָ֔ה וּמִכֹּ֖ל חַיַּ֣ת הַשָּׂדֶ֑ה
// עַל־גְּחֹנְךָ֣ תֵלֵ֔ךְ // וְעָפָ֥ר תֹּאכַ֖ל כָּל־יְמֵ֥י חַיֶּֽיךָ׃

וַיֹּאמֶר יְהוָה אֱלֹהִים אֶל־הַנָּחָשׁ (a) Textuality > conj paratactic expansion / Mood > declarative: past / Transitivity > verbal.

אֶל־הַנָּחָשׁ	יְהוָה אֱלֹהִים	וַיֹּאמֶר	**Constituents**
to the snake	*YHVH deity*	*and he said*	**Translation**
		Theme	**Textuality**
	Subject	Finite	**Mood**
Receiver	Sayer	Process	**Transitivity**

וַיֹּאמֶר. Theme: textual > clause conj + Theme: experiential / Finite > wayyiqtol 3ms / Process > qal **אמר**.

יְהוָה אֱלֹהִים. Subject > ms / Sayer > nominal group: noun proper ms + noun common mp.

אֶל־הַנָּחָשׁ. Receiver > prep phrase: prep - def art + noun common ms.

כִּי עָשִׂיתָ זֹּאת. (b) Textuality > conj hypotactic projection: quote / Mood > declarative: past / Transitivity > material: action.

זֹּאת	עָשִׂיתָ	כִּי	**Constituents**
this	*you did*	*because*	**Translation**
	Theme	Theme	**Textuality**
	Finite		**Mood**
Goal	Process		**Transitivity**

כִּי. Theme: textual > conj.

עָשִׂיתָ. Theme: experiential / Finite > qatal 2ms / Process > qal **עשׂה**.

זֹּאת. Goal > pronoun demonstrative fs, referent is the way the snake provoked the woman, not a specific fs textual antecedent.

אָרוּר אַתָּה מִכָּל־הַבְּהֵמָה וּמִכֹּל חַיַּת הַשָּׂדֶה. (c) Textuality > appositive paratactic projection: quote / Mood > declarative: non-past / Transitivity > relational: attribution. The declarative mood may best be viewed as a directive.

מִכָּל־הַבְּהֵמָה וּמִכֹּל חַיַּת הַשָּׂדֶה	אַתָּה	אָרוּר	**Constituents**
from all of the beastkind and from all of the animalkind of the field	*you*	*cursed*	**Translation**
		Theme	**Textuality**
	Subject	Complement	**Mood**
Range	Carrier	Attribute	**Transitivity**

אָרוּר. Theme: experiential / Complement > ms / Attribute > passive ptc ms qal ארר.

אַתָּה. Subject > 2ms / Carrier > pronoun suffix 2ms, antecedent is הַנָּחָשׁ, the Receiver of the quote.

מִכָּל־הַבְּהֵמָה וּמִכֹּל חַיַּת הַשָּׂדֶה. Range > prep phrase complex: two conjoined prep phrases.

מִכָּל־הַבְּהֵמָה. Range 1 > prep phrase: prep + noun common ms const - def art + noun common collective fs.

וּמִכֹּל חַיַּת הַשָּׂדֶה. Group conj + Range 2 > prep phrase: prep + noun common ms const | noun common collective fs const | def art + noun common ms.

עַל־גְּחֹנְךָ תֵלֵךְ. (d) Textuality > appositive paratactic projection: quote / Mood > declarative: non-past / Transitivity > material: action. The Subject / Actor is הַנָּחָשׁ, absent by ellipsis.

תֵלֵךְ	עַל־גְּחֹנְךָ	**Constituents**
you will go	*on your belly*	**Translation**
	Theme	**Textuality**
Finite		**Mood**
Process	Range	**Transitivity**

עַל־גְּחֹנְךָ. Range > prep phrase: prep - noun common ms const + pronoun suffix 2ms, antecedent is הַנָּחָשׁ *the snake*.

תֵלֵךְ. Finite > yiqtol 2ms / Process > qal הלך.

וְעָפָר תֹּאכַל כָּל־יְמֵי חַיֶּיךָ. (e) Textuality > conj paratactic projection: quote / Mood > declarative: non-past / Transitivity > material: action. Again, the Subject / Actor is הַנָּחָשׁ.

כָּל־יְמֵי חַיֶּיךָ	תֹּאכַל	וְעָפָר	**Constituents**
all the days of your life	*you will eat*	*and dust*	**Translation**
		Theme	**Textuality**
	Finite		**Mood**
Circumstance	Process	Goal	**Transitivity**

וְעָפָר. Theme: textual > clause conj + Theme: experiential / Goal > nominal group: noun common ms.

תֹּאכַל. Finite > yiqtol 2ms / Process > qal אכל.

כָּל־יְמֵי חַיֶּיךָ. Range > nominal group: noun common ms const - noun common mp const | noun common mp const + pronoun suffix 2ms, antecedent is הַנָּחָשׁ *the snake.*

3:15 // וְאֵיבָה | אָשִׁית בֵּינְךָ וּבֵין הָאִשָּׁה וּבֵין זַרְעֲךָ וּבֵין
זַרְעָהּ // הוּא יְשׁוּפְךָ רֹאשׁ // וְאַתָּה תְּשׁוּפֶנּוּ עָקֵב׃ ס

. וְאֵיבָה אָשִׁית בֵּינְךָ וּבֵין הָאִשָּׁה וּבֵין זַרְעֲךָ וּבֵין זַרְעָהּ
(a) Textuality > conj paratactic projection: quote / Mood > declarative: past / Transitivity > material: action. The Subject / Actor is the speaker יְהוָה אֱלֹהִים.

בֵּינְךָ וּבֵין הָאִשָּׁה וּבֵין זַרְעֲךָ וּבֵין זַרְעָהּ	אָשִׁית	וְאֵיבָה	**Constituents**
between you and between the woman and between your seedkind and between her seedkind	*I made*	*and enmity*	**Translation**
		Theme	**Textuality**
	Finite		**Mood**
Range	Process	Goal	**Transitivity**

וְאֵיבָה. Theme: textual > clause conj + Theme: experiential / Goal > nominal group: noun common fs.

אָשִׁית. Finite > qatal 1cs / Process > qal שׁית.

בֵּינְךָ וּבֵין הָאִשָּׁה וּבֵין זַרְעֲךָ וּבֵין זַרְעָהּ. Range > prep phrase complex: two conjoined prep phrase sub-complexes.

בֵּינְךָ וּבֵין הָאִשָּׁה. Range 1 > prep phrase sub-complex 1.

בֵּינְךָ. Prep phrase A > prep + pronoun suffix 2ms, antecedent is הַנָּחָשׁ *the snake,* the Receiver of the verbal process.

וּבֵין הָאִשָּׁה. Group conj + Prep phrase B > prep ı def art + noun common fs.

וּבֵין זַרְעֲךָ וּבֵין זַרְעָהּ. Range 2 > prep phrase sub-complex 2.

וּבֵין זַרְעֲךָ. Complex conj + Prep phrase A > prep ı noun common collective ms + pronoun suffix 2ms, antecedent is הַנָּחָשׁ *the snake.*

וּבֵין זַרְעָהּ. Group conj + Prep phrase B > prep + noun common collective ms const + pronoun suffix 3fs, antecedent is הָאִשָּׁה *the woman.*

הוּא יְשׁוּפְךָ רֹאשׁ. (b) Textuality > appositive paratactic projection: quote / Mood > declarative: non-past / Transitivity > material: action. The Subject / Actor is the collective זַרְעָהּ *her seed.*

רֹאשׁ	יְשׁוּפְךָ	הוּא	**Constituents**
head-wise	*he will strike you*	*he*	**Translation**
		Theme	**Textuality**
	Finite	Subject	**Mood**
Scope	Process + Goal	Actor	**Transitivity**

הוּא. Theme: experiential / Subject > ms / Actor > pronoun personal 3ms, antecedent is זַרְעָהּ *her seed.* This is a collective noun, so it is translated as a plural.

יְשׁוּפְךָ. Finite > yiqtol 3ms / Process > qal שׁוּף + Goal > pronoun suffix 2ms, antecedent is the Receiver, הַנָּחָשׁ *the snake.*

רֹאשׁ. Scope > nominal group: noun common ms. NRSV is representative of the translation tradition: *he will strike your head.* But notice precisely how the clause is worded. The Goal, the thing struck, is הַנָּחָשׁ, represented by the pronoun suffix on the verb. The structure of the clause suggests רֹאשׁ specifies the Scope: the snake will be struck on the head. The Scope of a material process is a circumstantial element, here the location of the blow, that is disguised as a Participant.

וְאַתָּה תְּשׁוּפֶנּוּ עָקֵב. (c) Textuality > conj paratactic projection: quote / Mood > declarative: non-past / Transitivity > material: action.

עָקֵב	תְּשׁוּפֶנּוּ	וְאַתָּה	**Constituents**
heel-wise	*you will strike him*	*and you*	**Translation**
		Theme	**Textuality**
	Finite	Subject	**Mood**
Scope	Process + Goal	Actor	**Transitivity**

וְאַתָּה. Theme: textual > clause conj + Theme: experiential / Subject > 2ms / Actor > pronoun personal 2ms, antecedent is the Receiver, הַנָּחָשׁ *the snake.*

תְּשׁוּפֶנּוּ. Finite > yiqtol 2ms / Process > qal שׁוּף + Goal > pronoun suffix 3ms, antecedent is זַרְעָהּ *her seed*. The Goal is singular because the noun is singular, but it designates a collectivity, so it is translated plural.

עָקֵב. Scope > nominal group: noun common ms: *on the heel.* Compare NRSV: *and you will strike his heel*, which does not precisely capture the Hebrew syntax. See the discussion of Scope in the preceding clause.

3:16 // אֶל־הָאִשָּׁה אָמַר // הַרְבָּה אַרְבֶּה עִצְּבוֹנֵךְ
וְהֵרֹנֵךְ // בְּעֶצֶב תֵּלְדִי בָנִים // וְאֶל־אִישֵׁךְ תְּשׁוּקָתֵךְ
// וְהוּא יִמְשָׁל־בָּךְ׃ ס

With each of the quoted clauses in this verse (clauses b through e), the process is the second component in its clause and each is a yiqtol form. Only the last two clauses are introduced with a clause-level conjunction.

אֶל־הָאִשָּׁה אָמַר. (a) Textuality > appositive paratactic expansion / Mood > declarative: past / Transitivity > verbal. The Subject / Sayer is יְהוָה אֱלֹהִים, absent here by ellipsis.

אָמַר	אֶל־הָאִשָּׁה	**Constituents**
he said	*to the woman*	**Translation**
	Theme	**Textuality**
Finite		**Mood**
Process	Receiver	**Transitivity**

אֶל־הָאִשָּׁה. Theme: experiential / Receiver > prep phrase: prep - def art + noun common fs.

אָמַר. Finite > qatal 3ms / Process > qal אמר.

הַרְבָּה אַרְבֶּה עִצְּבוֹנֵךְ וְהֵרֹנֵךְ. (b) Textuality > appositive paratactic projection: quote / Mood > declarative: non-past / Transitivity > material: action.

עִצְּבוֹנֵךְ וְהֵרֹנֵךְ	אַרְבֶּה	הַרְבָּה	**Constituents**
your pain and your conceiving	*I will increase*	*increasing*	**Translation**
	Theme	Theme	Textuality
	Finite	Adjunct	Mood
Goal	Process		Transitivity

הַרְבָּה. Theme: interpersonal / Adjunct: interpersonal > modal: inf abs hifil רבה. This component of the interpersonal system reinforces the certainty of the material process.

אַרְבֶּה. Theme: experiential / Finite > yiqtol 1cs / Process > hifil רבה.

עִצְּבוֹנֵךְ וְהֵרֹנֵךְ. Goal > nominal group complex: two nominal groups. The NRSV Translation *your pangs in childbearing* does not accurately represent the structure of the text, which is two coordinated but separate nouns. There is a good bit of interpretation in the NRSV's translation. Friedman is truer to the structure: *I will make your suffering and your labor pain great.*

עִצְּבוֹנֵךְ. Goal 1 > nominal group: noun common ms const + pronoun suffix 2fs, antecedent is הָאִשָּׁה, the Receiver of the verbal process in clause (a).

וְהֵרֹנֵךְ. Group conj + Goal 2 > nominal group: noun common ms const + pronoun suffix 2fs, antecedent is הָאִשָּׁה *the woman.*

בְּעֶצֶב תֵּלְדִי בָנִים. (c) Textuality > appositive paratactic projection: quote / Mood > declarative: non-past / Transitivity > material: action.

בָנִים	תֵּלְדִי	בְּעֶצֶב	**Constituents**
sons	*you will bear*	*in pain*	**Translation**
		Theme	**Textuality**
	Finite		**Mood**
Goal	Process	Circumstance	**Transitivity**

בְּעֶצֶב. Circumstance: manner, quality > prep phrase: prep + noun common ms.

תֵּלְדִי. Finite > yiqtol 2fs / Process > qal ילד.

בָנִים. Goal > nominal group: noun common mp.

וְאֶל־אִישֵׁךְ תְּשׁוּקָתֵךְ. (d) Textuality > conj paratactic projection: quote / Mood > declarative: non-past / Transitivity > relational: attribution. This clause does not appear to be a curse so much as a statement of fact. Perhaps this is an example of grammatical metaphor, in which case a declarative clause is really a command directive.

תְּשׁוּקָתֵךְ	וְאֶל־אִישֵׁךְ	**Constituents**
your desire	*and to your man*	**Translation**
	Theme	**Textuality**
Subject	Complement	**Mood**
Carrier	Attribute	**Transitivity**

וְאֶל־אִישֵׁךְ. Theme: textual > clause conj + Theme: experiential / Complement / Attribute > prep phrase: prep - noun common ms const + pronoun suffix 2fs, antecedent is the Receiver, הָאִשָּׁה *the woman.*

תְּשׁוּקָתֵךְ. Subject > fs / Carrier > nominal group: noun common fs const + pronoun suffix 2fs, antecedent is the Receiver, הָאִשָּׁה *the woman.*

וְהוּא יִמְשָׁל־בָּךְ. (e) Textuality > conj paratactic projection: quote / Mood > declarative: non-past / Transitivity > material: action.

בָּךְ	יִמְשָׁל־	וְהוּא	**Constituents**
over you	*will exercise rule*	*and he*	**Translation**
		Theme	**Textuality**
	Finite	Subject	**Mood**
Range	Process	Actor	**Transitivity**

וְהוּא. Theme: textual > clause conj + Behaver: pronoun 3ms, antecedent is אִישֵׁךְ *your man.*

יִמְשָׁל־. Finite > yiqtol 3ms / Process > qal משׁל.

בָּךְ. Range > prep phrase: prep + pronoun suffix 2fs, antecedent is הָאִשָּׁה *the woman.* The woman is traditionally understood as the Goal or object that the man would rule. Because this is a prepositional phrase rather than a nominal group, it may instead designate the domain or Range over which the man exercises rule.

3:17 וּלְאָדָ֣ם אָמַ֗ר // כִּֽי־שָׁמַעְתָּ֮ לְק֣וֹל אִשְׁתֶּךָ֒ // וַתֹּ֙א־
כַל֙ מִן־הָעֵ֔ץ אֲשֶׁ֤ר צִוִּיתִ֙יךָ֙ לֵאמֹ֔ר // לֹ֥א תֹאכַ֖ל מִמֶּ֑נּוּ
// אֲרוּרָ֤ה הָֽאֲדָמָה֙ בַּעֲבוּרֶ֔ךָ // בְּעִצָּבוֹן֙ תֹּֽאכֲלֶ֔נָּה
כֹּ֖ל יְמֵ֥י חַיֶּֽיךָ׃

וּלְאָדָם אָמַר. (a) Textuality > conj paratactic expansion / Mood > declarative: past / Transitivity > verbal.

אָמַר	וּלְאָדָם	Constituents
he said	*and to 'Adam*	**Translation**
	Theme	**Textuality**
Finite		**Mood**
Process	Receiver	**Transitivity**

וּלְאָדָם. Theme: textual > clause conj + Theme: experiential / Receiver > prep phrase: prep + noun proper ms. Here *'Adam* rather than *the human*. The noun does not have an attached definite article.

אָמַר. Finite > qatal 3ms / Process > qal אמר.

כִּי־שָׁמַעְתָּ לְקוֹל אִשְׁתֶּךָ. (b) Textuality > conj hypotactic projection: quote / Mood > declarative: past / Transitivity > behavioral.

לְקוֹל אִשְׁתֶּךָ	שָׁמַעְתָּ	כִּי־	Constituents
to the voice of your woman	*you listened*	*because*	**Translation**
	Theme	Theme	**Textuality**
	Finite		**Mood**
Range	Process		**Transitivity**

כִּי־. Theme: textual > conj. This signals a logical relationship with clause (d). The כִּי governs both clauses (b) and (c).

שָׁמַעְתָּ. Theme: experiential / Finite > qatal 2ms / Process > qal שׁמע: *listened to, gave heed to.* The process structure שָׁמַע plus לְ indicating Range is behavioral, while שָׁמַע plus אֶת marking the Goal is a mental process of perception. It is the difference between listening to and hearing.

לְקוֹל אִשְׁתֶּךָ. Range > prep phrase: prep + noun ms const | noun fs const + pronoun suffix 2ms, antecedent is the Receiver, אָדָם *'Adam.*

וַתֹּאכַל מִן־הָעֵץ [[אֲשֶׁר צִוִּיתִיךָ לֵאמֹר לֹא תֹאכַל מִמֶּנּוּ]]. (c) Textuality > conj hypotactic projection: quote / Mood > declarative: past / Transitivity > material: action.

Constituents	וַתֹּאכַל	מִן־הָעֵץ [[אֲשֶׁר צִוִּיתִיךָ לֵאמֹר לֹא תֹאכַל מִמֶּנּוּ]]
Translation	*and you ate*	*from the tree which I commanded you by saying not you will eat from him*
Textuality	Theme	
Mood	Finite	
Transitivity	Process	Range

וַתֹּאכַל. Theme: textual > clause conj + Theme: experiential / Finite > wayyiqtol 2ms / Process > qal אכל.

מִן־הָעֵץ [[אֲשֶׁר צִוִּיתִיךָ לֵאמֹר לֹא תֹאכַל מִמֶּנּוּ]]. Range > prep phrase complex: Head + Post-modifier.

מִן־הָעֵץ. Head > prep phase: def art + noun common ms.

אֲשֶׁר צִוִּיתִיךָ לֵאמֹר [[לֹא תֹאכַל מִמֶּנּוּ]]. (i) Post-modifier >> Textuality > embedded expansion: relative clause / Transitivity > verbal.

Constituents	אֲשֶׁר	צִוִּיתִיךָ	לֵאמֹר	[[לֹא תֹאכַל מִמֶּנּוּ]]
Translation	*which*	*I commanded you*	*by saying*	*not you will eat from him*
Textuality	Theme			
Mood		Finite		
Transitivity	Range	Process + Receiver	Circumstance	Verbiage

אֲשֶׁר. Theme: textual and experiential > pronoun relative / Range > antedecent הָעֵץ *the tree.*

צִוִּיתִיךָ. Finite > qatal 1cs / Process > piel צוה + Receiver > pronoun suffix 2ms, antecedent is אָדָם *'Adam.*

לֵאמֹר. Circumstance: manner > prep phrase: prep + inf const qal אמר.

לֹא תֹאכַל מִמֶּנּוּ. (a') Verbiage >> Textuality > embedded projection: quote / Mood > directive: imperative / Transitivity > material: action.

מִמֶּנּוּ	תֹאכַל	לֹא	**Constituents**
from him	*you will eat*	*not*	**Translation**
	Theme	Theme	**Textuality**
	Finite	Adjunct	**Mood**
Range	Process		**Transitivity**

לֹא. Theme: interpersonal / Adjunct: interpersonal > polarity: negative.

תֹאכַל. Theme: experiential / Finite > yiqtol 2ms / Process > qal אכל. The negative adjunct plus second person yiqtol is conventional for a directive, the negative imperative.

מִמֶּנּוּ. Range > prep phrase: prep + pronoun suffix 3ms, antecedent is הָעֵץ *the tree.*

אֲרוּרָה הָאֲדָמָה בַּעֲבוּרֶךָ. (d) Textuality > appositive paratactic projection: quote / Mood > declarative: non-past / Transitivity > relational: attribution. This is the dominant clause upon which the כִּי clauses (b) and (c) logically depend.

בַּעֲבוּרֶךָ	הָאֲדָמָה	אֲרוּרָה	**Constituents**
on account of you	*the ground*	*cursed*	**Translation**
		Theme	**Textuality**
	Subject	Complement	**Mood**
Circumstance	Carrier	Attribute	**Transitivity**

אֲרוּרָה. Theme: experiential / Complement > fs / Attribute > passive ptc fs qal ארר.

הָאֲדָמָה. Subject > fs / Carrier > nominal group: def art + noun common fs.

בַּעֲבוּרֶךָ. Circumstance: cause, reason > prep phrase: prep + pronoun suffix 2ms, antecedent is the Receiver, אָדָם *'Adam. On account of you* in the sense of *because of what you did.*

בְּעִצָּבוֹן תֹּאכְלֶנָּה כֹּל יְמֵי חַיֶּיךָ. (e) Textuality > appositive paratactic projection: quote / Mood > declarative: non-past / Transitivity > material: action.

כֹּל יְמֵי חַיֶּיךָ	תֹּאכְלֶנָּה	בְּעִצָּבוֹן	**Constituents**
all the days of your life	*you will eat her*	*in pain*	**Translation**
		Theme	**Textuality**
	Finite		**Mood**
Range	Process + Goal	Circumstance	**Transitivity**

בְּעִצָּבוֹן. Circumstance: manner > prep phrase: prep + noun common ms.

תֹּאכְלֶנָּה. Finite > yiqtol 2ms / Process > qal אכל + Goal > pronoun suffix 3fs, antecedent is הָאֲדָמָה—but, of course, he would not eat the ground itself, but what comes from the ground.

כֹּל יְמֵי חַיֶּיךָ. Range > nominal group: noun common ms const | noun common mp const | noun common mp const + pronoun suffix 2ms, antecedent is the Receiver, אָדָם *'Adam*.

3:18 // וְקוֹץ וְדַרְדַּר תַּצְמִיחַ לָךְ // וְאָכַלְתָּ אֶת־עֵשֶׂב הַשָּׂדֶה׃

וְקוֹץ וְדַרְדַּר תַּצְמִיחַ לָךְ. (a) Textuality > conj paratactic projection: quote / Mood > declarative: non-past / Transitivity > material: action. The Subject / Actor is הָאֲדָמָה *the ground*, absent here by ellipsis.

לָךְ	תַּצְמִיחַ	וְקוֹץ וְדַרְדַּר	**Constituents**
for you	*she will grow*	*thorn and thistle*	**Translation**
		Theme	**Textuality**
	Finite		**Mood**
Beneficiary	Process	Goal	**Transitivity**

וְקוֹץ וְדַרְדַּר. Theme: textual > clause conj + Goal > nominal group: noun common collective ms | group conj + noun common collective ms.

תַּצְמִיחַ. Finite > yiqtol 3fs / Process > hifil צמח.

לָךְ. Beneficiary > prep phrase: prep + pronoun suffix 2ms, antecedent is the Receiver, אָדָם *'Adam*. The vocalization of לָךְ has it looking like 2fs. But 2ms לְךָ becomes לָךְ under pausal stress, as here with the *'atnach*.

וְאָכַלְתָּ אֶת־עֵשֶׂב הַשָּׂדֶה. (b) Textuality > conj paratactic projection: quote / Mood > declarative: non-past / Transitivity > material: action. The Subject / Actor is the Receiver, אָדָם *'Adam*, absent by ellipsis. The Actor of this clause represents a change of Actor from the prior clause. Yet אָדָם is the antecedent of the pronoun of לָךְ, which immediately precedes this clause, so it is easily retrievable within the textual structure of the text.

אֶת־עֵשֶׂב הַשָּׂדֶה	וְאָכַלְתָּ	**Constituents**
the plantkind of the field	*and you will eat*	**Translation**
	Theme	**Textuality**
	Finite	**Mood**
Goal	Process	**Transitivity**

וְאָכַלְתָּ. Finite > weqatal 2ms / Process > qal אכל.

אֶת־עֵשֶׂב הַשָּׂדֶה. Goal > nominal group: goal marker - noun common collective ms const | def art + noun common ms. This clause appears to be a bit out of place structurally and semantically. It employs a weqatal form in contrast to the preceding yiqtol forms, and it does not sound like a curse, as do the other clauses. Or, maybe this vegetarianism is a curse, if the writer and his world were used to eating meat.

3:19 // בְּזֵעַת אַפֶּיךָ תֹּאכַל לֶחֶם עַד שׁוּבְךָ אֶל־הָאֲדָמָה /
כִּי מִמֶּנָּה לֻקָּחְתָּ // כִּי־עָפָר אַתָּה / וְאֶל־עָפָר תָּשׁוּב׃

בְּזֵעַת אַפֶּיךָ תֹּאכַל לֶחֶם עַד שׁוּבְךָ אֶל־הָאֲדָמָה. (a) Textuality > appositive paratactic projection: quote / Mood > declarative: non-past / Transitivity > material: action. The Subject / Actor of this and the subsequent three clauses is the Receiver of the quote, אָדָם *'Adam*, absent here by ellipsis.

עַד שׁוּבְךָ אֶל־הָאֲדָמָה	לֶחֶם	תֹּאכַל	בְּזֵעַת אַפֶּיךָ	**Constituents**
until your return to the ground	*bread*	*you will eat*	*by the sweat of your nostrils*	**Translation**
			Theme	**Textuality**
		Finite		**Mood**
Circumstance	Goal	Process	Circumstance	**Transitivity**

בְּזֵעַת אַפֶּיךָ. Circumstance: manner > prep phrase: prep + noun common fs const | noun common mp const + pronoun suffix 2ms, antecedent is the Receiver, אָדָם *'Adam*.

תֹּאכַל. Finite > yiqtol 2ms / Process > qal אכל.

לֶחֶם. Goal > nominal group: noun common collective ms. *Bread*, and perhaps more broadly, *food*.

עַד שׁוּבְךָ אֶל־הָאֲדָמָה. (i) Circumstance: extent, time >> Textuality > embedded extension: prep clause / Transitivity > material: action. This clause extends the meaning of the main clausc process תֹּאכַל by specifying the duration of the activity.

אֶל־הָאֲדָמָה	שׁוּבְךָ	עַד	**Constituents**
to the ground	*your return*	*until*	**Translation**
	Theme	Theme	**Textuality**
Circumstance	Process + Actor		**Transitivity**

עַד. Theme: textual > prep.

שׁוּבְךָ. Theme: experiential / Process > inf const qal שׁוב + Actor > pronoun suffix 2ms, antecedent is the Receiver, אָדָם *'Adam*.

אֶל־הָאֲדָמָה. Circumstance: location, place > prep phrase: prep - def art + noun common fs.

כִּי מִמֶּנָּה לֻקָּחְתָּ. (b) Textuality > conj hypotactic projection: quote / Mood > declarative: past / Transitivity > material: action. This clause extends the meaning of the prior clause.

לֻקָּחְתָּ	מִמֶּנָּה	כִּי	**Constituents**
you were taken	*from her*	*because*	**Translation**
	Theme	Theme	**Textuality**
Finite			**Mood**
Process	Circumstance		**Transitivity**

כִּי. Theme: textual > conj. This signals logical dependency, in this case, on the prior clause.

מִמֶּנָּה. Circumstance: location, place > prep phrase: prep + pronoun suffix 3fs, antecedent is הָאֲדָמָה *the ground.*

לֻקָּחְתָּ. Finite > qatal 2ms / Process > qal passive or pual לקח. The interpersonal Subject of the passive verb is אָדָם, who is then functionally the Goal of the material process.

כִּי־עָפָר אַתָּה. (c) Textuality > conj hypotactic projection: quote / Mood > declarative: non-past / Transitivity > relational: attribution. This clause is hypotactically related to the following clause.

אַתָּה	עָפָר	כִּי־	**Constituents**
you	*dust*	*because*	**Translation**
	Theme	Theme	**Textuality**
Subject	Complement		**Mood**
Carrier	Attribute		**Transitivity**

כִּי־. Theme: textual > conj. This signals logical dependency on the following clause, textually reinforced by the repetition of עָפָר *dust.*

עָפָר. Complement > ms / Attribute > noun common ms.

אַתָּה. Carrier > pronoun personal 2ms, antecedent is אָדָם *'Adam.*

וְאֶל־עָפָר תָּשׁוּב. (d) Textuality > conj paratactic projection: quote / Mood > declarative: non-past / Transitivity > material: action. We expect this to be a dominant clause, because the prior **כִּי** *because* clause sets up an expected dependency.

תָּשׁוּב	וְאֶל־עָפָר	**Constituents**
you will return	*and to dust*	**Translation**
	Theme	**Textuality**
Finite		**Mood**
Process	Range	**Transitivity**

וְאֶל־עָפָר. Theme: textual > clause conj + Theme: experiential / Range > prep phrase: prep - noun common ms.

תָּשׁוּב. Finite > yiqtol 2ms / Process > qal **שׁוּב**.

Genesis 3:20-21

[20]And the human called the name of his woman Chavva, because she was mother of all alive. [21]And YHVH deity made for 'Adam and for his woman garments of skin. And he clothed them.

3:20 /// וַיִּקְרָא הָאָדָם שֵׁם אִשְׁתּוֹ חַוָּה / כִּי הִוא הָיְתָה
אֵם כָּל־חָי׃

וַיִּקְרָא הָאָדָם שֵׁם אִשְׁתּוֹ חַוָּה. (a) Textuality > conj paratactic expansion / Mood > declarative: past / Transitivity > verbal.

חַוָּה	שֵׁם אִשְׁתּוֹ	הָאָדָם	וַיִּקְרָא	**Constituents**
Chavva	*the name of his woman*	*the human*	*and he called*	**Translation**
			Theme	**Textuality**
		Subject	Finite	**Mood**
Verbiage	Target	Sayer	Process	**Transitivity**

וַיִּקְרָא. Theme: textual > clause conj + Theme: experiential / Finite > wayyiqtol 3ms / Process > qal קרא.

הָאָדָם. Subject > ms / Sayer > nominal group: def art + noun common.

שֵׁם אִשְׁתּוֹ. Target > nominal group: noun common ms const ׀ noun common fs const + pronoun suffix 3ms, antecedent is הָאָדָם *the human*. Notice how the text reverts back to the generic term after having used the proper noun since 3:17(a).

חַוָּה. Verbiage > nominal group: noun proper fs.

כִּי הִוא הָיְתָה אֵם כָּל־חָי. (b) Textuality > conj hypotactic expansion / Mood > declarative: past / Transitivity > relational: attribution. This clause has logical dependency on clause (a).

אֵם כָּל־חָי	הָיְתָה	הִוא	כִּי	**Constituents**
mother of all alive	*she was*	*she*	*because*	**Translation**
		Theme	Theme	**Textuality**
Complement	Finite	Subject		**Mood**
Attribute	Process	Carrier		**Transitivity**

כִּי. Theme: textual > conj.

הִוא. Theme: experiential / Subject > 3fs / Carrier > pronoun personal 3fs, antecedent is אִשְׁתּוֹ *his woman*.

הָיְתָה. Finite > qatal 3fs / Process > qal היה.

אֵם כָּל־חָי. Complement > fs (אֵם) / Attribute > nominal group: noun common fs const ׀ noun common collective ms const + adj ms: *a mother of all living*. Though NRSV renders this nominal group *the mother of all living*, there is no indicator of definiteness in it.

3:21 // וַיַּעַשׂ יְהוָה אֱלֹהִים לְאָדָם וּלְאִשְׁתּוֹ כָּתְנוֹת עוֹר
// וַיַּלְבִּשֵׁם׃ פ

וַיַּעַשׂ יְהוָה אֱלֹהִים לְאָדָם וּלְאִשְׁתּוֹ כָּתְנוֹת עוֹר. (a) Textuality > conj paratactic expansion / Mood > declarative: past / Transitivity > material: action.

כָּתְנוֹת עוֹר	לְאָדָם וּלְאִשְׁתּוֹ	יְהוָה אֱלֹהִים	וַיַּעַשׂ	**Constituents**
garments of skin	*for 'Adam and for his woman*	*YHVH deity*	*and he made*	**Translation**
			Theme	**Textuality**
		Subject	Finite	**Mood**
Goal	Beneficiary	Actor	Process	**Transitivity**

וַיַּעַשׂ. Theme: textual > clause conj + Theme: experiential / Finite > wayyiqtol 3ms / Process > qal עשׂה.

יְהוָה אֱלֹהִים. Subject > ms / Actor > nominal group: noun proper ms + noun common mp.

לְאָדָם וּלְאִשְׁתּוֹ. Beneficiary: prep phrase complex: prep + noun common ms ו group conj + prep + noun common fs const + pronoun suffix 3ms, antecedent is אָדָם *'Adam*.

כָּתְנוֹת עוֹר. Goal > nominal group: noun common fp const + noun common ms.

וַיַּלְבִּשֵׁם. (b) Textuality > conj paratactic expansion / Mood > declarative: past / Transitivity > material: action. The Subject / Actor is יְהוָה אֱלֹהִים *YHVH deity*, absent here by ellipsis.

וַיַּלְבִּשֵׁם	**Constituents**
and he clothed them	**Translation**
Theme	**Textuality**
Finite	**Mood**
Process + Goal	**Transitivity**

וַיַּלְבִּשֵׁם. Theme: textual > clause conj + Theme: experiential / Finite > wayyiqtol 3ms / Process > hifil לבשׁ + Goal > pronoun suffix 3mp, antecedent is אָדָם וְאִשְׁתּוֹ *'Adam and his woman*.

Genesis 3:22-24

[22]And YHVH deity said, "This the human became like one of us knowing good and bad." And now, lest he will extend his hand and he will take also from the tree of the living and he will eat and he will live to eternity, [23]YHVH deity sent him from the garden of Eden to work the ground, from which he was taken. [24]And he expelled the human. And he settled east of the garden of Eden the cherubs and the flame of the rotating sword to guard the way of the tree of the living.

3:22 /// וַיֹּאמֶר | יְהוָה אֱלֹהִים // הֵן הָאָדָם הָיָה כְּאַחַד
מִמֶּנּוּ לָדַעַת טוֹב וָרָע // וְעַתָּה | פֶּן־יִשְׁלַח יָדוֹ
וְלָקַח גַּם מֵעֵץ הַחַיִּים וְאָכַל וָחַי לְעֹלָם׃

וַיֹּאמֶר יְהוָה אֱלֹהִים. (a) Textuality > conj paratactic expansion / Mood > declarative: past / Transitivity > verbal.

יְהוָה אֱלֹהִים	וַיֹּאמֶר	**Constituents**
YHVH deity	*and he said*	**Translation**
	Theme	**Textuality**
Subject	Finite	**Mood**
Sayer	Process	**Transitivity**

וַיֹּאמֶר. Theme: textual > clause conj + Theme: experiential / Finite > wayyiqtol 3ms / Process > qal אמר.

יְהוָה אֱלֹהִים. Subject > ms / Sayer > nominal group: noun proper ms + noun common mp.

הֵן הָאָדָם הָיָה כְּאַחַד מִמֶּנּוּ [[לָדַעַת טוֹב וָרָע]]. (b) Textuality > appositive paratactic projection: quote / Mood > declarative: past / Transitivity > relational: attribution.

כְּאַחַד מִמֶּנּוּ [[לָדַעַת טוֹב וָרָע]]	הָיָה	הָאָדָם	הֵן	**Constituents**
like one from us, to know good-and-bad	*was / became*	*the human*	*now*	**Translation**
		Theme	Theme	**Textuality**
	Finite	Subject		**Mood**
Attribute	Process	Carrier		**Transitivity**

הֵן. Theme: interpersonal / Adjunct: textual > contra-expectation. This textual adjunct, cognate with הִנֵּה, signals an unexpected and undesirable development. See the explanation attached to 1:29(a).

הָאָדָם. Theme: experiential / Subject > ms / Carrier > nominal group: def art + noun common ms.

הָיָה. Finite > qatal 3ms / Process > qal היה. Instead of *was*, some render the process *became.*

כְּאַחַד מִמֶּנּוּ [[לָדַעַת טוֹב וָרָע]]. Attribute > prep phrase complex: prep - Head + Post-modifier.

כְּאַחַד. Prep + Head > numeral ms.

מִמֶּנּוּ לָדַעַת טוֹב וָרָע. Post-modifier > prep - Head + Post-modifier.

מִמֶּנּוּ. Prep + Head > pronoun suffix 1cp, antecedent is יְהוָה אֱלֹהִים *YHVH deity.*

לָדַעַת טוֹב וָרָע. (i) Post-modifier >> Textuality > embedded expansion: prep clause / Transitivity > mental: perception. This clause extends the meaning of כְּ by specifying in what way the human is like one of the gods.

טוֹב וָרָע	לָדַעַת	**Constituents**
good and bad	*to know*	**Translation**
	Theme	**Textuality**
Phenomenon	Process	**Transitivity**

לָדַ֫עַת. Theme: textual > prep + Theme: experiential / Process > inf const qal ידע.

ט֥וֹב וָרָ֑ע. Phenomenon > nominal group: adj ms | group conj + adj ms. Note again the hendiadys conjunction uniting the two components of this constituent.

וְעַתָּ֣ה ׀ פֶּן־יִשְׁלַ֣ח יָד֗וֹ. (c) Textuality > conj hypotactic expansion / Mood > declarative: non-past / Transitivity > material: action. Actor is הָאָדָם, absent by ellipsis. This is the first clause of four clauses that are dependent on clause 3:23(a).

יָד֗וֹ	יִשְׁלַ֣ח	פֶּן־	וְעַתָּ֣ה	Constituents
his hand	*he will extend*	*lest*	*and now*	**Translation**
	Theme	Theme	Theme	Textuality
	Finite	Adjunct		Mood
Goal	Process			Transitivity

וְעַתָּ֣ה. Theme: textual > conj adjunct. וְעַתָּה *and now* is typically used to mark the beginning of a new clause complex, but in such a way that it is a continuation of the prior clause complex. Note that NRSV interprets this clause as a continuation of the prior quote clause. We view it as an expansion, not a projection.

פֶּן־. Theme: interpersonal / Adjunct: interpersonal > polarity: negative. The word פֶּן *so that not* is typically followed by a yiqtol Finite. We interpret this clause, along with the next three clauses, as all determined by this פֶּן *lest* and dependent upon 3:23(a), which is the dominant clause of this clause complex.

יִשְׁלַ֣ח. Theme: experiential / Finite > yiqtol 3ms / Process > qal שׁלח.

יָד֗וֹ. Goal > noun common ms const + pronoun suffix 3ms, antecedent is הָאָדָם *the human* in 3:22(b).

וְלָקַח֙ גַּ֚ם מֵעֵ֣ץ הַֽחַיִּ֔ים. (d) Textuality > conj paratactic expansion / Mood > declarative: non-past / Transitivity > material: action.

Actor is הָאָדָם, absent by ellipsis. This is the second clause that is dependent on clause 3:23(a).

מֵעֵץ הַחַיִּים	גַּם	וְלָקַח	**Constituents**
from the tree of the living	*also*	*and he will take*	**Translation**
	Adjunct	Theme	**Textuality**
		Finite	**Mood**
Range/Goal		Process	**Transitivity**

וְלָקַח. Theme: textual > clause conj + Theme: experiential / Finite > weqatal 3ms / Process > qal לקח.

גַּם. Adjunct: textual > additive, meaning also. This references the earlier text event when something else was taken from a different tree, as told in 3:6(e). As such it functions within the textual system.

מֵעֵץ הַחַיִּים. Range > prep phrase: prep + noun common ms const | def art + noun common mp. Or Goal; see 2:16(b).

וְאָכַל. (e) Textuality > conj paratactic expansion / Mood > declarative: non-past / Transitivity > material: action. Both the Subject / Actor and the Goal are absent by ellipsis. This is the third clause that is dependent on clause 3:23(a).

וְאָכַל	**Constituents**
and he will eat	**Translation**
Theme	**Textuality**
Finite	**Mood**
Process	**Transitivity**

וְאָכַל. Theme: textual > clause conj + Theme: experiential / Finite > weqatal 3ms / Process > qal אכל.

וָחַי לְעֹלָם. (f) Textuality > conj paratactic expansion / Mood > declarative: non-past / Transitivity > material: action. This is the fourth and last clause that is dependent on clause 3:23(a).

לְעֹלָם	וָחַי	**Constituents**
to eternity	*and he will live*	**Translation**
	Theme	**Textuality**
	Finite	**Mood**
Circumstance	Process	**Transitivity**

וָחַי. Theme: textual > clause conj + Theme: experiential / Finite > weqatal 3ms / Process > qal חיה.

לְעֹלָם. Circumstance: extent, time > prep phrase: prep + noun common ms.

3:23 / וַיְשַׁלְּחֵהוּ יְהוָה אֱלֹהִים מִגַּן־עֵדֶן לַעֲבֹד אֶת־הָאֲדָ־
מָה אֲשֶׁר לֻקַּח מִשָּׁם׃

וַיְשַׁלְּחֵהוּ יְהוָה אֱלֹהִים מִגַּן־עֵדֶן [[לַעֲבֹד אֶת־הָאֲדָמָה [[אֲשֶׁר לֻקַּח מִשָּׁם]]]]. (a) Textuality > conj paratactic expansion / Mood > declarative: past / Transitivity > material: action.

[[לַעֲבֹד אֶת־הָאֲדָמָה [[אֲשֶׁר לֻקַּח מִשָּׁם]]]]	מִגַּן־עֵדֶן	יְהוָה אֱלֹהִים	וַיְשַׁלְּחֵהוּ	**Constituents**
to work the ground which he was taken from there	*from the garden of Eden*	*YHVH deity*	*and he sent him*	**Translation**
			Theme	**Textuality**
		Subject	Finite	**Mood**
Circumstance	Circumstance	Actor	Process + Goal	**Transitivity**

וַיְשַׁלְּחֵהוּ. Theme: textual > clause conj + Theme: experiential / Finite > wayyiqtol 3ms / Process > qal שלח + Goal > pronoun suffix 3ms, antecedent is הָאָדָם *the human*. Both Process and Goal are thematized.

יְהוָה אֱלֹהִים. Subject > ms / Actor > nominal group: noun proper ms + noun common mp.

מִגַּן־עֵדֶן. Circumstance: location, place > prep phrase: prep + noun common ms const - noun proper.

לַעֲבֹד אֶת־הָאֲדָמָה [[אֲשֶׁר לֻקַּח מִשָּׁם]]. (i) Circumstance: cause, purpose >> Textuality > embedded expansion: prep clause / Transitivity > material: action. The Subject / Actor is הָאָדָם *the human*, manifest as the Goal > pronoun suffix 3ms of clause (a).

אֶת־הָאֲדָמָה [[אֲשֶׁר לֻקַּח מִשָּׁם]]	לַעֲבֹד	**Constituents**
the ground which he was taken from there	*to work*	**Translation**
	Theme	**Textuality**
Goal	Process	**Transitivity**

לַעֲבֹד. Theme: textual > prep + Process > inf const qal עבד.

אֶת־הָאֲדָמָה [[אֲשֶׁר לֻקַּח מִשָּׁם]]. Goal > nominal group complex: goal marker - Head + Post-modifier.

הָאֲדָמָה. Head > def art + noun common fs.

אֲשֶׁר לֻקַּח מִשָּׁם. (a') Post-modifier >> Textuality > embedded expansion: relative clause / Mood > declarative: past / Transitivity > material: action. The Subject / Actor is הָאָדָם *the human*, which is also the Goal of the Process, absent here by ellipsis.

מִשָּׁם	לֻקַּח	אֲשֶׁר	**Constituents**
from there	*he was taken*	*which*	**Translation**
		Theme	**Textuality**
	Finite		**Mood**
Circumstance	Process	Goal	**Transitivity**

אֲשֶׁר. Theme: textual and experiential > pronoun relative / Goal > antecedent הָאֲדָמָה *the ground.*

לֻקַּח. Finite > qatal 3ms / Process > pual לקח.

מִשָּׁם. Circumstance: location, place > prep phrase: prep + Adjunct: experiential > circumstance, place. This adjunct serves as a type of pronoun in so far as its antecedent is הָאֲדָמָה.

3:24 // וַיְגָ֖רֶשׁ אֶת־הָֽאָדָ֑ם // וַיַּשְׁכֵּן֩ מִקֶּ֨דֶם לְגַן־עֵ֜דֶן
אֶת־הַכְּרֻבִ֗ים וְאֵ֨ת לַ֤הַט הַחֶ֨רֶב֙ הַמִּתְהַפֶּ֔כֶת לִשְׁמֹ֕ר
אֶת־דֶּ֖רֶךְ עֵ֥ץ הַֽחַיִּֽים׃ ס

וַיְגָ֖רֶשׁ אֶת־הָֽאָדָ֑ם. (a) Textuality > conj paratactic expansion / Mood > declarative: past / Transitivity > material: action. The Subject / Actor is יְהוָה אֱלֹהִים from 3:23(a), absent here by ellipsis.

אֶת־הָאָדָם	וַיְגָרֶשׁ	**Constituents**
the human	*and he expelled*	**Translation**
	Theme	Textuality
	Finite	Mood
Goal	Process	Transitivity

וַיְגָרֶשׁ. Theme: textual > clause conj + Theme: experiential / Finite > wayyiqtol 3ms / Process > qal גרשׁ.

אֶת־הָאָדָם. Goal > goal marker - def art + noun common ms.

וַיַּשְׁכֵּן מִקֶּדֶם לְגַן־עֵדֶן אֶת־הַכְּרֻבִים וְאֵת לַהַט הַחֶרֶב הַמִּתְהַפֶּכֶת [[לִשְׁמֹר אֶת־דֶּרֶךְ עֵץ הַחַיִּים]]. (b) Textuality > conj paratactic expansion / Mood > declarative: past / Transitivity > material: action. The Subject / Actor is יְהוָה אֱלֹהִים from 3:23(a), absent here by ellipsis.

[[לִשְׁמֹר אֶת־דֶּרֶךְ עֵץ הַחַיִּים]]	אֶת־הַכְּרֻבִים וְאֵת לַהַט הַחֶרֶב הַמִּתְהַפֶּכֶת	מִקֶּדֶם לְגַן־עֵדֶן	וַיַּשְׁכֵּן	**Constituents**
to guard the way of the tree of the living	*the cherubs and the flame of the rotating sword*	*from east to the garden of Eden*	*and he settled*	**Translation**
			Theme	**Textuality**
			Finite	**Mood**
Circumstance	Goal	Circumstance	Process	**Transitivity**

וַיַּשְׁכֵּן. Theme: textual > clause conj + Theme: experiential / Finite > wayyiqtol 3ms / Process > hifil שׁכן.

מִקֶּדֶם לְגַן־עֵדֶן. Circumstance: location, place > prep phrase complex: prep + noun common ms | prep + noun ms const + noun proper.

אֶת־הַכְּרֻבִים וְאֵת לַהַט הַחֶרֶב הַמִּתְהַפֶּכֶת. Goal > nominal group complex: two nominal groups.

אֶת־הַכְּרֻבִים. Goal 1 > nominal group: goal marker - def art + noun common mp.

וְאֵת לַהַט הַחֶרֶב הַמִּתְהַפֶּכֶת. Group conj + Goal 2 > nominal group: goal marker | noun common ms const | def art + noun common fs | def art + ptc fs hitpael הפך. The hitpael stem is often associated with reflexive or reciprocal activity. See WO chapter 26. In the case of the sword here, it may suggest either rotation or a back-and-forth oscillating motion.

לִשְׁמֹר אֶת־דֶּרֶךְ עֵץ הַחַיִּים. (i) Circumstance: cause, purpose >> Textuality > embedded expansion: prep clause / Transitivity > material: action.

אֶת־דֶּרֶךְ עֵץ הַחַיִּים	לִשְׁמֹר	**Constituents**
the way of the tree of the living	*to guard*	**Translation**
	Theme	**Textuality**
Goal	Process	**Transitivity**

לִשְׁמֹר. Theme: textual > prep + Theme: experiential / Process > inf const qal שׁמר.

אֶת־דֶּרֶךְ עֵץ הַחַיִּים. Goal > nominal group: goal marker - noun common cs const | noun common ms const | def art + noun common mp.

Genesis 4:1-7

*[1]And the human knew Chavva his woman. And she conceived. And
she birthed Qayin. And she said, "I got a man with YHVH." [2]She did it
again, bearing his brother Hevel. And Hevel was a tender of sheep. And
Qayin was a worker of ground. [3]And it happened days afterward, and
Qayin brought from the fruit of the ground an offering to YHVH. [4]And
Hevel, he also brought from the firstborn of his flock and from their fats.
And YHVH looked to Hevel and to his offering. [5]And to Qayin and to his
offering he looked not. And Qayin was very hot. And his face fell. [6]And
YHVH said to Qayin, "Why were you hot? And why fell your face? [7]Is it
not so?—If you will do good, acceptance. And if you will not do good, sin
is a lurker at the door. And to you is its desire. And you will rule over it."*

4:1 /// וְהָאָדָם יָדַע אֶת־חַוָּה אִשְׁתּוֹ // וַתַּהַר // וַתֵּלֶד
אֶת־קַיִן // וַתֹּאמֶר // קָנִיתִי אִישׁ אֶת־יְהוָה׃

וְהָאָדָם יָדַע אֶת־חַוָּה אִשְׁתּוֹ. (a) Textuality > conj paratactic expansion / Mood > declarative: past / Transitivity > mental: cognition, which is actually an Actor + Material Process + Goal transitivity structure. The mental process *know* is a metaphor or euphemism for a material process, namely, *have intercourse*. Also in 4:25(a).

אֶת־חַוָּה אִשְׁתּוֹ	יָדַע	וְהָאָדָם	**Constituents**
Chavva his woman	*knew*	*and the human*	**Translation**
		Theme	**Textuality**
	Finite	Subject	**Mood**
Phenomenon	Process	Senser	**Transitivity**

וְהָאָדָם. Theme: textual > clause conj + Theme: experiential / Subject > ms / Senser > nominal group: def art + noun common.

יָדַע. Finite > qatal 3ms / Process > qal ידע.

אֶת־חַוָּה אִשְׁתּוֹ. Goal > nominal group: goal marker - noun proper | noun fs const + pronoun suffix 3ms, antecedent is הָאָדָם *the human*.

וַתַּהַר. (b) Textuality > conj paratactic expansion / Mood > declarative: past / Transitivity > material: action. Subject / Actor is חַוָּה *Chavva*, absent by ellipsis.

וַתַּהַר	**Constituents**
and she conceived	**Translation**
Theme	**Textuality**
Finite	**Mood**
Process	**Transitivity**

וַתַּהַר. Theme: experiential / Finite > wayyiqtol 3fs / Process > qal הרה.

וַתֵּלֶד אֶת־קַיִן. (c) Textuality > conj paratactic expansion / Mood > declarative: past / Transitivity > material: action.

אֶת־קַיִן	וַתֵּלֶד	**Constituents**
Qayin	*and she birthed*	**Translation**
	Theme	**Textuality**
	Finite	**Mood**
Goal	Process	**Transitivity**

וַתֵּלֶד. Finite > wayyiqtol 3fs / Process > qal ילד.

אֶת־קָיִן. Goal > nominal group: goal marker - noun proper.

וַתֹּאמֶר. (d) Textuality > conj paratactic expansion / Mood > declarative: past / Transitivity > verbal.

וַתֹּאמֶר	**Constituents**
and she said	**Translation**
Theme	**Textuality**
Finite	**Mood**
Process	**Transitivity**

וַתֹּאמֶר. Theme: experiential / Finite > wayyiqtol 3fs / Process > qal אמר.

קָנִיתִי אִישׁ אֶת־יְהוָה. (e) Textuality > appositive paratactic projection: quote / Mood > declarative: past / Transitivity > material: action. The Actor is חַוָּה, absent by ellipsis. This is a rather strange clause, for a number of reasons. The transitivity structure appears to have as its goal אֶת־יְהוָה, but presumably this cannot be, for logical reasons. So אִישׁ is rendered as the Goal, and the אֶת of אֶת־יְהוָה is rendered as the preposition *with*. The literal meaning of קָנָה is *buy, purchase*, but it is traditionally interpreted metaphorically as *get, acquire*. The semantics of this clause have a certain forced and tortured quality, which may be due to the attempt to provide the proper name קַיִן with an etymology. Lastly, this is a strange first appearance of the divine name יְהוָה detached from the common noun אֱלֹהִים, which has been paired with it to this point in the text.

אֶת־יְהוָה	אִישׁ	קָנִיתִי	**Constituents**
with YHVH	*a man*	*I got*	**Translation**
		Theme	**Textuality**
		Finite	**Mood**
Circumstance	Goal	Process	**Transitivity**

קָנִיתִי. Finite > qatal 1cs / Process > qal קנה.

אִישׁ. Goal > nominal group: noun common ms.

אֶת־יְהוָה. Circumstance > prep phase: prep - noun proper ms.

4:2 // וַתֹּסֶף לָלֶדֶת אֶת־אָחִיו אֶת־הָבֶל // וַיְהִי־הֶבֶל
רֹעֵה צֹאן // וְקַיִן הָיָה עֹבֵד אֲדָמָה׃

וַתֹּסֶף לָלֶדֶת אֶת־אָחִיו אֶת־הָבֶל. (a) Textuality > conj paratactic expansion / Mood > declarative: past / Transitivity > material: action.The Actor is חַוָּה, absent by ellipsis. As did 4:1(d), this clause presents structures that have not appeared in the text before. The Finite verb expresses the existential process of doing something again, and the embedded extension clause is the one that expresses the material process of birthing. This creates cohesion with the prior account of the birth of קַיִן by introducing another birthing episode. The first verb, וַתֹּסֶף, is structurally dominant, but the second verb, לָלֶדֶת is semantically dominant. This process could have been worded simply וַתֵּלֶד as in 4:1(c), so we might want to ask why *doing again* is the Theme rather than *giving birth*. Here is a suggested rendering: *she did it again, bearing his brother, Hevel.*

אֶת־אָחִיו אֶת־הָבֶל	לָלֶדֶת	וַתֹּסֶף	**Constituents**
his brother Hevel	*birthed*	*and she again*	**Translation**
		Theme	**Textuality**
		Finite	**Mood**
Goal		Process	**Transitivity**

וַתֹּסֶף לָלֶדֶת. Theme: textual > clause conj + Theme: experiential > verbal group complex: Finite + Non-finite. Functional grammar calls this structure a verbal group complex, which is a way of combining two processes into one; see 4:26(c) and Thompson 124.

וַתֹּסֶף. Finite > wayyiqtol 3fs / Process > hiphil יסף.

לָלֶדֶת. Non-finite > prep phrase: prep + Process > inf const qal ילד.

אֶת־אָחִיו אֶת־הָבֶל. Goal > nominal group: Head + Post-modifier.

אֶת־אָחִיו. Head > nominal group: goal marker - noun ms const + pronoun suffix 3ms, antecedent is קַיִן *Qayin*.

אֶת־הָבֶל. Post-modifier > nominal group: goal marker - noun proper. This nominal group extends the meaning of the Head by specifying the name of Qayin's brother.

וַיְהִי־הֶבֶל רֹעֵה צֹאן. (b) Textuality > conj paratactic expansion / Mood > declarative: past / Transitivity > relational: attribution.

רֹעֵה צֹאן	הֶבֶל	וַיְהִי־	**Constituents**
a tender of sheep	*Hevel*	*and he was*	**Translation**
		Theme	**Textuality**
Complement	Subject	Finite	**Mood**
Attribute	Carrier	Process	**Transitivity**

וַיְהִי־. Theme: textual > clause conj + Theme: experiential / Finite > wayyiqtol 3ms / Process > qal היה.

הֶבֶל. Subject > ms / Carrier > nominal group: noun proper.

רֹעֵה צֹאן. (i) Complement > ms / Attribute: nominal group >> Textuality > embedded ptc clause / Transitivity > material: action.

צֹאן	רֹעֵה	**Constituents**
sheep	*one tending*	**Translation**
	Theme	**Textuality**
Goal	Actor / Process	**Transitivity**

רֹעֵה. Theme: experiential / Actor > ptc ms / Process > qal רעה.

צֹאן. Goal > nominal group: noun common collective cs.

וְקַיִן הָיָה עֹבֵד אֲדָמָה. (c) Textuality >conj paratactic expansion / Mood > declarative: past / Transitivity > relational: attribution. The experiential structure of this clause matches that of clause (b), though the order of Constituents changes. The transposition of Process and Carrier in clause (c) is a function of the textual system. By not using a wayyiqtol, which signals past sequential activity, clause (c) is presented as simultaneous with clause (b).

עֹבֵד אֲדָמָה	הָיָה	וְקַיִן	**Constituents**
a worker of ground	*he was*	*and Qayin*	**Translation**
		Theme	**Textuality**
Complement	Finite	Subject	**Mood**
Attribute	Process	Carrier	**Transitivity**

וְקַיִן. Theme: textual > clause conj + Theme: experiential / Subject > ms / Carrier > nominal group: noun proper.

הָיָה. Finite > qatal 3ms / Process > qal היה.

עֹבֵד אֲדָמָה. (i) Complement > ms / Attribute: nominal group >> Textuality > embedded ptc clause / Transitivity > material: action.

אֲדָמָה	עֹבֵד	**Constituents**
ground	*one working*	**Translation**
	Theme	**Textuality**
Goal	Actor / Process	**Transitivity**

עֹבֵד. Theme: experiential / Actor > ptc ms / Process > qal עָבַד.

אֲדָמָה. Goal > nominal group: noun common fs.

4:3 // וַֽיְהִ֖י מִקֵּ֣ץ יָמִ֑ים / וַיָּבֵ֨א קַ֜יִן מִפְּרִ֧י הָאֲדָמָ֛ה מִנְחָ֖ה
לַֽיהוָֽה׃

וַֽיְהִי מִקֵּץ יָמִים. (a) Textuality > conj hypotactic expansion / Mood > declarative: past / Transitivity > existential. This clause posits the setting for the following narrative sequence.

מִקֵּץ יָמִים	וַיְהִי	**Constituents**
from end of days	*and he was*	**Translation**
	Theme	**Textuality**
	Finite	**Mood**
Circumstance	Process	**Transitivity**

וַיְהִי. Theme: textual > clause conj + Theme: experiential / Finite > wayyiqtol 3ms / Process > qal היה.

מִקֵּץ יָמִים. Circumstance: location, time > prep phrase: prep + noun ms const ׀ noun mp. *Days afterward*, lit. *from end of days.*

וַיָּבֵא קַיִן מִפְּרִי הָאֲדָמָה מִנְחָה לַיהוָה. (b) Textuality > conj paratactic expansion / Mood > declarative: past / Transitivity > material: action.

לַיהוָה	מִנְחָה	מִפְּרִי הָאֲדָמָה	קַיִן	וַיָּבֵא	**Constituents**
to YHVH	*offering*	*from the fruit of the ground*	*Qayin*	*and he brought*	**Translation**
				Theme	**Textuality**
			Subject	Finite	**Mood**
Beneficiary	Goal	Range	Actor	Process	**Transitivity**

וַיָּבֵא. Theme: textual > clause conj + Theme: experiential / Finite > wayyiqtol 3ms / Process > hifil בוא.

קַיִן. Subject > ms / Actor > nominal group: noun proper.

מִפְּרִי הָאֲדָמָה. Range > prep phrase: prep + noun common collective ms const ׀ def art + noun common fs.

מִנְחָה. Goal > nominal group: noun common fs.

לַיהוָה. Beneficiary > prep phrase: prep + noun proper ms.

4:4 // וְהֶ֨בֶל הֵבִ֥יא גַם־ה֛וּא מִבְּכֹר֥וֹת צֹאנ֖וֹ וּמֵֽחֶלְבֵהֶ֑ן //
וַיִּ֣שַׁע יְהוָ֔ה אֶל־הֶ֖בֶל וְאֶל־מִנְחָתֽוֹ׃

וְהֶבֶל הֵבִיא גַם־הוּא מִבְּכֹרוֹת צֹאנוֹ וּמֵחֶלְבֵהֶן. (a) Textuality > conj paratactic expansion / Mood > declarative: past / Transitivity > material: action. The Goal is מִנְחָה and the Beneficiary is לַיהוָה from 4:3(b); both are absent here by ellipsis.

מִבְּכֹרוֹת צֹאנוֹ וּמֵחֶלְבֵהֶן	הוּא	גַם־	הֵבִיא	וְהֶבֶל	**Constituents**
from the firstborn of his flock and from their fats	*he*	*also*	*he brought*	*and Hevel*	**Translation**
		Adjunct		Theme	**Textuality**
	Subject		Finite	Subject	**Mood**
Range	Actor		Process	Actor	**Transitivity**

וְהֶבֶל. Theme: textual > clause conj + Theme: experiential / Subject > ms / Actor > noun proper ms. This is a preposed Theme, substituted later by the personal pronoun הוּא.

הֵבִיא. Finite > qatal 3ms / Process > hifil בוא.

גַם־. Adjunct: textual > addition. This establishes an analogy with the episode in 4:3(b).

הוּא. Subject > ms / Actor > pronoun personal 3ms, antecedent is הֶבֶל.

מִבְּכֹרוֹת צֹאנוֹ וּמֵחֶלְבֵהֶן. Range > prep phrase complex: two conjoined prep phrases.

מִבְּכֹרוֹת צֹאנוֹ. Range 1 > prep phrase: prep + noun fp const | noun cs const + pronoun suffix 3ms, antecedent is הֶבֶל.

וּמֵחֶלְבֵהֶן. Group conj + Range 2 > prep phrase: prep + noun common mp const + pronoun suffix 3fp, antecedent is בְּכֹרוֹת *firstborns.*

וַיִּשַׁע יְהוָה אֶל־הֶבֶל וְאֶל־מִנְחָתוֹ. (b) Textuality > conj paratactic expansion / Mood > declarative: past / Transitivity > behavioral. The process is rendered as a behavioral one (*looked toward*) rather than as a mental one (*saw something*), because the clause contains prepositional phrases rather than goals.

אֶל־הֶבֶל וְאֶל־מִנְחָתוֹ	יְהוָה	וַיִּשַׁע	**Constituents**
to Hevel and to his offering	*YHVH*	*and he looked*	**Translation**
		Theme	**Textuality**
	Subject	Finite	**Mood**
Range	Behaver	Process	**Transitivity**

וַיִּשַׁע. Theme: textual > clause conj + Theme: experiential / Finite > wayyiqtol 3ms / Process > qal שׁעה. This is considered a behavioral process having the meaning *give attention to* or *pay attention to.*

יְהוָה. Subject > ms / Behaver > nominal group: noun proper.

אֶל־הֶבֶל וְאֶל־מִנְחָתוֹ. Range > prep phrase complex: two conjoined prep phrases.

אֶל־הֶבֶל. Range 1 > prep phrase: prep - noun proper ms.

וְאֶל־מִנְחָתוֹ. Group conj + Range 2 > prep - noun common fs const + pronoun suffix 3ms, antecedent is הֶבֶל *Hevel.*

4:5 וְאֶל־קַיִן וְאֶל־מִנְחָתוֹ לֹא שָׁעָה // וַיִּחַר לְקַיִן //
מְאֹד // וַיִּפְּלוּ פָּנָיו׃

וְאֶל־קַיִן וְאֶל־מִנְחָתוֹ לֹא שָׁעָה. (a) Textuality > conj paratactic expansion / Mood > declarative: past / Transitivity > behavioral. The Behaver is יְהוָה from 4:5(b) and is absent by ellipsis.

שָׁעָה	לֹא	וְאֶל־קַיִן וְאֶל־מִנְחָתוֹ	**Constituents**
he looked	*not*	*and to Qayin and to his offering*	**Translation**
		Theme	**Textuality**
Finite	Adjunct		**Mood**
Process		Range	**Transitivity**

וְאֶל־קַיִן וְאֶל־מִנְחָתוֹ. Clause conj + Range > prep phrase complex: two conjoined prep phrases.

אֶל־קַיִן. Range 1 > prep phrase: prep - noun proper ms.

וְאֶל־מִנְחָתוֹ. Group conj + Range 2 > prep phrase: prep - noun common fs const + pronoun suffix 3ms, antecedent is קַיִן *Qayin*.

לֹא. Adjunct: interpersonal > polarity: negative.

שָׁעָה. Finite > qatal 3ms / Process > qal שׁעה.

וַיִּחַר לְקַיִן מְאֹד. (b) Textuality > conj paratactic expansion / Mood > declarative: past / Transitivity > relational: attribution. Literally, *it was very hot to Qayin*, which is taken to mean, *Qayin was very hot, Qayin was very angry*. In the transitivity structure, *Qayin* is not the Actor but the Carrier of the process. The emotion is portrayed as an attributive relational process rather than directly as a mental process of emotion. The Subject / Actor of the process is textually unspecified.

מְאֹד	לְקַיִן	וַיִּחַר	**Constituents**
very	*to Qayin*	*and he was hot*	**Translation**
		Theme	**Textuality**
Adjunct		Finite	**Mood**
	Carrier	Process	**Transitivity**

וַיִּחַר. Theme: textual > clause conj + Theme: experiential / Finite > wayyiqtol 3ms / Process > qal חרה. The attribute is the Process, not an independent adjective as with most attributive relational clauses.

לְקַיִן. Carrier > prep phrase: prep + noun proper ms.

מְאֹד. Adjunct: interpersonal > modal: extent. This modal adjunct indicates the extent of the Finite: how hot, how angry.

וַיִּפְּלוּ פָּנָיו. (c) Textuality > conj paratactic expansion / Mood > declarative: past / Transitivity > material: action. As in clause (b), a mental process is depicted as a physical or physiological one. And the Actor is worded as a body part rather than as a person.

פָּנָיו	וַיִּפְּלוּ	**Constituents**
his face	*and they fell*	**Translation**
	Theme	**Textuality**
Subject	Finite	**Mood**
Actor	Process	**Transitivity**

וַיִּפְּלוּ. Theme: textual > clause conj + Theme: experiential / Finite > wayyiqtol 3mp / Process > qal נפל. The Finite is plural because the word for *face*, פָּנִים, is plural.

פָּנָיו. Subject > mp / Actor > nominal group: noun common mp const + pronoun suffix 3ms, antecedent is קָיִן in clause (b).

4:6 // וַיֹּאמֶר יְהוָה אֶל־קָיִן // לָמָּה חָרָה לָךְ // וְלָמָּה
נָפְלוּ פָנֶיךָ׃

וַיֹּאמֶר יְהוָה אֶל־קָיִן. (a) Textuality > conj paratactic expansion / Mood > declarative: past / Transitivity > verbal.

אֶל־קָיִן	יְהוָה	וַיֹּאמֶר	**Constituents**
to Qayin	*YHVH*	*and he said*	**Translation**
		Theme	**Textuality**
	Subject	Finite	**Mood**
Receiver	Sayer	Process	**Transitivity**

וַיֹּאמֶר. Theme: textual > clause conj + Theme: experiential / Finite > wayyiqtol 3ms / Process > qal אמר.

יְהוָה. Subject > ms / Sayer > nominal group: noun proper.

אֶל־קָיִן. Receiver > prep phrase: prep - noun proper ms.

לָמָּה חָרָה לָךְ. (b) Textuality > appositive paratactic projection: quote / Mood > interrogative / Transitivity > relational: attribution.

לָךְ	חָרָה	לָמָּה	**Constituents**
to you	*he was hot*	*why*	**Translation**
		Theme	**Textuality**
	Finite	Adjunct	**Mood**
Carrier	Process	Circumstance	**Transitivity**

לָמָּה. Theme: interpersonal / Adjunct: interpersonal > interrogative: wh- / Circumstance: cause, reason > prep phrase: prep + pronoun interrogative, literally, *for what*.

חָרָה. Finite > qatal 3ms / Process > qal חרה.

לָךְ. Carrier > prep phrase: prep + pronoun suffix 2ms, antecedent is the Receiver of the quote, קַיִן. This is pausal form: לְךָ becomes לָךְ when it receives major stress as the last word of the verse.

וְלָמָּה נָפְלוּ פָנֶיךָ. (c) Textuality > conj paratactic projection: quote / Mood > interrogative / Transitivity > material: action.

פָנֶיךָ	נָפְלוּ	וְלָמָּה	**Constituents**
your face	*they fell*	*and why*	**Translation**
		Theme	**Textuality**
Subject	Finite		**Mood**
Actor	Process	Circumstance	**Transitivity**

וְלָמָּה. Theme: textual > clause conj + Theme: experiential / Circumstance: cause, purpose > pronoun interrogative: wh-.

נָפְלוּ. Finite > qatal 3mp / Process > qal נפל.

פָנֶיךָ. Subject > mp / Actor > nominal group: noun mp const + pronoun suffix 2 ms, antecedent is קַיִן in clause (a).

4:7 // הֲלוֹא // אִם־תֵּיטִיב // שְׂאֵת // וְאִם לֹא תֵיטִיב
// לַפֶּתַח חַטָּאת רֹבֵץ // וְאֵלֶיךָ תְּשׁוּקָתוֹ // וְאַתָּה
תִּמְשָׁל־בּוֹ׃

הֲלוֹא. (a) Textuality > appositive paratactic projection: quote / Mood > interrogative / Transitivity > existential. This is a yes/no interrogative clause that is posed as a rhetorical question. It expects a "yes" answer from the Receiver: *Is it not? ... Yes, it is*. We could translate: *Is it not the case?* or *Is it not so?* This clause asserts the truth value of the following two clauses. As such it is purely modal with no expressed experiential constituent, though the transitivity designation *existential* may be appropriate.

לוֹא	הֲ	**Constituents**
not	?	**Translation**
Theme	Theme	**Textuality**
Adjunct	Adjunct	**Mood**
		Transitivity

הֲלוֹא. Theme: interpersonal / Adjunct: interpersonal > interrogative: yes/no + Adjunct: interpersonal > polarity: negative.

אִם־תֵּיטִיב. (b) Textuality > appositive hypotactic projection: quote / Mood > declarative: non-past / Transitivity > material: action. The Subject / Actor is קַיִן, the Receiver of the quote. The presumed Beneficiary is *Hevel*. Clause (b) is dependent on clause (c) in a conditional clause complex: *if you will do good, then acceptance*.

תֵּיטִיב	אִם־	**Constituents**
you will do good	*if*	**Translation**
Theme	Theme	**Textuality**
Finite		**Mood**
Process		**Transitivity**

אִם־. Theme: textual > conj.

תֵּיטִיב. Theme: experiential / Finite > yiqtol 2ms / Process > hifil יטב. The qal and the hifil of יטב differ in Transitivity structure: qal is attributive relational (Process = Attribute + Carrier), *be good;* hifil is material (Process + Actor + Beneficiary), *do good.*

שְׂאֵת. (c) Textuality > appositive paratactic projection: quote / Mood > declarative: non-past / Transitivity > existential. This one word clause consists solely of a nominalized verb. The clause is interpreted as an existential process: *acceptance is*. Because it lacks a proper Process, it is called a minor clause.

שְׂאֵת	**Constituents**
acceptance	**Translation**
Theme	**Textuality**
Subject	**Mood**
Existent	**Transitivity**

שְׂאֵת. Theme: experiential / Existent > ms / Process > inf const qal **נשׂא**. Literally, *acceptance*, presumably in the sense *you will find acceptance*. This is a highly elliptical clause that retains only the barest transitivity structure in the form of an infinitive construct. The one doing the accepting is unspecified, though apparently it is the Sayer of the quote, יְהוָה *YHVH*.

וְאִם לֹא תֵיטִיב. (d) Textuality > conj hypotactic projection: quote / Mood > declarative: non-past / Transitivity > material: action. Again, the Subject / Actor is קַיִן, the Receiver of the quote. Clause (d) is dependent on clause (e) in a conditional clause complex: *if ... then*, as with clauses (b) and (c).

תֵיטִיב	לֹא	וְאִם	**Constituents**
you will do good	*not*	*and if*	**Translation**
Theme	Theme	Theme	**Textuality**
Finite	Adjunct		**Mood**
Process			**Transitivity**

וְאִם. Theme: textual > clause conj + conj.

לֹא. Theme: interpersonal / Adjunct: interpersonal > polarity: negative.

תֵּיטִיב. Theme: experiential / Finite > yiqtol 2ms / Process > hifil יטב.

לַפֶּתַח חַטָּאת רֹבֵץ. (e) Textuality > conj paratactic projection: quote / Mood > declarative: non-past / Transitivity > relational: attribution. Literally, *To the door sin is a lurker.* The transitivity structure of this clause has proven rather difficult to unravel. Each word individually has a discernible meaning. How they function together is the issue. The grammatical mismatch between the Subject, which is fs, and the Complement, which is ms, only adds to the troubles.

רֹבֵץ	חַטָּאת	לַפֶּתַח	**Constituents**
lurker / is lurking	*sin*	*to the door*	**Translation**
		Theme	**Textuality**
Complement	Subject		**Mood**
Attribute	Carrier	Circumstance	**Transitivity**

לַפֶּתַח. Theme: experiential / Circumstance: location, place > prep phrase: prep + def art + noun common ms.

חַטָּאת. Subject > fs / Carrier > nominal group: noun common. Notice how sin, an abstract concept, is personified by being presented as acting in a material process. As noted above, the Subject and Complement are not grammatically congruent. Perhaps the personification of the term חַטָּאת transformed it from feminine to masculine in the mind of the Sayer. That it was actually considered masculine in gender is further supported by the next clause in which the pronoun suffix on תְּשׁוּקָתוֹ is masculine; on logical-semantic grounds the pronoun presumably refers to חַטָּאת, but could be referring to רֹבֵץ.

רֹבֵץ. Complement > ms / Attribute > ptc qal רבץ: *something or someone who lurks, a lurker.*

וְאֵלֶיךָ תְּשׁוּקָתוֹ. (f) Textuality > conj paratactic projection: quote / Mood > declarative: non-past / Transitivity > relational: attribution. *And toward you is its desire (i.e. the desire of the one who lurks).* This clause has exactly the same structure and vocabulary as 3:16(d).

תְּשׁוּקָתוֹ	וְאֵלֶיךָ	**Constituents**
his desire	*and to you*	**Translation**
	Theme	**Textuality**
Subject	Complement	**Mood**
Carrier	Attribute	**Transitivity**

וְאֵלֶיךָ. Theme: textual > clause conj + Theme: experiential / Complement / Attribute > prep phrase: prep + pronoun suffix 2ms, antecedent is קָיִן *Qayin* in 4:6(a).

תְּשׁוּקָתוֹ. Subject > fs / Carrier > nominal group: noun common fs const + pronoun suffix 3ms, antecedent is difficult to identify because it should be masculine. NRSV and NJPS render this clause as if חַטָּאת *sin* in clause (e) were the antecedent, but that would be formally incorrect. If חַטָּאת is not the antecedent, there is only one other viable option given the grammatical forms, and that is רֹבֵץ in clause (e).

וְאַתָּה תִּמְשָׁל־בּוֹ. (g) Textuality > conj paratactic projection: quote / Mood > declarative: non-past / Transitivity > material: action.

בּוֹ	תִּמְשָׁל־	וְאַתָּה	**Constituents**
in him	*you will rule*	*and you*	**Translation**
		Theme	**Textuality**
	Finite	Subject	**Mood**
Range	Process	Actor	**Transitivity**

וְאַתָּה. Theme: textual > clause conj + Theme: experiential / Subject > 2ms / Actor > pronoun personal 2ms, antecedent is קָיִן *Qayin* in 4:6(a).

תִּמְשָׁל־. Finite > yiqtol 2ms / Process > qal משׁל.

בּוֹ. Range > prep phrase: prep + pronoun suffix 3ms, antecedent is masculine. See the discussion regarding the gender of חַטָּאת in clauses (e) and (f). The grammatically congruent antecedent would be רֹבֵץ, but the versions most often interpret the antecedent as חַטָּאת in clause (e), and this might be preferable.

Genesis 4:8-12

[8]And Qayin spoke to Hevel his brother. And when they were in the field, Qayin stood up to Hevel his brother. And he killed him. [9]And YHVH said to Qayin, "Where is Hevel your brother?" And he said, "I knew not. Am I the keeper of my brother?" [10]And he said, "What did you do? The voice of the blood of your brother cries out to me from the ground. [11]And now, cursed are you from the ground, which opened her mouth to take the blood of your brother from your hand. [12]If you will work the ground, it will not again give her strength to you. A fugitive and a wanderer you will be on the earth."

4:8 /// וַיֹּ֥אמֶר קַ֖יִן אֶל־הֶ֣בֶל אָחִ֑יו // וַֽיְהִי֙ בִּהְיוֹתָ֣ם
בַּשָּׂדֶ֔ה // וַיָּ֥קָם קַ֛יִן אֶל־הֶ֥בֶל אָחִ֖יו // וַיַּהַרְגֵֽהוּ׃

וַיֹּ֥אמֶר קַ֖יִן אֶל־הֶ֣בֶל אָחִ֑יו. (a) Textuality > conj paratactic expansion / Mood > declarative: past / Transitivity > behavioral. This is the way quote clauses are typically introduced, yet this one is not followed by a quote. This has led some translations, e.g. NRSV, to insert a quote clause on the the basis of the Targum. See also NJPS footnote to Genesis 4:8. Given the absence of a quote, the process might better be interpreted as behavioral than verbal and rendered: *And Qayin spoke to Hevel his brother.*

אֶל־הֶ֣בֶל אָחִ֑יו	קַ֖יִן	וַיֹּ֥אמֶר	**Constituents**
to Hevel his brother	*Qayin*	*and he spoke*	**Translation**
		Theme	**Textuality**
	Subject	Finite	**Mood**
Target	Behaver	Process	**Transitivity**

וַיֹּאמֶר. Theme: textual > clause conj + Theme: experiential / Finite > wayyiqtol 3ms / Process > qal אמר.

קַיִן. Subject > ms / Behaver > nominal group: noun proper ms.

אֶל־הֶבֶל אָחִיו. Target > prep phrase: prep + nominal group: Head + Post-modifier.

הֶבֶל. Head > noun proper ms.

אָחִיו. Post-modifier > noun common ms const + pronoun suffix 3ms, antecedent is הֶבֶל. The second noun expands the meaning of the first.

[[בִּהְיוֹתָם בַּשָּׂדֶה]] וַיְהִי. (b) Textuality > conj hypotactic expansion / Mood > declarative: past / Transitivity > existential. This is a typical structure of temporal clauses.

[[בִּהְיוֹתָם בַּשָּׂדֶה]]	וַיְהִי	**Constituents**
in their being in the field	*and he was*	**Translation**
	Theme	**Textuality**
Subject	Finite	**Mood**
Existent	Process	**Transitivity**

וַיְהִי. Theme: textual > clause conj + Theme: experiential / Finite > wayyiqtol 3ms / Process > qal היה. The Subject / Existent is not a textual component, but rather the embedded clause.

בִּהְיוֹתָם בַּשָּׂדֶה. (i) Existent >> Textuality > embedded prep clause / Transitivity > existential. This clause establishes the temporal circumstance of the following clause.

בַּשָּׂדֶה	בִּהְיוֹתָם	**Constituents**
in the field	*in their being*	**Translation**
	Theme	**Textuality**
Circumstance	Process + Existent	**Transitivity**

בִּהְיוֹתָם. Theme: textual > prep + Theme: experiential / Process > inf const qal היה + Existent > pronoun suffix 3mp, antecedent is קַיִן and הֶבֶל in clause (a).

בַּשָּׂדֶה. Circumstance > prep phrase: prep + def art + noun common ms.

וַיָּקָם קַיִן אֶל־הֶבֶל אָחִיו. (c) Textuality > conj paratactic expansion / Mood > declarative: past / Transitivity > material: action.

אֶל־הֶבֶל אָחִיו	קַיִן	וַיָּקָם	**Constituents**
to Hevel his brother	*Qayin*	*and he rose*	**Translation**
		Theme	**Textuality**
	Subject	Finite	**Mood**
Range	Actor	Process	**Transitivity**

וַיָּקָם. Theme: textual > clause conj + Theme: experiential / Finite > wayyiqtol 3ms / Process > qal קום. The Process + Range *rise to* is similar to the English locution *stand up to, confront, challenge*; compare 1 Samuel 22:13 and 24:8 for the same combination.

קַיִן. Subject > ms / Actor > noun proper ms.

אֶל־הֶבֶל אָחִיו. Range > prep phrase: prep + nominal group complex: Head + Post-modifier.

הֶבֶל. Head > noun proper ms.

אָחִיו. Post-modifier > noun common ms const + pronoun suffix 3ms, antecedent is קַיִן. This noun extends the meaning of the previous one by providing further specification.

וַיַּהַרְגֵהוּ. (d) Textuality >conj paratactic expansion / Mood > declarative: past / Transitivity > material: action. The Subject / Actor is קַיִן, continuous with clause (c) where it was also Subject / Actor, absent here by ellipsis.

וַיַּהַרְגֵהוּ	Constituents
and he killed him	**Translation**
Theme	**Textuality**
Finite	**Mood**
Process + Goal	**Transitivity**

וַיַּהַרְגֵהוּ. Theme: textual > clause conj + Theme: experiential / Finite > wayyiqtol 3ms / Process > qal הרג + Goal > pronoun suffix 3ms, antecedent is הֶבֶל in clause (c).

4:9 // וַיֹּאמֶר יְהוָה אֶל־קַיִן // אֵי הֶבֶל אָחִיךָ // וַיֹּאמֶר
// לֹא יָדַעְתִּי // הֲשֹׁמֵר אָחִי אָנֹכִי׃

וַיֹּאמֶר יְהוָה אֶל־קַיִן. (a) Textuality > conj paratactic expansion / Mood > declarative: past / Transitivity > verbal.

אֶל־קַיִן	יְהוָה	וַיֹּאמֶר	Constituents
to Qayin	*YHVH*	*and he said*	**Translation**
		Theme	**Textuality**
	Subject	Finite	**Mood**
Receiver	Sayer	Process	**Transitivity**

וַיֹּאמֶר. Theme: textual > clause conj + Theme: experiential / Finite > wayyiqtol 3ms / Process > qal אמר.

יְהוָה. Subject > ms / Sayer > nominal group: noun proper.

אֶל־קַיִן. Receiver > prep phrase: prep - noun proper ms.

אֵי הֶבֶל אָחִיךָ. (b) Textuality > appositive paratactic projection: quote / Mood > interrogative / Transitivity > relational: attribution.

הֶבֶל אָחִיךָ	אֵי	**Constituents**
Hevel your brother	*where*	**Translation**
	Theme	**Textuality**
Subject	Complement	**Mood**
Carrier	Attribute	**Transitivity**

אֵי. Theme: experiential / Complement / Attribute > pronoun interrogative: wh-. The Attribute seeks to identify the locational Circumstance of the Carrier.

הֶבֶל אָחִיךָ. Subject > ms / Carrier > nominal group: noun proper ms | noun common ms const + pronoun suffix 2ms, antecedent is the Receiver of the quote, קַיִן in clause (a).

וַיֹּאמֶר. (c) Textuality > conj paratactic expansion / Mood > declarative: past / Transitivity > verbal. The Subject / Sayer is קַיִן in clause (a), absent here by ellipsis.

וַיֹּאמֶר	**Constituents**
and he said	**Translation**
Theme	**Textuality**
Finite	**Mood**
Process	**Transitivity**

וַיֹּאמֶר. Theme: textual > clause conj + Theme: experiential / Finite > wayyiqtol 3ms / Process > qal **אמר**.

לֹא יָדַעְתִּי. (d) Textuality > conj paratactic projection: quote / Mood > declarative: past / Transitivity > mental: cognition.

יָדַעְתִּי	לֹא	**Constituents**
I knew	*not*	**Translation**
Theme	Theme	**Textuality**
Finite	Adjunct	**Mood**
Process		**Transitivity**

לֹא. Theme: interpersonal / Adjunct: interpersonal > polarity: negative.

יָדַעְתִּי. Theme: experiential / Finite > qatal 1cs / Process > qal ידע. The mental process of cognition of the root ידע *knowing* has a durative rather than a punctual internal semantic structure. In other words, when we know something, the point at which we come to know it may be identifiable, but the knowing of it lasts to the present (unless, of course, we forget it). In this case, the text has Qayin use the past tense with knowing to indicate, so he claims, that he never came to know what happened to his brother, and so does not now know it.

הֲשֹׁמֵר אָחִי אָנֹכִי. (e) Textuality > conj paratactic projection: quote / Mood > interrogative / Transitivity > relational: attribution. *The one guarding my brother am I?* Formally, the Mood is interrogative, but functionally it is declarative; it is a rhetorical question with the implied answer *no, I am not.*

אָנֹכִי	שֹׁמֵר אָחִי	הֲ	**Constituents**
I	*the keeper of my brother*	*?*	**Translation**
	Theme	Theme	**Textuality**
Subject	Complement	Adjunct	**Mood**
Identified	Identifier		**Transitivity**

הֲ. Theme: interpersonal / Adjunct: interpersonal > interrogative: yes/no.

שֹׁמֵר אָחִי. (i) Theme: experiential / Complement > ms / Identifier > nominal group >> embedded ptc clause / Transitivity > material: action. *The one keeping/watching/guarding my brother.*

אָחִי	שֹׁמֵר	**Constituents**
my brother	*keeper*	**Translation**
	Theme	**Textuality**
Goal	Actor / Process	**Transitivity**

שֹׁמֵר. Theme: experiential / Actor > ptc ms / Process > qal **שמר**.

אָחִי. Goal > nominal group: noun common ms const + pronoun suffix 1cs, antecedent is קַיִן, the Sayer of clauses (d) and (e).

אָנֹכִי. Subject > 1cs / Identified > pronoun personal 1cs, antecedent is קַיִן.

4:10 // וַיֹּ֖אמֶר // מֶ֣ה עָשִׂ֑יתָ // ק֚וֹל דְּמֵ֣י אָחִ֔יךָ צֹעֲקִ֥ים אֵלַ֖י מִן־הָֽאֲדָמָֽה׃

וַיֹּאמֶר. (a) Textuality > conj paratactic expansion / Mood > declarative: past / Transitivity > verbal. Subject / Sayer is יְהוָה from 4:9(a), absent here by ellipsis. The Receiver is קַיִן, also absent by ellipsis. *And he said.*

וַיֹּאמֶר	**Constituents**
and he said	**Translation**
Theme	**Textuality**
Finite	**Mood**
Process	**Transitivity**

וַיֹּאמֶר. Theme: textual > clause conj + Theme: experiential / Finite > wayyiqtol 3ms / Process > qal **אמר**.

מֶה עָשִׂיתָ. (b) Textuality > appositive paratactic projection: quote / Mood > interrogative / Transitivity > material: action. Actor is קַיִן, the Receiver of the quote. *What did you do?*

עָשִׂיתָ	מֶה	**Constituents**
you did	*what*	**Translation**
	Theme	**Textuality**
Finite	Adjunct	**Mood**
Process	Goal	**Transitivity**

מָה. Theme: interpersonal / Adjunct: interpersonal > interrogative: wh- / Goal > pronoun interrogative.

עָשִׂיתָ. Finite > qatal 2ms / Process > qal עשׂה.

קוֹל דְּמֵי אָחִיךָ צֹעֲקִים אֵלַי מִן־הָאֲדָמָה. (c) Textuality > appositive paratactic projection: quote / Mood > declarative: non-past / Transitivity > verbal. There is a grammatical incongruity in so far as the Sayer קוֹל *voice* is singular and the Process צֹעֲקִים *cries* is plural. Compare NRSV: *Listen; your brother's blood is crying out to me from the ground!* Perhaps the logical Subject was thought to be דְּמֵי *blood of*, which is mp.

מִן־הָאֲדָמָה	אֵלַי	צֹעֲקִים	קוֹל דְּמֵי אָחִיךָ	**Constituents**
from the ground	*to me*	*cries out*	*the voice of the blood of your brother*	**Translation**
			Theme	**Textuality**
		Finite	Subject	**Mood**
Circumstance	Receiver	Process	Sayer	**Transitivity**

קוֹל דְּמֵי אָחִיךָ. Theme: experiential / Subject > ms! (קוֹל) / Sayer > nominal group: noun common ms const | noun common mp const | noun common ms const + pronoun suffix 2ms, antecedent is הֶבֶל in 4:9(c).

צֹעֲקִים. Finite > ptc mp! / Process > qal צעק.

אֵלַי. Receiver > prep phrase: prep + pronoun suffix 1cs, antecedent is יְהוָה in 4:9(a).

מִן־הָאֲדָמָה. Circumstance: location, place > prep phrase: prep - def art + noun common fs.

4:11 // וְעַתָּה אָרוּר אָתָּה מִן־הָאֲדָמָה אֲשֶׁר פָּצְתָה אֶת־
פִּיהָ לָקַחַת אֶת־דְּמֵי אָחִיךָ מִיָּדֶךָ׃

וְעַתָּה אָרוּר אָתָּה מִן־הָאֲדָמָה [[אֲשֶׁר פָּצְתָה אֶת־פִּיהָ [[לָקַחַת אֶת־דְּמֵי אָחִיךָ מִיָּדֶךָ]]]]. (a) Textuality > conj paratactic projection: quote / Mood > declarative: non-past / Transitivity > relational: attribution.

מִן־הָאֲדָמָה [[אֲשֶׁר פָּצְתָה אֶת־פִּיהָ [[לָקַחַת אֶת־דְּמֵי אָחִיךָ מִיָּדֶךָ]]]]	אָתָּה	אָרוּר	וְעַתָּה	**Constituents**
from the ground, which she opened her mouth to take the blood of your brother from your hand	*you*	*cursed*	*and now*	**Translation**
		Theme	Theme	**Textuality**
	Subject	Complement		**Mood**
Range	Carrier	Attribute		**Transitivity**

וְעַתָּה. Theme: textual > clause conj + Adjunct: textual > conj. The conjunctive adjunct עַתָּה *now* suggests that what follows is not only temporally successive but also causally a consequence of prior activity.

אָרוּר. Theme: experiential / Complement > ms / Attribute > ptc passive qal ערר.

אָתָּה. Subject > 2ms / Carrier > pronoun personal 2ms, antecedent is קַיִן.

מִן־הָאֲדָמָה [[אֲשֶׁר פָּצְתָה אֶת־פִּיהָ [[לָקַחַת אֶת־דְּמֵי אָחִיךָ מִיָּדֶךָ]]]]. Range > prep phrase complex: prep + Head + Post-modifier.

הָאֲדָמָה. Head > nominal group: def art + noun common fs.

אֲשֶׁר פָּצְתָה אֶת־פִּיהָ [[לָקַחַת אֶת־דְּמֵי אָחִיךָ מִיָּדֶךָ]]. (i) Post-modifier >> Textuality > embedded expansion: relative clause / Transitivity > material: action.

[[לָקַחַת אֶת־דְּמֵי אָחִיךָ מִיָּדֶךָ]]	אֶת־פִּיהָ	פָּצְתָה	אֲשֶׁר	**Constituents**
to take the blood of your brother from your hand	*her mouth*	*she opened*	*which*	**Translation**
			Theme	**Textuality**
		Finite	Subject	**Mood**
Circumstance	Goal	Process	Actor	**Transitivity**

אֲשֶׁר. Theme: textual and experiential / Subject > fs / Actor > pronoun relative, the antecedent הָאֲדָמָה is the Subject.

פָּצְתָה. Finite > qatal 3fs / Process > qal פצה.

אֶת־פִּיהָ. Goal > nominal group: goal marker - noun common ms const + pronoun suffix 3fs, antecedent is הָאֲדָמָה.

לָקַחַת אֶת־דְּמֵי אָחִיךָ מִיָּדֶךָ. (a') Circumstance: cause, purpose >> Textuality > embedded prep clause / Transitivity > material: action. The Subject / Actor is הָאֲדָמָה. This embedded clause extends the meaning of the prior embedded clause by specifying the purpose of the ground's opening her mouth.

מִיָּדֶךָ	אֶת־דְּמֵי אָחִיךָ	לָקַחַת	**Constituents**
from your hand	*the blood of your brother*	*to take*	**Translation**
		Theme	**Textuality**
Circumstance	Goal	Process	**Transitivity**

לָקַחַת. Theme: textual > prep + Theme: experiential / Process > inf const qal לקח.

אֶת־דְּמֵי אָחִיךָ. Goal > nominal group: goal marker + noun common mp const ׀ noun common ms const + pronoun suffix 2ms, antecedent is קַיִן.

מִיָּדֶךָ. Circumstance: location, place > prep phrase: prep + noun common fs const + pronoun suffix 2ms, antecedent is the Receiver of the quote, קָיִן.

4:12 // כִּ֤י תַעֲבֹד֙ אֶת־הָֽאֲדָמָ֔ה / לֹֽא־תֹסֵ֥ף תֵּת־כֹּחָ֖הּ לָ֑ךְ
// נָ֥ע וָנָ֖ד תִּֽהְיֶ֥ה בָאָֽרֶץ׃

Clauses (a) and (b) are a clause complex in which clause (a) is the conditional clause and clause (b) is the consequence clause.

כִּי תַעֲבֹד אֶת־הָאֲדָמָה. (a) Textuality > conj hypotactic projection: quote / Mood > declarative: non-past / Transitivity > material: action. The Subject / Actor is קָיִן, the Receiver of the quote.

אֶת־הָאֲדָמָה	תַעֲבֹד	כִּי	**Constituents**
the ground	*you will work*	*if*	**Translation**
	Theme	Theme	**Textuality**
	Finite		**Mood**
Goal	Process		**Transitivity**

כִּי. Theme: textual > conj / Adjunct: textual > condition.

תַעֲבֹד. Theme: experiential / Finite > yiqtol 2ms / Process > qal עבד.

אֶת־הָאֲדָמָה. Goal > nominal group: goal marker - def art + noun common fs.

לֹא־תֹסֵף תֵּת־כֹּחָהּ לָךְ. (b) Textuality > quote / Mood > declarative / Transitivity > material: action. The Process is a verbal group complex consisting of the Finite תֹסֵף and the non-finite verb תֵּת. The main material process is expressed in the non-finite verb. The Actor of the Finite verb, and hence of the entire verbal group complex, is הָאֲדָמָה from clause (a).

לָֽךְ	כֹּחָהּ	תֵּת־	תֹסֵף	לֹא־	**Constituents**
to you	*her strength*	*give*	*she will again*	*not*	**Translation**
			Theme	Theme	**Textuality**
			Finite	Adjunct	**Mood**
Beneficiary	Goal	Process	Process		**Transitivity**

לֹא־. Theme: interpersonal / Adjunct: interpersonal > polarity: negative.

תֹסֵף תֵּת־. Process > verbal group complex: Finite + Non-finite.

תֹסֵף. Theme: experiential / Finite > yiqtol 3fs / Process > qal יסף.

תֵּת־. Non-finite > inf const qal נתן.

כֹּחָהּ. Goal > nominal group: noun common ms const + pronoun suffix 3fs, antecedent is הָאֲדָמָה.

לָֽךְ. Beneficiary > prep phrase: prep + pronoun suffix 2ms, antecedent is קַיִן, the Receiver of the verbal process. Note the pausal lengthening of the suffix vowel due to the *'atnach*.

נָע וָנָד תִּהְיֶה בָאָרֶץ. (c) Textuality > appositive paratactic projection: quote / Mood > declarative: non-past / Transitivity > relational: attribution.

בָאָרֶץ	תִּהְיֶה	נָע וָנָד	**Constituents**
in the earth	*you will be*	*a fugitive and a wanderer*	**Translation**
		Theme	**Textuality**
	Finite	Complement	**Mood**
Circumstance	Process	Attribute	**Transitivity**

נָע וָנָד. Theme: experiential / Complement / Attribute > nominal group: two conjoined nominal groups forming one constituent unit. Note the use of the hendiadys conjunction וָ. Note that this is not labeled a nominal group complex, because the two nouns are effectively one unit.

נָע. Attribute 1 > ptc ms qal נוע.

וָנָד. Group conj + Attribute 2 > ptc ms qal נוד.

תִּהְיֶה. Finite > yiqtol 2ms / Process > qal היה.

בָאָרֶץ. Circumstance: location, place > prep phrase: prep + def art + noun common fs.

Genesis 4:13-16

[13]And Qayin said to YHVH, "My iniquity is bigger than I can carry. [14]Now you expelled me today from the face of the ground. And from your face I will hide. And I will be a fugitive and a wanderer in the earth. And it will be: all finding me will kill me." [15]And YHVH said to him, "So then, all killer of Qayin will be punished double seven. And YHVH made a sign for Qayin so all finding him not smite him. [16]And Qayin went out from before YHVH. And he lived in the land of Nod, east of Eden."

4:13 // וַיֹּ֥אמֶר קַ֖יִן אֶל־יְהוָ֑ה // גָּד֥וֹל עֲוֺנִ֖י מִנְּשֹֽׂא׃

וַיֹּאמֶר קַיִן אֶל־יְהוָה. (a) Textuality > conj paratactic expansion / Mood > declarative: past / Transitivity > verbal.

אֶל־יְהוָה	קַיִן	וַיֹּאמֶר	**Constituents**
to YHVH	*Qayin*	*and he said*	**Translation**
		Theme	**Textuality**
	Subject	Finite	**Mood**
Receiver	Sayer	Process	**Transitivity**

וַיֹּאמֶר. Theme: textual > clause conj + Theme: experiential / Finite > wayyiqtol 3ms / Process > qal אמר.

קַיִן. Subject > ms / Sayer > nominal group: noun proper.

אֶל־יְהוָה. Receiver > prep phrase: prep - noun proper ms.

גָּדוֹל עֲוֺנִי מִנְּשֹׂא. (b) Textuality > appositive paratactic projection: quote / Mood > declarative: non-past / Transitivity > relational: attribution.

מִנְּשֹׂא	עֲוֺנִי	גָּדוֹל	**Constituents**
from carrying	*my iniquity*	*big*	**Translation**
		Theme	**Textuality**
	Subject	Complement	**Mood**
Range	Carrier	Attribute	**Transitivity**

גָּדוֹל. Theme: experiential / Complement > ms / Attribute > adjective group: adj.

עֲוֺנִי. Subject > ms / Carrier > nominal group: noun common ms const + pronoun suffix 1cs, antecedent is the Sayer, קַיִן *Qayin.*

מִנְּשֹׂא. Range > prep phrase: prep + Process > inf const qal נשׂא. The construction X מִן Y is often comparative. In this setting it could be understood as *My sin is bigger than carrying (i.e. than I can carry).* The inf const is essentially an embedded clausal process with קַיִן as the implied Actor of the material Process, and with עֲוֺנִי as the implicit Goal.

4:14 // הֵן גֵּרַשְׁתָּ אֹתִי הַיּוֹם מֵעַל פְּנֵי הָאֲדָמָה // וּמִפָּנֶיךָ אֶסָּתֵר // וְהָיִיתִי נָע וָנָד בָּאָרֶץ // וְהָיָה כָל־מֹצְאִי יַהַרְגֵנִי׃

הֵן גֵּרַשְׁתָּ אֹתִי הַיּוֹם מֵעַל פְּנֵי הָאֲדָמָה. (a) Textuality > appositive paratactic projection: quote / Mood > declarative: past / Transitivity > material: action.

מֵעַל פְּנֵי הָאֲדָמָה	הַיּוֹם	אֹתִי	גֵּרַשְׁתָּ	הֵן	**Constituents**
from on the face of the ground	*today*	*me*	*you expelled*	*now*	**Translation**
			Theme	Theme	**Textuality**
			Finite		**Mood**
Circumstance	Circumstance	Goal	Process		**Transitivity**

הֵן. Theme: textual / Adjunct: textual > contra-expectation. This textual adjunct communicates Qayin's shock and surprise at this unexpected and fearful turn of events. See also 3:22(b) and 1:29(b).

גֵּרַשְׁתָּ. Theme: experiential / Finite > qatal 2ms / Process > piel גרשׁ.

אֹתִי. Goal > nominal group: goal marker + pronoun suffix 1cs, antecedent is the Sayer of the quote.

הַיּוֹם. Circumstance: location, time > nominal group: def art + noun common ms.

מֵעַל פְּנֵי הָאֲדָמָה. Circumstance: location, place > prep phrase: prep + prep | noun common mp const | def art + noun common fs.

וּמִפָּנֶיךָ אֶסָּתֵר. (b) Textuality > conj paratactic projection: quote / Mood > declarative: non-past / Transitivity > behavioral.

אֶסָּתֵר	וּמִפָּנֶיךָ	**Constituents**
I will hide	*and from your face*	**Translation**
	Theme	**Textuality**
Finite		**Mood**
Process	Range	**Transitivity**

וּמִפָּנֶיךָ. Theme: textual > clause conj + Theme: experiential / Range > prep phrase: prep + noun common mp const + pronoun suffix 2ms, antecedent is יְהוָה, the Receiver of the verbal process.

אֶסָּתֵר. Finite > yiqtol 1cs / Process > nifal **סתר**. The nifal process is middle voice and not passive, and so seems consistent with a behavioral, rather than a material, process.

וְהָיִיתִי נָע וָנָד בָּאָרֶץ. (c) Textuality > conj paratactic projection: quote / Mood > declarative: non-past / Transitivity > relational: attribution.

בָּאָרֶץ	נָע וָנָד	וְהָיִיתִי	**Constituents**
in the earth	*a fugitive and a wanderer*	*and I will be*	**Translation**
		Theme	**Textuality**
	Complement	Finite	**Mood**
Circumstance	Attribute	Process	**Transitivity**

וְהָיִיתִי. Theme: textual > clause conj + Theme: experiential / Finite > weqatal 1cs / Process > qal **הָיָה**. The Subject / Carrier is implicit in the verb form; it is the Sayer of the quote, **קַיִן**.

נָע וָנָד. Complement / Attribute > nominal group: two conjoined nominal groups. Note the use of the hendiadys conjunction **וָ**. See 4:12(c).

נָע. Attribute 1 > ptc ms qal **נוע**.

וָנָד. Group conj + Attribute 2 > ptc ms qal **נוד**.

בָּאָרֶץ. Circumstance: location, place > prep phrase: prep + def art + noun common fs.

וְהָיָה [[כָל־מֹצְאִי]] [[יַהַרְגֵנִי]]. (d) Textuality > conj paratactic projection: quote / Mood > declarative: non-past / Transitivity > existential. The string of four words constituting this clause is challenging to sort out. There are two finite verbs and one non-finite verb in this short span. *And he (it) will be: all who find me will kill me.*

[[[[כָּל־מֹצְאִי]] יַהַרְגֵנִי]]	וְהָיָה	**Constituents**
all finding me, he will kill me	*and he will be*	**Translation**
	Theme	**Textuality**
Subject	Finite	**Mood**
Existent	Process	**Transitivity**

וְהָיָה. Theme: textual > clause conj + Theme: experiential / Finite > weqatal 3ms / Process > qal היה. The verb וְהָיָה is here interpreted as an existential process that is asserting the future inevitability of the scenario contained in the following embedded clause.

[[כָּל־מֹצְאִי]] יַהַרְגֵנִי. (i) Existent >> Textuality > embedded Finite clause / Mood > declarative: non-past / Transitivity > material: action. This is a dependent embedded clause that serves as the Existent of the existential clause that contains it.

יַהַרְגֵנִי	[[כָּל־מֹצְאִי]]	**Constituents**
he will kill me	*all finding me*	**Translation**
	Theme	**Textuality**
Finite	Subject	**Mood**
Process + Goal	Actor	**Transitivity**

כָּל־מֹצְאִי. (i) Theme: experiential / Subject > ms (כָּל) / Actor >> Textuality > embedded ptc clause: nominal / Transitivity > material: action. This embedded clause functions as the Subject / Actor of the clause that contains it.

מֹצְאִי	כָּל־	**Constituents**
finding me	*all of*	**Translation**
	Theme	**Textuality**
Finite	Subject	**Mood**
Process + Goal	Actor	**Transitivity**

כָּל־. Theme: experiential / Subject > ms / Actor > nominal group: noun common ms const.

מֹצְאִי. Finite > ptc ms / Process >qal מצא + Goal > pronoun suffix 1cs, antecedent is קַיִן, the Sayer of the verbal process.

יַהַרְגֵנִי. Finite > yiqtol 3ms / Process > qal הרג + Goal > pronoun suffix 1cs, antecedent is the Sayer of the quote, קַיִן.

4:15 // וַיֹּאמֶר לוֹ יְהוָה // לָכֵן כָּל־הֹרֵג קַיִן שִׁבְעָתַיִם
יֻקָּם // וַיָּשֶׂם יְהוָה לְקַיִן אוֹת לְבִלְתִּי הַכּוֹת־אֹתוֹ
כָּל־מֹצְאוֹ׃

וַיֹּאמֶר לוֹ יְהוָה. (a) Textuality > conj paratactic expansion / Mood > declarative: past / Transitivity > verbal.

יְהוָה	לוֹ	וַיֹּאמֶר	**Constituents**
YHVH	*to him*	*and he said*	**Translation**
		Theme	**Textuality**
Subject		Finite	**Mood**
Sayer	Receiver	Process	**Transitivity**

וַיֹּאמֶר. Theme: textual > clause conj + Theme: experiential / Finite > wayyiqtol 3ms / Process > qal אמר.

לוֹ. Receiver > prep phrase: prep + pronoun suffix 3ms, antecedent is קַיִן.

יְהוָה. Subject > ms / Sayer > nominal group: noun proper.

לָכֵן [[כָּל־הֹרֵג קַיִן]] שִׁבְעָתַיִם יֻקָּם. (b) Textuality > conj paratactic expansion: quote / Mood > declarative: non-past / Transitivity > material: action

יֻקָּם	שִׁבְעָתַיִם	[[כָּל־הֹרֵג קַיִן]]	לָכֵן	**Constituents**
he will be punished	*double seven*	*all killing Qayin*	*so then*	**Translation**
		Theme	Theme	**Textuality**
Finite	Adjunct	Subject		**Mood**
Process		Goal		**Transitivity**

לָכֵן. Theme: textual / Adjunct: textual > conj. This is a conjunctive adjunct introducing a clause that is a response to the quotes in 4:13(b)-14.

כָּל־הֹרֵג קַיִן. (i) Theme: experiential / Subject > ms (כָּל) / Goal > nominal group >> Textuality > embedded ptc clause / Transitivity > material: action.

קַיִן	הֹרֵג	כָּל־	**Constituents**
Qayin	*killing*	*all*	**Translation**
		Theme	**Textuality**
	Finite	Subject	**Mood**
Goal	Process	Actor	**Transitivity**

כָּל־. Theme: experiential / Subject > 3ms / Actor > nominal group: noun common collective ms.

הֹרֵג. Finite > ptc ms / Process > qal הרג.

קַיִן. Goal > nominal group: noun proper ms.

שִׁבְעָתַיִם. Adjunct: interpersonal > intensity: numeral fd. Literally, *double seven.* Often translated seven-fold, but the form is a dual.

יֻקָּם. Finite > yiqtol 3ms / Process > hofal (or qal passive) נקם. The Goal of this Process (that which is acted upon) is also the interpersonal Subject of the verb. Goal = Subject is the typical structure of passive processes.

וַיָּשֶׂם יְהוָה לְקַיִן אוֹת [[לְבִלְתִּי הַכּוֹת־אֹתוֹ [[כָּל־מֹצְאוֹ]]]].

(c) Textuality > conj paratactic expansion / Mood > declarative: past / Transitivity > material: action.

לְבִלְתִּי]] הַכּוֹת־אֹתוֹ [[כָּל־מֹצְאוֹ]]	אוֹת	לְקַיִן	יְהוָה	וַיָּשֶׂם	**Constituents**
so all finding him not smite him	*a sign*	*for Qayin*	*YHVH*	*and he made*	**Translation**
				Theme	**Textuality**
			Subject	Finite	**Mood**
Circumstance	Goal	Beneficiary	Actor	Process	**Transitivity**

וַיָּשֶׂם. Theme: textual > clause conj + Theme: experiential / Finite > wayyiqtol 3ms / Process > qal שׂים.

יְהוָה. Subject > ms / Actor > nominal group: noun proper.

לְקַיִן. Beneficiary > prep phrase: prep + noun proper ms. Typically translated *on Qayin*, for example NRSV: *And the Lord put a mark on Cain*. This makes it sound like a tatoo. Yet the structure looks more like a Beneficiary than a Circumstance of location, which might be expected to use prep בְּ or עַל.

אוֹת. Goal > nominal group: noun common ms.

לְבִלְתִּי הַכּוֹת־אֹתוֹ [[כָּל־מֹצְאוֹ]]. (i) Circumstance >> Textuality > embedded prep clause: purpose / Transitivity > material: action. This embedded clause provides the purpose of the אוֹת *sign*.

[[כָּל־מֹצְאוֹ]]	אֹתוֹ	הַכּוֹת־	לְבִלְתִּי	**Constituents**
all finding him	*him*	*smite*	*to not*	**Translation**
		Theme	Theme	**Textuality**
Subject		Complement	Adjunct	**Mood**
Actor	Goal	Process		**Transitivity**

לְבִלְתִּי. Theme: textual > prep + Theme: interpersonal / Adjunct:

interpersonal > polarity: negative. This particular adjunct negates only infinitive construct forms.

הַכּוֹת־. Theme: experiential / Complement / Process > inf const hifil נכה.

אֹתוֹ. Goal > nominal group: goal marker + pronoun suffix 3ms, antecedent is קַיִן.

כָּל־מֹצְאוֹ. (a') Subject > ms (כָּל) / Actor > nominal group >> Textuality > embedded ptc clause / Transitivity > material: action. As with 4:14(d), this nominal group complex is an embedded clause.

מֹצְאוֹ	כָּל־	**Constituents**
finding him	*all*	**Translation**
	Theme	**Textuality**
Finite	Subject	**Mood**
Process + Goal	Actor	**Transitivity**

כָּל־. Theme: experiential / Subject > ms / Actor > noun common collective ms const.

מֹצְאוֹ. Finite > ptc ms / Process > qal מצא + Goal > pronoun suffix 3ms, antecedent is קַיִן.

4:16 // וַיֵּצֵא קַיִן מִלִּפְנֵי יְהוָה // וַיֵּשֶׁב בְּאֶרֶץ־נוֹד קִדְמַת־עֵדֶן׃

וַיֵּצֵא קַיִן מִלִּפְנֵי יְהוָה. (a) Textuality > conj paratactic expansion / Mood > declarative: past / Transitivity > material: action.

מִלִּפְנֵי יְהוָה	קַיִן	וַיֵּצֵא	**Constituents**
from before YHVH	*Qayin*	*and he went out*	**Translation**
		Theme	Textuality
	Subject	Finite	**Mood**
Circumstance	Actor	Process	**Transitivity**

וַיֵּצֵא. Theme: textual > clause conj + Theme: experiential / Finite > wayyiqtol 3ms / Process > qal יצא.

קַיִן. Subject > ms / Actor > nominal group: noun proper.

מִלִּפְנֵי יְהוָה. Circumstance: location, place > prep phrase: prep + prep | noun common mp const | noun proper ms.

וַיֵּשֶׁב בְּאֶרֶץ־נוֹד קִדְמַת־עֵדֶן. (b) Textuality > conj paratactic expansion / Mood > declarative: past / Transitivity > material: action. The Subject / Actor is קַיִן, absent here by ellipsis.

בְּאֶרֶץ־נוֹד קִדְמַת־עֵדֶן	וַיֵּשֶׁב	Constituents
in the land of Nod, east of Eden	*and he lived*	**Translation**
	Theme	**Textuality**
	Finite	**Mood**
Circumstance	Process	**Transitivity**

וַיֵּשֶׁב. Theme: textual > clause conj + Theme: experiential / Finite > wayyiqtol 3ms / Process > qal ישׁב.

בְּאֶרֶץ־נוֹד קִדְמַת־עֵדֶן. Circumstance: location, place > prep phrase: prep + Head + Post-modifier.

אֶרֶץ־נוֹד. Head > nominal group: noun common fs const - noun proper fs.

קִדְמַת־עֵדֶן. Post-modifier > nominal group: noun common fs const + noun proper. This group expands the meaning of the prior nominal group in the prep phrase by specifying its relative location.

Genesis 4:17-24

17And Qayin knew his woman. And she conceived. And she bore Cha-
nokh. And he was a builder of a city. And he called the name of the city
like the name of his son Chanokh. 18And 'Irad was born to Chanokh.
And 'Irad fathered Mechuya'el. And Mechiya'el fathered Metusha'el.
And Metusha'el fathered Lemekh. 19 And Lemekh took for himself two
women. The name of the one is 'Adah. The name of the second is Tsilla.

[20]And 'Ada birthed Yaval. He was father of tent dwelling and livestock. [21]And the name of his brother was Yuval. He was father of all playing lyre and pipe. [22] And Tsilla, she also birthed Tuval Qayin, sharpener of all engraving-thing of bronze and iron. And the sister of Tuval-Qayin is Na'ama. [23]And Lemekh said to his women, "'Adah and Tsilla, hear my voice. Women of Lemekh, heed my word, that I killed a man for my bruise and a boy for my wound. [24] If double seven Qayin will be avenged, then Lemekh seventy and seven."

4:17 /// וַיֵּ֤דַע קַ֙יִן֙ אֶת־אִשְׁתּ֔וֹ // וַתַּ֖הַר // וַתֵּ֣לֶד אֶת־חֲנ֑וֹךְ // וַֽיְהִי֙ בֹּ֣נֶה עִ֔יר // וַיִּקְרָא֙ שֵׁ֣ם הָעִ֔יר כְּשֵׁ֖ם בְּנ֥וֹ חֲנֽוֹךְ׃

וַיֵּדַע קַיִן אֶת־אִשְׁתּוֹ. (a) Textuality > conj paratactic expansion / Mood > declarative: past / Transitivity > mental: cognition. This mental process is a metaphor for a material process.

אֶת־אִשְׁתּוֹ	קַיִן	וַיֵּדַע	**Constituents**
his woman	*Qayin*	*and he knew*	**Translation**
		Theme	**Textuality**
	Subject	Finite	**Mood**
Phenomenon	Senser	Process	**Transitivity**

וַיֵּדַע. Finite > wayyiqtol 3ms / Process > qal ידע. This, of course, is a euphemism for sexual intercourse.

קַיִן. Subject > ms / Actor > nominal group: noun proper.

אֶת־אִשְׁתּוֹ. Goal > nominal group: goal marker - noun common fs const + pronoun suffix 3ms, antecedent is קַיִן.

וַתַּהַר. (b) Textuality > conj paratactic expansion / Mood > declarative: past / Transitivity > material: action. The Subject / Actor is אִשְׁתּוֹ in clause (a), absent here by ellipsis.

וַתַּהַר	**Constituents**
and she conceived	**Translation**
Theme	**Textuality**
Finite	**Mood**
Process	**Transitivity**

וַתַּהַר. Theme: textual > clause conj + Theme: experiential / Finite > wayyiqtol 3fs / Process > qal הרה.

וַתֵּלֶד אֶת־חֲנוֹךְ. (c) Textuality > conj paratactic expansion / Mood > declarative: past / Transitivity > material: action. Same Subject / Actor as the prior clause.

אֶת־חֲנוֹךְ	וַתֵּלֶד	**Constituents**
Chanokh	*and she bore*	**Translation**
	Theme	**Textuality**
	Finite	**Mood**
Goal	Process	**Transitivity**

וַתֵּלֶד. Theme: textual > clause conj + Theme: experiential / Finite > wayyiqtol 3fs / Process > qal ילד.

אֶת־חֲנוֹךְ. Goal > nominal group: goal marker - noun proper ms.

וַיְהִי [[בֹּנֶה עִיר]]. (d) Textuality > conj paratactic expansion / Mood > declarative: past / Transitivity > relational: attribution. The Subject / Carrier is *he*, the implicit ms Subject of the verb form. The nearest ms match would be חֲנוֹךְ from clause (c). However, this might not enable clause (e) to make good sense. Therefore, קַיִן *Qayin*, the Actor of clause (a), may be the better match. Still, some interpreters do see it the other way, with *Chanokh* as the Carrier.

[[בֹּנֶה עִיר]]	וַיְהִי	**Constituents**
builder of a city	*and he was*	**Translation**
	Theme	**Textuality**
Complement	Finite	**Mood**
Attribute	Process	**Transitivity**

וַיְהִי. Theme: textual > clause conj + Theme: experiential / Finite > wayyiqtol 3ms / Process > qal היה.

בֹּנֶה עִיר. (i) Complement > ms (בֹּנֶה) / Attribute > nominal group >> Textuality > embedded ptc clause / Transitivity > material: action.

עִיר	בֹּנֶה	**Constituents**
city	*builder*	**Translation**
	Theme	**Textuality**
	Finite	**Mood**
Goal	Process	**Transitivity**

בֹּנֶה. Theme: experiential / Finite > ms / Process > ptc qal בנה.

עִיר. Goal > nominal group: noun common fs.

וַיִּקְרָא שֵׁם הָעִיר כְּשֵׁם בְּנוֹ חֲנוֹךְ׃. (e) Textuality > conj paratactic extension / Mood > declarative: past / Transitivity > verbal. The Subject / Sayer is taken to be קַיִן. See the discussion under clause (d) regarding the difficulty of identifying the Subject.

כְּשֵׁם בְּנוֹ חֲנוֹךְ	שֵׁם הָעִיר	וַיִּקְרָא	**Constituents**
as the name of his son Chanokh	*the name of the city*	*and he called*	**Translation**
		Theme	**Textuality**
		Finite	**Mood**
Verbiage	Target	Process	**Transitivity**

וַיִּקְרָא. Theme: textual > clause conj + Theme: experiential / Finite > wayyiqtol 3ms / Process > qal קרא.

שֵׁם הָעִיר. Target > nominal group: noun common ms const | def art + noun common fs.

כְּשֵׁם בְּנוֹ חֲנוֹךְ. Verbiage > prep phrase: prep + Head + Post-modifier.

שֵׁם בְּנוֹ. Head > nominal group: noun common ms const | noun common ms const + pronoun suffix 3ms, antecedent is קַיִן *Qayin*, probably the Sayer of the verbal process.

חֲנוֹךְ. Post-modifier > noun proper ms. This appositive noun adds specificity to the prior nominal group. However, those who interpret *Chanokh* as the Carrier in clause (d) read חֲנוֹךְ *Chanokh* here as the Sayer of clause (e).

4:18 // וַיִּוָּלֵד לַחֲנוֹךְ אֶת־עִירָד // וְעִירָד יָלַד אֶת־
מְחוּיָאֵל // וּמְחִיָּיאֵל יָלַד אֶת־מְתוּשָׁאֵל //
וּמְתוּשָׁאֵל יָלַד אֶת־לָמֶךְ׃

וַיִּוָּלֵד לַחֲנוֹךְ אֶת־עִירָד. (a) Textuality > conj paratactic expansion / Mood > declarative: past / Transitivity > material: action. *And was born to Chanokh 'Irad.* Compare this structure using the passive voice to that of the following clauses in this verse, all with active voice.

אֶת־עִירָד	לַחֲנוֹךְ	וַיִּוָּלֵד	**Constituents**
'Irad	*to Chanokh*	*and he was born*	**Translation**
		Theme	**Textuality**
Subject		Finite	**Mood**
Goal	Beneficiary	Process	**Transitivity**

וַיִּוָּלֵד. Theme: textual > clause conj + Theme: experiential / Finite > wayyiqtol 3ms / Process > nifal ילד. This is a passive Process. The experiential Goal is also the interpersonal Subject of the verb. The use of the passive leaves the paternity of 'Irad under-specified.

לַחֲנוֹךְ. Beneficiary > prep phrase: prep + noun proper ms.

אֶת־עִירָד. Goal > nominal group: goal marker - noun proper ms.

וְעִירָד יָלַד אֶת־מְחוּיָאֵל. (b) Textuality > conj paratactic expansion / Mood > declarative: past / Transitivity > material: action.

אֶת־מְחוּיָאֵל	יָלַד	וְעִירָד	**Constituents**
Mechuya'el	*he fathered*	*and 'Irad*	**Translation**
		Theme	**Textuality**
	Finite	Subject	**Mood**
Goal	Process	Actor	**Transitivity**

וְעִירָד. Theme: textual > clause conj + Theme: experiential / Subject > ms / Actor > nominal group: noun proper.

יָלַד. Finite > qatal 3ms / Process > qal ילד.

אֶת־מְחוּיָאֵל. Goal > nominal group: goal marker – noun proper ms.

וּמְחִיָּיאֵל יָלַד אֶת־מְתוּשָׁאֵל. (c) Textuality > conj paratactic expansion / Mood > declarative: past / Transitivity > material: action.

אֶת־מְתוּשָׁאֵל	יָלַד	וּמְחִיָּיאֵל	**Constituents**
Metusha'el	*he fathered*	*and Mechiya'el*	**Translation**
		Theme	**Textuality**
	Finite	Subject	**Mood**
Goal	Process	Actor	**Transitivity**

וּמְחִיָּיאֵל. Theme: textual > clause conj + Theme: experiential / Subject > ms / Actor > nominal group: noun proper. Presumably the same name as in clause (b) but spelled with a י here in place of a ו there.

יָלַד. Finite > qatal 3ms / Process > qal ילד.

אֶת־מְתוּשָׁאֵל. Goal > nominal group: goal marker - noun proper ms.

וּמְתוּשָׁאֵל יָלַד אֶת־לָמֶךְ. (d) Textuality > conj paratactic expansion / Mood > declarative: past / Transitivity > material: action.

אֶת־לָמֶךְ	יָלַד	וּמְתוּשָׁאֵל	**Constituents**
Lemech	*he fathered*	*and Metusha'el*	**Translation**
		Theme	**Textuality**
	Finite	Subject	**Mood**
Goal	Process	Actor	**Transitivity**

וּמְתוּשָׁאֵל. Theme: textual > clause conj + Theme: experiential / Subject > ms / Actor > nominal group: noun proper.

יָלַד. Finite > qatal 3ms / Process > qal ילד.

אֶת־לָמֶךְ. Goal > nominal group: goal marker - noun proper ms.

4:19 // וַיִּקַּח־לוֹ לֶמֶךְ שְׁתֵּי נָשִׁים // שֵׁם הָאַחַת עָדָה //
וְשֵׁם הַשֵּׁנִית צִלָּה׃

וַיִּקַּח־לוֹ לֶמֶךְ שְׁתֵּי נָשִׁים. (a) Textuality > conj paratactic expansion / Mood > declarative: past / Transitivity > material: action.

שְׁתֵּי נָשִׁים	לֶמֶךְ	לוֹ	וַיִּקַּח־	**Constituents**
two women	*Lemekh*	*for himself*	*and he took*	**Translation**
			Theme	**Textuality**
	Subject		Finite	**Mood**
Goal	Actor	Beneficiary	Process	**Transitivity**

וַיִּקַּח־. Theme: textual > clause conj + Theme: experiential / Finite > wayyiqtol 3ms / Process > qal לקח.

לוֹ. Beneficiary > prep phrase: prep + pronoun suffix 3ms, antecedent is לֶמֶךְ in 4:19(d), though it is also cataphoric to the following word in the present clause.

לֶמֶךְ. Subject > ms / Actor > nominal group: noun proper.

שְׁתֵּי נָשִׁים. Goal > nominal group: numeral fp const | noun common fp.

שֵׁם הָאַחַת עָדָה. (b) Textuality > appositive paratactic expansion / Mood > declarative: non-past / Transitivity > relational: identification.

עָדָה	שֵׁם הָאַחַת	**Constituents**
'Ada	*the name of the one*	**Translation**
	Theme	**Textuality**
Subject	Complement	**Mood**
Identifier	Identified	**Transitivity**

שֵׁם הָאַחַת. Identified > nominal group: noun common ms const | def art + numeral fs.

עָדָה. Identifier > nominal group: noun proper fs.

וְשֵׁם הַשֵּׁנִית צִלָּה. (c) Textuality > conj paratactic expansion / Mood > declarative: non-past / Transitivity > relational: identification.

צִלָּה	וְשֵׁם הַשֵּׁנִית	**Constituents**
Tsilla	*and the name of the second*	**Translation**
	Theme	**Textuality**
Subject	Complement	**Mood**
Identifier	Identified	**Transitivity**

וְשֵׁם הַשֵּׁנִית. Theme: textual > clause conj + Theme: experiential / Complement > ms / Identified > nominal group: noun common ms const | def art + numeral fs.

צִלָּה. Subject > fs / Identifier > nominal group: noun proper.

4:20 // וַתֵּ֥לֶד עָדָ֖ה אֶת־יָבָ֑ל // ה֣וּא הָיָ֔ה אֲבִ֕י יֹשֵׁ֥ב אֹ֖הֶל וּמִקְנֶֽה׃

וַתֵּ֥לֶד עָדָ֖ה אֶת־יָבָ֑ל. (a) Textuality > conj paratactic expansion / Mood > declarative: past / Transitivity > material: action.

אֶת־יָבָל	עָדָה	וַתֵּלֶד	**Constituents**
Yaval	*'Ada*	*and she birthed*	**Translation**
		Theme	**Textuality**
	Subject	Finite	**Mood**
Goal	Actor	Process	**Transitivity**

וַתֵּלֶד. Theme: textual > clause conj + Theme: experiential / Finite > wayyiqtol 3fs / Process > qal ילד.

עָדָה. Subject > fs / Actor > nominal group: noun proper.

אֶת־יָבָל. Goal > nominal group: goal marker + noun proper ms.

הוּא הָיָה אֲבִי [[יֹשֵׁב אֹהֶל]] וּמִקְנֶה. (b) Textuality > appositive paratactic expansion / Mood > declarative: past / Transitivity > relational: identification.

אֲבִי [[יֹשֵׁב אֹהֶל]] וּמִקְנֶה	הָיָה	הוּא	**Constituents**
father of tent dwelling and livestock	*he was*	*he*	**Translation**
		Theme	**Textuality**
	Finite	Subject	**Mood**
Identifier	Process	Identified	**Transitivity**

הוּא. Theme: experiential / Subject > ms / Identified > pronoun personal 3ms, antecedent is יָבָל *Yaval* in the preceding clause.

הָיָה. Finite > qatal 3ms / Process > qal היה.

אֲבִי [[יֹשֵׁב אֹהֶל]] וּמִקְנֶה. Identifier > nominal group: Head + Post-modifler.

אֲבִי. Head > noun common ms const. As a construct noun, it controls the following nominal group.

יֹשֵׁב אֹהֶל וּמִקְנֶה. Post-modifier > nominal group complex: two nominal groups.

יֹשֵׁב אֹהֶל. (i) Post-modifier 1 >> Textuality > embedded ptc clause / Transitivity > material: action. Literally, *a dweller of tent, a tent-dweller.* It is a minor embedded clause that means *one who dwells in a tent.*

אֹהֶל	יֹשֵׁב	Constituents
tent	*dweller of*	**Translation**
	Theme	**Textuality**
Circumstance	Actor / Process	**Transitivity**

יֹשֵׁב. Theme: experiential / Actor > ptc ms / Process > qal **ישׁב**. As a nominal form, this should probably be understood as a construct bound to the following noun.

אֹהֶל. Circumstance: location, place > nominal group: noun common ms.

וּמִקְנֶה. Group-level conj + Post-modifier 2 > nominal group: noun common collective ms.

וְשֵׁם אָחִיו יוּבָל // הוּא הָיָה אֲבִי כָּל־תֹּפֵשׂ כִּנּוֹר וְעוּגָב׃ // 4:21

וְשֵׁם אָחִיו יוּבָל. (a) Textuality > conj paratactic expansion / Mood > declarative: non-past / Transitivity > relational: identification.

יוּבָל	וְשֵׁם אָחִיו	Constituents
Yuval	*and the name of his brother*	**Translation**
	Theme	**Textuality**
Subject	Complement	**Mood**
Identifier	Identified	**Transitivity**

וְשֵׁם אָחִיו. Theme: textual > clause conj + Theme: experiential / Complement > ms / Identified > nominal group: noun common ms const | noun common ms const + pronoun suffix 3ms, antecedent is **יָבָל** *Yaval* in 4:20(a).

יוּבָל. Subject > ms / Identifier > nominal group: noun proper.

הוּא הָיָה [[אֲבִי כָּל־תֹּפֵשׂ כִּנּוֹר וְעוּגָב]]. (b) Textuality > appositive paratactic expansion / Mood > declarative: past / Transitivity > relational: identification. Compare 4:20(b).

אֲבִי [[כָּל־תֹּפֵשׂ כִּנּוֹר וְעוּגָב]]	הָיָה	הוּא	**Constituents**
father of all playing lyre and pipe	*he was*	*he*	**Translation**
		Theme	**Textuality**
	Finite	Subject	**Mood**
Identifier	Process	Identified	**Transitivity**

הוּא. Theme: experiential / Subject > ms / Identified > pronoun personal 3ms, antecedent is יוּבָל *Yuval.*

הָיָה. Finite > qatal 3ms / Process > qal היה.

[[כָּל־תֹּפֵשׂ כִּנּוֹר וְעוּגָב]] אֲבִי. Identifier > nominal group: Head + Post-modifier.

אֲבִי. Head > noun common ms const. As a construct noun, it controls the following nominal group.

כָּל־תֹּפֵשׂ כִּנּוֹר וְעוּגָב. (i) Post-modifier >> Textuality > embedded ptc clause / Transitivity > material: action.

כִּנּוֹר וְעוּגָב	תֹּפֵשׂ	כָּל־	**Constituents**
lyre and pipe	*playing*	*all*	**Translation**
		Theme	**Textuality**
	Finite	Subject	**Mood**
Goal	Process	Actor	**Transitivity**

כָּל־. Theme: experiential / Subject > ms (כָּל) / Actor > nominal group: noun common collection ms const.

תֹּפֵשׂ. Finite > ptc ms / Process > qal תפשׂ.

כִּנּוֹר וְעוּגָב. Goal > nominal group complex: noun common ms | group conj + noun common ms.

4:22 // וְצִלָּה גַם־הִוא יָלְדָה אֶת־תּוּבַל קַיִן לֹטֵשׁ כָּל־
חֹרֵשׁ נְחֹשֶׁת וּבַרְזֶל // וַאֲחוֹת תּוּבַל־קַיִן נַעֲמָה׃

וְצִלָּה גַם־הִוא יָלְדָה אֶת־תּוּבַל קַיִן [[לֹטֵשׁ [[כָּל־חֹרֵשׁ נְחֹשֶׁת וּבַרְזֶל]]]]. (a) Textuality > conj paratactic expansion / Mood > declarative: past / Transitivity > material: action.

Constituents	וְצִלָּה	גַם־	הִוא	יָלְדָה	אֶת־תּוּבַל קַיִן [[לֹטֵשׁ [[כָּל־חֹרֵשׁ נְחֹשֶׁת וּבַרְזֶל]]]]
Translation	*and Tsilla*	*also*	*she*	*she birthed*	*Tuval Qayin, sharpener of all engraving-thing of bronze and iron*
Textuality	Theme	Adjunct			
Mood	Subject		Subject	Finite	
Transitivity	Actor		Actor	Process	Goal

וְצִלָּה. Theme: textual > clause conj + Theme: experiential / Subject > fs / Actor > nominal group: noun proper fs. This is a preposed Theme, substituted later in the clause by הִוא.

גַם־. Adjunct: textual > addition. The גַם references the fact that Tsilla's co-wife 'Adah had given birth, and that Tsilla now likewise did; see 4:20(a). The additive applies to the Actor.

הִוא. Subject > 3fs / Actor > pronoun personal 3fs, antecedent is צִלָּה.

יָלְדָה. Finite > qatal 3fs / Process > qal ילד.

[[[[כָּל־חֹרֵשׁ נְחֹשֶׁת וּבַרְזֶל]] לֹטֵשׁ]] אֶת־תּוּבַל קַיִן. Goal > nominal group: Head + Post-modifier.

אֶת־תּוּבַל קַיִן. Head > nominal group > goal marker - noun proper ms | noun proper ms. The two proper nouns are generally rendered as a hyphenated name, though they may exist in a construct relationship: *Tuval of Qayin.*

[[כָּל־חֹרֵשׁ נְחֹשֶׁת וּבַרְזֶל]] לֹטֵשׁ. (i) Post-modifier >> Textuality > embedded ptc clause / Transitivity > material: action. *One who sharpens all engraving-thing of bronze and iron.* This embedded clause is a post-modifier, extending the meaning of תּוּבַל קַיִן *Tuval Qayin* by describing him. Notice that, unlike his brothers, he is not the אֲבִי *father of* those doing something. This embedded clause contains within it another embedded clause as its Goal.

[[כָּל־חֹרֵשׁ נְחֹשֶׁת וּבַרְזֶל]]	לֹטֵשׁ	**Constituents**
all engraving-thing of bronze and iron	*sharpener of*	**Translation**
	Theme	**Textuality**
Goal	Actor / Process	**Transitivity**

לֹטֵשׁ. Actor > ptc ms / Process > qal לטשׁ.

כָּל־חֹרֵשׁ נְחֹשֶׁת וּבַרְזֶל. Goal > nominal group: Head + Post-modifier.

כָּל־. Head > noun common ms const.

חֹרֵשׁ נְחֹשֶׁת וּבַרְזֶל. (a) Post-modifier >> Textuality > embedded ptc clause / Transitivity > material: action. *Engraving-thing of bronze and iron.*

נְחֹשֶׁת וּבַרְזֶל	חֹרֵשׁ	**Constituents**
bronze and iron	*engraving-thing*	**Translation**
	Theme	**Textuality**
Circumstance	Actor / Process	**Transitivity**

חֹרֵשׁ. Actor > ptc ms / Process > qal חרשׁ.

נְחֹשֶׁת וּבַרְזֶל. Circumstance: material > nominal group complex: noun common fs | group conj + noun common ms.

וַאֲחוֹת תּוּבַל־קַיִן נַעֲמָה. (b) Textuality > conj paratactic extension / Mood > declarative: non-past / Transitivity > relational: identification.

נַעֲמָה	וַאֲחוֹת תּוּבַל־קַיִן	Constituents
Na'ama	*and the sister of Tuval-Qayin*	**Translation**
	Theme	**Textuality**
Subject	Complement	**Mood**
Identifier	Identified	**Transitivity**

וַאֲחוֹת תּוּבַל־קַיִן. Theme: textual > clause conj + Theme: experiential / Complement > fs / Identified > nominal group: noun common fs const | noun proper ms - noun proper ms.

נַעֲמָה. Subject > fs / Identifier > nominal group: noun proper.

4:23 // וַיֹּאמֶר לֶמֶךְ לְנָשָׁיו // עָדָה וְצִלָּה שְׁמַעַן קוֹלִי //
נְשֵׁי לֶמֶךְ הַאְזֵנָּה אִמְרָתִי / כִּי אִישׁ הָרַגְתִּי לְפִצְעִי
וְיֶלֶד לְחַבֻּרָתִי׃

וַיֹּאמֶר לֶמֶךְ לְנָשָׁיו. (a) Textuality > conj paratactic expansion / Mood > declarative: past / Transitivity > verbal.

לְנָשָׁיו	לֶמֶךְ	וַיֹּאמֶר	Constituents
to his women	*Lemekh*	*and he said*	**Translation**
		Theme	**Textuality**
	Subject	Finite	**Mood**
Receiver	Sayer	Process	**Transitivity**

וַיֹּאמֶר. Finite > wayyiqtol 3ms / Process > qal אמר.

לֶמֶךְ. Subject > ms / Sayer > nominal group: noun proper.

לְנָשָׁיו. Receiver > prep phrase: prep + noun common fp const + pronoun suffix 3ms, antecedent is לֶמֶךְ *Lemekh*.

עָדָה וְצִלָּה שְׁמַעַן קוֹלִי. (b) Textuality > appositive paratactic projection: quote / Mood > directive: imperative / Transitivity > mental: perception.

קוֹלִי	שְׁמַעַן	עָדָה וְצִלָּה	Constituents
my voice	*you hear*	*'Ada and Tsilla*	**Translation**
		Theme	**Textuality**
	Finite	Subject	**Mood**
Phenomenon	Process	Senser	**Transitivity**

עָדָה וְצִלָּה. Theme: experiential / Subject > fp / Senser > nominal group complex: noun proper fs ı group conj + noun proper fs. This is a marked Theme in so far as an imperative is typically the first constituent in a directive clause. Ordinarily it is not necessary to specify the Receiver. The Subject of the clause is the Senser of the Process and the Receiver of the quote, and this is evident by the context of the situation.

שְׁמַעַן. Finite > impv fp / Process > qal שׁמע.

קוֹלִי. Phenomenon > nominal group: noun common ms const + pronoun suffix 1cs, antecedent is לֶמֶךְ, the Sayer of the verbal process.

נְשֵׁי לֶמֶךְ הַאְזֵנָּה אִמְרָתִי. (c) Textuality > appositive paratactic projection: quote / Mood > directive: imperative / Transitivity > mental: perception.

אִמְרָתִי	הַאְזֵנָּה	נְשֵׁי לֶמֶךְ	Constituents
my word	*give ear*	*women of Lemekh*	**Translation**
		Theme	**Textuality**
	Finite	Subject	**Mood**
Phenomenon	Process	Senser	**Transitivity**

נְשֵׁי לֶמֶךְ. Theme: experiential / Subject > fp / Senser > nominal group: noun common fp const | noun proper ms. Again, this is a marked Theme.

הַאְזֵנָּה. Finite > impv fp / Process > hifil אזן.

אִמְרָתִי. Phenomenon > nominal group: noun common fs const + pronoun suffix 1cs, antecedent is לֶמֶךְ, the Sayer of the verbal process.

כִּי אִישׁ הָרַגְתִּי לְפִצְעִי. (d) Textuality > conj hypotactic projection: report / Mood > declarative: past / Transitivity > material: action. The Subject / Actor is לֶמֶךְ *Lemekh*, referenced by the verb form.

לְפִצְעִי	הָרַגְתִּי	אִישׁ	כִּי	**Constituents**
for my bruise	*I killed*	*a man*	*that*	**Translation**
		Theme	Theme	**Textuality**
	Finite			**Mood**
Circumstance	Process	Goal		**Transitivity**

כִּי. Theme: textual > conj. It introduces the report clause that contains the content of אִמְרָתִי *my word* in clause (c).

אִישׁ. Theme: experiential / Goal > nominal group: noun common ms.

הָרַגְתִּי. Finite > qatal 1cs / Process > qal הרג.

לְפִצְעִי. Circumstance: cause, reason > prep phrase: prep + noun common ms const + pronoun suffix 1cs, antecedent is the Sayer, לֶמֶךְ *Lemekh*.

וְיֶלֶד לְחַבֻּרָתִי. (e) Textuality > conj paratactic projection: report / Mood > declarative: past / Transitivity > material: action. The material Process is הָרַגְתִּי *I killed* from the prior clause, but it is absent here by ellipsis, making this a minor clause. Ellipsis routinely happens with Participants, but this clause illustrates that it might also happen with Processes. *And (I killed) a boy for my wound.* These two words could also be analyzed as Constituents of clause (d), providing a second Goal and Circumstance, rather than as a separate clause.

לְחַבֻּרָתִי	וְיֶלֶד	**Constituents**
for my wound	*and a boy*	**Translation**
	Theme	**Textuality**
	Subject	**Mood**
Circumstance	Goal	**Transitivity**

וְיֶלֶד. Theme: textual > clause conj + Theme: experiential / Goal > nominal group: noun common ms.

לְחַבֻּרָתִי. Circumstance: cause, reason > prep phrase: prep + noun common fs const + pronoun suffix 1cs, antecedent is the Sayer, לֶמֶךְ.

4:24 // כִּי שִׁבְעָתַיִם יֻקַּם־קָיִן / וְלֶמֶךְ שִׁבְעִים וְשִׁבְעָה׃

כִּי שִׁבְעָתַיִם יֻקַּם־קָיִן. (a) Textuality > conj hypotactic projection: quote / Mood > declarative: non-past / Transitivity > material: action.

קָיִן	יֻקַּם־	שִׁבְעָתַיִם	כִּי	**Constituents**
Qayin	*he will be avenged*	*double seven*	*if*	**Translation**
		Theme	Theme	**Textuality**
Subject	Finite	Adjunct		**Mood**
Goal	Process			**Transitivity**

כִּי. Theme: textual / Adjunct: textual > conj.

שִׁבְעָתַיִם. Adjunct: interpersonal > intensity: numeral fd. See 4:15(b).

יֻקַּם־. Finite > yiqtol 3ms / Process > hofal נקם.

קָיִן. Goal > nominal group: noun proper ms. The Goal of a passive is also the interpersonal Subject of the clause.

וְלֶמֶךְ שִׁבְעִים וְשִׁבְעָה. (b) Textuality > conj paratactic projection: quote / Mood > declarative: non-past / Transitivity > material: action. *Then Lemekh (will be avenged) seventy and seven times.* The material Process is יֻקַּם from clause (a), absent here by ellipsis.

שִׁבְעִים וְשִׁבְעָה	וְלֶמֶךְ	**Constituents**
seventy and seven	*and Lemekh*	**Translation**
	Theme	**Textuality**
Adjunct	Subject	**Mood**
	Goal	**Transitivity**

וְלֶמֶךְ. > Theme: textual > clause conj + Theme: experiential / Goal > noun proper ms.

שִׁבְעִים וְשִׁבְעָה. Adjunct: interpersonal > intensity: numeral mp | group conj + numeral ms.

Genesis 4:25-26

[25]And 'Adam again knew his woman. And she birthed a son. And she called his name Shet. "Because deity gave me other seed in place of Hevel," because Qayin killed him. [26]And also to Shet was born a son. And he called his name 'Enosh. Then was begun to call on the name of YHVH.

4:25 /// וַיֵּ֨דַע אָדָ֥ם עוֹד֙ אֶת־אִשְׁתּ֔וֹ // וַתֵּ֣לֶד בֵּ֔ן //
וַתִּקְרָ֥א אֶת־שְׁמ֖וֹ שֵׁ֑ת / כִּ֣י שָֽׁת־לִ֤י אֱלֹהִים֙ זֶ֣רַע
אַחֵ֔ר תַּ֣חַת הֶ֔בֶל / כִּ֥י הֲרָג֖וֹ קָֽיִן׃

וַיֵּ֨דַע אָדָ֥ם עוֹד֙ אֶת־אִשְׁתּ֔וֹ. (a) Textuality > conj paratactic expansion / Mood > declarative: past / Transitivity > mental: perception, which is actually a material process. See 4:1(a).

אֶת־אִשְׁתּוֹ	עוֹד	אָדָם	וַיֵּדַע	**Constituents**
his woman	*more*	*'Adam*	*and he knew*	**Translation**
	Adjunct		Theme	**Textuality**
		Subject	Finite	**Mood**
Phenomenon		Senser	Process	**Transitivity**

וַיֵּדַע. Theme: textual > clause conj + Theme: experiential / Finite > wayyiqtol 3ms / Process > qal ידע.

אָדָם. Subject > ms / Actor > nominal group: noun proper.

עוֹד. Adjunct: textual > recurrence. This references prior text to indicate that the material process described in this clause also happened earlier. See 4:1(a).

אֶת־אִשְׁתּוֹ. Goal > nominal group: goal marker - noun common fs const + pronoun suffix 3ms, antecedent is אָדָם *'Adam*.

וַתֵּלֶד בֵּן. (b) Textuality > conj paratactic expansion / Mood > declarative: past / Transitivity > material: action. The Subject / Actor is אִשְׁתּוֹ *his woman* in the preceding clause.

בֵּן	וַתֵּלֶד	**Constituents**
a son	*and she birthed*	**Translation**
	Theme	**Textuality**
	Finite	**Mood**
Goal	Process	**Transitivity**

וַתֵּלֶד. Theme: textual > clause conj + Theme: experiential / Finite > wayyiqtol 3fs / Process > qal ילד.

בֵּן. Goal > nominal group: noun common ms.

וַתִּקְרָא אֶת־שְׁמוֹ שֵׁת. (c) Textuality > conj paratactic expansion / Mood > declarative: past / Transitivity > verbal. The Subject / Sayer is אִשְׁתּוֹ *his wife* from clause (a).

שֵׁת	אֶת־שְׁמוֹ	וַתִּקְרָא	**Constituents**
Shet	*his name*	*and she called*	**Translation**
		Theme	**Textuality**
		Finite	**Mood**
Verbiage	Target	Process	**Transitivity**

וַתִּקְרָא. Theme: textual > clause conj + Theme: experiential / Finite > wayyiqtol 3fs / Process > qal קרא.

אֶת־שְׁמוֹ. Target > nominal group: goal marker - noun common ms const + pronoun suffix 3ms, antecedent is בֵּן *son* from clause (b).

שֵׁת. Verbiage > nominal group: noun proper ms.

כִּי שָׁת־לִי אֱלֹהִים זֶרַע אַחֵר תַּחַת הֶבֶל. (d) Textuality > conj hypotactic projection: quote / Mood > declarative: past / Transitivity > material: action. *Because deity gave me other seed in place of Hevel.* This is clearly projected as a quote, though there is no proper projecting clause, that is, a verbal process clause such as *and she said.* This has led, for example, NRSV to insert "for she said."

תַּחַת הֶבֶל	זֶרַע אַחֵר	אֱלֹהִים	לִי	שָׁת־	כִּי	**Constituents**
under Hevel	*other seed*	*deity*	*to me*	*he gave*	*because*	**Translation**
				Theme	Theme	**Textuality**
		Subject		Finite		**Mood**
Circumstance	Goal	Actor	Beneficiary	Process		**Transitivity**

כִּי. Theme: textual > conj.

שָׁת־. Theme: experiential / Finite > qatal 3ms / Process > qal שׁית.

לִי. Beneficiary > prep phrase: prep + pronoun suffix, antecedent is אִשְׁתּוֹ *his wife.*

אֱלֹהִים. Subject > mp / Actor > nominal group: noun common.

זֶרַע אַחֵר. Goal > nominal group: noun common ms | adj ms.

תַּחַת הֶבֶל. Circumstance: cause, reason > prep phrase: prep | noun proper ms. This Circumstance is worded as a locational one, but really fits the category of cause, and more specifically the reason why, and means *in place of, to replace.*

כִּי הֲרָגוֹ קָיִן. (e) Textuality > conj hypotactic expansion / Mood > declarative: past / Transitivity > material: action. This appears not to be a continuation of the quote. Rather, it appears to be a gloss to the preceding quote added by the narrator.

קָיִן	הֲרָגוֹ	כִּי	**Constituents**
Qayin	*he killed him*	*because*	**Translation**
	Theme	Theme	**Textuality**
Subject	Finite		**Mood**
Actor	Process + Goal		**Transitivity**

כִּי. Theme: textual > conj.

הֲרָגוֹ. Theme: experiential / Finite > qatal 3ms / Process > qal הרג + Goal > pronoun suffix 3ms, antecedent is הֶבֶל *Hevel*.

קָיִן. Subject > ms / Actor > nominal group: noun proper.

4:26 // וּלְשֵׁת גַּם־הוּא יֻלַּד־בֵּן // וַיִּקְרָא אֶת־שְׁמוֹ אֱנוֹשׁ
// אָז הוּחַל לִקְרֹא בְּשֵׁם יְהוָה׃ פ

וּלְשֵׁת גַּם־הוּא יֻלַּד־בֵּן. (a) Textuality > conj paratactic expansion / Mood > declarative: past / Transitivity > material: action.

בֵּן	יֻלַּד־	הוּא	גַּם־	וּלְשֵׁת	**Constituents**
a son	*he was born*	*he*	*also*	*and to Shet*	**Translation**
			Adjunct	Theme	**Textuality**
Subject	Finite				**Mood**
Goal	Process	Beneficiary		Beneficiary	**Transitivity**

וּלְשֵׁת. Theme: textual > clause conj + Theme: experiential / Beneficiary > prep phrase: prep + noun proper ms. This is a preposed Theme, substituted later in the clause by הוּא.

גַּם־. Adjunct: textual > addition. It references a prior event, in this case, that a son was also born to 'Adam in 4:25(a-b).

הוּא. Beneficiary > pronoun suffix 3ms, antecedent is שֵׁת *Shet*. This is an interesting clause feature, because הוּא *he* is typically a Subject personal pronoun, but here it is used as a Beneficiary, which is normally configured as a לְ prepositional phrase. One might have expected it be worded לוֹ rather than הוּא.

יֻלַּד־. Finite > qatal 3ms / Process > pual or qal passive ילד.

בֵּן. Goal > nominal group: noun common ms. Also, the interpersonal Subject of the preceding passive verb.

וַיִּקְרָא אֶת־שְׁמוֹ אֱנוֹשׁ. (b) Textuality > conj paratactic expansion / Mood > declarative: past / Transitivity > verbal. The Subject / Sayer is שֵׁת *Shet*, the Beneficiary in the preceding clause, absent here by ellipsis.

אֱנוֹשׁ	אֶת־שְׁמוֹ	וַיִּקְרָא	**Constituents**
'Enosh	*his name*	*and he called*	**Translation**
		Theme	**Textuality**
		Finite	**Mood**
Verbiage	*Target*	*Process*	**Transitivity**

וַיִּקְרָא. Theme: textual > clause conj + Theme: experiential / Finite > wayyiqtol 3ms / Process > qal קרא.

אֶת־שְׁמוֹ. Target > nominal group: goal marker - noun common ms const + pronoun suffix 3ms, antecedent is בֵּן, the son born as reported in the preceding clause.

אֱנוֹשׁ. Verbiage > nominal group: noun common/proper ms. The word אֱנוֹשׁ means *man* and is here appropriated as a personal name, yet another indication of the typological character of these early narratives.

אָז הוּחַל [[לִקְרֹא בְּשֵׁם יְהוָה]]. (c) Textuality > conj paratactic expansion / Mood > declarative: past / Transitivity > existential.

Then was begun to call on the name of YHVH. The existential process is passive.

[[לִקְרֹא בְּשֵׁם יְהוָה]]	הוּחַל	אָז	**Constituents**
to call in the name of YHVH	*he was begun*	*then*	**Translation**
		Theme	**Textuality**
Subject	Finite		**Mood**
Existent	Process		**Transitivity**

אָז. Theme: textual > conj. This is an explicit indicator of sequence, perhaps with the added connotation that this is the first time such a thing was done, reinforced by the Process.

הוּחַל לִקְרֹא. Verbal group complex > Finite + Non-finite.

הוּחַל. Theme: experiential / Finite > qatal 3ms / Process > hofal חלל I. This is a passive process. The following clause, containing its own process, is what was begun, or what came into being for the first time. The structure הוּחַל לִקְרֹא *was begun to call* is termed a verbal group complex. The first verb in a verbal group complex typically qualifies the second verb by saying something about its modality (its usuality or frequency) including starting (חלל) and continuing (יסף). The Finite form הוּחַל here provides the parameter *begin* for the main semantic process of the clause *call*, which is indicated by the non-finite form קְרֹא. Note that the infinitive can also be construed as the Head of an embedded clause.

לִקְרֹא בְּשֵׁם יְהוָה. (i) Subject / Existent >> Textuality > embedded inf clause / Transitivity > verbal. The Subject / Sayer of this embedded verbal process does not have a textual referent. NRSV translates *At that time people began to invoke the name of the LORD.*

בְּשֵׁם יְהוָה	לִקְרֹא	**Constituents**
in the name of YHVH	*to call*	**Translation**
	Theme	**Textuality**
Circumstance	Process	**Transitivity**

לִקְרֹא. Theme: textual > prep + Theme: experiential / Process > inf const qal קרא.

בְּשֵׁם יְהוָה. Circumstance > prep phrase: prep + noun common ms const | noun proper ms.

Genesis 5:1-5

[1]*This is the book of the outcomes of 'Adam. In the day deity created 'Adam, in the likeness of deity he made him.* [2]*Male and female he created them. And he blessed them. And he called their name humankind in the day they were created.* [3]*And 'Adam lived 130 years. And he fathered in his likeness as his image. And he called his name Shet.* [4]*And the days of 'Adam, after his fathering Shet, were 800 years. And he fathered sons and daughters.* [5]*And all the days of 'Adam, which he is alive, were 930 years. And he died.*

5:1 /// זֶה סֵפֶר תּוֹלְדֹת אָדָם // בְּיוֹם בְּרֹא אֱלֹהִים אָדָם בִּדְמוּת אֱלֹהִים עָשָׂה אֹתוֹ׃

זֶה סֵפֶר תּוֹלְדֹת אָדָם. (a) Textuality > appositive paratactic expansion / Mood > declarative: non-past / Transitivity > relational: identification.

סֵפֶר תּוֹלְדֹת אָדָם	זֶה	**Constituents**
the book of the outcomes of 'Adam	*this*	**Translation**
	Theme	**Textuality**
Complement	Subject	**Mood**
Identifier	Identified	**Transitivity**

זֶה. Theme > 3ms / Subject > ms / Identified > pronoun demonstrative: near. This pronoun is cataphoric, rather than anaphoric, and points to the following clause complex.

סֵפֶר תּוֹלְדֹת אָדָם. Complement > ms (סֵפֶר) / Identifier > nominal group: noun common ms const | noun common fp const | noun proper ms. It may be an open question whether **אָדָם** is *'Adam* or *humankind* in the clause complex of which this clause is a part. In clause (b) following, the Goal **אֹתוֹ**, referencing **אָדָם**, is 3ms. But in 5:2(a-c) the pronouns referencing **אָדָם** are 3mp, perhaps indicating that **אָדָם** is now being understood in a plural collective sense. Regarding the translation *outcomes* for **תּוֹלְדֹת**, see 2:4(a).

[[בְּיוֹם בְּרֹא אֱלֹהִים אָדָם]] בִּדְמוּת אֱלֹהִים עָשָׂה אֹתוֹ.

(b) Textuality > appositive paratactic expansion / Mood > declarative: past / Transitivity > material: action.

אֹתוֹ	עָשָׂה	בִּדְמוּת אֱלֹהִים	[[בְּיוֹם בְּרֹא אֱלֹהִים אָדָם]]	**Constituents**
him	*he made*	*in the likeness of deity*	*in the day of deity's creating 'Adam*	**Translation**
			Theme	**Textuality**
	Finite			**Mood**
Goal	Process	Circumstance	Circumstance	**Transitivity**

בְּיוֹם בְּרֹא אֱלֹהִים אָדָם. (i) Circumstance: location, time >> Textuality > embedded prep clause / Transitivity > material: action. This embedded clause is built from what otherwise might be an independent clause: *deity created 'Adam.* With the addition of **בְּיוֹם** this clause process is transformed such that it becomes a prepositional phrase, which then functions as the Circumstance of the independent clause that contains it. The embedded clause retains a fully expressed Transitivity structure, with a Process and Participants. Additionally, we could say that this embedded clause functions as the Theme of the clause that contains it; as Theme it situates the containing clause in relation to prior text that detailed the story of Adam's creation.

אָדָם	אֱלֹהִים	בְּרֹא	בְּיוֹם	Constituents
'Adam	*deity*	*the creating of*	*in the day of*	**Translation**
			Theme	**Textuality**
Goal	Actor	Process	Circumstance	**Transitivity**

בְּיוֹם. Theme: textual > prep phrase: prep + noun common ms const.

בְּרֹא. Theme: experiential / Process > inf const qal ברא.

אֱלֹהִים. Actor > nominal group: noun common.

אָדָם. Goal > nominal group: noun proper ms.

בִּדְמוּת אֱלֹהִים. Circumstance: role > prep phrase: prep + noun common fs const | noun common mp. Compare 1:26(b) and 1:27(a-b).

עָשָׂה. Finite > 3ms / Process > qal עשׂה.

אֹתוֹ. Goal > goal marker + pronoun suffix 3ms, antecedent is אֱלֹהִים *deity.*

5:2 // זָכָר וּנְקֵבָה בְּרָאָם // וַיְבָרֶךְ אֹתָם // וַיִּקְרָא אֶת־
שְׁמָם אָדָם בְּיוֹם הִבָּרְאָם׃ ס

זָכָר וּנְקֵבָה בְּרָאָם. (a) Textuality > appositive paratactic expansion / Mood > declarative: past / Transitivity > material: action. The Subject / Actor is אֱלֹהִים *deity*, absent here by ellipsis.

בְּרָאָם	זָכָר וּנְקֵבָה	Constituents
he created them	*male and female*	**Translation**
	Theme	**Textuality**
Finite		**Mood**
Process + Goal	Scope	**Transitivity**

זָכָר וּנְקֵבָה. Theme: experiential / Scope > nominal group: noun common ms | group conj + noun common fs.

בְּרָאָם. Finite > qatal 3ms / Process > qal ברא + Goal > pronoun suffix 3mp, antecedent is presumably אָדָם, now taken in a plural sense.

וַיְבָרֶךְ אֹתָם. (b) Textuality > conj paratactic expansion / Mood > declarative: past / Transitivity > material: action. The Subject / Actor is אֱלֹהִים *deity*, absent here by ellipsis.

אֹתָם	וַיְבָרֶךְ	**Constituents**
them	*and he blessed*	**Translation**
	Theme	**Textuality**
	Finite	**Mood**
Goal	Process	**Transitivity**

וַיְבָרֶךְ. Theme: textual > clause conj + Theme: experiential / Finite > wayyiqtol 3ms / Process > piel ברך.

אֹתָם. Goal > goal marker + pronoun suffix 3mp, antecedent is אָדָם *humankind*.

וַיִּקְרָא אֶת־שְׁמָם אָדָם [[בְּיוֹם הִבָּרְאָם]]. (c) Textuality > conj paratactic expansion / Mood > declarative: past / Transitivity > verbal. The Subject / Sayer is אֱלֹהִים *deity*, absent here by ellipsis.

[[בְּיוֹם הִבָּרְאָם]]	אָדָם	אֶת־שְׁמָם	וַיִּקְרָא	**Constituents**
in the day of their having been created	*humankind*	*their name*	*and he called*	**Translation**
			Theme	**Textuality**
			Finite	**Mood**
Circumstance	Verbiage	Target	Process	**Transitivity**

וַיִּקְרָא. Theme: textual > clause conj + Theme: experiential / Finite > wayyiqtol 3ms / Process > qal קרא.

אֶת־שְׁמָם. Target > nominal group: goal marker + noun common ms const + pronoun suffix 3mp, antecedent is presumably אָדָם *humankind*, which then means this clause makes a strange kind of sense: *and he called humankind's name "humankind/'Adam" in the day they were created.*

אָדָם. Verbiage > nominal group: noun common collective ms = noun proper ms.

בְּיוֹם הִבָּרְאָם. (i) Circumstance: location, time >> Textuality > embedded prep clause / Transitivity > material: action.

הִבָּרְאָם	בְּיוֹם	**Constituents**
their having been created	*in the day of*	**Translation**
	Theme	**Textuality**
Process + Goal	Circumstance	**Transitivity**

בְּיוֹם. Theme: textual > prep + Theme: experiential / Circumstance > noun common ms const.

הִבָּרְאָם. Process > inf const nifal ברא + Goal > pronoun suffix 3mp, antecedent is אָדָם *humankind.*

5:3 // וַיְחִי אָדָם שְׁלֹשִׁים וּמְאַת שָׁנָה // וַיּוֹלֶד בִּדְמוּתוֹ
כְּצַלְמוֹ // וַיִּקְרָא אֶת־שְׁמוֹ שֵׁת׃

וַיְחִי אָדָם שְׁלֹשִׁים וּמְאַת שָׁנָה. (a) Textuality > conj paratactic expansion / Mood > declarative: past / Transitivity > material: event.

שְׁלֹשִׁים וּמְאַת שָׁנָה	אָדָם	וַיְחִי	**Constituents**
thirty and a hundred years	*'Adam*	*and he lived*	**Translation**
		Theme	**Textuality**
	Subject	Finite	**Mood**
Scope	Actor	Process	**Transitivity**

וַיְחִי. Theme: textual > clause conj + Theme: experiential / Finite > wayyiqtol 3ms / Process > qal חיה.

אָדָם. Subject > ms / Actor > noun proper.

שְׁלֹשִׁים וּמְאַת שָׁנָה. Scope > nominal group: numeral ׀ group conj + numeral fs const ׀ noun common fs.

וַיּוֹלֶד בִּדְמוּתוֹ כְּצַלְמוֹ. (b) Textuality > conj paratactic expansion / Mood > declarative / Transitivity > material: action. Subject / Actor is אָדָם *'Adam*, absent here by ellipsis. The Goal, presumably a *son*, is not made explicit in this clause. This is an observation made more interesting because the non-explicit son is presumably the antecedent of *his* in אֶת־שְׁמוֹ *his name* in the next clause.

כְּצַלְמוֹ	בִּדְמוּתוֹ	וַיּוֹלֶד	**Constituents**
as his image	*in his likeness*	*and he fathered*	**Translation**
		Theme	**Textuality**
		Finite	**Mood**
	Circumstance	Process	**Transitivity**

וַיּוֹלֶד. Theme: textual > clause conj + Theme: experiential / Finite > wayyiqtol 3ms / Process > hifil ילד. This process in this construction would normally be followed by a Goal, either the name of a son or the phrase בָּנִים וּבָנוֹת *sons and daughters*; see 5:6(b) and 5:4(b) respectively, and many other examples in this chapter. Here there is no explicit Goal.

בִּדְמוּתוֹ כְּצַלְמוֹ. Circumstance: role > prep phrase complex. The two prepositional phrases are not connected by a group conjunction. The second one may then be an appositive expansion of the first one, rather than its synonym.

בִּדְמוּתוֹ. Prep phrase 1 > prep + noun common fs const + pronoun suffix 3ms, antecedent is אָדָם *'Adam*.

כְּצַלְמוֹ. Prep phrase 2 > prep + noun common ms const + pronoun suffix 3ms, antecedent is אָדָם *'Adam*.

וַיִּקְרָא אֶת־שְׁמוֹ שֵׁת. (c) Textuality > conj paratactic expansion / Mood > declarative: past / Transitivity > verbal. Subject / Actor is אָדָם *'Adam*, absent here by ellipsis.

שֵׁת	אֶת־שְׁמוֹ	וַיִּקְרָא	**Constituents**
Shet	*his name*	*and he called*	**Translation**
		Theme	**Textuality**
		Finite	**Mood**
Verbiage	Target	Process	**Transitivity**

וַיִּקְרָא. Theme: textual > clause conj + Theme: experiential / Finite > wayyiqtol 3ms / Process > qal קרא.

אֶת־שְׁמוֹ. Target > nominal group: goal marker - noun common ms const + pronoun suffix 3ms; the antecedent is presumably *son*, though *son* is not explicit in the preceding clause; see comments to clause (b).

שֵׁת. Verbiage > nominal group: noun proper ms.

5:4 // וַיִּהְיוּ יְמֵי־אָדָם אַחֲרֵי הוֹלִידוֹ אֶת־שֵׁת שְׁמֹנֶה
מֵאֹת שָׁנָה // וַיּוֹלֶד בָּנִים וּבָנוֹת׃

וַיִּהְיוּ יְמֵי־אָדָם [[אַחֲרֵי הוֹלִידוֹ אֶת־שֵׁת]] שְׁמֹנֶה מֵאֹת שָׁנָה. (a) Textuality > conj paratactic expansion / Mood > declarative: past / Transitivity > relational: attribution.

שְׁמֹנֶה מֵאֹת שָׁנָה	[[אַחֲרֵי הוֹלִידוֹ אֶת־שֵׁת]]	יְמֵי־אָדָם	וַיִּהְיוּ	**Constituents**
eight hundred years	*after his fathering Shet*	*the days of 'Adam*	*and they were*	**Translation**
			Theme	**Textuality**
		Subject	Finite	**Mood**
Attribute	Circumstance	Carrier	Process	**Transitivity**

וַיִּהְיוּ. Theme: textual > clause conj + Theme: experiential / Finite > wayyiqtol 3mp / Process > qal היה.

יְמֵי־אָדָם. Subject > mp / Carrier > nominal group: noun common mp const - noun proper ms.

אַחֲרֵי הוֹלִידוֹ אֶת־שֵׁת. (i) Circumstance >> Textuality > embedded prep clause / Transitivity > material: action.

אֶת־שֵׁת	הוֹלִידוֹ	אַחֲרֵי	**Constituents**
Shet	*his fathering*	*after*	**Translation**
	Theme	Theme	**Textuality**
Goal	Process + Actor		**Transitivity**

אַחֲרֵי. Theme: textual > prep.

הוֹלִידוֹ. Theme: experiential / Process > inf const hifil ילד + Actor > pronoun suffix 3ms, antecedent is the אָדָם *'Adam* preceding the embedded clause.

אֶת־שֵׁת. Goal > nominal group: goal marker - noun proper ms.

שְׁמֹנֶה מֵאֹת שָׁנָה. Attribute > nominal group: numeral ms ו numeral fp const ו noun common fs.

וַיּוֹלֶד בָּנִים וּבָנוֹת. (b) Textuality > conj paratactic expansion / Mood > declarative: past / Transitivity > material: action.

בָּנִים וּבָנוֹת	וַיּוֹלֶד	**Constituents**
sons and daughters	*and he fathered*	**Translation**
	Theme	**Textuality**
	Finite	**Mood**
Goal	Process	**Transitivity**

וַיּוֹלֶד. Theme: textual > clause conj + Theme: experiential / Finite > wayyiqtol 3ms / Process > hifil ילד.

בָּנִים וּבָנוֹת. Goal > nominal group complex: noun common mp ו group conj + noun common fp.

5:5 // וַיִּֽהְי֞וּ כָּל־יְמֵ֤י אָדָם֙ אֲשֶׁר־חַ֔י תְּשַׁ֤ע מֵאוֹת֙ שָׁנָ֔ה
וּשְׁלֹשִׁ֖ים שָׁנָ֑ה // וַיָּמֹֽת׃ ס

וַיִּהְיוּ כָּל־יְמֵי אָדָם [[אֲשֶׁר־חַי]] תְּשַׁע מֵאוֹת שָׁנָה וּשְׁלֹשִׁים שָׁנָה. (a) Textuality > conj paratactic expansion / Mood declarative: past / Transitivity > relational: attribution.

תְּשַׁע מֵאוֹת שָׁנָה וּשְׁלֹשִׁים שָׁנָה	כָּל־יְמֵי אָדָם [[אֲשֶׁר־חַי]]	וַיִּהְיוּ	**Constituents**
nine hundred years and thirty years	*all of the days of 'Adam, which alive*	*and they were*	**Translation**
		Theme	**Textuality**
	Subject	Finite	**Mood**
Attribute	Carrier	Process	**Transitivity**

וַיִּהְיוּ. Theme: textual > clause conj + Theme: experiential / Finite > wayyiqtol 3mp / Process > qal היה.

כָּל־יְמֵי אָדָם [[אֲשֶׁר־חַי]]. Subject > mp / Carrier > nominal group: Head + Post-modifier.

כָּל־יְמֵי אָדָם. Head > noun common collective ms const - noun common mp const | noun proper ms. The Finite is 3mp whereas the presumed proper Subject is כָּל *all*, the head noun of the Head nominal group, which is ms—though it is a collective noun, which may account for the plural verb. Or, the semantic subject was considered to be יְמֵי *days of*, which is a construct plural.

אֲשֶׁר־חַי. (i) Post-modifier >> Textuality > embedded expansion: relative clause / Mood > declarative: past / Transitivity > relational: attribution.

חַי	אֲשֶׁר־	**Constituents**
alive	*which*	**Translation**
	Theme	**Textuality**
Attribute	Carrier	**Transitivity**

אֲשֶׁר־. Theme: textual > pronoun relative + Theme: experiential / Carrier > antecedent אָדָם *'Adam.*

חַי. Attribute > adjective group: adj ms.

תְּשַׁע מֵאוֹת שָׁנָה וּשְׁלֹשִׁים שָׁנָה. Attribute > nominal group complex: numeral fs | numeral fp | noun common fs | group conj + numeral fp | noun common fs.

וַיָּמֹת. (b) Textuality > conj paratactic expansion / Mood > declarative: past / Transitivity > material: event.

וַיָּמֹת	**Constituents**
and he died	**Translation**
Theme	**Textuality**
Finite	**Mood**
Process	**Transitivity**

וַיָּמֹת. Theme: textual > clause conj + Theme: experiential / Finite > wayyiqtol 3ms / Process > qal מות.

Genesis 5:6-8

[6]Shet lived 105 years. And he fathered 'Enosh. [7]And Shet lived, after his fathering 'Enosh, 807 years. And he fathered sons and daughters. [8]And all the days of Shet were 912 years. And he died.

5:6 /// וַיְחִי־שֵׁ֕ת חָמֵ֥שׁ שָׁנִ֖ים וּמְאַ֣ת שָׁנָ֑ה // וַיּ֖וֹלֶד
אֶת־אֱנֽוֹשׁ׃

וַיְחִי־שֵׁת חָמֵשׁ שָׁנִים וּמְאַת שָׁנָה. (a) Textuality > conj paratactic expansion / Mood > declarative: past / Transitivity > material: event.

חָמֵשׁ שָׁנִים וּמְאַת שָׁנָה	שֵׁת	וַיְחִי־	**Constituents**
five years and a hundred years	*Shet*	*and he lived*	**Translation**
		Theme	**Textuality**
	Subject	Finite	**Mood**
Scope	Actor	Process	**Transitivity**

וַיְחִי־. Theme: textual > clause conj + Theme: experiential / Finite > wayyiqtol 3ms / Process > qal חיה.

שֵׁת. Subject > ms / Actor > nominal group: noun proper.

חָמֵשׁ שָׁנִים וּמְאַת שָׁנָה. Scope > nominal group complex: numeral ms | noun common fp | group conj + numeral fs const | noun common fs.

וַיּוֹלֶד אֶת־אֱנוֹשׁ. (b) Textuality > conj paratactic expansion / Mood > declarative: past / Transitivity > material: action.

אֶת־אֱנוֹשׁ	וַיּוֹלֶד	**Constituents**
'Enosh	*and he fathered*	**Translation**
	Theme	**Textuality**
	Finite	**Mood**
Goal	Process	**Transitivity**

וַיּוֹלֶד. Theme: textual > clause conj + Theme: experiential / Finite > wayyiqtol 3ms / Process > hifil ילד.

אֶת־אֱנוֹשׁ. Goal > nominal group: goal marker - noun proper ms.

5:7 // וַיְחִי־שֵׁת אַחֲרֵי הוֹלִידוֹ אֶת־אֱנוֹשׁ שֶׁבַע שָׁנִים
וּשְׁמֹנֶה מֵאוֹת שָׁנָה // וַיּוֹלֶד בָּנִים וּבָנוֹת׃

וַיְחִי־שֵׁת [[אַחֲרֵי הוֹלִידוֹ אֶת־אֱנוֹשׁ]] שֶׁבַע שָׁנִים וּשְׁמֹנֶה מֵאוֹת שָׁנָה. (a) Textuality > conj paratactic expansion / Mood > declarative: past / Transitivity > material: event.

שֶׁבַע שָׁנִים וּשְׁמֹנֶה מֵאוֹת שָׁנָה	[[אַחֲרֵי הוֹלִידוֹ אֶת־אֱנוֹשׁ]]	שֵׁת	וַיְחִי־	**Constituents**
seven years and eight hundred years	*after his fathering 'Enosh*	*Shet*	*and he lived*	**Translation**
			Theme	**Textuality**
		Subject	Finite	**Mood**
Scope	Circumstance	Actor	Process	**Transitivity**

וַיְחִי־. Theme: textual > clause conj + Theme: experiential / Finite > wayyiqtol 3ms / Process > qal חיה.

שֵׁת. Subject > ms / Actor > nominal group: noun proper.

אַחֲרֵי הוֹלִידוֹ אֶת־אֱנוֹשׁ. (i) Circumstance >> Textuality > embedded prep clause / Transitivity > material: action.

אֶת־אֱנוֹשׁ	הוֹלִידוֹ	אַחֲרֵי	**Constituents**
'Enosh	*his fathering*	*after*	**Translation**
	Theme	Theme	**Textuality**
Goal	Process + Actor		**Transitivity**

אַחֲרֵי. Theme: textual > prep.

הוֹלִידוֹ. Theme: experiential / Process > inf const hifil ילד + Actor > pronoun suffix 3ms, antecedent is שֵׁת *Shet* preceding the embedded clause.

אֶת־אֱנוֹשׁ. Goal > nominal group: goal marker - noun proper ms.

שֶׁבַע שָׁנִים וּשְׁמֹנֶה מֵאוֹת שָׁנָה. Scope > nominal group complex: numeral ı noun common fp ı group conj + numeral fs ı numeral fp ı noun common fs.

וַיּוֹלֶד בָּנִים וּבָנוֹת. (b) Textuality > conj paratactic expansion / Mood > declarative: past / Transitivity > material: action.

בָּנִים וּבָנוֹת	וַיּוֹלֶד	**Constituents**
sons and daughters	*and he fathered*	**Translation**
	Theme	**Textuality**
	Finite	**Mood**
Goal	Process	**Transitivity**

וַיּוֹלֶד. Theme: textual > clause conj + Theme: experiential / Finite > wayyiqtol 3ms / Process > hifil ילד.

בָּנִים וּבָנוֹת. Goal > nominal group complex: noun common mp ו group conj + noun common fp.

5:8 // וַיִּהְיוּ כָּל־יְמֵי־שֵׁת שְׁתֵּים עֶשְׂרֵה שָׁנָה וּתְשַׁע
מֵאוֹת שָׁנָה // וַיָּמֹת׃ ס

וַיִּהְיוּ כָּל־יְמֵי־שֵׁת שְׁתֵּים עֶשְׂרֵה שָׁנָה וּתְשַׁע מֵאוֹת שָׁנָה.
(a) Textuality > conj paratactic expansion / Mood > declarative: past / Transitivity > relational: attribution.

שְׁתֵּים עֶשְׂרֵה שָׁנָה וּתְשַׁע מֵאוֹת שָׁנָה	כָּל־יְמֵי־שֵׁת	וַיִּהְיוּ	**Constituents**
twelve years and nine hundred years	*all the days of Shet*	*and they were*	**Translation**
		Theme	**Textuality**
	Subject	Finite	**Mood**
Attribute	Carrier	Process	**Transitivity**

וַיִּהְיוּ. Theme: textual > clause conj + Theme: experiential / Finite > wayyiqtol 3mp / Process > qal היה.

כָּל־יְמֵי־שֵׁת. Subject > mp / Carrier > nominal group: noun common collective ms const - noun common mp const - noun proper ms. See comments to 5:5(a).

שְׁתֵּים עֶשְׂרֵה שָׁנָה וּתְשַׁע מֵאוֹת שָׁנָה. Attribute > nominal group complex: numeral fs | numeral fs | noun common fs | group conj + numeral fs | numeral fp | noun common fs.

וַיָּמֹת. (b) Textuality > conj paratactic expansion / Mood > declarative: past / Transitivity > material: event.

וַיָּמֹת	**Constituents**
and he died	**Translation**
Theme	**Textuality**
Finite	**Mood**
Process	**Transitivity**

וַיָּמֹת. Theme: textual > clause conj + Theme: experiential / Finite > wayyiqtol 3ms / Process > qal מות.

Genesis 5:9-11

[9]And 'Enosh lived 90 years. And he fathered Qenan. [10]And 'Enosh lived, after his fathering Qenan, 815 years. And he fathered sons and daughters. [11]And all the days of 'Enosh were 905 years. And he died.

5:9 /// וַיְחִי אֱנוֹשׁ תִּשְׁעִים שָׁנָה // וַיּוֹלֶד אֶת־קֵינָן׃

וַיְחִי אֱנוֹשׁ תִּשְׁעִים שָׁנָה. (a) Textuality > conj paratactic expansion / Mood > declarative: past / Transitivity > material: event.

תִּשְׁעִים שָׁנָה	אֱנוֹשׁ	וַיְחִי	**Constituents**
ninety years	*'Enosh*	*and he lived*	**Translation**
		Theme	**Textuality**
	Subject	Finite	**Mood**
Scope	Actor	Process	**Transitivity**

וַיְחִי. Theme: textual > clause conj + Theme: experiential / Finite > wayyiqtol 3ms / Process > qal חיה.

אֱנוֹשׁ. Subject > ms / Actor > nominal group: noun proper.

תִּשְׁעִים שָׁנָה. Scope > nominal group: numeral mp ׀ noun common fs.

וַיּוֹלֶד אֶת־קֵינָן. (b) Textuality > conj paratactic expansion / Mood > declarative: past / Transitivity > material: action.

אֶת־קֵינָן	וַיּוֹלֶד	**Constituents**
Qenan	*and he fathered*	**Translation**
	Theme	**Textuality**
	Finite	**Mood**
Goal	Process	**Transitivity**

וַיּוֹלֶד. Theme: textual > clause conj + Theme: experiential / Finite > wayyiqtol 3ms / Process > hifil ילד.

אֶת־קֵינָן. Goal > nominal group: goal marker - noun proper.

5:10 // וַיְחִי אֱנוֹשׁ אַחֲרֵי הוֹלִידוֹ אֶת־קֵינָן חֲמֵשׁ עֶשְׂרֵה
שָׁנָה וּשְׁמֹנֶה מֵאוֹת שָׁנָה // וַיּוֹלֶד בָּנִים וּבָנוֹת׃

וַיְחִי אֱנוֹשׁ [[אַחֲרֵי הוֹלִידוֹ אֶת־קֵינָן]] חֲמֵשׁ עֶשְׂרֵה שָׁנָה וּשְׁמֹנֶה מֵאוֹת שָׁנָה. (a) Textuality > conj paratactic expansion / Mood > declarative: past / Transitivity > material: event.

חֲמֵשׁ עֶשְׂרֵה שָׁנָה וּשְׁמֹנֶה מֵאוֹת שָׁנָה	[[אַחֲרֵי הוֹלִידוֹ אֶת־קֵינָן]]	אֱנוֹשׁ	וַיְחִי	**Constituents**
fifteen years and eight hundred years	*after his fathering Qenan*	*'Enosh*	*and he lived*	**Translation**
			Theme	**Textuality**
		Subject	Finite	**Mood**
Scope	Circumstance	Actor	Process	**Transitivity**

וַיְחִי. Theme: textual > clause conj + Theme: experiential / Finite > wayyiqtol 3ms / Process > qal חיה.

אֱנוֹשׁ. Subject > ms / Actor > nominal group: noun proper.

אַחֲרֵי הוֹלִידוֹ אֶת־קֵינָן. (i) Circumstance >> Textuality > embedded prep clause / Transitivity > material: action.

אֶת־קֵינָן	הוֹלִידוֹ	אַחֲרֵי	**Constituents**
Qenan	*his fathering*	*after*	**Translation**
	Theme	Theme	**Textuality**
Goal	Process + Actor		**Transitivity**

אַחֲרֵי. Theme: textual > prep.

הוֹלִידוֹ. Theme: experiential / Process > inf const hifil ילד + Actor > pronoun suffix 3ms, antecedent is אֱנוֹשׁ *'Enosh* preceding the embedded clause.

אֶת־קֵינָן. Goal > nominal group: goal marker - noun proper ms.

חֲמֵשׁ עֶשְׂרֵה שָׁנָה וּשְׁמֹנֶה מֵאוֹת שָׁנָה. Scope > nominal group complex: numeral | numeral | noun common fs | group conj + numeral | numeral | noun common fs.

וַיּוֹלֶד בָּנִים וּבָנוֹת. (b) Textuality > conj paratactic expansion / Mood > declarative: past / Transitivity > material: action.

בָּנִים וּבָנוֹת	וַיּוֹלֶד	**Constituents**
sons and daughters	*and he fathered*	**Translation**
	Theme	**Textuality**
	Finite	**Mood**
Goal	Process	**Transitivity**

וַיּוֹלֶד. Theme: textual > clause conj + Theme: experiential / Finite > wayyiqtol 3ms / Process > hifil ילד.

בָּנִים וּבָנוֹת. Goal > nominal group complex: noun common mp | group conj + noun common fp.

5:11 // וַיִּהְיוּ כָּל־יְמֵי אֱנוֹשׁ חָמֵשׁ שָׁנִים וּתְשַׁע מֵאוֹת
שָׁנָה // וַיָּמֹת׃ ס

וַיִּהְיוּ כָּל־יְמֵי אֱנוֹשׁ חָמֵשׁ שָׁנִים וּתְשַׁע מֵאוֹת שָׁנָה. (a) Textuality > conj paratactic expansion / Mood > declarative: past / Transitivity > relational: attribution.

חָמֵשׁ שָׁנִים וּתְשַׁע מֵאוֹת שָׁנָה	כָּל־יְמֵי אֱנוֹשׁ	וַיִּהְיוּ	**Constituents**
five years and nine hundred years	*all the days of 'Enosh*	*and they were*	**Translation**
		Theme	**Textuality**
	Subject	Finite	**Mood**
Attribute	Carrier	Process	**Transitivity**

וַיִּהְיוּ. Theme: textual > clause conj + Theme: experiential / Finite > wayyiqtol 3mp / Process > qal היה.

כָּל־יְמֵי אֱנוֹשׁ. Subject > mp / Carrier > nominal group: noun common collective ms const - noun common mp const - noun proper ms. See comments to 5:5(a).

חָמֵשׁ שָׁנִים וּתְשַׁע מֵאוֹת שָׁנָה. Attribute > nominal group complex: numeral fs | noun common fp | group conj + numeral fs | numeral fp | noun common fs.

וַיָּמֹת. (b) Textuality > conj paratactic expansion / Mood > declarative: past / Transitivity > material: event.

וַיָּמֹת	**Constituents**
and he died	**Translation**
Theme	**Textuality**
Finite	**Mood**
Process	**Transitivity**

וַיָּמֹת. Theme: textual > clause conj + Theme: experiential / Finite > wayyiqtol 3ms / Process > qal מות.

Genesis 5:12-14

[12]And Qenan lived 70 years. And he fathered Mahalal'el. [13]And Qenan lived, after his fathering Mahalal'el, 840 years. And he fathered sons and daughters. [14]And all the days of Qenan were 910 years. And he died.

5:12 /// וַיְחִי קֵינָן שִׁבְעִים שָׁנָה // וַיּוֹלֶד אֶת־מַהֲלַלְאֵל׃

וַיְחִי קֵינָן שִׁבְעִים שָׁנָה. (a) Textuality > conj paratactic expansion / Mood > declarative: past / Transitivity > material: event.

שִׁבְעִים שָׁנָה	קֵינָן	וַיְחִי	**Constituents**
seventy years	*Qenan*	*and he lived*	**Translation**
		Theme	**Textuality**
	Subject	Finite	**Mood**
Scope	Actor	Process	**Transitivity**

וַיְחִי. Theme: textual > clause conj + Theme: experiential / Finite > wayyiqtol 3ms / Process > qal חיה.

קֵינָן. Subject > ms / Actor > nominal group: noun proper.

תִּשְׁעִים שָׁנָה. Scope > nominal group: numeral mp | noun common fs.

וַיּוֹלֶד אֶת־מַהֲלַלְאֵל. (b) Textuality > conj paratactic expansion / Mood > declarative: past / Transitivity > material: action.

אֶת־מַהֲלַלְאֵל	וַיּוֹלֶד	**Constituents**
Mehalal'el	*and he fathered*	**Translation**
	Theme	**Textuality**
	Finite	**Mood**
Goal	Process	**Transitivity**

וַיּ֫וֹלֶד. Theme: textual > clause conj + Theme: experiential / Finite > wayyiqtol 3ms / Process > hifil ילד.

אֶת־מַהֲלַלְאֵל. Goal > nominal group: goal marker - noun proper ms.

5:13 // וַיְחִ֣י קֵינָ֗ן אַחֲרֵי֙ הוֹלִיד֣וֹ אֶת־מַֽהֲלַלְאֵ֔ל אַרְבָּעִ֣ים
שָׁנָ֔ה וּשְׁמֹנֶ֥ה מֵא֖וֹת שָׁנָ֑ה // וַיּ֥וֹלֶד בָּנִ֖ים וּבָנֽוֹת׃

וַיְחִי קֵינָן [[אַחֲרֵי הוֹלִידוֹ אֶת־מַהֲלַלְאֵל]] אַרְבָּעִים שָׁנָה וּשְׁמֹנֶה מֵאוֹת שָׁנָה. (a) Textuality > conj paratactic expansion / Mood > declarative: past / Transitivity > material: event.

אַרְבָּעִים שָׁנָה וּשְׁמֹנֶה מֵאוֹת שָׁנָה	[[אַחֲרֵי הוֹלִידוֹ אֶת־מַהֲלַלְאֵל]]	קֵינָן	וַיְחִי	**Constituents**
forty years and eight hundred years	*after his fathering Mahalal'el*	*Qenan*	*and he lived*	**Translation**
			Theme	**Textuality**
		Subject	Finite	**Mood**
Scope	Circumstance	Actor	Process	**Transitivity**

וַיְחִי. Theme: textual > clause conj + Theme: experiential / Finite > wayyiqtol 3ms / Process > qal חיה.

קֵינָן. Subject > ms / Actor > nominal group: noun proper.

אַחֲרֵי הוֹלִידוֹ אֶת־מַהֲלַלְאֵל. (i) Circumstance >> Textuality > embedded prep clause / Transitivity > material: action.

אֶת־מַהֲלַלְאֵל	הוֹלִידוֹ	אַחֲרֵי	**Constituents**
Mahalal'el	*his fathering*	*after*	**Translation**
	Theme	Theme	**Textuality**
Goal	Process + Actor		**Transitivity**

אַחֲרֵי. Theme: textual > prep.

הוֹלִידוֹ. Theme: experiential / Process > inf const hifil ילד + Actor > pronoun suffix 3ms, antecedent is קֵינָן *Qenan* preceding the embedded clause.

אֶת־מַהֲלַלְאֵל. Goal > nominal group: goal marker - noun proper ms.

אַרְבָּעִים שָׁנָה וּשְׁמֹנֶה מֵאוֹת שָׁנָה. Scope > nominal group complex: numeral fp | noun common fs | group conj + numeral fs | numeral fp | noun common fs.

וַיּוֹלֶד בָּנִים וּבָנוֹת. (b) Textuality > conj paratactic expansion / Mood > declarative: past / Transitivity > material: action.

בָּנִים וּבָנוֹת	וַיּוֹלֶד	**Constituents**
sons and daughters	*and he fathered*	**Translation**
	Theme	**Textuality**
	Finite	**Mood**
Goal	Process	**Transitivity**

וַיּוֹלֶד. Theme: textual > clause conj + Theme: experiential / Finite > wayyiqtol 3ms / Process > hifil ילד.

בָּנִים וּבָנוֹת. Goal > nominal group complex: noun common mp | group conj + noun common fp.

5:14 // וַיִּהְיוּ כָּל־יְמֵי קֵינָן עֶשֶׂר שָׁנִים וּתְשַׁע מֵאוֹת שָׁנָה
// וַיָּמֹת׃ ס //

וַיִּהְיוּ כָּל־יְמֵי קֵינָן עֶשֶׂר שָׁנִים וּתְשַׁע מֵאוֹת שָׁנָה. (a) Textuality > conj paratactic expansion / Mood > declarative: past / Transitivity > relational: attribution.

עֶשֶׂר שָׁנִים וּתְשַׁע מֵאוֹת שָׁנָה	כָּל־יְמֵי קֵינָן	וַיִּהְיוּ	**Constituents**
ten years and nine hundred years	*all the days of Qenan*	*and they were*	**Translation**
		Theme	**Textuality**
	Subject	Finite	**Mood**
Attribute	Carrier	Process	**Transitivity**

וַיִּהְיוּ. Theme: textual > clause conj + Theme: experiential / Finite > wayyiqtol 3mp / Process > qal היה.

כָּל־יְמֵי קֵינָן. Subject > ms / Carrier > nominal group: noun common collective ms const - noun common mp const - noun proper ms. See comments to 5:5(a).

עֶשֶׂר שָׁנִים וּתְשַׁע מֵאוֹת שָׁנָה. Scope > nominal group complex: numeral fs | noun common fp | group conj + numeral fs | numeral fp | noun common fs.

וַיָּמֹת. (b) Textuality > conj paratactic expansion / Mood > declarative: past / Transitivity > material: event.

וַיָּמֹת	**Constituents**
and he died	**Translation**
Theme	**Textuality**
Finite	**Mood**
Process	**Transitivity**

וַיָּמֹת. Theme: textual > clause conj + Theme: experiential / Finite > wayyiqtol 3ms / Process > qal מות.

Genesis 5:15-17

[15]And Mahalal'el lived 65 years. And he fathered Yered. [16]And Mahalal'el lived, after his fathering Yered, 830 years. And he fathered sons and daughters. [17]And all the days of Mahalal'el were 895 years. And he died.

5:15 /// וַיְחִי מַהֲלַלְאֵל חָמֵשׁ שָׁנִים וְשִׁשִּׁים שָׁנָה //
וַיּוֹלֶד אֶת־יָרֶד׃

וַיְחִי מַהֲלַלְאֵל חָמֵשׁ שָׁנִים וְשִׁשִּׁים שָׁנָה. (a) Textuality > conj paratactic expansion / Mood > declarative: past / Transitivity > material: event.

חָמֵשׁ שָׁנִים וְשִׁשִּׁים שָׁנָה	מַהֲלַלְאֵל	וַיְחִי	**Constituents**
five years and sixty years	*Mahalal'el*	*and he lived*	**Translation**
		Theme	**Textuality**
	Subject	Finite	**Mood**
Scope	Actor	Process	**Transitivity**

וַיְחִי. Theme: textual > clause conj + Theme: experiential / Finite > wayyiqtol 3ms / Process > qal חיה.

מַהֲלַלְאֵל. Subject > ms / Actor > nominal group: noun proper.

חָמֵשׁ שָׁנִים וְשִׁשִּׁים שָׁנָה. Scope > nominal group complex: numeral ms ׀ noun common fp ׀ group conj + numeral fp ׀ noun common fs.

וַיּוֹלֶד אֶת־יָרֶד. (b) Textuality > conj paratactic expansion / Mood > declarative: past / Transitivity > material: action.

אֶת־יָרֶד	וַיּוֹלֶד	**Constituents**
Yered	*and he fathered*	**Translation**
	Theme	**Textuality**
	Finite	**Mood**
Goal	Process	**Transitivity**

וַיּוֹלֶד. Theme: textual > clause conj + Theme: experiential / Finite > wayyiqtol 3ms / Process > hifil ילד.

אֶת־יָרֶד. Goal > nominal group: goal marker - noun proper ms.

5:16 וַֽיְחִי מַֽהֲלַלְאֵ֗ל אַֽחֲרֵי֙ הוֹלִיד֣וֹ אֶת־יֶ֔רֶד שְׁלֹשִׁ֣ים // שָׁנָ֔ה וּשְׁמֹנֶ֥ה מֵא֖וֹת שָׁנָ֑ה // וַיּ֥וֹלֶד בָּנִ֖ים וּבָנֽוֹת׃

וַיְחִי מַהֲלַלְאֵל [[אַחֲרֵי הוֹלִידוֹ אֶת־יֶרֶד]] שְׁלֹשִׁים שָׁנָה וּשְׁמֹנֶה מֵאוֹת שָׁנָה. (a) Textuality > conj paratactic expansion / Mood > declarative: past / Transitivity > material: event.

שְׁלֹשִׁים שָׁנָה וּשְׁמֹנֶה מֵאוֹת שָׁנָה	[[אַחֲרֵי הוֹלִידוֹ אֶת־יֶרֶד]]	מַהֲלַלְאֵל	וַיְחִי	**Constituents**
thirty years and eight hundred years	*after his fathering Yered*	*Mahalal'el*	*and he lived*	**Translation**
			Theme	**Textuality**
		Subject	Finite	**Mood**
Scope	Circumstance	Actor	Process	**Transitivity**

וַיְחִי. Theme: textual > clause conj + Theme: experiential / Finite > wayyiqtol 3ms / Process > qal חיה.

מַהֲלַלְאֵל. Subject > ms / Actor > nominal group: noun proper.

אַחֲרֵי הוֹלִידוֹ אֶת־יֶרֶד. (i) Circumstance >> Textuality > embedded prep clause / Transitivity > material: action.

אֶת־יֶרֶד	הוֹלִידוֹ	אַחֲרֵי	**Constituents**
Yered	*his fathering*	*after*	**Translation**
	Theme	Theme	**Textuality**
Goal	Process + Actor		**Transitivity**

אַחֲרֵי. Theme: textual > prep.

הוֹלִידוֹ. Theme: experiential / Process > inf const hifil ילד + Actor > pronoun suffix 3ms, antecedent is מַהֲלַלְאֵל *Mahalal'el* preceding the embedded clause.

אֶת־יֶרֶד. Goal > nominal group: goal marker - noun proper ms.

שְׁלֹשִׁים שָׁנָה וּשְׁמֹנֶה מֵאוֹת שָׁנָה. Scope > nominal group complex: numeral fs ı noun common fs ı group conj + numeral fs ı numeral fp ı noun common fs.

וַיּוֹלֶד בָּנִים וּבָנוֹת. (b) Textuality > conj paratactic expansion / Mood > declarative: past / Transitivity > material: action.

בָּנִים וּבָנוֹת	וַיּוֹלֶד	**Constituents**
sons and daughters	*and he fathered*	**Translation**
	Theme	**Textuality**
	Finite	**Mood**
Goal	Process	**Transitivity**

וַיּוֹלֶד. Theme: textual > clause conj + Theme: experiential / Finite > wayyiqtol 3ms / Process > hifil ילד.

בָּנִים וּבָנוֹת. Goal > nominal group complex: noun common mp ı group conj + noun common fp.

5:17 // וַיִּהְיוּ֙ כָּל־יְמֵ֣י מַהֲלַלְאֵ֔ל חָמֵ֤שׁ וְתִשְׁעִים֙ שָׁנָ֔ה
וּשְׁמֹנֶ֥ה מֵא֖וֹת שָׁנָ֑ה // וַיָּמֹֽת׃ ס

וַיִּהְיוּ כָּל־יְמֵי מַהֲלַלְאֵל חָמֵשׁ וְתִשְׁעִים שָׁנָה וּשְׁמֹנֶה מֵאוֹת שָׁנָה. (a) Textuality > conj paratactic expansion / Mood > declarative: past / Transitivity > relational: attribution.

חָמֵשׁ וְתִשְׁעִים שָׁנָה וּשְׁמֹנֶה מֵאוֹת שָׁנָה	כָּל־יְמֵי מַהֲלַלְאֵל	וַיִּהְיוּ	**Constituents**
five and ninety years and eight hundred years	*all the days of Mahalal'el*	*and they were*	**Translation**
		Theme	**Textuality**
	Subject	Finite	**Mood**
Attribute	Carrier	Process	**Transitivity**

וַיִּהְיוּ. Theme: textual > clause conj + Theme: experiential / Finite > wayyiqtol 3mp / Process > qal היה.

כָּל־יְמֵי מַהֲלַלְאֵל. Subject > ms / Carrier > nominal group: noun common collective ms const - noun common mp const - noun proper ms. See comments to 5:5(a).

חָמֵשׁ וְתִשְׁעִים שָׁנָה וּשְׁמֹנֶה מֵאוֹת שָׁנָה. Scope > nominal group complex: numeral fs ׀ group conj + numeral fs ׀ noun common fs ׀ group conj + numeral fs ׀ numeral fp ׀ noun common fs.

וַיָּמֹת. (b) Textuality > conj paratactic expansion / Mood > declarative: past / Transitivity > material: event.

וַיָּמֹת	**Constituents**
and he died	**Translation**
Theme	**Textuality**
Finite	**Mood**
Process	**Transitivity**

וַיָּמֹת. Theme: textual > clause conj + Theme: experiential / Finite > wayyiqtol 3ms / Process > qal מות.

Genesis 5:18-20

[18]And Yered lived 162 years. And he fathered Chanokh. [19]And Yered lived, after his fathering Chanokh, 800 years. And he fathered sons and daughters. [20]And all the days of Yered were 962 years. And he died.

5:18 /// וַיְחִי־יֶ֕רֶד שְׁתַּ֧יִם וְשִׁשִּׁ֛ים שָׁנָ֖ה וּמְאַ֣ת שָׁנָ֑ה //
וַיּ֖וֹלֶד אֶת־חֲנֽוֹךְ׃

וַיְחִי־יֶרֶד שְׁתַּיִם וְשִׁשִּׁים שָׁנָה וּמְאַת שָׁנָה. (a) Textuality > conj paratactic expansion / Mood > declarative: past / Transitivity > material: event.

שְׁתַּיִם וְשִׁשִּׁים שָׁנָה וּמְאַת שָׁנָה	יֶרֶד	וַיְחִי־	**Constituents**
two and sixty years and a hundred years	*Yered*	*and he lived*	**Translation**
		Theme	**Textuality**
	Subject	Finite	**Mood**
Scope	Actor	Process	**Transitivity**

וַיְחִי־. Theme: textual > clause conj + Theme: experiential / Finite > wayyiqtol 3ms / Process > qal חיה.

יֶרֶד. Subject > ms / Actor > nominal group: noun proper.

שְׁתַּיִם וְשִׁשִּׁים שָׁנָה וּמְאַת שָׁנָה. Scope > nominal group complex: numeral fd ı group conj + numeral fs ı noun common fs ı group conj + numeral fs ı noun common fs.

וַיּוֹלֶד אֶת־חֲנוֹךְ. (b) Textuality > conj paratactic expansion / Mood > declarative: past / Transitivity > material: action.

אֶת־חֲנוֹךְ	וַיּוֹלֶד	**Constituents**
Chanokh	*and he fathered*	**Translation**
	Theme	**Textuality**
	Finite	**Mood**
Goal	Process	**Transitivity**

וַיּוֹלֶד. Theme: textual > clause conj + Theme: experiential / Finite > wayyiqtol 3ms / Process > hifil ילד.

אֶת־חֲנוֹךְ. Goal > nominal group: goal marker - noun proper ms.

5:19 // וַיְחִי־יֶרֶד אַחֲרֵי הוֹלִידוֹ אֶת־חֲנוֹךְ שְׁמֹנֶה מֵאוֹת
שָׁנָה // וַיּוֹלֶד בָּנִים וּבָנוֹת׃

וַיְחִי־יֶרֶד [[אַחֲרֵי הוֹלִידוֹ אֶת־חֲנוֹךְ]] שְׁמֹנֶה מֵאוֹת שָׁנָה. (a) Textuality > conj paratactic expansion / Mood > declarative: past / Transitivity > material: event.

שְׁמֹנֶה מֵאוֹת שָׁנָה	[[אַחֲרֵי הוֹלִידוֹ אֶת־חֲנוֹךְ]]	יֶרֶד	וַיְחִי־	**Constituents**
eight hundred years	*after his fathering Chanokh*	*Yered*	*and he lived*	**Translation**
			Theme	**Textuality**
	Subject	Finite		**Mood**
Scope	Circumstance	Actor	Process	**Transitivity**

וַיְחִי־. Theme: textual > clause conj + Theme: experiential / Finite > wayyiqtol 3ms / Process > qal חיה.

יֶרֶד. Subject > ms / Actor > nominal group: noun proper.

אַחֲרֵי הוֹלִידוֹ אֶת־חֲנוֹךְ. (i) Circumstance >> Textuality > embedded prep clause / Transitivity > material: action.

אֶת־חֲנוֹךְ	הוֹלִידוֹ	אַחֲרֵי	**Constituents**
Chanokh	*his fathering*	*after*	**Translation**
	Theme	Theme	**Textuality**
Goal	Process + Actor		**Transitivity**

אַחֲרֵי. Theme: textual > prep.

הוֹלִידוֹ. Theme: experiential / Process > inf const hifil ילד + Actor > pronoun suffix 3ms, antecedent is יֶרֶד *Yered* preceding the embedded clause.

אֶת־חֲנוֹךְ. Goal > nominal group: goal marker - noun proper ms.

שְׁמֹנֶה מֵאוֹת שָׁנָה. Scope > nominal group: numeral fs ו numeral fp ו noun common fs.

וַיּוֹלֶד בָּנִים וּבָנוֹת. (b) Textuality > conj paratactic expansion / Mood > declarative: past / Transitivity > material: action.

בָּנִים וּבָנוֹת	וַיּוֹלֶד	**Constituents**
sons and daughters	*and he fathered*	**Translation**
	Theme	**Textuality**
	Finite	**Mood**
Goal	Process	**Transitivity**

וַיּוֹלֶד. Theme: textual > clause conj + Theme: experiential / Finite > wayyiqtol 3ms / Process > hifil ילד.

בָּנִים וּבָנוֹת. Goal > nominal group complex: noun common mp | group conj + noun common fp.

5:20 // וַיִּהְיוּ כָּל־יְמֵי־יֶרֶד שְׁתַּיִם וְשִׁשִּׁים שָׁנָה וּתְשַׁע
מֵאוֹת שָׁנָה // וַיָּמֹת׃ פ

וַיִּהְיוּ כָּל־יְמֵי־יֶרֶד שְׁתַּיִם וְשִׁשִּׁים שָׁנָה וּתְשַׁע מֵאוֹת שָׁנָה. (a) Textuality > conj paratactic expansion / Mood > declarative: past / Transitivity > relational: attribution.

שְׁתַּיִם וְשִׁשִּׁים שָׁנָה וּתְשַׁע מֵאוֹת שָׁנָה	כָּל־יְמֵי־יֶרֶד	וַיִּהְיוּ	**Constituents**
two and sixty years and nine hundred years	*all the days of Yered*	*and they were*	**Translation**
		Theme	**Textuality**
	Subject	Finite	**Mood**
Attribute	Carrier	Process	**Transitivity**

וַיִּהְיוּ. Theme: textual > clause conj + Theme: experiential / Finite > wayyiqtol 3mp / Process > qal היה.

כָּל־יְמֵי־יֶרֶד. Subject > ms / Carrier > nominal group: noun common collective ms const - noun common mp const - noun proper ms. See comments to 5:5(a).

שְׁתַּיִם וְשִׁשִּׁים שָׁנָה וּתְשַׁע מֵאוֹת שָׁנָה. Scope > nominal group complex: numeral fd | group conj + numeral fp | noun common fs | group conj + numeral fs | numeral fp | noun common fs.

וַיָּמֹת. (b) Textuality > conj paratactic expansion / Mood > declarative: past / Transitivity > material: event.

וַיָּמֹת	Constituents
and he died	**Translation**
Theme	**Textuality**
Finite	**Mood**
Process	**Transitivity**

וַיָּמֹת. Theme: textual > clause conj + Theme: experiential / Finite > wayyiqtol 3ms / Process > qal מות.

Genesis 5:21-24

[21]And Chanokh lived 65 years. And he fathered Metushalach. [22]And Chanokh walked with the deity, after his fathering Metushalach, 300 years. And he fathered sons and daughters. [23]And all the days of Chanokh were 365 years. [24]And Chanokh walked with the deity. And he is not, because deity took him.

5:21 /// וַיְחִי חֲנוֹךְ חָמֵשׁ וְשִׁשִּׁים שָׁנָה // וַיּוֹלֶד אֶת־
מְתוּשָׁלַח׃

וַיְחִי חֲנוֹךְ. (a) Textuality > conj paratactic expansion / Mood > declarative: past / Transitivity > material: event.

חָמֵשׁ וְשִׁשִּׁים שָׁנָה	חֲנוֹךְ	וַיְחִי	Constituents
five years and sixty years	*Chanokh*	*and he lived*	**Translation**
		Theme	**Textuality**
	Subject	Finite	**Mood**
Scope	Actor	Process	**Transitivity**

וַיְחִי. Theme: textual > clause conj + Theme: experiential / Finite > wayyiqtol 3ms / Process > qal חיה.

חֲנוֹךְ. Subject > ms / Actor > nominal group: noun proper.

חָמֵשׁ וְשִׁשִּׁים שָׁנָה. Scope > nominal group: numeral fs ׀ group conj + numeral fp ׀ noun common fs.

וַיּוֹלֶד אֶת־מְתוּשָׁלַח. (b) Textuality > conj paratactic expansion / Mood > declarative: past / Transitivity > material: action.

אֶת־מְתוּשָׁלַח	וַיּוֹלֶד	**Constituents**
Metushalach	*and he fathered*	**Translation**
	Theme	**Textuality**
	Finite	**Mood**
Goal	Process	**Transitivity**

וַיּוֹלֶד. Theme: textual > clause conj + Theme: experiential / Finite > wayyiqtol 3ms / Process > hifil ילד.

אֶת־מְתוּשָׁלַח. Goal > nominal group: goal marker - noun proper ms.

5:22 // וַיִּתְהַלֵּךְ חֲנוֹךְ אֶת־הָאֱלֹהִים אַחֲרֵי הוֹלִידוֹ אֶת־
מְתוּשֶׁלַח שְׁלֹשׁ מֵאוֹת שָׁנָה // וַיּוֹלֶד בָּנִים וּבָנוֹת׃

וַיִּתְהַלֵּךְ חֲנוֹךְ אֶת־הָאֱלֹהִים אַחֲרֵי הוֹלִידוֹ אֶת־מְתוּשֶׁלַח שְׁלֹשׁ מֵאוֹת שָׁנָה. (a) Textuality > conj paratactic expansion / Mood > declarative: past / Transitivity > material: action.

שְׁלֹשׁ מֵאוֹת שָׁנָה	[[אַחֲרֵי הוֹלִידוֹ אֶת־מְתוּשֶׁלַח]]	אֶת־הָאֱלֹהִים	חֲנוֹךְ	וַיִּתְהַלֵּךְ	**Constituents**
three hundred years	*after his fathering Metushelach*	*with the deity*	*Chanokh*	*and he walked*	**Translation**
				Theme	**Textuality**
			Subject	Finite	**Mood**
Scope	Circumstance	Circumstance	Actor	Process	**Transitivity**

וַיִּתְהַלֵּךְ. Theme: textual > clause conj + Theme: experiential / Finite > wayyiqtol 3ms / Process > hitpael הלך.

חֲנוֹךְ. Subject > ms / Actor > nominal group: noun proper.

אֶת־הָאֱלֹהִים. Circumstance: accompaniment > prep phrase: prep - def art + noun common mp. Notice that the definite article defines *deity* or *deities* here.

אַחֲרֵי הוֹלִידוֹ אֶת־מְתוּשֶׁלַח. (i) Circumstance >> Textuality > embedded prep clause / Transitivity > material: action.

אֶת־מְתוּשֶׁלַח	הוֹלִידוֹ	אַחֲרֵי	**Constituents**
Metushelach	*his fathering*	*after*	**Translation**
	Theme	Theme	**Textuality**
Goal	Process + Actor		**Transitivity**

אַחֲרֵי. Theme: textual > prep.

הוֹלִידוֹ. Theme: experiential / Process > inf const hifil ילד + Actor > pronoun suffix 3ms, antecedent is חֲנוֹךְ *Chanokh* preceding the embedded clause.

אֶת־מְתוּשֶׁלַח. Goal > nominal group: goal marker - noun proper ms.

שְׁלֹשׁ מֵאוֹת שָׁנָה. Scope > nominal group: numeral fs | numeral fp | noun common fs.

וַיּוֹלֶד בָּנִים וּבָנוֹת. (b) Textuality > conj paratactic expansion / Mood > declarative: past / Transitivity > material: action.

בָּנִים וּבָנוֹת	וַיּוֹלֶד	**Constituents**
sons and daughters	*and he fathered*	**Translation**
	Theme	**Textuality**
	Finite	**Mood**
Goal	Process	**Transitivity**

וַיּוֹלֶד. Theme: textual > clause conj + Theme: experiential / Finite > wayyiqtol 3ms / Process > hifil ילד.

בָּנִים וּבָנוֹת. Goal > nominal group complex: noun common mp | group conj + noun common fp.

5:23 // וַיְהִ֖י כָּל־יְמֵ֣י חֲנ֑וֹךְ חָמֵ֤שׁ וְשִׁשִּׁים֙ שָׁנָ֔ה וּשְׁלֹ֥שׁ מֵא֖וֹת שָׁנָֽה׃

וַיְהִי כָּל־יְמֵי חֲנוֹךְ חָמֵשׁ וְשִׁשִּׁים שָׁנָה וּשְׁלֹשׁ מֵאוֹת שָׁנָה. (a) Textuality > conj paratactic expansion / Mood > declarative: past / Transitivity > relational: attribution.

חָמֵשׁ וְשִׁשִּׁים שָׁנָה וּשְׁלֹשׁ מֵאוֹת שָׁנָה	כָּל־יְמֵי חֲנוֹךְ	וַיְהִי	**Constituents**
five and sixty years and three hundred years	*all the days of Chanokh*	*and he was*	**Translation**
		Theme	**Textuality**
	Subject	Finite	**Mood**
Attribute	Carrier	Process	**Transitivity**

וַיְהִי. Theme: textual > clause conj + Theme: experiential / Finite > wayyiqtol 3ms / Process > qal היה.

כָּל־יְמֵי חֲנוֹךְ. Subject > ms (כָּל) / Carrier > nominal group: noun common collective ms const - noun common mp const - noun proper

3ms. The ms Subject כָּל is congruent with the 3ms Finite וַיְהִי; this is also the case in the analogous clause 5:31(a) which also has כָּל־יְמֵי as its Carrier. However, in 5:5(a) and seven other clauses in chapter 5 which have כָּל־יְמֵי as the Carrier, the Finite is וַיִּהְיוּ. There appears, then, to be some variability in whether the ms כָּל was considered to be the grammatical Subject or the mp יְמֵי. Or, כָּל, being a collective noun, was considered oftentimes to be plural.

חָמֵשׁ וְשִׁשִּׁים שָׁנָה וּשְׁלֹשׁ מֵאוֹת שָׁנָה. Scope > nominal group complex: numeral fs ı group conj + numeral fp ı noun common fs ı group conj + numeral fs ı numeral fp ı noun common fs.

5:24 // וַיִּתְהַלֵּךְ חֲנוֹךְ אֶת־הָאֱלֹהִים | וְאֵינֶנּוּ / כִּי־לָקַח אֹתוֹ אֱלֹהִים׃ פ

וַיִּתְהַלֵּךְ חֲנוֹךְ אֶת־הָאֱלֹהִים. (a) Textuality > conj paratactic expansion / Mood > declarative: past / Transitivity > material: action.

אֶת־הָאֱלֹהִים	חֲנוֹךְ	וַיִּתְהַלֵּךְ	**Constituents**
with the deity	*Chanokh*	*and he walked*	**Translation**
		Theme	**Textuality**
	Subject	Finite	**Mood**
Circumstance	Actor	Process	**Transitivity**

וַיִּתְהַלֵּךְ. Theme: textual > clause conj + Theme: experiential / Finite > wayyiqtol 3ms / Process > hitpael of הלך.

חֲנוֹךְ. Subject > ms / Actor > nominal group: noun proper.

אֶת־הָאֱלֹהִים. Circumstance: accompaniment > prep phrase: prep - def art + noun common mp. *Deity* is again found with the definite article; see 5:22(a).

וְאֵינֶנּוּ. (b) Textuality > conj paratactic expansion / Mood > declarative: non-past / Transitivity > existential.

וְאֵינֶנּוּ	**Constituents**
and he is not	**Translation**
Theme	**Textuality**
Subject	**Mood**
Process + Existent	**Transitivity**

וְאֵינֶנּוּ. Theme: textual > clause conj + Theme: experiential / Process > negative adjunct + Existent > pronoun suffix 3ms, antecedent is חֲנוֹךְ *Chanokh* in the prior clause.

כִּי־לָקַח אֹתוֹ אֱלֹהִים. (c) Textuality > conj hypotactic expansion / Mood > declarative: past / Transitivity > material: action.

אֱלֹהִים	אֹתוֹ	לָקַח	כִּי־	**Constituents**
deity	*him*	*he took*	*because*	**Translation**
		Theme	Theme	**Textuality**
Subject		Finite		**Mood**
Actor	Goal	Process		**Transitivity**

כִּי־. Theme: textual > conj.

לָקַח. Theme: experiential / Finite > qatal 3ms / Process > qal לקח.

אֹתוֹ. Goal > goal marker + pronoun suffix 3ms, antecedent is חֲנוֹךְ *Chanokh* in clause (a).

אֱלֹהִים. Subject > mp / Actor > nominal group: noun common mp. *Deity* does not have the definite article in this instance.

Genesis 5:25-27

[25]And Metushelach lived 187 years. And he fathered Lemekh. [26]And Metushelach lived, after his fathering Lemekh, 782 years. And he fathered sons and daughters. [27]And all the days of Metushelach were 969 years. And he died.

5:25 /// וַיְחִי מְתוּשֶׁלַח שֶׁבַע וּשְׁמֹנִים שָׁנָה וּמְאַת שָׁנָה
// וַיּוֹלֶד אֶת־לָמֶךְ׃

וַיְחִי מְתוּשֶׁלַח. (a) Textuality > conj paratactic expansion / Mood > declarative: past / Transitivity > material: event.

שֶׁבַע וּשְׁמֹנִים שָׁנָה וּמְאַת שָׁנָה	מְתוּשֶׁלַח	וַיְחִי	**Constituents**
seven and eighty years and a hundred years	*Metushelach*	*and he lived*	**Translation**
		Theme	**Textuality**
	Subject	Finite	**Mood**
Scope	Actor	Process	**Transitivity**

וַיְחִי. Theme: textual > clause conj + Theme: experiential / Finite > wayyiqtol 3ms / Process > qal חיה.

מְתוּשֶׁלַח. Subject > ms / Actor > nominal group: noun proper.

שֶׁבַע וּשְׁמֹנִים שָׁנָה וּמְאַת שָׁנָה. Scope > nominal group complex: numeral fs | group conj + numeral fp | noun common fs | numeral fs | noun common fs.

וַיּוֹלֶד אֶת־לָמֶךְ. (b) Textuality > conj paratactic expansion / Mood > declarative: past / Transitivity > material: action.

אֶת־לָמֶךְ	וַיּוֹלֶד	**Constituents**
Lemekh	*and he fathered*	**Translation**
	Theme	**Textuality**
	Finite	**Mood**
Goal	Process	**Transitivity**

וַיּוֹלֶד. Theme: textual > clause conj + Theme: experiential / Finite > wayyiqtol 3ms / Process > hifil ילד.

אֶת־לָמֶךְ. Goal > nominal group: goal marker - noun proper ms. The *qamets* is due to stress lengthening.

5:26 // וַיְחִ֣י מְתוּשֶׁ֗לַח אַחֲרֵי֙ הוֹלִיד֣וֹ אֶת־לֶ֔מֶךְ שְׁתַּ֤יִם
וּשְׁמוֹנִים֙ שָׁנָ֔ה וּשְׁבַ֥ע מֵא֖וֹת שָׁנָ֑ה // וַיּ֥וֹלֶד בָּנִ֖ים
וּבָנֽוֹת׃

וַיְחִי מְתוּשֶׁלַח [[אַחֲרֵי הוֹלִידוֹ אֶת־לֶמֶךְ]] שְׁתַּיִם וּשְׁמוֹנִים שָׁנָה וּשְׁבַע מֵאוֹת שָׁנָה. (a) Textuality > conj paratactic expansion / Mood > declarative: past / Transitivity > material: event.

שְׁתַּיִם וּשְׁמוֹנִים שָׁנָה וּשְׁבַע מֵאוֹת שָׁנָה	[[אַחֲרֵי הוֹלִידוֹ אֶת־לֶמֶךְ]]	מְתוּשֶׁלַח	וַיְחִי	**Constituents**
two and eighty years and seven hundred years	*after his fathering Lemekh*	*Metushelach*	*and he lived*	**Translation**
			Theme	**Textuality**
		Subject	Finite	**Mood**
Scope	Circumstance	Actor	Process	**Transitivity**

וַיְחִי. Theme: textual > clause conj + Theme: experiential / Finite > wayyiqtol 3ms / Process > qal חיה.

מְתוּשֶׁלַח. Subject > ms / Actor > nominal group: noun proper.

אַחֲרֵי הוֹלִידוֹ אֶת־לֶמֶךְ. (i) Circumstance >> Textuality > embedded prep clause / Transitivity > material: action.

אֶת־לֶמֶךְ	הוֹלִידוֹ	אַחֲרֵי	**Constituents**
Lemekh	*his fathering*	*after*	**Translation**
	Theme	Theme	**Textuality**
Goal	Process + Actor		**Transitivity**

אַחֲרֵי. Theme: textual > prep.

הוֹלִידוֹ. Theme: experiential / Process > inf const hifil ילד + Actor > pronoun suffix 3ms, antecedent is מְתוּשֶׁלַח *Metushelach* preceding the embedded clause.

אֶת־לֶמֶךְ. Goal > nominal group: goal marker - noun proper ms.

שְׁתַּיִם וּשְׁמוֹנִים שָׁנָה וּשְׁבַע מֵאוֹת שָׁנָה. Scope > nominal group complex: numeral fd | group conj + numeral fp | noun common fs | group conj + numeral fs | numeral fp | noun common fs.

וַיּוֹלֶד בָּנִים וּבָנוֹת. (b) Textuality > conj paratactic expansion / Mood > declarative: past / Transitivity > material: action.

בָּנִים וּבָנוֹת	וַיּוֹלֶד	**Constituents**
sons and daughters	*and he fathered*	**Translation**
	Theme	**Textuality**
	Finite	**Mood**
Goal	Process	**Transitivity**

וַיּוֹלֶד. Theme: textual > clause conj + Theme: experiential / Finite > wayyiqtol 3ms / Process > hifil ילד.

בָּנִים וּבָנוֹת. Goal > nominal group complex: noun common mp | group conj + noun common fp.

5:27 // וַיִּהְיוּ כָּל־יְמֵי מְתוּשֶׁלַח תֵּשַׁע וְשִׁשִּׁים שָׁנָה וּתְשַׁע
מֵאוֹת שָׁנָה // וַיָּמֹת: פ

וַיִּהְיוּ כָּל־יְמֵי מְתוּשֶׁלַח. (a) Textuality > conj paratactic expansion / Mood > declarative: past / Transitivity > relational: attribution.

תֵּשַׁע וְשִׁשִּׁים שָׁנָה וּתְשַׁע מֵאוֹת שָׁנָה	כָּל־יְמֵי מְתוּשֶׁלַח	וַיִּהְיוּ	**Constituents**
nine and sixty years and nine hundred years	*all the days of Metushelach*	*and they were*	**Translation**
		Theme	**Textuality**
	Subject	Finite	**Mood**
Attribute	Carrier	Process	**Transitivity**

וַיִּֽהְיוּ. Theme: textual > clause conj + Theme: experiential / Finite > wayyiqtol 3mp / Process > qal היה.

כָּל־יְמֵי מְתוּשֶׁלַח. Subject > ms / Carrier > nominal group: noun common collective ms const - noun common mp const - noun proper ms. See comments to 5:5(a).

תֵּשַׁע וְשִׁשִּׁים שָׁנָה וּתְשַׁע מֵאוֹת שָׁנָה. Scope > nominal group complex: numeral fs ׀ group conj + numeral fp ׀ noun common fs ׀ group conj + numeral fs ׀ numeral fp ׀ noun common fs.

וַיָּמֹת. (b) Textuality > conj paratactic expansion / Mood > declarative: past / Transitivity > material: event.

וַיָּמֹת	**Constituents**
and he died	**Translation**
Theme	**Textuality**
Finite	**Mood**
Process	**Transitivity**

וַיָּמֹת. Theme: textual > clause conj + Theme: experiential / Finite > wayyiqtol 3ms / Process > qal מות.

Genesis 5:28-31

[28]And Lemekh lived 182 years. And he fathered a son. [29]And he called his name Noach saying, "This one will comfort us from our work and from the toil of our hands, from the ground, which YHVH cursed." [30]And Lemekh lived, after his fathering Noach, 575 years. And he fathered sons and daughters. [31]And all the days of Lemekh were 777 years. And he died.

5:28 /// וַֽיְחִי־לֶ֕מֶךְ שְׁתַּ֧יִם וּשְׁמֹנִ֛ים שָׁנָ֖ה וּמְאַ֣ת שָׁנָ֑ה // וַיּ֖וֹלֶד בֵּֽן׃

וַיְחִי־לֶמֶךְ שְׁתַּיִם וּשְׁמֹנִים שָׁנָה וּמְאַת שָׁנָה. (a) Textuality >

conj paratactic expansion / Mood > declarative: past / Transitivity > material: event.

שְׁתַּיִם וּשְׁמֹנִים שָׁנָה וּמְאַת שָׁנָה	לֶמֶךְ	וַיְחִי־	**Constituents**
two and eighty years and a hundred years	*Lemekh*	*and he lived*	**Translation**
		Theme	**Textuality**
	Subject	Finite	**Mood**
Scope	Actor	Process	**Transitivity**

וַיְחִי־. Theme: textual > clause conj + Theme: experiential / Finite > wayyiqtol 3ms / Process > qal חיה.

לֶמֶךְ. Subject > ms / Actor > nominal group: noun proper.

שְׁתַּיִם וּשְׁמֹנִים שָׁנָה וּמְאַת שָׁנָה. Scope > nominal group complex: numeral fd | group conj + numeral fp | noun common fs | group conj + numeral fs | noun common fs.

וַיּוֹלֶד בֵּן. (b) Textuality > conj paratactic expansion / Mood > declarative: past / Transitivity > material: action.

בֵּן	וַיּוֹלֶד	**Constituents**
a son	*and he fathered*	**Translation**
	Theme	**Textuality**
	Finite	**Mood**
Goal	Process	**Transitivity**

וַיּוֹלֶד. Theme: textual > clause conj + Theme: experiential / Finite > wayyiqtol 3ms / Process > hifil ילד.

בֵּן. Goal > nominal group: noun common ms.

5:29 // וַיִּקְרָא אֶת־שְׁמוֹ נֹחַ לֵאמֹר // זֶה יְנַחֲמֵנוּ
מִמַּעֲשֵׂנוּ וּמֵעִצְּבוֹן יָדֵינוּ מִן־הָאֲדָמָה אֲשֶׁר אֵרְרָהּ
יְהוָה׃

וַיִּקְרָא אֶת־שְׁמוֹ נֹחַ לֵאמֹר. (a) Textuality > conj paratactic expansion / Mood > declarative: past / Transitivity > verbal.

לֵאמֹר	נֹחַ	אֶת־שְׁמוֹ	וַיִּקְרָא	**Constituents**
by saying	*Noach*	*his name*	*and he called*	**Translation**
			Theme	**Textuality**
			Finite	**Mood**
Circumstance	Verbiage	Target	Process	**Transitivity**

וַיִּקְרָא. Theme: textual > clause conj + Theme: experiential / Finite > wayyiqtol 3ms / Process > qal **קרא**.

אֶת־שְׁמוֹ. Target > nominal group: goal marker - noun common ms const + pronoun suffix 3ms, antecedent is בֵּן *son* in the prior clause.

נֹחַ. Verbiage > nominal group: noun proper ms.

לֵאמֹר. Circumstance: manner, means > prep phrase: prep + Process > inf const qal **אמר**. In origin this is an embedded clause; it has been grammaticalized as a quote marker. It is not found before every quote, but is limited in distribution. See Miller (1996).

זֶה יְנַחֲמֵנוּ מִמַּעֲשֵׂנוּ וּמֵעִצְּבוֹן יָדֵינוּ מִן־הָאֲדָמָה [[אֲשֶׁר אֵרְרָהּ יְהוָה]]. (b) Textuality > appositive paratactic projection: quote / Mood > declarative: non-past / Transitivity > material: action.

מִמַּעֲשֵׂנוּ וּמֵעִצְּבוֹן יָדֵינוּ מִן־הָאֲדָמָה [[אֲשֶׁר אֵרְרָהּ יְהוָה]]	יְנַחֲמֵנוּ	זֶה	**Constituents**
from our work and from the toil of our hands, from the ground, which YHVH cursed her	*he will comfort us*	*this*	**Translation**
		Theme	**Textuality**
	Finite	Subject	**Mood**
Scope	Process + Beneficiary	Actor	**Transitivity**

זֶה. Theme: experiential / Subject > ms / Actor > pronoun demonstrative, antecedent is **נֹחַ** *Noach* in the prior clause.

יְנַחֲמֵנוּ. Finite > yiqtol 3ms / Process > piel **נחם** + Beneficiary > pronoun suffix 1cp, antecedent is **לֶמֶךְ** *Lemekh*, and since it is plural, presumably he is speaking also for all of humankind.

מִמַּעֲשֵׂנוּ וּמֵעִצְּבוֹן יָדֵינוּ מִן־הָאֲדָמָה [[אֲשֶׁר אֵרְרָהּ יְהוָה]]. Scope > prep phrase complex: this complex consists of three **מִן** prep phrases. The first two are sub-grouped together, and the third appears to be an appositive expansion of the preceding sub-group. The third prep phrase is itself expanded by an embedded relative clause.

מִמַּעֲשֵׂנוּ וּמֵעִצְּבוֹן יָדֵינוּ. Prep phrase complex: prep phrase 1 + prep phase 2.

מִמַּעֲשֵׂנוּ. Prep phrase 1 > prep + noun common fs const + pronoun suffix 1cp, antecedent is **לֶמֶךְ** *Lemekh* and all humankind.

וּמֵעִצְּבוֹן יָדֵינוּ. Prep phrase 2 > group conj + prep + noun common ms const | noun common fem dual const + pronoun suffix 1cp, antecedent is **לֶמֶךְ** *Lemekh* and all humankind.

מִן־הָאֲדָמָה [[אֲשֶׁר אֵרְרָהּ יְהוָה]]. Prep phrase complex > Head (prep phrase 3) + Post-modifier (expansion). This appositive complex expands the meaning of the preceding prep phrase complex by giving it greater specificity; by so doing it connects this clause to Genesis 3:17 and 4:11, both of which mention **ארר** and **הָאֲדָמָה**, and 3:17 additionally mentions **עִצָּבוֹן**.

מִן־הָאֲדָמָה. Prep phrase 3 > prep - def art + noun common fs.

אֲשֶׁר אֵרְרָהּ יְהוָה. (i) Expansion >> Textuality > embedded expansion: relative clause / Mood > declarative: past / Process > verbal. The embedded clause gives greater specificity to its antecedent **הָאֲדָמָה**.

יְהוָה	אֵרְרָהּ	אֲשֶׁר	**Constituents**
YHVH	*he cursed her*	*which*	**Translation**
		Theme	**Textuality**
Subject	Finite		**Mood**
Sayer	Process + Target	Target	**Transitivity**

אֲשֶׁר. Theme: textual > pronoun relative / Target > antecedent הָאֲדָמָה *the ground* immediately preceding. This functions as a type of preposed Theme. Of course, structurally it has to be first in the clause, but it is substituted later by the pronoun suffix on אֵרְרָהּ, which gives it that preposed feel.

אֵרְרָהּ. Finite > qatal 3ms / Process > piel ארר + Target > pronoun suffix 3fs, antecedent is again הָאֲדָמָה *the ground.*

יְהוָה. Subject > ms / Sayer > nominal group: noun proper.

5:30 // וַֽיְחִי־לֶ֗מֶךְ אַֽחֲרֵי֙ הוֹלִיד֣וֹ אֶת־נֹ֔חַ חָמֵ֤שׁ וְתִשְׁעִים֙
שָׁנָ֔ה וַחֲמֵ֥שׁ מֵאֹ֖ת שָׁנָ֑ה // וַיּ֥וֹלֶד בָּנִ֖ים וּבָנֽוֹת׃

וַיְחִי־לֶמֶךְ [[אַחֲרֵי הוֹלִידוֹ אֶת־נֹחַ]] חָמֵשׁ וְתִשְׁעִים שָׁנָה וַחֲמֵשׁ מֵאֹת שָׁנָה. (a) Textuality > conj paratactic expansion / Mood > declarative: past / Transitivity > material: event.

חָמֵשׁ וְתִשְׁעִים שָׁנָה וַחֲמֵשׁ מֵאֹת שָׁנָה	[[אַחֲרֵי הוֹלִידוֹ אֶת־נֹחַ]]	לֶמֶךְ	וַיְחִי־	**Constituents**
five and seventy years and five hundred years	*after his fathering Noach*	*Lemekh*	*and he lived*	**Translation**
			Theme	**Textuality**
		Subject	Finite	**Mood**
Scope	Circumstance	Actor	Process	**Transitivity**

וַיְחִי־. Theme: textual > clause conj + Theme: experiential / Finite > wayyiqtol 3ms / Process > qal חיה.

לֶמֶךְ. Subject > ms / Actor > nominal group: noun proper.

אַחֲרֵי הוֹלִידוֹ אֶת־נֹחַ. (i) Circumstance >> Textuality > embedded prep clause / Transitivity > material: action.

אֶת־נֹחַ	הוֹלִידוֹ	אַחֲרֵי	**Constituents**
Noach	*his fathering*	*after*	**Translation**
	Theme	Theme	**Textuality**
Goal	Process + Actor		**Transitivity**

אַחֲרֵי. Theme: textual > prep.

הוֹלִידוֹ. Theme: experiential / Process > inf const hifil ילד + Actor > pronoun suffix 3ms, antecedent is לֶמֶךְ *Lemekh* preceding the embedded clause.

אֶת־נֹחַ. Goal > nominal group: goal marker - noun proper ms.

חָמֵשׁ וְתִשְׁעִים שָׁנָה וַחֲמֵשׁ מֵאֹת שָׁנָה. Scope > nominal group complex: numeral | group conj + numeral | noun common fs | group conj + numeral | numeral | noun common fs.

וַיּוֹלֶד בָּנִים וּבָנוֹת. (b) Textuality > conj paratactic expansion / Mood > declarative: past / Transitivity > material: action.

בָּנִים וּבָנוֹת	וַיּוֹלֶד	**Constituents**
sons and daughters	*and he fathered*	**Translation**
	Theme	**Textuality**
	Finite	**Mood**
Goal	Process	**Transitivity**

וַיּוֹלֶד. Theme: textual > clause conj + Theme: experiential / Finite > wayyiqtol 3ms / Process > hifil ילד.

בָּנִים וּבָנוֹת. Goal > nominal group complex: noun common mp | group conj + noun common fp.

5:31 // וַיְהִי֙ כָּל־יְמֵי־לֶ֔מֶךְ שֶׁ֤בַע וְשִׁבְעִים֙ שָׁנָ֔ה וּשְׁבַ֥ע
מֵא֖וֹת שָׁנָ֑ה // וַיָּמֹֽת׃ ס

וַיְהִי כָּל־יְמֵי־לֶמֶךְ שֶׁבַע וְשִׁבְעִים שָׁנָה וּשְׁבַע מֵאוֹת שָׁנָה. (a) Textuality > conj paratactic expansion / Mood > declarative: past / Transitivity > relational: attribution.

שֶׁבַע וְשִׁבְעִים שָׁנָה וּשְׁבַע מֵאוֹת שָׁנָה	כָּל־יְמֵי־לֶמֶךְ	וַיְהִי	**Constituents**
seven and seventy years and seven hundred years	*all of the days of Lemekh*	*and he was*	**Translation**
		Theme	**Textuality**
	Subject	Finite	**Mood**
Attribute	Carrier	Process	**Transitivity**

וַיְהִי. Theme: textual > clause conj + Theme: experiential / Finite > wayyiqtol 3ms / Process > qal היה.

כָּל־יְמֵי־לֶמֶךְ. Subject > ms / Carrier > nominal group: noun common collective ms const - noun common mp const - noun proper ms. See comments to 5:5(a).

שֶׁבַע וְשִׁבְעִים שָׁנָה וּשְׁבַע מֵאוֹת שָׁנָה. Attribute > nominal group complex: numeral fs ı group conj + numeral fp ı noun common fs ı group conj + numeral fs ı numeral fp ı noun common fs.

וַיָּמֹת. (b) Textuality > conj paratactic expansion / Mood > declarative: past / Transitivity > material: event.

וַיָּמֹת	**Constituents**
and he died	**Translation**
Theme	**Textuality**
Finite	**Mood**
Process	**Transitivity**

וַיָּמֹת. Theme: textual > clause conj + Theme: experiential / Finite > wayyiqtol 3ms / Process > qal מות.

Genesis 5:32

[32]And Noach was 500 years old. And Noach fathered Shem, Cham, and Yefet.

5:32 /// וַֽיְהִי־נֹ֕חַ בֶּן־חֲמֵ֥שׁ מֵא֖וֹת שָׁנָ֑ה // וַיּ֣וֹלֶד נֹ֔חַ אֶת־
שֵׁ֖ם אֶת־חָ֥ם וְאֶת־יָֽפֶת׃

וַיְהִי־נֹחַ בֶּן־חֲמֵשׁ מֵאוֹת שָׁנָה. (a) Textuality > conj paratactic expansion / Mood > declarative: past / Transitivity > relational: attribution.

בֶּן־חֲמֵשׁ מֵאוֹת שָׁנָה	נֹחַ	וַיְהִי־	**Constituents**
a son of five hundred years	*Noach*	*and he was*	**Translation**
	Theme	Theme	**Textuality**
	Subject	Finite	**Mood**
Attribute	Carrier	Process	**Transitivity**

וַיְהִי־. Theme: textual > clause conj + Theme: experiential / Finite > wayyiqtol 3ms / Process > qal היה.

נֹחַ. Subject > ms / Carrier > nominal group: noun proper.

בֶּן־חֲמֵשׁ מֵאוֹת שָׁנָה. Attribute > nominal group: noun common fs const - numeral fs | numeral fp | noun common fs.

וַיּוֹלֶד נֹחַ אֶת־שֵׁם אֶת־חָם וְאֶת־יָפֶת. (b) Textuality > conj paratactic expansion / Mood > declarative: past / Transitivity > material: action.

אֶת־שֵׁם אֶת־חָם וְאֶת־יָפֶת	נֹחַ	וַיּוֹלֶד	**Constituents**
Shem Cham and Yefet	*Noach*	*and he fathered*	**Translation**
		Theme	**Textuality**
	Subject	Finite	**Mood**
Goal	Actor	Process	**Transitivity**

וַיּוֹלֶד. Theme: textual > clause conj + Theme: experiential / Finite > wayyiqtol 3ms / Process > hifil ילד.

נֹחַ. Subject > ms / Actor > nominal group: noun proper.

אֶת־שֵׁם אֶת־חָם וְאֶת־יָפֶת. Goal > nominal group complex: goal marker - noun proper ׀ goal marker - noun proper ׀ group conj + goal marker - noun proper ms. The *qamets* in יָפֶת is due to stress lengthening.

Genesis 6:1-4

[1]And it was, when humankind began to multiply on the face of the ground, and daughters were born to them, [2]and the sons of the deity saw the daughters of the humankind, that they are good. And they took for themselves women from all which they chose. [3]And YHVH said, "My spirit will not remain in the humankind forever. Since also he is flesh, his days will be 120 years." [4]And the Nefilim were in the earth in those days —and also afterwards—when the sons of the deity come to the daughters of the humankind and they bear for them. They are the warriors, who from eternity are the men of the name.

6:1 /// וַיְהִי֙ // כִּֽי־הֵחֵ֣ל הָֽאָדָ֔ם לָרֹ֖ב עַל־פְּנֵ֣י הָֽאֲדָמָ֑ה //
וּבָנ֖וֹת יֻלְּד֥וּ לָהֶֽם׃

וַיְהִי֙. (a) Textuality > conj paratactic expansion / Mood > declarative: past / Transitivity > existential process. There is no explicit Subject / Existent in this clause and no prior component that may be absent by ellipsis. This clause functions as the Theme, so to speak, of the clause complex which it introduces. As Theme, it indicates that the following episode happened. It is, after all, a rather strange event, maybe so even in the day of the narrator, and its happenedness needed to be asserted.

וַיְהִי	**Constituents**
and it was	**Translation**
Theme	**Textuality**
Finite	**Mood**
Process	**Transitivity**

וַיְהִי. Theme: textual > clause conj + Theme: experiential / Finite > wayyiqtol 3ms / Process > qal היה.

כִּי־הֵחֵל הָאָדָם לָרֹב עַל־פְּנֵי הָאֲדָמָה. (b) Textuality > conj hypotactic expansion: temporal / Mood > declarative: past / Transitivity > material: action.

עַל־פְּנֵי הָאֲדָמָה	לָרֹב	הָאָדָם	הֵחֵל	כִּי־	**Constituents**
on the face of the ground	*to multiply*	*the human-kind*	*he began*	*when*	**Translation**
				Theme	**Textuality**
		Subject	Finite		**Mood**
Circumstance	Process	Actor	Process		**Transitivity**

כִּי־. Theme: textual > conj.

הֵחֵל. Theme: experiential / Finite > qatal 3ms / Process > hifil חלל. Along with לָרֹב it forms a verbal group complex. Typically the two components of a verbal group complex (Finite + Non-finite) are not separated by another constituent, but here the Subject / Actor intervenes. The first verb in a verbal group complex often relates the manner in which the main process unfolds, such as beginning, adding, continuing, and stopping. In this clause הֵחֵל *he* (i.e. *they*) *began* relates the start of the main process לָרֹב *to multiply.*

הָאָדָם. Subject > ms / Actor > nominal group: noun common collective.

לָרֹב. Prep + Process > inf const qal רבב.

עַל־פְּנֵי הָאֲדָמָה. Circumstance > prep phrase: prep - noun common mp const | def art + noun common fs.

וּבָנוֹת יֻלְּדוּ לָהֶם. (c) Textuality > conj hypotactic expansion / Mood > declarative: past / Transitivity > material: action. This clause is coordinated with the prior clause, and together they are a hypotactic clause complex that is dependent on clause 6:1(d). The process in clause (c) is expressed using a passive stem, the pual. We might ask ourselves why the representational meaning of this clause was not expressed using an active stem, such as *and they had daughters,* with הָאָדָם *the humankind* as the Subject / Actor. The reason may lie in transitivity structures. With males, ילד is used in the hifil stem; with females it is used in the qal stem. Perhaps to avoid specifying agency and to be gender inclusive, pual was chosen as the most appropriate stem.

לָהֶם	יֻלְּדוּ	וּבָנוֹת	**Constituents**
to them	*they were born*	*and daughters*	**Translation**
		Theme	**Textuality**
	Finite	Subject	**Mood**
Beneficiary	Process	Goal	**Transitivity**

וּבָנוֹת. Theme: textual > clause conj + Theme: experiential / Subject > fp / Goal > nominal group: noun common.

יֻלְּדוּ. Finite > qatal 3fp / Process > pual ילד.

לָהֶם. Beneficiary > prep phrase: prep + pronoun suffix 3mp, antecedent is הָאָדָם *the humankind* in the prior clause. It seems that when the collective term הָאָדָם appears explicitly in a clause, it is treated as singular by the Finite verb in that clause. But when it is later referenced, as it is here by לָהֶם *to them*, it is treated as a plural.

6:2 // וַיִּרְאוּ בְנֵי־הָאֱלֹהִים אֶת־בְּנוֹת הָאָדָם / כִּי טֹבֹת
הֵנָּה // וַיִּקְחוּ לָהֶם נָשִׁים מִכֹּל אֲשֶׁר בָּחָרוּ׃

וַיִּרְאוּ בְנֵי־הָאֱלֹהִים אֶת־בְּנוֹת הָאָדָם. (a) Textuality > conj paratactic expansion / Mood > declarative: past / Transitivity > mental: perception.

אֶת־בְּנוֹת הָאָדָם	בְנֵי־הָאֱלֹהִים	וַיִּרְאוּ	**Constituents**
the daughters of the humankind	*the sons of the deity*	*and they saw*	**Translation**
		Theme	**Textuality**
	Subject	Finite	**Mood**
Phenomenon	Senser	Process	**Transitivity**

וַיִּרְאוּ. Theme: textual > clause conj + Theme: experiential / Finite > wayyiqtol 3mp / Process > qal ראה.

בְנֵי־הָאֱלֹהִים. Subject > mp (בְּנֵי) / Senser > nominal group: noun common mp const - def art + noun common mp.

אֶת־בְּנוֹת הָאָדָם. Phenomenon > nominal group: goal marker - noun common fp const | def art + noun common collective ms.

כִּי טֹבֹת הֵנָּה. (b) Textuality > conj hypotactic projection: report / Mood > declarative: non-past / Transitivity > relational: attribution.

הֵנָּה	טֹבֹת	כִּי	**Constituents**
they	*good*	*that*	**Translation**
	Theme	Theme	**Textuality**
Subject	Complement		**Mood**
Carrier	Attribute		**Transitivity**

כִּי. Theme: textual > conj.

טֹבֹת. Theme: experiential / Complement > fp / Attribute > adj fp.

הֵנָּה. Subject > 3fp / Carrier > pronoun personal.

וַיִּקְחוּ לָהֶם נָשִׁים מִכֹּל [[אֲשֶׁר בָּחָרוּ]]. (c) Textuality > conj paratactic expansion / Mood > declarative: past / Transitivity > material: action. Subject / Actor is בְנֵי־הָאֱלֹהִים *the sons of the deity*, absent here by ellipsis.

נָשִׁים מִכֹּל [[אֲשֶׁר בָּחָרוּ]]	לָהֶם	וַיִּקְחוּ	**Constituents**
women from all which they chose	*for themselves*	*and they took*	**Translation**
		Theme	**Textuality**
		Finite	**Mood**
Goal	Beneficiary	Process	**Transitivity**

וַיִּקְחוּ. Theme: textual > clause conj + Theme: experiential / Finite > wayyiqtol 3mp / Process > qal לקח.

לָהֶם. Beneficiary > prep phrase: prep + pronoun suffix 3mp, antecedent is בְנֵי־הָאֱלֹהִים *the sons of the deity* in clause (a).

נָשִׁים מִכֹּל [[אֲשֶׁר בָּחָרוּ]]. Goal > nominal group: Head + Post-modifier. It is somewhat challenging to sort out this nominal group, in particular, to make sense of its prepositional phrase מִכֹּל *from all*. The relevant question is, from all of what? *All* is typically followed by another nominal, and we would seem to have two choices here: the nominal is either the embedded relative clause, or it is a noun which is absent by ellipsis. If it is the relative clause, it would result in a redundant statement something like *women from all of the women which they chose*. If it is elliptical, the logical antecedent is בְּנוֹת הָאָדָם *the daughters of the humankind* in clause (a), resulting in a meaning for the nominal group: *women from all (the daughters of humankind) which they chose* i.e *whichever women from all (the daughters of humankind) they chose.* The latter seems the logical choice.

נָשִׁים. Head > noun common fp.

מִכֹּל [[אֲשֶׁר בָּחָרוּ]]. Post-modifier > prep phrase complex: prep phrase + embedded clause.

מִכֹּל. Prep phrase > prep + noun common collective ms const.

אֲשֶׁר בָּחָרוּ. (i) Embedded clause >> Textuality > embedded: relative / Mood > declarative: past / Transitivity > material: action.

בָּחָרוּ	אֲשֶׁר	**Constituents**
they chose	*which*	**Translation**
	Theme	**Textuality**
Finite		**Mood**
Process	Goal	**Transitivity**

אֲשֶׁר. Theme: textual > pronoun relative + Theme: experiential / Goal > antecedent כֹּל *all.*

בָּחָרוּ. Finite > qatal 3mp / Process > qal בחר.

6:3 // וַיֹּאמֶר יְהוָה // לֹא־יָדוֹן רוּחִי בָאָדָם לְעֹלָם /
בְּשַׁגַּם הוּא בָשָׂר // וְהָיוּ יָמָיו מֵאָה וְעֶשְׂרִים שָׁנָה׃

וַיֹּאמֶר יְהוָה. (a) Textuality > conj paratactic expansion / Mood > declarative: past / Transitivity > verbal.

יְהוָה	וַיֹּאמֶר	**Constituents**
YHVH	*and he said*	**Translation**
	Theme	**Textuality**
Subject	Finite	**Mood**
Sayer	Process	**Transitivity**

וַיֹּאמֶר. Theme: textual > clause conj + Theme: experiential / Finite > wayyiqtol 3ms / Process > qal אמר.

יְהוָה. Subject > ms / Sayer > noun proper.

לֹא־יָדוֹן רוּחִי בָאָדָם לְעֹלָם. (b) Textuality > appositive paratactic projection: quote / Mood > declarative: non-past / Transitivity > material: action.

לְעֹלָם	בָאָדָם	רוּחִי	יָדוֹן	לֹא־	**Constituents**
to forever	*in the human-kind*	*my spirit*	*he will remain*	*not*	**Translation**
			Theme	Theme	**Textuality**
		Subject	Finite	Adjunct	**Mood**
Circumstance	Circumstance	Actor	Process		**Transitivity**

לֹא־. Theme: interpersonal / Adjunct: interpersonal > polarity: negative.

יָדוֹן. Theme > experiential / Finite > yiqtol 3ms / Process > qal דון. This word is a so-called *hapax legomenon* in biblical Hebrew, which is to say, a word from this root is found only here. The lexical meaning of this form is disputed, but converging lines of evidence suggest it means *abide*, *remain*.

רוּחִי. Subject > cs / Actor > nominal group: noun common cs + pronoun suffix 1cs, antecedent is יְהוָה *YHVH*.

בָאָדָם. Circumstance: location, place > prep phrase: prep + def art + noun common collective ms.

לְעֹלָם. Circumstance: location, time > prep phrase: prep + noun common ms.

בְּשַׁגַּם הוּא בָשָׂר. (c) Textuality > conj hypotactic expansion / Mood > declarative: non-past / Transitivity > relational: attribution. This clause has traditionally been interpreted as dependent on the prior clause. NRSV: *My spirit shall not abide in mortals forever, for they are flesh.* We are rendering it as dependent on the following clause, giving reason for a finite life span.

בָשָׂר	הוּא	בְּשַׁגַּם	**Constituents**
flesh	*he*	*in which also*	**Translation**
	Theme	Theme	**Textuality**
Complement	Subject		**Mood**
Attribute	Carrier		**Transitivity**

בְּשַׁגַּם. Theme: textual > prep phrase: prep + pronoun relative + adjunct. This word has three identifiable components, but their cumulative meaning is uncertain. It has traditionally been interpreted as a subordinating conjunction, hence the reason for reading this clause as hypotactic. NRSV translates it *for*.

הוּא. Theme: experiential / Subject > ms / Carrier > pronoun personal, antecedent is presumably אָדָם *humankind* in the prior clause, but in 6:1(c) the collective אָדָם was construed grammatically as a plural, attested by לָהֶם *to them*.

בָשָׂר. Complement > ms / Attribute > nominal group: noun common collective.

וְהָיוּ יָמָיו מֵאָה וְעֶשְׂרִים שָׁנָה. (d) Textuality > conj paratactic expansion / Mood > declarative: non-past / Transitivity > relational: attribution.

מֵאָה וְעֶשְׂרִים שָׁנָה	יָמָיו	וְהָיוּ	**Constituents**
a hundred and twenty years	*his days*	*and they will be*	**Translation**
		Theme	**Textuality**
	Subject	Finite	**Mood**
Attribute	Carrier	Process	**Transitivity**

וְהָיוּ. Theme: textual > clause conj + Theme: experiential / Finite > weqatal 3mp / Process > qal היה.

יָמָיו. Subject > mp / Carrier > nominal group: noun common const + pronoun suffix 3ms, antecedent is אָדָם *humankind*.

מֵאָה וְעֶשְׂרִים שָׁנָה. Attribute > nominal group: numeral fs ǀ group conj + numeral fp ǀ noun common fs.

6:4 // הַנְּפִלִים הָיוּ בָאָרֶץ בַּיָּמִים הָהֵם וְגַם אַחֲרֵי־כֵן
אֲשֶׁר יָבֹאוּ בְּנֵי הָאֱלֹהִים אֶל־בְּנוֹת הָאָדָם וְיָלְדוּ
לָהֶם // הֵמָּה הַגִּבֹּרִים אֲשֶׁר מֵעוֹלָם אַנְשֵׁי הַשֵּׁם׃ פ

(a) הַנְּפִלִים הָיוּ בָאָרֶץ בַּיָּמִים הָהֵם << וְגַם אַחֲרֵי־כֵן >> [[אֲשֶׁר יָבֹאוּ בְּנֵי הָאֱלֹהִים אֶל־בְּנוֹת הָאָדָם וְיָלְדוּ לָהֶם]]. Textuality > appositive paratactic expansion / Mood > declarative: past / Transitivity > existential.

בַּיָּמִים הָהֵם << וְגַם אַחֲרֵי־כֵן >> [[אֲשֶׁר יָבֹאוּ בְּנֵי הָאֱלֹהִים אֶל־בְּנוֹת הָאָדָם וְיָלְדוּ לָהֶם]]	בָאָרֶץ	הָיוּ	הַנְּפִלִים	**Constituents**
in those days—and also after so—when the sons of the deity come to the daughters of the humankind and they bore for them	*in the earth*	*they were*	*the Nefilim*	**Translation**
			Theme	**Textuality**
		Finite	Subject	**Mood**
Circumstance	Circumstance	Process	Existent	**Transitivity**

הַנְּפִלִים. Theme: experiential / Subject > mp / Existent > nominal group: def art + noun common. The attached definite article implies that these figures were well known to the hearers. They were not mentioned before, yet they are not otherwise accounted for.

הָיוּ. Finite > qatal 3mp / Process > qal היה.

בָּאָרֶץ. Circumstance: location, place > prep phrase: prep + def art + noun common fs.

בַּיָּמִים הָהֵם « וְגַם אַחֲרֵי־כֵן » [[אֲשֶׁר יָבֹאוּ בְּנֵי הָאֱלֹהִים אֶל־בְּנוֹת הָאָדָם וְיָלְדוּ לָהֶם]]. Circumstance: location, time > prep phrase complex: prep phrase + included clause + embedded clause.

בַּיָּמִים הָהֵם. Prep phrase > prep + def art + noun common mp | def art + pronoun demonstrative 3mp, antecedent is not a specific term but the prior account of events.

וְגַם אַחֲרֵי־כֵן. Minor clause > aside. There is no Process in this clause, and for this reason it is termed a minor clause. An included clause is contained within another clause, but it does not have a structural role in the clause that encloses it. This included clause is related to the clause that contains it only by non-structural cohesive reference. In this case the cohesive connection is established by גַּם *also* and by כֵּן *so, such*. This minor clause in its highly compressed form stands for this meaning: *and also the Nefilim/fallen ones were in the earth after those days.* This clause was most likely inserted at some later date by someone who considered the *Nefilim* still to be around.

וְגַם. Theme: textual > clause conj + Adjunct: textual > addition.

אַחֲרֵי־כֵן. Circumstance > prep phrase: prep - substitute. The word כֵּן *so, such* is a substitute for הַיָּמִים הָהֵם *those days*. This element is a conjunctive adjunct often used to refer to a prior clause complex.

אֲשֶׁר יָבֹאוּ בְּנֵי הָאֱלֹהִים אֶל־בְּנוֹת הָאָדָם. (i) Textuality > embedded expansion: relative clause / Mood > declarative: non-past / Process > material: action.

אֶל־בְּנוֹת הָאָדָם	בְּנֵי הָאֱלֹהִים	יָבֹאוּ	אֲשֶׁר	**Constituents**
to the daughters of the humankind	*the sons of the deity*	*they will go in*	*which*	**Translation**
			Theme	**Textuality**
	Subject	Finite		**Mood**
Circumstance	Actor	Process	Circumstance	**Transitivity**

אֲשֶׁר. Theme: textual > pronoun relative + Theme: experiential / Circumstance: location, time > antecedent הַיָּמִים הָהֵם *those days.*

יָבֹאוּ. Finite > yiqtol 3mp / Process > qal בוא.

בְּנֵי הָאֱלֹהִים. Subject > mp / Actor > nominal group: noun common mp const | def art + noun common mp.

אֶל־בְּנוֹת הָאָדָם. Circumstance: location, place > prep phrase: prep - noun common fp const | def art + noun common collective ms. The clause process is encoded as movement to a place, but presumably is a euphemism for sexual intercourse.

וְיָלְדוּ לָהֶם. (ii) Textuality > conj paratactic expansion of the first clause of the embedded relative clause / Mood > declarative: non-past / Transitivity > material: action. This clause, along with clause (a.i), constitutes the embedded relative clause. The Subject / Actor of the clause process is left unspecified and the verb form has common gender; logically it is בְּנוֹת הָאָדָם *the daughters of the humankind* in the preceding clause, and absent here by ellipsis.

לָהֶם	וְיָלְדוּ	**Constituents**
for them	*and they will bear*	**Translation**
	Theme	**Textuality**
	Finite	**Mood**
Beneficiary	Process	**Transitivity**

וְיָלְדוּ. Theme: textual > clause conj + Theme: experiential / Finite > weqatal 3cp / Process > qal ילד.

לָהֶם. Beneficiary > prep phrase: prep + pronoun suffix 3mp, antecedent is בְּנֵי הָאֱלֹהִים *the sons of the deity* in the preceding clause.

הֵמָּה הַגִּבֹּרִים [[אֲשֶׁר מֵעוֹלָם אַנְשֵׁי הַשֵּׁם]]. (c) Textuality > appositive paratactic expansion / Mood > declarative: non-past / Transitivity > relational: identification.

הַגִּבֹּרִים [[אֲשֶׁר מֵעוֹלָם אַנְשֵׁי הַשֵּׁם]]	הֵמָּה	**Constituents**
the warriors who from forever are the men of the name	*they*	**Translation**
	Theme	**Textuality**
Complement	Subject	**Mood**
Identifier	Identified	**Transitivity**

הֵמָּה. Theme: experiential / Subject > 3mp / Identified > pronoun personal.

הַגִּבֹּרִים [[אֲשֶׁר מֵעוֹלָם אַנְשֵׁי הַשֵּׁם]]. Complement > mp / Identifier > nominal group: Head + Post-modifier.

הַגִּבֹּרִים. Head > def art + noun common mp.

אֲשֶׁר מֵעוֹלָם אַנְשֵׁי הַשֵּׁם. (i) Post-modifier >> Textuality > embedded expansion: relative clause / Mood > declarative: non-past / Transitivity > relational: identification.

אַנְשֵׁי הַשֵּׁם	מֵעוֹלָם	אֲשֶׁר	**Constituents**
the men of the name	*from forever*	*who*	**Translation**
		Theme	**Textuality**
Complement		Subject	**Mood**
Identifier	Circumstance	Identified	**Transitivity**

אֲשֶׁר. Theme > structural / Subject > mp / Identified > pronoun relative, antecedent is הַגִּבֹּרִים *the warriors*.

מֵעוֹלָם. Circumstance: extent, time > prep phrase: prep + noun common ms.

אַנְשֵׁי הַשֵּׁם. Complement > mp / Identifier > nominal group: noun common mp const | def art + noun common ms. While הַשֵּׁם, the second noun, is definite and as such is presumed to be known or identifiable, it is not obvious to what this *name* makes reference. It is often taken in the sense *reputation* or *renown* (as NRSV translates it). Could הַשֵּׁם *the name* be a reference to deity or YHVH, as is apparently the case in Leviticus 24:11 and generally within Rabbinic Judaism? See HALOT s.v. שֵׁם definition 3 "*name*, as designation of God." Then, could the phrase be *the men of God*, on analogy with אִישׁ אֱלֹהִים and בְּנֵי אֱלֹהִים?

Genesis 6:5-8

[5]And YHVH saw that great is the evil of the humankind in the earth. And all impulse, the plans of his heart, are only bad all day. [6]And YHVH regretted that he made the humankind in the earth. And he grieved to his heart. [7]And YHVH said, "I will destroy the humankind, which I created, from on the face of the ground, from humankind to beastkind to creeper-kind and to fowl of the heavens, because I regretted that I made them." [8]And Noach found grace in the eyes of YHVH.

/// וַיַּ֣רְא יְהוָ֔ה / כִּ֥י רַבָּ֛ה רָעַ֥ת הָאָדָ֖ם בָּאָ֑רֶץ // 6:5
וְכָל־יֵ֙צֶר֙ מַחְשְׁבֹ֣ת לִבּ֔וֹ רַ֥ק רַ֖ע כָּל־הַיּֽוֹם׃

וַיַּ֣רְא יְהוָ֔ה. (a) Textuality > conj paratactic expansion / Mood > declarative: past / Transitivity > mental: perception.

יְהוָ֔ה	וַיַּ֣רְא	**Constituents**
YHVH	*and he saw*	**Translation**
	Theme	**Textuality**
Subject	Finite	**Mood**
Senser	Process	**Transitivity**

וַיַּרְא. Theme: textual > clause conj + Theme: experiential / Finite > wayyiqtol 3ms / Process > qal ראה.

יְהוָה. Subject > ms / Senser > nominal group: noun proper.

כִּי רַבָּה רָעַת הָאָדָם בָּאָרֶץ. (b) Textuality > conj hypotactic projection: report / Mood > declarative: past / Transitivity > relational: attribution.

בָּאָרֶץ	רָעַת הָאָדָם	רַבָּה	כִּי	**Constituents**
in the earth	*the evil of the humankind*	*great*	*that*	**Translation**
		Theme	Theme	**Textuality**
	Subject	Complement		**Mood**
Circumstance	Carrier	Attribute		**Transitivity**

כִּי. Theme: textual > conj.

רַבָּה. Theme: experiential / Complement > fs / Attribute > adjective group: adjective.

רָעַת הָאָדָם. Subject > fs / Carrier > nominal group: noun common fs const | def art + noun common ms.

בָּאָרֶץ. Circumstance: location, place > prep phrase: prep + def article + noun common fs.

וְכָל־יֵצֶר מַחְשְׁבֹת לִבּוֹ רַק רַע כָּל־הַיּוֹם. (c) Textuality > conj paratactic expansion / Mood > declarative: non-past / Transitivity > relational: attribution.

כָּל־הַיּוֹם	רַק רַע	וְכָל־יֵצֶר מַחְשְׁבֹת לִבּוֹ	**Constituents**
all the day	*only bad*	*and all impulse, the plans of his heart*	**Translation**
		Theme	**Textuality**
	Complement	Subject	**Mood**
Range	Attribute	Carrier	**Transitivity**

וְכָל־יֵצֶר מַחְשְׁבֹת לִבּוֹ. Theme: textual > clause conj + Subject

> ms / Carrier > nominal group: Head + Post-modifier. We are interpreting the second nominal group to be an appositive expansion of the first nominal group. As a Post-modifier expansion, it provides further description and specification of the Head nominal group.

כָּל־יֵצֶר. Head > nominal group 1: noun common ms const - noun common ms.

מַחְשְׁבֹת לִבּוֹ. Post-modifier > nominal group 2: noun common fs const | noun common ms const + pronoun suffix 3ms, antecedent is הָאָדָם *the humankind* in the prior clause.

רַק רַע. Complement > ms / Attribute > Pre-modifier + Head.

רַק. Pre-modifier > restrictor. רַק is a particle that does not inflect or otherwise change its form as an adjective might, in order to agree with a noun or adjective it conditions. The word רַק stands before the element is conditions, which then takes on a exclusive sense: *only bad, totally bad, completely bad.*

רַע. Head > adjective group: adj ms.

כָּל־הַיּוֹם. Range > nominal group: noun common ms const - def art + noun common ms. This is not a Circumstance, which might designate a point in time, but it indicates the extent in time, or duration, of the process.

6:6 // וַיִּנָּחֶם יְהוָה / כִּי־עָשָׂה אֶת־הָאָדָם בָּאָרֶץ //
וַיִּתְעַצֵּב אֶל־לִבּוֹ׃

וַיִּנָּחֶם יְהוָה. (a) Textuality > conj paratactic expansion / Mood > declarative: past / Transitivity > mental: cognition.

יְהוָה	וַיִּנָּחֶם	**Constituents**
YHVH	*and he regretted*	**Translation**
	Theme	**Textuality**
Subject	Finite	**Mood**
Senser	Process	**Transitivity**

וַיִּנָּחֶם. Theme: textual > clause conj + Theme: experiential / Finite > wayyiqtol 3ms / Process > nifal **נחם**.

יְהוָה. Subject > ms / Senser > noun proper.

כִּי־עָשָׂה אֶת־הָאָדָם בָּאָרֶץ. (b) Textuality > conj hypotactic projection: report / Mood > declarative: past / Transitivity > material: action.

בָּאָרֶץ	אֶת־הָאָדָם	עָשָׂה	כִּי־	**Constituents**
in the earth	*the humankind*	*he made*	*that*	**Translation**
		Theme	Theme	**Textuality**
		Finite		**Mood**
Circumstance	Goal	Process		**Transitivity**

כִּי־. Theme: textual > conj.

עָשָׂה. Theme: experiential / Finite > qatal 3ms / Process > qal **עשׂה**.

אֶת־הָאָדָם. Goal > nominal group: goal marker - def art + noun common collective ms.

בָּאָרֶץ. Circumstance: location, place > prep phrase: prep + def art + noun common fs.

וַיִּתְעַצֵּב אֶל־לִבּוֹ. (c) Textuality > conj paratactic expansion / Mood > declarative: past / Transitivity > mental: emotion.

אֶל־לִבּוֹ	וַיִּתְעַצֵּב	**Constituents**
to his heart	*and he grieved*	**Translation**
	Theme	**Textuality**
	Finite	**Mood**
Scope	Process	**Transitivity**

וַיִּתְעַצֵּב. Theme: textual > clause conj + Theme: experiential / Finite > wayyiqtol 3ms / Process > hitpael **עצב**. The hitpael stem is reflexive here. The transitivity structure of the hitpael has the Actor function also as the Beneficiary: *he grieved himself to his heart.*

אֶל־לִבּוֹ. Scope > prep phrase: prep - noun common ms const + pronoun suffix 3ms, antecedent is יְהוָה *YHVH.*

6:7 // וַיֹּאמֶר יְהוָה // אֶמְחֶה אֶת־הָאָדָם אֲשֶׁר־בָּרָאתִי
מֵעַל פְּנֵי הָאֲדָמָה מֵאָדָם עַד־בְּהֵמָה עַד־רֶמֶשׂ וְעַד־
עוֹף הַשָּׁמָיִם / כִּי נִחַמְתִּי / כִּי עֲשִׂיתִם׃

וַיֹּאמֶר יְהוָה. (a) Textuality > conj paratactic expansion / Mood > declarative: past / Transitivity > verbal process.

יְהוָה	וַיֹּאמֶר	**Constituents**
YHVH	*and he said*	**Translation**
	Theme	**Textuality**
Subject	Finite	**Mood**
Sayer	Process	**Transitivity**

וַיֹּאמֶר. Theme > structural + Theme: experiential / Finite > wayyiqtol 3ms / Process > qal אמר.

יְהוָה. Subject > ms / Sayer > nominal group: noun proper.

אֶמְחֶה אֶת־הָאָדָם [[אֲשֶׁר־בָּרָאתִי]] מֵעַל פְּנֵי הָאֲדָמָה מֵאָדָם עַד־בְּהֵמָה עַד־רֶמֶשׂ וְעַד־עוֹף הַשָּׁמָיִם. (b) Textuality > appositive paratactic projection: quote / Mood > declarative: non-past / Transitivity > material: action.

מֵאָדָם עַד־בְּהֵמָה עַד־רֶמֶשׂ וְעַד־עוֹף הַשָּׁמָיִם	מֵעַל פְּנֵי הָאֲדָמָה	אֶת־הָאָדָם [[אֲשֶׁר־בָּרָאתִי]]	אֶמְחֶה	**Constituents**
from humankind to beastkind to creeper-kind and to fowl of the heavens	*from on the face of the ground*	*the human-kind which I created*	*I will destroy*	**Translation**
			Theme	**Textuality**
			Finite	**Mood**
Scope	Circumstance	Goal	Process	**Transitivity**

אֶמְחֶה. Theme: experiential / Finite > yiqtol 1cs / Process > qal מחה.

אֶת־הָאָדָם [[אֲשֶׁר־בָּרָאתִי]]. Goal > nominal group: Head + Post-modifier.

אֶת־הָאָדָם. Head > nominal group: goal marker - def art + noun common collective ms.

אֲשֶׁר־בָּרָאתִי. (i) Post-modifier >> Textuality > embedded expansion: relative clause / Mood > declarative: past / Transitivity > material: action.

בָּרָאתִי	אֲשֶׁר־	**Constituents**
I created	*which*	**Translation**
	Theme	**Textuality**
Finite		**Mood**
Process	Goal	**Transitivity**

אֲשֶׁר־. Theme > textual > pronoun relative / Goal > antecedent הָאָדָם *the humankind.*

בָּרָאתִי. Finite > qatal 1cs / Process > qal ברא.

מֵעַל פְּנֵי הָאֲדָמָה. Circumstance: location, place > prep phrase: prep + prep ו noun common mp const ו def art + noun common fs.

מֵאָדָם עַד־בְּהֵמָה עַד־רֶמֶשׂ וְעַד־עוֹף הַשָּׁמָיִם. Scope > prep phrase complex: four prep phrases, the last three all with עַד forming a collection.

מֵאָדָם. Prep phrase 1 > prep + noun common collective ms.

עַד־בְּהֵמָה. Prep phrase 2 > prep - noun common collective fs.

עַד־רֶמֶשׂ. Prep phase 3 > prep - noun common collective ms.

וְעַד־עוֹף הַשָּׁמָיִם. Prep phrase 4 > group conj + prep - noun common collective ms const | def art + noun common mp.

כִּי נִחַמְתִּי. (c) Textuality > conj hypotactic projection: quote / Mood > declarative: past / Transitivity > mental: cognition.

נִחַמְתִּי	כִּי	**Constituents**
I regretted	*because*	**Translation**
Theme	Theme	**Textuality**
Finite		**Mood**
Process		**Transitivity**

כִּי. Theme: textual > conj.

נִחַמְתִּי. Theme: experiential / Finite > qatal 1cs / Process > nifal נחם.

כִּי עֲשִׂיתִם. (d) Textuality > conj hypotactic projection: quote / Mood > declarative: past / Transitivity > material: action. The Subject / Actor is the Sayer of the quote, יְהוָה *YHVH* in clause (a).

עֲשִׂיתִם	כִּי	**Constituents**
I made them	*that*	**Translation**
Theme	Theme	**Textuality**
Finite		**Mood**
Process + Goal		**Transitivity**

כִּי. Theme: textual > conj.

עֲשִׂיתִם. Theme: experiential / Finite > qatal 1cs / Process > qal

עשׂה + Goal > pronoun suffix 3mp, antecedent goes back to clause (b) and could simply be הָאָדָם *the humankind* taken as plural, or it could be the entire Scope of clause (b) that includes four types of living things.

6:8 // וְנֹ֕חַ מָ֥צָא חֵ֖ן בְּעֵינֵ֥י יְהוָֽה׃ פ

וְנֹחַ מָצָא חֵן בְּעֵינֵי יְהוָה. (a) Textuality > conj paratactic expansion / Mood > declarative: past / Transitivity > material: action.

בְּעֵינֵי יְהוָה	חֵן	מָצָא	וְנֹחַ	**Constituents**
in the eyes of YHVH	*grace*	*found*	*and Noach*	**Translation**
			Theme	**Textuality**
		Finite	Subject	**Mood**
Circumstance	Goal	Process	Actor	**Transitivity**

וְנֹחַ. Theme textual > clause conj + Theme: experiential / Subject > ms / Actor > nominal group: noun proper. Noach was last mentioned in 5:32 and here is brought back into the narration. He is the Theme of this clause, which is non-sequential in relation to the preceding, and stands in contrast to הָאָדָם *the humankind.*

מָצָא. Finite > qatal 3ms / Process > qal מצא.

חֵן. Goal > nominal group: noun common ms.

בְּעֵינֵי יְהוָה. Circumstance: location, place > prep phrase: prep + noun common mp const | noun proper.

Genesis 6:9-10

[9]These are the outcomes of Noach. Noach is a righteous man. He was blameless in his generations. With the deity Noach walked. [10]And Noach fathered three sons: Shem, Cham, and Yefet.

6:9 /// אֵ֚לֶּה תּוֹלְדֹ֣ת נֹ֔חַ // נֹ֗חַ אִ֥ישׁ צַדִּ֛יק // תָּמִ֥ים
הָיָ֖ה בְּדֹֽרֹתָ֑יו // אֶת־הָאֱלֹהִ֖ים הִֽתְהַלֶּךְ־נֹֽחַ׃

אֵלֶּה תּוֹלְדֹת נֹחַ. (a) Textuality > appositive paratactic expansion / Mood > declarative: non-past / Transitivity > relational: identification.

תּוֹלְדֹת נֹחַ	אֵלֶּה	**Constituents**
the outcomes of Noach	*these*	**Translation**
	Theme	**Textuality**
Complement	Subject	**Mood**
Identifier	Identified	**Transitivity**

אֵלֶּה. Theme: experiential / Subject > 3cp / Identified > pronoun demonstrative, cataphoric referent is the clause complex following this clause.

תּוֹלְדֹת נֹחַ. Complement > fp / Identifier > nominal group: noun common fp const | noun proper ms.

נֹחַ אִישׁ צַדִּיק. (b) Textuality > appositive paratactic expansion / Mood > declarative: non-past / Transitivity > relational: attribution.

אִישׁ צַדִּיק	נֹחַ	**Constituents**
a righteous man	*Noach*	**Translation**
	Theme	**Textuality**
Complement	Subject	**Mood**
Attribute	Carrier	**Transitivity**

נֹחַ. Theme: experiential / Subject > ms / Carrier > nominal group: noun proper.

אִישׁ צַדִּיק. Complement > ms / Attribute > nominal group: noun common ms | adj ms.

תָּמִים הָיָה בְּדֹרֹתָיו. (c) Textuality > appositive paratactic expansion / Mood > declarative: past / Transitivity > relational: attribution. The Subject / Carrier is נֹחַ, absent by ellipsis.

בְּדֹרֹתָיו	הָיָה	תָּמִים	**Constituents**
in his generations	*he was*	*blameless*	**Translation**
		Theme	**Textuality**
	Finite		**Mood**
Circumstance	Process	Attribute	**Transitivity**

תָּמִים. Theme: experiential / Attribute > adjective group: adj ms.

הָיָה. Finite > qatal 3ms / Process > qal היה.

בְּדֹרֹתָיו. Circumstance: extent, place > prep phrase: prep + noun common fp const + pronoun suffix 3ms, antecedent is נֹחַ *Noach*.

אֶת־הָאֱלֹהִים הִתְהַלֶּךְ־נֹחַ. (d) Textuality > appositive paratactic expansion / Mood > declarative: past / Transitivity > material: action.

נֹחַ	הִתְהַלֶּךְ־	אֶת־הָאֱלֹהִים	**Constituents**
Noach	*he walked*	*with the deity*	**Translation**
		Theme	**Textuality**
Subject	Finite		**Mood**
Actor	Process	Circumstance	**Transitivity**

אֶת־הָאֱלֹהִים. Theme: experiential / Circumstance: accompaniment > prep phrase: prep - def art + noun common mp.

הִתְהַלֶּךְ־. Finite > qatal 3ms / Process > hitpael הלך.

נֹחַ. Subject > ms / Actor > nominal group: noun proper.

6:10 // וַיּ֥וֹלֶד נֹ֖חַ שְׁלֹשָׁ֣ה בָנִ֑ים אֶת־שֵׁ֖ם אֶת־חָ֥ם וְאֶת־
יָֽפֶת׃

וַיּוֹלֶד נֹחַ שְׁלֹשָׁה בָנִים אֶת־שֵׁם אֶת־חָם וְאֶת־יָפֶת. (a) Textuality > conj paratactic expansion / Mood > declarative: past / Transitivity > material: action.

שְׁלֹשָׁה בָנִים אֶת־שֵׁם אֶת־חָם וְאֶת־יָפֶת	נֹחַ	וַיּוֹלֶד	**Constituents**
three sons: Shem, Cham, and Yefet	*Noach*	*and he fathered*	**Translation**
		Theme	**Textuality**
	Subject	Finite	**Mood**
Goal	Actor	Process	**Transitivity**

וַיּוֹלֶד. Theme: textual > clause conj + Theme: experiential / Finite > wayyiqtol 3ms / Process > hifil ילד.

נֹחַ. Subject > ms / Actor > nominal group: noun proper.

שְׁלֹשָׁה בָנִים אֶת־שֵׁם אֶת־חָם וְאֶת־יָפֶת. Goal > nominal group complex: Head + Post-modifier. The second nominal group expands the meaning of the first group by specifying the three individuals.

שְׁלֹשָׁה בָנִים. Head > nominal group: numeral ms | noun common mp.

אֶת־שֵׁם אֶת־חָם וְאֶת־יָפֶת. Post-modifier > nominal group complex: goal marker - noun proper | goal marker - noun proper | group conj + goal marker - noun proper.

Genesis 6:11-16

[11]And the earth was spoiled before the deity. And the earth was filled with violence. [12]And deity saw the earth, that truly spoiled it was, because all flesh spoiled its way on the earth. [13]And deity said to Noach, "An end of all flesh came to me, because the earth is full of violence because of them. And I am the one spoiling them with the earth. [14]Make yourself an ark of cyprus wood. You will make the ark with nests. And you will cover it inside and outside in tar. [15]And this is what you will make it: 300 cubits is the length of the ark, 50 cubits is its width, and 30 cubits is its height. [16]You will make a roof for the ark. And you will finish it to a cubit from

the top. And the door of the ark you will put in its side. With under decks, second-level decks, and third-level decks you will make her."

6:11 וַתִּשָּׁחֵ֥ת הָאָ֖רֶץ לִפְנֵ֣י הָאֱלֹהִ֑ים // וַתִּמָּלֵ֥א הָאָ֖רֶץ /// חָמָֽס׃

וַתִּשָּׁחֵת הָאָרֶץ לִפְנֵי הָאֱלֹהִים. (a) Textuality > conj paratactic expansion / Mood > declarative: past / Transitivity > material: happening or doing.

לִפְנֵי הָאֱלֹהִים	הָאָרֶץ	וַתִּשָּׁחֵת	**Constituents**
before the deity	*the earth*	*and she was spoiled*	**Translation**
		Theme	**Textuality**
	Subject	Finite	**Mood**
Circumstance	Actor or Goal	Process	**Transitivity**

וַתִּשָּׁחֵת. Theme: textual > clause conj + Theme: experiential / Finite > wayyiqtol 3fs / Process > nifal שׁחת. This nifal verb process can be interpreted as middle voice (*spoiled*, *became spoiled*) or passive voice (*was spoiled* by someone or something else).

הָאָרֶץ. Subject > fs / Actor (if middle voice) or Goal (if passive voice) > nominal group: def art + noun common fs.

לִפְנֵי הָאֱלֹהִים. Circumstance: location, place > prep phrase: prep + noun common mp const | def art + noun common mp.

וַתִּמָּלֵא הָאָרֶץ חָמָס. (b) Textuality > conj paratactic expansion / Mood > declarative: past / Transitivity > material: action or relational: attribution. Arguably the process is presented as a material one, but it could also be interpreted as attributive relational. The clause looks to express that violence characterized the earth, that is, the earth was completely violent. Since BH does not have an adjective *violent* to match the noun *violence*, the verb *was full* is used to bring *the earth* and *violence* into relationship; *the earth is/was violence* would not be an acceptable wording.

חָמָס	הָאָרֶץ	וַתִּמָּלֵא	**Constituents**
violence	*the earth*	*and she was full of / was filled with*	**Translation**
		Theme	**Textuality**
	Subject	Finite	**Mood**
Attribute or Scope	Carrier or Goal	Process	**Transitivity**

וַתִּמָּלֵא. Theme: textual > clause conj + Theme: experiential / Finite > wayyiqtol 3fs / Process > nifal **מלא**. Either *was full* (middle voice) or *was filled* (passive voice).

הָאָרֶץ. Subject > fs / Carrier (if middle voice) or Goal (if passive voice) > nominal group: def art + noun common.

חָמָס. Attribute (if middle voice) or Scope (if passive voice) > nominal group: noun common ms.

6:12 // וַיַּ֧רְא אֱלֹהִ֛ים אֶת־הָאָ֖רֶץ // וְהִנֵּ֣ה נִשְׁחָ֑תָה //
כִּֽי־הִשְׁחִ֧ית כָּל־בָּשָׂ֛ר אֶת־דַּרְכּ֖וֹ עַל־הָאָֽרֶץ׃ ס

וַיַּרְא אֱלֹהִים אֶת־הָאָרֶץ. (a) Textuality > conj paratactic expansion / Mood > declarative: past / Transitivity > mental: perception.

אֶת־הָאָרֶץ	אֱלֹהִים	וַיַּרְא	**Constituents**
the earth	*deity*	*and he saw*	**Translation**
		Theme	**Textuality**
	Subject	Finite	**Mood**
Phenomenon	Senser	Process	**Transitivity**

וַיַּרְא. Theme: textual > clause conj + Theme: experiential / Finite > wayyiqtol 3ms / Process > qal **ראה**.

אֱלֹהִים. Subject > mp / Senser > nominal group: noun proper.

אֶת־הָאָרֶץ. Phenomenon > nominal group: goal marker - def art + noun common fs.

וְהִנֵּה נִשְׁחָתָה. (b) Textuality > conj hypotactic projection: report / Mood > declarative: past / Transitivity > relational: attribution. The Carrier of the relational process is הָאָרֶץ *the earth* from the prior clause, absent here by ellipsis.

נִשְׁחָתָה	וְהִנֵּה	**Constituents**
she was spoiled	*and now*	**Translation**
Theme	Theme	**Textuality**
Finite		**Mood**
Process		**Transitivity**

וְהִנֵּה. Theme: textual > clause conj + Adjunct: textual > contra-expectation. The הִנֵּה textual adjunct is used to thematize the word that follows it so as to assert its unexpected and undesirable state. The sequence ראה followed by הִנֵּה evidenced here is analogous to ראה followed by כִּי in other clauses, such as 1:4(a-b) and 8:13(d-e). Both hypotactic clause structures consist of report projections following a mental process of perception. The הִנֵּה adds the element of contra-expectation and surprise to the report.

נִשְׁחָתָה. Theme: experiential / Finite > qatal 3fs / Process > nifal שׁחת. This verb is one that attributes a quality to the Carrier.

כִּי־הִשְׁחִית כָּל־בָּשָׂר אֶת־דַּרְכּוֹ עַל־הָאָרֶץ. (c) Textuality > conj hypotactic expansion / Mood > declarative: past / Transitivity > material: action.

עַל־הָאָרֶץ	אֶת־דַּרְכּוֹ	כָּל־בָּשָׂר	הִשְׁחִית	כִּי־	**Constituents**
on the earth	*his way*	*all of flesh*	*he spoiled*	*because*	**Translation**
			Theme	Theme	**Textuality**
		Subject	Finite		**Mood**
Circumstance	Goal	Actor	Process		**Transitivity**

כִּי־. Theme: textual > conj.

הִשְׁחִית. Theme: experiential / Finite > qatal 3ms / Process > hifil שׁחת.

כָּל־בָּשָׂר. Subject > ms / Actor > nominal group: noun common ms const - noun common collective ms.

אֶת־דַּרְכּוֹ. Goal > nominal group: goal marker - noun common collective m/fs const + pronoun suffix 3ms, antecedent could be כָּל *all* or בָּשָׂר *flesh*, since both are ms.

עַל־הָאָרֶץ. Circumstance: location, place > prep phrase: prep - def art + noun common fs.

6:13 // וַיֹּאמֶר אֱלֹהִים לְנֹחַ // קֵץ כָּל־בָּשָׂר בָּא לְפָנַי /
כִּי־מָלְאָה הָאָרֶץ חָמָס מִפְּנֵיהֶם // וְהִנְנִי מַשְׁחִיתָם
אֶת־הָאָרֶץ׃

וַיֹּאמֶר אֱלֹהִים לְנֹחַ. (a) Textuality > conj paratactic expansion / Mood > declarative: past / Transitivity > verbal.

לְנֹחַ	אֱלֹהִים	וַיֹּאמֶר	**Constituents**
to Noach	*deity*	*and he said*	**Translation**
		Theme	**Textuality**
	Subject	Finite	**Mood**
Recipient	Sayer	Process	**Transitivity**

וַיֹּאמֶר. Theme: textual > clause conj + Theme: experiential / Finite > wayyiqtol 3ms / Process > qal אמר.

אֱלֹהִים. Subject > mp / Sayer > nominal group: noun common.

לְנֹחַ. Recipient > prep phrase: prep + noun proper.

קֵץ כָּל־בָּשָׂר בָּא לְפָנַי. (b) Textuality > appositive paratactic expansion: quote / Mood > declarative: past / Transitivity > material: action. The thought contained in this clause is expressed, for example, by the NRSV as *I have determined to make an end of all flesh*, and by the NJPS as *I have decided to put an end to all flesh.* But it is not encoded that way in Hebrew. Deity is not the Subject of the clause, nor is a verb of cognition (determine or decide) used. Instead, the meaning of this clause is encoded with a material process that expresses movement, as if the notion of the demise of all flesh passed before deity and so made itself evident. In fact, the Hebrew construction distances deity from the decision making process, almost as if this outcome was inevitable.

לְפָנַי	בָּא	קֵץ כָּל־בָּשָׂר	**Constituents**
before me	*came* (or *comes*)	*an end of all of flesh*	**Translation**
		Theme	**Textuality**
	Finite	Subject	**Mood**
Circumstance	Process	Actor	**Transitivity**

קֵץ כָּל־בָּשָׂר. Theme: experiential / Subject > ms (קֵץ) / Actor > nominal group: noun common ms const | noun common collective ms const - noun common collective ms.

בָּא. Finite > qatal 3ms (or ptc ms) / Process > qal בוא. Both qatal and ptc have the same form. As participle it may signal imminent action, that is, action which is about to occur; see MNK 162.

לְפָנַי. Circumstance: location, place > prep phrase: prep + noun common mp const + pronoun suffix 1cs, antecedent is the Sayer of the quote, אֱלֹהִים *deity.*

כִּי־מָלְאָה הָאָרֶץ חָמָס מִפְּנֵיהֶם. (c) Textuality > conj paratactic projection: quote / Mood > declarative: past / Transitivity > relational: attribution. See 6:11(b) for an interpretation of this clause as attributive relational.

מִפְּנֵיהֶם	חָמָס	הָאָרֶץ	מָלְאָה	כִּי־	**Constituents**
from before them	*violence*	*the earth*	*is full*	*because*	**Translation**
			Theme	Theme	**Textuality**
		Subject	Finite		**Mood**
Circumstance	Attribute	Carrier	Process		**Transitivity**

כִּי־. Theme: textual > conj.

מָלְאָה. Theme: experiential / Finite > qatal 3fs / Process > qal מלא.

הָאָרֶץ. Subject > fs / Carrier > nominal group: noun common.

חָמָס. Attribute > nominal group: noun common ms.

מִפְּנֵיהֶם. Circumstance: cause, reason > prep phrase: prep + noun common mp const + pronoun suffix 3mp, antecedent is כָּל־ *all* or בָּשָׂר *flesh*, taken as plural. Perhaps to be taken in the sense *because of them*.

וְהִנְנִי מַשְׁחִיתָם אֶת־הָאָרֶץ. (d) Textuality > conj paratactic projection: quote / Mood > declarative: non-past / Transitivity > material: action.

אֶת־הָאָרֶץ	מַשְׁחִיתָם	וְהִנְנִי	**Constituents**
with the earth	*am spoiling them*	*and now I*	**Translation**
		Theme	**Textuality**
	Finite	Subject	**Mood**
Circumstance	Process + Goal	Actor	**Transitivity**

וְהִנְנִי. Theme: textual > clause conj + Adjunct: textual > contra-expectation + Subject > 1cs / Actor > pronoun suffix, antecedent is the Sayer, אֱלֹהִים *deity*. This textual adjunct signals that the tables, so to speak, have been turned. In an ironic move, deity is going to spoil all flesh because humankind spoiled the earth.

מַשְׁחִיתָם. Finite > ptc ms / Process > hifil שׁחת + Goal > pronoun suffix 3mp, antecedent is כָּל־ *all*, or בָּשָׂר *flesh* taken as plural.

The participle used as a Finite verb may signal imminent action: *and now I am about to spoil them with the earth*; see 6:13(b). Regarding the meaning of this root, compare שחת here with its use in 6:11(a) and 6:12(b). שחת can variously be translated *corrupt*, *spoil*, *destroy*, *ruin*. The important feature to notice in this narrative is that this root is used in different stems: nifal in 6:11(a) and 6:12(b), and hifil in 6:12(c) and 6:13(d), as well as in 9:11(c) and 9:15(b). The connection is lost in both the NRSV and NJPS, as the nifal and the hifil in 6:12(c) are translated *corrupt*, but the hifil in 6:13(d) is translated *destroy*. We render all instances of שחת *spoil* in order to maintain the connection.

אֶת־הָאָֽרֶץ. Circumstance: accompaniment > prep phrase: prep - def art + noun common fs.

6:14 // עֲשֵׂה לְךָ֙ תֵּבַ֣ת עֲצֵי־גֹ֔פֶר // קִנִּ֖ים תַּעֲשֶׂ֣ה אֶת־הַתֵּבָ֑ה // וְכָפַרְתָּ֥ אֹתָ֛הּ מִבַּ֥יִת וּמִח֖וּץ בַּכֹּֽפֶר׃

עֲשֵׂה לְךָ֙ תֵּבַ֣ת עֲצֵי־גֹ֔פֶר. (a) Textuality > appositive paratactic projection: quote / Mood > directive: imperative / Transitivity > material: action.

תֵּבַת עֲצֵי־גֹפֶר	לְךָ	עֲשֵׂה	**Constituents**
an ark of wood of cyprus	*for yourself*	*make*	**Translation**
		Theme	**Textuality**
		Finite	**Mood**
Goal	Beneficiary	Process	**Transitivity**

עֲשֵׂה. Theme: experiential / Finite > impv ms / Process > qal עשׂה.

לְךָ֙. Beneficiary > prep phrase: prep + pronoun suffix 2ms, antecedent is נֹחַ *Noach* in 6:13(a).

תֵּבַ֣ת עֲצֵי־גֹ֔פֶר. Goal > nominal group: noun common fs const ı noun common mp const - noun common collective ms.

קִנִּ֖ים תַּעֲשֶׂ֣ה אֶת־הַתֵּבָ֑ה. (b) Textuality > appositive paratactic projection: quote / Mood > declarative: non-past → directive / Transitivity > material: action. The Subject/Actor is נֹחַ *Noach*, absent here by ellipsis. A yiqtol clause following an imperative clause is typically rendered as a second imperative clause.

אֶת־הַתֵּבָה	תַּעֲשֶׂה	קִנִּים	**Constituents**
the ark	*you will make*	*nests*	**Translation**
		Theme	**Textuality**
	Finite		**Mood**
Goal	Process	Scope	**Transitivity**

קִנִּים. Theme: experiential / Scope > nominal group: noun common mp.

תַּעֲשֶׂה. Finite > yiqtol 2ms / Process > qal עשׂה. The Transitivity structure of this clause is a bit unusual, as if the clause process has two Goals, or is doubly transitive (to use a traditional term). The sense is fairly clear, especially in combination with the preceding clause: you will make yourself an ark such that it will have nests.

אֶת־הַתֵּבָה. Goal > nominal group: goal marker - def art + noun common fs.

וְכָפַרְתָּ אֹתָהּ מִבַּיִת וּמִחוּץ בַּכֹּפֶר. (c) Textuality > conj paratactic projection: quote / Mood > declarative: non-past → directive / Transitivity > material: action.

בַּכֹּפֶר	מִבַּיִת וּמִחוּץ	אֹתָהּ	וְכָפַרְתָּ	**Constituents**
in the tar	*from house and from outside*	*her*	*and you will cover*	**Translation**
			Theme	**Textuality**
			Finite	**Mood**
Circumstance	Scope	Goal	Process	**Transitivity**

וְכָפַרְתָּ. Theme: textual > clause conj + Theme: experiential / Finite > weqatal 2ms / Process > qal כפר.

אֹתָהּ. Goal > nominal group: goal marker + pronoun suffix 3fs, antecedent is הַתֵּבָה, *the ark*.

מִבַּיִת וּמִחוּץ. Scope > prep phrase complex: prep phrase 1 + prep phrase 2.

מִבַּיִת. Prep phrase 1 > prep + noun common ms.

וּמִחוּץ. Group conj + Prep phrase 2 > prep + noun common ms.

בַּכֹּפֶר. Circumstance: manner, means > prep phrase: prep + def art + noun common ms.

6:15 /// וְזֶ֕ה אֲשֶׁ֥ר תַּעֲשֶׂ֖ה אֹתָ֑הּ // שְׁלֹ֨שׁ מֵא֤וֹת אַמָּה֙
אֹ֣רֶךְ הַתֵּבָ֔ה // חֲמִשִּׁ֤ים אַמָּה֙ רָחְבָּ֔הּ // וּשְׁלֹשִׁ֥ים
אַמָּ֖ה קוֹמָתָֽהּ׃

וְזֶה [[אֲשֶׁר תַּעֲשֶׂה אֹתָהּ]]. (a) Textuality > conj paratactic projection: quote / Mood > declarative: non-past / Transitivity > relational: identification. This type of clause is called a thematic equative, because the Theme equals the Rheme; see Thompson, 150. Though connected to the preceding clauses by the pronoun suffix on אֹתָהּ, this clause stands at the head of a clause complex that extends from 6:15(a) to (d).

[[אֲשֶׁר תַּעֲשֶׂה אֹתָהּ]]	וְזֶה	**Constituents**
what you will make it	*and this*	**Translation**
Rheme	Theme	**Textuality**
Complement	Subject	**Mood**
Identified	Identifier	**Transitivity**

וְזֶה. Theme: textual > clause conj + Theme: experiential / Subject > ms / Identifier > pronoun demonstrative, referent is the following three clauses that specify the dimensions for the ark. This demonstrative pronoun is cataphoric, meaning that it looks ahead to the following text.

אֲשֶׁר תַּעֲשֶׂה אֹתָהּ. (i) Textuality > embedded: relative clause / Mood > declarative: non-past / Process > material: action.

אֹתָהּ	תַּעֲשֶׂה	אֲשֶׁר	**Constituents**
it	*you will make*	*what*	**Translation**
		Theme	**Textuality**
	Finite		**Mood**
Goal	Process	Scope	**Transitivity**

אֲשֶׁר. Theme: textual > pronoun relative / Scope > cataphoric clause complex. The *what* is the specification that follows, clauses (b) through (d).

תַּעֲשֶׂה. Finite > yiqtol 2ms / Process > qal עשׂה.

אֹתָהּ. Goal > nominal group: goal marker + pronoun suffix 3fs, antecedent is הַתֵּבָה *the ark* in 6:14(a).

שְׁלֹשׁ מֵאוֹת אַמָּה אֹרֶךְ הַתֵּבָה. (b) Textuality > appositive paratactic projection: quote / Mood > declarative: non-past / Transitivity > relational: attribution. This is the first clause of a three clause complex that provides the dimensions of the ark.

אֹרֶךְ הַתֵּבָה	שְׁלֹשׁ מֵאוֹת אַמָּה	**Constituents**
the length of the ark	*three hundred cubits*	**Translation**
	Theme	**Textuality**
Subject	Complement	**Mood**
Carrier	Attribute	**Transitivity**

שְׁלֹשׁ מֵאוֹת אַמָּה. Theme: experiential / Complement > fs / Attribute > nominal group: numeral fs | numeral fp | noun common fs.

אֹרֶךְ הַתֵּבָה. Subject > ms / Carrier > nominal group: noun common ms const | def art + noun common fs.

חֲמִשִּׁים אַמָּה רָחְבָּהּ. (c) Textuality > appositive paratactic projection: quote / Mood > declarative: non-past / Transitivity > relational: attribution. This is the second clause of a three clause complex that provides the dimensions of the ark.

רָחְבָּהּ	חֲמִשִּׁים אַמָּה	**Constituents**
its width	*fifty cubits*	**Translation**
	Theme	**Textuality**
Subject	Complement	**Mood**
Carrier	Attribute	**Transitivity**

חֲמִשִּׁים אַמָּה. Theme: experiential / Complement > fs / Attribute > nominal group: numeral fp | noun common fs.

רָחְבָּהּ. Subject > ms / Carrier > nominal group: noun ms const + pronoun suffix 3fs, antecedent is הַתֵּבָה *the ark.*

וּשְׁלֹשִׁים אַמָּה קוֹמָתָהּ. (d) Textuality > conj paratactic projection: quote / Mood > declarative: non-past / Transitivity > relational: attribution. This is the third clause of a three clause complex that provides the dimensions of the ark.

קוֹמָתָהּ	וּשְׁלֹשִׁים אַמָּה	**Constituents**
its height	*and thirty cubits*	**Translation**
	Theme	**Textuality**
Subject	Complement	**Mood**
Carrier	Attribute	**Transitivity**

וּשְׁלֹשִׁים אַמָּה. Theme: textual > group conj + Theme: experiential / Complement > fs / Attribute > nominal group: numeral fp | noun common fs.

קוֹמָתָהּ. Subject > ms / Carrier > nominal group: noun common fs const + pronoun suffix 3fs, antecedent is הַתֵּבָה *the ark.*

6:16 // צֹ֣הַר ׀ תַּעֲשֶׂ֣ה לַתֵּבָ֗ה // וְאֶל־אַמָּה֙ תְּכַלֶּ֣נָּה
מִלְמַ֔עְלָה // וּפֶ֥תַח הַתֵּבָ֖ה בְּצִדָּ֣הּ תָּשִׂ֑ים // תַּחְתִּיִּ֛ם
שְׁנִיִּ֥ם וּשְׁלִשִׁ֖ים תַּעֲשֶֽׂהָ׃

צֹהַר תַּעֲשֶׂה לַתֵּבָה. (a) Textuality > appositive paratactic projection: quote / Mood > declarative: non-past / Transitivity > material: action.

לַתֵּבָה	תַּעֲשֶׂה	צֹהַר	**Constituents**
for the ark	*you will make*	*a roof*	**Translation**
		Theme	**Textuality**
	Finite		**Mood**
Beneficiary	Process	Goal	**Transitivity**

צֹהַר. Theme: experiential / Goal > noun common m/fs. BDB identifies this *hapax legomenon* as feminine in gender, but does not provide evidence. One might surmise that the 3fs pronoun suffix on תְּכַלֶּנָּה is the evidence, which, if so, would be rather circular. HALOT does not provide a gender designation.

תַּעֲשֶׂה. Finite > yiqtol 2ms / Process > qal עשׂה.

לַתֵּבָה. Beneficiary > prep phrase: prep + def art + noun common fs.

וְאֶל־אַמָּה תְּכַלֶּנָּה מִלְמַעְלָה. (b) Textuality > conj paratactic projection: quote / Mood > declarative: non-past / Transitivity > material: action.

מִלְמַעְלָה	תְּכַלֶּנָּה	וְאֶל־אַמָּה	**Constituents**
from to above	*you will finish her*	*and to a cubit*	**Translation**
		Theme	**Textuality**
		Finite	**Mood**
Circumstance	Process + Goal	Circumstance	**Transitivity**

וְאֶל־אַמָּה. Theme: textual > clause conj + Theme: experiential / Circumstance: extent, place > prep phrase: prep - noun common fs.

תְּכַלֶּנָּה. Finite > yiqtol 2ms / Process > piel כלה + Goal > pronoun suffix 3fs, antecedent could match הַתֵּבָה *the ark* or צֹהַר *roof* (if it is feminine) in the prior clause, though the former seems more likely. It is not clear exactly what is meant by this process, or what the clause as a whole intends to depict. If the antecedent is הַתֵּבָה, then the clause may be suggesting that the wall of the ark will be solid until it gets within a cubit of the roof, leaving an opening for light and ventilation. If the antecedent is צֹהַר, then perhaps it is saying that the roof will overhang the top of the ark by one cubit, meaning it will have about a 1.5 foot overhang.

מִלְמַעְלָה. Circumstance: location, place > prep phrase: prep + prep + adverb. Literally, *from to above.*

וּפֶתַח הַתֵּבָה בְּצִדָּהּ תָּשִׂים. (c) Textuality > conj paratactic projection: quote / Mood > declarative: non-past / Transitivity > material: action.

תָּשִׂים	בְּצִדָּהּ	וּפֶתַח הַתֵּבָה	**Constituents**
you will put	*in her side*	*and the door of the ark*	**Translation**
		Theme	**Textuality**
	Finite		**Mood**
Process	Circumstance	Goal	**Transitivity**

וּפֶתַח הַתֵּבָה. Theme: textual > clause conj + Theme: experiential / Goal > nominal group: noun common ms const | def art + noun common fs.

בְּצִדָּהּ. Circumstance: location, place > prep phrase: prep + noun common ms const + pronoun suffix 3fs, antecedent is הַתֵּבָה *the ark.*

תָּשִׂים. Finite > yiqtol 2ms / Process > qal שִׂים.

תַּחְתִּיִּם שְׁנִיִּם וּשְׁלִשִׁים תַּעֲשֶׂהָ. (d) Textuality > appositive paratactic projection: quote / Mood > declarative: non-past / Transitivity > material: action.

תַּעֲשֶׂהָ	תַּחְתִּיִּם שְׁנִיִּם וּשְׁלִשִׁים	Constituents
you will make her	*unders seconds and thirds*	**Translation**
	Theme	**Textuality**
Finite		**Mood**
Process + Goal	Scope	**Transitivity**

תַּחְתִּיִּם שְׁנִיִּם וּשְׁלִשִׁים. Theme: experiential / Scope > nominal group: noun common mp ǀ noun common mp ǀ group conj + noun common mp.

תַּעֲשֶׂהָ. Finite > yiqtol 2ms / Process > qal עשׂה + Goal > pronoun suffix 3fs, antecedent is הַתֵּבָה *the ark*. The Transitivity structure encodes the process as making the ark (Goal) to have multi-level decks. For a similar construction using a material process (same verb עשׂה) with Goal and Scope, see 6:14(b).

Genesis 6:17-22

[17] "And I, now I, am bringing the flood, water, on the earth to spoil all flesh, in which is spirit of life, from under the heavens. All which is on the earth will perish. [18]And I will establish my covenant with you. And you will go to the ark, you and your sons and your woman and the women of your sons with you. [19]And from all alive from all flesh, two from all you will bring to the ark to keep alive with you. Male and female they will be. [20]From the fowl for its kind and from the beastkind for its kind, from all of the creeperkind of the earth for its kind, two from all will go to you to keep alive. [21]And you take for yourself from all foodstuff, which will be eaten. And you will gather to yourself. And it will be for you and for them for food." [22]And Noach did. Such as all which deity commanded him, so he did.

6:17 /// וַאֲנִי הִנְנִי מֵבִיא אֶת־הַמַּבּוּל מַיִם עַל־הָאָרֶץ
לְשַׁחֵת כָּל־בָּשָׂר אֲשֶׁר־בּוֹ רוּחַ חַיִּים מִתַּחַת הַשָּׁמָיִם
// כֹּל אֲשֶׁר־בָּאָרֶץ יִגְוָע׃

(a) וַאֲנִי הִנְנִי מֵבִיא אֶת־הַמַּבּוּל מַיִם עַל־הָאָרֶץ [[לְשַׁחֵת כָּל־בָּשָׂר [[אֲשֶׁר־בּוֹ רוּחַ חַיִּים]] מִתַּחַת הַשָּׁמָיִם]]. Textuality > conj paratactic expansion / Mood > declarative: non-past / Transitivity > material: action.

[[לְשַׁחֵת כָּל־בָּשָׂר [[אֲשֶׁר־בּוֹ רוּחַ חַיִּים]] מִתַּחַת הַשָּׁמָיִם]]	עַל־הָאָרֶץ	אֶת־הַמַּבּוּל מַיִם	מֵבִיא	וַאֲנִי הִנְנִי	**Constituents**
to spoil all of flesh, which in it is spirit of life, from under the heavens	*on the earth*	*the flood, water*	*am bringing*	*and I now I*	**Translation**
				Theme	**Textuality**
			Finite	Subject	**Mood**
Circumstance	Circumstance	Goal	Process	Actor	**Transitivity**

וַאֲנִי הִנְנִי. Theme: textual > clause conj + Theme: experiential / Subject > 1cs / Actor > pronoun personal + Adjunct: textual > contra-expectation + pronoun suffix 1cs, antecedent is אֲנִי *I*.

מֵבִיא. Finite > ptc ms / Process > hifil בוא. Possibly the participle of imminent action.

אֶת־הַמַּבּוּל מַיִם. Goal > nominal group: Head + Post-modifier.

אֶת־הַמַּבּוּל. Head > nominal group: goal marker - def art + noun common ms.

מַיִם. Post-modifier > nominal group: noun common mp.

עַל־הָאָרֶץ. Circumstance > prep phrase: prep - def art + noun common fs.

לְשַׁחֵת כָּל־בָּשָׂר [[אֲשֶׁר־בּוֹ רוּחַ חַיִּים]] מִתַּחַת הַשָּׁמָיִם. (i) Circumstance: cause, purpose >> Textuality > embedded expansion: ptc clause / Process > material: action.

מִתַּחַת הַשָּׁמָיִם	כָּל־בָּשָׂר [[אֲשֶׁר־בּוֹ רוּחַ חַיִּים]]	לְשַׁחֵת	**Constituents**
from under the heavens	*all of flesh which in it is spirit of life*	*to spoil*	**Translation**
		Theme	**Textuality**
Circumstance	Goal	Process	**Transitivity**

לְשַׁחֵת. Theme: textual > prep + Theme: experiential / Process > inf const piel שחת.

[[אֲשֶׁר־בּוֹ רוּחַ חַיִּים]] כָּל־בָּשָׂר. Goal > nominal group: Head + Post-modifier.

כָּל־בָּשָׂר. Head > nominal group: noun common collective ms const - noun common collective ms.

אֲשֶׁר־בּוֹ רוּחַ חַיִּים. (a') Textuality > embedded expansion: relative clause / Mood > declarative: non-past / Transitivity > relational: attribution. The clause before embedding would be *spirit of life is in all flesh.* When it is repurposed for use as a relative clause it becomes *all flesh which in it is spirit of life.* Is this a restrictive (defining) or non-restrictive relative clause? If it is a restrictive relative clause, this would imply two categories: flesh with a spirit of life and flesh without it. If it is a non-restrictive relative clause, it is providing further description of *all flesh.* More likely it is the latter.

רוּחַ חַיִּים	בּוֹ	אֲשֶׁר־	**Constituents**
spirit of life	*in him*	*which*	**Translation**
	Theme	Theme	**Textuality**
Subject	Complement		**Mood**
Carrier	Attribute		**Transitivity**

אֲשֶׁר־. Theme: textual > pronoun relative, antecedent כָּל־בָּשָׂר *all flesh.*

בּוֹ. Theme: experiential / Complement / Attribute > prep phrase: prep + pronoun suffix 3ms, antecedent is כָּל־בָּשָׂר *all flesh.*

רוּחַ חַיִּים. Subject > fs / Carrier > nominal group: noun common fs const | noun common mp.

מִתַּחַת הַשָּׁמָיִם. Circumstance: location, place > prep phrase: prep + prep | def art + noun common mp. This Circumstance has a role in the Transitivity structure of the embedded purpose clause (i), and not in the immediately preceding embedded relative clause (a').

כֹּל [[אֲשֶׁר־בָּאָרֶץ]] יִגְוָע. (b) Textuality > appositive paratactic projection: quote / Mood > declarative: non-past / Transitivity > material: action.

יִגְוָע	כֹּל [[אֲשֶׁר־בָּאָרֶץ]]	**Constituents**
will perish	*all which is on the earth*	**Translation**
	Theme	**Textuality**
Finite	Subject	**Mood**
Process	Actor	**Transitivity**

כֹּל [[אֲשֶׁר־בָּאָרֶץ]]. Theme: experiential / Subject > ms / Actor > nominal group: Head + Post-modifier.

כֹּל. Head > noun common collective ms.

אֲשֶׁר־בָּאָרֶץ. Post-modifier. (i) Textuality > embedded expansion: relative clause / Mood > declarative: non-past / Transitivity > relational: attribution.

בָּאָרֶץ	אֲשֶׁר־	**Constituents**
on the earth	*which*	**Translation**
	Theme	**Textuality**
Complement	Subject	**Mood**
Attribute	Carrier	**Transitivity**

אֲשֶׁר־. Theme: textual > pronoun relative / Subject > ms (כֹּל) / Carrier > antecedent כֹּל *all.*

בָּאָרֶץ. Complement / Attribute > prep phrase: prep + def art + noun common fs.

יִגְוָע. Finite > yiqtol 3ms / Process > qal גוע.

6:18 // וַהֲקִמֹתִי אֶת־בְּרִיתִי אִתָּךְ // וּבָאתָ אֶל־הַתֵּבָה אַתָּה וּבָנֶיךָ וְאִשְׁתְּךָ וּנְשֵׁי־בָנֶיךָ אִתָּךְ׃

וַהֲקִמֹתִי אֶת־בְּרִיתִי אִתָּךְ. (a) Textuality > conj paratactic projection: quote / Mood > declarative: non-past / Transitivity > material: action.

אִתָּךְ	אֶת־בְּרִיתִי	וַהֲקִמֹתִי	**Constituents**
with you	*my covenant*	*and I will establish*	**Translation**
		Theme	**Textuality**
		Finite	**Mood**
Beneficiary	Goal	Process	**Transitivity**

וַהֲקִמֹתִי. Theme: textual > clause conj + Theme: experiential / Finite > weqatal 1cs / Process > hifil קום.

אֶת־בְּרִיתִי. Goal > nominal group: goal marker - noun common fs const + pronoun suffix 1cs, antecedent is the Sayer, אֱלֹהִים *deity* in 6:13(a).

אִתָּךְ. Beneficiary > prep phrase: prep + pronoun suffix 2ms, antecedent is the Receiver of the quote, נֹחַ *Noach* in 6:13(a).

וּבָאתָ אֶל־הַתֵּבָה אַתָּה וּבָנֶיךָ וְאִשְׁתְּךָ וּנְשֵׁי־בָנֶיךָ אִתָּךְ. (b) Textuality > conj paratactic projection: quote / Mood > declarative: non-past / Transitivity > material: action.

אַתָּה וּבָנֶיךָ וְאִשְׁתְּךָ וּנְשֵׁי־בָנֶיךָ אִתָּךְ	אֶל־הַתֵּבָה	וּבָאתָ	**Constituents**
you and your sons and your woman and the women of your sons with you	*to the ark*	*and you will go*	**Translation**
		Theme	**Textuality**
Subject		Finite	**Mood**
Actor	Circumstance	Process	**Transitivity**

וּבָאתָ. Theme: textual > clause conj + Theme: experiential / Finite > weqatal 2ms / Process > qal בוא.

אֶל־הַתֵּבָה. Circumstance: location, place > prep phrase: prep - def art + noun common fs.

אַתָּה וּבָנֶיךָ וְאִשְׁתְּךָ וּנְשֵׁי־בָנֶיךָ אִתָּךְ. Subject > 2ms (אַתָּה) / Actor > nominal group complex: Head + Addition + Post-modifier.

אַתָּה. Head > pronoun personal 2ms. Notice that this is the grammatical Subject of the Finite, which is singular.

וּבָנֶיךָ וְאִשְׁתְּךָ וּנְשֵׁי־בָנֶיךָ. Addition > group conj + noun common mp const + pronoun suffix 2ms, antecedent is אַתָּה *you* | group conj + noun common fs const + pronoun suffix 2ms, antecedent is אַתָּה *you* | group conj + noun common fp const - noun common mp const + pronoun suffix 2ms, antecedent is אַתָּה *you.*

אִתָּךְ. Post-modifier > prep phrase: prep + pronoun suffix 2ms, antecedent is אַתָּה *you.* This is a compressed relative clause: *who are with you.*

6:19 // וּמִכָּל־הָחַי מִכָּל־בָּשָׂר שְׁנַיִם מִכֹּל תָּבִיא אֶל־
הַתֵּבָה לְהַחֲיֹת אִתָּךְ // זָכָר וּנְקֵבָה יִהְיוּ׃

וּמִכָּל־הָחַי מִכָּל־בָּשָׂר שְׁנַיִם מִכֹּל תָּבִיא אֶל־הַתֵּבָה [[לְהַחֲיֹת אִתָּךְ]]. (a) Textuality > conj paratactic projection: quote

/ Mood > declarative: non-past / Transitivity > material: action. The Subject / Actor is אַתָּה *you* from the prior clause.

[[לְהַחֲיֹת אִתָּךְ]]	אֶל־הַתֵּבָה	תָּבִיא	שְׁנַיִם מִכֹּל	וּמִכָּל־הָחַי מִכָּל־בָּשָׂר	**Constituents**
to keep alive with you	*to the ark*	*you will bring*	*two from all*	*and from all of the alive from all of flesh*	**Translation**
				Theme	**Textuality**
		Finite			**Mood**
Circum-stance	Circum-stance	Process	Goal	Range	**Transitivity**

וּמִכָּל־הָחַי מִכָּל־בָּשָׂר. Theme: textual > clause conj + Theme: experiential / Range > prep phrase complex: Head + Post-modifier. The second prep phrase adds specificity to the first one.

מִכָּל־הָחַי. Prep phrase 1 > prep + noun common collective ms const - def art + noun common ms. This is the more general of the two.

מִכָּל־בָּשָׂר. Prep phrase 2 > prep + noun common collective ms const - noun common collective ms. This is more specific, specifying which alive things of what kind will be brought into the ark.

שְׁנַיִם מִכֹּל. Goal > Head + Post-modifier.

שְׁנַיִם. Head > noun common m dual.

מִכֹּל. Post-modifier > prep phrase: prep + noun common collective ms. The כֹּל here references the specification in the preceding Range prep phrase complex.

תָּבִיא. Finite > yiqtol 2ms / Process > hifil בוא.

אֶל־הַתֵּבָה. Circumstance: location, place > prep phrase: prep - def art + noun common fs.

לְהַחֲיֹת אִתָּךְ. (i) Circumstance: cause, purpose >> Textuality > embedded expansion: prep clause / Transitivity > material: action.

אִתָּךְ	לְהַחֲיֹת	**Constituents**
with you	*to keep alive*	**Translation**
	Theme	**Textuality**
Circumstance	Process	**Transitivity**

לְהַחֲיֹת. Theme: textual > prep + Theme: experiential / Process > inf const hifil חיה.

אִתָּךְ. Circumstance: accompaniment > prep phrase: prep + pronoun suffix 2ms, antecedent is the Receiver of the quote, אַתָּה *you.*

זָכָר וּנְקֵבָה יִהְיוּ. (b) Textuality > appositive paratactic projection: quote / Mood > declarative: non-past / Transitivity > relational: attribution. Subject / Carrier is שְׁנַיִם *two* from 6:19(a), absent here by ellipsis.

יִהְיוּ	זָכָר וּנְקֵבָה	**Constituents**
they will be	*male and female*	**Translation**
	Theme	**Textuality**
Finite		**Mood**
Process	Attribute	**Transitivity**

זָכָר וּנְקֵבָה. Theme: experiential / Attribute > nominal group complex: noun common ms | group conj + noun common fs.

יִהְיוּ. Finite > yiqtol 3mp / Process > qal היה.

6:20 // מֵהָעוֹף לְמִינֵהוּ וּמִן־הַבְּהֵמָה לְמִינָהּ מִכֹּל רֶמֶשׂ
הָאֲדָמָה לְמִינֵהוּ שְׁנַיִם מִכֹּל יָבֹאוּ אֵלֶיךָ לְהַחֲיוֹת׃

מֵהָעוֹף לְמִינֵהוּ וּמִן־הַבְּהֵמָה לְמִינָהּ מִכֹּל רֶמֶשׂ הָאֲדָמָה לְמִינֵהוּ שְׁנַיִם מִכֹּל יָבֹאוּ אֵלֶיךָ [[לְהַחֲיוֹת]]. (a) Textuality > appositive paratactic projection: quote / Mood > declarative: non-past / Transitivity > material: action.

לְהַחֲיוֹת	אֵלֶיךָ	יָבֹאוּ	שְׁנַיִם מִכֹּל	מֵהָעוֹף לְמִינֵהוּ וּמִן־הַבְּהֵמָה לְמִינָהּ מִכֹּל רֶמֶשׂ הָאֲדָמָה לְמִינֵהוּ	**Constituents**
to keep alive	*to you*	*they will go*	*two from all*	*from the fowl for his kind and from the beastkind for her kind, from all of the creeperkind of the earth for his kind*	**Translation**
				Theme	**Textuality**
		Finite	Subject		**Mood**
Expan-sion	Circum-stance	Process	Actor	Range	**Transitivity**

מֵהָעוֹף לְמִינֵהוּ וּמִן־הַבְּהֵמָה לְמִינָהּ מִכֹּל רֶמֶשׂ הָאֲדָמָה לְמִינֵהוּ. Theme: experiential / Range > prep phrase complex: it consists of three prepositional phrase complexes. The first two prepositional phrase complexes are joined by the conjunction, but not the third one, which raises the question of how that third one is related within the larger complex. In a series, usually the third item has the conjunction, or all items after the first have the conjunction, but not usually just the second and not the third.

מֵהָעוֹף לְמִינֵהוּ. Prep phrase complex 1 > prep phrase: prep + def art + noun common collective ms | prep phrase: prep + noun common ms const + pronoun suffix 3ms, antecedent is הָעוֹף *the fowl.*

וּמִן־הַבְּהֵמָה לְמִינָהּ. Group conj + Prep phrase complex 2 > prep - def art + noun common collective fs | prep phrase: prep + noun common ms const + pronoun suffix 3fs, antecedent is הַבְּהֵמָה *the beastkind.*

מִכֹּל רֶמֶשׂ הָאֲדָמָה לְמִינֵהוּ. Prep phrase complex 3 > prep phrase: prep + noun common collective ms const | noun common collective ms const | def art + noun common fs | prep phrase: prep + noun common ms const + pronoun suffix 3ms, antecedent is רֶמֶשׂ *creeperkind.*

שְׁנַיִם מִכֹּל. Subject > mp / Actor > nominal group: Head + Post-modifier.

שְׁנַיִם. Head > noun common m dual.

מִכֹּל. Post-modifier > prep phrase: prep + noun common ms.

יָבֹאוּ. Finite > yiqtol 3mp / Process > qal בוא.

אֵלֶיךָ. Circumstance: location, place > prep phrase: prep + pronoun suffix 2ms, antecedent is the Receiver of the quote, אַתָּה *you.*

לְהַחֲיוֹת. (i) Circumstance: cause, purpose >> Textuality > embedded expansion: prep clause / Transitivity > material: action.

לְהַחֲיוֹת	**Constituents**
to keep alive	**Translation**
Theme	**Textuality**
Process	**Transitivity**

לְהַחֲיוֹת. Theme: textual > prep / Theme: experiential / Process > inf const hifil חיה.

6:21 // וְאַתָּ֣ה קַח־לְךָ֗ מִכָּל־מַאֲכָל֙ אֲשֶׁ֣ר יֵאָכֵ֔ל //
וְאָסַפְתָּ֖ אֵלֶ֑יךָ // וְהָיָ֥ה לְךָ֛ וְלָהֶ֖ם לְאָכְלָֽה׃

וְאַתָּה קַח־לְךָ מִכָּל־מַאֲכָל [[אֲשֶׁר יֵאָכֵל]]. (a) Textuality > conj paratactic projection: quote / Mood > directive: imperative / Transitivity > material: action.

מִכָּל־מַאֲכָל [[אֲשֶׁר יֵאָכֵל]]	לְךָ	קַח־	וְאַתָּה	**Constituents**
from all foodstuff, which will be eaten	*for yourself*	*take*	*and you*	**Translation**
			Theme	**Textuality**
		Finite	Subject	**Mood**
Goal	Beneficiary	Process	Actor	**Transitivity**

וְאַתָּה. Theme: textual > clause conj + Theme: experiential / Subject > 2ms / Actor > pronoun personal. This is a special thematic structure; the imperative alone and in first position is the unmarked structure for such directive clauses. Making the Subject of the imperative explicit and placing it first thematizes it.

קַח־. Finite > impv ms / Process > qal לקח.

לְךָ. Beneficiary > prep phrase: prep + pronoun suffix 2ms, antecedent is אַתָּה *you*.

מִכָּל־מַאֲכָל [[אֲשֶׁר יֵאָכֵל]]. Goal > prep phrase + Post-modifier. Normally a prep phrase complex would not be a Participant in the Transitivity structure of a clause, but here it is. This construction can be referred to as the partitive usage of מִן, meaning *some of.*

מִכָּל־מַאֲכָל. Prep phrase > prep + noun common collective ms const - noun common ms.

אֲשֶׁר יֵאָכֵל. (i) Post-modifier >> Textuality > embedded expansion: relative clause / Mood > declarative: non-past / Transitivity > material: action.

יֵאָכֵל	אֲשֶׁר	**Constituents**
it will be eaten	*which*	**Translation**
	Theme	**Textuality**
Finite	Subject	**Mood**
Process	Goal	**Transitivity**

אֲשֶׁר. Theme: textual > pronoun relative / Subject > ms / Goal > antecedent כָּל־מַאֲכָל *all of food*.

יֵאָכֵל. Finite > yiqtol 3ms / Process > nifal אכל.

וְאָסַפְתָּ אֵלֶיךָ. (b) Textuality > conj paratactic projection: quote / Mood > declarative: non-past / Transitivity > material: action. The Goal of the process is מִכָּל־מַאֲכָל *from all foodstuff*, absent here by ellipsis.

אֵלֶיךָ	וְאָסַפְתָּ	**Constituents**
to yourself	*and you will gather*	**Translation**
	Theme	**Textuality**
	Finite	**Mood**
Circumstance	Process	**Transitivity**

וְאָסַפְתָּ. Theme: textual > clause conj + Theme: experiential / Finite > weqatal 2ms / Process > qal אסף.

אֵלֶיךָ. Circumstance: location, place > prep phrase: prep + pronoun suffix 2ms, antecedent is אַתָּה *you*.

וְהָיָה לְךָ וְלָהֶם לְאָכְלָה. (c) Textuality > conj paratactic projection: quote / Mood > declarative: non-past / Transitivity > relational: attribution. The Subject / Carrier of the relational process is כָּל־מַאֲכָל *all foodstuff*.

לְאָכְלָה	לְךָ וְלָהֶם	וְהָיָה	**Constituents**
for food	*for you and for them*	*and it will be*	**Translation**
		Theme	**Textuality**
		Finite	**Mood**
Attribute	Beneficiary	Process	**Transitivity**

וְהָיָה. Theme: textual > clause conj + Theme: experiential / Finite > weqatal 3ms / Process > qal היה.

לְךָ וְלָהֶם. Beneficiary > prep phrase complex: prep phrase 1 + prep phrase 2.

לְךָ. Prep phrase 1 > prep + pronoun suffix 2ms, antecedent is אַתָּה *you.*

וְלָהֶם. Group conj + Prep phrase 2 > prep + pronoun suffix 3mp, antecedent is all the animals and humans mentioned in 6:18-20.

לְאָכְלָה. Attribute > prep phrase: prep + noun common fs.

6:22 // וַיַּעַשׂ נֹחַ // כְּכֹל אֲשֶׁר צִוָּה אֹתוֹ אֱלֹהִים כֵּן עָשָׂה׃ ס

וַיַּעַשׂ נֹחַ. (a) Textuality > conj paratactic expansion / Mood > declarative: past / Transitivity > material: action. The Goal of the material process is not specified but can be assumed to be the series of instructions contained in the prior clauses. The MT *'atnach* accent indicates that the following כְּ constituent is to be structured as part of the following clause rather than as a part of this clause.

נֹחַ	וַיַּעַשׂ	**Constituents**
Noach	*and he did*	**Translation**
	Theme	**Textuality**
Subject	Finite	**Mood**
Actor	Process	**Transitivity**

וַיַּעַשׂ. Theme: textual > clause conj + Theme: experiential / Finite > wayyiqtol 3ms / Process > qal עשׂה.

נֹחַ. Subject > ms / Actor > noun proper.

כְּכֹל [[אֲשֶׁר צִוָּה אֹתוֹ אֱלֹהִים]] כֵּן עָשָׂה. (b) Textuality > appositive paratactic expansion/ Mood > declarative: past / Transitivity > material: action. This clause employs a special thematizing structure called the preposed Theme. A preposed Theme is a marked structure that announces the Theme of the clause as a separate constituent which is substituted by a pronoun later in the clause, in this case by כֵּן *so.* This preposed Theme structure of כְּכֹל אֲשֶׁר followed by כֵּן plus עשׂה is found elsewhere in the Hebrew Bible: see, for example, Ex. 25:9, 39:32, and 42. The Subject / Actor of this clause process is נֹחַ *Noach* in the prior clause, absent here by ellipsis. This clause is clearly designed to be the concluding clause of a clause complex.

עָשָׂה	כֵּן	כְּכֹל [[אֲשֶׁר צִוָּה אֹתוֹ אֱלֹהִים]]	**Constituents**
he did	*so*	*such as all which deity commanded him*	**Translation**
		Theme	**Textuality**
Finite			**Mood**
Process	Goal	Circumstance	**Transitivity**

כְּכֹל [[אֲשֶׁר צִוָּה אֹתוֹ אֱלֹהִים]]. Theme: experiential / Circumstance: manner > prep phrase: Head + Post-modifier.

כְּכֹל. Head > prep + noun common ms.

אֲשֶׁר צִוָּה אֹתוֹ אֱלֹהִים. (i) Post-modifier >> Textuality > embedded expansion: relative clause / Mood > declarative: past / Transitivity > verbal.

אֱלֹהִים	אֹתוֹ	צִוָּה	אֲשֶׁר	**Constituents**
deity	*him*	*he commanded*	*which*	**Translation**
			Theme	**Textuality**
Subject		Finite		**Mood**
Sayer	Receiver	Process	Verbiage	**Transitivity**

אֲשֶׁר. Theme: textual and experiential > pronoun relative / Verbiage > antecedent כֹּל *all.*

צִוָּה. Finite > qatal 3ms / Process > piel צוה.

אֹתוֹ. Receiver > goal marker + pronoun suffix 3ms, antecedent is נֹחַ *Noach.*

אֱלֹהִים. Subject > mp / Sayer > noun common.

כֵּן. Goal > text pronoun, antecedent is the prior Theme / Circumstance.

עָשָׂה. Finite > qatal 3ms / Process > qal עשׂה.

Genesis 7:1-5

[1]And YHVH said to Noach, "Go you and all of your house to the ark.
You I saw, that you are righteous before me in this generation. [2]From
all the clean beastkind you will take for yourself man and his woman by
sevens. And from the beastkind which is not clean, man and his woman
by pairs. [3]Also from the fowl of the heavens, male and female by sevens
to preserve seed on the face of all the earth. [4]Because in seven more days I
make it rain on the earth forty days and forty nights. And I will eliminate
all of the substance which I made from on the face of the ground." [5]And
Noach did all which YHVH commanded him.

7:1 /// וַיֹּאמֶר יְהוָה לְנֹחַ // בֹּא־אַתָּה וְכָל־בֵּיתְךָ אֶל־הַתֵּבָה / כִּי־אֹתְךָ רָאִיתִי צַדִּיק לְפָנַי בַּדּוֹר הַזֶּה׃

וַיֹּאמֶר יְהוָה לְנֹחַ. (a) Textuality > conj paratactic expansion / Mood > declarative: past / Transitivity > verbal. This clause has a fully explicit transitivity structure as befits the first clause of a new clause complex.

לְנֹחַ	יְהוָה	וַיֹּאמֶר	**Constituents**
to Noach	*YHVH*	*and he said*	**Translation**
		Theme	**Textuality**
	Subject	Finite	**Mood**
Receiver	Sayer	Process	**Transitivity**

וַיֹּאמֶר. Theme: textual > clause conj + Theme: experiential / Finite > wayyiqtol 3ms / Process > qal אמר.

יְהוָה. Subject > ms / Sayer > nominal group: noun proper.

לְנֹחַ. Receiver > prep phrase: prep + noun proper ms.

בֹּא־אַתָּה וְכָל־בֵּיתְךָ אֶל־הַתֵּבָה. (b) Textuality > appositive paratactic projection: quote / Mood > directive: imperative / Transitivity > material: action.

אֶל־הַתֵּבָה	אַתָּה וְכָל־בֵּיתְךָ	בֹּא־	**Constituents**
to the ark	*you and all of your house*	*go*	**Translation**
		Theme	**Textuality**
	Subject	Finite	**Mood**
Circumstance	Actor	Process	**Transitivity**

בֹּא־. Theme: experiential / Finite > impv ms / Process > qal בוא.

אַתָּה וְכָל־בֵּיתְךָ. Subject > 2ms (אַתָּה) / Actor > nominal group complex: Head + Addition.

אַתָּה. Head > pronoun personal 2ms, antecedent is נֹחַ *Noach*, the Receiver in the prior clause. The Head portion of the Goal matches the Finite verb, not the entire nominal group. This maintains the focus on Noach. This indicates that the quote was addressed only to Noach.

וְכָל־בֵּיתְךָ. Group conj + Addition > nominal group: noun common ms const - noun common ms const + pronoun suffix 2ms, antecedent is נֹחַ *Noach*.

אֶל־הַתֵּבָה. Circumstance: location, place > prep phrase: prep - def art + noun common fs.

כִּי־אֹתְךָ רָאִיתִי צַדִּיק לְפָנַי בַּדּוֹר הַזֶּה. (c) Textuality > conj hypotactic projection: quote / Mood > declarative: past / Transitivity > mental: perception. The experiential meaning of the clause is this: *I saw that you are righteous before me in this generation*. The structure that would be congruent with this meaning and with mental processes generally is to have two clauses: a dominant mental process clause and a hypotactic report clause. The Phenomenon of the mental perception process would be the hypotactic relational clause *you are righteous....* But in the present clause, the expected word order has been remapped in order to thematize *you* in a strong way. Thematizing *you* establishes a stark contrast between Noach and the rest of his generation. Most translations view the כִּי as a causal conjunctive adjunct, linking it to the prior clause. But the logical relationship between *Go!* and *because I saw* is not immediately evident. More likely, the כִּי introduces the report clause of the mental process. The mental process verb was displaced from the head of the clause when אֹתְךָ *you* was thematized: *that you, I saw, are righteous before me in this generation. You* אֹתְךָ is, in fact, thematized in two ways: in addition to being made the first clause Participant in serial order, it is rendered as a constituent in the main mental process (the Goal of ראה) rather than as the Carrier of the dependent (hypotactic) report clause. To communicate both thematic effects, the clause could be rendered: *You I saw, that you are righteous before me in this generation*. See Bandstra (1982) for the syntax of כִּי in BH.

בַּדּוֹר הַזֶּה	לְפָנַי	צַדִּיק	רָאִיתִי	אֹתְךָ	כִּי־	**Constituents**
in this generation	*before me*	*righteous*	*I saw*	*you*	*that*	**Translation**
				Theme	Theme	**Textuality**
			Finite			**Mood**
Range	Circumstance	Attribute	Process	Goal + Carrier		**Transitivity**

כִּי־. Theme: textual > conj.

אֹתְךָ. Theme: experiential / Goal (of the dominant clause) + Carrier (of the dependent clause) > goal marker + pronoun suffix 2ms, antecedent is אַתָּה *you* in the dominant clause.

רָאִיתִי. Finite > qatal 1cs / Process > qal ראה.

צַדִּיק. Attribute > adjective group: adj 3ms.

לְפָנַי. Circumstance: location, place > prep phrase: prep + noun common mp const + pronoun suffix 1cs, antecedent is the Sayer of the quote, יְהוָה *YHVH*.

בַּדּוֹר הַזֶּה. Range > prep phrase: prep + def art + noun common ms | def art + pronoun demonstrative: near 3ms.

7:2 // מִכֹּ֣ל ׀ הַבְּהֵמָ֣ה הַטְּהוֹרָ֗ה תִּֽקַּח־לְךָ֛ שִׁבְעָ֥ה
שִׁבְעָ֖ה אִ֣ישׁ וְאִשְׁתּ֑וֹ // וּמִן־הַבְּהֵמָ֡ה אֲ֠שֶׁר לֹ֣א
טְהֹרָ֥ה הִ֛וא שְׁנַ֖יִם אִ֥ישׁ וְאִשְׁתּֽוֹ׃

מִכֹּל הַבְּהֵמָה הַטְּהוֹרָה תִּקַּח־לְךָ שִׁבְעָה שִׁבְעָה אִישׁ וְאִשְׁתּוֹ. (a) Textuality > appositive paratactic projection: quote / Mood > declarative: non-past / Transitivity > material: action. The Subject / Actor is the Receiver of the quote, נֹחַ *Noach*.

אִישׁ וְאִשְׁתּוֹ	שִׁבְעָה שִׁבְעָה	לְךָ	תִּקַּח־	מִכֹּל הַבְּהֵמָה הַטְּהוֹרָה	**Constituents**
man and his woman	*seven seven*	*for yourself*	*you will take*	*from all the clean beast-kind*	**Translation**
				Theme	**Textuality**
			Finite		**Mood**
Goal	Scope	Beneficiary	Process	Range	**Transitivity**

מִכֹּל הַבְּהֵמָה הַטְּהוֹרָה. Theme: experiential / Range > prep phrase: prep + noun common ms const | def art + noun common collective fs | def art + adj fs.

תִּקַּח־. Finite > yiqtol 2ms / Process > qal לקח.

לְךָ. Beneficiary > prep phrase: prep + pronoun suffix 2ms, antecedent is אַתָּה *you*.

שִׁבְעָה שִׁבְעָה. Scope > nominal group: numeral ms | numeral ms. The item counted is הַבְּהֵמָה *the beast. Seven seven*, no conjunction, presumably means seven pairs; Hebrew does not otherwise have a word for *pair*. A constituent that functions as Scope is typically a constituent that looks like a participant, as here, but that really serves to specify something about how the process will be carried out.

אִישׁ וְאִשְׁתּוֹ. Goal > nominal group complex: noun common ms | group conj + noun common fs const + pronoun suffix 3ms, antecedent is אִישׁ *man*. The phrase does not reference humans but the male and female mates of the animal kingdom.

וּמִן־הַבְּהֵמָה [[אֲשֶׁר לֹא טְהֹרָה הִוא]] שְׁנַיִם אִישׁ וְאִשְׁתּוֹ. (b) Textuality > conj paratactic projection: quote / Mood > declarative: non-past / Transitivity > material: action. This string does not have a Finite, so it could be interpreted as a continuation of the preceding clause. Or, the Process + Beneficiary תִּקַּח־לְךָ *you will take for yourself* could be inferred from the prior clause, and be considered absent here due to ellipsis.

אִישׁ וְאִשְׁתּוֹ	שְׁנַיִם	וּמִן־הַבְּהֵמָה [[אֲשֶׁר לֹא טְהֹרָה הִוא]]	**Constituents**
man and his woman	*twos*	*and from the beast, which not clean she*	**Translation**
		Theme	**Textuality**
			Mood
Goal	Scope	Range	**Transitivity**

וּמִן־הַבְּהֵמָה [[אֲשֶׁר לֹא טְהֹרָה הִוא]]. Theme: textual > clause conj + Theme: experiential / Range > prep phrase: Head + Post-modifier.

מִן־הַבְּהֵמָה. Head > prep phrase: prep - def art + noun common fs.

אֲשֶׁר לֹא טְהֹרָה הִוא. (i) Post-modifier >> Textuality > embedded expansion: relative clause / Mood > declarative: non-past / Transitivity > relational: attribution.

הִוא	טְהֹרָה	לֹא	אֲשֶׁר	**Constituents**
she	*clean*	*not*	*which*	**Translation**
			Theme	**Textuality**
Subject	Complement	Adjunct	Subject	**Mood**
Carrier	Attribute		Carrier	**Transitivity**

אֲשֶׁר. Theme: textual > pronoun relative / Subject > fs / Carrier > antecedent הַבְּהֵמָה *the beast.* The Subject / Carrier is substituted later in the clause by הִוא.

לֹא. Adjunct: interpersonal > polarity: negative.

טְהֹרָה. Complement / Attribute > adjective group: adj fs.

הִוא. Carrier > pronoun personal 3fs, antecedent is הַבְּהֵמָה *the beast.*

שְׁנַיִם. Scope > nominal group: numeral md.

אִישׁ וְאִשְׁתּוֹ. Goal > nominal group complex: noun common ms | group conj + noun common fs const + pronoun suffix 3ms, antecedent is אִישׁ *man.*

7:3 // גַּם מֵעוֹף הַשָּׁמַיִם שִׁבְעָה שִׁבְעָה זָכָר וּנְקֵבָה
לְחַיּוֹת זֶרַע עַל־פְּנֵי כָל־הָאָרֶץ׃

גַּם מֵעוֹף הַשָּׁמַיִם שִׁבְעָה שִׁבְעָה זָכָר וּנְקֵבָה לְחַיּוֹת זֶרַע עַל־פְּנֵי כָל־הָאָרֶץ. (a) Textuality > appositive paratactic projection: quote / Mood > declarative: non-past / Transitivity > material: action. As with 7:2(b), we read this string as a clause, but one which is missing an explicit Finite. As before, the Process + Beneficiary is תִּקַּח־לְךָ *you will take for yourself,* which is retrieved from 7:2(a), and is considered absent here due to ellipsis. The effect of this repeated ellipsis is the creation of a cohesive clause complex.

[[לְחַיּוֹת זֶרַע עַל־פְּנֵי כָל־הָאָרֶץ]]	זָכָר וּנְקֵבָה	שִׁבְעָה שִׁבְעָה	מֵעוֹף הַשָּׁמַיִם	גַּם	**Constituents**
to keep alive seed on the face of all the earth	*male and female*	*seven seven*	*from the fowl of the heavens*	*also*	**Translation**
			Theme	Adjunct	**Textuality**
					Mood
Circumstance	Goal	Scope	Range		**Transitivity**

גַּם. Theme: textual / Adjunct: textual > addition. Indicates that this is a continuation of the clause complex, and it specifically conditions the following prep phrase.

מֵעוֹף הַשָּׁמַיִם. Theme: experiential / Range > prep phrase: prep + noun common collective ms const | def art + noun common mp.

שִׁבְעָה שִׁבְעָה. Scope > nominal group: numeral ms + numeral ms.

זָכָר וּנְקֵבָה. Goal > nominal group: noun common ms | group conj + noun common fs.

לְחַיּוֹת זֶרַע עַל־פְּנֵי כָל־הָאָרֶץ. (i) Circumstance: cause, purpose >> Textuality > embedded extension: prep clause / Transitivity > material: event.

עַל־פְּנֵי כָל־הָאָרֶץ	זֶרַע	לְחַיּוֹת	**Constituents**
on the face of all the earth	*seed*	*to preserve*	**Translation**
		Theme	**Textuality**
Circumstance	Goal	Process	**Transitivity**

לְחַיּוֹת. Theme > textual + Theme: experiential / Non-finite: inf const / Process > piel חיה.

זֶרַע. Goal > nominal group: noun common collective ms.

עַל־פְּנֵי כָל־הָאָרֶץ. Circumstance: location, place > prep phrase: prep - noun common mp const | noun common collective ms const - def art + noun common fs.

7:4 / כִּ֣י לְיָמִ֞ים ע֣וֹד שִׁבְעָ֗ה אָנֹכִי֙ מַמְטִ֣יר עַל־הָאָ֔רֶץ
אַרְבָּעִ֣ים י֔וֹם וְאַרְבָּעִ֖ים לָ֑יְלָה // וּמָחִ֗יתִי אֶֽת־כָּל־
הַיְקוּם֙ אֲשֶׁ֣ר עָשִׂ֔יתִי מֵעַ֖ל פְּנֵ֥י הָאֲדָמָֽה׃

כִּי לְיָמִים עוֹד שִׁבְעָה אָנֹכִי מַמְטִיר עַל־הָאָרֶץ אַרְבָּעִים יוֹם

וְאַרְבָּעִים לָיְלָה. (a) Textuality > conj hypotactic projection: quote / Mood > declarative: non-past / Transitivity > material: action.

אַרְבָּעִים יוֹם וְאַרְבָּעִים לָיְלָה	עַל־הָאָרֶץ	מַמְטִיר	אָנֹכִי	לְיָמִים עוֹד שִׁבְעָה	כִּי	**Constituents**
forty days and forty nights	*on the earth*	*am making rain*	*I*	*to days again seven*	*because*	**Translation**
				Theme	Theme	**Textuality**
		Finite	Subject			**Mood**
Scope	Circum-stance	Process	Actor	Circum-stance		**Transitivity**

כִּי. Theme: textual > conj.

לְיָמִים עוֹד שִׁבְעָה. Theme: experiential / Circumstance: extent, time > prep phrase: prep + noun common mp + circumstantial adjunct + numeral ms. This phrase indicates that the rain will arrive seven days from the time of speaking.

עוֹד. Adjunct: textual > recurrence. The **עוֹד** *again* qualifies *seven*: *seven more days, seven days from now*. Here the textual adjunct intervenes between *days* and *seven*. Normally **עוֹד** stands before the Circumstance. Compare 8:10(a) and 8:12(a). However, the Circumstance is a prepositional phrase here in contrast to the examples in chapter 8.

אָנֹכִי. Subject > 1cs / Actor > pronoun personal, antecedent is the Sayer, **יְהוָה** *YHVH*, last specified in 7:1(a).

מַמְטִיר. Finite > ptc ms / Process > hifil **מטר**. This is a ptc of imminent action.

עַל־הָאָרֶץ. Circumstance: location, place > prep phrase: prep - def art + noun common fs.

אַרְבָּעִים יוֹם וְאַרְבָּעִים לָיְלָה. Scope > nominal group: numeral cp | noun common ms | group conj + numeral cp | noun common fs.

וּמָחִיתִי אֶת־כָּל־הַיְקוּם [[אֲשֶׁר עָשִׂיתִי]] מֵעַל פְּנֵי הָאֲדָמָה. (b) Textuality > conj paratactic projection: quote / Mood > declarative: non-past / Transitivity > material: action. The Subject / Actor is the Sayer of the quote, יְהוָה *YHVH*.

מֵעַל פְּנֵי הָאֲדָמָה	אֶת־כָּל־הַיְקוּם [[אֲשֶׁר עָשִׂיתִי]]	וּמָחִיתִי	**Constituents**
from on the face of the ground	*all of the substance, which I made*	*and I will eliminate*	**Translation**
		Theme	**Textuality**
		Finite	**Mood**
Circumstance	Goal	Process	**Transitivity**

וּמָחִיתִי. Theme: textual > clause conj + Theme: experiential / Finite > weqatal 1cs / Process > qal מחה.

אֶת־כָּל־הַיְקוּם [[אֲשֶׁר עָשִׂיתִי]]. Goal > nominal group complex: Head + Post-modifier.

אֶת־כָּל־הַיְקוּם. Head > nominal group: goal marker - noun common collective ms const - def art + noun common ms.

אֲשֶׁר עָשִׂיתִי. (i) Post-modifier >> Textuality > embedded expansion: relative clause / Mood > declarative: past / Transitivity > material: action.

עָשִׂיתִי	אֲשֶׁר	**Constituents**
I made	*which*	**Translation**
	Theme	**Textuality**
Finite		**Mood**
Process	Goal	**Transitivity**

אֲשֶׁר. Theme: textual and experiential > pronoun relative / Goal > antecedent כָּל־הַיְקוּם *all of the substance.*

עָשִׂיתִי. Finite > qatal 1cs / Process > qal עשׂה.

מֵעַל פְּנֵי הָאֲדָמָה. Circumstance: location, place > prep phrase: prep + prep | noun common mp const | def art + noun common fs.

7:5 // וַיַּעַשׂ נֹחַ כְּכֹל אֲשֶׁר־צִוָּהוּ יְהוָה׃

וַיַּעַשׂ נֹחַ כְּכֹל [[אֲשֶׁר־צִוָּהוּ יְהוָה]]. (a) Textuality > conj paratactic expansion / Mood > declarative: past / Transitivity > material: action. This fulfillment clause completes the clause complex.

כְּכֹל [[אֲשֶׁר־צִוָּהוּ יְהוָה]]	נֹחַ	וַיַּעַשׂ	**Constituents**
such as all which YHVH commanded him	*Noach*	*and he did*	**Translation**
		Theme	**Textuality**
	Subject	Finite	**Mood**
Circumstance	Actor	Process	**Transitivity**

וַיַּעַשׂ. Theme: textual > clause conj + Theme: experiential / Finite > wayyiqtol 3ms / Process > qal עשׂה.

נֹחַ. Subject > ms / Actor > nominal group: noun proper.

כְּכֹל [[אֲשֶׁר־צִוָּהוּ יְהוָה]]. Circumstance: manner > prep phrase: Head + Post-modifier.

כְּכֹל. Head > prep phrase: prep + noun common ms.

אֲשֶׁר־צִוָּהוּ יְהוָה. (i) Post-modifier >> Textuality > embedded expansion: relative clause / Mood > declarative: past / Transitivity > verbal.

יְהוָה	צִוָּהוּ	אֲשֶׁר־	**Constituents**
YHVH	*he commanded him*	*which*	**Translation**
		Theme	**Textuality**
Subject	Finite		**Mood**
Sayer	Process + Receiver	Verbiage	**Transitivity**

אֲשֶׁר־. Theme: textual and experiential > pronoun relative / Verbiage > antecedent כֹּל *all.*

צִוָּהוּ. Finite > qatal 3ms / Process > piel צוה + Receiver > pronoun suffix 3ms, antecedent is נֹחַ *Noach.*

יְהוָה. Subject > ms / Sayer > nominal group: noun proper.

Genesis 7:6-10

[6]And Noach is six hundred years old. And the flood was water on the earth. [7]And Noach and his sons and his woman and his sons' women with him came to the ark from the face of the waters of the flood. [8]From the clean beastkind and from the beastkind which it is not clean and from the fowl and all which creeps on the ground, [9]by twos they came to Noach to the ark, male and female, as deity commanded Noach. [10]The seven days happened, and the waters of the flood were on the earth.

7:6 /// וְנֹחַ בֶּן־שֵׁשׁ מֵאוֹת שָׁנָה // וְהַמַּבּוּל הָיָה מַיִם
עַל־הָאָרֶץ׃

וְנֹחַ בֶּן־שֵׁשׁ מֵאוֹת שָׁנָה. (a) Textuality > conj paratactic expansion / Mood > declarative: non-past / Transitivity > relational: attribution.

בֶּן־שֵׁשׁ מֵאוֹת שָׁנָה	וְנֹחַ	**Constituents**
a son of six hundred years	*and Noach*	**Translation**
	Theme	**Textuality**
Complement	Subject	**Mood**
Attibute	Carrier	**Transitivity**

וְנֹחַ. Theme: textual > clause conj + Theme: experiential / Subject > ms / Carrier > nominal group: noun proper.

בֶּן־שֵׁשׁ מֵאוֹת שָׁנָה. Complement > 3ms (בֶּן) / Attribute > nominal group: noun common ms const - numeral ms | numeral fp | noun common fs.

וְהַמַּבּוּל הָיָה מַיִם עַל־הָאָֽרֶץ. (b) Textuality > conj paratactic expansion / Mood > declarative: past / Transitivity > relational: attribution.

עַל־הָאָֽרֶץ	מַיִם	הָיָה	וְהַמַּבּוּל	**Constituents**
on the earth	*water*	*he was*	*and the flood*	**Translation**
			Theme	**Textuality**
		Finite	Subject	**Mood**
Circumstance	Attribute	Process	Carrier	**Transitivity**

וְהַמַּבּוּל. Theme: textual > clause conj + Theme: experiential / Subject > ms / Carrier > nominal group: def art + noun common ms.

הָיָה. Finite > qatal 3ms / Process > qal היה.

מַיִם. Attribute > nominal group: noun common mp.

עַל־הָאָֽרֶץ. Circumstance: location, place > prep phrase: prep - def art + noun common fs.

7:7 // וַיָּ֣בֹא נֹ֗חַ וּ֠בָנָיו וְאִשְׁתּ֧וֹ וּנְשֵֽׁי־בָנָ֛יו אִתּ֖וֹ אֶל־הַתֵּבָ֑ה
מִפְּנֵ֖י מֵ֥י הַמַּבּֽוּל׃

וַיָּבֹא נֹחַ וּבָנָיו וְאִשְׁתּוֹ וּנְשֵׁי־בָנָיו אִתּוֹ אֶל־הַתֵּבָה מִפְּנֵי מֵי הַמַּבּוּל. (a) Textuality > conj paratactic expansion / Mood > declarative: past / Transitivity > material: action.

מִפְּנֵי מֵי הַמַּבּוּל	אֶל־הַתֵּבָה	נֹחַ וּבָנָיו וְאִשְׁתּוֹ וּנְשֵׁי־בָנָיו אִתּוֹ	וַיָּבֹא	**Constituents**
from the face of the waters of the flood	*to the ark*	*Noach and his sons and his woman and the women of his sons with him*	*and he came*	**Translation**

			Theme	**Textuality**
		Subject	Finite	**Mood**
Range	Circumstance	Actor	Process	**Transitivity**

וַיָּבֹא. Theme: textual > clause conj + Theme: experiential / Finite > wayyiqtol 3ms / Process > qal בוא.

נֹחַ וּבָנָיו וְאִשְׁתּוֹ וּנְשֵׁי־בָנָיו אִתּוֹ. Subject > ms / Actor > nominal group complex: Head + Post-modifier.

נֹחַ. Head > nominal group: noun proper ms.

וּבָנָיו וְאִשְׁתּוֹ וּנְשֵׁי־בָנָיו אִתּוֹ. Group conj + Post-modifier > nominal group 1 + nominal group 2 + nominal group 3 + Post-modifier.

וּבָנָיו. Group conj + Nominal group 1 > noun common mp const + pronoun suffix 3ms, antecedent is נֹחַ *Noach.*

וְאִשְׁתּוֹ. Group conj + Nominal group 2 > noun common fs const + pronoun suffix 3ms, antecedent is נֹחַ *Noach.*

וּנְשֵׁי־בָנָיו. Group conj + Nominal group 3 > noun common fp const - noun common mp const + pronoun suffix 3ms, antecedent is נֹחַ *Noach.*

אִתּוֹ. Post-modifier > prep + pronoun suffix 3ms, antecedent is נֹחַ *Noach.*

אֶל־הַתֵּבָה. Circumstance: location, place > prep - def art + noun common fs.

מִפְּנֵי מֵי הַמַּבּוּל. Range > prep phrase: prep + noun common mp const | noun common mp const | def art + noun common ms. This constituent could be considered a compressed embedded purpose clause with an elliptical process, along the lines of *in order to escape from the waters of the flood.*

7:8-9 // מִן־הַבְּהֵמָה֙ הַטְּהוֹרָ֔ה וּמִן־הַבְּהֵמָ֔ה אֲשֶׁ֥ר אֵינֶ֖נָּה טְהֹרָ֑ה וּמִן־הָע֕וֹף וְכֹ֥ל אֲשֶׁר־רֹמֵ֖שׂ עַל־הָאֲדָמָֽה׃

שְׁנַ֨יִם שְׁנַ֜יִם בָּ֧אוּ אֶל־נֹ֛חַ אֶל־הַתֵּבָ֖ה זָכָ֣ר וּנְקֵבָ֑ה // כַּאֲשֶׁ֛ר צִוָּ֥ה אֱלֹהִ֖ים אֶת־נֹֽחַ׃

מִן־הַבְּהֵמָה הַטְּהוֹרָה וּמִן־הַבְּהֵמָה [[אֲשֶׁר אֵינֶנָּה טְהֹרָה]] וּמִן־הָעוֹף וְכֹל [[אֲשֶׁר־רֹמֵשׂ עַל־הָאֲדָמָה]] שְׁנַיִם שְׁנַיִם בָּאוּ אֶל־נֹחַ אֶל־הַתֵּבָה זָכָר וּנְקֵבָה. (a) Textuality > appositive paratactic expansion / Mood > declarative: past / Transitivity > material: action. This is a very long clause that spans a verse and a half in the MT: 7:8-9(a). The clause contains within it two embedded relative clauses and other enhancements, including an expansion of the Subject / Actor that is separated from its Head and placed at the very end of the clause, perhaps suggesting an afterthought.

זָכָר וּנְקֵבָה	אֶל־נֹחַ אֶל־הַתֵּבָה	בָּאוּ	שְׁנַיִם שְׁנַיִם	מִן־הַבְּהֵמָה הַטְּהוֹרָה וּמִן־הַבְּהֵמָה [[אֲשֶׁר אֵינֶנָּה טְהֹרָה]] וּמִן־הָעוֹף וְכֹל [[אֲשֶׁר־רֹמֵשׂ עַל־הָאֲדָמָה]]	**Constituents**
male and female	*to Noach to the ark*	*they came*	*twos twos*	*from the clean beastkind and from the beastkind which it is not clean and from the fowl and all which creeps on the ground*	**Translation**
				Theme	**Textuality**
Subject		Finite	Subject		**Mood**
Actor	Circumstance	Process	Actor	Scope	**Transitivity**

מִן־הַבְּהֵמָה הַטְּהוֹרָה וּמִן־הַבְּהֵמָה [[אֲשֶׁר אֵינֶנָּה טְהֹרָה]] וּמִן־הָעוֹף וְכֹל [[אֲשֶׁר־רֹמֵשׂ עַל־הָאֲדָמָה]]. Theme: experiential / Range > prep phrase complex [prep phrase 1 + prep phrase 2 + prep phrase 3 + nominal group complex.

מִן־הַבְּהֵמָה הַטְּהוֹרָה. Prep phrase 1 > prep - def art + noun common collective fs ׀ def art + adj fs.

וּמִן־הַבְּהֵמָה [[אֲשֶׁר אֵינֶנָּה טְהֹרָה]]. Group conj + Prep phrase 2 > prep phrase + Post-modifier.

מִן־הַבְּהֵמָה. Prep phrase > prep - def art + noun common collective fs.

אֲשֶׁר אֵינֶנָּה טְהֹרָה. (i) Post-modifier >> Textuality > embedded expansion: relative clause / Mood > declarative: non-past / Transitivity > relational: attribution. This clause adds specification to the object of the preposition, הַבְּהֵמָה *the beast.*

טְהֹרָה	אֵינֶנָּה	אֲשֶׁר	**Constituents**
clean	*she is not*	*which*	**Translation**
		Theme	**Textuality**
Attribute	Process + Carrier	Carrier	**Transitivity**

אֲשֶׁר. Theme: textual and experiential > pronoun relative / Carrier > antecedent הַבְּהֵמָה *the beast.*

אֵינֶנָּה. Process > negative adjunct + Carrier > pronoun suffix 3fs, antecedent is הַבְּהֵמָה *the beast.*

טְהֹרָה. Attribute > adjective group: adj fs.

וּמִן־הָעוֹף. Group conj + Prep phrase 3 > prep - def art + noun common collective ms.

וְכֹל [[אֲשֶׁר־רֹמֵשׂ עַל־הָאֲדָמָה]]. Group conj + nominal group > Head + Post-modifier.

כֹּל. Head > noun common ms. This group does not follow a preposition מִן as the preceding do. The preposition could be assumed on the basis of ellipsis, or its omission was deliberate, perhaps to separate off this class of creature from the rest, because this class did not pair up in a gendered way as did the other classes.

אֲשֶׁר־רֹמֵשׂ עַל־הָאֲדָמָה. (i) Post-modifier >> Textuality > embedded relative clause / Mood > declarative: non-past / Transitivity > material: action.

עַל־הָאֲדָמָה	רֹמֵשׂ	אֲשֶׁר־	**Constituents**
on the ground	*he creeps*	*which*	**Translation**
		Theme	**Textuality**
	Finite	Subject	**Mood**
Circumstance	Process	Actor	**Transitivity**

אֲשֶׁר־. Theme > textual and experiential / Subject > ms / Actor > antecedent כֹּל *all.*

רֹמֵשׂ. Finite > ptc ms / Process > qal רמשׂ.

עַל־הָאֲדָמָה. Circumstance: location, place > prep phrase: prep - def art + noun common fs.

שְׁנַיִם שְׁנַיִם. Subject > mp / Actor > nominal group: numeral ms | numeral ms.

בָּאוּ. Finite > qatal 3mp / Process > qal בוא.

אֶל־נֹחַ אֶל־הַתֵּבָה. Circumstance: location, place > prep phase complex: Head + Post-modifier.

אֶל־נֹחַ. Head > prep phrase: prep - noun proper.

אֶל־הַתֵּבָה. Post-modifier > prep phrase: prep - def art + noun common fs. This prepositional phrase adds specificity to the prior prepositional phrase.

זָכָר וּנְקֵבָה. Subject > cp / Actor > nominal group complex: noun common ms | group conj + noun common fs. This nominal group appears to further define the first articulation of the Subject / Actor by defining what kind of *twos*: *male and female.*

כַּאֲשֶׁר צִוָּה אֱלֹהִים אֶת־נֹחַ. (b) Textuality > conj hypotactic expansion / Mood > declarative: past / Transitivity > verbal.

אֶת־נֹחַ	אֱלֹהִים	צִוָּה	כַּאֲשֶׁר	**Constituents**
Noach	*deity*	*he commanded*	*as which*	**Translation**
			Theme	**Textuality**
	Subject	Finite		**Mood**
Receiver	Sayer	Process	Circumstance	**Transitivity**

כַּאֲשֶׁר. Theme: textual > conj adjunct / Circumstance: matter > antecedent is the prior series of commands given to Noach. This is labeled Matter rather than Verbiage because it is a general back reference to the stated commands, rather than explicit spoken words.

צִוָּה. Finite > qatal 3ms / Process > piel צוה.

אֱלֹהִים. Subject > mp / Sayer > nominal group: noun common.

אֶת־נֹחַ. Receiver > nominal group: goal marker - noun proper 3ms.

7:10 // וַיְהִי לְשִׁבְעַת הַיָּמִים // וּמֵי הַמַּבּוּל הָיוּ עַל־
הָאָרֶץ׃

וַיְהִי לְשִׁבְעַת הַיָּמִים. (a) Textuality > conj paratactic expansion / Mood > declarative: past / Transitivity > existential. We are interpreting this as an existential process to this effect: *the seven days happened*. The clause structure thematizes the fact that the seven days had transpired.

לְשִׁבְעַת הַיָּמִים	וַיְהִי	**Constituents**
to the seven days	*and he was*	**Translation**
	Theme	**Textuality**
	Finite	**Mood**
Existent	Process	**Transitivity**

וַיְהִי. Finite > wayyiqtol 3ms / Process > qal היה. The verb היה plus לְ means *become*, which in the past means *became, happened*.

לְשִׁבְעַת הַיָּמִים. Existent > prep phrase: prep + numeral fs const | def art + noun common mp. The object of the preposition is definite —הַיָּמִים; this prompts us to retrieve its earlier referent, which is in לְיָמִים עוֹד שִׁבְעָה in 7:4(a).

וּמֵי הַמַּבּוּל הָיוּ עַל־הָאָרֶץ. (b) Textuality > conj paratactic expansion / Mood > declarative: past / Transitivity > existential process.

עַל־הָאָרֶץ	הָיוּ	וּמֵי הַמַּבּוּל	**Constituents**
on the earth	*they were*	*and the waters of the flood*	**Translation**
		Theme	**Textuality**
	Finite	Subject	**Mood**
Circumstance	Process	Existent	**Transitivity**

וּמֵי הַמַּבּוּל. Theme: textual > clause conj + Theme: experiential / Subject > mp (מֵי) / Existent > nominal group: noun common mp const | def art + noun common ms.

הָיוּ. Finite > qatal 3mp / Process > qal היה.

עַל־הָאָרֶץ. Circumstance: location, place > prep phrase: prep - def art + noun common fs.

Genesis 7:11-16

[11]In the six hundredth year of the life of Noach, in the second month, in the seventeenth day to the month, in this day, all the sources of great deep-water split. And the windows of the heavens opened. [12]And the rain was on the earth forty days and forty nights. [13]In this very same day Noach, and Shem and Cham and Yefet, the sons of Noach, and the three women of his sons with them came to the ark, [14]they and all of the livingkind for its kind and all of the beastkind for its kind and all of the creeperkind, the creeperkind on the earth for its kinds and all of the fowl for its kinds, all birdkind and all wingedkind. [15]And they came to Noach to the ark by twos from all the flesh in which is spirit of life. [16]And the ones coming are male and female. From all flesh they came, as deity commanded him. And YHVH closed up behind him.

7:11 // בִּשְׁנַ֨ת שֵׁשׁ־מֵא֤וֹת שָׁנָה֙ לְחַיֵּי־נֹ֔חַ בַּחֹ֙דֶשׁ֙ הַשֵּׁנִ֔י
בְּשִׁבְעָֽה־עָשָׂ֥ר י֖וֹם לַחֹ֑דֶשׁ בַּיּ֣וֹם הַזֶּ֗ה נִבְקְעוּ֙ כָּֽל־
מַעְיְנֹת֙ תְּה֣וֹם רַבָּ֔ה // וַאֲרֻבֹּ֥ת הַשָּׁמַ֖יִם נִפְתָּֽחוּ׃

בִּשְׁנַת שֵׁשׁ־מֵאוֹת שָׁנָה לְחַיֵּי־נֹחַ בַּחֹדֶשׁ הַשֵּׁנִי בְּשִׁבְעָה־עָשָׂר יוֹם לַחֹדֶשׁ בַּיּוֹם הַזֶּה נִבְקְעוּ כָּל־מַעְיְנֹת תְּהוֹם רַבָּה. (a) Textuality > appositive paratactic expansion / Mood > declarative: past / Transitivity > material: event.

כָּל־מַעְיְנֹת תְּהוֹם רַבָּה	נִבְקְעוּ	בִּשְׁנַת שֵׁשׁ־מֵאוֹת שָׁנָה לְחַיֵּי־נֹחַ בַּחֹדֶשׁ הַשֵּׁנִי בְּשִׁבְעָה־עָשָׂר יוֹם לַחֹדֶשׁ בַּיּוֹם הַזֶּה	**Constituents**
all sources of great deep-water	*they split*	*in the year of six hundred, a year to the life of Noach, in the second month, in the seventeenth day to the month, in this day*	**Translation**
		Theme	**Textuality**
Subject	Finite		**Mood**
Actor	Process	Circumstance	**Transitivity**

בִּשְׁנַת שֵׁשׁ־מֵאוֹת שָׁנָה לְחַיֵּי־נֹחַ בַּחֹדֶשׁ הַשֵּׁנִי בְּשִׁבְעָה־עָשָׂר יוֹם לַחֹדֶשׁ בַּיּוֹם הַזֶּה. Circumstance: location, time > prep phrase complex: [prep phrase 1 + Post-modifier] + prep phrase 2 + [prep phrase 3 + Post-modifier] + prep phrase 4.

בִּשְׁנַת שֵׁשׁ־מֵאוֹת שָׁנָה לְחַיֵּי־נֹחַ. Prep phrase 1 + Post-modifier.

בִּשְׁנַת שֵׁשׁ־מֵאוֹת. Prep phrase 1 > prep + noun common fs const | numeral fs - numeral fs.

שָׁנָה לְחַיֵּי־נֹחַ. Post-modifier > nominal group: noun common fs | prep phrase: prep + noun common mp const - noun proper.

בַּחֹדֶשׁ הַשֵּׁנִי. Prep phrase 2 > prep + noun common ms | def art + numeral ms.

בְּשִׁבְעָה־עָשָׂר יוֹם לַחֹדֶשׁ. Prep phrase 3 + Post-modifier.

בְּשִׁבְעָה־עָשָׂר יוֹם. Prep phrase 3 > prep + numeral ms - numeral ms | noun common ms.

לַחֹדֶשׁ. Post-modifier > prep phrase: prep + def art + noun common ms.

בַּיּוֹם הַזֶּה. Prep phrase 4 > prep + noun common ms | def art + pronoun demonstrative ms.

נִבְקְעוּ. Finite > qatal 3cp / Process > nifal בקע. The verb is taken as middle voice rather than passive, since no agent is specified.

כָּל־מַעְיְנֹת תְּהוֹם רַבָּה. Subject > mp / Actor > nominal group: noun common collective ms const - noun common fp const | noun common fs | adj fs. The Subject / Actor is כָּל־ *all* in a plural sense, or it could be מַעְיְנֹת, since the verb is common gender.

וַאֲרֻבֹּת הַשָּׁמַיִם נִפְתָּחוּ. (b) Textuality > conj paratactic expansion / Mood > declarative: past / Transitivity > material: event.

נִפְתָּחוּ	וַאֲרֻבֹּת הַשָּׁמַיִם	**Constituents**
they opened	*and the windows of the heavens*	**Translation**
	Theme	**Textuality**
Finite	Subject	**Mood**
Process	Actor	**Transitivity**

וַאֲרֻבֹּת הַשָּׁמַיִם. Theme: textual > clause conj + Theme: experiential / Subject > 3fp / Actor > nominal group: noun common fp const | def art + noun common mp.

נִפְתָּחוּ. Finite > qatal 3cp / Process > nifal פתח. Again, the verb is taken to be in the middle voice.

7:12 // וַיְהִי הַגֶּשֶׁם עַל־הָאָרֶץ אַרְבָּעִים יוֹם וְאַרְבָּעִים
לָיְלָה׃

(a) וַיְהִי הַגֶּשֶׁם עַל־הָאָרֶץ אַרְבָּעִים יוֹם וְאַרְבָּעִים לָיְלָה.
Textuality > conj paratactic expansion / Mood > declarative: past / Transitivity > existential.

Constituents	וַיְהִי	הַגֶּשֶׁם	עַל־הָאָרֶץ	אַרְבָּעִים יוֹם וְאַרְבָּעִים לָיְלָה
Translation	*and he was*	*the rain*	*on the earth*	*forty days and forty nights*
Textuality	Theme			
Mood	Finite	Subject		
Transitivity	Process	Existent	Circumstance	Scope

וַיְהִי. Theme: textual > clause conj + Theme: experiential / Finite > wayyiqtol 3ms / Process > qal היה.

הַגֶּשֶׁם. Subject > ms / Existent > nominal group: def art + noun common.

עַל־הָאָרֶץ. Circumstance: location, place > prep phrase: prep - def art + noun common fs.

אַרְבָּעִים יוֹם וְאַרְבָּעִים לָיְלָה. Scope > nominal group: numeral cp | noun common ms | group conj + numeral cp | noun common fs.

7:13 // בְּעֶצֶם הַיּוֹם הַזֶּה בָּא נֹחַ וְשֵׁם־וְחָם וָיֶפֶת בְּנֵי־נֹחַ
וְאֵשֶׁת נֹחַ וּשְׁלֹשֶׁת נְשֵׁי־בָנָיו אִתָּם אֶל־הַתֵּבָה׃

7:14 הֵמָּה וְכָל־הַחַיָּה לְמִינָהּ וְכָל־הַבְּהֵמָה לְמִינָהּ וְכָל־
הָרֶמֶשׂ הָרֹמֵשׂ עַל־הָאָרֶץ לְמִינֵהוּ וְכָל־הָעוֹף לְמִינֵהוּ
כֹּל צִפּוֹר כָּל־כָּנָף׃

בְּעֶצֶם הַיּוֹם הַזֶּה בָּא נֹחַ וְשֵׁם־וְחָם וָיֶפֶת בְּנֵי־נֹחַ וְאֵשֶׁת נֹחַ
וּשְׁלֹשֶׁת נְשֵׁי־בָנָיו אִתָּם אֶל־הַתֵּבָה הֵמָּה וְכָל־הַחַיָּה לְמִינָהּ

וְכָל־הַבְּהֵמָה לְמִינָהּ וְכָל־הָרֶמֶשׂ הָרֹמֵשׂ עַל־הָאָרֶץ לְמִינֵהוּ וְכָל־הָעוֹף לְמִינֵהוּ כֹּל צִפּוֹר כָּל־כָּנָף. (a) Textuality > appositive paratactic expansion / Mood > declarative: past / Transitivity > material: action. This clause spans two entire verses. It is the longest single clause in Genesis 1–11, made more remarkable by the fact that it has no embedded clauses, just two very long Subject / Actor complexes.

הֵמָּה וְכָל־הַחַיָּה לְמִינָהּ וְכָל־הַבְּהֵמָה לְמִינָהּ וְכָל־הָרֶמֶשׂ הָרֹמֵשׂ עַל־הָאָרֶץ לְמִינֵהוּ וְכָל־הָעוֹף לְמִינֵהוּ כֹּל צִפּוֹר כָּל־כָּנָף	אֶל־הַתֵּבָה	נֹחַ וְשֵׁם־וְחָם וָיֶפֶת בְּנֵי־נֹחַ וְאֵשֶׁת נֹחַ וּשְׁלֹשֶׁת נְשֵׁי־בָנָיו אִתָּם	בָּא	בְּעֶצֶם הַיּוֹם הַזֶּה	**Constituents**
they and all of the livingkind for her kind and all of the beastkind for her kind and all of the creeperkind, the creeper on the earth, for his kinds, and all of the fowl for his kinds, all birdkind and all winged-kind	*to the ark*	*Noach and Shem and Cham and Yefet, the sons of Noach, and the three women of his sons with them*	*he came*	*in the very same of this day*	**Translation**

				Theme	**Textuality**
Subject		Subject	Finite		**Mood**
Actor	Circum-stance	Actor	Process	Circum-stance	**Transitivity**

בְּעֶצֶם הַיּוֹם הַזֶּה. Theme: experiential / Circumstance: location, time > prep phrase: prep + adjunct | def art + noun common ms | def art + pronoun near demonstrative ms. The textual adjunct עֶצֶם *very same* references the preceding clause and suggests the remarkable timing of events laid out in this sequence.

בָּא. Finite > qatal 3ms / Process > qal בוא.

נֹחַ וְשֵׁם־וְחָם וָיֶפֶת בְּנֵי־נֹחַ וְאֵשֶׁת נֹחַ וּשְׁלֹשֶׁת נְשֵׁי־בָנָיו אִתָּם. Subject > ms (נֹחַ) / Actor > nominal group complex: nominal group complex 1 + nominal group complex 2. This long Subject is a complex of complexes. This is an example, notable for its length but structurally not unusual, of how the Subject of a material clause is not necessarily coextensive with its Actor.

[nominal group 1 + Post-modifier] + [nominal group 2 + nominal group 3 + Post-modifier].

נֹחַ וְשֵׁם־וְחָם וָיֶפֶת בְּנֵי־נֹחַ. Nominal group complex 1 > Head + Post-modifier.

נֹחַ וְשֵׁם־וְחָם וָיֶפֶת. Head > nominal group complex: noun proper | group conj + noun proper | group conj + noun proper | group conj + noun proper.

בְּנֵי־נֹחַ. Post-modifier > nominal group: noun common mp const - noun proper. This nominal group further identifies the preceding one.

וְאֵשֶׁת נֹחַ וּשְׁלֹשֶׁת נְשֵׁי־בָנָיו אִתָּם. Group conj + nominal group complex 2 > Head + Post-modifier.

אֵשֶׁת נֹחַ וּשְׁלֹשֶׁת נְשֵׁי־בָנָיו. Head > nominal group complex: nominal group 1 + nominal group 2.

אֵ֣שֶׁת נֹ֔חַ. Nominal group 1 > noun common fs const | noun proper.

וּשְׁלֹ֥שֶׁת נְשֵֽׁי־בָנָ֛יו. Group conj + Nominal group 2 > numeral | noun common f pl const - noun common mp const + pronoun suffix 3ms, antecedent is נֹחַ *Noach.*

אִתָּ֖ם. Post-modifier > prep phrase: prep + pronoun suffix 3mp, antecedent is either just בָנָיו *his sons,* or combined נֹחַ and בָנָיו; there is no formal way to decide.

אֶל־הַתֵּבָֽה. Circumstance: location, place > prep phrase: prep - def art + noun common fs.

הֵ֜מָּה וְכָל־הַֽחַיָּ֣ה לְמִינָ֗הּ וְכָל־הַבְּהֵמָה֙ לְמִינָ֔הּ וְכָל־הָרֶ֛מֶשׂ הָֽרֹמֵ֥שׂ עַל־הָאָ֖רֶץ לְמִינֵ֑הוּ וְכָל־הָע֣וֹף לְמִינֵ֔הוּ כֹּ֖ל צִפּ֥וֹר כָּל־כָּנָֽף. Subject > mp / Actor > nominal group complex: six nominal groups.

הֵ֜מָּה. Nominal group 1 > pronoun personal 3mp, antecedent is the prior Subject / Actor nominal group complex that specified all the human beings that would board the ark. What follows now is all the non-human terrestrial life.

וְכָל־הַֽחַיָּ֣ה לְמִינָ֗הּ. Group conj + Nominal group 2 > Head: noun common collective ms const - def art + noun common collective fs + Post-modifier: prep phrase: prep + noun common ms const + pronoun suffix 3fs, antecedent is הַחַיָּה *the life.*

וְכָל־הַבְּהֵמָה֙ לְמִינָ֔הּ. Group conj + Nominal group 3 > Head: noun common collective ms const - def art + noun common collective fs + Post-modifier: prep phrase: prep + noun common ms const + pronoun suffix 3fs, antecedent is הַבְּהֵמָה *the beast.*

וְכָל־הָרֶ֛מֶשׂ [[הָֽרֹמֵ֥שׂ עַל־הָאָ֖רֶץ]] לְמִינֵ֑הוּ. Group conj + Nominal group 4 > Head: noun common collective ms const - def art + noun common collective ms + Post-modifier 1: embedded relative clause + Post-modifier 2: prep + noun common mp const + pronoun suffix 3ms, antecedent is הָרֶמֶשׂ *the creepingkind.*

הָרֹמֵשׂ עַל־הָאָרֶץ. (i) Post-modifier 1 >> Textuality > embedded expansion: relative clause / Mood > declarative: non-past / Transitivity > material: action. An asyndetic relative clause that adds specification to the preceding nominal group כָּל־הָרֶמֶשׂ.

עַל־הָאָרֶץ	הָרֹמֵשׂ	**Constituents**
on the earth	*the one creeping*	**Translation**
	Theme	**Textuality**
	Finite = Subject	**Mood**
Circumstance	Process = Actor	**Transitivity**

הָרֹמֵשׂ. Finite = Subject = Actor > ptc ms / Process > qal רמשׂ.

עַל־הָאָרֶץ. Circumstance: location, place > prep phrase: prep - def art + noun common fs.

וְכָל־הָעוֹף לְמִינֵהוּ. Group conj + Nominal group 5 > Head: noun common collective ms const - def art + noun common collective ms + Post-modifier: prep phrase: prep + noun common mp const + pronoun suffix 3fs, antecedent is הָעוֹף *the fowl.*

כֹּל צִפּוֹר כָּל־כָּנָף. Nominal group 6 > Nominal group A: noun common collective m/f s const + noun common ms + Nominal group B: noun common collective ms const - noun common fs, taking the appositive Nominal group B not as a new group, but as a specification of the preceding Nominal group A. Nominal group 6 appears to be an afterthought post-modifier to הָעוֹף in Nominal group 5, though it is difficult to catch the precise way in which *all birdkind, all wingedkind* qualifies *all fowl.*

וַיָּבֹאוּ אֶל־נֹחַ אֶל־הַתֵּבָה שְׁנַיִם שְׁנַיִם מִכָּל־ // 7:15
הַבָּשָׂר אֲשֶׁר־בּוֹ רוּחַ חַיִּים׃

וַיָּבֹאוּ אֶל־נֹחַ אֶל־הַתֵּבָה שְׁנַיִם שְׁנַיִם מִכָּל־הַבָּשָׂר [[אֲשֶׁר־

[[בּוֹ רוּחַ חַיִּים]]. (a) Textuality > conj paratactic expansion / Mood > declarative: past / Transitivity > material: action.

מִכָּל־הַבָּשָׂר [[אֲשֶׁר־בּוֹ רוּחַ חַיִּים]]	שְׁנַיִם שְׁנַיִם	אֶל־נֹחַ אֶל־הַתֵּבָה	וַיָּבֹאוּ	**Constituents**
twos twos from all of the flesh which in him is spirit of life		*to Noach to the Ark*	*and they came*	**Translation**
			Theme	**Textuality**
	Subject		Finite	**Mood**
Scope	Actor	Circumstance	Process	**Transitivity**

וַיָּבֹאוּ. Theme: textual > clause conj + Theme: experiential / Finite > wayyiqtol 3mp / Process > qal בוא.

אֶל־נֹחַ אֶל־הַתֵּבָה. Circumstance: location > prep phrase complex: prep phrase 1 + prep phrase 2.

אֶל־נֹחַ. Prep phrase 1 > prep - noun proper.

אֶל־הַתֵּבָה. Prep phrase 2 > prep - def art + noun common fs.

שְׁנַיִם שְׁנַיִם. Subject > mp / Actor > nominal group: numeral md | numeral md.

מִכָּל־הַבָּשָׂר [[אֲשֶׁר־בּוֹ רוּחַ חַיִּים]]. Scope > prep phrase complex: Head + Post-modifier.

מִכָּל־הַבָּשָׂר. Head > prep phrase: prep + noun common collective ms const - def art + noun common ms.

אֲשֶׁר־בּוֹ רוּחַ חַיִּים. (i) Post-modifier >> Textuality > embedded expansion: relative clause / Mood > declarative: non-past / Transitivity > relational: attribution. This clause adds specificity to the preceding nominal group כָּל־הַבָּשָׂר.

רוּחַ חַיִּים	בּוֹ	אֲשֶׁר־	**Constituents**
spirit of life	*in him*	*which*	**Translation**
	Theme	Theme	**Textuality**
Subject	Complement		**Mood**
Carrier	Attribute		**Transitivity**

אֲשֶׁר־. Theme: textual > pronoun relative, antecedent is הַבָּשָׂר *the flesh.*

בּוֹ. Theme: experiential / Complement / Attribute > prep phrase: prep + pronoun suffix 3ms, antecedent is הַבָּשָׂר *the flesh.*

רוּחַ חַיִּים. Subject > 3fs (רוּחַ) / Carrier > nominal group: noun common fs const | def art + noun common mp.

7:16 // וְהַבָּאִים זָכָר וּנְקֵבָה // מִכָּל־בָּשָׂר בָּאוּ / כַּאֲשֶׁר
צִוָּה אֹתוֹ אֱלֹהִים // וַיִּסְגֹּר יְהוָה בַּעֲדוֹ׃

וְהַבָּאִים זָכָר וּנְקֵבָה. (a) Textuality > conj paratactic expansion / Mood > declarative: non-past / Transitivity > relational: attribution. This clause could be construed instead as a nominal group that functions as the Subject / Actor of what we have separated off as clause (b). The problem with such an analysis is the redundancy in the use of **בוא** that would result: *and the ones **coming**, male and female from all flesh, **came**.*

זָכָר וּנְקֵבָה	וְהַבָּאִים	**Constituents**
male and female	*and the ones coming*	**Translation**
	Theme	**Textuality**
Complement	Subject	**Mood**
Attribute	Carrier	**Transitivity**

וְהַבָּאִים. Theme: textual > clause conj + Theme: experiential / Subject > mp / Carrier > nominal group: def art + ptc mp qal **בוא**.

זָכָר וּנְקֵבָה. Complement > cp / Attribute > nominal group: noun common ms ı group conj + noun common fs.

מִכָּל־בָּשָׂר בָּאוּ. (b) Textuality > appositive paratactic expansion / Mood > declarative: past / Transitivity > material: action. Rendering the clauses of 7:16 this way leaves clause (b) without an explicit Subject / Actor, so one has to be assumed from prior text. In this case it would presumably be זָכָר וּנְקֵבָה *male and female,* or the sum total of living beings detailed in the clause complex.

בָּאוּ	מִכָּל־בָּשָׂר	**Constituents**
they came	*from all of flesh*	**Translation**
	Theme	**Textuality**
Finite		**Mood**
Process	Scope	**Transitivity**

מִכָּל־בָּשָׂר. Theme: experiential / Scope > prep phrase: prep + noun common collective ms const - noun common ms.

בָּאוּ. Finite > qatal 3cp / Process > qal בוא.

כַּאֲשֶׁר צִוָּה אֹתוֹ אֱלֹהִים. (c) Textuality > conj paratactic expansion / Mood > declarative: past / Transitivity > verbal.

אֱלֹהִים	אֹתוֹ	צִוָּה	כַּאֲשֶׁר	**Constituents**
deity	*him*	*he commanded*	*as which*	**Translation**
			Theme	**Textuality**
Subject		Finite		**Mood**
Sayer	Receiver	Process	Matter	**Transitivity**

כַּאֲשֶׁר. Theme: textual > conj adjunct.

צִוָּה. Finite > qatal 3ms / Process > piel צוה.

אֹתוֹ. Receiver > nominal group: goal marker + pronoun suffix 3ms, antecedent is נֹחַ *Noach* in 7:15(a).

אֱלֹהִים. Subject > mp / Sayer > noun common.

וַיִּסְגֹּר יְהוָה בַּעֲדוֹ. (d) Textuality > conj paratactic expansion / Mood > declarative: past / Transitivity > material: action. The Goal of the clause process is left unspecified, but most likely is הַתֵּבָה *the ark*, last mentioned in 7:15(a).

בַּעֲדוֹ	יְהוָה	וַיִּסְגֹּר	**Constituents**
behind him	*YHVH*	*and he closed*	**Translation**
		Theme	**Textuality**
	Subject	Finite	**Mood**
Circumstance	Actor	Process	**Transitivity**

וַיִּסְגֹּר. Theme: textual > clause conj + Theme: experiential / Finite > wayyiqtol 3ms / Process > qal סגר.

יְהוָה. Subject > ms / Actor > nominal group: noun proper.

בַּעֲדוֹ. Circumstance: location, place > prep phrase: prep + pronoun suffix 3ms, antecedent is נֹחַ *Noach*, last mentioned in 7:15(a).

Genesis 7:17-24

[17]And the flood was forty days on the earth. And the waters increased. And they raised the ark. And it ascended from on the earth. [18]And the waters deepened. And they increased greatly on the earth. And the ark moved about on the face of the waters. [19]And the waters deepened very greatly on the earth. And all the high mountains, which are under all the heavens, were covered. [20]The waters deepened fifteen cubits over the top. And the mountains were covered. [21]And they perished, all flesh, the creeperkind on the earth: among fowl and among beastkind and among animalkind and among all the swarmingkind, the swarmerkind on the earth, and all of the humankind. [22]All which breath of spirit of life is in their nostrils, from all which is in the dry-land, they died. [23]And he eliminated all of the substance which is on the face of the ground, from humankind to beastkind to creeperkind and to the fowl of the heavens. And they were eliminated from the earth. And just Noah and who were with him in the ark remained. [24]And the waters deepened on the earth one hundred and fifty days.

7:17 וַיְהִ֧י הַמַּבּ֛וּל אַרְבָּעִ֥ים י֖וֹם עַל־הָאָ֑רֶץ /// וַיִּרְבּ֣וּ //
הַמַּ֗יִם // וַיִּשְׂאוּ֙ אֶת־הַתֵּבָ֔ה // וַתָּ֖רָם מֵעַ֥ל הָאָֽרֶץ׃

וַיְהִי הַמַּבּוּל אַרְבָּעִים יוֹם עַל־הָאָרֶץ. (a) Textuality > conj paratactic expansion / Mood > declarative: past / Transitivity > existential.

עַל־הָאָרֶץ	אַרְבָּעִים יוֹם	הַמַּבּוּל	וַיְהִי	**Constituents**
on the earth	*forty days*	*the flood*	*and he was*	**Translation**
			Theme	**Textuality**
		Subject	Finite	**Mood**
Circumstance	Scope	Existent	Process	**Transitivity**

וַיְהִי. Theme: textual > clause conj + Theme: experiential / Finite > wayyiqtol 3ms / Process > qal היה.

הַמַּבּוּל. Subject > ms / Carrier > nominal group: def art + noun common ms.

אַרְבָּעִים יוֹם. Scope > nominal group: numeral | noun common ms.

עַל־הָאָרֶץ. Circumstance: location, place > prep phrase: prep - def art + noun common fs.

וַיִּרְבּוּ הַמַּיִם. (b) Textuality > conj paratactic expansion / Mood > declarative: past / Transitivity > material: event.

הַמַּיִם	וַיִּרְבּוּ	**Constituents**
the waters	*and they increased*	**Translation**
	Theme	**Textuality**
Subject	Finite	**Mood**
Actor	Process	**Transitivity**

וַיִּרְבּוּ. Theme: textual > clause conj + Theme: experiential / Finite > wayyiqtol 3mp / Process > qal רבה.

הַמַּ֫יִם. Subject > mp / Actor > nominal group: def art + noun common.

וַיִּשְׂאוּ֙ אֶת־הַתֵּבָ֔ה. (c) Textuality > conj paratactic expansion / Mood > declarative: past / Transitivity > material: action. The Subject / Actor is הַמַּ֫יִם *the waters* in the preceding clause, absent here by ellipsis.

אֶת־הַתֵּבָה	וַיִּשְׂאוּ	**Constituents**
the ark	*and they raised*	**Translation**
	Theme	**Textuality**
	Finite	**Mood**
Goal	Process	**Transitivity**

וַיִּשְׂאוּ. Theme: textual > clause conj + Theme: experiential / Finite > wayyiqtol 3mp / Process > qal **נשׂא**.

אֶת־הַתֵּבָה. Goal > nominal group: goal marker - def art + noun common fs.

וַתָּ֖רָם מֵעַ֥ל הָאָֽרֶץ. (d) Textuality > conj paratactic expansion / Mood > declarative: past / Transitivity > material: event. The Subject / Actor is הַתֵּבָה *the ark* in the preceding clause, absent here by ellipsis.

מֵעַל הָאָרֶץ	וַתָּרָם	**Constituents**
from on the earth	*and she ascended*	**Translation**
	Theme	**Textuality**
	Finite	**Mood**
Circumstance	Process	**Transitivity**

וַתָּרָם. Theme: textual > clause conj + Theme: experiential / Finite > wayyiqtol 3fs / Process > qal **רום**.

מֵעַל הָאָרֶץ. Circumstance: location, place > prep phrase: prep + prep | def art + noun common fs.

7:18 וַיִּגְבְּרוּ הַמַּיִם // וַיִּרְבּוּ מְאֹד עַל־הָאָרֶץ // וַתֵּלֶךְ // הַתֵּבָה עַל־פְּנֵי הַמָּיִם׃

וַיִּגְבְּרוּ הַמַּיִם. (a) Textuality > conj paratactic expansion / Mood > declarative: past / Transitivity > material: event.

הַמַּיִם	וַיִּגְבְּרוּ	**Constituents**
the waters	*and they strengthened*	**Translation**
	Theme	**Textuality**
Subject	Finite	**Mood**
Actor	Process	**Transitivity**

וַיִּגְבְּרוּ. Theme: textual > clause conj + Theme: experiential / Finite > wayyiqtol 3mp / Process > qal גבר. *Strengthened* takes on the meaning *deepened* in this clause complex.

הַמַּיִם. Subject > mp / Actor > nominal group: def art + noun common.

וַיִּרְבּוּ מְאֹד עַל־הָאָרֶץ. (b) Textuality > conj paratactic expansion / Mood > declarative: past / Transitivity > material: action.

עַל־הָאָרֶץ	מְאֹד	וַיִּרְבּוּ	**Constituents**
on the earth	*greatly*	*and they increased*	**Translation**
		Theme	**Textuality**
	Adjunct	Finite	**Mood**
Circumstance		Process	**Transitivity**

וַיִּרְבּוּ. Theme: textual > clause conj + Theme: experiential / Finite > wayyiqtol 3mp / Process > qal רבה.

מְאֹד. Adjunct: interpersonal > modal: extent. This modal adjunct specifies the extent of the Finite.

עַל־הָאָרֶץ. Circumstance: location, place > prep phrase: prep - def art + noun common ms.

וַתֵּלֶךְ הַתֵּבָה עַל־פְּנֵי הַמָּיִם. (c) Textuality > conj paratactic expansion / Mood > declarative: past / Transitivity > material: event.

עַל־פְּנֵי הַמָּיִם	הַתֵּבָה	וַתֵּלֶךְ	**Constituents**
on the face of the waters	*the ark*	*and she went*	**Translation**
		Theme	**Textuality**
	Subject	Finite	**Mood**
Circumstance	Actor	Process	**Transitivity**

וַתֵּלֶךְ. Theme: textual > clause conj + Theme: experiential / Finite > wayyiqtol 3fs / Process > qal הלך.

הַתֵּבָה. Subject > fs / Actor > nominal group: def art + noun common.

עַל־פְּנֵי הַמָּיִם. Circumstance: location > prep phrase: prep - noun common mp const | def art + noun common mp.

7:19 // וְהַמַּיִם גָּבְרוּ מְאֹד מְאֹד עַל־הָאָרֶץ // וַיְכֻסּוּ כָּל־
הֶהָרִים הַגְּבֹהִים אֲשֶׁר־תַּחַת כָּל־הַשָּׁמָיִם׃

וְהַמַּיִם גָּבְרוּ מְאֹד מְאֹד עַל־הָאָרֶץ. (a) Textuality > conj paratactic expansion / Mood > declarative: past / Transitivity > material: event.

עַל־הָאָרֶץ	מְאֹד מְאֹד	גָּבְרוּ	וְהַמַּיִם	**Constituents**
on the earth	*greatly greatly*	*strengthened*	*and the waters*	**Translation**
			Theme	**Textuality**
	Adjunct	Finite	Subject	**Mood**
Circumstance		Process	Actor	**Transitivity**

וְהַמַּיִם. Theme: textual > clause conj + Theme: experiential / Subject > mp / Actor > nominal group: def art + noun common.

גָּבְרוּ. Finite > qatal 3cp / Process > qal גבר.

מְאֹד מְאֹד. Adjunct: interpersonal > modal: extent. The repetition of מְאֹד doubles the extent of the strengthening process.

עַל־הָאָרֶץ. Circumstance: location, place > prep phrase: prep - def art + noun common fs.

וַיְכֻסּוּ כָּל־הֶהָרִים הַגְּבֹהִים [[אֲשֶׁר־תַּחַת כָּל־הַשָּׁמָיִם]]. (b) Textuality > conj paratactic expansion / Mood > declarative: past / Transitivity > material: action.

כָּל־הֶהָרִים הַגְּבֹהִים [[אֲשֶׁר־תַּחַת כָּל־הַשָּׁמָיִם]]	וַיְכֻסּוּ	**Constituents**
all of the high mountains, which are under all of the heavens	*and they were covered*	**Translation**
	Theme	**Textuality**
Subject	Finite	**Mood**
Goal	Process	**Transitivity**

וַיְכֻסּוּ. Theme > textual + Theme: experiential / Finite > wayyiqtol 3mp / Process > pual כסה.

כָּל־הֶהָרִים הַגְּבֹהִים [[אֲשֶׁר־תַּחַת כָּל־הַשָּׁמָיִם]]. Subject > mp (הֶהָרִים) / Goal > nominal group: Head + Post-modifier. Apparently הֶהָרִים *the mountains* is the Subject, rather than כָּל *all*, because the Finite is 3mp. Normally the first element of a nominal group is the grammatical Subject.

כָּל־הֶהָרִים הַגְּבֹהִים. Head > nominal group: noun common ms const - def art + noun common mp | def art + adj mp.

אֲשֶׁר־תַּחַת כָּל־הַשָּׁמָיִם. (i) Post-modifier >> Textuality > embedded expansion: relative clause / Mood > declarative: non-past / Transitivity > relational: attribution.

תַּחַת כָּל־הַשָּׁמָיִם	אֲשֶׁר־	**Constituents**
under all of the heavens	*which*	**Translation**
	Theme	**Textuality**
Complement	Subject	**Mood**
Attribute	Carrier	**Transitivity**

אֲשֶׁר־. Theme: textual and experiential > pronoun relative / Subject > mp / Carrier > the preceding nominal group.

תַּחַת כָּל־הַשָּׁמָיִם. Complement / Attribute > prep phrase: prep | noun common ms const - def art + noun common mp.

7:20 // חֲמֵשׁ עֶשְׂרֵה אַמָּה מִלְמַעְלָה גָּבְרוּ הַמָּיִם //
וַיְכֻסּוּ הֶהָרִים׃

חֲמֵשׁ עֶשְׂרֵה אַמָּה מִלְמַעְלָה גָּבְרוּ הַמָּיִם. (a) Textuality > appositive paratactic expansion / Mood > declarative: past / Transitivity > material: action.

הַמָּיִם	גָּבְרוּ	חֲמֵשׁ עֶשְׂרֵה אַמָּה מִלְמַעְלָה	**Constituents**
the waters	*they strengthened*	*fifteen cubits from to above*	**Translation**
		Theme	**Textuality**
Subject	Finite		**Mood**
Actor	Process	Scope	**Transitivity**

חֲמֵשׁ עֶשְׂרֵה אַמָּה מִלְמַעְלָה. Theme > existential / Scope > nominal group: Head + Post-modifier.

חֲמֵשׁ עֶשְׂרֵה אַמָּה. Head > nominal group: numeral | numeral | noun common fs.

מִלְמַעְלָה. Post-modifier > prep phrase: prep + prep + noun common fs.

גָּבְרוּ. Finite > qatal 3cp / Process > qal גבר.

הַמָּיִם. Subject > mp / Actor > nominal group: def art + noun common.

וַיְכֻסּוּ הֶהָרִים. (b) Textuality > conj paratactic expansion / Mood > declarative: past / Transitivity > material process: action.

הֶהָרִים	וַיְכֻסּוּ	**Constituents**
the mountains	*and they were covered*	**Translation**
	Theme	**Textuality**
Subject	Finite	**Mood**
Goal	Process	**Transitivity**

וַיְכֻסּוּ. Theme: textual > clause conj + Theme: experiential / Finite > wayyiqtol 3mp / Process > pual of כסה.

הֶהָרִים. Subject > mp / Goal > nominal group: def art + noun common.

7:21 // וַיִּגְוַ֞ע כָּל־בָּשָׂ֣ר ׀ הָרֹמֵ֣שׂ עַל־הָאָ֗רֶץ בָּעֹוף֙
וּבַבְּהֵמָה֙ וּבַֽחַיָּ֔ה וּבְכָל־הַשֶּׁ֖רֶץ הַשֹּׁרֵ֣ץ עַל־הָאָ֑רֶץ וְכֹ֖ל
הָאָדָֽם׃

וַיִּגְוַע כָּל־בָּשָׂר הָרֹמֵשׂ עַל־הָאָרֶץ בָּעוֹף וּבַבְּהֵמָה וּבַחַיָּה וּבְכָל־הַשֶּׁרֶץ הַשֹּׁרֵץ עַל־הָאָרֶץ וְכֹל הָאָדָם. (a) Textuality > conj paratactic expansion / Mood > declarative: past / Transitivity > material: event.

כָּל־בָּשָׂר [[הָרֹמֵשׂ עַל־הָאָרֶץ]] בָּעוֹף וּבַבְּהֵמָה וּבַחַיָּה וּבְכָל־הַשֶּׁרֶץ [[הַשֹּׁרֵץ עַל־הָאָרֶץ]] וְכֹל הָאָדָם	וַיִּגְוַע	**Constituents**
all flesh, the creeperkind on the earth: in fowl and in beastkind and in animalkind and in all the swarmingkind, the swarmerkind on the earth, and all of the humankind	*and he perished*	**Translation**

	Theme	**Textuality**
Subject	Finite	**Mood**
Actor	Process	**Transitivity**

וַיִּגְוַע. Theme: textual > clause conj + Theme: experiential / Finite > wayyiqtol 3ms / Process > qal גוע.

כָּל־בָּשָׂר הָרֹמֵשׂ עַל־הָאָרֶץ בָּעוֹף וּבַבְּהֵמָה וּבַחַיָּה וּבְכָל־הַשֶּׁרֶץ הַשֹּׁרֵץ עַל־הָאָרֶץ וְכֹל הָאָדָם. Subject > ms (כָּל) / Actor > nominal group complex: nominal group 1 + nominal group 2. The head of the Subject / Actor is כָּל־בָּשָׂר *all flesh* ... וְכֹל הָאָדָם *and all humanity*. The rest is an expansion on the first term *all flesh*.

כָּל־בָּשָׂר [[הָרֹמֵשׂ עַל־הָאָרֶץ]] בָּעוֹף וּבַבְּהֵמָה וּבַחַיָּה וּבְכָל־הַשֶּׁרֶץ [[הַשֹּׁרֵץ עַל־הָאָרֶץ]]. Nominal group 1: Head (nominal group) + Post-modifier 1 (relative clause) + Post-modifier 2 (prep phrase complex) + Post-modifier 3 (relative clause).

כָּל־בָּשָׂר. Head > nominal group: noun common collective ms const - noun common ms.

הָרֹמֵשׂ עַל־הָאָרֶץ. (i) Post-modifier 1 >> Textuality > embedded expansion: relative clause / Mood > declarative: non-past / Transitivity > material: action. The antecedent of this relative clause is כָּל־בָּשָׂר *all flesh*, or just *flesh*.

עַל־הָאָרֶץ	הָרֹמֵשׂ	**Constituents**
on the earth	*the creeperkind*	**Translation**
	Theme	**Textuality**
Complement	Subject	**Mood**
Circumstance	Actor	**Transitivity**

הָרֹמֵשׂ. Theme: experiential / Subject > ms / Actor > def art + ptc qal רמשׂ.

עַל־הָאָרֶץ. Complement / Circumstance: location, place > prep phrase: prep - def art + noun common fs.

בָּעוֹף וּבַבְּהֵמָה וּבַחַיָּה וּבְכָל־הַשֶּׁרֶץ [[הַשֹּׁרֵץ עַל־הָאָרֶץ]]. Post-modifier 2 > prep phase group + relative clause.

בָּעוֹף וּבַבְּהֵמָה וּבַחַיָּה וּבְכָל־הַשֶּׁרֶץ. Prep phrase group > prep + noun common collective ms | group conj + prep + noun common collective ms | group conj + prep + def art + noun common collective fs + group conj + prep + noun common collective ms - def art + noun common collective ms.

הַשֹּׁרֵץ עַל־הָאָרֶץ. (ii) Post-modifier 3 >> Textuality > embedded expansion: relative clause / Mood > declarative: non-past / Transitivity > material: action. This relative clause modifies only the object of the preposition of the last prep phrase in the group. The antcecedent of this relative clause is כָּל־הַשֶּׁרֶץ *all the swarming kind.*

עַל־הָאָרֶץ	הַשֹּׁרֵץ	**Constituents**
on the earth	*the swarmerkind*	**Translation**
	Theme	**Textuality**
Complement	Subject	**Mood**
Circumstance	Actor	**Transitivity**

הַשֹּׁרֵץ. Theme: experiential / Subject > ms / Actor > nominal group: def art + ptc qal שׁרץ.

עַל־הָאָרֶץ. Complement / Circumstance > prep phrase: prep - def art + noun common fs.

וְכֹל הָאָדָם. Group conj + Nominal group 2 > noun common collective ms const | def art + noun common collective ms. This is one of the two head elements of the Subject / Actor.

7:22 // כֹּל אֲשֶׁר נִשְׁמַת־רוּחַ חַיִּים בְּאַפָּיו מִכֹּל אֲשֶׁר בֶּחָרָבָה מֵתוּ׃

כֹּל [[אֲשֶׁר נִשְׁמַת־רוּחַ חַיִּים בְּאַפָּיו]] מִכֹּל [[אֲשֶׁר

מֵתוּ]] בֶּחָרָבָה. (a) Textuality > appositive paratactic expansion / Mood > declarative: past / Transitivity > material: event.

מֵתוּ	כֹּל]] אֲשֶׁר נִשְׁמַת־רוּחַ חַיִּים בְּאַפָּיו]] מִכֹּל]] אֲשֶׁר בֶּחָרָבָה]]	**Constituents**
they died	*all, which breath of spirit of life is in his nostrils, from all, which is in the dry-land*	**Translation**
	Theme	**Textuality**
Finite	Subject	**Mood**
Process	Actor	**Transitivity**

כֹּל אֲשֶׁר נִשְׁמַת־רוּחַ חַיִּים בְּאַפָּיו מִכֹּל אֲשֶׁר בֶּחָרָבָה. Theme: experiential / Subject > ms (כֹּל) / Actor > nominal group: Head (nominal group) + Post-modifier 1 (relative clause) + Post-modifier 2 (prep phrase).

כֹּל. Head > nominal group: noun common collective ms.

אֲשֶׁר נִשְׁמַת־רוּחַ חַיִּים בְּאַפָּיו. (i) Post-modifier 1 >> Textuality > embedded expansion: relative clause / Mood > declarative: non-past / Transitivity > relational: attribution.

בְּאַפָּיו	נִשְׁמַת־רוּחַ חַיִּים	אֲשֶׁר	**Constituents**
in his nostrils	*breath of spirit of life*	*which*	**Translation**
		Theme	**Textuality**
Complement	Subject		**Mood**
Attribute	Carrier		**Transitivity**

אֲשֶׁר. Theme: textual and experiential / Subject > ms / Carrier > antecedent כֹּל.

נִשְׁמַת־רוּחַ חַיִּים. Subject > fs / Carrier > nominal group: noun common fs const - noun common fs const | noun common mp.

בְּאַפָּיו. Complement / Attribute > prep phrase: prep + noun common fd const + pronoun suffix 3ms, antecedent is כֹּל.

מִכֹּל אֲשֶׁר בֶּחָרָבָה. Post-modifier 2 > prep phrase complex: Head + Post-modifier 2a. This complex modifies כֹּל, the Subject / Actor of clause (a).

מִכֹּל. Head > prep phrase: prep + noun common collective ms.

אֲשֶׁר בֶּחָרָבָה. (a') Post-modifier 2a >> Textuality > embedded expansion: relative clause / Mood > declarative: non-past / Transitivity > relational: attribution.

בֶּחָרָבָה	אֲשֶׁר	**Constituents**
in the dry-land	*which*	**Translation**
	Theme	**Textuality**
Complement	Subject	**Mood**
Attribute	Carrier	**Transitivity**

אֲשֶׁר. Theme > textual and experiential / Subject > ms / Carrier > antecedent כֹּל.

בֶּחָרָבָה. Complement and Attribute > prep phrase: prep + def art + noun common fs.

מֵתוּ. Finite > qatal 3cp / Process > qal מות. The grammatical Subject / Actor is כֹּל, a collective ms noun, which is here matched to a plural Finite even though they are incongruent.

7:23 // וַיִּמַח אֶת־כָּל־הַיְקוּם | אֲשֶׁר | עַל־פְּנֵי הָאֲדָמָה
מֵאָדָם עַד־בְּהֵמָה עַד־רֶמֶשׂ וְעַד־עוֹף הַשָּׁמַיִם //
וַיִּמָּחוּ מִן־הָאָרֶץ // וַיִּשָּׁאֶר אַךְ־נֹחַ וַאֲשֶׁר אִתּוֹ
בַּתֵּבָה׃

וַיִּמַח אֶת־כָּל־הַיְקוּם [[אֲשֶׁר עַל־פְּנֵי הָאֲדָמָה]] מֵאָדָם עַד־בְּהֵמָה עַד־רֶמֶשׂ וְעַד־עוֹף הַשָּׁמַיִם. (a) Textuality > conj paratactic expansion / Mood > declarative: past / Transitivity > material: action. Compare 7:4(b). The closest divine Subject / Actor is YHVH in 7:16(d).

אֶת־כָּל־הַיְקוּם [[אֲשֶׁר עַל־פְּנֵי הָאֲדָמָה]] מֵאָדָם עַד־בְּהֵמָה עַד־רֶמֶשׂ וְעַד־עוֹף הַשָּׁמַיִם	וַיִּמַח	**Constituents**
all of the substance which is on the face of the ground, from humankind to beastkind to creeper-kind and to the fowl of the heavens	*and he eliminated*	**Translation**
	Theme	**Textuality**
	Finite	**Mood**
Goal	Process	**Transitivity**

וַיִּמַח. Theme: textual > clause conj + Theme: experiential / Finite > wayyiqtol 3ms / Process > qal מחה.

אֶת־כָּל־הַיְקוּם [[אֲשֶׁר עַל־פְּנֵי הָאֲדָמָה]] מֵאָדָם עַד־בְּהֵמָה עַד־רֶמֶשׂ וְעַד־עוֹף הַשָּׁמַיִם. Goal > nominal group: Head + Post-modifier 1 (relative clause) + Post-modifier 2 (prep phrase complex).

אֶת־כָּל־הַיְקוּם. Head > nominal group: goal marker - noun common collective ms const - def art + noun common ms.

אֲשֶׁר עַל־פְּנֵי הָאֲדָמָה. (i) Post-modifier 1 >> Textuality > embedded expansion: relative clause / Mood > declarative: non-past / Transitivity > relational: attribution.

עַל־פְּנֵי הָאֲדָמָה	אֲשֶׁר	**Constituents**
on the face of the ground	*which*	**Translation**
	Theme	**Textuality**
Complement	Subject	**Mood**
Attribute	Carrier	**Transitivity**

אֲשֶׁר. Theme: textual and experiential > pronoun relative / Subject > ms / Carrier > antecedent כָּל־הַיְקוּם *all of the substance.*

עַל־פְּנֵי הָאֲדָמָה. Complement / Attribute > prep phrase: prep - noun common mp const | def art + noun common fs.

מֵאָדָם עַד־בְּהֵמָה עַד־רֶמֶשׂ וְעַד־עוֹף הַשָּׁמַיִם. Post-modifier 2 > prep phrase complex: prep phrase 1 + prep phrase 2 + prep phrase 3 + prep phrase 4.

מֵאָדָם. Prep phrase 1 > prep + noun common collective ms.

עַד־בְּהֵמָה. Prep phrase 2 > prep - noun common collective fs.

עַד־רֶמֶשׂ. Prep phrase 3 > prep - noun common collective ms.

וְעַד־עוֹף הַשָּׁמַיִם. Group conj + Prep phrase 4 > prep - noun common collective ms const | def art + noun common mp.

וַיִּמָּחוּ מִן־הָאָרֶץ. (b) Textuality > conj paratactic expansion / Mood > declarative: past / Transitivity > material: action. The Subject / Goal of the process is כָּל־הַיְקוּם *all the substance* in clause (a), absent here by ellipsis. Since the verbal process is passive, the Subject is the Goal, not the Actor. The Actor is a divine agent. Deity was last mentioned in 7:16(c) and YHVH was last mentioned in 7:16(d).

מִן־הָאָרֶץ	וַיִּמָּחוּ	**Constituents**
from the earth	*and they were eliminated*	**Translation**
	Theme	**Textuality**
	Finite	**Mood**
Circumstance	Process	**Transitivity**

וַיִּמָּחוּ. Theme: textual > clause conj + Theme: experiential / Finite > wayyiqtol 3mp / Process > nifal מחה.

מִן־הָאָרֶץ. Circumstance > prep phrase: prep - def art + noun common fs.

וַיִּשָּׁאֶר אַךְ־נֹחַ וַאֲשֶׁר אִתּוֹ בַּתֵּבָה. (c) Textuality > conj paratactic expansion / Mood > declarative: past / Transitivity > existential.

נֹחַ וַאֲשֶׁר אִתּוֹ בַּתֵּבָה	אַךְ־	וַיִּשָּׁאֶר	**Constituents**
Noach and which with him in the ark	*just*	*and he remained*	**Translation**
	Adjunct	Theme	**Textuality**
Subject		Finite	**Mood**
Existent		Process	**Transitivity**

וַיִּשָּׁאֶר. Theme: textual > clause conj + Theme: experiential / Finite > wayyiqtol 3ms / Process > nifal שׁאר. The verb is interpreted as middle voice.

אַךְ־. Adjunct: textual > limitation. This is a textual rather than experiential or interpersonal component which, like הִנֵּה, precedes the constituent that it qualifies. This is a textual adjunct because it defines a subgroup in relation to a previously defined larger group: *all flesh* in 21(a)–23(b). As such, it presupposes those clauses. MNK 311–12 calls this a focus particle.

נֹחַ וַאֲשֶׁר אִתּוֹ בַּתֵּבָה. Subject > ms (נֹחַ) / Existent > nominal group complex: Head + Post-modifier. The relative clause is without an explicit antecedent. Both together are the Existent of the clause process, though the Process grammatically matches only נֹחַ *Noach.*

נֹחַ. Head > nominal group: noun proper ms.

וַאֲשֶׁר אִתּוֹ בַּתֵּבָה. Group conj + (i) Post-modifier >> Textuality > embedded expansion: relative clause / Mood > declarative: non-past / Transitivity > relational: attribution.

בַּתֵּבָה	אִתּוֹ	וַאֲשֶׁר	**Constituents**
in the ark	*with him*	*and which*	**Translation**
		Theme	**Textuality**
	Complement	Subject	**Mood**
Circumstance	Attribute	Carrier	**Transitivity**

וַאֲשֶׁר. Theme: textual > group conj + Theme: experiential > relative pronoun / Subject > ms / Carrier > there is no explicit antecedent, though perhaps כֹּל *all* can be presumed: *all which with him in the ark.*

אִתּוֹ. Complement / Attribute > prep phrase: prep + pronoun suffix 3ms, antecedent is נֹחַ *Noach.*

בַּתֵּבָה. Circumstance: location, place > prep phrase: prep + def art + noun common fs.

7:24 // וַיִּגְבְּרוּ הַמַּיִם עַל־הָאָרֶץ חֲמִשִּׁים וּמְאַת יוֹם׃

וַיִּגְבְּרוּ הַמַּיִם עַל־הָאָרֶץ חֲמִשִּׁים וּמְאַת יוֹם. (a) Textuality > conj paratactic expansion / Mood > declarative: past / Transitivity > material: event.

חֲמִשִּׁים וּמְאַת יוֹם	עַל־הָאָרֶץ	הַמַּיִם	וַיִּגְבְּרוּ	**Constituents**
fifty and a hundred days	*on the earth*	*the waters*	*and they strengthened*	**Translation**
			Theme	**Textuality**
		Subject	Finite	**Mood**
Scope	Circumstance	Actor	Process	**Transitivity**

וַיִּגְבְּרוּ. Theme: textual > clause conj + Theme: experiential / Finite > wayyiqtol 3mp / Process > qal גבר.

הַמַּיִם. Subject > mp / Actor > nominal group: def art + noun common.

עַל־הָאָרֶץ. Circumstance: location, place > prep phrase: prep - def art + noun common fs.

חֲמִשִּׁים וּמְאַת יוֹם. Scope > nominal group: numeral mp | numeral cs | noun common ms.

Genesis 8:1-5

[1]*And deity remembered Noach and all the animalkind and all the beastkind which were with him in the ark. And deity passed a wind over*

the earth. And the waters abated. [2] *And the springs of deep-water and the windows of the heavens were plugged. And the rain was held back from the heavens.* [3]*And the waters receded from on the earth apace. And the waters diminished by the end of a hundred and fifty days.* [4]*And the ark rested in the seventh month in the seventeenth day to the month on the mountains of 'Ararat.* [5]*And the waters were diminishing apace until the tenth month. In the tenth month in the first to the month, the heads of the mountains were seen.*

8:1 /// וַיִּזְכֹּר אֱלֹהִים אֶת־נֹחַ וְאֵת כָּל־הַחַיָּה וְאֶת־כָּל־
הַבְּהֵמָה אֲשֶׁר אִתּוֹ בַּתֵּבָה // וַיַּעֲבֵר אֱלֹהִים רוּחַ
עַל־הָאָרֶץ // וַיָּשֹׁכּוּ הַמָּיִם׃

וַיִּזְכֹּר אֱלֹהִים אֶת־נֹחַ וְאֵת כָּל־הַחַיָּה וְאֶת־כָּל־הַבְּהֵמָה [[אֲשֶׁר אִתּוֹ בַּתֵּבָה]]. (a) Textuality > conj paratactic expansion / Mood > declarative: past / Transitivity > mental: cognition.

אֶת־נֹחַ וְאֵת כָּל־הַחַיָּה וְאֶת־כָּל־הַבְּהֵמָה [[אֲשֶׁר אִתּוֹ בַּתֵּבָה]]	אֱלֹהִים	וַיִּזְכֹּר	**Constituents**
Noach and all the animalkind and all the beastkind which were with him in the ark	*deity*	*and he remembered*	**Translation**
		Theme	**Textuality**
	Subject	Finite	**Mood**
Phenomenon	Senser	Process	**Transitivity**

וַיִּזְכֹּר. Theme: textual > clause conj + Theme: experiential / wayyiqtol 3ms / Process > qal זכר.

אֱלֹהִים. Subject > mp / Senser > noun common mp.

אֶת־נֹחַ וְאֵת כָּל־הַחַיָּה וְאֶת־כָּל־הַבְּהֵמָה [[אֲשֶׁר אִתּוֹ בַּתֵּבָה]]. Phenomenon > nominal group complex: Head (nominal group complex) + Post-modifier (relative clause).

אֶת־נֹחַ וְאֵת כָּל־הַחַיָּה וְאֶת־כָּל־הַבְּהֵמָה. Head > nominal group complex: nominal group 1 + nominal group 2 + nominal group 3.

אֶת־נֹחַ. Nominal group 1 > goal marker - noun proper ms.

וְאֵת כָּל־הַחַיָּה. Group conj + Nominal group 2 > goal marker - noun common collective ms const - def art + noun common collective fs.

וְאֶת־כָּל־הַבְּהֵמָה. Group conj + Nominal group 3 > goal marker - noun common collective ms const - def art + noun common fs.

אֲשֶׁר אִתּוֹ בַּתֵּבָה. (i) Post-modifier >> Textuality > embedded expansion: relative clause / Mood > declarative: non-past / Transitivity > relational: attribution.

בַּתֵּבָה	אִתּוֹ	אֲשֶׁר	**Constituents**
in the ark	*with him*	*which*	**Translation**
		Theme	**Textuality**
	Complement	Subject	**Mood**
Circumstance	Attribute	Carrier	**Transitivity**

אֲשֶׁר. Theme: textual and experiential > pronoun relative / Subject > 3cp / Carrier > antecedent כָּל־הַחַיָּה *all the animalkind* and כָּל־הַבְּהֵמָה *all the beastkind.*

אִתּוֹ. Complement / Attribute > prep phrase: prep + pronoun suffix 3ms, antecedent is נֹחַ *Noach.*

בַּתֵּבָה. Circumstance: location, place > prep phrase: prep + def art + noun common fs.

וַיַּעֲבֵר אֱלֹהִים רוּחַ עַל־הָאָרֶץ. (b) Textuality > conj paratactic expansion / Mood > declarative: past / Transitivity > material: action.

עַל־הָאָרֶץ	רוּחַ	אֱלֹהִים	וַיַּעֲבֵר	**Constituents**
on the earth	*a wind*	*deity*	*and he passed*	**Translation**
			Theme	**Textuality**
		Subject	Finite	**Mood**
Circumstance	Goal	Actor	Process	**Transitivity**

וַיַּעֲבֵר. Theme: textual > clause conj + Theme: experiential / Finite > wayyiqtol 3ms / Process > hifil עבר.

אֱלֹהִים. Subject > mp / Actor > noun common ms.

רוּחַ. Goal > noun common fs.

עַל־הָאָרֶץ. Circumstance: location, place > prep phrase: prep - def art + noun common fs.

וַיָּשֹׁכּוּ הַמָּיִם. (c) Textuality > conj paratactic expansion / Mood > declarative: past / Transitivity > material: event.

הַמָּיִם	וַיָּשֹׁכּוּ	**Constituents**
the waters	*and they abated*	**Translation**
	Theme	**Textuality**
Subject	Finite	**Mood**
Actor	Process	**Transitivity**

וַיָּשֹׁכּוּ. Theme: textual > clause conj + Theme: experiential / Finite > wayyiqtol 3mp / Process > qal שׁכך.

הַמָּיִם. Subject > mp / Actor > nominal group: def art + noun common mp.

8:2 // וַיִּסָּכְרוּ מַעְיְנֹת תְּהוֹם וַאֲרֻבֹּת הַשָּׁמָיִם // וַיִּכָּלֵא
הַגֶּשֶׁם מִן־הַשָּׁמָיִם׃

וַיִּסָּכְרוּ מַעְיְנֹת תְּהוֹם וַאֲרֻבֹּת הַשָּׁמָיִם. (a) Textuality > conj paratactic expansion / Mood > declarative: past / Transitivity > material: action.

מַעְיְנֹת תְּהוֹם וַאֲרֻבֹּת הַשָּׁמָיִם	וַיִּסָּכְרוּ	**Constituents**
the springs of deep-water and the windows of the heavens	*and they were plugged*	**Translation**
	Theme	**Textuality**
Subject	Finite	**Mood**
Goal	Process	**Transitivity**

וַיִּסָּכְרוּ. Theme: textual > clause conj + Theme: experiential / Finite > wayyiqtol 3mp / Process > nifal סכר.

מַעְיְנֹת תְּהוֹם וַאֲרֻבֹּת הַשָּׁמָיִם. Subject > 3fp (אֲרֻבֹּת and מַעְיְנֹת) / Goal > nominal group complex: nominal group 1 + nominal group 2. Whereas the Head of each nominal group is 3fp, the Finite is 3mp.

מַעְיְנֹת תְּהוֹם. Nominal group 1 > noun common fp const ו noun proper. The parallel structure of the nominal group complex suggests that תְּהוֹם is definite, since הַשָּׁמָיִם is. As a proper noun, תְּהוֹם would be definite; this is an argument in favor of reading this term as the Hebrew analog of the Babylonian antagonist of the Enuma Elish, Tiamat.

וַאֲרֻבֹּת הַשָּׁמָיִם. Group conj + Nominal group 2 > noun common fp const ו def art + noun common mp.

וַיִּכָּלֵא הַגֶּשֶׁם מִן־הַשָּׁמָיִם. (b) Textuality > conj paratactic expansion / Mood > declarative: past / Transitivity > material: action.

מִן־הַשָּׁמָיִם	הַגֶּשֶׁם	וַיִּכָּלֵא	**Constituents**
from the heavens	*the rain*	*and he was held back*	**Translation**
		Theme	**Textuality**
	Subject	Finite	**Mood**
Circumstance	Goal	Process	**Transitivity**

וַיִּכָּלֵא. Theme: textual > clause conj + Theme: experiential / Finite > wayyiqtol 3ms / Process > nifal כלא.

הַגֶּשֶׁם. Subject > ms / Goal > nominal group: def art + noun common ms.

מִן־הַשָּׁמָיִם. Circumstance > prep phrase: prep - def art + noun common mp.

8:3 // וַיָּשֻׁבוּ הַמַּיִם מֵעַל הָאָרֶץ הָלוֹךְ וָשׁוֹב // וַיַּחְסְרוּ
הַמַּיִם מִקְצֵה חֲמִשִּׁים וּמְאַת יוֹם׃

וַיָּשֻׁבוּ הַמַּיִם מֵעַל הָאָרֶץ הָלוֹךְ וָשׁוֹב. (a) Textuality > conj paratactic expansion / Mood > declarative: past / Transitivity > material: action.

הָלוֹךְ וָשׁוֹב	מֵעַל הָאָרֶץ	הַמַּיִם	וַיָּשֻׁבוּ	**Constituents**
going and returning	*from on the earth*	*the waters*	*and they returned*	**Translation**
			Theme	**Textuality**
		Subject	Finite	**Mood**
Circumstance	Circumstance	Actor	Process	**Transitivity**

וַיָּשֻׁבוּ. Theme: textual > clause conj + Theme: experiential / Finite > wayyiqtol 3mp / Process > qal שׁוב.

הַמַּיִם. Subject > mp / Actor > nominal group: def art + noun common mp.

מֵעַל הָאָרֶץ. Circumstance: location > prep phrase: prep + prep ׀ def art + noun common fs.

הָלוֹךְ וָשׁוֹב. Circumstance: manner, quality > nominal group: inf abs qal הלך ׀ group conj + inf abs qal שׁוב. These infinitives are analyzed as a nominal group that functions as a circumstantial adjunct of manner, indicating the progress of the verbal process. Notice the hendiadys conjunction, which effectively renders this a nominal group rather a nominal group complex.

וַיַּחְסְרוּ הַמַּיִם מִקְצֵה חֲמִשִּׁים וּמְאַת יוֹם. (b) Textuality > conj paratactic expansion / Mood > declarative: past / Transitivity > material: event.

מִקְצֵה חֲמִשִּׁים וּמְאַת יוֹם	הַמַּיִם	וַיַּחְסְרוּ	**Constituents**
from the end of fifty and a hundred days	*the waters*	*and they diminished*	**Translation**
		Theme	**Textuality**
	Subject	Finite	**Mood**
Circumstance	Actor	Process	**Transitivity**

וַיַּחְסְרוּ. Theme: textual > clause conj + Theme: experiential / Finite > wayyiqtol 3mp / Process > qal חסר.

הַמַּיִם. Subject > mp / Actor > noun common mp.

מִקְצֵה חֲמִשִּׁים וּמְאַת יוֹם. Circumstance: extent, time > prep phrase: prep + noun common ms const | numeral cp | group conj + numeral cs | noun common ms.

8:4 // וַתָּ֤נַח הַתֵּבָה֙ בַּחֹ֣דֶשׁ הַשְּׁבִיעִ֔י בְּשִׁבְעָֽה־עָשָׂ֥ר י֖וֹם
לַחֹ֑דֶשׁ עַ֖ל הָרֵ֥י אֲרָרָֽט׃

וַתָּנַח הַתֵּבָה בַּחֹדֶשׁ הַשְּׁבִיעִי בְּשִׁבְעָה־עָשָׂר יוֹם לַחֹדֶשׁ עַל הָרֵי אֲרָרָט. (a) Textuality > conj paratactic expansion / Mood > declarative: past / Transitivity > material: event.

עַל הָרֵי אֲרָרָט	בַּחֹדֶשׁ הַשְּׁבִיעִי בְּשִׁבְעָה־עָשָׂר יוֹם לַחֹדֶשׁ	הַתֵּבָה	וַתָּנַח	**Constituents**
on the mountains of 'Ararat	*in the seventh month in the seventeenth day to the month*	*the ark*	*and she rested*	**Translation**

			Theme	**Textuality**
		Subject	Finite	**Mood**
Circumstance	Circumstance	Actor	Process	**Transitivity**

וַתָּנַח. Theme: textual > clause conj + Theme: experiential / Finite > wayyiqtol 3ms / Process > qal נוח.

הַתֵּבָה. Subject > 3fs / Actor > def art + noun common fs.

בַּחֹדֶשׁ הַשְּׁבִיעִי בְּשִׁבְעָה־עָשָׂר יוֹם לַחֹדֶשׁ. Circumstance: location, time > prep phrase complex: Head + Post-modifier. The movement in meaning is from general to more specific.

בַּחֹדֶשׁ הַשְּׁבִיעִי. Head > prep phrase: prep + def art + noun common ms | def art + numeral, ordinal.

בְּשִׁבְעָה־עָשָׂר יוֹם לַחֹדֶשׁ. Post-modifier > Head + Post-modifier.

בְּשִׁבְעָה־עָשָׂר יוֹם. Head > prep phase: prep + numeral-numeral, ordinal | noun common ms.

לַחֹדֶשׁ. Post-modifier > prep phrase: prep + def art + noun common ms.

עַל הָרֵי אֲרָרָט. Circumstance: location, place > prep phrase: prep | noun common ms const | noun proper.

8:5 // וְהַמַּיִם הָיוּ הָלוֹךְ וְחָסוֹר עַד הַחֹדֶשׁ הָעֲשִׂירִי //
בָּעֲשִׂירִי בְּאֶחָד לַחֹדֶשׁ נִרְאוּ רָאשֵׁי הֶהָרִים׃

וְהַמַּיִם הָיוּ הָלוֹךְ וְחָסוֹר עַד הַחֹדֶשׁ הָעֲשִׂירִי. (a) Textuality > conj paratactic expansion / Mood > declarative: past / Transitivity > material: event.

עַד הַחֹדֶשׁ הָעֲשִׂירִי	הָלוֹךְ וְחָסוֹר	הָיוּ	וְהַמַּיִם	**Constituents**
until the tenth month	*going and diminishing*	*they were*	*and the waters*	**Translation**
			Theme	**Textuality**
		Finite	Subject	**Mood**
Circumstance	Circumstance	Process	Actor	**Transitivity**

וְהַמַּיִם. Theme: textual > clause conj / Theme: experiential / Subject > mp / Actor > nominal group: def art + noun, common.

הָיוּ. Finite > qatal 3mp / Process > qal היה.

הָלוֹךְ וְחָסוֹר. Circumstance: manner, quality > nominal group: inf abs qal הלך | group conj + inf abs qal חסר. See 8:3(a).

עַד הַחֹדֶשׁ הָעֲשִׂירִי. Circumstance > prep phrase: prep | def art + noun, common ms | def art + numeral ms.

בָּעֲשִׂירִי בְּאֶחָד לַחֹדֶשׁ נִרְאוּ רָאשֵׁי הֶהָרִים. (b) Textuality > appositive paratactic expansion / Mood > declarative: past / Transitivity > mental: perception.

רָאשֵׁי הֶהָרִים	נִרְאוּ	בָּעֲשִׂירִי בְּאֶחָד לַחֹדֶשׁ	**Constituents**
the heads of the mountains	*they were seen*	*in the tenth in first to the month*	**Translation**
		Theme	**Textuality**
Subject	Finite		**Mood**
Goal	Process	Circumstance	**Transitivity**

בָּעֲשִׂירִי בְּאֶחָד לַחֹדֶשׁ. Circumstance: location, time > prep phrase complex: Head + Post-modifier.

בָּעֲשִׂירִי. Head > prep phrase: prep + def art + numeral, ordinal. The noun that עֲשִׂירִי *tenth* modifies is חֹדֶשׁ *month*, which is textually absent but can be assumed.

בְּאֶחָד לַחֹדֶשׁ. Post-modifier > Head + Post-modifier.

בְּאֶחָד. Head > prep phrase: prep + numeral, cardinal. Here אֶחָד *one*, which is a cardinal number, is used to mean *first*, an ordinal number.

לַחֹדֶשׁ. Post-modifier > prep phrase: prep + def art + noun common ms.

נִרְאוּ. Finite > qatal 3cp / Process > nifal ראה.

רָאשֵׁי הֶהָרִים. Subject > mp (רָאשֵׁי) / Goal > nominal group: noun common mp const | def art + noun common mp.

Genesis 8:6-12

[6]And it was at the end of forty days, and Noach opened the window of the ark which he made. [7]And he sent forth the raven. And he went out going back and forth until the waters dried from on the earth. [8]And he sent forth the dove from him to see whether the water subsided from on the face of the ground. [9]And the dove found not rest for the sole of her foot. And she returned to him to the ark, because water is on the face of all the earth. And he extended his hand. And he took her. And he brought her to him to the ark. [10]And he waited some more, seven additional days. And again he sent the dove from the ark. [11]And the dove came to him at evening time. And now a plucked olive leaf is in its mouth. And Noach knew that the waters subsided from on the earth. [12]And he waited some more, seven additional days. And he sent the dove. And she returned no more to him again.

8:6 /// וַיְהִי מִקֵּץ אַרְבָּעִים יוֹם // וַיִּפְתַּח נֹחַ אֶת־חַלּוֹן
הַתֵּבָה אֲשֶׁר עָשָׂה׃

וַיְהִי מִקֵּץ אַרְבָּעִים יוֹם. (a) Textuality > conj paratactic expansion / Mood > declarative: past / Transitivity > relational: attribution. While this is a temporal clause indicating that a forty day span of time has elapsed, it is not clear what the reference point is.

מִקֵּץ אַרְבָּעִים יוֹם	וַיְהִי	**Constituents**
from end of forty days	*and it was*	**Translation**
	Theme	**Textuality**
	Finite	**Mood**
Circumstance	Process	**Transitivity**

וַיְהִי. Theme: textual > clause conj + Theme: experiential / Finite > wayyiqtol 3ms / Process > qal היה.

מִקֵּץ אַרְבָּעִים יוֹם. Circumstance: extent, time > prep phrase: prep + noun common ms const | numeral | noun common ms.

וַיִּפְתַּח נֹחַ אֶת־חַלּוֹן הַתֵּבָה [[אֲשֶׁר עָשָׂה]]. (b) Textuality > conj paratactic expansion / Mood > declarative: past / Transitivity > material: action.

אֶת־חַלּוֹן הַתֵּבָה [[אֲשֶׁר עָשָׂה]]	נֹחַ	וַיִּפְתַּח	**Constituents**
the window of the ark which he made	*Noach*	*and he opened*	**Translation**
		Theme	**Textuality**
	Subject	Finite	**Mood**
Goal	Actor	Process	**Transitivity**

וַיִּפְתַּח. Theme: textual > clause conj + Theme: experiential / Finite > wayyiqtol 3ms / Process > qal פתח.

נֹחַ. Subject > ms / Actor > noun proper.

אֶת־חַלּוֹן הַתֵּבָה [[אֲשֶׁר עָשָׂה]]. Goal > nominal group complex: Head + Post-modifier.

אֶת־חַלּוֹן הַתֵּבָה. Head > nominal group: goal marker - noun common ms const | def art + noun common fs.

אֲשֶׁר עָשָׂה. (i) Post-modifier >> Textuality > embedded expansion: relative clause / Mood > declarative: past / Transitivity > material: action. The Subject / Actor of the process is נֹחַ *Noach* in the dominant clause.

עָשָׂה	אֲשֶׁר	**Constituents**
he made	*which*	**Translation**
	Theme	**Textuality**
Finite		**Mood**
Process	Goal	**Transitivity**

אֲשֶׁר. Theme: textual and experiential > pronoun relative / Goal > antecedent חַלּוֹן הַתֵּבָה *window of the ark.*

עָשָׂה. Finite > qatal 3ms / Process > qal עשׂה.

8:7 // וַיְשַׁלַּח אֶת־הָעֹרֵב // וַיֵּצֵא יָצוֹא וָשׁוֹב עַד־יְבֹשֶׁת
הַמַּיִם מֵעַל הָאָרֶץ׃

וַיְשַׁלַּח אֶת־הָעֹרֵב. (a) Textuality > conj paratactic expansion / Mood > declarative: past / Transitivity > material: action. The Subject / Actor is נֹחַ *Noach*, absent here by ellipsis.

אֶת־הָעֹרֵב	וַיְשַׁלַּח	**Constituents**
the raven	*and he sent*	**Translation**
	Theme	**Textuality**
	Finite	**Mood**
Goal	Process	**Transitivity**

וַיְשַׁלַּח. Theme: textual > clause conj + Theme: experiential / Finite > wayyiqtol 3ms / Process > piel שׁלח.

אֶת־הָעֹרֵב. Goal > goal marker - def art + noun commn ms. The noun is marked definite, though it had not been mentioned before. Perhaps sending *the raven* was such a well-known motif in ancient flood stories that it could be presumed; it is also present in the Gilgamesh Epic, Tablet 11.

וַיֵּצֵא יָצוֹא וָשׁוֹב עַד־יְבֹשֶׁת הַמַּיִם מֵעַל הָאָרֶץ. (b) Textuality > conj paratactic expansion / Mood > declarative: past / Transitivity > material: action. The Subject / Actor is הָעֹרֵב *the raven* in the prior clause, textually absent here by ellipsis.

מֵעַל הָאָרֶץ	עַד־יְבֹשֶׁת הַמַּיִם	יָצוֹא וָשׁוֹב	וַיֵּצֵא	**Constituents**
from on the earth	*until the drying of the waters*	*going out and returning*	*and he went out*	**Translation**
			Theme	**Textuality**
			Finite	**Mood**
Circumstance	Circumstance	Circumstance	Process	**Transitivity**

וַיֵּצֵא. Theme: textual > clause conj + Theme: experiential / Finite > wayyiqtol 3mp / Process > qal יצא.

יָצוֹא וָשׁוֹב. Circumstance: manner, quality > nominal group: inf abs qal יצא | group conj + inf abs qal שׁוב. A hendiadys group; compare 8:3(a).

עַד־יְבֹשֶׁת הַמַּיִם. Circumstance: extent, time > prep phrase: prep - inf const qal יבשׁ | def art + noun common mp. The object of the preposition is יְבֹשֶׁת הַמַּיִם, a nominal group. The first member of the group is an infinitive construct of יבשׁ. Implicit in this nominal group is a material process in the middle voice: Actor (*water*) + Process (*dry*), *the waters dried up*. When this is nominalized so that it can become the object of the preposition, it becomes *the drying up of the waters*. Functional grammar analyzes prepositional phrases in general as clauses that have been condensed down to phrases. See Thompson 23–24. This is a good example of such a transformation.

מֵעַל הָאָרֶץ. Circumstance: location, place > prep phase: prep + prep | def art + noun common fs. This is a Circumstance to the Process in the preceding prep phrase.

8:8 // וַיְשַׁלַּח אֶת־הַיּוֹנָה מֵאִתּוֹ לִרְאוֹת הֲקַלּוּ הַמַּיִם
מֵעַל פְּנֵי הָאֲדָמָה׃

וַיְשַׁלַּח אֶת־הַיּוֹנָה מֵאִתּוֹ [[לִרְאוֹת הֲקַלּוּ הַמַּיִם מֵעַל פְּנֵי הָאֲדָמָה]]. (a) Textuality > conj paratactic expansion / Mood > declarative: past / Transitivity > material: action.

[[לִרְאוֹת הֲקַלּוּ הַמַּיִם מֵעַל פְּנֵי הָאֲדָמָה]]	מֵאִתּוֹ	אֶת־הַיּוֹנָה	וַיְשַׁלַּח	**Constituents**
to see whether the water subsided from on the face of the ground	*from with him*	*the dove*	*and he sent*	**Translation**
			Theme	**Textuality**
			Finite	**Mood**
Circumstance	Circum-stance	Goal	Process	**Transitivity**

וַיְשַׁלַּח. Theme: textual > clause conj + Theme: experiential / Finite > wayyiqtol 3ms / Process > piel שׁלח.

אֶת־הַיּוֹנָה. Goal > nominal group: goal marker - def art + noun common fs. The dove, like the raven in the preceding verse, is definite. A dove is also found in the Gilgamesh Epic.

מֵאִתּוֹ. Circumstance: location, place > prep phrase: prep + prep + pronoun suffix 3ms, antecedent is נֹחַ *Noach*, last textually explicit in 8:6(b).

לִרְאוֹת הֲקַלּוּ הַמַּיִם מֵעַל פְּנֵי הָאֲדָמָה. (i) Circumstance: cause, purpose >> Textuality > embedded expansion: prep clause / Transitivity > mental: perception. The embedded purpose clause itself contains a report clause.

[[הֲקַלּוּ הַמַּיִם מֵעַל פְּנֵי הָאֲדָמָה]]	לִרְאוֹת	**Constituents**
had the water subsided from on the face of the ground?	*to see*	**Translation**
	Theme	**Textuality**
Phenomenon	Process	**Transitivity**

לִרְאוֹת. Theme: textual > prep + Theme: experiential / Process > inf const (qal ראה).

הֲקַלּוּ הַמַּיִם מֵעַל פְּנֵי הָאֲדָמָה. (a') Phenomenon >> Textuality > paratactic projection: report / Mood > interrogative: yes-no / Transitivity > material: action.

מֵעַל פְּנֵי הָאֲדָמָה	הַמַּיִם	קַלּוּ	הֲ	**Constituents**
from on the face of the ground	*the water*	*subsided*	?	**Translation**
		Theme	Theme	**Textuality**
	Subject	Finite	Adjunct	**Mood**
Circumstance	Actor	Process		**Transitivity**

הֲ. Theme: interpersonal > Adjunct: interpersonal > modal.

קַלּוּ. Theme: experiential / Finite > qatal 3cp / Process > qal קלל.

הַמַּיִם. Subject > mp / Actor > def art + noun common mp.

מֵעַל פְּנֵי הָאֲדָמָה. Circumstance: extent, place > prep phrase: prep + prep | noun common mp const | def art + noun common fs.

8:9 // וְלֹא־מָצְאָה הַיּוֹנָה מָנוֹחַ לְכַף־רַגְלָהּ // וַתָּשָׁב
אֵלָיו אֶל־הַתֵּבָה / כִּי־מַיִם עַל־פְּנֵי כָל־הָאָרֶץ //
וַיִּשְׁלַח יָדוֹ // וַיִּקָּחֶהָ // וַיָּבֵא אֹתָהּ אֵלָיו אֶל־
הַתֵּבָה׃

וְלֹא־מָצְאָה הַיּוֹנָה מָנוֹחַ לְכַף־רַגְלָהּ. (a) Textuality > conj paratactic expansion / Mood > declarative: past / Transitivity > material: action.

לְכַף־רַגְלָהּ	מָנוֹחַ	הַיּוֹנָה	מָצְאָה	וְלֹא־	**Constituents**
for the sole of her foot	*rest*	*the dove*	*she found*	*and not*	**Translation**
			Theme	Theme	**Textuality**
		Subject	Finite	Adjunct	**Mood**
Beneficiary	Goal	Actor	Process		**Transitivity**

וְלֹא־. Theme: textual > clause conj + Theme: interpersonal > Adjunct: interpersonal > polarity: negative.

מָצְאָה. Theme: experiential / Finite > qatal 3fs / Process > qal מצא.

הַיּוֹנָה. Subject > 3fs / Actor > def art + noun common fs.

מָנוֹחַ. Goal > noun common fs.

לְכַף־רַגְלָהּ. Beneficiary > prep phrase: prep + noun common fs const - noun common fs const + pronoun suffix 3fs, antecedent is הַיּוֹנָה *the dove.*

וַתָּשָׁב אֵלָיו אֶל־הַתֵּבָה. (b) Textuality > conj paratactic expansion / Mood > declarative: past / Transitivity > material: action. The Subject / Actor is הַיּוֹנָה *the dove*, textually absent by ellipsis.

אֵלָיו אֶל־הַתֵּבָה	וַתָּשָׁב	**Constituents**
to him to the ark	*and she returned*	**Translation**
	Theme	**Textuality**
	Finite	**Mood**
Circumstance	Process	**Transitivity**

וַתָּשָׁב. Theme: textual > clause conj + Theme: experiential / Finite > wayyiqtol 3ms / Process > qal שׁוב.

אֵלָיו אֶל־הַתֵּבָה. Circumstance: location, place > prep phrase group: Head + Post-modifier.

אֵלָיו. Head > prep phrase: prep + pronoun suffix 3ms, antecedent is נֹחַ *Noach.*

אֶל־הַתֵּבָה. Post-modifier > prep phrase: prep - def art + noun common fs.

כִּי־מַיִם עַל־פְּנֵי כָל־הָאָרֶץ. (c) Textuality > conj hypotactic expansion: purpose / Mood > declarative: past / Transitivity > relational: attribution.

עַל־פְּנֵי כָל־הָאָרֶץ	מַיִם	כִּי־	**Constituents**
on the face of all the earth	*water*	*because*	**Translation**
	Theme	Theme	**Textuality**
Complement	Subject		**Mood**
Attribute	Carrier		**Transitivity**

כִּי־מַיִם. Theme: textual > conj + Theme: experiential / Subject > mp / Carrier > noun common mp.

עַל־פְּנֵי כָל־הָאָרֶץ. Complement / Attribute > prep phrase: prep + noun common mp const | noun common ms - def art + noun common fs.

וַיִּשְׁלַח יָדוֹ. (d) Textuality > conj paratactic expansion / Mood > declarative: past / Transitivity > material: action. Subject / Actor is נֹחַ *Noach*, textually absent here by ellipsis.

יָדוֹ	וַיִּשְׁלַח	**Constituents**
his hand	*and he extended*	**Translation**
	Theme	**Textuality**
	Finite	**Mood**
Goal	Process	**Transitivity**

וַיִּשְׁלַח. Theme: textual > clause conj + Theme: experiential / Finite > wayyiqtol 3ms / Process > qal שׁלח.

יָדוֹ. Goal > noun common fs const + pronoun suffix 3ms, antecedent is נֹחַ *Noach*.

וַיִּקָּחֶהָ. (e) Textuality > conj paratactic expansion / Mood > declarative: past / Transitivity > material: action.

וַיִּקָּחֶהָ	**Constituents**
and he took her	**Translation**
Theme	**Textuality**
Finite	**Mood**
Process + Goal	**Transitivity**

וַיִּקָּחֶהָ. Theme: textual > clause conj + Theme: experiential / Finite > wayyiqtol 3ms / Process > qal לקח + Goal > pronoun suffix 3fs, antecedent is הַיּוֹנָה *the dove*. By combining Goal with Process, both become components of the Theme.

וַיָּבֵא אֹתָהּ אֵלָיו אֶל־הַתֵּבָה. (f) Textuality > conj paratactic expansion / Mood > declarative: past / Transitivity > material: action.

אֵלָיו אֶל־הַתֵּבָה	אֹתָהּ	וַיָּבֵא	**Constituents**
to him to the ark	her	and he brought	**Translation**
		Theme	**Textuality**
		Finite	**Mood**
Circumstance	Goal	Process	**Transitivity**

וַיָּבֵא. Theme: textual > clause conj + Theme: experiential / Finite > wayyiqtol 3ms / Process > hifil בוא.

אֹתָהּ. Goal > goal marker + pronoun suffix 3fs, antecedent is הַיּוֹנָה the dove.

אֵלָיו אֶל־הַתֵּבָה. Circumstance: location, place > Head + Post-modifier.

אֵלָיו. Head > prep phrase: prep + pronoun suffix 3ms, antecedent is נֹחַ Noach.

אֶל־הַתֵּבָה. Post-modifier > prep phrase: prep - def art + noun common fs.

8:10 // וַיָּחֶל עוֹד שִׁבְעַת יָמִים אֲחֵרִים // וַיֹּסֶף שַׁלַּח
אֶת־הַיּוֹנָה מִן־הַתֵּבָה׃

וַיָּ֣חֶל ע֔וֹד שִׁבְעַ֥ת יָמִ֖ים אֲחֵרִ֑ים. (a) Textuality > conj paratactic expansion / Mood > declarative: past / Transitivity > material: action.

שִׁבְעַת יָמִים אֲחֵרִים	עוֹד	וַיָּחֶל	**Constituents**
seven additional days	*more*	*and he waited*	**Translation**
	Adjunct	Theme	**Textuality**
		Finite	**Mood**
Circumstance		Process	**Transitivity**

וַיָּחֶל. Theme: textual > clause conj + Theme: experiential / Finite > wayyiqtol 3ms / Process > qal חיל.

עוֹד. Adjunct: textual > recurrence. This textual adjunct indicates that a period of time has elapsed in relation to a prior point in time.

שִׁבְעַת יָמִים אֲחֵרִים. Circumstance: extent, time > nominal group: numeral | noun common mp | adj mp. Compare 7:4(a). Here and in 8:12(a) the Circumstance of time is a nominal group rather than, as is typical, a prepositional phrase.

וַיֹּ֛סֶף שַׁלַּ֥ח אֶת־הַיּוֹנָ֖ה מִן־הַתֵּבָֽה. (b) Textuality > conj paratactic expansion / Mood > declarative: past / Transitivity > material: action. Subject / Actor is נֹחַ Noach, textually absent here by ellipsis.

מִן־הַתֵּבָה	אֶת־הַיּוֹנָה	שַׁלַּח	וַיֹּסֶף	**Constituents**
from the ark	*the dove*	*sent*	*and he again*	**Translation**
			Theme	**Textuality**
		Complement	Finite	**Mood**
Circumstance	Goal	Process	Process	**Transitivity**

וַיֹּסֶף שַׁלַּח. Theme: textual > clause conj + verbal group complex: Finite + Complement.

יֹסֶף. Theme: experiential / Finite > wayyiqtol 3ms / Process > qal יסף. This component defines the unfolding of the Process.

שַׁלַּח. Complement > inf const / Process > piel שׁלח. This component expresses the main clause Process.

אֶת־הַיּוֹנָה. Goal > nominal group: goal marker - def art + noun common fs.

מִן־הַתֵּבָה. Circumstance: location, place > prep - def art + noun common fs.

8:11 וַתָּבֹא אֵלָיו הַיּוֹנָה לְעֵת עֶרֶב // וְהִנֵּה עֲלֵה־זַיִת //
טָרָף בְּפִיהָ // וַיֵּדַע נֹחַ / כִּי־קַלּוּ הַמַּיִם מֵעַל הָאָרֶץ:

וַתָּבֹא אֵלָיו הַיּוֹנָה לְעֵת עֶרֶב. (a) Textuality > conj paratactic expansion / Mood > declarative: past / Transitivity > material: action.

לְעֵת עֶרֶב	הַיּוֹנָה	אֵלָיו	וַתָּבֹא	**Constituents**
to time of evening	*the dove*	*to him*	*and she came*	**Translation**
			Theme	**Textuality**
	Subject		Finite	**Mood**
Circumstance	Actor	Circumstance	Process	**Transitivity**

וַתָּבֹא. Theme: textual > clause conj + Theme: experiential / Finite > wayyiqtol 3fs / Process > qal בוא.

אֵלָיו. Circumstance: location, place > prep + pronouns suffix 3ms, antecedent is נֹחַ *Noach.*

הַיּוֹנָה. Subject > 3fs / Actor > def art + noun common fs.

לְעֵת עֶרֶב. Circumstance: location, time > prep + noun common ms const | noun common ms.

וְהִנֵּה עֲלֵה־זַיִת טָרָף בְּפִיהָ. (b) Textuality > conj paratactic expansion / Mood > declarative: non-past / Transitivity > relational: attribution.

בְּפִיהָ	עֲלֵה־זַיִת טָרָף	וְהִנֵּה	**Constituents**
in its mouth	*a plucked leaf of olive*	*and now*	**Translation**
	Theme	Theme	**Textuality**
Complement	Subject		**Mood**
Attribute	Carrier		**Transitivity**

וְהִנֵּה. Theme: textual > clause conj + Adjunct: textual > contra-expectation.

עֲלֵה־זַיִת טָרָף. Theme: experiential / Subject > ms / Carrier > nominal group: noun common ms const - noun common ms | adj ms.

בְּפִיהָ. Complement / Attribute > prep phrase: prep + noun common ms const + pronoun suffix 3fs, antecedent is הַיּוֹנָה *the dove.*

וַיֵּדַע נֹחַ. (c) Textuality > conj paratactic expansion / Mood > declarative: past / Transitivity > mental: cognition. The Phenomenon of this mental process is the following clause.

נֹחַ	וַיֵּדַע	**Constituents**
Noach	*and he knew*	**Translation**
	Theme	**Textuality**
Subject	Finite	**Mood**
Senser	Process	**Transitivity**

וַיֵּדַע. Theme: textual > clause conj + Theme: experiential / Finite > wayyiqtol 3ms / Process > qal ידע.

נֹחַ. Subject > ms / Actor > noun proper.

כִּי־קַלּוּ הַמַּיִם מֵעַל הָאָרֶץ. (d) Textuality > conj hypotactic projection: idea / Mood > declarative: past / Transitivity > material: action.

מֵעַל הָאָרֶץ	הַמַּיִם	קַלּוּ	כִּי־	**Constituents**
from on the earth	*the waters*	*they subsided*	*that*	**Translation**
		Theme	Theme	**Textuality**
	Subject	Finite		**Mood**
Circumstance	Actor	Process		**Transitivity**

כִּי־. Theme: textual > conj.

קַלּוּ. Theme: experiential / Finite > qatal 3cp / Process > qal קלל.

הַמַּיִם. Subject > mp / Actor > def art + noun common mp.

מֵעַל הָאָרֶץ. Circumstance: extent, place > prep phrase: prep + prep ׀ def art + noun common fs.

8:12 וַיִּיָּחֶל עֹוד שִׁבְעַת יָמִים אֲחֵרִים // וַיְשַׁלַּח אֶת־
הַיֹּונָה // וְלֹא־יָסְפָה שׁוּב־אֵלָיו עֹוד׃

וַיִּיָּחֶל עוֹד שִׁבְעַת יָמִים אֲחֵרִים. (a) Textuality > conj paratactic expansion / Mood > declarative: past / Transitivity > material: action. Compare 8:10(a).

שִׁבְעַת יָמִים אֲחֵרִים	עוֹד	וַיִּיָּחֶל	**Constituents**
seven additional days	*more*	*and he waited*	**Translation**
	Adjunct	Theme	**Textuality**
		Finite	**Mood**
Circumstance		Process	**Transitivity**

וַיִּיָּחֶל. Theme: textual > clause conj + Theme: experiential / Finite > wayyiqtol 3ms / Process > nifal יחל. Notice that in 8:10(a) the root is חיל and here it is יחל. Both are rendered *wait.*

עוֹד. Adjunct: textual > recurrence. See comment to עוֹד in 8:10(a).

שִׁבְעַת יָמִים אֲחֵרִים. Circumstance: extent, time > nominal group: numeral ׀ noun common mp ׀ adj mp.

וַיְשַׁלַּח אֶת־הַיּוֹנָה. (b) Textuality > conj paratactic expansion / Mood > declarative: past / Transitivity > material: action.

אֶת־הַיּוֹנָה	וַיְשַׁלַּח	**Constituents**
the dove	*and he sent*	**Translation**
	Theme	**Textuality**
	Finite	**Mood**
Goal	Process	**Transitivity**

וַיְשַׁלַּח. Theme: textual > clause conj + Theme: experiential / Finite > wayyiqtol 3ms / Process > piel שׁלח.

אֶת־הַיּוֹנָה. Goal > nominal group: goal marker - def art + noun common fs.

וְלֹא־יָסְפָה שׁוּב־אֵלָיו עוֹד. (c) Textuality > conj paratactic expansion / Mood > declarative: past / Transitivity > material: action.

עוֹד	אֵלָיו	שׁוּב־	יָסְפָה	וְלֹא־	**Constituents**
again	*to him*	*returned*	*she more*	*and not*	**Translation**
Adjunct			Theme	Theme	**Textuality**
		Complement	Finite	Adjunct	**Mood**
	Circumstance	Process	Process		**Transitivity**

וְלֹא־. Theme: textual > clause conj + Theme: interpersonal / Adjunct: interpersonal > polarity: negative.

יָסְפָה שׁוּב־. Verbal group complex: Finite + Complement.

יָסְפָה. Theme: experiential / Finite > qatal 3fs / Process > qal יסף. This defines the unfolding of the main Process.

שׁוּב. Complement > inf const / Process > qal שׁוּב. This expresses the main Process of the clause.

אֵלָיו. Circumstance: location, place > prep + pronoun suffix 3ms, antecedent is נֹחַ *Noach*.

עוֹד. Adjunct: textual > repetitive. Before, the dove would go and return, but not again.

Genesis 8:13-14

[13]And it was in the six hundredth and first year in the first month in the first to the month, the waters dried from on the earth. And Noach removed the covering of the ark. And he saw, and the face of the ground really was dry. [14]And in the second month in the seventeenth day to the month the earth was dry.

8:13 /// וַיְהִי בְּאַחַת וְשֵׁשׁ־מֵאוֹת שָׁנָה בָּרִאשׁוֹן בְּאֶחָד
לַחֹדֶשׁ חָרְבוּ הַמַּיִם מֵעַל הָאָרֶץ // וַיָּסַר נֹחַ אֶת־
מִכְסֵה הַתֵּבָה // וַיַּרְא / וְהִנֵּה חָרְבוּ פְּנֵי הָאֲדָמָה׃

(a) וַיְהִי בְּאַחַת וְשֵׁשׁ־מֵאוֹת שָׁנָה בָּרִאשׁוֹן בְּאֶחָד לַחֹדֶשׁ. Textuality > conj paratactic expansion / Mood > declarative: past / Transitivity > relational: attribution.

בְּאַחַת וְשֵׁשׁ־מֵאוֹת שָׁנָה בָּרִאשׁוֹן בְּאֶחָד לַחֹדֶשׁ	וַיְהִי	**Constituents**
in one and six hundred years, in the first, in one to the month	*and it was*	**Translation**
	Theme	**Textuality**
	Finite	**Mood**
Circumstance	Process	**Transitivity**

וַיְהִי. Theme: textual > clause conj + Theme: experiential / Finite > wayyiqtol 3ms / Process > qal היה.

בְּאַחַת וְשֵׁשׁ־מֵאוֹת שָׁנָה בָּרִאשׁוֹן בְּאֶחָד לַחֹדֶשׁ. Circumstance: location, time > prep phrase complex: Head + Post-modifier. This is a series of four prepositional phrases. Each successive one makes the one preceding it more specific.

בְּאַחַת וְשֵׁשׁ־מֵאוֹת שָׁנָה. Head > prep phrase: prep + numeral ordinal ׀ group conj + numeral ordinal - numeral ordinal ׀ noun common fs.

בָּרִאשׁוֹן בְּאֶחָד לַחֹדֶשׁ. Post-modifier > prep phrase complex: Head + Post-modifier.

בָּרִאשׁוֹן. Head > prep phrase: prep + def art + numeral ordinal.

בְּאֶחָד לַחֹדֶשׁ. Post-modifier > prep phrase complex: Head + Post-modifier.

בְּאֶחָד. Head > prep phrase: prep + numeral ms.

לַחֹדֶשׁ. Post-modifier > prep phrase: prep + def art + noun common ms.

חָרְבוּ הַמַּיִם מֵעַל הָאָרֶץ. (b) Textuality > appositive paratactic expansion / Mood > declarative: past / Transitivity > material: event.

מֵעַל הָאָרֶץ	הַמַּיִם	חָרְבוּ	**Constituents**
from on the earth	*the waters*	*and they dried*	**Translation**
		Theme	**Textuality**
	Subject	Finite	**Mood**
Circumstance	Actor	Process	**Transitivity**

חָרְבוּ. Theme: experiential / Finite > qatal 3cp / Process > qal חרב.

הַמַּיִם. Subject > mp / Actor > def art + noun common mp.

מֵעַל הָאָרֶץ. Circumstance: extent, place > prep phrase: prep + prep + def art + noun common fs.

וַיָּסַר נֹחַ אֶת־מִכְסֵה הַתֵּבָה. (c) Textuality > conj paratactic expansion / Mood > declarative: past / Transitivity > material: action.

אֶת־מִכְסֵה הַתֵּבָה	נֹחַ	וַיָּסַר	**Constituents**
the covering of the ark	*Noach*	*and he removed*	**Translation**
		Theme	**Textuality**
	Subject	Finite	**Mood**
Goal	Actor	Process	**Transitivity**

וַיָּסַר. Theme: textual > clause conj + Theme: experiential / Finite > wayyiqtol 3ms / Process > qal סור.

נֹחַ. Subject > ms / Actor > noun proper.

אֶת־מִכְסֵה הַתֵּבָה. Goal > goal marker - noun common ms const | def art + noun common fs.

וַיַּרְא. (d) Textuality > conj paratactic expansion / Mood > declarative: past / Transitivity > mental: perception. The Subject / Senser is **נֹחַ** *Noach* from the preceding clause, absent here by ellipsis.

וַיַּרְא	**Constituents**
and he saw	**Translation**
Theme	**Textuality**
Finite	**Mood**
Process	**Transitivity**

וַיַּרְא. Theme: textual > clause conj + Theme: experiential / Finite > wayyiqtol 3ms / Process > qal **ראה**.

וְהִנֵּה חָרְבוּ פְּנֵי הָאֲדָמָה. (e) Textuality > conj hypotactic projection: idea / Mood > declarative: past / Transitivity > material: action. This clause is analyzed as the Phenomenon of the preceding mental process of perception clause.

פְּנֵי הָאֲדָמָה	חָרְבוּ	וְהִנֵּה	**Constituents**
the faces of the ground	*they were dry*	*and now*	**Translation**
	Theme	Theme	**Textuality**
Subject	Finite		**Mood**
Actor	Process		**Transitivity**

וְהִנֵּה. Theme: textual > clause conj + Adjunct: textual > contra-expectation.

חָרְבוּ. Theme: experiential / Finite > qatal 3cp / Process > qal **חרב**.

פְּנֵי הָאֲדָמָה. Subject > mp (פְּנֵי) / Actor > nominal group: noun common mp const | def art + noun common fs.

8:14 // וּבַחֹ֙דֶשׁ֙ הַשֵּׁנִ֔י בְּשִׁבְעָ֧ה וְעֶשְׂרִ֛ים י֖וֹם לַחֹ֑דֶשׁ
יָבְשָׁ֖ה הָאָֽרֶץ׃ ס

וּבַחֹדֶשׁ הַשֵּׁנִי בְּשִׁבְעָה וְעֶשְׂרִים יוֹם לַחֹדֶשׁ יָבְשָׁה הָאָרֶץ.
(a) Textuality > conj paratactic expansion / Mood > declarative: past / Transitivity > relational: attribution.

הָאָרֶץ	יָבְשָׁה	וּבַחֹדֶשׁ הַשֵּׁנִי בְּשִׁבְעָה וְעֶשְׂרִים יוֹם לַחֹדֶשׁ	**Constituents**
the earth	*was dry*	*and in the second month, in the seven and tenth day to the month*	**Translation**
		Theme	**Textuality**
Subject	Finite		**Mood**
Carrier	Attribute	Circumstance	**Transitivity**

וּבַחֹדֶשׁ הַשֵּׁנִי בְּשִׁבְעָה וְעֶשְׂרִים יוֹם לַחֹדֶשׁ. Theme: textual > clause conj + Theme: experiential / Circumstance: location, time > prep phrase complex: Head + Post-modifier.

בַחֹדֶשׁ הַשֵּׁנִי. Head > prep phrase: prep + def art + noun common ms | def art + numeral, ordinal.

בְּשִׁבְעָה וְעֶשְׂרִים יוֹם לַחֹדֶשׁ. Post-modifier > prep phrase complex: Head + Post-modifier.

בְּשִׁבְעָה וְעֶשְׂרִים יוֹם. Head > prep phrase: prep + numeral cardinal | group conj + numeral ordinal | noun common ms.

לַחֹדֶשׁ. Post-modifier > prep phrase: prep + def art + noun common ms.

יָבְשָׁה. Finite > qatal 3fs / Process = Attribute > qal יבשׁ. So-called stative verbs, such as this one, indicate the state of the Subject. As such, they are essentially realizing an attributive relational process.

הָאָרֶץ. Subject > 3fs / Carrier > def art + noun common fs.

Genesis 8:15-19

[15]And deity spoke to Noach by saying, [16]"Exit from the ark, you and
your woman and your sons and your sons' women with you. [17]All the liv-
ingkind which is with you from all flesh: among the fowl and among the
beastkind and among all the creepingkind, the creeperkind on the earth,
bring them out with you. And they will swarm in the earth. And they will
bear fruit. And they will multiply on the earth." [18]And Noach and his sons
and his woman and his sons' women with him exited. [19]All the livingkind,
all the creepingkind and all the fowl, all creeperkind on the earth, for
their families they exited from the ark.

8:15 /// וַיְדַבֵּ֥ר אֱלֹהִ֖ים אֶל־נֹ֥חַ לֵאמֹֽר׃

וַיְדַבֵּר אֱלֹהִים אֶל־נֹחַ לֵאמֹר. (a) Textuality > conj paratactic expansion / Mood > declarative: past / Transitivity > verbal. Notice the fully articulated Transitivity structure, with Process plus explicit Sayer and Receiver. This is indicative of the beginning of a new clause complex.

לֵאמֹר	אֶל־נֹחַ	אֱלֹהִים	וַיְדַבֵּר	**Constituents**
saying	*to Noach*	*deity*	*and he spoke*	**Translation**
			Theme	**Textuality**
		Subject	Finite	**Mood**
Circumstance	Receiver	Sayer	Process	**Transitivity**

וַיְדַבֵּר. Theme: textual > clause conj + Theme: experiential / Finite > wayyiqtol 3ms / Process > piel **דבר**.

אֱלֹהִים. Subject > mp / Sayer > noun common mp.

אֶל־נֹחַ. Receiver > prep phrase: prep - noun proper ms.

לֵאמֹר. Circumstance: manner, means > prep phrase: prep + Process > inf const qal **אמר**.

8:16 // צֵא מִן־הַתֵּבָה אַתָּה וְאִשְׁתְּךָ וּבָנֶיךָ וּנְשֵׁי־בָנֶיךָ אִתָּךְ׃

(a) .צֵא מִן־הַתֵּבָה אַתָּה וְאִשְׁתְּךָ וּבָנֶיךָ וּנְשֵׁי־בָנֶיךָ אִתָּךְ Textuality > appositive paratactic projection: quote / Mood > directive: imperative / Transitivity > material: action.

אַתָּה וְאִשְׁתְּךָ וּבָנֶיךָ וּנְשֵׁי־בָנֶיךָ אִתָּךְ	מִן־הַתֵּבָה	צֵא	**Constituents**
you and your woman and your sons and the women of your sons with you	*from the ark*	*exit*	**Translation**
		Theme	**Textuality**
Subject		Finite	**Mood**
Actor	Circumstance	Process	**Transitivity**

.צֵא Theme: experiential / Finite > impv ms / Process > qal יצא.

.מִן־הַתֵּבָה Circumstance: location, place > prep phrase: prep - def art + noun common fs.

.אַתָּה וְאִשְׁתְּךָ וּבָנֶיךָ וּנְשֵׁי־בָנֶיךָ אִתָּךְ Subject > 2 ms (אַתָּה) / Actor > nominal group complex: Head + Post-modifier.

.אַתָּה Head > pronoun personal 2 ms, antecedent is נֹחַ *Noach.*

.וְאִשְׁתְּךָ וּבָנֶיךָ וּנְשֵׁי־בָנֶיךָ אִתָּךְ Group conj + Post-modifier > nominal group complex: Head + Post-modifier.

.אִשְׁתְּךָ וּבָנֶיךָ וּנְשֵׁי־בָנֶיךָ Head > nominal group: noun common fs const + pronoun suffix 2 ms, antecedent is נֹחַ | group conj + noun common mp const + pronoun suffix 2 ms, antecedent is נֹחַ | group conj + noun common fp const - noun common mp const + pronoun suffix 2 ms, antecedent is נֹחַ.

.אִתָּךְ Post-modifier > prep phrase: prep + pronoun suffix 2 ms, antecedent is נֹחַ.

8:17 // כָּל־הַחַיָּ֨ה אֲשֶׁר־אִתְּךָ֜ מִכָּל־בָּשָׂ֗ר בָּע֧וֹף וּבַבְּהֵמָ֛ה
וּבְכָל־הָרֶ֛מֶשׂ הָרֹמֵ֥שׂ עַל־הָאָ֖רֶץ הוֹצֵא [הַיְצֵ֣א] אִתָּ֑ךְ
// וְשָׁרְצ֣וּ בָאָ֔רֶץ // וּפָר֥וּ // וְרָב֖וּ עַל־הָאָֽרֶץ׃

כָּל־הַחַיָּה [[אֲשֶׁר־אִתְּךָ]] מִכָּל־בָּשָׂר בָּעוֹף וּבַבְּהֵמָה וּבְכָל־הָרֶמֶשׂ [[הָרֹמֵשׂ עַל־הָאָרֶץ]] הוֹצֵא [הַיְצֵא] אִתָּךְ.
(a) Textuality > appositive paratactic projection / Mood > directive / Transitivity > material: action.

אִתָּךְ	הוֹצֵא [הַיְצֵא]	כָּל־הַחַיָּה [[אֲשֶׁר־אִתְּךָ]] מִכָּל־בָּשָׂר בָּעוֹף וּבַבְּהֵמָה וּבְכָל־הָרֶמֶשׂ [[הָרֹמֵשׂ עַל־הָאָרֶץ]]	**Constituents**
with you	*bring out*	*all the livingkind which is with you from all flesh, in fowl and in beastkind and in all the creepingkind, the creeperkind on the earth*	**Translation**
		Theme	**Textuality**
	Finite		**Mood**
Circumstance	Process	Goal	**Transitivity**

כָּל־הַחַיָּה [[אֲשֶׁר־אִתְּךָ]] מִכָּל־בָּשָׂר בָּעוֹף וּבַבְּהֵמָה וּבְכָל־הָרֶמֶשׂ [[הָרֹמֵשׂ עַל־הָאָרֶץ]]. Theme: experiential / Goal > nominal group complex: Head + Post-modifier. This is a rather intricate complex in which the head nominal group (כָּל־הַחַיָּה) is directly post-modified in two ways, first by a relative clause and then by a prep phrase. Then, the post-modifier prep phrase is qualified by a series of prep phrases, the last of which is then modified by a relative clause.

כָּל־הַחַיָּה [[אֲשֶׁר־אִתְּךָ]] מִכָּל־בָּשָׂר. Head > nominal group complex: Head + Post-modifier 1 + Post-modifier 2.

כָּל־הַחַיָּה. Head > noun common collective ms const - def art + noun common collective fs.

אֲשֶׁר־אִתְּךָ. (i) Post-modifier 1 >> Textuality > embedded expansion: relative clause / Mood > declarative: non-past / Transitivity > relational: attribution.

אִתְּךָ	אֲשֶׁר־	**Constituents**
with you	*which*	**Translation**
	Theme	**Textuality**
Complement	Subject	**Mood**
Attribute	Carrier	**Transitivity**

אֲשֶׁר־. Theme: textual / Subject > ms (כָּל) / Carrier > pronoun relative, antecedent is כָּל־הַחַיָּה *all the living.*

אִתְּךָ. Complement / Attribute > prep phrase: prep + pronoun suffix 2 ms, antecedent is נֹחַ *Noach.*

מִכָּל־בָּשָׂר. Post-modifier 2 > prep phrase: prep + noun common collective ms const - noun common collective ms.

בָּעוֹף וּבַבְּהֵמָה וּבְכָל־הָרֶמֶשׂ [[הָרֹמֵשׂ עַל־הָאָרֶץ]]. Post-modifier > prep phrase complex: prep phrase 1 + prep phrase 2 + prep phrase 3.

בָּעוֹף. Prep phrase 1 > prep + def art + noun common collective ms.

וּבַבְּהֵמָה. Group conj + Prep phrase 2 > prep + def art + noun common collective fs.

וּבְכָל־הָרֶמֶשׂ [[הָרֹמֵשׂ עַל־הָאָרֶץ]]. Group conj + Prep phrase 3 > Head + Post-modifier.

בְּכָל־הָרֶמֶשׂ. Head > prep phrase: prep + noun common collective ms const - def art + noun common collective ms.

הָרֹמֵשׂ עַל־הָאָרֶץ. (a') Post-modifier >> Textuality > embedded expansion: relative clause / Mood > declarative: non-past / Transitivity > relational: attribution.

עַל־הָאָרֶץ	הָרֹמֵשׂ	**Constituents**
on the earth	*the creeperkind*	**Translation**
	Theme	**Textuality**
Attribute	Carrier / Process	**Transitivity**

הָרֹמֵשׂ. Theme: experiential / Carrier > ptc ms / Process > qal רמשׂ.

עַל־הָאָרֶץ. Complement / Attribute > prep phrase: prep - def art + noun fs.

הוֹצֵא. Finite > impv ms / Process > hifil יצא. The MT has the unusual Qere form הַיְצֵא, which appears to be an impv formed as if it were a 1-yod verb on the pattern of ישׁר (see GKC 69v, 70b). The Ketiv form appears to be preferable.

אִתָּךְ. Circumstance: location, place > prep phrase: prep + pronoun suffix 2 ms, antecedent is *Noach*.

וְשָׁרְצוּ בָאָרֶץ. (b) Textuality > conj paratactic projection / Mood > declarative: non-past / Transitivity > material: event. The Subject / Actor is כָּל־הַחַיָּה *all the living* from the preceding clause.

בָאָרֶץ	וְשָׁרְצוּ	**Constituents**
in the earth	*and they will swarm*	**Translation**
	Theme	**Textuality**
	Finite	**Mood**
Circumstance	Process	**Transitivity**

וְשָׁרְצוּ. Theme: textual > clause conj + Theme: experiential / Finite > weqatal 3cp / Process > qal שׁרץ.

בָאָרֶץ. Circumstance: location, place > prep phrase: prep + def art + noun common fs.

וּפָרוּ. (c) Textuality > conj paratactic projection / Mood > declarative: non-past / Transitivity > material: action. The Subject / Actor is כָּל־הַחַיָּה *all the living* from clause (a).

וּפָרוּ	Constituents
and they will bear fruit	**Translation**
Theme	**Textuality**
Finite	**Mood**
Process	**Transitivity**

וּפָרוּ. Theme: textual > clause conj + Theme: experiential / Finite > weqatal 3cp / Process > qal פרה.

וְרָבוּ עַל־הָאָרֶץ. (d) Textuality > conj paratactic projection / Mood > declarative: non-past / Transitivity > material: event. The Subject / Actor is כָּל־הַחַיָּה *all the living* from clause (a).

עַל־הָאָרֶץ	וְרָבוּ	Constituents
on the earth	*and they will multiply*	**Translation**
	Theme	**Textuality**
	Finite	**Mood**
Circumstance	Process	**Transitivity**

וְרָבוּ. Theme: textual > clause conj + Theme: experiential / Finite > weqatal 3cp / Process > qal רבה.

עַל־הָאָרֶץ. Circumstance: location, place > prep phrase: prep - def art + noun common fs.

8:18 // וַיֵּצֵא־נֹחַ וּבָנָיו וְאִשְׁתּוֹ וּנְשֵׁי־בָנָיו אִתּוֹ׃

וַיֵּצֵא־נֹחַ וּבָנָיו וְאִשְׁתּוֹ וּנְשֵׁי־בָנָיו אִתּוֹ. (a) Textuality > conj paratactic expansion / Mood > declarative: past / Transitivity > material: action.

נֹחַ וּבָנָיו וְאִשְׁתּוֹ וּנְשֵׁי־בָנָיו אִתּוֹ	וַיֵּצֵא־	**Constituents**
Noach and his sons and his woman and the women of his sons with him	*and he exited*	**Translation**
	Theme	**Textuality**
Subject	Finite	**Mood**
Actor	Process	**Transitivity**

וַיֵּצֵא־. Theme: textual > clause conj + Theme: experiential / Finite > wayyiqtol 3ms / Process > qal יצא.

נֹחַ וּבָנָיו וְאִשְׁתּוֹ וּנְשֵׁי־בָנָיו אִתּוֹ. Subject > ms (נֹחַ) / Actor > nominal group complex: Head + Post-modifier.

נֹחַ. Head > noun proper ms.

וּבָנָיו וְאִשְׁתּוֹ וּנְשֵׁי־בָנָיו אִתּוֹ. Post-modifier > Head + Post-modifier.

וּבָנָיו וְאִשְׁתּוֹ וּנְשֵׁי־בָנָיו. Head > nominal group complex > nominal group 1 + nominal group 2 + nominal group 3.

וּבָנָיו. Nominal group 1 > Group conj + noun common mp const + pronoun suffix 3ms, antecedent is נֹחַ *Noach.*

וְאִשְׁתּוֹ. Nominal group 2 > Group conj + noun common fs const + pronoun suffix 3ms, antecedent is נֹחַ *Noach.*

וּנְשֵׁי־בָנָיו. Nominal group 3 > Group conj + noun common fp const - noun common mp const + pronoun suffix 3ms, antecedent is נֹחַ *Noach.*

אִתּוֹ. Post-modifier > prep phrase: prep + pronoun suffix 3ms, antecedent is נֹחַ *Noach.*

8:19 // כָּל־הַחַיָּה כָּל־הָרֶמֶשׂ וְכָל־הָעוֹף כֹּל רוֹמֵשׂ עַל־
הָאָרֶץ לְמִשְׁפְּחֹתֵיהֶם יָצְאוּ מִן־הַתֵּבָה׃

כָּל־הַחַיָּה כָּל־הָרֶמֶשׂ וְכָל־הָעוֹף כֹּל [[רוֹמֵשׂ עַל־הָאָרֶץ]]

לְמִשְׁפְּחֹתֵיהֶם יָצְאוּ מִן־הַתֵּבָה. (a) Textuality > appositive paratactic expansion / Mood > declarative: past / Transitivity > material: action.

מִן־הַתֵּבָה	יָצְאוּ	לְמִשְׁפְּחֹתֵיהֶם	כָּל־הַחַיָּה כָּל־הָרֶמֶשׂ וְכָל־הָעוֹף כֹּל [[רוֹמֵשׂ עַל־הָאָרֶץ]]	**Constituents**
from the ark	*they exited*	*for their families*	*all the livingkind, all the creepingkind and all the fowl, all creeperkind on the earth*	**Translation**
			Theme	**Textuality**
	Finite		Subject	**Mood**
Circumstance	Process	Beneficiary	Actor	**Transitivity**

כָּל־הַחַיָּה כָּל־הָרֶמֶשׂ וְכָל־הָעוֹף כֹּל [[רוֹמֵשׂ עַל־הָאָרֶץ]]. Theme: experiential / Subject > ms (כָּל־) / Actor > nominal group complex: Head + Post-modifier 1 + Post-modifier 2. The nominal group כָּל־הַחַיָּה is interpreted as the Head, here a general category of living things, which is specified by the following post-modifiers.

כָּל־הַחַיָּה. Head > nominal group: noun common collective ms const - def art + noun common collective fs.

כָּל־הָרֶמֶשׂ וְכָל־הָעוֹף. Post-modifier 1 > nominal group complex: nominal group 1 + nominal group 2.

כָּל־הָרֶמֶשׂ. Nominal group 1 > noun common collective ms const - def art + noun common collective ms.

וְכָל־הָעוֹף. Group conj + Nominal group 2 > noun common collective ms const - def art + noun common collective ms.

כֹּל [[רוֹמֵשׂ עַל־הָאָרֶץ]]. Post-modifier 2 > Head + Post-modifier. Nominal group 2, וְכָל־הָעוֹף, looks to be an intrusion. Compare 7:14(a) and 8:17(a) where כָּל־הָרֶמֶשׂ הָרֹמֵשׂ עַל־הָאָרֶץ is found as a contiguous nominal group.

כֹּל. Head > noun common collective ms.

רוֹמֵשׂ עַל־הָאָרֶץ. Post-modifier >> Textuality > embedded expansion: relative clause / Mood > declarative: non-past / Transitivity > relational: attribution. An asyndetic relative clause.

עַל־הָאָרֶץ	רוֹמֵשׂ	**Constituents**
on the earth	*creepingkind*	**Translation**
	Theme	**Textuality**
Complement	Subject	**Mood**
Attribute	Carrier	**Transitivity**

רוֹמֵשׂ. Theme: experiential / Subject > ms / Carrier > ptc ms qal רמשׂ.

עַל־הָאָרֶץ. Complement / Attribute > prep phrase: prep - def art + noun common fs.

לְמִשְׁפְּחֹתֵיהֶם. Beneficiary > prep phrase: prep + noun common fp const + pronoun suffix 3mp, antecedent is the first כָּל or the final כֹּל.

יָצְאוּ. Finite > qatal 3cp / Process > qal יצא.

מִן־הַתֵּבָה. Circumstance: location, place > prep phrase: prep - def art + noun common fs.

Genesis 8:20-22

[20]And Noach built an altar to YHVH. And he took from all the clean beastkind and from all the clean fowl. And he offered offerings on the altar. [21]And YHVH smelled the smell of the consolation. And YHVH said to his heart, "Not again will I again curse the ground on account of the humankind, because the impulse of the heart of the humankind is evil from his youth. And not again will I any more strike all alive, such as I did. [22]From now on, all the days of the earth, seed and harvest, and cold and heat, and summer and winter, and day and night, they will not cease."

8:20 /// וַיִּ֤בֶן נֹ֙חַ֙ מִזְבֵּ֖חַ לַֽיהוָ֑ה // וַיִּקַּ֞ח מִכֹּ֣ל ׀ הַבְּהֵמָ֣ה
הַטְּהוֹרָ֗ה וּמִכֹּל֙ הָע֣וֹף הַטָּהֹ֔ר // וַיַּ֥עַל עֹלֹ֖ת בַּמִּזְבֵּֽחַ׃

וַיִּבֶן נֹחַ מִזְבֵּחַ לַיהוָה. (a) Textuality > conj paratactic expansion / Mood > declarative: past / Transitivity > material: action.

לַיהוָ	מִזְבֵּחַ	נֹחַ	וַיִּבֶן	**Constituents**
to YHVH	*an altar*	*Noach*	*and he built*	**Translation**
			Theme	**Textuality**
		Subject	Finite	**Mood**
Beneficiary	Goal	Actor	Process	**Transitivity**

וַיִּבֶן. Theme: textual > clause conj + Theme: experiential / Finite > wayyiqtol 3ms / Process > qal בנה.

נֹחַ. Subject > ms / Actor > nominal group: noun proper.

מִזְבֵּחַ. Goal > nominal group: noun common ms.

לַיהוָה. Beneficiary > prep phrase: prep + noun proper ms.

וַיִּקַּח מִכֹּל הַבְּהֵמָה הַטְּהוֹרָה וּמִכֹּל הָעוֹף הַטָּהֹר. (b) Textuality > conj paratactic expansion / Mood > declarative: past / Transitivity > material: action. Subject / Actor is נֹחַ *Noach*, absent by ellipsis.

מִכֹּל הַבְּהֵמָה הַטְּהוֹרָה וּמִכֹּל הָעוֹף הַטָּהֹר	וַיִּקַּח	**Constituents**
from all the clean beastkind and from all the clean fowl	*and he took*	**Translation**
	Theme	**Textuality**
	Finite	**Mood**
Range	Process	**Transitivity**

וַיִּקַּח. Theme: textual > clause conj + Theme: experiential / Finite > wayyiqtol 3ms / Process > qal לקח.

מִכֹּל הַבְּהֵמָה הַטְּהוֹרָה וּמִכֹּל הָעוֹף הַטָּהֹר. Range > prep phrase group: prep phrase 1 + prep phrase 2.

מִכֹּל הַבְּהֵמָה הַטְּהוֹרָה. Prep phrase 1 > prep + noun common collective ms const | def art + noun common collective fs | def art + adj fs.

וּמִכֹּל הָעוֹף הַטָּהֹר. Group conj + Prep phrase 2 > prep + noun common collective ms const | def art + noun common collective ms | def art + adj ms.

וַיַּעַל עֹלֹת בַּמִּזְבֵּחַ. (c) Textuality > conj paratactic expansion / Mood > declarative: past / Transitivity > material: action. Subject / Actor is נֹחַ *Noach*, absent by ellipsis.

בַּמִּזְבֵּחַ	עֹלֹת	וַיַּעַ	**Constituents**
on the altar	*offerings*	*and he offered*	**Translation**
		Theme	**Textuality**
		Finite	**Mood**
Circumstance	Goal	Process	**Transitivity**

וַיַּעַל. Theme: textual > clause conj + Theme: experiential / Finite > wayyiqtol 3ms / Process > qal עלה.

עֹלֹת. Goal > nominal group: noun common fp.

בַּמִּזְבֵּחַ. Circumstance: location, place > prep phrase: prep + def art + noun common ms.

8:21 // וַיָּרַח יְהוָה אֶת־רֵיחַ הַנִּיחֹחַ // וַיֹּאמֶר יְהוָה
אֶל־לִבּוֹ // לֹא־אֹסִף לְקַלֵּל עוֹד אֶת־הָאֲדָמָה בַּעֲבוּר
הָאָדָם / כִּי יֵצֶר לֵב הָאָדָם רַע מִנְּעֻרָיו // וְלֹא־אֹסִף
עוֹד לְהַכּוֹת אֶת־כָּל־חַי / כַּאֲשֶׁר עָשִׂיתִי׃

וַיָּרַח יְהוָה אֶת־רֵיחַ הַנִּיחֹחַ. (a) Textuality > conj paratactic expansion / Mood > declarative: past / Transitivity > mental: perception.

אֶת־רֵיחַ הַנִּיחֹחַ	יְהוָה	וַיָּרַח	**Constituents**
the smell of the consolation	*YHVH*	*and he smelled*	**Translation**
		Theme	**Textuality**
	Subject	Finite	**Mood**
Phenomenon	Senser	Process	**Transitivity**

וַיָּרַח. Theme: textual > clause conj + Theme: experiential / Finite > wayyiqtol 3ms / Process > hifil רוח.

יְהוָה. Subject > ms / Senser > nominal group: noun proper.

אֶת־רֵיחַ הַנִּיחֹחַ. Phenomenon > nominal group: goal marker - noun common ms const | def art + noun common ms. Notice the word play on the name נֹחַ *Noach*, and compare 5:29.

וַיֹּאמֶר יְהוָה אֶל־לִבּוֹ. (b) Textuality > conj paratactic expansion / Mood > declarative: past / Transitivity > verbal.

אֶל־לִבּוֹ	יְהוָה	וַיֹּאמֶר	**Constituents**
to his heart	*YHVH*	*and he said*	**Translation**
		Theme	**Textuality**
	Subject	Finite	**Mood**
Receiver	Sayer	Process	**Transitivity**

וַיֹּאמֶר. Theme: textual > clause conj + Theme: experiential / Finite > wayyiqtol 3ms / Process > qal אמר.

יְהוָה. Subject > ms / Sayer > nominal group: noun proper.

אֶל־לִבּוֹ. Receiver > prep phrase: prep - noun common ms const + pronoun suffix 3ms, antecedent is יְהוָה *YHVH*.

לֹא־אֹסִף לְקַלֵּל עוֹד אֶת־הָאֲדָמָה בַּעֲבוּר הָאָדָם. (c) Textuality > appositive paratactic projection: quote / Mood > declarative: non-past / Transitivity > verbal. Sayer of the quote is יְהוָה *YHVH*.

בַּעֲבוּר הָאָדָם	אֶת־הָאֲדָמָה	עוֹד	לְקַלֵּל	אֹסִף	לֹא־	**Constituents**
on account of the humankind	*the ground*	*more*	*curse*	*I will again*	*not*	**Translation**
		Adjunct		Theme	Theme	**Textuality**
			Com-plement	Finite	Adjunct	**Mood**
Circum-stance	Goal		Process	Process		**Transitivity**

לֹא־. Theme: interpersonal / Adjunct: interpersonal > polarity: negative.

אֹסִף לְקַלֵּל. Process > verbal group complex: Finite + Complement.

אֹסִף. Theme: experiential / Finite > yiqtol 1cs / Process > hifil אסף.

לְקַלֵּל. Complement > prep phrase: prep + Process > inf const piel קלל. Semantically speaking, this is the main process of the clause.

עוֹד. Adjunct: textual > recurrence. This reinforces the sense of the Finite in this clause (again curse), and implicitly recollects the times the ground had been cursed: 3:17(d), 4:11(a), and 5:29(b).

אֶת־הָאֲדָמָה. Goal > nominal group: goal marker - def art + noun common fs.

בַּעֲבוּר הָאָדָם. Circumstance: cause, reason > prep phrase: prep + def art + noun common collective ms.

כִּי יֵצֶר לֵב הָאָדָם רַע מִנְּעֻרָיו. (d) Textuality > conj hypotactic projection: quote / Mood > declarative: non-past / Transitivity > relational: attribution. Sayer of the quote is יְהוָה *YHVH*.

מִנְּעֻרָיו	רַע	יֵצֶר לֵב הָאָדָם	כִּי	Constituents
from his youth	*evil*	*the impulse of the heart of the human*	*because*	**Translation**
		Theme	Theme	**Textuality**
	Complement	Subject		**Mood**
Circumstance	Attribute	Carrier		**Transitivity**

כִּי. Theme: textual > conj.

יֵצֶר לֵב הָאָדָם. Theme: experiential / Subject > ms (יֵצֶר) / Carrier > nominal group: noun common ms const | noun common ms const | def art + noun common collective ms.

רַע. Complement / Attribute > adjective group: adj ms.

מִנְּעֻרָיו. Circumstance: extent, time > prep phrase: prep + noun common mp const + pronoun suffix 3ms, antecedent is הָאָדָם *the humankind.*

וְלֹא־אֹסִף עוֹד לְהַכּוֹת אֶת־כָּל־חַי. (e) Textuality > conj paratactic projection: quote / Mood > declarative: non-past / Transitivity > material: action. Sayer of the quote is יְהוָה *YHVH.*

אֶת־כָּל־חַי	לְהַכּוֹת	עוֹד	אֹסִף	וְלֹא־	Constituents
all alive	*strike*	*again*	*I will more*	*and not*	**Translation**
		Adjunct	Theme	Theme	**Textuality**
	Complement		Finite	Adjunct	**Mood**
Goal	Process		Process		**Transitivity**

וְלֹא־. Theme: textual > clause conj + Theme: interpersonal / Adjunct: interpersonal > polarity: negative.

אֹסִף. Theme: experiential / Finite > yiqtol 1cs / Process > hifil **אסף**. This is the first component of the verbal group complex. It is structured the same way as 8:21(c), except that the circumstantial adjunct עוֹד stands between the two components of the group.

עוֹד. Adjunct: textual > repetition.

לְהַכּוֹת. Complement > prep phrase: prep + Process > inf const hifil נכה. Semantically speaking, this is the main process of the clause.

אֶת־כָּל־חַי. Goal > nominal group: goal marker - noun common collective ms - adj ms.

כַּאֲשֶׁר עָשִׂיתִי. (f) Textuality > conj hypotactic projection: quote / Mood > declarative: past / Transitivity > material: action. This temporal clause qualifies the immediately preceding clause (e).

עָשִׂיתִי	כַּאֲשֶׁר	**Constituents**
I did	*such as which*	**Translation**
	Theme	**Textuality**
Finite		**Mood**
Process	Goal	**Transitivity**

כַּאֲשֶׁר. Theme: textual > prep + Theme: experiential > pronoun relative/ Goal > antecedent is the preceding clause complex.

עָשִׂיתִי. Finite > qatal 1cs / Process > qal עשׂה.

8:22 // עֹ֖ד כָּל־יְמֵ֣י הָאָ֑רֶץ זֶ֡רַע וְקָצִיר֩ וְקֹ֨ר וָחֹ֜ם וְקַ֧יִץ
וָחֹ֛רֶף וְי֥וֹם וָלַ֖יְלָה לֹ֥א יִשְׁבֹּֽתוּ׃

עֹד כָּל־יְמֵי הָאָרֶץ זֶרַע וְקָצִיר וְקֹר וָחֹם וְקַיִץ וָחֹרֶף וְיוֹם וָלַיְלָה לֹא יִשְׁבֹּתוּ. (a) Textuality > appositive paratactic expansion / Mood > declarative: non-past / Transitivity > material: action.

יִשְׁבֹּתוּ	לֹא	זֶרַע וְקָצִיר וְקֹר וָחֹם וְקַיִץ וָחֹרֶף וְיוֹם וָלַיְלָה	כָּל־יְמֵי הָאָרֶץ	עֹד	**Constituents**
they will cease	*not*	*seed and harvest, and cold and heat, and summer and winter, and day and night*	*all of the days of the earth*	*more*	**Translation**
			Theme	Adjunct	**Textuality**
Finite	Adjunct	Subject			**Mood**
Process		Actor	Circumstance		**Transitivity**

עֹד. Theme: textual / Adjunct: textual > recurrence. This textual adjunct signals that from now, the point of speaking, and into the indefinite future, these things will not cease.

כָּל־יְמֵי הָאָרֶץ. Theme: experiential / Circumstance: extent, time > nominal group: noun common collective ms const - noun common mp const | def art + noun common fs.

זֶרַע וְקָצִיר וְקֹר וָחֹם וְקַיִץ וָחֹרֶף וְיוֹם וָלַיְלָה. Subject > mp / Actor > nominal group complex: nominal group 1 + nominal group 2 + nominal group 3 + nominal group 4. Notice how the conjunctions linking the four groups are all in the form וְ and, after the first group, the conjunctions within each group are the וָ hendiadys form of the conjunction.

זֶרַע וְקָצִיר. Nominal group 1 > noun common ms | group conj + noun common ms.

וְקֹר וָחֹם. Group conj + Nominal group 2 > noun common ms | group conj + noun common ms.

וְקַיִץ וָחֹרֶף. Group conj + Nominal group 3 > noun common ms |

group conj + noun common ms.

וְיוֹם וָלַיְלָה. Group conj + Nominal group 4 > noun common ms | group conj + noun common ms.

לֹא. Adjunct: interpersonal > polarity: negative.

יִשְׁבֹּתוּ. Finite > yiqtol 3mp / Process > qal שׁבת.

Genesis 9:1-7

[1]And deity blessed Noach and his sons. And he said to them, "Bear fruit. And be many. And fill the earth. [2]Fear of you and dread of you will be on all the animalkind of the earth and on all the fowl of the heavens, in all with which the ground creeps and in all the fish of the sea. Into your hand they were put. [3]All creeperkind which is alive will be for food for you. As grass greens I gave all to you. [4]Just flesh in its life, its blood, you will not eat. [5]And just your blood I will require for the sake of your lives. I will require it from the hand of all animalkind. And from the hand of humankind, from a man's hand of his brother, I will require the life of humankind." [6]One shedding the blood of humankind, by humankind will his blood be shed, because into an image of deity he made humankind. [7]"And you, bear fruit. And multiply. And swarm in the earth. And multiply in it."

9:1 /// וַיְבָרֶךְ אֱלֹהִים אֶת־נֹחַ וְאֶת־בָּנָיו // וַיֹּאמֶר לָהֶם
// פְּרוּ // וּרְבוּ // וּמִלְאוּ אֶת־הָאָרֶץ׃

וַיְבָרֶךְ אֱלֹהִים אֶת־נֹחַ וְאֶת־בָּנָיו. (a) Textuality > conj paratactic expansion / Mood > declarative: past / Transitivity > material: action.

אֶת־נֹחַ וְאֶת־בָּנָיו	אֱלֹהִים	וַיְבָרֶךְ	**Constituents**
Noach and his sons	*deity*	*and he blessed*	**Translation**
		Theme	**Textuality**
	Subject	Finite	**Mood**
Goal	Actor	Process	**Transitivity**

וַיְבָ֫רֶךְ. Theme: textual > clause conj + Theme: experiential / Finite > wayyiqtol 3ms / Process > piel ברך.

אֱלֹהִים. Subject > mp / Actor > nominal group: noun common.

אֶת־נֹחַ וְאֶת־בָּנָיו. Goal > nominal group: goal marker - noun proper ms | group conj + goal marker - noun common mp const + pronoun suffix 3ms, antecedent is נֹחַ *Noach.*

וַיֹּאמֶר לָהֶם. (b) Textuality > conj paratactic expansion / Mood > declarative: past / Transitivity > verbal. Subject / Sayer is אֱלֹהִים *deity* from the preceding clause.

לָהֶם	וַיֹּאמֶר	Constituents
to them	*and he said*	**Translation**
	Theme	**Textuality**
	Finite	**Mood**
Receiver	Process	**Transitivity**

וַיֹּאמֶר. Theme: textual > clause conj + Theme: experiential / Finite > wayyiqtol 3ms / Process > qal אמר.

לָהֶם. Receiver > prep phrase: prep + pronoun suffix 3mp, antecedent is נֹחַ *Noach* and בָּנָיו *his sons.*

פְּרוּ. (c) Textuality > appositive paratactic projection: quote / Mood > directive: imperative / Transitivity > material: action.

פְּרוּ	Constituents
bear fruit	**Translation**
Theme	**Textuality**
Finite	**Mood**
Process	**Transitivity**

פְּרוּ. Theme: experiential / Finite > impv mp / Process > qal פרה.

וּרְבוּ. (d) Textuality > conj paratactic projection: quote / Mood > directive: imperative / Transitivity > material: event.

וּרְבוּ	Constituents
and be many	**Translation**
Theme	**Textuality**
Finite	**Mood**
Process	**Transitivity**

וּרְבוּ. Theme: textual > clause conj + Theme: experiential / Finite > impv mp / Process > qal רבה.

וּמִלְאוּ אֶת־הָאָרֶץ. (e) conj paratactic projection: quote / Mood > directive: imperative / Transitivity > material: action.

אֶת־הָאָרֶץ	וּמִלְאוּ	Constituents
the earth	*and fill*	**Translation**
	Theme	**Textuality**
	Finite	**Mood**
Goal	Process	**Transitivity**

וּמִלְאוּ. Theme: textual > clause conj + Theme: experiential / Finite > impv mp / Process > qal מלא.

אֶת־הָאָרֶץ. Goal > nominal group: goal marker - def art + noun common fs.

9:2 // וּמוֹרַאֲכֶם וְחִתְּכֶם יִהְיֶה עַל כָּל־חַיַּת הָאָרֶץ וְעַל
כָּל־עוֹף הַשָּׁמָיִם בְּכֹל אֲשֶׁר תִּרְמֹשׂ הָאֲדָמָה וּבְכָל־
דְּגֵי הַיָּם // בְּיֶדְכֶם נִתָּנוּ׃

וּמוֹרַאֲכֶם וְחִתְּכֶם יִהְיֶה עַל כָּל־חַיַּת הָאָרֶץ וְעַל כָּל־עוֹף הַשָּׁמָיִם בְּכֹל [[אֲשֶׁר תִּרְמֹשׂ הָאֲדָמָה]] וּבְכָל־דְּגֵי הַיָּם. (a) Textuality > conj paratactic projection: quote / Mood > declarative: non-past / Transitivity > relational: attribution.

עַל כָּל־חַיַּת הָאָרֶץ וְעַל כָּל־עוֹף הַשָּׁמָיִם בְּכֹל [[אֲשֶׁר תִּרְמֹשׂ הָאֲדָמָה]] וּבְכָל־דְּגֵי הַיָּם	יִהְיֶה	וּמוֹרַאֲכֶם וְחִתְּכֶם	**Constituents**
on all the animalkind of the earth and on all the fowl of the heavens, in all with which the ground creeps and in all the fish of the sea	*he will be*	*fear of you and dread of you*	**Translation**
		Theme	**Textuality**
	Finite	Subject	**Mood**
Attribute	Process	Carrier	**Transitivity**

וּמוֹרַאֲכֶם וְחִתְּכֶם. Theme: textual > clause conj + Theme: experiential / Subject > mp / Carrier > nominal group complex: nominal group 1 + nominal group 2.

מוֹרַאֲכֶם. Nominal group 1 > noun common ms const + pronoun suffix 2mp, antecedent is נֹחַ *Noach* and בָּנָיו *his sons,* the Receiver from 9:1(a): *fear of you.* The pronoun indicates not the one doing the fearing (the so-called subject, or subjective genitive), but the object of the process, the ones being feared (called the objective genitive).

וְחִתְּכֶם. Group conj + Nominal group 1 > noun common ms const + pronoun suffix 2mp, antecedent is the same as the preceding nominal group.

יִהְיֶה. Finite > yiqtol 3ms / Process > qal היה. The Subject is presumably plural, consisting as it does of two conjoined nouns, but the Finite is singular in form. This is the first grammatical anomaly in this clause.

עַל כָּל־חַיַּת הָאָרֶץ וְעַל כָּל־עוֹף הַשָּׁמָיִם בְּכֹל אֲשֶׁר תִּרְמֹשׂ הָאֲדָמָה וּבְכָל־דְּגֵי הַיָּם. Attribute > prep phrase complex: prep phrase 1 + prep phrase 2 + prep phrase 3 + prep phrase 4. The first two are עַל phrases joined by the conjunction, and the second two are בְּ phrases joined by the conjunction.

עַל כָּל־חַיַּת הָאָרֶץ. Prep phrase 1 > prep | noun common collective ms const - noun common collective fs const | def art + noun common fs.

וְעַל כָּל־עוֹף הַשָּׁמָיִם. Group conj + Prep phrase 2 > prep | noun common collective ms const - noun common collective ms const | def art + noun common mp.

בְּכֹל אֲשֶׁר תִּרְמֹשׂ הָאֲדָמָה. Prep phrase 3 > prep + Head + Post-modifier.

כֹּל. Head > nominal group: noun common collective ms.

אֲשֶׁר תִּרְמֹשׂ הָאֲדָמָה. (i) Post-modifier >> Textuality > embedded expansion: relative clause / Mood > declarative: non-past / Transitivity > material: action. This embedded clause contains the second grammatical anomaly. Compare Leviticus 20:25 which contains the same embedded relative clause. The NRSV of the relevant portions of that verse reads: *by anything with which the ground teems.* Would we not expect כֹּל to be the Subject / Actor, and הָאֲדָמָה to be the circumstance: *all which will creep on the ground*? Instead, הָאֲדָמָה is the Subject / Actor.

הָאֲדָמָה	תִּרְמֹשׂ	אֲשֶׁר	**Constituents**
the ground	*she will creep*	*which*	**Translation**
		Theme	**Textuality**
Subject	Finite		**Mood**
Actor	Process		**Transitivity**

אֲשֶׁר. Theme: textual and experiential > pronoun relative, antecedent is כֹּל *all.*

תִּרְמֹשׂ. Finite > yiqtol 3fs / Process > qal רמשׂ.

הָאֲדָמָה. Subject > fs / Actor > nominal group: def art + noun common.

וּבְכָל־דְּגֵי הַיָּם. Group conj + Prep phrase 4 > prep + noun common ms const - noun common mp const | def art + noun common ms.

בְּיֶדְכֶם נִתָּנוּ. (b) Textuality > appositive paratactic projection: quote / Mood > declarative: past / Transitivity > material: action.

נִתָּנוּ	בְּיֶדְכֶם	**Constituents**
they were given	*in your hand*	**Translation**
	Theme	**Textuality**
Finite		**Mood**
Process	Circumstance	**Transitivity**

בְּיֶדְכֶם. Theme: experiential / Circumstance: location, place > prep phrase: prep + noun common fs const + pronoun suffix 2mp, antecedent is נֹחַ *Noach* and בָּנָיו *his sons.*

נִתָּנוּ. Finite > qatal 3cp / Process > nifal נתן.

9:3 // כָּל־רֶמֶשׂ אֲשֶׁר הוּא־חַי לָכֶם יִהְיֶה לְאָכְלָה /
כְּיֶרֶק עֵשֶׂב נָתַתִּי לָכֶם אֶת־כֹּל׃

כָּל־רֶמֶשׂ [[אֲשֶׁר הוּא־חַי]] לָכֶם יִהְיֶה לְאָכְלָה. (a) Textuality > appositive paratactic projection: quote / Mood > declarative: non-past / Transitivity > relational: attribution.

לְאָכְלָה	יִהְיֶה	לָכֶם	כָּל־רֶמֶשׂ [[אֲשֶׁר הוּא־חַי]]	**Constituents**
for food	*he will be*	*to you*	*all creeperkind which he is alive*	**Translation**
			Theme	**Textuality**
	Finite		Subject	**Mood**
Attribute	Process	Beneficiary	Carrier	**Transitivity**

כָּל־רֶמֶשׂ [[אֲשֶׁר הוּא־חַי]]. Theme: experiential / Subject > ms (כָּל) / Carrier > nominal group complex: Head + Post-modifier.

כָּל־רֶמֶשׂ. Head > nominal group: noun common collective ms const - noun common collective ms.

אֲשֶׁר הוּא־חַי. (i) Post-modifier >> Textuality > embedded expansion: relative clause / Mood > declarative: non-past / Transitivity > relational: attribution.

חַי	הוּא־	אֲשֶׁר	**Constituents**
alive	*he*	*which*	**Translation**
		Theme	**Textuality**
Complement	Subject	Subject	**Mood**
Attribute	Carrier	Carrier	**Transitivity**

אֲשֶׁר. Theme: textual / Subject > ms / Carrier > pronoun relative, antecedent is כֹּל *all*, but could also be רֶמֶשׂ *creeperkind.*

הוּא־. Theme: experiential / Subject > ms / Carrier > pronoun personal 3ms, antecedent is the same as that of אֲשֶׁר. The personal pronoun appears to be grammatically redundant.

חַי. Complement / Attribute > adjective group: adj ms.

לָכֶם. Beneficiary > prep phrase: prep + pronoun suffix 2mp, antecedent is נֹחַ *Noach* and בָּנָיו *his sons.*

יִהְיֶה. Finite > yiqtol 3ms / Process > qal היה.

לְאָכְלָה. Attribute > prep phrase: prep + noun common fs.

כְּיֶרֶק עֵשֶׂב נָתַתִּי לָכֶם אֶת־כֹּל. (b) Textuality > conj hypotactic projection: quote / Mood > declarative: past / Transitivity > material: action.

אֶת־כֹּל	לָכֶם	נָתַתִּי	כְּיֶרֶק עֵשֶׂב	**Constituents**
all	*to you*	*I gave*	*as greens of grass*	**Translation**
			Theme	**Textuality**
		Finite		**Mood**
Goal	Beneficiary	Process	Circumstance	**Transitivity**

כְּיֶרֶק עֵשֶׂב. Theme: experiential / Circumstance: manner, comparison > prep phrase: prep + noun common collective ms const |

noun common collective ms. Is this prepositional phrase an abbreviated clause? Compare NRSV which translates this phrase *and just as I gave you the green plants*. Since this phrase does not have a predicator, it is unlikely that this is a viable reading, and it would assume a large amount of elliptical material. As it stands, the phrase merely compares animal substance to vegetable substance as a source of food.

נָתַתִּי. Finite > qatal 1cs / Process > qal נתן.

לָכֶם. Beneficiary > prep phrase: prep + pronoun suffix 2mp, antecedent is נֹחַ *Noach* and בָּנָיו *his sons.*

אֶת־כֹּל. Goal > nominal group: goal marker - noun common collective ms.

9:4 // אַךְ־בָּשָׂר בְּנַפְשׁוֹ דָמוֹ לֹא תֹאכֵלוּ׃

אַךְ־בָּשָׂר בְּנַפְשׁוֹ דָמוֹ לֹא תֹאכֵלוּ. (a) Textuality > appositive paratactic projection: quote / Mood > declarative: non-past / Transitivity > material: action. Subject / Actor is נֹחַ *Noach* and בָּנָיו *his sons*, absent by ellipsis.

תֹאכֵלוּ	לֹא	בָּשָׂר בְּנַפְשׁוֹ דָמוֹ	אַךְ־	**Constituents**
you will eat	*not*	*flesh in its life, its blood*	*just*	**Translation**
		Theme	Adjunct	**Textuality**
Finite	Adjunct			**Mood**
Process		Goal		**Transitivity**

אַךְ־. Theme: textual > Adjunct: textual > restriction. This introduces an exception to the allowance of eating flesh. It is a textual adjunct because it places a restriction on a prior statement, and in this function then presumes the prior statement.

בָּשָׂר בְּנַפְשׁוֹ דָמוֹ. Theme: experiential / Goal > nominal group: Head + Post-modifier. *Flesh in its life, its blood*, meaning, flesh with its life-blood still in it.

בָּשָׂר. Head > nominal group: noun ms.

בְּנַפְשׁוֹ דָמוֹ. Post-modifier > prep phrase complex: Head + Post-modifier.

בְּנַפְשׁוֹ. Head > prep phrase > prep + noun common fs const + pronoun suffix 3ms, antecedent is בָּשָׂר *flesh.*

דָמוֹ. Post-modifier > nominal group: noun common ms const + pronoun suffix 3ms, antecedent is בָּשָׂר *flesh.*

לֹא. Adjunct: interpersonal > polarity: negative.

תֹאכֵלוּ. Finite > yiqtol 2mp / Process > qal אכל.

9:5 // וְאַךְ אֶת־דִּמְכֶם לְנַפְשֹׁתֵיכֶם אֶדְרֹשׁ // מִיַּד כָּל־
חַיָּה אֶדְרְשֶׁנּוּ // וּמִיַּד הָאָדָם מִיַּד אִישׁ אָחִיו אֶדְרֹשׁ
אֶת־נֶפֶשׁ הָאָדָם׃

וְאַךְ אֶת־דִּמְכֶם לְנַפְשֹׁתֵיכֶם אֶדְרֹשׁ. (a) Textuality > conj paratactic projection: quote / Mood > declarative: non-past / Transitivity > material: action.

אֶדְרֹשׁ	לְנַפְשֹׁתֵיכֶם	אֶת־דִּמְכֶם	וְאַךְ	**Constituents**
I will require	*for your lives*	*your blood*	*and just*	**Translation**
		Theme	Adjunct	**Textuality**
Finite				**Mood**
Process	Beneficiary	Goal		**Transitivity**

וְאַךְ. Theme: textual > clause conj + Theme: textual / Adjunct: textual > restriction. Again, a restrictive adjunct, this time placing a restriction or qualification on a prior restriction. In effect, it is authorizing the eating of living flesh as long as it is not eaten with blood in it, with the exception of human flesh, which if taken, the deity will require the shedding of blood.

אֶת־דִּמְכֶם. Goal > nominal group: goal marker - noun common ms const + pronoun suffix 2mp, antecedent is נֹחַ *Noach* and בָּנָיו *his sons.*

לְנַפְשֹׁתֵיכֶם. Beneficiary > prep phrase: prep + noun common fp const + pronoun suffix 2mp, antecedent is נֹחַ *Noach* and בָּנָיו *his sons.*

אֶדְרֹשׁ. Finite > yiqtol 1cs / Process > qal דּרשׁ.

מִיַּד כָּל־חַיָּה אֶדְרְשֶׁנּוּ. (b) Textuality > appositive paratactic projection: quote / Mood > declarative: non-past / Transitivity > material: action.

אֶדְרְשֶׁנּוּ	מִיַּד כָּל־חַיָּה	**Constituents**
I will require him	*from the hand of all animalkind*	**Translation**
	Theme	**Textuality**
Finite		**Mood**
Process + Goal	Scope	**Transitivity**

מִיַּד כָּל־חַיָּה. Scope > prep phrase: prep + noun common fs const | noun common collective ms const - noun common fs.

אֶדְרְשֶׁנּוּ. Finite > yiqtol 1cs / Process > qal דּרשׁ + Goal > pronoun suffix 3ms, antecedent is דָּם *blood* in the preceding clause.

וּמִיַּד הָאָדָם מִיַּד אִישׁ אָחִיו אֶדְרֹשׁ אֶת־נֶפֶשׁ הָאָדָם. (c) Textuality > conj paratactic projection: quote / Mood > declarative: non-past / Transitivity > material: action. This clause has presented difficulties because it appears somewhat compressed, especially the phrase מִיַּד אִישׁ אָחִיו.

אֶת־נֶפֶשׁ הָאָדָם	אֶדְרֹשׁ	וּמִיַּד הָאָדָם מִיַּד אִישׁ אָחִיו	**Constituents**
the life of the humankind	*I will require*	*and from the hand of the humankind, from a man's hand his brother*	**Translation**
		Theme	**Textuality**
	Finite		**Mood**
Goal	Process	Scope	**Transitivity**

וּמִיַּד הָאָדָם מִיַּד אִישׁ אָחִיו. Theme: textual > clause conj + Theme: experiential / Scope > prep phrase group: Head + Post-modifier.

מִיַּד הָאָדָם. Head > prep phrase: prep + noun common fs const | def art + noun common collective ms. This prep phrase identifies what this injunction has to do with—humankind—in distinction from clause (b), which has to do with animalkind.

מִיַּד אִישׁ אָחִיו. Post-modifier > prep phrase: prep + noun common fs const | noun common ms const | noun common ms const + pronoun suffix 3ms, antecedent is **אִישׁ** *man*. This appears to be a prep phrase that adds specification to the Head by individuating it: *regarding humankind, when a man takes the life-blood of his brother. ...* The part about *takes the life-blood of* would then have to be assumed.

אֶדְרֹשׁ. Finite > yiqtol 1cs / Process > qal דרשׁ.

אֶת־נֶפֶשׁ הָאָדָם. Goal > nominal group: goal marker - noun common fs const | def + noun common collective ms.

9:6 // שֹׁפֵךְ דַּם הָאָדָם בָּאָדָם דָּמוֹ יִשָּׁפֵךְ / כִּי בְּצֶלֶם
אֱלֹהִים עָשָׂה אֶת־הָאָדָם׃

[[שֹׁפֵךְ דַּם הָאָדָם]] בָּאָדָם דָּמוֹ יִשָּׁפֵךְ. (a) Textuality > appositive paratactic projection: quote or appositive paratactic expansion / Mood > declarative: non-past / Transitivity > material: action. This clause may be part of a third person explanatory insertion into the quote. See the discussion of the following clause for the explanation.

יִשָּׁפֵךְ	דָּמוֹ	בָּאָדָם	[[שֹׁפֵךְ דַּם הָאָדָם]]	**Constituents**
will be shed	*his blood*	*by the humankind*	*one shedding the blood of the humankind*	**Translation**
		Theme	Theme	**Textuality**
Finite	Subject			**Mood**
Process	Goal	Circumstance	Goal	**Transitivity**

[[שֹׁפֵךְ דַּם הָאָדָם]]. (i) Theme: experiential / Goal >> Textuality > embedded participle clause / Mood > declarative: non-past / Transitivity > material: action. This structure is called a preposed Theme. The embedded participle clause identifies one of the participants of the main clause. This participant reappears within the transitivity structure of the main clause as the 3ms pronoun suffix on the Subject / Goal.

דַּם הָאָדָם	שֹׁפֵךְ	**Constituents**
the blood of the human	*one shedding*	**Translation**
	Theme	**Textuality**
Goal	Actor / Process	**Transitivity**

שֹׁפֵךְ. Theme: experiential / Actor > ptc ms / Process > qal שׁפך.

דַּם הָאָדָם. Goal > nominal group: noun common ms const | def art + noun common collective ms.

בָּאָדָם. Circumstance: manner, means > prep phrase: prep + def art + noun common collective ms.

דָּמוֹ. Subject > ms / Goal > nominal group: noun common ms const + pronoun suffix 3ms, antecedent is שֹׁפֵךְ *one shedding* specifically, and by extension the entire preposed theme.

יִשָּׁפֵךְ. Finite > yiqtol 3ms / Process > nifal שׁפך.

כִּי בְּצֶלֶם אֱלֹהִים עָשָׂה אֶת־הָאָדָם. (b) Textuality > conj hypotactic expansion / Mood > declarative: past / Transitivity > material: action. This clause for sure, and possibly the preceding clause along with it, are an expansion inserted into the quote. The Finite states in the third person that deity made humankind, and the Circumstance refers to deity in the third person; both are inconsistent with a quote spoken by deity. NRSV mistakenly treats this clause as part of the quote. NJPS formats 6(a-b) as a poetic interlude within the quote, but still part of the quote.

אֶת־הָאָדָם	עָשָׂה	בְּצֶלֶם אֱלֹהִים	כִּי	**Constituents**
the humankind	*he made*	*in an image of deity*	*because*	**Translation**
		Theme	Theme	**Textuality**
	Finite			**Mood**
Goal	Process	Circumstance		**Transitivity**

כִּי. Theme: textual > conj.

בְּצֶלֶם אֱלֹהִים. Theme: experiential / Circumstance: role, product > prep phrase: prep + noun common ms const ו noun common mp.

עָשָׂה. Finite > qatal 3ms / Process > qal עשׂה.

אֶת־הָאָדָם. Goal > nominal group: goal marker - def art + noun common collective ms.

9:7 // וְאַתֶּם פְּרוּ // וּרְבוּ // שִׁרְצוּ בָאָרֶץ // וּרְבוּ־בָהּ׃
ס

וְאַתֶּם פְּרוּ. (a) Textuality > conj paratactic projection: quote / Mood > directive: imperative / Transitivity > material: action.

פְּרוּ	וְאַתֶּם	**Constituents**
bear fruit	*and you*	**Translation**
	Theme	**Textuality**
Finite	Subject	**Mood**
Process	Actor	**Transitivity**

וְאַתֶּם. Theme: textual > clause conj + Theme: experiential / Subject > 2mp / Actor > pronoun personal 2mp. This is a marked Theme in so far as imperatives typically come first in their clauses, and Subject pronouns are not necessary and are normally not textually expressed. The second person pronoun, as a marked Theme, effectively returns the text to quotation from the third person explanatory insertion of the preceding clause.

פְּרוּ. Finite > impv mp / Process > qal פרה.

וּרְבוּ. (b) Textuality > conj paratactic projection: quote / Mood > directive: imperative / Transitivity > material: action.

וּרְבוּ	**Constituents**
and multiply	**Translation**
Theme	**Textuality**
Finite	**Mood**
Process	**Transitivity**

וּרְבוּ. Theme: textual > clause conj + Finite > impv mp / Process > qal רבה.

שִׁרְצוּ בָאָרֶץ. (c) Textuality > appositive paratactic projection: quote / Mood > directive: imperative / Transitivity > material: action.

בָאָרֶץ	שִׁרְצוּ	**Constituents**
in the earth	*swarm*	**Translation**
	Theme	**Textuality**
	Finite	**Mood**
Circumstance	Process	**Transitivity**

שִׁרְצוּ. Theme: experiential / Finite > impv mp / Process > qal שרץ.

בָאָרֶץ. Circumstance: location, place > prep phrase: prep + def art + noun common fs.

וּרְבוּ־בָהּ. (d) Textuality > conj paratactic projection: quote / Mood > directive: imperative / Transitivity > material: action.

בָהּ	וּרְבוּ־	**Constituents**
in her	*and multiply*	**Translation**
	Theme	**Textuality**
	Finite	**Mood**
Circumstance	Process	**Transitivity**

וּרְבוּ־. Theme: textual > clause conj + Theme: experiential / Finite > impv mp / Process > qal רבה.

בָהּ. Circumstance: location, place > prep phrase: prep + pronoun suffix 3fs, antecedent is הָאָרֶץ *the earth* in clause (c).

Genesis 9:8-11

[8]And deity said to Noach and to his sons with him by saying, [9]"And I now I am establishing my covenant with you and your seed after you [10]and all living being which is with you, in the fowl and in the beastkind and in all the animalkind of the earth with you, from all the ones exiting the ark to all the animalkind of the earth. [11]And I will establish my covenant with you. And all flesh will not be cut again from the waters of the flood. And a flood will not be again to destroy the earth."

9:8 /// וַיֹּ֤אמֶר אֱלֹהִים֙ אֶל־נֹ֔חַ וְאֶל־בָּנָ֥יו אִתּ֖וֹ לֵאמֹֽר׃

וַיֹּאמֶר אֱלֹהִים אֶל־נֹחַ וְאֶל־בָּנָיו אִתּוֹ לֵאמֹר. (a) Textuality > conj paratactic expansion / Mood > declarative: past / Transitivity > verbal.

לֵאמֹר	אֶל־נֹחַ וְאֶל־בָּנָיו אִתּוֹ	אֱלֹהִים	וַיֹּאמֶר	**Constituents**
by saying	*to Noach and to his sons with him*	*deity*	*and he said*	**Translation**
			Theme	**Textuality**
		Subject	Finite	**Mood**
Circumstance	Receiver	Sayer	Process	**Transitivity**

וַיֹּאמֶר. Theme: textual > clause conj + Theme: experiential / Finite > wayyiqtol 3ms / Process > qal אמר.

אֱלֹהִים. Subject > mp / Sayer > nominal group: noun common.

אֶל־נֹחַ וְאֶל־בָּנָיו אִתּוֹ. Receiver > prep phrase complex: two conjoined prep phrases.

אֶל־נֹחַ. Prep phrase 1 > prep - noun proper ms.

וְאֶל־בָּנָיו אִתּוֹ. Group conj + Prep phrase 2 > Head + Post-modifier.

אֶל־בָּנָיו. Head > prep phrase: prep - noun common mp const + pronoun suffix 3ms, antecedent is נֹחַ *Noach.*

אִתּוֹ. Post-modifier > prep phrase: prep + pronoun suffix 3ms, antecedent is נֹחַ *Noach.*

לֵאמֹר. Circumstance: manner, means > prep phrase: prep + inf const qal אמר.

9:9 // וַאֲנִי הִנְנִי מֵקִים אֶת־בְּרִיתִי אִתְּכֶם וְאֶת־זַרְעֲכֶם
אַחֲרֵיכֶם׃ 9:10 וְאֵת כָּל־נֶפֶשׁ הַחַיָּה אֲשֶׁר אִתְּכֶם
בָּעוֹף בַּבְּהֵמָה וּבְכָל־חַיַּת הָאָרֶץ אִתְּכֶם מִכֹּל יֹצְאֵי
הַתֵּבָה לְכֹל חַיַּת הָאָרֶץ׃

וַאֲנִי הִנְנִי מֵקִים אֶת־בְּרִיתִי אִתְּכֶם וְאֶת־זַרְעֲכֶם אַחֲרֵיכֶם וְאֵת כָּל־נֶפֶשׁ הַחַיָּה [[אֲשֶׁר אִתְּכֶם בָּעוֹף בַּבְּהֵמָה וּבְכָל־חַיַּת הָאָרֶץ אִתְּכֶם מִכֹּל יֹצְאֵי הַתֵּבָה לְכֹל חַיַּת הָאָרֶץ. (a) Textuality > conj paratactic projection: quote / Mood > declarative: non-past / Transitivity > material: action. The Beneficiary of the process is incredibly long and layered. This clause has a Theme structure that reinforces the doer of the process.

אִתְּכֶם וְאֶת־זַרְעֲכֶם אַחֲרֵיכֶם וְאֵת כָּל־נֶפֶשׁ הַחַיָּה אֲשֶׁר אִתְּכֶם בָּעוֹף בַּבְּהֵמָה וּבְכָל־חַיַּת הָאָרֶץ אִתְּכֶם מִכֹּל יֹצְאֵי הַתֵּבָה לְכֹל חַיַּת הָאָרֶץ	אֶת־בְּרִיתִי	מֵקִים	הִנְנִי	וַאֲנִי	**Constituents**

with you and your seed after you and all living being which is with you, in the fowl and in the beastkind and in all the animalkind of the earth with you, from all the ones exiting the ark to all the animal-kind of the earth	*my cov-enant*	*am estab-lishing*	*now I*	*and I*	**Translation**
			Theme	Theme	**Textuality**
		Finite	Adjunct	Subject	**Mood**
Beneficiary	Goal	Process		Actor	**Transitivity**

וַאֲנִי. Theme: textual > clause conj + Theme: experiential / Subject > 1cs / Actor > pronoun personal 1cs.

הִנְנִי. Theme: interpersonal / Adjunct: interpersonal > modal + pronoun suffix 1cs, antecedent is the Subject / Actor of this clause.

מֵקִים. Finite > ptc ms / Process > hifil קום.

אֶת־בְּרִיתִי. Goal > nominal group: goal marker - noun common fs const + pronoun suffix 1cs, antecedent is אֲנִי *I*.

אִתְּכֶם וְאֶת־זַרְעֲכֶם אַחֲרֵיכֶם וְאֵת כָּל־נֶפֶשׁ הַחַיָּה [[אֲשֶׁר אִתְּכֶם]] בָּעוֹף בַּבְּהֵמָה וּבְכָל־חַיַּת הָאָרֶץ אִתְּכֶם מִכֹּל יֹצְאֵי הַתֵּבָה לְכֹל חַיַּת הָאָרֶץ. Beneficiary > prep phrase complex consisting of three sub-complexes. The antecedent of all the pronoun suffixes is *Noach and his sons*; see 9:1(a).

אִתְּכֶם וְאֶת־זַרְעֲכֶם אַחֲרֵיכֶם וְאֵת כָּל־נֶפֶשׁ הַחַיָּה [[אֲשֶׁר אִתְּכֶם]]. Prep complex 1 > three prep phrases, the last with an embedded relative clause post-modifier.

אִתְּכֶם. Prep phrase: prep + pronoun suffix 2mp.

וְאֶת־זַרְעֲכֶם אַחֲרֵיכֶם. Group conj + Prep phrase: prep - noun common collective + pronoun suffix 2mp | adj + pronoun suffix 2mp.

וְאֵת כָּל־נֶפֶשׁ הַחַיָּה [[אֲשֶׁר אִתְּכֶם]]. Group conj + Prep phrase: prep | noun common collective ms const - noun common fs const | def art + noun common collective fs + Post-modifier.

אֲשֶׁר אִתְּכֶם. (i) Post-modifier >> Textuality > embedded expansion: relative clause / Mood > declarative: non-past / Transitivity > relational: attribution.

אִתְּכֶם	אֲשֶׁר	**Constituents**
with you	*which*	**Translation**
	Theme	**Textuality**
Complement	Subject	**Mood**
Attribute	Carrier	**Transitivity**

אֲשֶׁר. Theme: textual and experiential / Subject > ms (כָּל) / Carrier > pronoun relative, antecedent is כָּל־נֶפֶשׁ הַחַיָּה *all the life of the animal.*

אִתְּכֶם. Complement / Attribute > prep phrase: prep + pronoun suffix 2mp.

בָּעוֹף בַּבְּהֵמָה וּבְכָל־חַיַּת הָאָרֶץ אִתְּכֶם. Prep complex 2 > three prep phrases, the last with a post-modifier.

בָּעוֹף. Prep phrase: prep + def art + noun common collective ms.

בַּבְּהֵמָה. Prep phrase: prep + def art + noun common collective fs.

וּבְכָל־חַיַּת הָאָרֶץ אִתְּכֶם. Group conj + Head > prep phrase: prep + noun common collective ms const - noun common collective fs const | def art + noun common fs + Post-modifier > prep phrase: prep + pronoun suffix 2mp.

מִכֹּל יֹצְאֵי הַתֵּבָה לְכֹל חַיַּת הָאָרֶץ. Prep complex 3 > two prep phrases.

מִכֹּל יֹצְאֵי הַתֵּבָה. Prep phrase: prep + noun common collective ms const | ptc mp const qal **יצא** | def art + noun common fs.

לְכֹל חַיַּת הָאָרֶץ. Prep phrase: prep + noun common ms const | noun common fs const | def art + noun common fs.

9:11 // וַהֲקִמֹתִ֤י אֶת־בְּרִיתִי֙ אִתְּכֶ֔ם // וְלֹֽא־יִכָּרֵ֧ת כָּל־
בָּשָׂ֛ר ע֖וֹד מִמֵּ֣י הַמַּבּ֑וּל // וְלֹֽא־יִהְיֶ֥ה ע֛וֹד מַבּ֖וּל
לְשַׁחֵ֥ת הָאָֽרֶץ׃

וַהֲקִמֹתִי אֶת־בְּרִיתִי אִתְּכֶם. (a) Textuality > conj paratactic projection: quote / Mood > declarative: non-past / Transitivity > material: action. The Subject / Actor is the Sayer of the quote, **אֱלֹהִים** *deity*.

אִתְּכֶם	אֶת־בְּרִיתִי	וַהֲקִמֹתִי	**Constituents**
with you	*my covenant*	*and I will establish*	**Translation**
		Theme	**Textuality**
		Finite	**Mood**
Beneficiary	Goal	Process	**Transitivity**

וַהֲקִמֹתִי. Theme: textual > clause conj + Theme: experiential / Finite > wayyiqtol 1cs / Process > hifil **קום**.

אֶת־בְּרִיתִי. Goal > nominal group: goal marker - noun common fs const + pronoun suffix 1cs, antecedent is **אֱלֹהִים** *deity*.

אִתְּכֶם. Beneficiary > prep phrase: prep + pronoun suffix 2mp, antecedent is Noach and his sons.

וְלֹא־יִכָּרֵת כָּל־בָּשָׂר עוֹד מִמֵּי הַמַּבּוּל. (b) Textuality > conj paratactic projection: quote / Mood > declarative: non-past / Transitivity > material: action.

מִמֵּי הַמַּבּוּל	עוֹד	כָּל־בָּשָׂר	יִכָּרֵת	וְלֹא־	**Constituents**
from the waters of the flood	*more*	*all flesh*	*will be cut*	*and not*	**Translation**
	Adjunct		Theme	Theme	**Textuality**
		Subject	Finite	Adjunct	**Mood**
Circumstance		Goal	Process		**Transitivity**

וְלֹא־יִכָּרֵת. Theme: textual > clause conj + Theme: interpersonal / Adjunct: interpersonal > polarity: negative + Theme: experiential / Finite > yiqtol 3ms / Process > nifal **כרת**. This verb *cut* is often translated *cut off* (NRSV and NJPS: *all flesh be cut off*). But *cut back*, or *truncated* might be more appropriate. All flesh was not in fact cut off by the flood the first time. Noah and his family survived, along with many other animals.

כָּל־בָּשָׂר. Subject > ms (כָּל) / Goal > nominal group: noun common ms const - noun common collective ms.

עוֹד. Adjunct: textual > recurrence. This is a textual adjunct because it implies that something happened before.

מִמֵּי הַמַּבּוּל. Circumstance: manner, means > prep phrase: prep + noun common ms const | def art + noun common ms. Not *from* in the sense of location, but in the sense of *by means of*.

וְלֹא־יִהְיֶה עוֹד מַבּוּל [[לְשַׁחֵת הָאָרֶץ]]. (c) Textuality > conj paratactic projection: quote / Mood > declarative: non-past / Transitivity > existential.

[[לְשַׁחֵת הָאָרֶץ]]	מַבּוּל	עוֹד	יִהְיֶה	וְלֹא־	**Constituents**
to spoil the earth	*a flood*	*again*	*he will be*	*and not*	**Translation**
		Adjunct		Theme	**Textuality**
	Subject		Finite	Adjunct	**Mood**
Circumstance	Existent		Process		**Transitivity**

וְלֹא־. Theme: textual > clause conj + Theme: interpersonal / Adjunct: interpersonal > polarity: negative.

יִהְיֶה. Theme: experiential / Finite > yiqtol 3ms / Process > qal היה.

עוֹד. Adjunct: textual > recurrence.

מַבּוּל. Subject > ms / Existent > nominal group: noun common.

לְשַׁחֵת הָאָרֶץ. (i) Circumstance: cause, purpose >> Textuality > embedded prep clause / Transitivity > material: action.

הָאָרֶץ	לְשַׁחֵת	**Constituents**
the earth	*to destroy*	**Translation**
	Theme	**Textuality**
Goal	Process	**Transitivity**

לְשַׁחֵת. Theme: textual > prep + Theme: experiential / Process > inf const piel שחת.

הָאָרֶץ. Goal > nominal group: def art + noun common fs.

Genesis 9:12-17

[12]*And deity said, "This is the sign of the covenant which I am giving between me and you and between all living being which is with you to generations of eternity.* [13]*My bow I put in the cloud cover. And it will be for a sign of the covenant between me and between the earth.* [14]*And it will be when I cloud cloud cover on the earth, the bow will be seen in the cloud cover.* [15]*And I will remember my covenant which is between me and between you and between all living being in all flesh. And the waters will not again become a flood to destroy all flesh.* [16]*And the bow will be in the cloud cover. And I will see it to remember a covenant of eternity between deity and between all living being in all flesh which is on the earth."* [17]*And deity said to Noach, "This is the sign of the covenant which I established between me and all flesh which is on the earth."*

9:12 /// וַיֹּאמֶר אֱלֹהִים // זֹאת אוֹת־הַבְּרִית אֲשֶׁר־אֲנִי

נֹתֵ֗ן בֵּינִי֙ וּבֵ֣ינֵיכֶ֔ם וּבֵ֛ין כָּל־נֶ֥פֶשׁ חַיָּ֖ה אֲשֶׁ֣ר אִתְּכֶ֑ם לְדֹרֹ֖ת עוֹלָֽם׃

וַיֹּאמֶר אֱלֹהִים. (a) Textuality > conj paratactic expansion / Mood > declarative: past / Transitivity > verbal. The Receiver is presumably still Noach and his sons from 9:8(a). This is reinforced by the 2mp pronoun suffix on **וּבֵינֵיכֶם** in the next clause.

אֱלֹהִים	וַיֹּאמֶר	**Constituents**
deity	*and he said*	**Translation**
	Theme	**Textuality**
Subject	Finite	**Mood**
Sayer	Process	**Transitivity**

וַיֹּאמֶר. Theme: textual > clause conj + Theme: experiential / Finite > wayyiqtol 3ms / Process > qal **אמר**.

אֱלֹהִים. Subject > mp / Sayer > nominal group: noun common.

זֹאת אוֹת־הַבְּרִית [[אֲשֶׁר־אֲנִי נֹתֵן בֵּינִי וּבֵינֵיכֶם וּבֵין כָּל־נֶפֶשׁ חַיָּה [[אֲשֶׁר אִתְּכֶם]]]] לְדֹרֹת עוֹלָם. (b) Textuality > appositive paratactic projection: quote / Mood > declarative: non-past / Transitivity > relational: identification. The Complement / Identifier presents an interesting structure that includes an embedded relative clause within an embedded relative clause.

לְדֹרֹת עוֹלָם	אוֹת־הַבְּרִית [[אֲשֶׁר־אֲנִי נֹתֵן בֵּינִי וּבֵינֵיכֶם וּבֵין כָּל־נֶפֶשׁ חַיָּה [[אֲשֶׁר אִתְּכֶם]]]]	זֹאת	**Constituents**
to generations of eternity	*the sign of the covenant which I am giving between me and between you and between all living being which is with you*	*this*	**Translation**
		Theme	**Textuality**

	Complement	Subject	**Mood**
Circumstance	Identifier	Identified	**Transitivity**

זֹאת. Theme: experiential / Subject > fs / Identified > pronoun demonstrative, referent is presumably **אוֹת** *sign*, which is the Head of the Identifier nominal group. But it could also be argued that the actual referent is 9:13(a), the placing the bow in the clouds.

אוֹת־הַבְּרִית [[אֲשֶׁר־אֲנִי נֹתֵן בֵּינִי וּבֵינֵיכֶם וּבֵין כָּל־נֶפֶשׁ חַיָּה [[אֲשֶׁר אִתְּכֶם]]]]. Identifier > nominal group complex: Head + Post-modifier.

אוֹת־הַבְּרִית. Head > nominal group: noun common cs - def art + noun common fs.

אֲשֶׁר־אֲנִי נֹתֵן בֵּינִי וּבֵינֵיכֶם וּבֵין כָּל־נֶפֶשׁ חַיָּה [[אֲשֶׁר אִתְּכֶם]]. (i) Post-modifier >> Textuality > embedded expansion: relative clause / Mood > declarative: non-past / Transitivity > material: action. There are three "betweens" in this relative clause, which presents a curiosity in so far as *between* is a binary relationship. Is deity related to Noah and his sons any differently from all the other living kind? Why the third *between*? This verges on over-analysis, but the third *between* may indicate that deity is in relationship equally with Noach's group and with all living being, in effect saying *between me and you all to whom I am speaking, and between me and all other living beings.*

בֵּינִי וּבֵינֵיכֶם וּבֵין כָּל־נֶפֶשׁ חַיָּה [[אֲשֶׁר אִתְּכֶם]]	נֹתֵן	אֲנִי	אֲשֶׁר־	**Constituents**
between me and between you and between all living being which is with you	*am giving*	*I*	*which*	**Translation**
			Theme	**Textuality**
	Finite	Subject		**Mood**
Beneficiary	Process	Actor	Goal	**Transitivity**

אֲשֶׁר־. Theme: textual and experiential / Goal > pronoun relative, antecedent is אות־הַבְּרִית *the sign of the covenant.*

אֲנִי. Subject > 1cs / Actor > pronoun personal, antecedent is אֱלֹהִים *deity.*

נֹתֵן. Finite > ptc ms / Process > qal נתן.

בֵּינִי וּבֵינֵיכֶם וּבֵין כָּל־נֶפֶשׁ חַיָּה [[אֲשֶׁר אִתְּכֶם]]. Beneficiary > prep phrase complex: three prep phrases, and the last one has an embedded relative clause.

בֵּינִי. Prep phrase 1 > prep + pronoun suffix 1cs, antecedent is the Sayer, אֱלֹהִים *deity.*

וּבֵינֵיכֶם. Group conj + Prep phrase 2 > prep + pronoun suffix 2mp, antecedent is *Noach and his sons* in 9:8(a).

וּבֵין כָּל־נֶפֶשׁ חַיָּה [[אֲשֶׁר אִתְּכֶם]]. Group conj + Prep phrase 3 > Head + Post-modifier.

בֵּין כָּל־נֶפֶשׁ חַיָּה. Head > prep ׀ noun common collective ms const - noun common collective fs ׀ adj fs.

אֲשֶׁר אִתְּכֶם. (a') Post-modifier >> Textuality > embedded expansion: relative clause / Mood > declarative: non-past / Transitivity > relational: attribution.

אִתְּכֶם	אֲשֶׁר	**Constituents**
with you	*which*	**Translation**
	Theme	**Textuality**
Complement	Subject	**Mood**
Attribute	Carrier	**Transitivity**

אֲשֶׁר. Theme: textual and experiential / Subject > ms (כָּל) / Carrier > pronoun relative, antecedent is כָּל־נֶפֶשׁ הַחַיָּה *all the life of the animal.*

אִתְּכֶם. Complement / Attribute > prep phrase: prep + pronoun suffix 2mp, antecedent is *Noach and his sons.*

לְדֹרֹת עוֹלָם. Circumstance: extent, time > prep phrase: prep + noun common mp const + noun common ms.

9:13 אֶת־קַשְׁתִּי נָתַתִּי בֶּעָנָן // וְהָיְתָה לְאוֹת בְּרִית //
בֵּינִי וּבֵין הָאָרֶץ׃

אֶת־קַשְׁתִּי נָתַתִּי בֶּעָנָן. (a) Textuality > appositive paratactic projection: quote / Mood > declarative: past / Transitivity > material: action.

בֶּעָנָן	נָתַתִּי	אֶת־קַשְׁתִּי	**Constituents**
in the cloud cover	*I put*	*my bow*	**Translation**
		Theme	**Textuality**
	Finite		**Mood**
Circumstance	Process	Goal	**Transitivity**

אֶת־קַשְׁתִּי. Theme: experiential / Goal > nominal group: goal marker - noun common fs const + pronoun suffix 1cs, antecedent is the Sayer, אֱלֹהִים *deity*. Having the Goal in Theme position is a marked constituent order. It is in this position to connect with **זֹאת אוֹת־הַבְּרִית** *this is the sign of the covenant* in 9:12(b) which has set up the logical expectation—what is the sign?—which is here fulfilled and answered.

נָתַתִּי. Finite > qatal 1cs / Process > qal נתן.

בֶּעָנָן. Circumstance: location, place > prep phrase: prep + def art + noun common collective ms.

וְהָיְתָה לְאוֹת בְּרִית בֵּינִי וּבֵין הָאָרֶץ. (b) Textuality > conj paratactic projection: quote / Mood > declarative: non-past / Transitivity > relational: attribution. The Subject / Carrier is קַשְׁתִּי *my bow* from the prior clause.

בֵּינִי וּבֵין הָאָרֶץ	לְאוֹת בְּרִית	וְהָיְתָה	Constituents
between me and between the earth	*for a sign of a covenant*	*and she will be*	**Translation**
		Theme	**Textuality**
		Finite	**Mood**
Beneficiary	Circumstance	Process	**Transitivity**

וְהָיְתָה. Theme: textual > clause conj + Theme: experiential / Finite > weqatal 3fs / Process > qal היה.

לְאוֹת בְּרִית. Circumstance: cause, purpose > prep phrase: prep + noun common fs const | noun common c s.

בֵּינִי וּבֵין הָאָרֶץ. Beneficiary > prep phrase group: prep phrase 1 + prep phrase 2.

בֵּינִי. Prep phrase 1: prep + pronoun suffix 1cs, antecedent is the Sayer, אֱלֹהִים *deity*.

וּבֵין הָאָרֶץ. Group conj + Prep phrase 2: prep | def art + noun common fs.

9:14 // וְהָיָה בְּעַנְנִי עָנָן עַל־הָאָרֶץ // וְנִרְאֲתָה הַקֶּשֶׁת בֶּעָנָן׃

וְהָיָה [[בְּעַנְנִי עָנָן עַל־הָאָרֶץ]]. (a) Textuality > conj hypotactic projection: quote / Mood > declarative: non-past / Transitivity > relational: attribution. This often employed היה plus בְּ construction is used to posit a temporal setting for a following clause complex.

[[בְּעַנְנִי עָנָן עַל־הָאָרֶץ]]	וְהָיָה	Constituents
in my clouding cloud cover on the earth	*and he will be*	**Translation**
	Theme	**Textuality**
	Finite	**Mood**
Circumstance	Process	**Transitivity**

וְהָיָה. Theme: textual > clause conj + Theme: experiential / Finite > weqatal 3ms / Process > qal היה.

בְּעַנְנִי עָנָן עַל־הָאָרֶץ. (i) Circumstance: location, time >> Textuality > embedded prep clause / Transitivity > material: action. This prepositional phrase has a fully explicit transitivity structure. The material Process, in effect, has been transformed from a Finite to an infinitive in order to transition the clause to a phrase. *I make cloud cover on the earth* (a clause) became *by my making cloud cover on the earth* (a phrase).

עַל־הָאָרֶץ	עָנָן	בְּעַנְנִי	**Constituents**
on the earth	*cloud cover*	*in my clouding*	**Translation**
		Theme	**Textuality**
Circumstance	Goal	Process + Subject	**Transitivity**

בְּעַנְנִי. Theme: textual > prep + Theme: experiential / Process > inf const qal ענן + Subject > pronoun suffix 1cs, antecedent is the Sayer, אֱלֹהִים *deity.*

עָנָן. Goal > nominal group: noun common collective ms. This Goal is a cognate of the material process ענן.

עַל־הָאָרֶץ. Circumstance: location, place > prep phrase: prep - def art + noun common fs.

וְנִרְאֲתָה הַקֶּשֶׁת בֶּעָנָן. (b) Textuality > conj paratactic projection: quote / Mood > declarative: non-past / Transitivity > mental: perception.

בֶּעָנָן	הַקֶּשֶׁת	וְנִרְאֲתָה	**Constituents**
in the cloud cover	*the bow*	*and she will be seen*	**Translation**
		Theme	**Textuality**
	Subject	Finite	**Mood**
Circumstance	Goal	Process	**Transitivity**

וְנִרְאֲתָה. Theme: textual > clause conj + Theme: experiential / Finite > weqatal 3fs / Process > nifal ראה.

הַקֶּשֶׁת. Subject > fs / Goal > nominal group: def art + noun common.

בֶּעָנָן. Circumstance: location, place > prep phrase: prep + def art + noun common collective ms.

9:15 // וְזָכַרְתִּי אֶת־בְּרִיתִי אֲשֶׁר בֵּינִי וּבֵינֵיכֶם וּבֵין כָּל־
נֶפֶשׁ חַיָּה בְּכָל־בָּשָׂר // וְלֹא־יִהְיֶה עוֹד הַמַּיִם לְמַבּוּל
לְשַׁחֵת כָּל־בָּשָׂר׃

וְזָכַרְתִּי אֶת־בְּרִיתִי [[אֲשֶׁר בֵּינִי וּבֵינֵיכֶם וּבֵין כָּל־נֶפֶשׁ חַיָּה בְּכָל־בָּשָׂר]]. (a) Textuality > conj paratactic projection: quote / Mood > declarative: non-past / Transitivity > mental: cognition. The Subject / Senser is the Sayer, אֱלֹהִים *deity*.

אֶת־בְּרִיתִי [[אֲשֶׁר בֵּינִי וּבֵינֵיכֶם וּבֵין כָּל־נֶפֶשׁ חַיָּה בְּכָל־בָּשָׂר]]	וְזָכַרְתִּי	**Constituents**
my covenant which is between me and between you and between all living being in all flesh	*and I will remember*	**Translation**
	Theme	**Textuality**
	Finite	**Mood**
Phenomenon	Process	**Transitivity**

וְזָכַרְתִּי. Theme: textual > clause conj + Theme: experiential / Finite > weqatal 1cs / Process > qal זכר.

אֶת־בְּרִיתִי [[אֲשֶׁר בֵּינִי וּבֵינֵיכֶם וּבֵין כָּל־נֶפֶשׁ חַיָּה בְּכָל־בָּשָׂר]]. Phenomenon > nominal group: Head + Post-modifier.

אֶת־בְּרִיתִי. Head > nominal group: goal marker - noun common fs const + pronoun suffix 1cs, antecedent is the Sayer, אֱלֹהִים *deity*.

אֲשֶׁר בֵּינִי וּבֵינֵיכֶם וּבֵין כָּל־נֶפֶשׁ חַיָּה בְּכָל־בָּשָׂר. (i) Post-modifier >> Textuality > embedded expansion: relative clause / Mood > declarative: non-past / Transitivity > relational: attribution.

בֵּינִי וּבֵינֵיכֶם וּבֵין כָּל־נֶפֶשׁ חַיָּה בְּכָל־בָּשָׂר	אֲשֶׁר	**Constituents**
between me and between you and between all living being in all flesh	*which*	**Translation**
	Theme	**Textuality**
Complement	Subject	**Mood**
Attribute	Carrier	**Transitivity**

אֲשֶׁר. Theme: textual / Subject > fs / pronoun relative, antecedent בְּרִיתִי *my covenant.*

בֵּינִי וּבֵינֵיכֶם וּבֵין כָּל־נֶפֶשׁ חַיָּה בְּכָל־בָּשָׂר. Complement / Attribute > prep phrase complex: three prep phrases, the last has a post-modifier prep phrase.

בֵּינִי. Prep phrase 1 > prep + pronoun suffix 1cs, antecedent is the Sayer, אֱלֹהִים *deity.*

וּבֵינֵיכֶם. Group conj + Prep phrase 2 > prep + pronoun suffix 2mp, antecedent is *Noach and his sons.*

וּבֵין כָּל־נֶפֶשׁ חַיָּה בְּכָל־בָּשָׂר. Group conj + Head + Post-modifier.

בֵּין כָּל־נֶפֶשׁ חַיָּה. Head > prep phrase 3: prep | noun common collective ms const - noun common fs const | adj fs.

בְּכָל־בָּשָׂר. Post-modifier > prep phrase 4: prep + noun common collective ms const - noun common ms.

וְלֹא־יִהְיֶה עוֹד הַמַּיִם לְמַבּוּל [[לְשַׁחֵת כָּל־בָּשָׂר]]. (b) Textuality > conj paratactic projection: quote / Mood > declarative: non-past / Transitivity > existential.

לְמַבּוּל [[לְשַׁחֵת כָּל־ בָּשָׂר]]	הַמַּיִם	עוֹד	יִהְיֶה	וְלֹא־	**Constituents**
for a flood to spoil all flesh	*the waters*	*again*	*he will become*	*and not*	**Translation**
		Adjunct		Theme	**Textuality**
	Subject		Finite	Adjunct	**Mood**
Circumstance	Existent		Process		**Transitivity**

וְלֹא־. Theme: textual > clause conj + Theme: interpersonal / Adjunct: interpersonal > polarity: negative.

יִהְיֶה. Theme: experiential / Finite > yiqtol 3ms / Process > qal היה. The verb היה plus the prep לְ is used here in the sense *become.*

עוֹד. Adjunct: textual > recurrence.

הַמַּיִם. Subject > mp / Existent > nominal group: def art + noun common. While the Subject is mp, the Finite is 3ms.

לְמַבּוּל [[לְשַׁחֵת כָּל־בָּשָׂר]]. Circumstance: cause, purpose > Head + Post-modifier.

לְמַבּוּל. Head > prep phrase: prep + noun common ms.

לְשַׁחֵת כָּל־בָּשָׂר. (i) Post-modifier >> Textuality > embedded expansion: prep clause / Transitivity > material: action.

כָּל־בָּשָׂר	לְשַׁחֵת	**Constituents**
all flesh	*to destroy*	**Translation**
	Theme	**Textuality**
Goal	Process	**Transitivity**

לְשַׁחֵת. Theme: textual > prep + Theme: experiential / Process > inf const piel שחת.

כָּל־בָּשָׂר. Goal > nominal group: noun common collective ms const - noun common ms.

9:16 // וְהָיְתָה הַקֶּשֶׁת בֶּעָנָן // וּרְאִיתִיהָ לִזְכֹּר בְּרִית
עוֹלָם בֵּין אֱלֹהִים וּבֵין כָּל־נֶפֶשׁ חַיָּה בְּכָל־בָּשָׂר אֲשֶׁר
עַל־הָאָרֶץ׃

וְהָיְתָה הַקֶּשֶׁת בֶּעָנָן. (a) Textuality > conj paratactic projection: quote / Mood > declarative: non-past / Transitivity > existential.

בֶּעָנָן	הַקֶּשֶׁת	וְהָיְתָה	**Constituents**
in the cloud cover	*the bow*	*and she will be*	**Translation**
		Theme	**Textuality**
	Subject	Finite	**Mood**
Circumstance	Existent	Process	**Transitivity**

וְהָיְתָה. Theme: textual > clause conj + Theme: experiential / Finite > weqatal 3fs / Process > qal היה.

הַקֶּשֶׁת. Subject > fs / Existent > nominal group: def art + noun common fs.

בֶּעָנָן. Circumstance: location, place > prep phrase: prep + def art + noun common collective ms.

וּרְאִיתִיהָ [[לִזְכֹּר בְּרִית עוֹלָם בֵּין אֱלֹהִים וּבֵין כָּל־נֶפֶשׁ חַיָּה בְּכָל־בָּשָׂר [[אֲשֶׁר עַל־הָאָרֶץ]]]]. (b) Textuality > conj paratactic projection: quote / Mood > declarative: non-past / Transitivity > mental: perception. The Subject / Senser is presumably the Sayer, אֱלֹהִים *deity*, see 9:12(a), though deity then refers to himself in the third person in the circumstantial embedded clause here.

[[לִזְכֹּר בְּרִית עוֹלָם בֵּין אֱלֹהִים וּבֵין כָּל־נֶפֶשׁ חַיָּה בְּכָל־בָּשָׂר [[אֲשֶׁר עַל־הָאָרֶץ]]]]	וּרְאִיתִיהָ	**Constituents**
to remember a covenant of eternity between deity and between all living being in all flesh which is on the earth	*and I will see her*	**Translation**

	Theme	**Textuality**
	Finite	**Mood**
Circumstance	Process + Phenomenon	**Transitivity**

וְרָאִיתִיהָ. Theme: textual > clause conj + Theme: experiential / Finite > weqatal 1cs / Process > qal ראה + Phenomenon > pronoun suffix 3fs, antecedent is הַקֶּשֶׁת *the bow* in the prior clause.

לִזְכֹּר בְּרִית עוֹלָם בֵּין אֱלֹהִים וּבֵין כָּל־נֶפֶשׁ חַיָּה בְּכָל־בָּשָׂר [[אֲשֶׁר עַל־הָאָרֶץ]]. (i) Circumstance: cause, purpose >> Textuality > embedded prep clause / Transitivity > mental: cognition. This embedded purpose clause has within it an embedded relative clause that expands the Head of the final prepositional phrase.

בְּרִית עוֹלָם בֵּין אֱלֹהִים וּבֵין כָּל־נֶפֶשׁ חַיָּה בְּכָל־בָּשָׂר [[אֲשֶׁר עַל־הָאָרֶץ]]	לִזְכֹּר	**Constituents**
a covenant of eternity between deity and between all living being in all flesh which is on the earth	*to remember*	**Translation**
	Theme	**Textuality**
Phenomenon	Process	**Transitivity**

לִזְכֹּר. Theme: textual > prep + Theme: experiential / Process > inf const qal זכר.

בְּרִית עוֹלָם בֵּין אֱלֹהִים וּבֵין כָּל־נֶפֶשׁ חַיָּה בְּכָל־בָּשָׂר [[אֲשֶׁר עַל־הָאָרֶץ]]. Phenomenon > nominal group: Head + Post-modifier.

בְּרִית עוֹלָם. Head > nominal group: noun common fs const + noun common ms.

בֵּין אֱלֹהִים וּבֵין כָּל־נֶפֶשׁ חַיָּה בְּכָל־בָּשָׂר [[אֲשֶׁר עַל־הָאָרֶץ]]. Post-modifier > prep phrase complex: prep phrase 1 + prep phrase 2 (prep phrase + Post-modifier). The presence of אֱלֹהִים *deity* here when we might expect a 1cs pronoun suffix, since this is part of a quote, may suggest this Post-modifier is a narrator's addition.

בֵּין אֱלֹהִים. Prep phrase 1 > prep | noun common mp.

וּבֵין כָּל־נֶפֶשׁ חַיָּה בְּכָל־בָּשָׂר אֲשֶׁר עַל־הָאָרֶץ. Group conj + Prep phrase 2 > Head + Post-modifier.

בֵּין כָּל־נֶפֶשׁ חַיָּה. Head > prep | noun common collective ms const - noun common fs | adj fs.

בְּכָל־בָּשָׂר אֲשֶׁר עַל־הָאָרֶץ. Post-modifier > Head + Post-modifier.

בְּכָל־בָּשָׂר. Head > prep phrase: prep + noun common collective ms const - noun common ms.

אֲשֶׁר עַל־הָאָרֶץ. (a') Post-modifier >> Textuality > embedded expansion: relative clause / Mood > declarative: non-past / Transitivity > relational: attribution.

עַל־הָאָרֶץ	אֲשֶׁר	**Constituents**
on the earth	*which*	**Translation**
	Theme	**Textuality**
Complement	Subject	**Mood**
Attribute	Carrier	**Transitivity**

אֲשֶׁר. Theme: textual and experiential / Subject > ms (כָּל) / Carrier > pronoun relative, antecedent is כָּל־בָּשָׂר *all flesh*.

עַל־הָאָרֶץ. Complement / Attribute > prep phrase: prep - def art + noun common fs.

9:17 // וַיֹּ֥אמֶר אֱלֹהִ֖ים אֶל־נֹ֑חַ // זֹ֤את אֽוֹת־הַבְּרִית֙ אֲשֶׁ֣ר
הֲקִמֹ֔תִי בֵּינִ֕י וּבֵ֥ין כָּל־בָּשָׂ֖ר אֲשֶׁ֥ר עַל־הָאָֽרֶץ׃ פ

וַיֹּאמֶר אֱלֹהִים אֶל־נֹחַ. (a) Textuality > conj paratactic expansion / Mood > declarative: past / Transitivity > verbal.

אֶל־נֹחַ	אֱלֹהִים	וַיֹּאמֶר	**Constituents**
to Noach	*deity*	*and he said*	**Translation**
		Theme	**Textuality**
	Subject	Finite	**Mood**
Receiver	Sayer	Process	**Transitivity**

וַיֹּאמֶר. Theme: textual > clause conj + Theme: experiential / Finite > wayyiqtol / Process > qal **אמר**.

אֱלֹהִים. Subject > mp / Sayer > nominal group: noun common.

אֶל־נֹחַ. Receiver > prep phrase: prep - noun proper ms.

זֹאת אוֹת־הַבְּרִית [[אֲשֶׁר הֲקִמֹתִי בֵּינִי וּבֵין כָּל־בָּשָׂר אֲשֶׁר עַל־הָאָרֶץ]]. (b) Textuality > appositive paratactic projection: quote / Mood > declarative: non-past / Transitivity > relational: identification. Compare 9:12(b) which has the same structure. *This is the covenant...* is found in that clause as in this clause.

אוֹת־הַבְּרִית [[אֲשֶׁר הֲקִמֹתִי בֵּינִי וּבֵין כָּל־בָּשָׂר אֲשֶׁר עַל־הָאָרֶץ]]	זֹאת	**Constituents**
the sign of the covenant which I established between me and between all flesh which on the earth	*this*	**Translation**
	Theme	**Textuality**
Complement	Subject	**Mood**
Identifier	Identified	**Transitivity**

זֹאת. Theme: experiential / Subject > 3fs / Identified > pronoun demonstrative, antecedent is **הַקֶּשֶׁת** *the bow*, in 9:16(a). NJPS translates the **זֹאת** in 9:12(b) *this* and the **זֹאת** in the present clause *that*, illustrating how **זֹאת** is a text pronoun, otherwise called a deictic pronoun, that can be cataphoric (forward pointing) or anaphoric (backward pointing).

אוֹת־הַבְּרִית [[אֲשֶׁר הֲקִמֹתִי בֵּינִי וּבֵין כָּל־בָּשָׂר [[אֲשֶׁר עַל־הָאָרֶץ]]]]. Complement > cs (אוֹת) / Identifier > nominal group: Head + Post-modifier.

אוֹת־הַבְּרִית. Head > nominal group: noun common cs const - def art + noun common fs.

(i) .אֲשֶׁר הֲקִמֹתִי בֵּינִי וּבֵין כָּל־בָּשָׂר [[אֲשֶׁר עַל־הָאָרֶץ]] Post-modifier >> Textuality > embedded expansion: relative clause / Mood > declarative: past / Transitivity > material: action. The Subject / Actor is the Sayer, אֱלֹהִים *deity*.

בֵּינִי וּבֵין כָּל־בָּשָׂר [[אֲשֶׁר עַל־הָאָרֶץ]]	הֲקִמֹתִי	אֲשֶׁר	**Constituents**
between me and between all flesh which on the earth	*I established*	*which*	**Translation**
		Theme	**Textuality**
	Finite		**Mood**
Beneficiary	Process	Goal	**Transitivity**

אֲשֶׁר. Theme: textual > pronoun relative and Theme: experiential / Goal > antecedent אוֹת־הַבְּרִית *the sign of the covenant.*

הֲקִמֹתִי. Finite > qatal 1cs / Process > hifil קום.

בֵּינִי וּבֵין כָּל־בָּשָׂר [[אֲשֶׁר עַל־הָאָרֶץ]]. Beneficiary > prep phrase complex: prep phrase 1 + prep phrase 2.

בֵּינִי. Prep phrase 1 > prep + pronoun suffix 1cs, antecedent is the Sayer, אֱלֹהִים *deity.*

וּבֵין כָּל־בָּשָׂר [[אֲשֶׁר עַל־הָאָרֶץ]]. Group conj + Prep phrase 2 > Head + Post-modifier.

בֵּין כָּל־בָּשָׂר. Head > prep | noun common ms const - noun common ms.

אֲשֶׁר עַל־הָאָרֶץ. (a') Post-modifier >> Textuality > embedded expansion: relative clause / Mood > declarative: non-past / Transitivity > relational: attribution.

עַל־הָאָרֶץ	אֲשֶׁר	**Constituents**
on the earth	*which*	**Translation**
	Theme	**Textuality**
Complement	Subject	**Mood**
Attribute	Carrier	**Transitivity**

אֲשֶׁר. Theme: textual > pronoun relative and Theme: experiential / Subject > ms / Carrier > antecedent כָּל־בָּשָׂר *all flesh.*

עַל־הָאָרֶץ. Complement / Attribute > prep phrase: prep + def art + noun common fs.

Genesis 9:18-19

[18]And the sons of Noach, the ones exiting from the ark, were Shem and Cham and Yefet. And Cham, he was the father of Kena'an. [19]These three are the sons of Noach. And from these all of the earth dispersed.

9:18 /// וַיִּהְי֣וּ בְנֵי־נֹ֗חַ הַיֹּֽצְאִים֙ מִן־הַתֵּבָ֔ה שֵׁ֖ם וְחָ֣ם וָיָ֑פֶת
// וְחָ֕ם ה֖וּא אֲבִ֥י כְנָֽעַן׃

(a) **וַיִּהְיוּ בְנֵי־נֹחַ [[הַיֹּצְאִים מִן־הַתֵּבָה]] שֵׁם וְחָם וָיָפֶת**. Textuality > conj paratactic expansion / Mood > declarative: past / Transitivity > relational: identification.

שֵׁם וְחָם וָיָפֶת	בְנֵי־נֹחַ [[הַיֹּצְאִים מִן־הַתֵּבָה]]	וַיִּהְיוּ	**Constituents**
Shem and Cham and Yefet	*the sons of Noach, the ones exiting from the ark*	*and they were*	**Translation**
		Theme	**Textuality**
	Subject	Finite	**Mood**
Identifier	Identified	Process	**Transitivity**

וַיִּהְיוּ. Theme: textual > clause conj + Theme: experiential / Finite > wayyiqtol 3mp / Process > qal היה.

בְּנֵי־נֹחַ הַיֹּצְאִים מִן־הַתֵּבָה. Subject > mp (בְּנֵי) / Identified > nominal group: Head + Post-modifier.

בְּנֵי־נֹחַ. Head > nominal group: noun common mp const - noun proper ms.

הַיֹּצְאִים מִן־הַתֵּבָה. (i) Post-modifier >> Textuality > embedded ptc clause / Mood > declarative: non-past / Transitivity > material: action.

מִן־הַתֵּבָה	הַיֹּצְאִים	**Constituents**
from the ark	*the ones exiting*	**Translation**
	Theme	**Textuality**
Circumstance	Actor / Process	**Transitivity**

הַיֹּצְאִים. Theme: experiential / Actor > ptc mp / Process > qal יצא.

מִן־הַתֵּבָה. Circumstance: location, place > prep phase: prep - def art + noun common fs.

שֵׁם וְחָם וָיָפֶת. Identifier > nominal group: noun proper ms ı group conj + noun proper ms ı group conj + noun proper ms.

וְחָם הוּא אֲבִי כְנָעַן. (b) Textuality > conj paratactic expansion / Mood > declarative: non-past / Transitivity > relational: identification.

אֲבִי כְנָעַן	הוּא	וְחָם	**Constituents**
the father of Kena'an	*he*	*and Cham*	**Translation**
		Theme	**Textuality**
Complement	Subject	Subject	**Mood**
Identifier	Identified	Identified	**Transitivity**

וְחָם. Theme: textual > clause conj + Theme: experiential / Subject > ms / Identified > noun proper ms. This structure is called a preposed Theme. Typically a preposed Theme is the subject of the clause, and later a pronoun substitutes for it at the normal place in the clause.

הוּא. Subject > ms / Identified > pronoun personal 3ms, antecedent is חָם *Cham*.

אֲבִי כְנָעַן. Complement > 3ms (אֲבִי) / Identifier > nominal group: noun common ms const ׀ noun proper ms.

9:19 // שְׁלֹשָׁה אֵלֶּה בְּנֵי־נֹחַ // וּמֵאֵלֶּה נָפְצָה כָל־הָאָרֶץ׃

שְׁלֹשָׁה אֵלֶּה בְּנֵי־נֹחַ. (a) Textuality > appositive paratactic expansion / Mood > declarative: non-past / Transitivity > relational: identification.

בְּנֵי־נֹחַ	שְׁלֹשָׁה אֵלֶּה	**Constituents**
the sons of Noach	*these three*	**Translation**
	Theme	**Textuality**
Complement	Subject	**Mood**
Identifier	Identified	**Transitivity**

שְׁלֹשָׁה אֵלֶּה. Theme: experiential / Subject > mp / Identified > nominal group: numeral ms ׀ pronoun demonstrative 3p, antecedent is שֵׁם וְחָם וָיָפֶת *Shem and Cham and Jefet* in 9:18(a).

בְּנֵי־נֹחַ. Complement > mp (בְּנֵי) / Identifier > nominal group: noun common mp const - noun proper ms.

וּמֵאֵלֶּה נָפְצָה כָל־הָאָרֶץ. (b) Textuality > conj paratactic expansion / Mood > declarative: past / Transitivity > material: event.

כָל־הָאָרֶץ	נָפְצָה	וּמֵאֵלֶּה	**Constituents**
all of the earth	*she dispersed*	*and from these*	**Translation**
		Theme	**Textuality**
Subject	Finite		**Mood**
Actor	Process	Circumstance	**Transitivity**

וּמֵאֵלֶּה. Theme: textual > clause conj + Theme: experiential / Circumstance: manner, means > prep phrase: prep + pronoun demonstrative 3p, antecedent is בְּנֵי־נֹחַ *sons of Noach.* It is unusual for a demonstrative pronoun to be the object of a preposition; ordinarily the referring word would be a pronoun suffix, in this case resulting in מֵהֶם.

נָפְצָה. Finite > qatal 3fs / Process > qal נפץ. GKC 67dd suggests this could be read as nifal of פוץ to provide a passive voice: *all of the earth was dispersed.*

כָל־הָאָרֶץ. Subject > ms (כָל) or fs (הָאָרֶץ) / Actor > nominal group: noun common collective ms const - def art + noun common fs. If this nominal group is, in fact, the Subject of the clause, the Mood structure would be incongruent. Normally, the first noun in a construct noun phrase is the grammatical Subject. But the Finite is 3fs. Most likely, then, הָאָרֶץ is the logical and grammatical Subject rather than כָל. In this context, *the earth* presumably means the people of the earth, or the inhabited earth.

Genesis 9:20-28

20 And Noach began to be a man of the ground. And he planted a vineyard. 21 And he drank from the wine. And he was drunk. And he uncovered himself inside his tent. 22 And Cham, the father of Kena'an, saw the nakedness of his father. And he told his two brothers outside. 23 And Shem and Yefet took the garment. And they put (it) on the shoulder of the two of them. And they walked backwards. And they covered the nakedness of their father. And their faces were backwards. And the nakedness of their father they saw not. 24 And Noach awoke from his wine. And he knew what his young son did to him. 25 And he said, "Cursed is Kena'an. Servant of servants he will be to his brothers." 26 And he said, "Blessed is YHVH, deity of Shem. May Kena'an be a servant to him. 27 May deity make space for Yefet. And may he dwell in the tents of Shem. And may Kena'an be a servant to him." 28 And Noach lived after the flood 350 years.

9:20 /// וַיָּ֥חֶל נֹ֖חַ אִ֣ישׁ הָאֲדָמָ֑ה // וַיִּטַּ֖ע כָּֽרֶם׃

וַיָּ֥חֶל נֹ֖חַ אִ֣ישׁ הָֽאֲדָמָ֑ה. (a) Textuality > conj paratactic expansion / Mood > declarative: past / Transitivity > relational: attribution.

אִ֣ישׁ הָֽאֲדָמָ֑ה	נֹ֖חַ	וַיָּ֥חֶל	**Constituents**
man of the ground	*Noach*	*and he began*	**Translation**
		Theme	**Textuality**
Complement	Subject	Finite	**Mood**
Attribute	Carrier	Process	**Transitivity**

וַיָּ֥חֶל. Theme: textual > clause conj + Theme: experiential / Finite > wayyiqtol 3ms / Process > hifil חלל. The notion of *begin* here could be taken in the sense of a cultural or civilizational first, or it could simply be that Noach became a man of the soil and began practicing what for him was a new vocation. After all, since the garden, people had been working the ground; see 2:5 and 2:15. This verb is typically found as the Finite element of a verbal group complex, followed by an infinitive construct. See 4:26(c) and 10:8(b) in our corpus, and more than twenty times elsewhere in the Hebrew Bible. Here no infinitive is present; if present presumably it would have been לִהְיוֹת as in 10:8(b). Its absence can be explained by the fact that the proposition *Noach is man of the ground* is essentially an attributive relational clause, for which an explicit verb form is not a requirement.

נֹ֖חַ. Subject > ms / Carrier > nominal group: noun proper.

אִ֣ישׁ הָֽאֲדָמָ֑ה. Complement > ms / Attribute > nominal group: noun common ms const ׀ def art + noun common fs. Normally, when the second element of a construct nominal group is definite, the first element is also definite. In this case however, the nominal group appears to provide a more generic characterization of Noach, such that he is *a man of the ground*, rather than *the man of the ground.*

וַיִּטַּ֖ע כָּֽרֶם. (b) Textuality > conj paratactic expansion / Mood > declarative: past / Transitivity > material: action. The Subject / Actor is נֹ֖חַ *Noach.*

כֶּרֶם	וַיִּטַּע	**Constituents**
a vineyard	*and he planted*	**Translation**
	Theme	**Textuality**
	Finite	**Mood**
Goal	Process	**Transitivity**

וַיִּטַּע. Theme: textual > clause conj + Theme: experiential / Finite > wayyiqtol 3ms / Process > qal נטע.

כֶּרֶם. Goal > nominal group: noun common ms.

9:21 // וַיֵּשְׁתְּ מִן־הַיַּיִן // וַיִּשְׁכָּר // וַיִּתְגַּל בְּתוֹךְ אָהֳלֹה׃

וַיֵּשְׁתְּ מִן־הַיַּיִן. (a) Textuality > conj paratactic expansion / Mood > declarative: past / Transitivity > material: action. The Subject / Actor is נֹחַ *Noach.*

מִן־הַיַּיִן	וַיֵּשְׁתְּ	**Constituents**
from the wine	*and he drank*	**Translation**
	Theme	**Textuality**
	Finite	**Mood**
Circumstance	Process	**Transitivity**

וַיֵּשְׁתְּ. Theme: textual > clause conj + Theme: experiential / Finite > 3ms / Process > qal שׁתה.

מִן־הַיַּיִן. Circumstance: location, place > prep phrase: prep - def art + noun common ms. This construction functions essentially as a Goal, though goals are typically nominal groups. Here we have a prep phrase, perhaps to be understood with מִן functioning as partitive, meaning *some of.*

וַיִּשְׁכָּר. (b) Textuality > conj paratactic expansion / Mood > declarative: past / Transitivity > relational: attribution. The Subject / Carrier is נֹחַ *Noach.*

וַיִּשְׁכָּר	**Constituents**
and he was drunk	**Translation**
Theme	**Textuality**
Finite	**Mood**
Process	**Transitivity**

וַיִּשְׁכָּר. Theme: textual > clause conj + Theme: experiential / Finite > 3ms / Process > qal שׁכר. This is a stative verb, which is a category of verb that encodes an attributive relational process.

וַיִּתְגַּל בְּתוֹךְ אָהֳלֹה. (c) Textuality > conj paratactic expansion / Mood > declarative: past / Transitivity > material: state. The Subject / Actor is נֹחַ *Noach*, and Actor = Goal.

בְּתוֹךְ אָהֳלֹה	וַיִּתְגַּל	**Constituents**
in the midst of his tent	*and he uncovered himself*	**Translation**
	Theme	**Textuality**
	Finite	**Mood**
Circumstance	Process	**Transitivity**

וַיִּתְגַּל. Theme: textual > clause conj + Theme: experiential / Finite > 3ms / Process > hitpael גלה. The transitivity structure of a hitpael process has the Actor also functioning as the Goal.

בְּתוֹךְ אָהֳלֹה. Circumstance: location, place > prep phrase: prep + noun common ms const | noun common ms const + pronoun suffix 3ms, antecedent is נֹחַ *Noach.*

9:22 וַיַּרְא חָם אֲבִי כְנַעַן אֵת עֶרְוַת אָבִיו // וַיַּגֵּד לִשְׁנֵי־
אֶחָיו בַּחוּץ׃

וַיַּרְא חָם אֲבִי כְנַעַן אֵת עֶרְוַת אָבִיו. (a) Textuality > conj paratactic expansion / Mood > declarative: past / Transitivity > mental: perception.

אֵת עֶרְוַת אָבִיו	חָם אֲבִי כְנַעַן	וַיַּרְא	Constituents
the nakedness of his father	*Cham, the father of Kena'an*	*and he saw*	**Translation**
		Theme	**Textuality**
	Subject	Finite	**Mood**
Phenomenon	Senser	Process	**Transitivity**

וַיַּרְא. Theme: textual > clause conj + Theme: experiential / Finite > wayyiqtol 3ms / Process > qal ראה.

חָם אֲבִי כְנַעַן. Subject > ms / Senser > nominal group: Head + Post-modifier.

חָם. Head > nominal group: noun proper ms.

אֲבִי כְנַעַן. Post-modifier > nominal group: noun common ms const | noun proper ms.

אֵת עֶרְוַת אָבִיו. Phenomenon > nominal group: goal marker | noun common fs const | noun common ms const + pronoun suffix 3ms, antecedent is נֹחַ *Noach.*

וַיַּגֵּד לִשְׁנֵי־אֶחָיו בַּחוּץ. (b) Textuality > conj paratactic expansion / Mood > declarative: past / Transitivity > verbal. The Subject / Sayer is חָם *Cham.* There is no explicit Verbiage in this clause, in other words, no record of the actual words that he said.

בַּחוּץ	לִשְׁנֵי־אֶחָיו	וַיַּגֵּד	Constituents
in the outside	*to the two of his brothers*	*and he told*	**Translation**
		Theme	**Textuality**
		Finite	**Mood**
Circumstance	Receiver	Process	**Transitivity**

וַיַּגֵּד. Theme: textual > clause conj + Theme: experiential / Finite > wayyiqtol 3ms / Process > hifil נגד.

לִשְׁנֵי־אֶחָיו. Receiver > prep phrase: prep + numeral mp const - noun common mp const + pronoun suffix 3ms, antecedent is חָם *Cham.*

בַּחוּץ. Circumstance: location, place > prep phrase: prep + noun common ms.

9:23 // וַיִּקַּח שֵׁם וָיֶפֶת אֶת־הַשִּׂמְלָה // וַיָּשִׂימוּ עַל־
שְׁכֶם שְׁנֵיהֶם // וַיֵּלְכוּ אֲחֹרַנִּית // וַיְכַסּוּ אֵת עֶרְוַת
אֲבִיהֶם // וּפְנֵיהֶם אֲחֹרַנִּית // וְעֶרְוַת אֲבִיהֶם לֹא
רָאוּ׃

וַיִּקַּח שֵׁם וָיֶפֶת אֶת־הַשִּׂמְלָה. (a) Textuality > conj paratactic expansion / Mood > declarative: past / Transitivity > material: action.

אֶת־הַשִּׂמְלָה	שֵׁם וָיֶפֶת	וַיִּקַּח	**Constituents**
the garment	*Shem and Yefet*	*and he took*	**Translation**
		Theme	**Textuality**
	Subject	Finite	**Mood**
Goal	Actor	Process	**Transitivity**

וַיִּקַּח. Theme: textual > clause conj + Theme: experiential / Finite > wayyiqtol 3ms / Process > qal לקח.

שֵׁם וָיֶפֶת. Subject > mp / Actor > nominal group: noun proper ms | group conj + noun proper ms. Notice that the Subject is logically plural in so far as it consists of both Shem and Yafet, while the Finite is 3ms in form. However, this pair of proper nouns is united with the hendiadys conjunction וָ which has the effect of creating a pair of words that function as a unit. This explains why it is labeled a nominal group rather than a nominal group complex. This may account for the singular verb.

אֶת־הַשִּׂמְלָה. Goal > nominal group: goal marker - def art + noun common fs. A definite noun, though no garment specifically had been mentioned before. However, if Noach uncovered himself, obviously a garment was left behind somewhere, presumably outside the tent given the action that follows. NJPS says they *took a cloth*.

וַיָּשִׂימוּ עַל־שְׁכֶם שְׁנֵיהֶם. (b) Textuality > conj paratactic expansion / Mood > declarative: past / Transitivity > material: action. The Subject / Actor is שֵׁם וָיֶפֶת *Shem and Yafet*. The Goal is הַשִּׂמְלָה *the garment* in the prior clause, absent here by ellipsis.

עַל־שְׁכֶם שְׁנֵיהֶם	וַיָּשִׂימוּ	**Constituents**
on the shoulder of the two of them	*and they put*	**Translation**
	Theme	**Textuality**
	Finite	**Mood**
Circumstance	Process	**Transitivity**

וַיָּשִׂימוּ. Theme: textual > clause conj + Theme: experiential / Finite > wayyiqtol 3mp / Process > qal שׂים.

עַל־שְׁכֶם שְׁנֵיהֶם. Circumstance: location, place > prep phrase: prep - noun common ms const | numeral mp + pronoun suffix 3mp, antecedent is שֵׁם וָיֶפֶת *Shem and Yafet*.

וַיֵּלְכוּ אֲחֹרַנִּית. (c) Textuality > conj paratactic expansion / Mood > declarative: past / Transitivity > material: action. The Subject / Actor is שֵׁם וָיֶפֶת *Shem and Yafet*.

אֲחֹרַנִּית	וַיֵּלְכוּ	**Constituents**
backwards	*and they walked*	**Translation**
	Theme	**Textuality**
	Finite	**Mood**
Adjunct	Process	**Transitivity**

וַיֵּלְכוּ. Theme: textual > clause conj + Theme: experiential / Finite > wayyiqtol 3mp / Process > qal הלך.

אֲחֹרַנִּית. Adjunct: experiential > circumstance: manner.

וַיְכַסּוּ אֵת עֶרְוַת אֲבִיהֶם. (d) Textuality > conj paratactic expansion / Mood > declarative: past / Transitivity > material: action. The Subject / Actor is שֵׁם וָיֶפֶת *Shem and Yafet*.

אֵת עֶרְוַת אֲבִיהֶם	וַיְכַסּוּ	**Constituents**
the nakedness of their father	*and they covered*	**Translation**
	Theme	**Textuality**
	Finite	**Mood**
Goal	Process	**Transitivity**

וַיְכַסּוּ. Theme: textual > clause conj + Theme: experiential / Finite > wayyiqtol 3mp / Process > piel כסה.

אֵת עֶרְוַת אֲבִיהֶם. Goal > nominal group: goal marker ׀ noun common fs const ׀ noun common ms const + pronoun suffix 3mp, antecedent is שֵׁם וָיֶפֶת *Shem and Yafet.*

וּפְנֵיהֶם אֲחֹרַנִּית. (e) Textuality > conj paratactic expansion / Mood > declarative: non-past / Transitivity > relational: attribution.

אֲחֹרַנִּית	וּפְנֵיהֶם	**Constituents**
backwards	*and their faces*	**Translation**
	Theme	**Textuality**
Complement	Subject	**Mood**
Adjunct = Attribute	Carrier	**Transitivity**

וּפְנֵיהֶם. Theme: textual > clause conj + Theme: experiential / Subject > mp / Carrier > nominal group: noun common mp const + pronoun suffix 3mp, antecedent is שֵׁם וָיֶפֶת *Shem and Yafet.*

אֲחֹרַנִּית. Complement / Attribute / Adjunct: experiential > circumstance: manner.

וְעֶרְוַת אֲבִיהֶם לֹא רָאוּ. (f) Textuality > conj paratactic expansion / Mood > declarative: past / Transitivity > mental: perception.

רָאוּ	לֹא	וְעֶרְוַת אֲבִיהֶם	**Constituents**
they saw	*not*	*and the nakedness of their father*	**Translation**
		Theme	**Textuality**
Finite	Adjunct		**Mood**
Process		Goal	**Transitivity**

וְעֶרְוַת אֲבִיהֶם. Theme: textual > clause conj + Theme: experiential / Goal > nominal group: noun common fs const | noun common ms const + pronoun suffix 3mp, antecedent is שֵׁם וָיֶפֶת *Shem and Yafet.*

לֹא. Adjunct: interpersonal > polarity: negative.

רָאוּ. Finite > qatal 3cp / Process > qal ראה.

9:24 // וַיִּ֥יקֶץ נֹ֖חַ מִיֵּינ֑וֹ // וַיֵּ֕דַע אֵ֥ת אֲשֶׁר־עָֽשָׂה־ל֖וֹ בְּנ֥וֹ
הַקָּטָֽן׃

וַיִּיקֶץ נֹחַ מִיֵּינוֹ. (a) Textuality > conj paratactic expansion / Mood > declarative: past / Transitivity > material: action.

מִיֵּינוֹ	נֹחַ	וַיִּיקֶץ	**Constituents**
from his wine	*Noach*	*and he awoke*	**Translation**
		Theme	**Textuality**
	Subject	Finite	**Mood**
Scope	Actor	Process	**Transitivity**

וַיִּיקֶץ. Theme: textual > clause conj + Theme: experiential / Finite > wayyiqtol 3ms / Process > qal יקץ.

נֹחַ. Subject > ms / Actor > nominal group: noun proper.

מִיֵּינוֹ. Scope > prep phrase: prep + noun common ms const + pronoun suffix 3ms, antecedent is נֹחַ *Noach.*

[[וַיֵּדַע אֵת]] אֲשֶׁר־עָשָׂה־לוֹ בְּנוֹ הַקָּטָן]]. (b) Textuality > conj paratactic expansion / Mood > declarative: past / Transitivity > mental: cognition. Subject / Senser is נֹחַ *Noach.*

אֵת [[אֲשֶׁר־עָשָׂה־לוֹ בְּנוֹ הַקָּטָן]]	וַיֵּדַע	**Constituents**
that which he did to him his young son	*and he knew*	**Translation**
	Theme	**Textuality**
	Finite	**Mood**
Phenomenon	Process	**Transitivity**

וַיֵּ֫דַע. Theme: textual > clause conj + Theme: experiential / Finite > wayyiqtol 3ms / Process > qal ידע.

אֵת [[אֲשֶׁר־עָשָׂה־לוֹ בְּנוֹ הַקָּטָן]]. Phenomenon > nominal group: (Head) + Post-modifier.

אֵת. (Head) > goal marker. This particle alone stands as the nominal group indicator. Actually, the following relative clause stands without a Head or antecedent. Normally a word such as כֹּל would stand as the Head.

אֲשֶׁר־עָשָׂה־לוֹ בְּנוֹ הַקָּטָן. (i) Post-modifier >> Textuality > embedded expansion: relative clause / Mood > declarative: past / Transitivity > material: action.

בְּנוֹ הַקָּטָן	לוֹ	עָשָׂה־	אֲשֶׁר־	**Constituents**
his young son	*to him*	*he did*	*which*	**Translation**
			Theme	**Textuality**
Subject		Finite		**Mood**
Actor	Beneficiary	Process	Goal	**Transitivity**

אֲשֶׁר־. Theme: textual > pronoun relative / Goal > the antecedent is the event narrated in 9:22(a) and cannot be tracked to a more specific word or phrase.

עָשָׂה־. Finite > qatal 3ms / Process > qal עשׂה.

לוֹ. Beneficiary > prep phrase: prep + pronoun suffix 3ms, antecedent is נֹחַ *Noach.*

בְּנוֹ הַקָּטָן. Subject > ms / Actor > nominal group: noun common ms const + pronoun suffix 3ms, antecedent is נֹחַ *Noach* + def art + adj ms.

9:25 // וַיֹּ֫אמֶר // אָרוּר כְּנָ֑עַן // עֶ֥בֶד עֲבָדִ֖ים יִֽהְיֶ֥ה לְאֶחָֽיו׃

וַיֹּ֫אמֶר. (a) Textuality > conj paratactic expansion / Mood > declarative: past / Transitivity > verbal. Even though reference to Cham is nearest (בְּנוֹ הַקָּטָן in the prior clause), the Subject / Sayer is presumably נֹחַ *Noach*. The reference to Cham is in an embedded clause. The most recent Subject of a dominant clause is Noach.

וַיֹּאמֶר	**Constituents**
and he said	**Translation**
Theme	**Textuality**
Finite	**Mood**
Process	**Transitivity**

וַיֹּאמֶר. Theme: textual > clause conj + Theme: experiential / Finite > wayyiqtol 3ms / Process > qal אמר.

אָרוּר כְּנָעַן. (b) Textuality > appositive paratactic projection: quote / Mood > declarative: non-past / Transitivity > relational: attribution. This clause is worded as a declarative statement. However, this is probably supposed to be understood as a directive rather than as a declarative. This is an example of grammatical metaphor. A grammatical metaphor utilizes one grammatical wording when it really intends a different one. In this case a declarative wording is intended to be a jussive directive.

כְּנָעַן	אָרוּר	**Constituents**
Kena'an	*cursed*	**Translation**
	Theme	**Textuality**
Subject	Complement	**Mood**
Carrier	Attribute	**Transitivity**

אָרוּר. Theme: experiential / Complement > ptc passive ms / Attribute > qal ארר.

כְּנָעַן. Subject > ms / Carrier > nominal group: noun proper.

עֶבֶד עֲבָדִים יִהְיֶה לְאֶחָיו. (c) Textuality > appositive paratactic projection: quote / Mood > declarative: non-past / Transitivity > relational: attribution. The Subject / Carrier is כְּנָעַן *Kena'an*.

לְאֶחָיו	יִהְיֶה	עֶבֶד עֲבָדִים	**Constituents**
to his brothers	*he will be*	*servant of servants*	**Translation**
		Theme	**Textuality**
	Finite		**Mood**
Beneficiary	Process	Attribute	**Transitivity**

עֶבֶד עֲבָדִים. Theme: experiential / Attribute > nominal group: noun common ms const | noun common mp.

יִהְיֶה. Finite > yiqtol 3ms / Process > qal היה.

לְאֶחָיו. Beneficiary > prep phrase: prep + noun common mp const + pronoun suffix 3ms, antecedent is כְּנָעַן *Kena'an*.

9:26 // וַיֹּאמֶר // בָּרוּךְ יְהוָה אֱלֹהֵי שֵׁם // וִיהִי כְנַעַן עֶבֶד לָמוֹ׃

וַיֹּאמֶר. (a) Textuality > conj paratactic expansion / Mood > declarative: past / Transitivity > verbal. The Subject / Sayer is נֹחַ *Noach*.

וַיֹּאמֶר	**Constituents**
and he said	**Translation**
Theme	**Textuality**
Finite	**Mood**
Process	**Transitivity**

וַיֹּאמֶר. Theme: textual > clause conj + Theme: experiential / Finite > wayyiqtol 3ms / Process > qal אמר.

בָּרוּךְ יְהוָה אֱלֹהֵי שֵׁם. (b) Textuality > appositive paratactic projection: quote / Mood > declarative: non-past / Transitivity > relational: attribution. Again, as with the curse clause, this clause is worded as a declarative statement but is a command; again, a grammatical metaphor.

יְהוָה אֱלֹהֵי שֵׁם	בָּרוּךְ	**Constituents**
YHVH deity of Shem	*blessed*	**Translation**
	Theme	**Textuality**
Subject	Complement	**Mood**
Carrier	Attribute	**Transitivity**

בָּרוּךְ. Theme: experiential / Complement > ptc passive ms / Attribute > qal ברך.

יְהוָה אֱלֹהֵי שֵׁם. Subject > ms (יְהוָה) / Carrier > nominal group: Head + Post-modifier.

יְהוָה. Head > noun proper ms.

אֱלֹהֵי שֵׁם. Post-modifier > nominal group: noun common mp const | noun proper ms.

וִיהִי כְנַעַן עֶבֶד לָמוֹ. (c) Textuality > conj paratactic projection: quote / Mood > directive: jussive / Transitivity > relational: attribution.

לָמוֹ	עֶבֶד	כְנַעַן	וִיהִי	**Constituents**
to him	*a servant*	*Kena'an*	*may he be*	**Translation**
			Theme	**Textuality**
		Subject	Finite	**Mood**
Beneficiary	Attribute	Carrier	Process	**Transitivity**

וִיהִי. Theme: textual > clause conj + Theme: experiential / Finite > jussive 3ms / Process > qal היה.

כְנַעַן. Subject > ms / Carrier > nominal group: noun proper.

עֶבֶד. Attribute > nominal group: noun common ms.

לָמוֹ. Beneficiary > prep phrase: prep + pronoun suffix 3ms, antecedent is שֵׁם *Shem* in the prior clause, though technically is could instead be יְהוָה in the preceding clause.

9:27 יַ֤פְתְּ אֱלֹהִים֙ לְיֶ֔פֶת // וְיִשְׁכֹּ֖ן בְּאָהֳלֵי־שֵׁ֑ם // וִיהִ֥י
כְנַ֖עַן עֶ֥בֶד לָֽמוֹ׃

יַ֤פְתְּ אֱלֹהִים֙ לְיֶ֔פֶת. (a) Textuality > appositive paratactic projection: quote / Mood > directive: jussive / Transitivity > material: action.

לְיֶ֔פֶת	אֱלֹהִים֙	יַ֤פְתְּ	**Constituents**
for Yefet	*deity*	*may he make space*	**Translation**
		Theme	**Textuality**
	Subject	Finite	**Mood**
Beneficiary	Actor	Process	**Transitivity**

יַ֤פְתְּ. Theme: textual > clause conj + Theme: experiential / Finite > jussive 3ms / Process > hifil פתה.

אֱלֹהִים֙. Subject > mp / Actor > nominal group: noun common.

לְיֶ֔פֶת. Beneficiary > prep phrase: prep + noun proper ms.

וְיִשְׁכֹּ֖ן בְּאָהֳלֵי־שֵׁ֑ם. (b) Textuality > conj paratactic projection: quote / Mood > declarative: non-past / Transitivity > material: action. The Subject / Actor is יֶ֫פֶת *Yefet.*

בְּאָהֳלֵי־שֵׁ֑ם	וְיִשְׁכֹּ֖ן	**Constituents**
in the tents of Shem	*and he will dwell / and may he dwell*	**Translation**
	Theme	**Textuality**
	Finite	**Mood**
Circumstance	Process	**Transitivity**

וְיִשְׁכֹּ֖ן. Theme: textual > clause conj + Theme: experiential / Finite > yiqtol 3ms / Process > qal שׁכן. The yiqtol form may be read also as a jussive, since both have the same form. The context of the clause complex argues for the jussive, which would translate as *and may he dwell.*

בְּאָהֳלֵי־שֵׁ֑ם. Circumstance: location, place > prep phrase: prep + noun common mp const - noun proper ms.

וְיהִי כְנַעַן עֶבֶד לָמוֹ. (c) Textuality > conj paratactic projection: quote / Mood > directive: jussive / Transitivity > relational: attribution.

לָמוֹ	עֶבֶד	כְנַעַן	וִיהִי	**Constituents**
to him	*a servant*	*Kena'an*	*and may he be*	**Translation**
			Theme	**Textuality**
		Subject	Finite	**Mood**
Beneficiary	Attribute	Carrier	Process	**Transitivity**

וִיהִי. Theme: textual > clause conj + Theme: experiential / Finite > jussive 3ms / Process > qal היה.

כְנַעַן. Subject > ms / Carrier > nominal group: noun proper.

עֶבֶד. Attribute > nominal group: noun common ms.

לָמוֹ. Beneficiary > prep phrase: prep + pronoun suffix 3ms, antecedent is שֵׁם *Shem*.

9:28 // וַיְחִי־נֹחַ אַחַר הַמַּבּוּל שְׁלֹשׁ מֵאוֹת שָׁנָה
וַחֲמִשִּׁים שָׁנָה׃

וַיְחִי־נֹחַ אַחַר הַמַּבּוּל שְׁלֹשׁ מֵאוֹת שָׁנָה וַחֲמִשִּׁים שָׁנָה. (a) Textuality > conj paratactic expansion / Mood > declarative: past / Transitivity > material: event.

שְׁלֹשׁ מֵאוֹת שָׁנָה וַחֲמִשִּׁים שָׁנָה	אַחַר הַמַּבּוּל	נֹחַ	וַיְחִי־	**Constituents**
three hundred years and fifty years	*after the flood*	*Noach*	*and he lived*	**Translation**
			Theme	**Textuality**
		Subject	Finite	**Mood**
Scope	Circumstance	Actor	Process	**Transitivity**

וַיְחִי־. Theme: textual > clause conj + Theme: experiential / Finite > wayyiqtol 3ms / Process > qal חיה.

נֹחַ. Subject > ms / Actor > nominal group: noun proper.

אַחַר הַמַּבּוּל. Circumstance: location, time > prep phrase: prep ׀ def art + noun common ms.

שְׁלֹשׁ מֵאוֹת שָׁנָה וַחֲמִשִּׁים שָׁנָה. Scope > nominal group: numeral ׀ numeral ׀ noun common fs ׀ group conj + numeral ׀ noun common fs.

9:29 // וַיִּהְיוּ כָּל־יְמֵי־נֹחַ תְּשַׁע מֵאוֹת שָׁנָה וַחֲמִשִּׁים שָׁנָה
וַיָּמֹת׃ פ

וַיִּהְיוּ כָּל־יְמֵי־נֹחַ תְּשַׁע מֵאוֹת שָׁנָה וַחֲמִשִּׁים שָׁנָה. (a) Textuality > conj paratactic expansion / Mood > declarative: past / Transitivity > relational: attribution.

תְּשַׁע מֵאוֹת שָׁנָה וַחֲמִשִּׁים שָׁנָה	כָּל־יְמֵי־נֹחַ	וַיִּהְיוּ	**Constituents**
nine hundred years and fifty years	*all the days of Noach*	*and they were*	**Translation**
		Theme	**Textuality**
	Subject	Finite	**Mood**
Attribute	Carrier	Process	**Transitivity**

וַיִּהְיוּ. Theme: textual > clause conj + Theme: experiential / Finite > wayyiqtol 3mp / Process > qal היה.

כָּל־יְמֵי־נֹחַ. Subject > ms / Carrier > nominal group: noun common collective ms const - noun common mp const - noun proper ms. The grammatical Subject, given the form of the Finite, is יְמֵי *the days of*, rather than the head of the construct noun phrase כָּל *all*, or *all* is understood in its distributive rather than collective sense. See also 5:5(a).

תְּשַׁע מֵאוֹת שָׁנָה וַחֲמִשִּׁים שָׁנָה. Attribute > nominal group complex: numeral fs | numeral fp | noun common fs | group conj + numeral fs | noun common fs.

וַיָּמֹת. (b) Textuality > conj paratactic expansion / Mood > declarative: past / Transitivity > material: event. The Subject / Actor is נֹחַ *Noach.*

וַיָּמֹת	**Constituents**
and he died	**Translation**
Theme	**Textuality**
Finite	**Mood**
Process	**Transitivity**

וַיָּמֹת. Theme: textual > clause conj + Theme: experiential / Finite > wayyiqtol 3ms / Process > qal מות.

Genesis 10:1

[1]And these are the outcomes of the sons of Noach, Shem Cham and Yefet. And sons were born to them after the flood.

10:1 /// וְאֵלֶּה תּוֹלְדֹת בְּנֵי־נֹחַ שֵׁם חָם וָיָפֶת // וַיִּוָּלְדוּ
לָהֶם בָּנִים אַחַר הַמַּבּוּל׃

וְאֵלֶּה תּוֹלְדֹת בְּנֵי־נֹחַ שֵׁם חָם וָיָפֶת. (a) Textuality > conj paratactic expansion / Mood > declarative: non-past / Transitivity > relational: identification.

תּוֹלְדֹת בְּנֵי־נֹחַ שֵׁם חָם וָיָפֶת	וְאֵלֶּה	**Constituents**
the outcomes of the sons of Noach, Shem Cham and Yefet	*and these*	**Translation**
	Theme	**Textuality**
Complement	Subject	**Mood**
Identifier	Identified	**Transitivity**

וְאֵלֶּה. Theme: textual > clause conj + Theme: experiential / Subject > 3cp / Identified > pronoun demonstrative, referent is the following clause complex.

תּוֹלְדֹת בְּנֵי־נֹחַ שֵׁם חָם וָיָפֶת. Complement / Identifier > nominal group: Head + Post-modifier.

תּוֹלְדֹת בְּנֵי־נֹחַ. Head > nominal group: noun common fp const | noun common mp const + noun proper ms.

שֵׁם חָם וָיָפֶת. Post-modifier > nominal group: noun proper ms | noun proper ms | group conj + noun proper ms. This appositive group specifically expands בְּנֵי־נֹחַ *the sons of Noach* in the preceding nominal group.

וַיִּוָּלְדוּ לָהֶם בָּנִים אַחַר הַמַּבּוּל. (b) Textuality > conj paratactic expansion / Mood > declarative: past / Transitivity > material: action.

אַחַר הַמַּבּוּל	בָּנִים	לָהֶם	וַיִּוָּלְדוּ	**Constituents**
after the flood	*sons*	*to them*	*and they were born*	**Translation**
			Theme	**Textuality**
	Subject		Finite	**Mood**
Circumstance	Goal	Beneficiary	Process	**Transitivity**

וַיִּוָּלְדוּ. Theme: textual > clause conj + Theme: experiential / Finite > wayyiqtol 3mp / Process > nifal ילד.

לָהֶם. Beneficiary > prep phrase: prep + pronoun suffix 3mp, antecedent is בְּנֵי־נֹחַ שֵׁם חָם וָיָפֶת *the sons of Noach, Shem Cham and Yefet.*

בָּנִים. Subject > mp / Goal > nominal group: noun common mp.

אַחַר הַמַּבּוּל. Circumstance: location, place > prep phrase: prep | def art + noun common ms.

Genesis 10:2-5

[2]The sons of Yefet are Gomer and Magog and Maday and Yavan and Tuval and Meshekh and Tiras. [3]And the sons of Gomer are 'Ashkenaz and Rifat and Togarma. [4]And the sons of Yavan are Elisha and Tarshish Kittim and Dodanim. [5]From these the islands of the nations were dispersed in their lands a man to his tongue to their families in their nations.

10:2 /// בְּנֵ֣י יֶ֔פֶת גֹּ֣מֶר וּמָג֔וֹג וּמָדַ֖י וְיָוָ֑ן וְתֻבָ֕ל וּמֶ֖שֶׁךְ וְתִירָֽס׃

בְּנֵי יֶפֶת גֹּמֶר וּמָגוֹג וּמָדַי וְיָוָן וְתֻבָל וּמֶשֶׁךְ וְתִירָס. (a) Textuality > appositive paratactic expansion / Mood > declarative: non-past / Transitivity > relational: identification. This is the first of a number of verses in this chapter which are identically structured as Identified > בְּנֵי + proper noun, followed by the Identifier which is a collection of proper nouns. In each case, with only a slight variation in 10:4, the Identifier collection of proper nouns uses the group conjunction to join the nouns into a constituent unit. In this type of relational clause structure, there is no obvious marker that separates the Identified from the Identifier. However, the fact that all the components of the Identifier are conjoined with the group conjunction, which serves to combine them into a unit, may serve at the same time to separate it from the Identified.

גֹּמֶר וּמָגוֹג וּמָדַי וְיָוָן וְתֻבָל וּמֶשֶׁךְ וְתִירָס	בְּנֵי יֶפֶת	**Constituents**
Gomer and Magog and Maday and Yavan and Tuval and Meshekh and Tiras	*the sons of Yefet*	**Translation**
	Theme	**Textuality**
Complement	Subject	**Mood**
Identifier	Identified	**Transitivity**

בְּנֵי יֶפֶת. Theme: experiential / Subject > mp / Identified > nominal group: noun common mp const | noun proper ms.

גֹּמֶר וּמָגוֹג וּמָדַי וְיָוָן וְתֻבָל וּמֶשֶׁךְ וְתִירָס. Complement / Identifier > nominal group: seven conjoined proper nouns. Notice the different forms of the group conjunction: normally וְ, but וּ before *bet*, *mem* or *pe* (the so-called *bumaf* rule).

10:3 // וּבְנֵי גֹּמֶר אַשְׁכְּנַז וְרִיפַת וְתֹגַרְמָה׃

וּבְנֵי גֹּמֶר אַשְׁכְּנַז וְרִיפַת וְתֹגַרְמָה. (a) Textuality > conj paratactic expansion / Mood > declarative: non-past / Transitivity > relational: identification.

אַשְׁכְּנַז וְרִיפַת וְתֹגַרְמָה	וּבְנֵי גֹּמֶר	**Constituents**
'Ashkenaz and Rifat and Togarma	*and the sons of Gomer*	**Translation**
	Theme	**Textuality**
Complement	Subject	**Mood**
Identifier	Identified	**Transitivity**

וּבְנֵי גֹּמֶר. Theme: textual > clause conj + Theme: experiential / Subject > mp / Identified > nominal group: noun common mp const | noun proper ms.

אַשְׁכְּנַז וְרִיפַת וְתֹגַרְמָה. Complement / Identifier > nominal group: three conjoined proper nouns.

10:4 // וּבְנֵי יָוָן אֱלִישָׁה וְתַרְשִׁישׁ כִּתִּים וְדֹדָנִים׃

וּבְנֵי יָוָן אֱלִישָׁה וְתַרְשִׁישׁ כִּתִּים וְדֹדָנִים. (a) Textuality > conj paratactic expansion / Mood > declarative: non-past / Transitivity > relational: identification.

אֱלִישָׁה וְתַרְשִׁישׁ כִּתִּים וְדֹדָנִים	וּבְנֵי יָוָן	**Constituents**
Elisha and Tarshish Kittim and Dodanim	*and the sons of Yavan*	**Translation**
	Theme	**Textuality**
Complement	Subject	**Mood**
Identifier	Identified	**Transitivity**

וּבְנֵי יָוָן. Theme: textual > clause conj + Theme: experiential / Subject > mp / Identified > nominal group: noun common mp const | noun proper ms.

אֱלִישָׁה וְתַרְשִׁישׁ כִּתִּים וְדֹדָנִים. Complement > mp / Identifier > nominal group complex: four proper nouns, conjoined in pairs.

10:5 // מֵאֵ֨לֶּה נִפְרְד֜וּ אִיֵּ֤י הַגּוֹיִם֙ בְּאַרְצֹתָ֔ם אִ֖ישׁ לִלְשֹׁנ֑וֹ
לְמִשְׁפְּחֹתָ֖ם בְּגוֹיֵהֶֽם׃

מֵאֵלֶּה נִפְרְדוּ אִיֵּי הַגּוֹיִם בְּאַרְצֹתָם אִישׁ לִלְשֹׁנוֹ לְמִשְׁפְּחֹתָם בְּגוֹיֵהֶם. (a) Textuality > appositive paratactic expansion / Mood > declarative: past / Transitivity > material: action. The last constituent is especially challenging; it is difficult to determine specifically what is expanding what.

בְּאַרְצֹתָם אִישׁ לִלְשֹׁנוֹ לְמִשְׁפְּחֹתָם בְּגוֹיֵהֶם	אִיֵּי הַגּוֹיִם	נִפְרְדוּ	מֵאֵלֶּה	**Constituents**
in their lands a man to his tongue to their families in their nations	*the islands of the nations*	*they were dispersed*	*from these*	**Translation**
			Theme	**Textuality**
	Subject	Finite		**Mood**
Circumstance	Goal	Process	Circumstance	**Transitivity**

מֵאֵלֶּה. Theme: experiential / Circumstance: location, place > prep phrase: prep + pronoun demonstrative, antecedent is either all of 10:2-4, or just 10:4. The אֵלֶּה in this clause is anaphoric; the אֵלֶּה in 10:1(a) was cataphoric.

נִפְרְדוּ. Finite > qatal 3cp / Process > nifal פרד.

אִיֵּי הַגּוֹיִם. Subject > mp (אִיֵּי) / Goal > nominal group: noun common mp const ı def art + noun common mp.

בְּאַרְצֹתָם אִישׁ לִלְשֹׁנוֹ לְמִשְׁפְּחֹתָם בְּגוֹיֵהֶם. Circumstance: location, place > prep phrase complex: Head + Post-modifier.

בְּאַרְצֹתָם אִישׁ לִלְשֹׁנוֹ. Head > Head + Post-modifier. *In their lands, each to its language.*

בְּאַרְצֹתָם. Head > prep phrase: prep + noun common fp const + pronoun suffix 3mp, antecedent is אִיֵּי הַגּוֹיִם *islands of the nations.*

אִישׁ לִלְשֹׁנוֹ. Post-modifier > head (noun common ms) + Post-modifier (prep phrase: prep + noun common ms const + pronoun suffix 3ms, antecedent is אִישׁ *man* or *each*). *Each to his tongue/language.*

לְמִשְׁפְּחֹתָם בְּגוֹיֵהֶם. Post-modifier > head (prep phrase: prep + noun common fp const + pronoun suffix 3mp, antecedent is אִיֵּי הַגּוֹיִם *islands of the nations*) + Post-modifier (prep phrase: prep + noun common mp const + pronoun suffix 3mp, antecedent is אִיֵּי הַגּוֹיִם *islands of the nations). To their families within their nations.*

Genesis 10:6-7

[6]And the sons of Cham are Kush and Mitsrayim and Put and Kena'an. [7]And the sons of Kush are Seva' and Chavila and Sabta and Ra'ma and Sabtekha'. And the sons of Ra'ma are Sheva' and Dedan.

10:6 /// וּבְנֵי חָם כּוּשׁ וּמִצְרַיִם וּפוּט וּכְנָעַן׃

וּבְנֵי חָם כּוּשׁ וּמִצְרַיִם וּפוּט וּכְנָעַן. (a) Textuality > conj paratactic expansion / Mood > declarative: non-past / Transitivity > relational: identification.

כּוּשׁ וּמִצְרַיִם וּפוּט וּכְנָעַן	וּבְנֵי חָם	**Constituents**
Kush and Mitsrayim and Put and Kena'an	*and the sons of Cham*	**Translation**
	Theme	**Textuality**
Complement	Subject	**Mood**
Identifier	Identified	**Transitivity**

וּבְנֵי חָם. Theme: textual > clause conj + Theme: experiential / Subject > mp / Identified > nominal group: noun common mp const | noun proper ms.

כּוּשׁ וּמִצְרַיִם וּפוּט וּכְנָעַן. Complement / Identifier > nominal group complex: four conjoined proper nouns.

10:7 // וּבְנֵ֣י כ֔וּשׁ סְבָא֙ וַחֲוִילָ֔ה וְסַבְתָּ֥ה וְרַעְמָ֖ה וְסַבְתְּכָ֑א
// וּבְנֵ֥י רַעְמָ֖ה שְׁבָ֥א וּדְדָֽן׃

וּבְנֵי כּוּשׁ סְבָא וַחֲוִילָה וְסַבְתָּה וְרַעְמָה וְסַבְתְּכָא. (a) Textuality > conj paratactic expansion / Mood > declarative: non-past / Transitivity > relational: identification.

סְבָא וַחֲוִילָה וְסַבְתָּה וְרַעְמָה וְסַבְתְּכָא	וּבְנֵי כּוּשׁ	**Constituents**
Seva' and Chavila and Sabta and Ra'ma and Sabtekha'	*and the sons of Kush*	**Translation**
	Theme	**Textuality**
Complement	Subject	**Mood**
Identifier	Identified	**Transitivity**

וּבְנֵי כּוּשׁ. Theme: textual > clause conj + Theme: experiential / Subject > mp / Identified > nominal group: noun common mp const | noun proper ms.

סְבָא וַחֲוִילָה וְסַבְתָּה וְרַעְמָה וְסַבְתְּכָא. Complement / Identifier > nominal group complex: five conjoined proper nouns.

וּבְנֵי רַעְמָה שְׁבָא וּדְדָן. (b) Textuality > conj paratactic expansion / Mood > declarative: non-past / Transitivity > relational: identification.

שְׁבָא וּדְדָן	וּבְנֵי רַעְמָה	Constituents
Sheva' and Dedan	*and the sons of Ra'ma*	**Translation**
	Theme	**Textuality**
Complement	Subject	**Mood**
Identifier	Identified	**Transitivity**

וּבְנֵי רַעְמָה. Theme: textual > clause conj + Theme: experiential / Subject > mp / Identified > nominal group: noun common mp const | noun proper ms.

שְׁבָא וּדְדָן. Complement / Identifier > nominal group complex: two conjoined proper nouns.

Genesis 10:8-12

[8]And Kush fathered Nimrod. He began to be a warrior in the earth.
[9]For such it will be said, "like Nimrod, a warrior of game, before YHVH."
[10]And the first of his kingdom was Babel and 'Erekh and 'Akkad and
Kalne in the land of Shinar. [11]And from that land 'Ashur exited. And he
built Nineve and Rechovot city and Kalach [12]and Resen between Nineve
and between Kalach. It is the big city.

10:8 /// וְכוּשׁ יָלַד אֶת־נִמְרֹד // הוּא הֵחֵל לִהְיוֹת גִּבֹּר בָּאָרֶץ׃

וְכוּשׁ יָלַד אֶת־נִמְרֹד. (a) Textuality > conj paratactic expansion / Mood > declarative: past / Transitivity > material: action.

אֶת־נִמְרֹד	יָלַד	וְכוּשׁ	**Constituents**
Nimrod	*fathered*	*and Kush*	**Translation**
		Theme	**Textuality**
	Finite	Subject	**Mood**
Goal	Process	Actor	**Transitivity**

וְכוּשׁ. Theme: textual > clause conj + Theme: experiential / Subject > ms / Actor > nominal group: noun proper ms.

יָלַד. Finite > qatal 3ms / Process > qal ילד.

אֶת־נִמְרֹד. Goal > nominal group: goal marker - noun proper ms.

הוּא הֵחֵל לִהְיוֹת גִּבֹּר בָּאָרֶץ. (b) Textuality > appositive paratactic expansion / Mood > declarative: past / Transitivity > relational: attribution.

בָּאָרֶץ	גִּבֹּר	לִהְיוֹת	הֵחֵל	הוּא	**Constituents**
in the earth	*a warrior*	*to be*	*began*	*he*	**Translation**
				Theme	**Textuality**
	Comple-ment	Comple-ment	Finite	Subject	**Mood**
Circumstance	Attribute	Process	Process	Carrier	**Transitivity**

הוּא. Theme: experiential / Subject > ms / Carrier > pronoun personal 3ms, antecedent is נִמְרֹד *Nimrod* in the preceding clause.

הֵחֵל לִהְיוֹת. Process > verbal group complex: Finite + Complement. As with most verbal group complexes, the non-finite form is the main semantic process in the clause.

הֵחֵל. Finite > qatal 3ms / Process > hifil חלל.

לִהְיוֹת. Complement > prep phrase: prep + Process > inf const qal היה.

גִּבֹּר. Attribute > noun common ms (*warrior*) or adj ms (*mighty*).

בָּאָרֶץ. Circumstance: location, place > prep phrase: prep + def art + noun common fs.

10:9 // הֽוּא־הָיָ֥ה גִבֹּֽר־צַ֖יִד לִפְנֵ֣י יְהוָ֑ה // עַל־כֵּן֙ יֵֽאָמַ֔ר //
כְּנִמְרֹ֛ד גִּבּ֥וֹר צַ֖יִד לִפְנֵ֥י יְהוָֽה׃

הֽוּא־הָיָ֥ה גִבֹּֽר־צַ֖יִד לִפְנֵ֣י יְהוָ֑ה. (a) Textuality > appositive paratactic expansion / Mood > declarative: past / Transitivity > relational: attribution.

לִפְנֵ֣י יְהוָ֑ה	גִבֹּֽר־צַ֖יִד	הָיָ֥ה	הֽוּא־	**Constituents**
before YHVH	*a warrior of game*	*he was*	*he*	**Translation**
			Theme	**Textuality**
	Complement	Finite	Subject	**Mood**
Circumstance	Attribute	Process	Carrier	**Transitivity**

הֽוּא־. Theme: experiential / Subject > ms / Carrier > pronoun personal 3ms, antecedent is presumably נִמְרֹד *Nimrod.*

הָיָ֥ה. Finite > qatal 3ms / Process > qal היה.

גִבֹּֽר־צַ֖יִד. Complement / Attribute > nominal group: noun common ms const - noun common ms.

לִפְנֵ֣י יְהוָ֑ה. Circumstance: location, place > prep phrase: prep + noun common mp const | noun proper ms.

עַל־כֵּן֙ יֵֽאָמַ֔ר. (b) Textuality > conj paratactic expansion / Mood > declarative: non-past / Transitivity > verbal.

יֵֽאָמַ֔ר	עַל־כֵּן֙	**Constituents**
he will be said	*on such*	**Translation**
	Theme	**Textuality**
Finite		**Mood**
Process		**Transitivity**

עַל־כֵּן֙. Theme: textual > conj adjunct. This references the preceding clause complex.

יֵאָמַר. Finite > yiqtol 3ms / Process > nifal אמר.

כְּנִמְרֹד גִּבּוֹר צַיִד לִפְנֵי יְהוָה. (c) Textuality > appositive paratactic projection: quote / Mood > declarative: non-past / Transitivity > relational: attribution. This is a clause fragment in so far as it lacks a process. But the prepositional group would probably be used as the Attribute in an attributive relational clause in which a Carrier is compared to this Nimrod. Apparently this group was a well-known saying that had application to a certain type of person.

לִפְנֵי יְהוָה	כְּנִמְרֹד גִּבּוֹר צַיִד	**Constituents**
before YHVH	*like Nimrod a warrior of game*	**Translation**
Circumstance	Attribute	**Transitivity**

כְּנִמְרֹד גִּבּוֹר צַיִד. Attribute > prep phrase: prep + Head + Post-modifier.

נִמְרֹד. Head > noun proper ms.

גִּבּוֹר צַיִד. Post-modifier > nominal group: noun common ms const - noun common ms.

לִפְנֵי יְהוָה. Circumstance: location, place > prep + noun common mp const | noun proper ms.

10:10 // וַתְּהִי רֵאשִׁית מַמְלַכְתּוֹ בָּבֶל וְאֶרֶךְ וְאַכַּד וְכַלְנֵה בְּאֶרֶץ שִׁנְעָר׃

וַתְּהִי רֵאשִׁית מַמְלַכְתּוֹ בָּבֶל וְאֶרֶךְ וְאַכַּד וְכַלְנֵה בְּאֶרֶץ שִׁנְעָר. (a) Textuality > conj paratactic expansion / Mood > declarative: past / Transitivity > relational: identification.

בְּאֶרֶץ שִׁנְעָר	בָּבֶל וְאֶרֶךְ וְאַכַּד וְכַלְנֵה	רֵאשִׁית מַמְלַכְתּוֹ	וַתְּהִי	**Constituents**
in the land of Shinar	*Babel and 'Erekh and 'Akkad and Kalne*	*the first of his kingdom*	*and she was*	**Translation**
			Theme	**Textuality**
		Subject	Finite	**Mood**
Circumstance	Identifier	Identified	Process	**Transitivity**

וַתְּהִי. Theme: textual > clause conj + Theme: experiential / Finite > wayyiqtol 3fs / Process > qal היה.

רֵאשִׁית מַמְלַכְתּוֹ. Subject > 3fs (רֵאשִׁית) / Identified > nominal group: numeral cardinal ו noun common fs const + pronoun suffix 3ms, antecedent is נִמְרֹד *Nimrod. First* may be intended in the sense of *best.*

בָּבֶל וְאֶרֶךְ וְאַכַּד וְכַלְנֵה. Identifier > nominal group complex: four conjoined proper nouns.

בְּאֶרֶץ שִׁנְעָר. Circumstance: location, place > prep phrase: prep + noun common fs const ו noun proper.

10:11-12 // מִן־הָאָרֶץ הַהִוא יָצָא אַשּׁוּר // וַיִּבֶן אֶת־
נִינְוֵה וְאֶת־רְחֹבֹת עִיר וְאֶת־כָּלַח׃ וְאֶת־רֶסֶן בֵּין
נִינְוֵה וּבֵין כָּלַח // הִוא הָעִיר הַגְּדֹלָה׃

מִן־הָאָרֶץ הַהִוא יָצָא אַשּׁוּר. (a) Textuality > appositive paratactic expansion / Mood > declarative: past / Transitivity > material: action.

אַשּׁוּר	יָצָא	מִן־הָאָרֶץ הַהִוא	**Constituents**
'Ashur	*he exited*	*from that land*	**Translation**
		Theme	**Textuality**
Subject	Finite		**Mood**
Actor	Process	Circumstance	**Transitivity**

מִן־הָאָ֫רֶץ הַהִוא. Theme: experiential / Circumstance: location, place > prep phrase: prep - def art + noun common fs | def art + pronoun demonstrative 3fs, antecedent is אֶרֶץ שִׁנְעָר *the land of Shinar* in the preceding clause.

יָצָא. Finite > qatal 3ms / Process > qal יצא.

אַשּׁוּר. Subject > ms / Actor > nominal group: noun proper.

וַיִּבֶן אֶת־נִינְוֵה וְאֶת־רְחֹבֹת עִיר וְאֶת־כָּלַח וְאֶת־רֶסֶן בֵּין נִינְוֵה וּבֵין כָּלַח. (b) Textuality > conj paratactic expansion / Mood > declarative: past / Transitivity > material: action.

אֶת־נִינְוֵה וְאֶת־רְחֹבֹת עִיר וְאֶת־כָּלַח וְאֶת־רֶסֶן בֵּין נִינְוֵה וּבֵין כָּלַח	וַיִּבֶן	**Constituents**
Nineve and Rechovot city and Kalach and Resen between Nineve and between Kalach.	*and he built*	**Translation**
	Theme	**Textuality**
	Finite	**Mood**
Goal	Process	**Transitivity**

וַיִּבֶן. Theme: textual > clause conj + Theme: experiential / Finite > wayyiqtol 3ms / Process > qal בנה.

אֶת־נִינְוֵה וְאֶת־רְחֹבֹת עִיר וְאֶת־כָּלַח וְאֶת־רֶסֶן בֵּין נִינְוֵה וּבֵין כָּלַח. Goal > nominal group complex: four conjoined nominal groups, the last post-modified by a prepositional group.

אֶת־נִינְוֵה. Nominal group 1 > goal marker - noun proper.

וְאֶת־רְחֹבֹת עִיר. Nominal group 2 > group conj + goal marker - noun proper.

וְאֶת־כָּלַח. Nominal group 3 > group conj + goal marker - noun proper.

וְאֶת־רֶסֶן בֵּין נִינְוֵה וּבֵין כָּלַח. Nominal group 4 > Head + Post-modifier.

וְאֶת־רֶסֶן. Head > group conj + goal marker - noun proper.

בֵּין נִינְוֵה וּבֵין כָּלַח. Post-modifier > prep phrase (prep | noun proper) + prep phrase (group conj + prep | noun proper).

הִוא הָעִיר הַגְּדֹלָה. (c) Textuality > appositive paratactic expansion / Mood > declarative: non-past / Transitivity > relational: identification.

הָעִיר הַגְּדֹלָה	הִוא	**Constituents**
the big city	*she*	**Translation**
	Theme	**Textuality**
Complement	Subject	**Mood**
Identifier	Identified	**Transitivity**

הִוא. Theme: experiential / Subject > 3fs / Identified > pronoun personal or demonstrative 3fs, antecedent is presumably רֶסֶן *Resen*, which is the last of the series of four in the preceding clause; or, it could be the last mentioned city in that clause, which is כָּלַח *Kalach*; or, it could go all the way back to *'Ashur* in 11(a), which was the capital of Assyria.

הָעִיר הַגְּדֹלָה. Complement / Identifier > nominal group: def art + noun common fs | def art + adj fs. Perhaps *big* in this context means head city or capital city.

Genesis 10:13-14

[13]And Egypt fathered Luds and 'Anams and Lehavs and Naftuchs [14]and Patruses and Kasluchs, from which Pelishts exited, and Kaftors.

10:13-14 /// וּמִצְרַ֡יִם יָלַ֞ד אֶת־לוּדִ֧ים וְאֶת־עֲנָמִ֛ים
וְאֶת־לְהָבִ֖ים וְאֶת־נַפְתֻּחִֽים׃ וְֽאֶת־פַּתְרֻסִ֞ים
וְאֶת־כַּסְלֻחִ֗ים אֲשֶׁ֨ר יָצְא֥וּ מִשָּׁ֛ם פְּלִשְׁתִּ֖ים וְאֶת־
כַּפְתֹּרִֽים׃ ס

וּמִצְרַיִם יָלַד אֶת־לוּדִים וְאֶת־עֲנָמִים וְאֶת־לְהָבִים וְאֶת־נַפְתֻּחִים וְאֶת־פַּתְרֻסִים וְאֶת־כַּסְלֻחִים [[אֲשֶׁר יָצְאוּ מִשָּׁם פְּלִשְׁתִּים]] וְאֶת־כַּפְתֹּרִים. (a) Textuality > conj paratactic expansion / Mood > declarative: past / Transitivity > material: action.

אֶת־לוּדִים וְאֶת־עֲנָמִים וְאֶת־לְהָבִים וְאֶת־נַפְתֻּחִים וְאֶת־פַּתְרֻסִים וְאֶת־כַּסְלֻחִים [[אֲשֶׁר יָצְאוּ מִשָּׁם פְּלִשְׁתִּים]] וְאֶת־כַּפְתֹּרִים	יָלַד	וּמִצְרַיִם	**Constituents**
Luds and 'Anams and Lehavs and Naftuchs and Patruses and Kasluchs, which exited from there Pelishts, and Kaftors	*fathered*	*and Egypt*	**Translation**
		Theme	**Textuality**
	Finite	Subject	**Mood**
Goal	Process	Actor	**Transitivity**

וּמִצְרַיִם. Theme: textual > clause conj + Theme: experiential / Subject > ms / Actor > noun proper.

יָלַד. Finite > qatal 3ms / Process > qal ילד.

אֶת־לוּדִים וְאֶת־עֲנָמִים וְאֶת־לְהָבִים וְאֶת־נַפְתֻּחִים וְאֶת־פַּתְרֻסִים וְאֶת־כַּסְלֻחִים [[אֲשֶׁר יָצְאוּ מִשָּׁם פְּלִשְׁתִּים]] וְאֶת־כַּפְתֹּרִים. Goal > nominal group complex: seven conjoined nominal groups; the penultimate one is expanded by a relative clause post-modifier. Each of the nominal groups is a gentilic noun, that is, a national or ethnic designation ending in the plural morpheme ־ִים.

אֶת־לוּדִים. Nominal group 1 > goal marker - noun proper.

וְאֶת־עֲנָמִים. Nominal group 2 > group conj + goal marker - noun proper.

וְאֶת־לְהָבִים. Nominal group 3 > group conj + goal marker - noun proper.

וְאֶת־נַפְתֻּחִים. Nominal group 4 > group conj + goal marker - noun proper.

וְאֶת־פַּתְרֻסִים. Nominal group 5 > group conj + goal marker - noun proper.

וְאֶת־כַּסְלֻחִים [[אֲשֶׁר יָצְאוּ מִשָּׁם פְּלִשְׁתִּים]]. Nominal group complex: Head + Post-modifier.

וְאֶת־כַּסְלֻחִים. Nominal group 6 > group conj + goal marker - noun proper.

אֲשֶׁר יָצְאוּ מִשָּׁם פְּלִשְׁתִּים. (i) Post-modifier >> Textuality > embedded expansion: relative clause / Mood > declarative: past / Transitivity > material: action.

פְּלִשְׁתִּים	מִשָּׁם	יָצְאוּ	אֲשֶׁר	**Constituents**
Pelishts	*from there*	*exited*	*which*	**Translation**
			Theme	**Textuality**
Subject		Finite		**Mood**
Actor	Circumstance	Process		**Transitivity**

אֲשֶׁר. Theme: textual > pronoun relative, antecedent is כַּסְלֻחִים *Kasluchs*, the preceding nominal group.

יָצְאוּ. Finite > qatal 3cp / Process > qal יצא.

מִשָּׁם. Circumstance: location, place > prep phrase: prep + Adjunct: experiential > circumstance, place. This points back to כַּסְלֻחִים *Kasluchs*.

פְּלִשְׁתִּים. Subject > mp / Actor > noun proper. The *Pelishts* are the Philistines.

וְאֶת־כַּפְתֹּרִים. Nominal group 7 > group conj + goal marker - noun proper. NRSV and NJPS read the preceding relative clause as post-modifying this nominal group. There is no linguistic justification for this, only an argument based on Amos 9:7, which connects the Philistines with Kaftor.

Genesis 10:15-20

[15]*And Kena'an fathered Tsidon his firstborn and Chet* [16]*and the*

Yevusite and the 'Amorite and the Girgashite [17]and the Chivite and the 'Arqite and the Sinite [18]and the 'Arvadite and the Tsemarite and the Chamatite. [19]And the border of the Kena'anite was from Sidon, your going to Gerar up to 'Azza, your going to Sedom and 'Amora and 'Adma and Tsevoyim up to Lasha'. [20]These are the sons of Cham to their families to their tongues in their lands in their nations.

10:15-18 /// וּכְנַ֕עַן יָלַ֛ד אֶת־צִידֹ֥ן בְּכֹר֖וֹ וְאֶת־חֵֽת׃ וְאֶת־
הַיְבוּסִי֙ וְאֶת־הָ֣אֱמֹרִ֔י וְאֵ֖ת הַגִּרְגָּשִֽׁי׃ וְאֶת־הַֽחִוִּ֥י
וְאֶת־הַֽעַרְקִ֖י וְאֶת־הַסִּינִֽי׃ וְאֶת־הָֽאַרְוָדִ֥י וְאֶת־
הַצְּמָרִ֖י וְאֶת־הַֽחֲמָתִ֑י // וְאַחַ֣ר נָפֹ֔צוּ מִשְׁפְּח֖וֹת
הַֽכְּנַעֲנִֽי׃

וּכְנַעַן יָלַד אֶת־צִידֹן בְּכֹרוֹ וְאֶת־חֵת וְאֶת־הַיְבוּסִי וְאֶת־הָאֱמֹרִי וְאֵת הַגִּרְגָּשִׁי וְאֶת־הַחִוִּי וְאֶת־הַעַרְקִי וְאֶת־הַסִּינִי וְאֶת־הָאַרְוָדִי וְאֶת־הַצְּמָרִי וְאֶת־הַחֲמָתִי. (a) Textuality > conj paratactic expansion / Mood > declarative: past / Transitivity > material: action.

אֶת־צִידֹן בְּכֹרוֹ וְאֶת־חֵת וְאֶת־הַיְבוּסִי וְאֶת־הָאֱמֹרִי וְאֵת הַגִּרְגָּשִׁי וְאֶת־הַחִוִּי וְאֶת־הַעַרְקִי וְאֶת־הַסִּינִי וְאֶת־הָאַרְוָדִי וְאֶת־הַצְּמָרִי וְאֶת־הַחֲמָתִי	יָלַד	וּכְנַעַן	**Constituents**
Tsidon his firstborn and Chet and the Yevusite and the 'Amorite and the Girgashite and the Chivite and the 'Arqite and the Sinite and the 'Arvadite and the Tsemarite and the Chamatite	*fathered*	*and Kena'an*	**Translation**
		Theme	**Textuality**
	Finite	Subject	**Mood**
Goal	Process	Actor	**Transitivity**

וּכְנַ֫עַן. Theme: textual > clause conj + Theme: experiential / Subject > ms / Actor > noun common ms.

יָלַד. Finite > qatal 3ms / Process > qal ילד.

אֶת־צִידֹן בְּכֹרוֹ וְאֶת־חֵת וְאֶת־הַיְבוּסִי וְאֶת־הָאֱמֹרִי וְאֵת הַגִּרְגָּשִׁי וְאֶת־הַחִוִּי וְאֶת־הַעַרְקִי וְאֶת־הַסִּינִי וְאֶת־הָאַרְוָדִי וְאֶת־הַצְּמָרִי וְאֶת־הַחֲמָתִי. Goal > nominal group complex: eleven conjoined nominal groups, the first of which has a post-modifier. The first two are proper nouns (names), and the nine nouns that follow are all singular gentilics with the definite article. Compare these to the plural gentilics without a definite article in 10:13(a).

אֶת־צִידֹן בְּכֹרוֹ. Nominal group 1 > Head (goal marker - noun proper) + Post-modifier (noun common ms const + pronoun suffix 3ms, antecedent is כְּנַעַן *Kena'an).*

וְאֶת־חֵת. Nominal group 2 > group conj + goal marker - noun proper.

וְאֶת־הַיְבוּסִי. Nominal group 3 > group conj + goal marker - def art + noun proper.

וְאֶת־הָאֱמֹרִי. Nominal group 4 > group conj + goal marker - def art + noun proper.

וְאֵת הַגִּרְגָּשִׁי. Nominal group 5 > group conj + goal marker ׀ def art + noun proper.

וְאֶת־הַחִוִּי. Nominal group 6 > group conj + goal marker - def art + noun proper.

וְאֶת־הַעַרְקִי. Nominal group 7 > group conj + goal marker - def art + noun proper.

וְאֶת־הַסִּינִי. Nominal group 8 > group conj + goal marker - def art + noun proper.

וְאֶת־הָאַרְוָדִי. Nominal group 9 > group conj + goal marker - def art + noun proper.

וְאֶת־הַצְּמָרִי. Nominal group 10 > group conj + goal marker - def art + noun proper.

וְאֶת־הַחֲמָתִי. Nominal group 11 > group conj + goal marker - def art + noun proper.

וְאַחַר נָפֹצוּ מִשְׁפְּחוֹת הַכְּנַעֲנִי. (b) Textuality > conj hypotactic expansion / Mood > declarative: past / Transitivity > material: action. NRSV and NJPS analyze this as an independent clause. Here it is analyzed as a hypotactic temporal clause dependent on the following clause, because **אַחַר** *after* followed by a Finite is often so used.

מִשְׁפְּחוֹת הַכְּנַעֲנִי	נָפֹצוּ	וְאַחַר	**Constituents**
the families of the Kena'anite	*they dispersed*	*and after*	**Translation**
		Theme	**Textuality**
Subject	Finite		**Mood**
Actor	Process	Adjunct	**Transitivity**

וְאַחַר. Theme: textual > clause conj + Theme: experiential / Adjunct: experiential > circumstance: time.

נָפֹצוּ. Finite > qatal 3cp / Process > nifal פוץ.

מִשְׁפְּחוֹת הַכְּנַעֲנִי. Subject > fp / Actor > nominal group: noun common fp const | def art + noun proper ms.

10:19 // וַיְהִ֞י גְּב֤וּל הַֽכְּנַעֲנִי֙ מִצִּידֹ֔ן בֹּאֲכָ֥ה גְרָ֖רָה עַד־עַזָּ֑ה
בֹּֽאֲכָ֞ה סְדֹ֧מָה וַעֲמֹרָ֛ה וְאַדְמָ֥ה וּצְבֹיִ֖ם עַד־לָֽשַׁע׃

וַיְהִי גְּבוּל הַכְּנַעֲנִי מִצִּידֹן בֹּאֲכָה גְרָרָה עַד־עַזָּה בֹּאֲכָה סְדֹמָה וַעֲמֹרָה וְאַדְמָה וּצְבֹיִם עַד־לָשַׁע. (a) Textuality > conj paratactic expansion / Mood > declarative: past / Transitivity > relational: attribution.

מִצִּידֹן בֹּאֲכָה גְרָרָה עַד־עַזָּה בֹּאֲכָה סְדֹמָה וַעֲמֹרָה וְאַדְמָה וּצְבֹיִם עַד־לָשַׁע	גְּבוּל הַכְּנַעֲנִי	וַיְהִי	**Constituents**
from Sidon, your going to Gerar up to 'Azza, your going to Sedom and 'Amora and 'Adma and Tsevoyim up to Lasha'	*the border of the Kena'anite*	*and he was*	**Translation**
		Theme	**Textuality**
	Subject	Finite	**Mood**
Attribute	Carrier	Process	**Transitivity**

וַיְהִי. Theme: textual > clause conj + Theme: experiential > Finite > wayyiqtol 3ms / Process > qal היה.

גְּבוּל הַכְּנַעֲנִי. Subject > ms (גְּבוּל) / Carrier > nominal group: noun common ms const ၊ def art + noun proper.

מִצִּידֹן בֹּאֲכָה גְרָרָה עַד־עַזָּה בֹּאֲכָה סְדֹמָה וַעֲמֹרָה וְאַדְמָה וּצְבֹיִם עַד־לָשַׁע. Attribute > prep phrase complex: Head + Post-modifier.

מִצִּידֹן. Head > prep phrase: prep + noun proper.

בֹּאֲכָה גְרָרָה עַד־עַזָּה בֹּאֲכָה סְדֹמָה וַעֲמֹרָה וְאַדְמָה וּצְבֹיִם עַד־לָשַׁע. Post-modifier > verbal group + verbal group. These two verbal groups use participle constructions to indicate geographical directions, and they do so in a form of direct address to the reader. This is how the first group might be rendered: *when you go toward Gerar as far as 'Azza.*

בֹּאֲכָה גְרָרָה עַד־עַזָּה. (i) Verbal group 1 >> Textuality > embedded expansion: ptc clause / Transitivity > material. action.

גְרָרָה עַד־עַזָּה	בֹּאֲכָה	**Constituents**
to Gerar up to 'Azza	*your going*	**Translation**
	Theme	**Textuality**
	Finite + Subject	**Mood**
Circumstance	Process + Actor	**Transitivity**

בֹּאֲכָה. Theme: experiential / Finite > ptc ms / Process > qal בוא + Subject > 2ms / Actor > pronoun suffix 2ms, referent is the audience.

גְרָרָה עַד־עַזָּה. Circumstance: extent, place > nominal group: Head + Post-modifier.

גְרָרָה. Head > nominal group: noun proper + directive adjunct.

עַד־עַזָּה. Post-modifier > prep phrase: prep - noun proper.

בֹּאֲכָה סְדֹמָה וַעֲמֹרָה וְאַדְמָה וּצְבֹיִם עַד־לָשַׁע. (ii) Verbal group 2 >> Textuality > embedded expansion: ptc clause / Transitivity > material: action.

סְדֹמָה וַעֲמֹרָה וְאַדְמָה וּצְבֹיִם עַד־לָשַׁע	בֹּאֲכָה	**Constituents**
to Sedom and 'Amora and 'Adma and Tsevoyim up to Lasha'	*your going*	**Translation**
	Theme	**Textuality**
	Finite + Subject	**Mood**
Circumstance	Process + Actor	**Transitivity**

בֹּאֲכָה. Theme: experiential / Finite > ptc ms / Process > qal בוא + Subject > 2ms / Actor > pronoun suffix 2ms, antecedent is the audience.

סְדֹמָה וַעֲמֹרָה וְאַדְמָה וּצְבֹיִם עַד־לָשַׁע. Circumstance: extent, place > nominal group complex: Head + Post-modifier.

סְדֹמָה וַעֲמֹרָה וְאַדְמָה וּצְבֹיִם. Head > nominal group complex: noun proper + directive adjunct | group conj + noun proper | group conj + noun proper | group conj + noun proper. Notice that the directive adjunct is attached only to the first of the four proper nouns in the series, yet has application to all four.

עַד־לָשַׁע. Post-modifier > prep phrase: prep - noun proper.

10:20// אֵלֶּה בְנֵי־חָם לְמִשְׁפְּחֹתָם לִלְשֹׁנֹתָם בְּאַרְצֹתָם בְּגוֹיֵהֶם׃ ס

(a) אֵלֶּה בְנֵי־חָם לְמִשְׁפְּחֹתָם לִלְשֹׁנֹתָם בְּאַרְצֹתָם בְּגוֹיֵהֶם. Textuality > appositive paratactic expansion / Mood > declarative: non-past / Transitivity > relational: identification.

בְּאַרְצֹתָם בְּגוֹיֵהֶם	לְמִשְׁפְּחֹתָם לִלְשֹׁנֹתָם	בְנֵי־חָם	אֵלֶּה	**Constituents**
in their lands in their nations	*to their families to their tongues*	*the sons of Cham*	*these*	**Translation**
			Theme	**Textuality**
		Comple-ment	Subject	**Mood**
Circum-stance	Range	Identifier	Identified	**Transitivity**

אֵלֶּה. Theme: experiential / Subject > 3cp / Identified > pronoun demonstrative, referent is the preceding clause complex; אֵלֶּה is anaphoric. This clause is a generalizing summary statement that draws the clause complex to a conclusion.

בְנֵי־חָם. Complement > mp (בְנֵי) / Identifier > nominal group: noun common mp const - noun proper.

לְמִשְׁפְּחֹתָם לִלְשֹׁנֹתָם. Range > prep phrase complex: Head + Post-modifier.

לְמִשְׁפְּחֹתָם. Head > prep phrase: prep + noun common fp const + pronoun suffix 3mp, antecedent is בְנֵי *the sons of (Cham).*

לִלְשֹׁנֹתָם. Post-modifier > prep phrase: prep + noun common fp const + pronoun suffix 3mp, antecedent is בְּנֵי *the sons of (Cham).*

בְּאַרְצֹתָם בְּגוֹיֵהֶם. Circumstance: location, place > prep phrase complex: Head + Post-modifier.

בְּאַרְצֹתָם. Head > prep phrase: prep + noun common fp const + pronoun suffix 3mp, antecedent is בְּנֵי *the sons of (Cham).*

בְּגוֹיֵהֶם. Post-modifier > prep phrase: prep + noun common mp const + pronoun suffix 3mp, antecedent is בְּנֵי *the sons of (Cham).*

Genesis 10:21-31

[21]And to Shem was born also he, the father of all of the sons of 'Ever, the big brother of Yefet. [22]The sons of Shem are 'Elam and 'Ashur and 'Arpakhshad and Lud and 'Aram. [23]And the sons of 'Aram are 'Uts and Chul and Geter and Mash. [24]And 'Arpakhshad fathered Shalach. And Shalach fathered 'Ever. [25]And to 'Ever was born two sons. The name of the one is Peleg, because in his days the earth was divided. And the name of his brother is Yoqtan. [26]And Yoqtan fathered 'Almodad and Shalef and Chatsarmavet and Yarach [27]and Hadoram and 'Uzal and Diqla [28]and 'Oval and 'Avima'el and Sheva' [29]and 'Ofir and Chavila and Yovav. All of these are the sons of Yoqtan. [30]And their dwelling was from Mesha' your going to Sefara, mountain of the east. [31]These are the sons of Shem to their families to their tongues in their lands to their nations.

10:21 /// וּלְשֵׁ֥ם יֻלַּ֖ד גַּם־ה֑וּא אֲבִי֙ כָּל־בְּנֵי־עֵ֔בֶר אֲחִ֖י יֶ֥פֶת הַגָּדֽוֹל׃

(a) וּלְשֵׁם יֻלַּד גַּם־הוּא אֲבִי כָּל־בְּנֵי־עֵבֶר אֲחִי יֶפֶת הַגָּדוֹל. Textuality > conj paratactic expansion / Mood > declarative: past / Transitivity > material: action. The Subject / Goal of the process is not specified and is assumed by NRSV and NJPS to be *children*, though this does not account for the 3ms form of the Finite.

גַּם־הוּא אֲבִי כָּל־בְּנֵי־עֵבֶר אֲחִי יֶפֶת הַגָּדוֹל	יֻלַּד	וּלְשֵׁם	**Constituents**
also he, the father of all of the sons of 'Ever, the big brother of Yefet	*he was born*	*and to Shem*	**Translation**
		Theme	**Textuality**
	Finite		**Mood**
Beneficiary	Process	Beneficiary	**Transitivity**

וּלְשֵׁם. Theme: textual > clause conj + Theme: experiential / Beneficiary > prep phrase: prep + noun proper.

יֻלַּד. Finite > qatal 3ms / Process > pual (or passive qal) ילד. The Subject / Goal is left unspecified. It is possible that the 3ms form of the Finite matches שֵׁם *Shem* as a logical Subject, rather than an assumed Subject such as *children*.

גַּם־הוּא אֲבִי כָּל־בְּנֵי־עֵבֶר אֲחִי יֶפֶת הַגָּדוֹל. Beneficiary > nominal group: Head + Post-modifier. This complex is an expansion of the Beneficiary שֵׁם expressed in the Theme.

גַּם־הוּא. Head > nominal group.

גַּם־. Adjunct: textual > addition. The textual adjunct גַּם *also* conditions the following word and implies that other children were born to other fathers, and indeed this is detailed in the preceding clause complex.

הוּא. Pronoun personal 3ms, antecedent is שֵׁם *Shem*. See 4:26(a) for a very similar structure.

אֲבִי כָּל־בְּנֵי־עֵבֶר אֲחִי יֶפֶת הַגָּדוֹל. Post-modifier > nominal group complex: two nominal groups linked by apposition.

אֲבִי כָּל־בְּנֵי־עֵבֶר. Nominal group > noun common ms const | noun common collective ms const - noun common mp const - noun proper.

אֲחִי יֶפֶת הַגָּדוֹל. Nominal group > noun common ms const | noun proper | def art + adj ms.

10:22 // בְּנֵ֥י שֵׁ֖ם עֵילָ֣ם וְאַשּׁ֑וּר וְאַרְפַּכְשַׁ֖ד וְל֥וּד וַאֲרָֽם׃

בְּנֵי שֵׁם עֵילָם וְאַשּׁוּר וְאַרְפַּכְשַׁד וְלוּד וַאֲרָם. (a) Textuality > appositive paratactic expansion / Mood > declarative: non-past / Transitivity > relational: identification.

עֵילָם וְאַשּׁוּר וְאַרְפַּכְשַׁד וְלוּד וַאֲרָם	בְּנֵי שֵׁם	**Constituents**
'Elam and 'Ashur and 'Arpakhshad and Lud and 'Aram	*the sons of Shem*	**Translation**
	Theme	**Textuality**
Complement	Subject	**Mood**
Identifier	Identified	**Transitivity**

בְּנֵי שֵׁם. Theme: experiential / Subject > mp (בְּנֵי) / Identified > nominal group: noun common mp const | noun proper ms.

עֵילָם וְאַשּׁוּר וְאַרְפַּכְשַׁד וְלוּד וַאֲרָם. Complement > mp / Identifier > nominal group complex: five conjoined proper nouns.

10:23 וּבְנֵ֖י אֲרָ֑ם ע֥וּץ וְח֖וּל וְגֶ֥תֶר וָֽמַשׁ׃

וּבְנֵי אֲרָם עוּץ וְחוּל וְגֶתֶר וָמַשׁ. (a) Textuality > conj paratactic expansion / Mood > declarative: non-past / Transitivity > relational: identification.

עוּץ וְחוּל וְגֶתֶר וָמַשׁ	וּבְנֵי אֲרָם	**Constituents**
'Uts and Chul and Geter and Mash	*and the sons of 'Aram*	**Translation**
	Theme	**Textuality**
Complement	Subject	**Mood**
Identifier	Identified	**Transitivity**

וּבְנֵי אֲרָם. Theme: textual > clause conj + Theme: experiential / Subject > mp (בְּנֵי) / Identified > nominal group: noun common mp const | noun proper ms.

עוּץ וְחוּל וְגֶתֶר וָמַשׁ. Complement / Identifier > nominal group complex: four conjoined proper nouns.

10:24 // וְאַרְפַּכְשַׁד יָלַד אֶת־שָׁלַח // וְשֶׁלַח יָלַד אֶת־עֵבֶר׃

וְאַרְפַּכְשַׁד יָלַד אֶת־שָׁלַח. (a) Textuality > conj paratactic expansion / Mood > declarative: past / Transitivity > material: action.

אֶת־שָׁלַח	יָלַד	וְאַרְפַּכְשַׁד	**Constituents**
Shalach	*fathered*	*and 'Arpakhshad*	**Translation**
		Theme	**Textuality**
	Finite	Subject	**Mood**
Goal	Process	Actor	**Transitivity**

וְאַרְפַּכְשַׁד. Theme: textual > clause conj + Theme: experiential / Subject > ms / Actor > nominal group: noun proper.

יָלַד. Finite > qatal 3ms / Process > qal ילד.

אֶת־שָׁלַח. Goal > nominal group: goal marker - noun proper ms.

וְשֶׁלַח יָלַד אֶת־עֵבֶר. (b) Textuality > conj paratactic expansion / Mood > declarative: past / Transitivity > material: action.

אֶת־עֵבֶר	יָלַד	וְשֶׁלַח	**Constituents**
'Ever	*fathered*	*and Shalach*	**Translation**
		Theme	**Textuality**
	Finite	Subject	**Mood**
Goal	Process	Actor	**Transitivity**

וְשֶׁלַח. Theme: textual > clause conj + Theme: experiential / Subject > ms / Actor > nominal group: noun proper.

יָלַד. Finite > qatal 3ms / Process > qal ילד.

אֶת־עֵבֶר. Goal > nominal group: goal marker - noun proper ms.

10:25 // וּלְעֵ֥בֶר יֻלַּ֖ד שְׁנֵ֣י בָנִ֑ים // שֵׁ֣ם הָאֶחָ֞ד פֶּ֗לֶג / כִּ֤י בְיָמָיו֙ נִפְלְגָ֣ה הָאָ֔רֶץ // וְשֵׁ֥ם אָחִ֖יו יָקְטָֽן׃

וּלְעֵבֶר יֻלַּד שְׁנֵי בָנִים. (a) Textuality > conj paratactic expansion / Mood > declarative: past / Transitivity > material: action. Compare 10:21(a) where the Finite also appears to match the Beneficiary.

שְׁנֵי בָנִים	יֻלַּד	וּלְעֵבֶר	**Constituents**
two sons	*he was born*	*and to 'Ever*	**Translation**
		Theme	**Textuality**
Subject	Finite		**Mood**
Goal	Process	Beneficiary	**Transitivity**

וּלְעֵבֶר. Theme: textual > clause conj + Theme: experiential / Beneficiary > prep phrase: prep + noun proper.

יֻלַּד. Finite > qatal 3ms / Process > pual (or passive qal) ילד. The Finite is singular but the Subject is plural.

שְׁנֵי בָנִים. Subject > md (שְׁנֵי) / Goal > nominal group: numeral md const ו noun common mp.

שֵׁם הָאֶחָד פֶּלֶג. (b) Textuality > appositive paratactic expansion / Mood > declarative: non-past / Transitivity > relational: identification.

פֶּלֶג	שֵׁם הָאֶחָד	**Constituents**
Peleg	*the name of the one*	**Translation**
	Theme	**Textuality**
Complement	Subject	**Mood**
Identifier	Identified	**Transitivity**

שֵׁם הָאֶחָד. Theme: experiential / Subject > ms / Identified > nominal group: noun common ms const ו def art + numeral ms. The cardinal numeral *one* here is used in the sense of the ordinal numeral *first*.

פֶּלֶג. Complement > ms / Identifier > nominal group: noun proper.

כִּי בְיָמָיו נִפְלְגָה הָאָרֶץ. (c) Textuality > conj hypotactic expansion / Mood > declarative: past / Transitivity > material: action.

הָאָרֶץ	נִפְלְגָה	בְיָמָיו	כִּי	**Constituents**
the earth	*she was divided*	*in his days*	*because*	**Translation**
		Theme	Theme	**Textuality**
Subject	Finite			**Mood**
Actor	Process	Circumstance		**Transitivity**

כִּי. Theme: textual > conj.

בְיָמָיו. Theme: experiential / Circumstance: location, time > prep phrase: prep + noun common mp const + pronoun suffix 3ms, antecedent is פֶּלֶג *Peleg*.

נִפְלְגָה. Finite > qatal 3fs / Process > nifal פלג.

הָאָרֶץ. Subject > fs / Actor > nominal group: def art + noun common fs.

וְשֵׁם אָחִיו יָקְטָן. (d) Textuality > conj paratactic expansion / Mood > declarative: non-past / Transitivity > relational: identification.

יָקְטָן	וְשֵׁם אָחִיו	**Constituents**
Yoqtan	*and the name of his brother*	**Translation**
	Theme	**Textuality**
Complement	Subject	**Mood**
Identifier	Identified	**Transitivity**

וְשֵׁם אָחִיו. Theme: textual > clause conj + Theme: experiential / Subject > ms (שֵׁם) / Identified > nominal group: noun common ms const | noun common ms const + pronoun suffix 3ms, antecedent is פֶּלֶג *Peleg*.

יָקְטָן. Complement > ms / Identifier > nominal group: noun proper.

10:26-29// וְיָקְטָ֣ן יָלַ֔ד אֶת־אַלְמוֹדָ֖ד וְאֶת־שָׁ֑לֶף וְאֶת־
חֲצַרְמָ֖וֶת וְאֶת־יָֽרַח׃ וְאֶת־הֲדוֹרָ֥ם וְאֶת־אוּזָ֖ל וְאֶת־
דִּקְלָֽה׃ וְאֶת־עוֹבָ֥ל וְאֶת־אֲבִֽימָאֵ֖ל וְאֶת־שְׁבָֽא׃
וְאֶת־אוֹפִ֥ר וְאֶת־חֲוִילָ֖ה וְאֶת־יוֹבָ֑ב // כָּל־אֵ֖לֶּה
בְּנֵ֥י יָקְטָֽן׃

וְיָקְטָן יָלַד אֶת־אַלְמוֹדָד וְאֶת־שָׁלֶף וְאֶת־חֲצַרְמָוֶת וְאֶת־יָרַח וְאֶת־הֲדוֹרָם וְאֶת־אוּזָל וְאֶת־דִּקְלָה וְאֶת־עוֹבָל וְאֶת־אֲבִימָאֵל וְאֶת־שְׁבָא וְאֶת־אוֹפִר וְאֶת־חֲוִילָה וְאֶת־יוֹבָב. (a) Textuality > conj paratactic expansion / Mood > declarative: past / Transitivity > material: action.

אֶת־אַלְמוֹדָד וְאֶת־שָׁלֶף וְאֶת־חֲצַרְמָוֶת וְאֶת־יָרַח וְאֶת־הֲדוֹרָם וְאֶת־אוּזָל וְאֶת־דִּקְלָה וְאֶת־עוֹבָל וְאֶת־אֲבִימָאֵל וְאֶת־שְׁבָא וְאֶת־אוֹפִר וְאֶת־חֲוִילָה וְאֶת־יוֹבָב	יָלַד	וְיָקְטָן	**Constituents**
'Almodad and Shalef and Chatsarmavet and Yarach and Hadoram and 'Uzal and Diqla and 'Oval and 'Avima'el and Sheva' and 'Ofir and Chavila and Yovav	*fathered*	*and Yoqtan*	**Translation**
		Theme	**Textuality**
	Finite	Subject	**Mood**
Goal	Process	Actor	**Transitivity**

וְיָקְטָן. Theme: textual > clause conj + Theme: experiential / Subject > ms / Actor > nominal group: noun proper.

יָלַד. Finite > qatal 3ms / Process > qal ילד.

אֶת־אַלְמוֹדָד וְאֶת־שָׁלֶף וְאֶת־חֲצַרְמָוֶת וְאֶת־יָרַח וְאֶת־הֲדוֹרָם וְאֶת־אוּזָל וְאֶת־דִּקְלָה וְאֶת־עוֹבָל וְאֶת־אֲבִימָאֵל

וְאֶת־שְׁבָא וְאֶת־אוֹפִר וְאֶת־חֲוִילָה וְאֶת־יוֹבָב. Goal > nominal group complex: thirteen conjoined nominal groups.

אֶת־אַלְמוֹדָד. Nominal group 1 > goal marker - noun proper.

וְאֶת־שָׁלֶף. Nominal group 2 > group conj + goal marker - noun proper.

וְאֶת־חֲצַרְמָוֶת. Nominal group 3 > group conj + goal marker - noun proper.

וְאֶת־יָרַח. Nominal group 4 > group conj + goal marker - noun proper.

וְאֶת־הֲדוֹרָם. Nominal group 5 > group conj + goal marker - noun proper.

וְאֶת־אוּזָל. Nominal group 6 > group conj + goal marker - noun proper.

וְאֶת־דִּקְלָה. Nominal group 7 > group conj + goal marker - noun proper.

וְאֶת־עוֹבָל. Nominal group 8 > group conj + goal marker - noun proper.

וְאֶת־אֲבִימָאֵל. Nominal group 9 > group conj + goal marker - noun proper.

וְאֶת־שְׁבָא. Nominal group 10 > group conj + goal marker - noun proper.

וְאֶת־אוֹפִר. Nominal group 11 > group conj + goal marker - noun proper.

וְאֶת־חֲוִילָה. Nominal group 12 > group conj + goal marker - noun proper.

וְאֶת־יוֹבָב. Nominal group 13 > group conj + goal marker - noun proper.

כָּל־אֵלֶּה בְּנֵי יָקְטָן. (b) Textuality > appositive paratactic expansion / Mood > declarative: non-past / Transitivity > relational: identification.

בְּנֵי יָקְטָן	כָּל־אֵלֶּה	**Constituents**
the sons of Yoqtan	*all of these*	**Translation**
	Theme	**Textuality**
Complement	Subject	**Mood**
Identifier	Identified	**Transitivity**

כָּל־אֵלֶּה. Theme: experiential / Subject > ms / Identified > nominal group: noun common collective ms const - pronoun demonstrative 3mp, antecedent is the Goal of the preceding clause. The pronoun אֵלֶּה is anaphoric.

בְּנֵי יָקְטָן. Complement > mp / Identifier > nominal group: noun common mp const ׀ noun proper.

10:30 // וַיְהִי מוֹשָׁבָם מִמֵּשָׁא בֹּאֲכָה סְפָרָה הַר הַקֶּדֶם׃

וַיְהִי מוֹשָׁבָם מִמֵּשָׁא בֹּאֲכָה סְפָרָה הַר הַקֶּדֶם. (a) Textuality > conj paratactic expansion / Mood > declarative: past / Transitivity > relational: attribution.

מִמֵּשָׁא בֹּאֲכָה סְפָרָה הַר הַקֶּדֶם	מוֹשָׁבָם	וַיְהִי	**Constituents**
from Mesha' your going to Sefara, mountain of the east	*their dwelling*	*and he was*	**Translation**
		Theme	**Textuality**
Complement	Subject	Finite	**Mood**
Attribute	Carrier	Process	**Transitivity**

וַיְהִי. Theme: textual > clause conj + Theme: experiential > Finite > wayyiqtol 3ms / Process > qal היה.

מוֹשָׁבָם. Subject > ms / Carrier > nominal group: noun common ms const + pronoun suffix 3mp, antecedent is בְּנֵי יָקְטָן *the sons of Yoqtan.*

מִמֵּשָׁא בֹּאֲכָה סְפָרָה הַר הַקֶּדֶם. Complement / Attribute > prep phrase complex: Head + Post-modifier.

מִמֵּשָׁא. Head > prep phrase: prep + noun proper.

בֹּאֲכָה סְפָרָה הַר הַקֶּדֶם. (i) Verbal group >> Textuality > embedded ptc clause / Transitivity > material: action.

סְפָרָה הַר הַקֶּדֶם	בֹּאֲכָה	**Constituents**
to Sefara, the mountain of the east	*your going*	**Translation**
	Theme	**Textuality**
Circumstance	Process + Actor	**Transitivity**

בֹּאֲכָה. Theme: experiential / Process > ptc ms qal בוא + Subject > 2ms / Actor > pronoun suffix 2ms, antecedent is the audience.

סְפָרָה הַר הַקֶּדֶם. Circumstance: extent, place > Head + Post-modifier.

סְפָרָה. Head > nominal group: noun proper + directive adjunct.

הַר הַקֶּדֶם. Post-modifier > nominal group: noun common ms const | def art + noun common ms. This nominal group is in apposition to the preceding one, giving it further specification.

10:31 // אֵלֶּה בְנֵי־שֵׁם לְמִשְׁפְּחֹתָם לִלְשֹׁנֹתָם בְּאַרְצֹתָם לְגוֹיֵהֶם׃

אֵלֶּה בְנֵי־שֵׁם לְמִשְׁפְּחֹתָם לִלְשֹׁנֹתָם בְּאַרְצֹתָם לְגוֹיֵהֶם. (a) Textuality > appositive paratactic expansion / Mood > declarative: non-past / Transitivity > relational: identification.

לְמִשְׁפְּחֹתָם לִלְשֹׁנֹתָם בְּאַרְצֹתָם לְגוֹיֵהֶם	בְנֵי־שֵׁם	אֵלֶּה	**Constituents**
to their families to their tongues in their lands to their nations	*the sons of Shem*	*these*	**Translation**
		Theme	**Textuality**
	Complement	Subject	**Mood**
Circumstance	Identifier	Identified	**Transitivity**

אֵ֣לֶּה. Theme: experiential / Subject > 3cp / Identified > pronoun demonstrative 3cp, referent is the preceding clause complex.

בְנֵי־שֵׁם. Complement > ms (בְּנֵי) / Identifier > nominal group: noun common mp const - noun proper.

לְמִשְׁפְּחֹתָם לִלְשֹׁנֹתָם בְּאַרְצֹתָם לְגוֹיֵהֶם. Circumstance: location, place > prep phrase complex: four prep phrases. This is virtually the same as the Circumstance in 10:20(a).

לְמִשְׁפְּחֹתָם. Prep phrase 1 > prep + noun common fp const + pronoun suffix 3mp, antecedent is בְּנֵי *the sons of (Shem).*

לִלְשֹׁנֹתָם. Prep phrase 2 > prep + noun common fp const + pronoun suffix 3mp, antecedent is בְּנֵי *the sons of (Shem).*

בְּאַרְצֹתָם. Prep phrase 3 > prep + noun common fp const + pronoun suffix 3mp, antecedent is בְּנֵי *the sons of (Shem).*

לְגוֹיֵהֶם. Prep phrase 4 > prep + noun common mp const + pronoun suffix 3mp, antecedent is בְּנֵי *the sons of (Shem).*

Genesis 10:32

[32]These are the families of the sons of Noach to their outcomes in their nations. And from these the nations were dispersed in the earth after the flood.

10:32 /// אֵ֣לֶּה מִשְׁפְּחֹ֧ת בְּנֵי־נֹ֛חַ לְתוֹלְדֹתָ֖ם בְּגוֹיֵהֶ֑ם //
וּמֵאֵ֜לֶּה נִפְרְד֧וּ הַגּוֹיִ֛ם בָּאָ֖רֶץ אַחַ֥ר הַמַּבּֽוּל׃ פ

אֵלֶּה מִשְׁפְּחֹת בְּנֵי־נֹחַ לְתוֹלְדֹתָם בְּגוֹיֵהֶם. (a) Textuality > appositive paratactic expansion / Mood > declarative: non-past / Transitivity > relational: identification.

לְתוֹלְדֹתָם בְּגוֹיֵהֶם	מִשְׁפְּחֹת בְּנֵי־נֹחַ	אֵלֶּה	**Constituents**
to their outcomes in their nations	*the families of the sons of Noach*	*these*	**Translation**
		Theme	**Textuality**
	Complement	Subject	**Mood**
Circumstance	Identifier	Identified	**Transitivity**

אֵלֶּה. Theme: experiential / Subject > 3cp / Identified > pronoun demonstrative. The pronoun is anaphoric and the referent is the entire chapter going back to 10:2. This clause forms an inclusion with 10:1(a) וְאֵלֶּה תּוֹלְדֹת בְּנֵי־נֹחַ שֵׁם חָם וָיָפֶת. The demonstrative pronoun אֵלֶּה in 10:1(a) is cataphoric and the one in 10:32(a) here is anaphoric.

מִשְׁפְּחֹת בְּנֵי־נֹחַ. Complement > fp (מִשְׁפְּחֹת) / Identifier > nominal group: noun common fp const ׀ noun common mp const - noun proper.

לְתוֹלְדֹתָם בְּגוֹיֵהֶם. Circumstance: location, place > prep phrase complex: two prep phrases.

לְתוֹלְדֹתָם. Prep phrase 1 > prep + noun common fp const + pronoun suffix 3mp, antecedent is מִשְׁפְּחֹת בְּנֵי־נֹחַ *the families of the sons of Noach.* Notice the occurrence of תּוֹלְדֹת *outcomes* here, which brackets its occurrence in 10:1(a).

בְּגוֹיֵהֶם. Prep phrase 2 > prep + noun common mp const + pronoun suffix 3mp, antecedent is מִשְׁפְּחֹת בְּנֵי־נֹחַ *the families of the sons of Noach.*

וּמֵאֵלֶּה נִפְרְדוּ הַגּוֹיִם בָּאָרֶץ אַחַר הַמַּבּוּל. (b) Textuality > conj paratactic expansion / Mood > declarative: past / Transitivity > material: action. This is the summary conclusion of the preceding clause complex. Notice how verbose and complete it is, with a fully articulated Transitivity structure: Circumstance + Process + Goal + Circumstance + Circumstance; and a complete Mood structure: Finite + Subject.

אַחַר הַמַּבּוּל	בָּאָרֶץ	הַגּוֹיִם	נִפְרְדוּ	וּמֵאֵלֶּה	**Constituents**
after the flood	*in the earth*	*the nations*	*they were dispersed*	*and from these*	**Translation**
				Theme	**Textuality**
		Subject	Finite		**Mood**
Circum-stance	Circum-stance	Goal	Process	Circum-stance	**Transitivity**

וּמֵאֵלֶּה. Theme: textual > clause conj + Theme: experiential / Circumstance: location, place > prep phrase: prep + pronoun demonstrative 3cp, antecedent is מִשְׁפְּחֹת בְּנֵי־נֹחַ *the families of the sons of Noach* in the preceding clause.

נִפְרְדוּ. Finite > qatal 3cp / Process > nifal פרד.

הַגּוֹיִם. Subject > mp / Goal > nominal group: def art + noun common mp.

בָּאָרֶץ. Circumstance: location, place > prep phrase: prep + def art + noun common fs.

אַחַר הַמַּבּוּל. Circumstance: location, time > prep phrase: prep + def art + noun common ms.

Genesis 11:1-2

[1]And all the earth was one language and the same words. [2]And it was when they traveled from east, and they found a valley in the land of Shinar. And they settled there.

11:1 /// וַיְהִי כָל־הָאָרֶץ שָׂפָה אֶחָת וּדְבָרִים אֲחָדִים׃

וַיְהִי כָל־הָאָרֶץ שָׂפָה אֶחָת וּדְבָרִים אֲחָדִים. (a) Textuality > conj paratactic expansion / Mood > declarative: past / Transitivity > relational: attribution. This clause is in effect the Theme of the clause complex. The form וַיְהִי is often used to posit a setting for following action, either with a relational process as here, or with a בְּ or כְּ embedded prep clause as in the next clause.

שָׂפָה אֶחָת וּדְבָרִים אֲחָדִים	כָל־הָאָרֶץ	וַיְהִי	**Constituents**
one lip and one words	*all the earth*	*and he was*	**Translation**
		Theme	**Textuality**
	Subject	Finite	**Mood**
Attribute	Carrier	Process	**Transitivity**

וַיְהִי. Theme: textual / clause conj + Theme: experiential / Finite > wayyiqtol 3ms / Process > qal היה.

כָל־הָאָרֶץ. Subject > ms (כָל) / Carrier > nominal group: noun common collective ms const - def art + noun common fs.

שָׂפָה אֶחָת וּדְבָרִים אֲחָדִים. Attribute > nominal group complex: noun common fs ׀ numeral cardinal fs ׀ group conj + noun common mp ׀ numeral cardinal mp. It is a bit strange for the numeral one to be found in the plural modifying a plural noun. Perhaps it has the sense here of *same*, as in the *same lip and same words*.

11:2 // וַיְהִי בְּנָסְעָם מִקֶּדֶם // וַיִּמְצְאוּ בִקְעָה בְּאֶרֶץ
שִׁנְעָר // וַיֵּשְׁבוּ שָׁם׃

וַיְהִי [[בְּנָסְעָם מִקֶּדֶם]]. (a) Textuality > conj hypotactic expansion / Mood > declarative: past / Transitivity > existential. וַיְהִי plus a בְּ prep phrase is a specialized thematic structure that creates a hypotactic temporal clause which conditions the following clause.

[[בְּנָסְעָם מִקֶּדֶם]]	וַיְהִי	**Constituents**
in their traveling from east	*and he was*	**Translation**
	Theme	**Textuality**
	Finite	**Mood**
Circumstance	Process	**Transitivity**

וַיְהִי. Theme: textual / clause conj + Theme: experiential / Finite > wayyiqtol 3ms / Process > qal היה. The Subject is not expressed and may be equivalent to the English *it*, used in similar English thematic structures.

בְּנָסְעָם מִקֶּדֶם. (i) Circumstance >> Textuality > embedded expansion: prep clause / Transitivity > material: action. Rendered as an independent clause before the embedding procedure it would have been *they traveled from east.*

מִקֶּדֶם	בְּנָסְעָם	**Constituents**
from east	*in their traveling*	**Translation**
	Theme	**Textuality**
	Complement + Subject	**Mood**
Circumstance	Process + Actor	**Transitivity**

בְּנָסְעָם. Theme: textual > prep + Theme: experiential / Complement > inf const / Process > qal נסע + Subject > mp / Actor > pronoun suffix 3mp, the antecedent of the pronoun suffix is presumably the collective noun כָּל *all* from 11:1(a); however, in that clause, it is treated as 3ms by the verb וַיְהִי.

מִקֶּדֶם. Circumstance: location, place > prep phrase: prep + noun common ms.

וַיִּמְצְאוּ בִקְעָה בְּאֶרֶץ שִׁנְעָר. (b) Textuality > conj paratactic expansion / Mood > declarative: past / Transitivity > material: action.

בְּאֶרֶץ שִׁנְעָר	בִקְעָה	וַיִּמְצְאוּ	**Constituents**
in the land of Shinar	*a valley*	*and they found*	**Translation**
		Theme	**Textuality**
		Finite	**Mood**
Circumstance	Goal	Process	**Transitivity**

וַיִּמְצְאוּ. Theme: textual / clause conj + Theme: experiential / Finite > wayyiqtol 3mp / Process > qal מצא.

בִקְעָה. Goal > nominal group: noun common fs.

בְּאֶרֶץ שִׁנְעָר. Circumstance > prep phrase: prep + noun common fs const ı noun proper.

וַיֵּשְׁבוּ שָׁם. (c) Textuality > conj paratactic expansion / Mood > declarative: past / Transitivity > material: action. A material process of happening does not take a Goal. Again, the Subject / Actor is כָּל *all* from 11:1(a), absent by ellipsis.

שָׁם	וַיֵּשְׁבוּ	**Constituents**
there	*and they settled*	**Translation**
	Theme	**Textuality**
	Finite	**Mood**
Circumstance	Process	**Transitivity**

וַיֵּשְׁבוּ. Theme: textual / clause conj + Theme: experiential / Finite > wayyiqtol 3mp / Process > qal ישׁב.

שָׁם. Circumstance: location, place > pronoun textual. The antecedent is אֶרֶץ שִׁנְעָר *land of Shinar* in the prior clause.

Genesis 11:3-4

[3]And a man said to his neighbor, "Come. Let us brick bricks. And let us burn (them) for a burning." And the brick for them became stone. And the tar became for them clay. [4]And they said, "Come. Let us build for ourselves a city and a tower and its head in the heavens. And let us make for ourselves a name, so that we not scatter on the face of all the earth."

/// וַיֹּאמְרוּ אִישׁ אֶל־רֵעֵהוּ // הָבָה // נִלְבְּנָה 11:3
לְבֵנִים // וְנִשְׂרְפָה לִשְׂרֵפָה // וַתְּהִי לָהֶם הַלְּבֵנָה
לְאָבֶן // וְהַחֵמָר הָיָה לָהֶם לַחֹמֶר׃

וַיֹּאמְרוּ אִישׁ אֶל־רֵעֵהוּ. (a) Textuality > conj paratactic expansion / Mood > declarative: past / Transitivity > verbal.

אֶל־רֵעֵהוּ	אִישׁ	וַיֹּאמְרוּ	**Constituents**
to his neighbor	*a man*	*and they said*	**Translation**
		Theme	**Textuality**
	Subject	Finite	**Mood**
Receiver	Sayer	Process	**Transitivity**

וַיֹּאמְרוּ. Theme: textual / clause conj + Theme: experiential / Finite > wayyiqtol 3mp / Process > qal אמר.

אִישׁ. Subject > ms / Sayer > noun common. Notice that the Subject is singular while the Finite is plural. This is presumably because the interlocutors are talking to each other, so more than one is talking.

אֶל־רֵעֵהוּ. Receiver > prep phrase: prep - noun common ms const + pronoun suffix 3ms, antecedent is אִישׁ *man*.

הָבָה. (b) Textuality > appositive paratactic projection: quote / Mood > directive: imperative / Transitivity > material: action. This Finite is singular, *you come*, directed as it is to the neighbor.

הָבָה	**Constituents**
come	**Translation**
Theme	**Textuality**
Finite	**Mood**
Process	**Transitivity**

הָבָה. Theme: experiential / Finite > impv ms / Process > qal יהב.

נִלְבְּנָה לְבֵנִים. (c) Textuality > appositive paratactic projection: quote / Mood > directive: cohortative / Transitivity > material: action. In contrast to the preceding clause, the Finite is now plural, *let us*. . . . and the Subject is a man and his neighbor.

לְבֵנִים	נִלְבְּנָה	**Constituents**
bricks	*let us brick*	**Translation**
	Theme	**Textuality**
	Finite	**Mood**
Goal	Process	**Transitivity**

נִלְבְּנָה. Theme: experiential / Finite > cohort 1cp / Process > qal לבן.

לְבֵנִים. Goal > noun common mp. Notice that the Goal is cognate with the Process, both being from the root לבן.

וְנִשְׂרְפָה לִשְׂרֵפָה. (d) Textuality > conj paratactic projection: quote / Mood > directive: cohortative / Transitivity > material: action. As with the prior clause, the Subject is a man and his neighbor. The Goal of the material process is לְבֵנִים from the prior clause, textually absent here by ellipsis.

לִשְׂרֵפָה	וְנִשְׂרְפָה	**Constituents**
for a burning	*let us burn*	**Translation**
	Theme	**Textuality**
	Finite	**Mood**
Range	Process	**Transitivity**

וְנִשְׂרְפָה. Theme: textual / clause conj + Theme: experiential / Finite > cohort 1cp / Process > qal שׂרף.

לִשְׂרֵפָה. Range > prep phrase: prep + noun common fs. The object of the prep here is cognate with the verb, both deriving from שׂרף. As Range, this prep phrase extends the force of the material process, *let us burn them for a burning*, suggesting, *let us fire them until they cannot be fired any more.*

וַתְּהִי לָהֶם הַלְּבֵנָה לְאָבֶן. (e) Textuality > conj paratactic expansion / Mood > declarative / Transitivity > relational: attribution. After three prior clauses of quotes, the text returns to narration.

לְאָבֶן	הַלְּבֵנָה	לָהֶם	וַתְּהִי	**Constituents**
for stone	*the brick*	*to them*	*and she was*	**Translation**
			Theme	**Textuality**
	Subject		Finite	**Mood**
Attribute	Carrier	Beneficiary	Process	**Transitivity**

וַתְּהִי. Theme: textual / clause conj + Theme: experiential / Finite > wayyiqtol 3fs / Process > qal היה. The verb היה with prep לְ is the process of becoming: *and brick became stone for them.*

לָהֶם. Beneficiary > prep phrase: prep + pronoun suffix 3mp, antecedent is man and his neighbor.

הַלְּבֵנָה. Subject > 3fs / Carrier > noun common.

לְאָבֶן. Attribute > prep phrase: prep + noun common fs. Notice the pausal lengthening: אֶבֶן to אָבֶן. *For stone* meaning, to be used for stone.

וְהַחֵמָר הָיָה לָהֶם לַחֹמֶר. (f) Textuality > conj paratactic expansion / Mood > declarative: past / Transitivity > relational: attribution.

לַחֹמֶר	לָהֶם	הָיָה	וְהַחֵמָר	**Constituents**
for clay	*to them*	*he was*	*and the tar*	**Translation**
			Theme	**Textuality**
		Finite	Subject	**Mood**
Attribute	Beneficiary	Process	Carrier	**Transitivity**

וְהַחֵמָר. Theme: textual / clause conj + Theme: experiential / Subject > ms / Carrier > def art + noun common. In contrast to the preceding clause, the Theme is not the Finite constituent, which necessitates the use of a qatal verb instead of a wayyiqtol verb. This designates temporal simultaneity rather than temporal sequence.

הָיָה. Finite > qatal 3ms / Process > qal היה.

לָהֶם. Beneficiary > prep phrase: prep + pronoun suffix 3mp, antecedent is man and his neighbor.

לַחֹמֶר. Attribute > prep phrase: prep + noun common ms.

11:4 // וַיֹּאמְרוּ // הָבָה | // נִבְנֶה־לָּנוּ עִיר וּמִגְדָּל //
וְרֹאשׁוֹ בַשָּׁמַיִם // וְנַעֲשֶׂה־לָּנוּ שֵׁם / פֶּן־נָפוּץ עַל־
פְּנֵי כָל־הָאָרֶץ׃

וַיֹּאמְרוּ. (a) Textuality > conj paratactic expansion / Mood > declarative: past / Transitivity > verbal.

וַיֹּאמְרוּ	**Constituents**
and they said	**Translation**
Theme	**Textuality**
Finite	**Mood**
Process	**Transitivity**

וַיֹּאמְרוּ. Theme: textual / clause conj + Theme: experiential / Finite > wayyiqtol 3mp / Verbal Process > qal אמר.

הָבָה. (b) Textuality > appositive paratactic projection: quote / Mood > directive: imperative / Transitivity > material: action. This Finite is singular, *you come*, directed as it is to the neighbor.

הָבָה	**Constituents**
come	**Translation**
Theme	**Textuality**
Finite	**Mood**
Process	**Transitivity**

הָבָה. Theme: experiential / Finite > impv ms / Process > qal יהב.

נִבְנֶה־לָּנוּ עִיר וּמִגְדָּל וְרֹאשׁוֹ בַשָּׁמַיִם. (c) Textuality > appositive paratactic projection: quote / Mood > directive: cohortative / Transitivity > material: action. The Subject is the speaker *we*, implicit in the Finite.

עִיר וּמִגְדָּל וְרֹאשׁוֹ בַשָּׁמַיִם	לָּנוּ	נִבְנֶה	**Constituents**
a city and a tower and his head in the heavens	*for ourselves*	*let us build*	**Translation**
		Theme	**Textuality**
		Finite	**Mood**
Goal	Beneficiary	Process	**Transitivity**

נִבְנֶה־. Theme: experiential / Finite > cohort 1cp / Process > qal בנה.

לָּנוּ. Beneficiary > prep phrase: prep + pronoun suffix 1cp, antecedent is the Subject of the Process, *we*. Notice the *dagesh lene* in the *lamed*; it, along with the *meteg*, binds the Beneficiary tightly to the Process.

עִיר וּמִגְדָּל וְרֹאשׁוֹ בַשָּׁמַיִם. Goal > nominal group complex: three goals realized as conjoined nominal groups.

עִיר. Goal 1 > nominal group: noun common fs.

וּמִגְדָּל. Group conj + Goal 2 > nominal group: noun common ms.

וְרֹאשׁוֹ בַשָּׁמַיִם . Group conj + Goal 3 > nominal group complex: Head + Post-modifier. This group almost has the look of an embedded attributive relational clause that has been inserted to expand מִגְדָּל: *and his head is in the heavens.* But it is worded as a third goal.

וְרֹאשׁוֹ. Head > nominal group: noun common ms + pronoun suffix 3ms, antecedent is מִגְדָּל *tower.*

בַשָּׁמַיִם. Post-modifier > prep phrase: prep + def art + noun common mp. The lack of *dagesh lene* in the *bet* binds this prep phrase closely to the preceding word.

וְנַעֲשֶׂה־לָּנוּ שֵׁם. (d) Textuality > conj paratactic projection: quote / Mood > directive: cohortative / Transitivity > material: action. The Subject / Sayer is the speaker *we*, implicit in the Finite.

שֵׁם	לָנוּ	וְנַעֲשֶׂה	**Constituents**
a name	*for ourselves*	*and let us make*	**Translation**
		Theme	**Textuality**
		Finite	**Mood**
Goal	Beneficiary	Process	**Transitivity**

וְנַעֲשֶׂה־. Theme: textual / clause conj + Theme: experiential / Finite > cohort 1cp / Process > qal עשׂה.

לָנוּ. Beneficiary > prep phrase: prep + pronoun suffix 1cp, antecedent is the Subject of the Process, *we*. See clause (c).

שֵׁם. Goal > nominal group: noun common ms.

פֶּן־נָפוּץ עַל־פְּנֵי כָל־הָאָרֶץ. (e) Textuality > conj hypotactic expansion / Mood > declarative: non-past / Transitivity > material: event. The Subject / Sayer is *we*, implicit in the Finite.

עַל־פְּנֵי כָל־הָאָרֶץ	נָפוּץ	פֶּן	**Constituents**
on the face of all the earth	*we will scatter*	*so that not*	**Translation**
	Theme	Theme	**Textuality**
	Finite	Adjunct	**Mood**
Circumstance	Process		**Transitivity**

פֶּן־. Theme: textual and interpersonal / Adjunct > negative.

נָפוּץ. Theme: experiential / Finite > yiqtol 1cp / Process > qal פוץ. NRSV translates *we shall be scattered*, but the verb is not passive in form. Rather, this is a material process of event (a so-called intransitive verb), which means the Actor is also the Goal of the Process. This is in distinction from a material process of doing, which has an expressed or implicit Goal distinct from the Actor.

עַל־פְּנֵי כָל־הָאָרֶץ. Circumstance > prep phrase: prep - noun common mp const | noun common ms const - def art + noun common fs.

Genesis 11:5-7

[5]And YHVH descended to see the city and the tower which the sons of humankind built. [6]And YHVH said, "One people! And they all have one language! And this is the beginning of what they will do. And now, all which they plan to make will not be insurmountable for them. [7]Come. Let us descend. And let us confuse there their language, which they will not hear, each man the language of his neighbor."

11:5 /// וַיֵּ֣רֶד יְהוָ֔ה לִרְאֹ֥ת אֶת־הָעִ֖יר וְאֶת־הַמִּגְדָּ֑ל אֲשֶׁ֥ר בָּנ֖וּ בְּנֵ֥י הָאָדָֽם׃

וַיֵּרֶד יְהוָה [[לִרְאֹת אֶת־הָעִיר וְאֶת־הַמִּגְדָּל [[אֲשֶׁר בָּנוּ בְּנֵי הָאָדָם]]]]. (a) Textuality > conj paratactic expansion / Mood > declarative: past / Transitivity > material: action.

[[לִרְאֹת אֶת־הָעִיר וְאֶת־הַמִּגְדָּל [[אֲשֶׁר בָּנוּ בְּנֵי הָאָדָם]]]]	יְהוָה	וַיֵּרֶד	**Constituents**
to see the city and the tower which the sons of the humankind built	*YHVH*	*and he descended*	**Translation**
		Theme	**Textuality**
	Subject	Finite	**Mood**
Circumstance	Actor	Process	**Transitivity**

וַיֵּרֶד. Theme: textual / clause conj + Theme: experiential / Finite > wayyiqtol 3ms / Process > qal ירד.

יְהוָה. Subject > ms / Actor > nominal group: noun proper.

[[לִרְאֹת אֶת־הָעִיר וְאֶת־הַמִּגְדָּל [[אֲשֶׁר בָּנוּ בְּנֵי הָאָדָם]]]]. (i) Circumstance: cause, purpose >> Textuality > embedded prep clause / Transitivity > mental: perception. The Subject / Senser of the mental process is יְהוָה *YHVH*, also the Subject of dominant clause (a). This embedded clause extends the meaning of the dominant clause by adding the purpose for YHVH's descending.

אֶת־הָעִיר וְאֶת־הַמִּגְדָּל [[אֲשֶׁר בָּנוּ בְּנֵי הָאָדָם]]	לִרְאֹת	**Constituents**
the city and the tower which the sons of the human built	*to see*	**Translation**
	Theme	**Textuality**
Phenomenon	Process	**Transitivity**

לִרְאֹת. Theme: textual > prep + Theme: experiential / Complement > inf const / Process > qal ראה.

אֶת־הָעִיר וְאֶת־הַמִּגְדָּל [[אֲשֶׁר בָּנוּ בְּנֵי הָאָדָם]]. Phenomenon > nominal group complex: Head + Post-modifier.

אֶת־הָעִיר וְאֶת־הַמִּגְדָּל. Head > goal marker - def art + noun common fs | group conj + goal marker - def art + noun common ms. This nominal group is the Phenomenon of the mental process (i.e. the thing seen) of the embedded clause, and is not a constituent of the dominant clause.

אֲשֶׁר בָּנוּ בְּנֵי הָאָדָם. (ii) Post-modifier >> Textuality > embedded expansion: relative clause / Mood > declarative: past / Transitivity > material: action. The Goal of the material process is the antecedent of the relative pronoun, אֶת־הָעִיר וְאֶת־הַמִּגְדָּל *the city and the tower*, from the prior embedded clause. Alternately, it is possible, though not likely, that the relative embedded clause modifies only הַמִּגְדָּל and not both Goal nouns. The dominant clause of this embedded clause is the prior embedded clause.

בְּנֵי הָאָדָם	בָּנוּ	אֲשֶׁר	**Constituents**
the sons of the humankind	*they built*	*which*	**Translation**
		Theme	**Textuality**
Subject	Finite		**Mood**
Actor	Process	Goal	**Transitivity**

אֲשֶׁר. Theme: textual > pronoun relative / Theme: experiential / Goal > antecedent אֶת־הָעִיר וְאֶת־הַמִּגְדָּל *the city and the tower* from the prior clause.

בָּנוּ. Finite > qatal 3p / Process > material doing: qal בנה.

בְּנֵי הָאָדָם. Subject > mp (בְּנֵי) / Actor > nominal group: noun common mp const | def art + noun common ms.

11:6 // וַיֹּ֣אמֶר יְהוָ֗ה // הֵ֣ן עַ֤ם אֶחָד֙ // וְשָׂפָ֤ה אַחַת֙
לְכֻלָּ֔ם // וְזֶ֖ה הַחִלָּ֣ם לַעֲשׂ֑וֹת // וְעַתָּה֙ לֹֽא־יִבָּצֵ֣ר
מֵהֶ֔ם כֹּ֛ל אֲשֶׁ֥ר יָזְמ֖וּ לַעֲשֽׂוֹת׃

וַיֹּאמֶר יְהוָה. (a) Textuality > conj paratactic expansion / Mood > declarative: past / Transitivity > verbal.

יְהוָה	וַיֹּאמֶר	**Constituents**
YHVH	*and he said*	**Translation**
	Theme	**Textuality**
Subject	Finite	**Mood**
Sayer	Process	**Transitivity**

וַיֹּאמֶר. Theme: textual / clause conj + Theme: experiential / Finite > wayyiqtol 3ms / Process > qal אמר.

יְהוָה. Subject > ms / Sayer > nominal group: noun proper ms.

הֵן עַם אֶחָד. (b) Textuality > appositive paratactic projection: quote / Mood > declarative: exclamative / Transitivity > N/A. This clause does not have a Transitivity structure, because there is no Process. It may be best to analyze it as an exclamative minor clause. The entire exclamative is thematic. *One people!*

עַם אֶחָד	הֵן	**Constituents**
one people	*now*	**Translation**
	Theme	**Textuality**
Subject		**Mood**
		Transitivity

הֵן. Theme: textual / Adjunct: textual > contra-expectation. This textual adjunct indicates that the following constituent represents a new and noteworthy development. It has a role in the Textual structure of the clause, but not in the Mood structure or the Transitivity structure (because there is none). See also 3:22(b), 4:14(a) and the discussion of הִנֵּה in 1:29(b).

עַם אֶחָד. Theme: interpersonal / Subject > nominal group: noun common collective ms ׀ numeral ms. Note that עַם is a non-definite noun, indicating it has not been defined in the text yet. In fact, this is the first time עַם occurs in Genesis.

וְשָׂפָה אַחַת לְכֻלָּם. (c) Textuality > conj paratactic projection: quote / Mood > declarative: non-past / Transitivity > relational: attribution. The prep לְ is used to establish a relationship of possession. *And to all of them is one lip*, i.e. *they all have one language.*

לְכֻלָּם	וְשָׂפָה אַחַת	**Constituents**
to all of them	*and one lip*	**Translation**
	Theme	**Textuality**
Complement	Subject	**Mood**
Attribute	Carrier	**Transitivity**

וְשָׂפָה אַחַת. Theme: textual / clause conj + Theme: experiential / Subject > 3fs / Carrier > nominal group: noun common fs ׀ numeral cardinal fs.

לְכֻלָּם. Complement / Attribute > prep phrase: prep + noun common collective ms const + pronoun suffix 3mp, antecedent is עַם *people* in the prior clause understood in its plural form.

וְזֶה הַחִלָּם לַעֲשׂוֹת. (d) Textuality > conj paratactic projection: quote / Mood > declarative: non-past / Transitivity > relational: attribution. *And this is their beginning to make,* i.e. *and this is the beginning of what they will do.*

הַחִלָּם לַעֲשׂוֹת	וְזֶה	**Constituents**
their beginning to make	*and this*	**Translation**
	Theme	**Textuality**
Complement	Subject	**Mood**
Attribute	Carrier	**Transitivity**

וְזֶה. Theme: textual / clause conj + Theme: experiential / Subject > ms / Carrier > pronoun demonstrative 3ms. The demonstrative pronoun *this* does not have a specific textual referent, rather it appears to reference the general situation that people have brought about with their building activities, as summarized in the preceding clause complex.

הַחִלָּם לַעֲשׂוֹת. (i) Complement / Attribute >> Textuality > embedded verbal group complex / Transitivity > material: action.

לַעֲשׂוֹת	הַחִלָּם	**Constituents**
to make	*their beginning*	**Translation**
	Theme	**Textuality**
Process		**Transitivity**

הַחִלָּם לַעֲשׂוֹת. Process > verbal group complex: Head + Complement.

הַחִלָּם. Head > def art + Process > inf const hifil חלל + Actor > pronoun suffix 3mp, antecedent is עַם *people* in clause (b).

לַעֲשׂוֹת. Complement > prep + Process > inf const qal עשׂה. The Complement is the core meaning of the Process.

וְעַתָּה לֹא־יִבָּצֵר מֵהֶם כֹּל אֲשֶׁר יָזְמוּ לַעֲשׂוֹת. (e) Textuality > conj paratactic projection: quote / Mood > declarative: non-past / Transitivity > material: action. This is a passive clause formation, and it puts כֹּל *all* in the 3ms Subject role.

כֹּל [[אֲשֶׁר יָזְמוּ לַעֲשׂוֹת]]	מֵהֶם	יִבָּצֵר	לֹא־	וְעַתָּה	**Constituents**
all which they plan to make	*from them*	*he will be insurmountable*	*not*	*and now*	**Translation**
				Theme	**Textuality**
Subject		Finite	Adjunct		**Mood**
Goal	Range	Process		Adjunct	**Transitivity**

וְעַתָּה. Theme: textual / clause conj + Theme: experiential / Adjunct: experiential > circumstance: time. *And now*, meaning, *from this point on*. The element וְעַתָּה comes to function as a conjunctive adjunct marking the beginning of a new clause complex that is temporally and logically consequent on the preceding clause complex.

לֹא־. Theme: interpersonal / Adjunct: interpersonal > polarity: negative.

יִבָּצֵר. Finite > yiqtol 3ms / Process > nifal בצר.

מֵהֶם. Range > prep phrase: prep + pronoun suffix 3mp, antecedent is the unified עַם *people* mentioned in 11:6(b).

כֹּל [[אֲשֶׁר יָזְמוּ לַעֲשׂוֹת]]. Subject > ms / Goal > nominal group complex: Head + Post-modifier. This is the Goal because the process in passive.

כֹּל. Head > noun common ms.

אֲשֶׁר יָזְמוּ לַעֲשׂוֹת. (i) Post-modifier >> Textuality > embedded expansion: relative clause / Mood > declarative: non-past / Transitivity > mental: cognition.

לַעֲשׂוֹת	יָזְמוּ	אֲשֶׁר	**Constituents**
to make	*they will plan*	*which*	**Translation**
		Theme	**Textuality**
Complement	Finite		**Mood**
Process	Process	Phenomenon	**Transitivity**

אֲשֶׁר. Theme: textual > relative pronoun / Phenomenon: antecedent כֹּל *all*, the Head of the Subject / Goal.

יָזְמוּ לַעֲשׂוֹת. Process > verbal group complex: Finite + Complement.

יָזְמוּ. Finite > yiqtol 3mp / Process > qal זמם.

לַעֲשׂוֹת. Complement > prep + Process > inf const qal עשׂה.

11:7 // הָבָה // נֵרְדָה // וְנָבְלָה שָׁם שְׂפָתָם אֲשֶׁר לֹא
יִשְׁמְעוּ אִישׁ שְׂפַת רֵעֵהוּ׃

הָבָה. (a) Textuality > appositive paratactic projection: quote / Mood > directive: imperative / Transitivity > material: action.

הָבָה	**Constituents**
come	**Translation**
Theme	**Textuality**
Finite	**Mood**
Process	**Transitivity**

הָבָה. Theme: experiential / Finite > impv ms / Process > qal יהב.

נֵרְדָה. (b) Textuality > appositive paratactic projection: quote / Mood > directive: cohortative / Transitivity > material: event.

נֵרְדָה	**Constituents**
let us descend	**Translation**
Theme	**Textuality**
Finite	**Mood**
Process	**Transitivity**

נֵרְדָה. Theme: experiential / Finite > cohort 1cp / Process > qal ירד.

וְנָבְלָה שָׁם שְׂפָתָם. (c) Textuality > conj paratactic projection: quote / Mood > directive: cohortative / Transitivity > material: action.

שְׂפָתָם [[אֲשֶׁר לֹא יִשְׁמְעוּ אִישׁ שְׂפַת רֵעֵהוּ]]	שָׁם	וְנָבְלָה	**Constituents**
their lip, which they will not hear, a man the lip of his neighbor	*there*	*and let us confuse*	**Translation**
		Theme	**Textuality**
		Finite	**Mood**
Goal	Circumstance	Process	**Transitivity**

וְנָבְלָה. Theme: textual > clause conj + Theme: experiential / Finite > cohort 1cp / Process > qal נבל.

שָׁם. Circumstance: location, place > pronoun textual, referring to the city and the tower of 11:5(a).

שְׂפָתָם [[אֲשֶׁר לֹא יִשְׁמְעוּ אִישׁ שְׂפַת רֵעֵהוּ]]. Goal > nominal group: Head + Post-modifier.

שְׂפָתָם. Head > nominal group: noun common fs const + pronoun suffix 3mp, antecedent is עַם in 11:6(b).

אֲשֶׁר לֹא יִשְׁמְעוּ אִישׁ שְׂפַת רֵעֵהוּ. (i) Post-modifier >> Textuality > embedded expansion: relative clause / Mood > declarative: non-past / Transitivity > mental: perception.

שְׂפַת רֵעֵהוּ	אִישׁ	יִשְׁמְעוּ	לֹא	אֲשֶׁר	**Constituents**
the lip of his neighbor	*a man*	*they will hear*	*not*	*which*	**Translation**
				Theme	**Textuality**
	Subject	Finite	Adjunct	Subject	**Mood**
Phenomenon	Actor	Process		Actor	**Transitivity**

אֲשֶׁר. Theme: textual and experiential > relative pronoun, antecedent is עַם / Subject > mp / Actor > antecedent *them*. The 3mp antecedent was most recently referenced by the pronoun suffix of the prior word שְׂפָתָם in clause (c).

לֹא. Adjunct: interpersonal > polarity: negative.

יִשְׁמְעוּ. Finite > yiqtol 3mp / Process > qal שׁמע. *Hear* in the sense of meaningfully hear, or *comprehend*.

אִישׁ. Subject > nominal group: noun common ms. This noun takes the plural Subject *they* and gives it a distributive meaning. *They will not hear, each man, the lip of his neighbor.*

שְׂפַת רֵעֵהוּ. Phenomenon > nominal group: noun common fs const | noun common ms const + pronoun suffix 3ms, antecedent is אִישׁ.

Genesis 11:8-9

[8]And YHVH scattered them from there on the face of all the earth. And they ceased to build the city. [9]Therefore he called its name Bavel, because there YHVH confused the language of all the earth. And from there YHVH scattered them upon the face of all the earth.

11:8 /// וַיָּפֶץ יְהוָה אֹתָם מִשָּׁם עַל־פְּנֵי כָל־הָאָרֶץ //
וַיַּחְדְּלוּ לִבְנֹת הָעִיר׃

וַיָּפֶץ יְהוָה אֹתָם מִשָּׁם עַל־פְּנֵי כָל־הָאָרֶץ. (a) Textuality > conj paratactic expansion / Mood > declarative: past / Transitivity > material: action.

עַל־פְּנֵי כָל־הָאָרֶץ	מִשָּׁם	אֹתָם	יְהוָה	וַיָּפֶץ	**Constituents**
on the face of all the earth	*from there*	*them*	*YHVH*	*and he scattered*	**Translation**
				Theme	**Textuality**
			Subject	Finite	**Mood**
Circum-stance	Circum-stance	Goal	Actor	Process	**Transitivity**

וַיָּפֶץ. Theme: textual / clause conj + Theme: experiential / Finite > wayyiqtol 3ms / Process > hifil פוץ.

יְהוָה. Subject > ms / Actor > noun proper.

אֹתָם. Goal > goal marker + pronoun suffix 3mp, antecedent is עַם.

מִשָּׁם. Circumstance: location, place > prep phrase: prep + Adjunct: experiential > circumstance: place.

עַל־פְּנֵי כָל־הָאָרֶץ. Circumstance: location, place > prep phrase: prep - noun common mp const | noun common ms const - def art + noun common fs.

וַיַּחְדְּלוּ לִבְנֹת הָעִיר. (b) Textuality > conj paratactic expansion / Mood > declarative: past / Transitivity > material: action. The Subject / Actor of this clause is textually absent by ellipsis.

הָעִיר	לִבְנֹת	וַיַּחְדְּלוּ	**Constituents**
the city	*to build*	*and they ceased*	**Translation**
		Theme	**Textuality**
	Complement	Finite	**Mood**
Goal	Process	Process	**Transitivity**

וַיַּחְדְּלוּ לִבְנֹת. Process > verbal group complex: Finite + Complement.

וַיַּחְדְּלוּ. Theme: textual > clause conj + Theme: experiential / Finite > wayyiqtol 3mp / Process > qal חדל.

לִבְנֹת. Complement / Process > inf const qal בנה.

הָעִיר. Goal > nominal group: def art + noun common fs.

11:9 // עַל־כֵּן קָרָא שְׁמָהּ בָּבֶל / כִּי־שָׁם בָּלַל יְהוָה
שְׂפַת כָּל־הָאָרֶץ // וּמִשָּׁם הֱפִיצָם יְהוָה עַל־פְּנֵי
כָּל־הָאָרֶץ׃ פ

עַל־כֵּן קָרָא שְׁמָהּ בָּבֶל. (a) Textuality > conj paratactic expansion / Mood > declarative: past / Transitivity > verbal. The Subject / Sayer is not textually expressed but presumes YHVH from 11:8(a), and is picked up again in clause (b) following.

בָּבֶל	שְׁמָהּ	קָרָא	עַל־כֵּן	**Constituents**
Bavel	*her name*	*he called*	*therefore*	**Translation**
		Theme	Adjunct	**Textuality**
		Finite		**Mood**
Verbiage	Target	Process		**Transitivity**

עַל־כֵּן. Theme: textual / Adjunct > prep phrase: prep + pronoun textual. Literally, *upon so.* This is a conjunctive adjunct. It signals that this clause is a consequence and conclusion of the preceding clauses in its clause complex.

קָרָא. Theme: experiential / Finite > qatal 3ms / Process > qal קרא.

שְׁמָהּ. Target > nominal group: noun common ms const + pronoun suffix 3fs, antecedent is הָעִיר in the prior clause.

בָּבֶל. Verbiage > nominal group: noun proper. This is the proper noun *Babylon.* Everywhere else בָּבֶל occurs in the Hebrew Bible, the versions translate it *Babylon.*

כִּי־שָׁם בָּלַל יְהוָה שְׂפַת כָּל־הָאָרֶץ. (b) Textuality > conj hypotactic expansion / Mood > declarative: past / Transitivity > material: action. In this clause all the functional roles of the process are specified.

שְׂפַת כָּל־הָאָרֶץ	יְהוָה	בָּלַל	שָׁם	כִּי־	**Constituents**
the lip of all the earth	*YHVH*	*he confused*	*there*	*because*	**Translation**
			Theme	Theme	**Textuality**
	Subject	Finite			**Mood**
Goal	Actor	Process	Circumstance		**Transitivity**

כִּי־. Theme: textual > conj.

שָׁם. Theme: experiential / Circumstance: location, place > pronoun textual, antecedent is בָּבֶל *Babylon.*

בָּלַל. Finite > qatal 3ms / Process > qal בלל.

יְהוָה. Subject > ms / Actor > noun proper.

שְׂפַת כָּל־הָאָרֶץ. Goal > nominal group: noun common fs const | noun common ms const - def art + noun common fs.

וּמִשָּׁם הֱפִיצָם יְהוָה עַל־פְּנֵי כָּל־הָאָרֶץ. (c) Textuality > conj paratactic expansion / Mood > declarative: past / Transitivity > material: action. This is the concluding clause of the clause complex in which it is found. Notice the fully explicit transitivity structure, with Process, Actor, Goal, and Circumstance. This is a characteristic of clauses that draw clause complexes and episodes to a conclusion.

עַל־פְּנֵי כָּל־הָאָרֶץ	יְהוָה	הֱפִיצָם	וּמִשָּׁם	**Constituents**
upon the face of all the earth	*YHVH*	*he scattered them*	*and from there*	**Translation**
			Theme	**Textuality**
	Subject	Finite		**Mood**
Circumstance	Actor	Process + Goal	Circumstance	**Transitivity**

וּמִשָּׁם. Theme: textual / clause conj + Theme: experiential / Circumstance: location, place > prep phrase: prep + pronoun textual, antecedent is בָּבֶל *Babylon*. Since the textual pronoun שָׁם is anaphoric, as is the Goal, this clause is paratactic with the preceding clauses in its complex. Making the Circumstance the Theme sublimates the notion of sequential action and focuses the clause on place, in particular Babylon.

הֱפִיצָם. Finite > qatal 3ms / Process > hifil פוץ + Goal > pronoun suffix 3mp, antecedent is עָם. Notice how long it has been since *them* has been identified or renominalized.

יְהוָה. Subject > ms / Actor > noun proper ms.

עַל־פְּנֵי כָּל־הָאָרֶץ. Circumstance: location, place > prep phrase: prep - noun common mp const | noun common ms const - def art + noun common fs.

Genesis 11:10-11

[10]*These are the outcomes of Shem. Shem is 100 years old. And he fathered 'Arpakhshad two years after the flood.* [11]*And Shem lived, after his fathering 'Arpakhshad, 500 years. And he fathered sons and daughters.*

11:10 /// אֵלֶּה תּוֹלְדֹת שֵׁם // שֵׁם בֶּן־מְאַת שָׁנָה // וַיּוֹלֶד אֶת־אַרְפַּכְשָׁד שְׁנָתַיִם אַחַר הַמַּבּוּל׃

אֵלֶּה תּוֹלְדֹת שֵׁם. (a) Textuality > appositive paratactic expansion / Mood > declarative: non-past / Transitivity > relational: identification. This אֵלֶּה clause functions as the Theme of its clause complex. Note that אֵלֶּה is cataphoric, befitting its role of introducing a text unit. In this case it introduces not just its own clause complex, but also the larger text unit that extends through verse 26.

תּוֹלְדֹת שֵׁם	אֵלֶּה	**Constituents**
the outcomes of Shem	*these*	**Translation**
	Theme	**Textuality**
Complement	Subject	**Mood**
Identified	Identifier	**Transitivity**

אֵלֶּה. Theme: experiential / Subject > 3cp / Identifier > pronoun demonstrative 3cp. *These* is congruent with תּוֹלְדֹת, and refers to the content of following clauses (b) and (c), and in an extended sense, all the subsequent generations up to and including Terach.

תּוֹלְדֹת שֵׁם. Complement / Identified > nominal group: noun common fs const | noun proper.

שֵׁם בֶּן־מְאַת שָׁנָה. (b) Textuality > appositive paratactic expansion / Mood > declarative: non-past / Transitivity > relational: attribution.

בֶּן־מְאַת שָׁנָה	שֵׁם	**Constituents**
a son of a hundred years	*Shem*	**Translation**
	Theme	**Textuality**
Complement	Subject	**Mood**
Attribute	Carrier	**Transitivity**

שֵׁם. Theme: experiential / Subject > ms / Carrier > noun proper.

בֶּן־מְאַת שָׁנָה. Complement > ms / Attribute > nominal group: noun common ms const - numeral fs const | noun common fs.

וַיּוֹלֶד אֶת־אַרְפַּכְשָׁד שְׁנָתַיִם אַחַר הַמַּבּוּל. (c) Textuality > conj paratactic expansion / Mood > declarative: past / Transitivity > material: action. The Subject / Actor שֵׁם *Shem* from the prior clause is textually absent here by ellipsis.

שְׁנָתַיִם אַחַר הַמַּבּוּל	אֶת־אַרְפַּכְשָׁד	וַיּוֹלֶד	**Constituents**
two years after the flood	*'Arpakhshad*	*and he fathered*	**Translation**
		Theme	**Textuality**
		Finite	**Mood**
Circumstance	Goal	Process	**Transitivity**

וַיּוֹלֶד. Theme: textual / clause conj + Theme: experiential / Finite > wayyiqtol 3ms / Process > hifil ילד.

אֶת־אַרְפַּכְשָׁד. Goal > nominal group: goal marker - noun proper.

שְׁנָתַיִם אַחַר הַמַּבּוּל. Circumstance: location, time > nominal group complex: Head + Post-modifier.

שְׁנָתַיִם. Head > nominal group: noun numeral fd.

אַחַר הַמַּבּוּל. Post-modifier > prep phrase: prep | def art + noun common ms.

11:11 // וַיְחִי־שֵׁ֗ם [[אַֽחֲרֵי֙ הוֹלִיד֣וֹ אֶת־אַרְפַּכְשָׁ֔ד]] חֲמֵ֥שׁ מֵא֖וֹת שָׁנָ֑ה // וַיּ֥וֹלֶד בָּנִ֖ים וּבָנֽוֹת׃ ס

וַיְחִי־שֵׁם [[אַחֲרֵי הוֹלִידוֹ אֶת־אַרְפַּכְשָׁד]] חֲמֵשׁ מֵאוֹת שָׁנָה. (a) Textuality > conj paratactic expansion / Mood > declarative: past / Transitivity > material: event.

Constituents	וַיְחִי־	שֵׁם	[[אַחֲרֵי הוֹלִידוֹ אֶת־אַרְפַּכְשָׁד]]	חֲמֵשׁ מֵאוֹת שָׁנָה
Translation	*and he lived*	*Shem*	*after his fathering 'Arpakhshad*	*five hundred years*
Textuality	Theme			
Mood	Finite	Subject		
Transitivity	Process	Actor	Circumstance	Range

וַיְחִי־. Theme: textual / clause conj + Theme: experiential / Finite > wayyiqtol 3ms / Process > qal חיה.

שֵׁם. Subject > ms / Actor > nominal group: noun proper.

אַחֲרֵי הוֹלִידוֹ אֶת־אַרְפַּכְשָׁד. (i) Circumstance: location, time >> Textuality > embedded prep clause / Transitivity > material: action.

Constituents	אַחֲרֵי	הוֹלִידוֹ	אֶת־אַרְפַּכְשָׁד
Translation	*after*	*his fathering*	*'Arpakhshad*
Textuality	Theme	Theme	
Transitivity		Process + Actor	Goal

אַחֲרֵי. Theme: textual > prep.

הוֹלִידוֹ. Theme: experiential / Process > inf const hifil ילד + Actor > pronoun suffix 3ms, antecedent is שֵׁם.

אֶת־אַרְפַּכְשָׁד. Goal > nominal group: goal marker - noun proper ms.

חֲמֵשׁ מֵאוֹת שָׁנָה. Range > nominal group: numeral fs const | noun common fp const | noun common fs. The first numeral conditions *hundreds* rather than *year*.

וַיּוֹלֶד בָּנִים וּבָנוֹת. (b) Textuality > conj paratactic expansion / Mood > declarative: past / Transitivity > material: action. The Subject / Actor is **שֵׁם**.

בָּנִים וּבָנוֹת	וַיּוֹלֶד	**Constituents**
sons and daughters	*and he fathered*	**Translation**
	Theme	**Textuality**
	Finite	**Mood**
Goal	Process	**Transitivity**

וַיּוֹלֶד. Theme: textual / clause conj + Theme: experiential / Finite > wayyiqtol 3ms / Process > hifil **ילד**.

בָּנִים וּבָנוֹת. Goal > nominal group: noun common mp | group conj + noun common fp.

Genesis 11:12-13

[12]And 'Arpakhshad is alive 35 years. And he fathered Shelach. [13]And 'Arpakhshad lived, after his fathering Shelach, 403 years. And he fathered sons and daughters.

11:12 /// וְאַרְפַּכְשַׁ֣ד חַ֔י חָמֵ֥שׁ וּשְׁלֹשִׁ֖ים שָׁנָ֑ה // וַיּ֖וֹלֶד
אֶת־שָֽׁלַח׃

וְאַרְפַּכְשַׁד חַי חָמֵשׁ וּשְׁלֹשִׁים שָׁנָה. (a) Textuality > conj paratactic expansion / Mood > declarative: past / Transitivity > relational: attribution. This clause does not specify tense, which is nonetheless clear from the context and from the fact that it has to do with the span of a life that obviously by then had already ended.

חָמֵשׁ וּשְׁלֹשִׁים שָׁנָה	חַי	וְאַרְפַּכְשַׁד	**Constituents**
five and thirty years	*alive*	*and 'Arpakhshad*	**Translation**
		Theme	**Textuality**
	Complement	Subject	**Mood**
Range	Attribute	Carrier	**Transitivity**

וְאַרְפַּכְשַׁד. Theme: experiential / Subject > ms / Carrier > nominal group: noun proper.

חַי. Complement > 3ms / Attribute > adj ms.

חָמֵשׁ וּשְׁלֹשִׁים שָׁנָה. Range > nominal group complex: numeral fs ı group conj + numeral fp ı noun common fs.

וַיּוֹלֶד אֶת־שָׁלַח. (b) Textuality > conj paratactic expansion / Mood > declarative: past / Transitivity > material: action. The Subject / Actor אַרְפַּכְשַׁד *'Arpakhshad* is not specified because it is presumed from the prior clause, absent here by ellipsis.

אֶת־שָׁלַח	וַיּוֹלֶד	**Constituents**
Shelach	*and he fathered*	**Translation**
	Theme	**Textuality**
	Finite	**Mood**
Goal	Process	**Transitivity**

וַיּוֹלֶד. Theme: textual / clause conj + Theme: experiential / Finite > wayyiqtol 3ms / Process > hifil ילד.

אֶת־שָׁלַח. Goal > nominal group: goal marker - noun proper ms. The *qamets* is due to stress lengthening.

11:13 // וַיְחִי אַרְפַּכְשַׁד אַחֲרֵי הוֹלִידוֹ אֶת־שֶׁלַח שָׁלֹשׁ
שָׁנִים וְאַרְבַּע מֵאוֹת שָׁנָה // וַיּוֹלֶד בָּנִים וּבָנוֹת׃ ס

וַיְחִי אַרְפַּכְשַׁד [[אַחֲרֵי הוֹלִידוֹ אֶת־שֶׁלַח]] שָׁלֹשׁ שָׁנִים

וְאַרְבַּע מֵאוֹת שָׁנָה. (a) Textuality > conj paratactic expansion / Mood > declarative: past / Transitivity > material: event.

שָׁלֹשׁ שָׁנִים וְאַרְבַּע מֵאוֹת שָׁנָה	[[אַחֲרֵי הוֹלִידוֹ אֶת־שָׁלַח]]	אַרְפַּכְשַׁד	וַיְחִי־	**Constituents**
three years and four hundred years	*after his fathering Shelach*	*'Arpakhshad*	*and he lived*	**Translation**
			Theme	**Textuality**
		Subject	Finite	**Mood**
Range	Circumstance	Actor	Process	**Transitivity**

וַיְחִי־. Theme: textual / clause conj + Theme: experiential / Finite > wayyiqtol 3ms / Process > qal חיה.

אַרְפַּכְשַׁד. Subject > ms / Actor > nominal group: noun proper.

אַחֲרֵי הוֹלִידוֹ אֶת־שָׁלַח. (i) Circumstance: location, time >> Textuality > embedded expansion: prep clause / Transitivity > matierial: action.

אֶת־שָׁלַח	הוֹלִידוֹ	אַחֲרֵי	**Constituents**
Shelach	*his fathering*	*after*	**Translation**
	Theme	Theme	**Textuality**
Goal	Process + Actor		**Transitivity**

אַחֲרֵי. Theme: textual > prep.

הוֹלִידוֹ. Theme: experiential / Process > inf const hifil ילד + Actor > pronoun suffix 3ms, antecedent is אַרְפַּכְשַׁד.

אֶת־שָׁלַח. Goal > nominal group: goal marker - noun proper ms.

שָׁלֹשׁ שָׁנִים וְאַרְבַּע מֵאוֹת שָׁנָה. Range > nominal group complex: numeral fs const | noun common fp const | numeral fs | numeral fp | noun common fs.

וַיּוֹלֶד בָּנִים וּבָנוֹת. (b) Textuality > conj paratactic expansion / Mood > declarative: past / Transitivity > material: action. The Subject / Actor is אַרְפַּכְשַׁד.

בָּנִים וּבָנוֹת	וַיּוֹלֶד	**Constituents**
sons and daughters	*and he fathered*	**Translation**
	Theme	**Textuality**
	Finite	**Mood**
Goal	Process	**Transitivity**

וַיּוֹלֶד. Theme: textual / clause conj + Theme: experiential / Finite > wayyiqtol 3ms / Process > hifil ילד.

בָּנִים וּבָנוֹת. Goal > nominal group: noun common mp | group conj + noun common fp.

Genesis 11:14-15

[14]And Shelach is alive 30 years. And he fathered 'Ever. [15]And Shelach lived, after his fathering 'Ever, 403 years. And he fathered sons and daughters.

11:14 /// וְשֶׁלַח חַי שְׁלֹשִׁים שָׁנָה // וַיּוֹלֶד אֶת־עֵבֶר׃

וְשֶׁלַח חַי שְׁלֹשִׁים שָׁנָה . (a) Textuality > conj paratactic expansion / Mood > declarative: past / Transitivity > relational: attribution.

שְׁלֹשִׁים שָׁנָה	חַי	וְשֶׁלַח	**Constituents**
thirty years	*alive*	*and Shelach*	**Translation**
		Theme	**Textuality**
		Subject	**Mood**
Range	Attribute	Carrier	**Transitivity**

וְשֶׁלַח. Theme: experiential / Subject > ms / Carrier > nominal group: noun proper.

חַי. Complement > 3ms / Attribute > adjective ms.

שְׁלֹשִׁים שָׁנָה. Range > nominal group: numeral fs ׀ noun common fs.

וַיּוֹלֶד אֶת־עֵבֶר. (b) Textuality > conj paratactic expansion / Mood > declarative: past / Transitivity > material: action.

אֶת־עֵבֶר	וַיּוֹלֶד	**Constituents**
'Ever	*and he fathered*	**Translation**
	Theme	**Textuality**
	Finite	**Mood**
Goal	Process	**Transitivity**

וַיּוֹלֶד. Theme: textual / clause conj + Theme: experiential / Finite > wayyiqtol 3ms / Process > hifil ילד.

אֶת־עֵבֶר. Goal > nominal group: goal marker - noun proper ms.

11:15 // וַֽיְחִי־שֶׁ֗לַח אַחֲרֵי֙ הוֹלִיד֣וֹ אֶת־עֵ֔בֶר שָׁלֹ֣שׁ שָׁנִ֔ים
וְאַרְבַּ֥ע מֵא֖וֹת שָׁנָ֑ה // וַיּ֥וֹלֶד בָּנִ֖ים וּבָנֽוֹת׃ ס

וַיְחִי־שֶׁלַח [[אַחֲרֵי הוֹלִידוֹ אֶת־עֵבֶר]] שָׁלֹשׁ שָׁנִים וְאַרְבַּע מֵאוֹת שָׁנָה. (a) Textuality > conj paratactic expansion / Mood > declarative: past / Transitivity > material: event.

שָׁלֹשׁ שָׁנִים וְאַרְבַּע מֵאוֹת שָׁנָה	[[אַחֲרֵי הוֹלִידוֹ אֶת־עֵבֶר]]	שֶׁלַח	וַיְחִי־	**Constituents**
three years and four hundred years	*after his fathering 'Ever*	*Shelach*	*and he lived*	**Translation**
			Theme	**Textuality**
		Subject	Finite	**Mood**
Range	Circumstance	Actor	Process	**Transitivity**

וַיְחִי־. Theme: textual / clause conj + Theme: experiential / Finite > wayyiqtol 3ms / Process > qal חיה.

שֶׁלַח. Subject > ms / Actor > nominal group: noun proper.

אַחֲרֵי הוֹלִידוֹ אֶת־עֵבֶר. (i) Circumstance: location, time >> Textuality > embedded expansion: prep clause / Transitivity > material: action.

אֶת־עֵבֶר	הוֹלִידוֹ	אַחֲרֵי	**Constituents**
'Ever	*his fathering*	*after*	**Translation**
	Theme	Theme	**Textuality**
Goal	Process + Actor		**Transitivity**

אַחֲרֵי. Theme: textual > prep.

הוֹלִידוֹ. Theme: experiential / Process > inf const hifil ילד + Actor > pronoun suffix 3ms, antecedent is שֶׁלַח.

אֶת־עֵבֶר. Goal > nominal group: goal marker - noun proper ms.

שָׁלֹשׁ שָׁנִים וְאַרְבַּע מֵאוֹת שָׁנָה. Range > nominal group complex: numeral fs const | noun common fp const | numeral fs | numeral fp | noun common fs.

וַיּוֹלֶד בָּנִים וּבָנוֹת. (b) Textuality > conj paratactic expansion / Mood > declarative: past / Transitivity > material: action. The Subject / Actor is שֶׁלַח.

בָּנִים וּבָנוֹת	וַיּוֹלֶד	**Constituents**
sons and daughters	*and he fathered*	**Translation**
	Theme	**Textuality**
	Finite	**Mood**
Goal	Process	**Transitivity**

וַיּוֹלֶד. Theme: textual / clause conj + Theme: experiential / Finite > wayyiqtol 3ms / Process > hifil ילד.

בָּנִים וּבָנוֹת. Goal > nominal group: noun common mp | group conj + noun common fp.

Genesis 11:16-17

[16]And 'Ever lived 34 years. And he fathered Peleg. [17]And 'Ever lived, after his fathering Peleg, 430 years. And he fathered sons and daughters.

11:16 /// וַֽיְחִי־עֵ֕בֶר אַרְבַּ֥ע וּשְׁלֹשִׁ֖ים שָׁנָ֑ה // וַיּ֖וֹלֶד אֶת־פָּֽלֶג׃

וַיְחִי־עֵבֶר אַרְבַּע וּשְׁלֹשִׁים שָׁנָה. (a) Textuality > conj paratactic expansion / Mood > declarative: past / Transitivity > material: event. Compare this to 11:14 etc. which use חַי rather than a verb. The verb construes a material rather than relational process.

אַרְבַּע וּשְׁלֹשִׁים שָׁנָה	עֵבֶר	וַיְחִי־	**Constituents**
four and thirty years	*'Ever*	*and he lived*	**Translation**
		Theme	**Textuality**
	Subject	Finite	**Mood**
Range	Actor	Process	**Transitivity**

וַיְחִי־. Theme: textual / clause conj + Theme: experiential / Finite > wayyiqtol 3ms / Process > qal חיה.

עֵבֶר. Subject > ms / Actor > nominal group: noun proper.

אַרְבַּע וּשְׁלֹשִׁים שָׁנָה. Range > nominal group complex: numeral fs ׀ group conj + numeral fp ׀ noun common fs.

וַיּוֹלֶד אֶת־פָּלֶג. (b) Textuality > conj paratactic expansion / Mood > declarative: past / Transitivity > material: action. The Subject / Actor is עֵבֶר.

אֶת־פָּלֶג	וַיּוֹלֶד	**Constituents**
Peleg	*and he fathered*	**Translation**
	Theme	**Textuality**
	Finite	**Mood**
Goal	Process	**Transitivity**

וַיּ֥וֹלֶד. Theme: textual / clause conj + Theme: experiential / Finite > wayyiqtol 3ms / Process > hifil ילד.

אֶת־פָּֽלֶג. Goal > nominal group: goal marker - noun proper ms.

11:17 // וַֽיְחִי־עֵ֗בֶר אַחֲרֵי֙ הוֹלִיד֣וֹ אֶת־פֶּ֔לֶג שְׁלֹשִׁ֣ים שָׁנָ֔ה
וְאַרְבַּ֥ע מֵא֖וֹת שָׁנָ֑ה // וַיּ֥וֹלֶד בָּנִ֖ים וּבָנֽוֹת׃ ס

וַיְחִי־עֵבֶר [[אַחֲרֵי הוֹלִידוֹ אֶת־פֶּלֶג]] שְׁלֹשִׁים שָׁנָה וְאַרְבַּע מֵאוֹת שָׁנָה. (a) Textuality > conj paratactic expansion / Mood > declarative: past / Transitivity > material: event.

שְׁלֹשִׁים שָׁנָה וְאַרְבַּע מֵאוֹת שָׁנָה	[[אַחֲרֵי הוֹלִידוֹ אֶת־פֶּלֶג]]	עֵבֶר	וַיְחִי־	**Constituents**
thirty years and four hundred years	*after his fathering Peleg*	*'Ever*	*and he lived*	**Translation**
			Theme	**Textuality**
		Subject	Finite	**Mood**
Range	Circumstance	Actor	Process	**Transitivity**

וַיְחִי־. Theme: textual / clause conj + Theme: experiential / Finite > wayyiqtol 3ms / Process > qal חיה.

עֵבֶר. Subject > ms / Actor > nominal group: noun proper.

אַחֲרֵי הוֹלִידוֹ אֶת־פֶּלֶג. (i) Circumstance: location, time >> Textuality > embedded expansion: prep clause / Transitivity > material: action.

אֶת־פֶּלֶג	הוֹלִידוֹ	אַחֲרֵי	**Constituents**
Peleg	*his fathering*	*after*	**Translation**
	Theme	Theme	**Textuality**
Goal	Process + Actor		**Transitivity**

אַחֲרֵי. Theme: textual > prep.

הוֹלִידוֹ. Theme: experiential / Process > inf const hifil ילד + Actor > pronoun suffix 3ms, antecedent is עֵבֶר.

אֶת־פֶּלֶג. Goal > nominal group: goal marker - noun proper ms.

שְׁלֹשִׁים שָׁנָה וְאַרְבַּע מֵאוֹת שָׁנָה. Range > nominal group complex: numeral fs ו noun common fs ו group conj + numeral fs ו numeral fp ו noun common fs. The numeral conditions *hundreds* rather than *year*.

וַיּוֹלֶד בָּנִים וּבָנוֹת. (b) Textuality > conj paratactic expansion / Mood > declarative: past / Transitivity > material: action. The Subject / Actor is עֵבֶר.

בָּנִים וּבָנוֹת	וַיּוֹלֶד	**Constituents**
sons and daughters	*and he fathered*	**Translation**
	Theme	**Textuality**
	Finite	**Mood**
Goal	Process	**Transitivity**

וַיּוֹלֶד. Theme: textual / clause conj + Theme: experiential / Finite > wayyiqtol 3ms / Process > hifil ילד.

בָּנִים וּבָנוֹת. Goal > nominal group: noun common mp ו group conj + noun common fp.

Genesis 11:18-19

[18]And Peleg lived 30 years. And he fathered Re'u. [19]And Peleg lived, after his fathering Re'u, 209 years. And he fathered sons and daughters.

11:18 /// וַיְחִי־פֶ֖לֶג שְׁלֹשִׁ֣ים שָׁנָ֑ה // וַיּ֖וֹלֶד אֶת־רְעֽוּ׃

וַיְחִי־פֶלֶג שְׁלֹשִׁים שָׁנָה. (a) Textuality > conj paratactic expansion / Mood > declarative: past / Transitivity > material: event.

שְׁלֹשִׁים שָׁנָה	פֶּלֶג	וַיְחִי־	**Constituents**
thirty years	*Peleg*	*and he lived*	**Translation**
		Theme	**Textuality**
	Subject	Finite	**Mood**
Range	Actor	Process	**Transitivity**

וַיְחִי־. Theme: textual / clause conj + Theme: experiential / Finite > wayyiqtol 3ms / Process > qal חיה.

עֵבֶר. Subject > ms / Actor > noun proper.

שְׁלֹשִׁים שָׁנָה. Range > nominal group: numeral fp ׀ noun common fs.

וַיּוֹלֶד אֶת־רְעוּ. (b) Textuality > conj paratactic expansion / Mood > declarative: past / Transitivity > material: action. The Subject / Actor is פֶּלֶג.

אֶת־רְעוּ	וַיּוֹלֶד	**Constituents**
Re'u	*and he fathered*	**Translation**
	Theme	**Textuality**
	Finite	**Mood**
Goal	Process	**Transitivity**

וַיּוֹלֶד. Theme: textual / clause conj + Theme: experiential / Finite > wayyiqtol 3ms / Process > hifil ילד.

אֶת־רְעוּ. Goal > nominal group: goal marker - noun proper ms.

11:19 // וַֽיְחִי־פֶ֗לֶג אַחֲרֵי֙ הוֹלִיד֣וֹ אֶת־רְע֔וּ תֵּ֧שַׁע שָׁנִ֛ים
וּמָאתַ֥יִם שָׁנָ֖ה // וַיּ֥וֹלֶד בָּנִ֖ים וּבָנֽוֹת׃ ס

וַיְחִי־פֶלֶג [[אַחֲרֵי הוֹלִידוֹ אֶת־רְעוּ]] תֵּשַׁע שָׁנִים וּמָאתַיִם שָׁנָה. (a) Textuality > conj paratactic expansion / Mood > declarative: past / Transitivity > material: event.

תְּשַׁע שָׁנִים וּמָאתַיִם שָׁנָה	[[אַחֲרֵי הוֹלִידוֹ אֶת־רְעוּ]]	פֶּלֶג	וַיְחִי־	**Constituents**
nine years and two hundred years	*after his fathering Re'u*	*Peleg*	*and he lived*	**Translation**
			Theme	**Textuality**
		Subject	Finite	**Mood**
Range	Circumstance	Actor	Process	**Transitivity**

וַיְחִי־. Theme: textual / clause conj + Theme: experiential / Finite > wayyiqtol 3ms / Process > qal חיה.

פֶּלֶג. Subject > ms / Actor > nominal group: noun proper.

אַחֲרֵי הוֹלִידוֹ אֶת־רְעוּ. (i) Circumstance: location, time >> Textuality > embedded expansion: prep clause / Transitivity > material: action.

אֶת־רְעוּ	הוֹלִידוֹ	אַחֲרֵי	**Constituents**
Re'u	*his fathering*	*after*	**Translation**
	Theme	Theme	**Textuality**
Goal	Process + Actor		**Transitivity**

אַחֲרֵי. Theme: textual > prep.

הוֹלִידוֹ. Theme: experiential / Process > inf const hifil ילד + Actor > pronoun suffix 3ms, antecedent is פֶּלֶג.

אֶת־רְעוּ. Goal > nominal group: goal marker - noun proper ms.

תְּשַׁע שָׁנִים וּמָאתַיִם שָׁנָה. Range > nominal group complex: numeral fs ׀ noun common fp ׀ group conj + numeral fd ׀ noun common fs.

וַיּוֹלֶד בָּנִים וּבָנוֹת. (b) Textuality > conj paratactic expansion / Mood > declarative: past / Transitivity > material: action. The Subject / Actor is פֶּלֶג.

בָּנִים וּבָנוֹת	וַיּ֖וֹלֶד	**Constituents**
sons and daughters	*and he fathered*	**Translation**
	Theme	**Textuality**
	Finite	**Mood**
Goal	Process	**Transitivity**

וַיּ֖וֹלֶד. Theme: textual / clause conj + Theme: experiential / Finite > wayyiqtol 3ms / Process > hifil ילד.

בָּנִים וּבָנוֹת. Goal > nominal group: noun common mp | group conj + noun common fp.

Genesis 11:20-21

[20]And Re'u lived 32 years. And he fathered Serug. [21]And Re'u lived, after his fathering Serug, 207 years. And he fathered sons and daughters.

11:20 /// וַיְחִ֣י רְע֔וּ שְׁתַּ֥יִם וּשְׁלֹשִׁ֖ים שָׁנָ֑ה // וַיּ֖וֹלֶד אֶת־
שְׂרֽוּג׃

וַיְחִי רְעוּ שְׁתַּיִם וּשְׁלֹשִׁים שָׁנָה. (a) Textuality > conj paratactic expansion / Mood > declarative: past / Transitivity > material: event.

שְׁתַּיִם וּשְׁלֹשִׁים שָׁנָה	רְעוּ	וַיְחִי־	**Constituents**
two and thirty years	*Re'u*	*and he lived*	**Translation**
		Theme	**Textuality**
	Subject	Finite	**Mood**
Range	Actor	Process	**Transitivity**

וַיְחִי־. Theme: textual / clause conj + Theme: experiential / Finite > wayyiqtol 3ms / Process > qal חיה.

רְעוּ. Subject > ms / Actor > nominal group: noun proper.

שְׁתַּיִם וּשְׁלֹשִׁים שָׁנָה. Range > nominal group: numeral fd | group conj + numeral fp | noun common fs.

וַיּוֹלֶד אֶת־שְׂרוּג. (b) Textuality > conj paratactic expansion / Mood > declarative: past / Transitivity > material: action. The Subject / Actor is רְעוּ.

אֶת־שְׂרוּג	וַיּוֹלֶד	**Constituents**
Serug	*and he fathered*	**Translation**
	Theme	**Textuality**
	Finite	**Mood**
Goal	Process	**Transitivity**

וַיּוֹלֶד. Theme: textual / clause conj + Theme: experiential / Finite > wayyiqtol 3ms / Process > hifil ילד.

אֶת־שְׂרוּג. Goal > nominal group: goal marker - noun proper ms.

11:21 // וַיְחִי רְעוּ אַחֲרֵי הוֹלִידוֹ אֶת־שְׂרוּג שֶׁבַע שָׁנִים
וּמָאתַיִם שָׁנָה // וַיּוֹלֶד בָּנִים וּבָנוֹת׃ ס

וַיְחִי רְעוּ [[אַחֲרֵי הוֹלִידוֹ אֶת־שְׂרוּג]] שֶׁבַע שָׁנִים וּמָאתַיִם שָׁנָה. (a) Textuality > conj paratactic expansion / Mood > declarative: past / Transitivity > material: event.

שֶׁבַע שָׁנִים וּמָאתַיִם שָׁנָה	[[אַחֲרֵי הוֹלִידוֹ אֶת־שְׂרוּג]]	רְעוּ	וַיְחִי־	**Constituents**
seven years and two hundred years	*after his fathering Serug*	*Re'u*	*and he lived*	**Translation**
			Theme	**Textuality**
		Subject	Finite	**Mood**
Range	Circumstance	Actor	Process	**Transitivity**

וַיְחִי־. Theme: textual / clause conj + Theme: experiential / Finite > wayyiqtol 3ms / Process > qal חיה.

רְעוּ. Subject > ms / Actor > nominal group: noun proper.

אַחֲרֵי הוֹלִידוֹ אֶת־שְׂרוּג. (i) Circumstance: location, time >> Textuality > embedded expansion: prep clause.

אֶת־שְׂרוּג	הוֹלִידוֹ	אַחֲרֵי	**Constituents**
Serug	*his fathering*	*after*	**Translation**
	Theme	Theme	**Textuality**
Goal	Process + Actor		**Transitivity**

אַחֲרֵי. Theme: textual > prep.

הוֹלִידוֹ. Theme: experiential / Process > inf const hifil ילד + Actor > pronoun suffix 3ms, antecedent is רְעוּ.

אֶת־שְׂרוּג. Goal > nominal group: goal marker - noun proper ms.

שֶׁבַע שָׁנִים וּמָאתַיִם שָׁנָה. Range > nominal group complex: numeral fs ı noun common fp ı group conj + numeral fd ı noun common fs.

וַיּוֹלֶד בָּנִים וּבָנוֹת. (b) Textuality > conj paratactic expansion / Mood > declarative: past / Transitivity > material: action. The Subject / Actor is רְעוּ.

בָּנִים וּבָנוֹת	וַיּוֹלֶד	**Constituents**
sons and daughters	*and he fathered*	**Translation**
	Theme	**Textuality**
	Finite	**Mood**
Goal	Process	**Transitivity**

וַיּוֹלֶד. Theme: textual / clause conj + Theme: experiential / Finite > wayyiqtol 3ms / Process > hifil ילד.

בָּנִים וּבָנוֹת. Goal > nominal group: noun common mp ı group conj + noun common fp.

Genesis 11:22-23

[22]And Serug lived 30 years. And he fathered Nachor. [23]And Serug lived, after his fathering Nachor, 200 years. And he fathered sons and daughters.

11:22 /// וַיְחִי שְׂרוּג שְׁלֹשִׁים שָׁנָה // וַיּוֹלֶד אֶת־נָחוֹר׃

וַיְחִי שְׂרוּג שְׁלֹשִׁים שָׁנָה. (a) Textuality > conj paratactic expansion / Mood > declarative: past / Transitivity > material: event.

שְׁלֹשִׁים שָׁנָה	שְׂרוּג	וַיְחִי־	**Constituents**
thirty years	*Serug*	*and he lived*	**Translation**
		Theme	**Textuality**
	Subject	Finite	**Mood**
Range	Actor	Process	**Transitivity**

וַיְחִי־. Theme: textual / clause conj + Theme: experiential / Finite > wayyiqtol 3ms / Process > qal חיה.

שְׂרוּג. Subject > ms / Actor > nominal group: noun proper.

שְׁלֹשִׁים שָׁנָה. Range > nominal group: numeral fp | noun common fs.

וַיּוֹלֶד אֶת־נָחוֹר. (b) Textuality > conj paratactic expansion / Mood > declarative: past / Transitivity > material: action. The Subject / Actor is שְׂרוּג.

אֶת־נָחוֹר	וַיּוֹלֶד	**Constituents**
Nachor	*and he fathered*	**Translation**
	Theme	**Textuality**
	Finite	**Mood**
Goal	Process	**Transitivity**

וַיּוֹלֶד. Theme: textual / clause conj + Theme: experiential / Finite > wayyiqtol 3ms / Process > hifil ילד.

אֶת־נָחוֹר. Goal > nominal group: goal marker - noun proper ms.

11:23 // וַיְחִי שְׂרוּג אַחֲרֵי הוֹלִידוֹ אֶת־נָחוֹר מָאתַיִם שָׁנָה
// וַיּוֹלֶד בָּנִים וּבָנוֹת׃ ס

(a) וַיְחִי שְׂרוּג [[אַחֲרֵי הוֹלִידוֹ אֶת־נָחוֹר]] מָאתַיִם שָׁנָה.
Textuality > conj paratactic expansion / Mood > declarative: past / Transitivity > material: event.

Constituents	וַיְחִי־	שְׂרוּג	[[אַחֲרֵי הוֹלִידוֹ אֶת־נָחוֹר]]	מָאתַיִם שָׁנָה
Translation	*and he lived*	*Serug*	*after his fathering Nachor*	*two hundred years*
Textuality	Theme	Theme		
Mood	Finite	Subject		
Transitivity	Process	Actor	Circumstance	Range

וַיְחִי־. Theme: textual / clause conj + Theme: experiential / Finite > wayyiqtol 3ms / Process > qal חיה.

שְׂרוּג. Subject > ms / Actor > nominal group: noun proper.

אַחֲרֵי הוֹלִידוֹ אֶת־נָחוֹר. (i) Circumstance: location, time >> Textuality > embedded expansion: prep clause / Transitivity > material: action.

Constituents	אַחֲרֵי	הוֹלִידוֹ	אֶת־נָחוֹר
Translation	*after*	*his fathering*	*Nachor*
Textuality	Theme	Theme	
Transitivity		Process + Actor	Goal

אַחֲרֵי. Theme: textual > prep.

הוֹלִידוֹ. Theme: experiential / Process > inf const hifil ילד + Actor > pronoun suffix 3ms, antecedent is שְׂרוּג.

אֶת־נָחוֹר. Goal > nominal group: goal marker - noun proper ms.

מָאתַ֥יִם שָׁנָ֑ה. Range > nominal group: numeral fd | noun common fs.

וַיּ֥וֹלֶד בָּנִ֖ים וּבָנֽוֹת. (b) Textuality > conj paratactic expansion / Mood > declarative: past / Transitivity > material: action. The Subject / Actor is שְׂרוּג.

בָּנִים וּבָנוֹת	וַיּוֹלֶד	**Constituents**
sons and daughters	*and he fathered*	**Translation**
	Theme	**Textuality**
	Finite	**Mood**
Goal	Process	**Transitivity**

וַיּוֹלֶד. Theme: textual / clause conj + Theme: experiential / Finite > wayyiqtol 3ms / Process > hifil ילד.

בָּנִים וּבָנוֹת. Goal > nominal group: noun common mp | group conj + noun common fp.

Genesis 11:24-25

[24]And Nachor lived 29 years. And he fathered Terach. [25]And Nachor lived, after his fathering Terach, 119 years. And he fathered sons and daughters.

11:24 /// וַיְחִ֣י נָח֔וֹר תֵּ֥שַׁע וְעֶשְׂרִ֖ים שָׁנָ֑ה // וַיּ֖וֹלֶד אֶת־
תָּֽרַח׃

וַיְחִי נָחוֹר תֵּשַׁע וְעֶשְׂרִים שָׁנָה. (a) Textuality > conj paratactic expansion / Mood > declarative: past / Transitivity > material: event.

תֵּשַׁע וְעֶשְׂרִים שָׁנָה	נָחוֹר	וַיְחִי־	**Constituents**
nine and twenty years	*Nachor*	*and he lived*	**Translation**
		Theme	**Textuality**
	Subject	Finite	**Mood**
Range	Actor	Process	**Transitivity**

וַיְחִי־. Theme: textual / clause conj + Theme: experiential / Finite > wayyiqtol 3ms / Process > qal חיה.

נָחוֹר. Subject > ms / Actor > nominal group: noun proper.

תֵּשַׁע וְעֶשְׂרִים שָׁנָה. Range > nominal group: numeral fp ǀ group conj + numeral fp ǀ noun common fs.

וַיּוֹלֶד אֶת־תָּרַח. (b) Textuality > conj paratactic expansion / Mood > declarative: past / Transitivity > material: action. The Subject / Actor is נָחוֹר.

אֶת־תָּרַח	וַיּוֹלֶד	**Constituents**
Terach	*and he fathered*	**Translation**
	Theme	**Textuality**
	Finite	**Mood**
Goal	Process	**Transitivity**

וַיּוֹלֶד. Theme: textual / clause conj + Theme: experiential / Finite > wayyiqtol 3ms / Process > hifil ילד.

אֶת־תָּרַח. Goal > nominal group: goal marker - noun proper ms.

11:25 // וַיְחִֽי נָח֗וֹר אַחֲרֵי֙ הוֹלִיד֣וֹ אֶת־תֶּ֔רַח תְּשַֽׁע־עֶשְׂרֵ֥ה
שָׁנָ֖ה וּמְאַ֣ת שָׁנָ֑ה // וַיּ֥וֹלֶד בָּנִ֖ים וּבָנֽוֹת׃ ס

וַיְחִי נָחוֹר [[אַחֲרֵי הוֹלִידוֹ אֶת־תֶּרַח]] תְּשַׁע־עֶשְׂרֵה שָׁנָה וּמְאַת שָׁנָה. (a) Textuality > conj paratactic expansion / Mood > declarative: past / Transitivity > material: event.

תְּשַׁע־עֶשְׂרֵה שָׁנָה וּמְאַת שָׁנָה	[[אַחֲרֵי הוֹלִידוֹ אֶת־תֶּרַח]]	נָחוֹר	וַיְחִי־	**Constituents**
nineteen years and a hundred years	*after his fathering Terach*	*Nachor*	*and he lived*	**Translation**
			Theme	**Textuality**
		Subject	Finite	**Mood**
Range	Circumstance	Actor	Process	**Transitivity**

וַיְחִי־. Theme: textual / clause conj + Theme: experiential / Finite > wayyiqtol 3ms / Process > qal חיה.

נָחוֹר. Subject > ms / Actor > nominal group: noun proper.

אַחֲרֵי הוֹלִידוֹ אֶת־תֶּרַח. (i) Circumstance: location, time >> Textuality > embedded expansion: prep clause / Transitivity > material: action.

אֶת־תֶּרַח	הוֹלִידוֹ	אַחֲרֵי	**Constituents**
Terach	*his fathering*	*after*	**Translation**
	Theme	Theme	**Textuality**
Goal	Process + Actor		**Transitivity**

אַחֲרֵי. Theme: textual > prep.

הוֹלִידוֹ. Theme: experiential / Process > inf const hifil ילד + Actor > pronoun suffix 3ms, antecedent is נָחוֹר.

אֶת־תֶּרַח. Goal > nominal group: goal marker - noun proper ms.

תְּשַׁע־עֶשְׂרֵה שָׁנָה וּמְאַת שָׁנָה. Range > nominal group complex: numeral fs - numeral fs ı noun common fs ı group conj + numeral fs ı noun common fs.

וַיּוֹלֶד בָּנִים וּבָנוֹת. (b) Textuality > conj paratactic expansion / Mood > declarative: past / Transitivity > material: action. The Subject / Actor is נָחוֹר.

בָּנִים וּבָנוֹת	וַיּוֹלֶד	Constituents
sons and daughters	*and he fathered*	**Translation**
	Theme	**Textuality**
	Finite	**Mood**
Goal	Process	**Transitivity**

וַיּוֹלֶד. Theme: textual / clause conj + Theme: experiential / Finite > wayyiqtol 3ms / Process > hifil ילד.

בָּנִים וּבָנוֹת. Goal > nominal group: noun common mp ׀ group conj + noun common fp.

Genesis 11:26

[26]And Terach lived 40 years. And he fathered 'Avram, Nachor, and Haran.

11:26 /// וַיְחִי־תֶרַח שִׁבְעִים שָׁנָה // וַיּוֹלֶד אֶת־אַבְרָם
אֶת־נָחוֹר וְאֶת־הָרָן׃

וַיְחִי־תֶרַח שִׁבְעִים שָׁנָה. (a) Textuality > conj paratactic expansion / Mood > declarative: past / Transitivity > material: event.

שִׁבְעִים שָׁנָה	תֶרַח	וַיְחִי־	Constituents
forty years	*Terach*	*and he lived*	**Translation**
		Theme	**Textuality**
	Subject	Finite	**Mood**
Range	Actor	Process	**Transitivity**

וַיְחִי־. Theme: textual / clause conj + Theme: experiential / Finite > wayyiqtol 3ms / Process > qal חיה.

תֶרַח. Subject > ms / Actor > nominal group: noun proper.

שִׁבְעִים שָׁנָה. Range > nominal group: numeral fp ׀ noun common fs.

וַיּוֹלֶד אֶת־אַבְרָם אֶת־נָחוֹר וְאֶת־הָרָן. (b) Textuality > conj paratactic expansion / Mood > declarative: past / Transitivity > material: action. The Subject / Actor is תֶּרַח.

אֶת־אַבְרָם אֶת־נָחוֹר וְאֶת־הָרָן	וַיּוֹלֶד	**Constituents**
'Avram Nachor and Haran	*and he fathered*	**Translation**
	Theme	**Textuality**
	Finite	**Mood**
Goal	Process	**Transitivity**

וַיּוֹלֶד. Theme: textual / clause conj + Theme: experiential / Finite > wayyiqtol 3ms / Process > hifil ילד.

אֶת־אַבְרָם אֶת־נָחוֹר וְאֶת־הָרָן. Goal > nominal group complex: goal marker - noun proper ms | goal marker - noun proper ms | group conj + goal marker - noun proper ms. Regarding the name נָחוֹר, the genealogy could get confusing in so far as this *Nachor* has a grandfather named *Nachor*; see 11:22-25.

Genesis 11:27-30

[27]And these are the outcomes of Terach. Terach fathered 'Avram, Nachor, and Haran. And Haran fathered Lot. [28]And Haran died before Terach his father in the land of his birth, in 'Ur of the Kasids. [29]And 'Avram and Nachor each took for themselves women. The name of the woman of 'Avram is Sarai. And the name of the woman of Nachor is Milka, daughter of Haran, father of Milka and father of Yiska. [30]And Sarai was barren. She has no boy.

11:27 /// וְאֵלֶּה תּוֹלְדֹת תֶּרַח // תֶּרַח הוֹלִיד אֶת־אַבְרָם
אֶת־נָחוֹר וְאֶת־הָרָן // וְהָרָן הוֹלִיד אֶת־לוֹט׃

וְאֵלֶּה תּוֹלְדֹת תֶּרַח. (a) Textuality > conj paratactic expansion / Mood > declarative: non-past / Transitivity > relational: identification. This clause serves to introduce a new clause complex and is not itself another moment in the narration of past happenings.

תּוֹלְדֹת תֶּרַח	וְאֵלֶּה	Constituents
the outcomes of Terach	*and these*	**Translation**
	Theme	**Textuality**
Complement	Subject	**Mood**
Identified	Identifier	**Transitivity**

וְאֵלֶּה. Theme: textual / clause conj + Theme: experiential / Subject > cp / Identifier > pronoun demonstrative. The referent of the pronoun is the content of the text that follows. This pronoun is cataphoric, meaning it looks forward, rather than anaphoric or backward looking, as is typical with pronouns.

תּוֹלְדֹת תֶּרַח. Complement > fp / Identified > nominal group: noun common fp const | noun proper ms.

תֶּרַח הוֹלִיד אֶת־אַבְרָם אֶת־נָחוֹר וְאֶת־הָרָן. (b) Textuality > appositive paratactic expansion / Mood > declarative: past / Transitivity > material: action. This clause articulates all constituents without ellipsis, and this is consistent with its status as the first clause of a clause complex.

אֶת־אַבְרָם אֶת־נָחוֹר וְאֶת־הָרָן	הוֹלִיד	תֶּרַח	Constituents
'Avram Nachor and Haran	*he fathered*	*Terach*	**Translation**
		Theme	**Textuality**
	Finite	Subject	**Mood**
Goal	Process	Actor	**Transitivity**

תֶּרַח. Theme: experiential / Subject > ms / Actor > nominal group: noun proper.

הוֹלִיד. Finite > qatal 3ms / Process > hifil ילד.

אֶת־אַבְרָם אֶת־נָחוֹר וְאֶת־הָרָן. Goal > nominal group complex: goal marker - noun proper ms ׀ goal marker - noun proper ms ׀ group conj + goal marker - noun proper ms.

וְהָרָן הוֹלִיד אֶת־לוֹט. (c) Textuality > conj paratactic expansion / Mood > declarative: past / Transitivity > material: action.

אֶת־לוֹט	הוֹלִיד	וְהָרָן	**Constituents**
Lot	*he fathered*	*and Haran*	**Translation**
		Theme	**Textuality**
	Finite	Subject	**Mood**
Goal	Process	Actor	**Transitivity**

וְהָרָן. Theme: textual / clause conj + Theme: experiential / Subject > ms / Actor > noun proper.

הוֹלִיד. Finite > qatal 3ms / Process > hifil ילד.

אֶת־לוֹט. Goal > nominal group: goal marker - noun proper ms.

11:28 // וַיָּ֣מָת הָרָ֔ן עַל־פְּנֵ֖י תֶּ֣רַח אָבִ֑יו בְּאֶ֥רֶץ מוֹלַדְתּ֖וֹ
בְּא֥וּר כַּשְׂדִּֽים׃

וַיָּמָת הָרָן עַל־פְּנֵי תֶּרַח אָבִיו בְּאֶרֶץ מוֹלַדְתּוֹ בְּאוּר כַּשְׂדִּים. (a) Textuality > conj paratactic expansion / Mood > declarative: past / Transitivity > material: event.

בְּאֶרֶץ מוֹלַדְתּוֹ בְּאוּר כַּשְׂדִּים	עַל־פְּנֵי תֶּרַח אָבִיו	הָרָן	וַיָּמָת	**Constituents**
in the land of his birth in 'Ur of the Kasids	*before Terach his father*	*Haran*	*and he died*	**Translation**
			Theme	**Textuality**
		Subject	Finite	**Mood**
Circumstance	Circumstance	Actor	Process	**Transitivity**

וַיָּמָת. Theme: textual / clause conj + Theme: experiential / Finite > wayyiqtol 3ms / Process > qal מות.

הָרָן. Subject > ms / Actor > nominal group: noun proper.

עַל־פְּנֵי תֶּרַח אָבִיו. Circumstance: location, time > prep phrase complex: prep + Head + Post-modifier.

עַל־פְּנֵי. Prep: prep - noun common mp const. *On the face of*, meaning, *before.*

תֶּרַח. Head > noun common mp const ׀ noun proper 3ms.

אָבִיו. Post-modifier > noun common ms const + pronoun suffix 3ms, antecedent is הָרָן *Haran.*

בְּאֶרֶץ מוֹלַדְתּוֹ בְּאוּר כַּשְׂדִּים. Circumstance: location, place > prep phrase complex: Head + Post-modifier.

בְּאֶרֶץ מוֹלַדְתּוֹ. Head > prep phrase 1: prep + noun common fs const ׀ noun common fs const + pronoun suffix 3ms, antecedent is הָרָן *Haran.*

בְּאוּר כַּשְׂדִּים. Post-modifier > prep phrase 2: prep + noun proper fs ׀ noun proper mp. This prep phrase is an expansion of the preceding prep phrase and gives it greater specificity.

11:29 // וַיִּקַּח אַבְרָם וְנָחוֹר לָהֶם נָשִׁים // שֵׁם אֵֽשֶׁת־
אַבְרָם֙ שָׂרָ֔י // וְשֵׁ֤ם אֵֽשֶׁת־נָחוֹר֙ מִלְכָּ֔ה בַּת־הָרָ֥ן
אֲבִֽי־מִלְכָּ֖ה וַאֲבִ֥י יִסְכָּֽה׃

וַיִּקַּח אַבְרָם וְנָחוֹר לָהֶם נָשִׁים. (a) Textuality > conj paratactic expansion / Mood > declarative: past / Transitivity > material: action. *And each took, 'Avram and Nachor, for themselves, women.*

נָשִׁים	לָהֶם	אַבְרָם וְנָחוֹר	וַיִּקַּח	**Constituents**
women	*for themselves*	*'Avram and Nachor*	*and he took*	**Translation**
			Theme	**Textuality**
		Subject	Finite	**Mood**
Goal	Beneficiary	Actor	Process	**Transitivity**

וַיִּקַּח. Theme: textual / clause conj + Theme: experiential / Finite > wayyiqtol 3ms / Process > qal לקח.

אַבְרָם וְנָחוֹר. Subject > mp! / Actor > nominal group complex: noun proper | group conj + noun proper. The Subject is logically plural in so far as it consists of two persons. Thus, we might be led to expect the Finite to be plural, but here it is singular. Perhaps we can infer that each, hence singular, took a wife for himself, and that the distributive sense of the process is indicated by the singular rather than a plural form. Compare 9:23(a).

לָהֶם. Beneficiary > prep phrase: prep + pronoun suffix 3mp, antecedent is אַבְרָם וְנָחוֹר *'Avram and Nachor.*

נָשִׁים. Goal > nominal group: noun common fp.

שֵׁם אֵשֶׁת־אַבְרָם שָׂרָי. (b) Textuality > appositive paratactic expansion / Mood > declarative: non-past / Transitivity > relational: identification.

שָׂרָי	שֵׁם אֵשֶׁת־אַבְרָם	**Constituents**
Sarai	*the name of the woman of 'Avram*	**Translation**
	Theme	**Textuality**
Subject	Complement	**Mood**
Identifier	Identified	**Transitivity**

שֵׁם אֵשֶׁת־אַבְרָם. Theme: experiential / Complement > ms (שֵׁם) / Identified > nominal group: noun common ms const | noun common fs const - noun proper ms.

שָׂרָי. Identifier > nominal group: noun proper fs.

וְשֵׁם אֵשֶׁת־נָחוֹר מִלְכָּה בַּת־הָרָן אֲבִי־מִלְכָּה וַאֲבִי יִסְכָּה. (c) Textuality > conj paratactic expansion / Mood > declarative: non-past / Transitivity > relational: identification.

מִלְכָּה בַּת־הָרָן אֲבִי־מִלְכָּה וַאֲבִי יִסְכָּה	וְשֵׁם אֵשֶׁת־נָחוֹר	Constituents
Milka, daughter of Haran, father of Milka and father of Yiska.	*and the name of the woman of Nachor*	**Translation**
	Theme	**Textuality**
Subject	Complement	**Mood**
Identifier	Identified	**Transitivity**

וְשֵׁם אֵשֶׁת־נָחוֹר. Theme: textual / clause conj + Theme: experiential / Complement > ms (שֵׁם) / Identified > nominal group: noun common ms const ı noun common fs const - noun proper ms.

מִלְכָּה בַּת־הָרָן אֲבִי־מִלְכָּה וַאֲבִי יִסְכָּה. Subject > fs (מִלְכָּה) / Identifier > nominal group complex: Head + Post-modifier 1 + Post-modifier 2.

מִלְכָּה. Head > noun proper fs.

בַּת־הָרָן. Post-modifier 1 > nominal group: noun common fs const - noun proper ms. This post-modifier group adds specification to the preceding noun מִלְכָּה *Milkah.*

אֲבִי־מִלְכָּה וַאֲבִי יִסְכָּה. Post-modifier 2 > nominal group complex: noun common ms const - noum proper fs ı group conj + noun common ms const ı noun proper fs. This post-modifier complex adds specification, not to the head of the Identifier complex, but to the immediately preceding proper noun הָרָן *Haran.*

11:30 // וַתְּהִי שָׂרַי עֲקָרָה // אֵין לָהּ וָלָד׃

וַתְּהִי שָׂרַי עֲקָרָה. (a) Textuality > conj paratactic extension / Mood > declarative: past / Transitivity > relational: attribution.

עֲקָרָה	שָׂרַי	וַתְּהִי	**Constituents**
barren	*Sarai*	*and she was*	**Translation**
		Theme	**Textuality**
	Subject	Finite	**Mood**
Attribute	Carrier	Process	**Transitivity**

וַתְּהִי. Theme: textual / clause conj + Theme: experiential / Finite > wayyiqtol 3fs / Process > qal היה.

שָׂרַי. Subject > fs / Carrier > nominal group: noun proper.

עֲקָרָה. Attribute > adj fs.

אֵין לָהּ וָלָד. (b) Textuality > apppositive paratactic expansion / Mood > declarative: non-past / Transitivity > existential. This concluding clause of its clause complex is not past sequential, but posits a notable, and what turns out to be enduring, condition.

וָלָד	לָהּ	אֵין	**Constituents**
a boy	*to her*	*is not*	**Translation**
		Theme	**Textuality**
Subject		Adjunct	**Mood**
Existent	Beneficiary	Process	**Transitivity**

אֵין. Theme: interpersonal and experiential / Adjunct: interpersonal > negative / Process > existential: negative.

לָהּ. Beneficiary > prep phrase: prep + pronoun suffix 3fs, antecedent is שָׂרַי *Sarai* in the prior clause.

וָלָד. Subject > ms / Existent > nominal group: noun common. This is a notable instance of the noun normally spelled יֶלֶד *boy*, in so far as it reflects a primitive Semitic form.

Genesis 11:31-32

31And Terach took 'Avram, his son, and Lot, the son of Haran, the son of his son, and Sarai, his daughter-in-law, the woman of 'Avram, his son.

And they departed with them from 'Ur of Kasids to go toward the land of Kena'an. And they came to Charan. And they dwelled there. [32]And the days of Terach were 205 years. And Terach died in Charan.

11:31 /// וַיִּקַּח תֶּרַח אֶת־אַבְרָם בְּנוֹ וְאֶת־לוֹט בֶּן־הָרָן
בֶּן־בְּנוֹ וְאֵת שָׂרַי כַּלָּתוֹ אֵשֶׁת אַבְרָם בְּנוֹ // וַיֵּצְאוּ
אִתָּם מֵאוּר כַּשְׂדִּים לָלֶכֶת אַרְצָה כְּנַעַן // וַיָּבֹאוּ
עַד־חָרָן // וַיֵּשְׁבוּ שָׁם׃

וַיִּקַּח תֶּרַח אֶת־אַבְרָם בְּנוֹ וְאֶת־לוֹט בֶּן־הָרָן בֶּן־בְּנוֹ וְאֵת שָׂרַי כַּלָּתוֹ אֵשֶׁת אַבְרָם בְּנוֹ. (a) Textuality > conj paratactic expansion / Mood > declarative: past / Transitivity > material: action. Notice the fully explicit transitivity structure that marks this initial clause of its complex. Also notice the elaborate Goal, which does not present new information, but gathers previous information together into a summarizing statement that connects to the prior clause complex in order to bring the narration to a new stage.

אֶת־אַבְרָם בְּנוֹ וְאֶת־לוֹט בֶּן־הָרָן בֶּן־בְּנוֹ וְאֵת שָׂרַי כַּלָּתוֹ אֵשֶׁת אַבְרָם בְּנוֹ	תֶּרַח	וַיִּקַּח	**Constituents**
'Avram, his son, and Lot, the son of Haran, the son of his son, and Sarai, his daughter-in-law, the woman of 'Avram, his son.	*Terach*	*and he took*	**Translation**
		Theme	**Textuality**
	Subject	Finite	**Mood**
Goal	Actor	Process	**Transitivity**

וַיִּקַּח. Theme: textual / clause conj + Theme: experiential / Finite > wayyiqtol 3ms / Process > qal לקח.

תֶּרַח. Subject > ms / Actor > noun proper.

אֶת־אַבְרָם | בְּנוֹ // וְאֶת־לוֹט | בֶּן־הָרָן | בֶּן־בְּנוֹ // וְאֵת

שָׂרַי | כַּלָּתוֹ | אֵשֶׁת אַבְרָם | בְּנוֹ. Goal > nominal group complex: nominal group complex 1 + nominal group complex 2 + nominal group complex 3. The structure of this nominal group complex is both intricate and elegant. The Goal consists of three nominal group complexes that constitutes one very large nominal group complex. Each of the three individual nominal group complexes is introduced with a goal marker, and the three complexes are both delineated by and conjoined with group conjunctions. Also, each nominal group complex is internally structured with one or more appositive nominal groups that expand the meaning of the head noun of the complex by specifying relatedness to Terach.

אֶת־אַבְרָם בְּנוֹ. Nominal group complex 1 > Head + Post-modifier.

אֶת־אַבְרָם. Head > goal marker - noun proper.

בְּנוֹ. Post-modifier > noun common ms const + pronoun suffix 3ms, antecedent is תֶּרַח *Terach.*

וְאֶת־לוֹט בֶּן־הָרָן בֶּן־בְּנוֹ. Nominal group complex 2 > Head + Post-modifier 1 + Post-modifier 2. Both post-modifier noun groups modify the head noun.

וְאֶת־לוֹט. Head > group conj + goal marker - noun proper ms.

בֶּן־הָרָן. Post-modifier 1 > noun common ms const - noun proper ms.

בֶּן־בְּנוֹ. Post-modifier 2 > noun common ms const - noun common ms const + pronoun suffix 3ms, antecedent is תֶּרַח *Terach.*

וְאֵת שָׂרַי כַּלָּתוֹ אֵשֶׁת אַבְרָם בְּנוֹ. Nominal group complex 3 > Head + Post-modifier 1 + Post-modifier 2.

וְאֵת שָׂרַי. Head > group conj + goal marker | noun proper fs.

כַּלָּתוֹ. Post-modifier 1 > noun common fs const + pronoun suffix 3ms, antecedent is תֶּרַח *Terach.*

אֵשֶׁת אַבְרָם בְּנוֹ. Post-modifier 2 > Head + Post-modifier.

אֵשֶׁת אַבְרָם. Head > nominal group: noun common fs const | noun proper ms.

בְּנוֹ. Post-modifier > nominal group: noun common ms const + pronoun suffix 3ms, antecedent תֶּרַח *Terach*. This post-modifier nominal group does not modify the head of nominal group complex 3, which is שָׂרַי *Sarai*, but rather it modifies the preceding proper noun אַבְרָם *Avram*.

(b) וַיֵּצְאוּ אִתָּם מֵאוּר כַּשְׂדִּים [[לָלֶכֶת אַרְצָה כְּנַעַן]]. Textuality > conj paratactic expansion / Mood > declarative: past / Transitivity > material: action. The Subject (3mp) / Actor is not specified but is easily constructed from the preceding clause and consists of *Terach*, *'Avram*, *Lot*, and *Sarai*.

[[לָלֶכֶת אַרְצָה כְּנַעַן]]	מֵאוּר כַּשְׂדִּים	אִתָּם	וַיֵּצְאוּ	**Constituents**
to go to the land of Kena'an	*from 'Ur of Kasids*	*with them*	*and they departed*	**Translation**
			Theme	**Textuality**
			Finite	**Mood**
Circumstance	Circumstance	Circumstance	Process	**Transitivity**

וַיֵּצְאוּ. Theme: textual / clause conj + Theme: experiential / Finite > wayyiqtol 3mp / Process > qal יצא.

אִתָּם. Circumstance: manner > prep phrase: prep + pronoun suffix 3mp, antecedent is opaque and difficult to identify with certainty. The problem of identifying *them* has given rise to text emendations, some of which find support in the versions (see Wenham 266, note 31d). If the existing text is to be the basis of interpretation, then there are at least two possibilities for identifying *them*: the עַם of the Babel/Babylon story, or the Kasdim of this clause. In other words, it may be implying that members of Terach's family left Babylon in a general dispersion, as part of a larger group.

מֵאוּר כַּשְׂדִּים. Circumstance: location, place > prep phrase: prep + noun proper | noun proper mp.

לָלֶכֶת אַרְצָה כְּנַעַן. (i) Circumstance: cause, purpose >> Textuality > embedded prep clause / Transitivity > material: action.

אַרְצָה כְּנַעַן	לָלֶכֶת	**Constituents**
to the land of Kena'an	*to go*	**Translation**
	Theme	**Textuality**
	Complement	**Mood**
Circumstance	Process	**Transitivity**

לָלֶכֶת. Theme: textual / prep + Theme: experiential / Complement > inf const / Process > qal הלך.

אַרְצָה כְּנַעַן. Circumstance: location, place > nominal group: noun common fs + directive suffix | noun proper. The post-positional ־ָה of אַרְצָה indicates direction toward.

וַיָּבֹאוּ עַד־חָרָן. (c) Textuality > conj paratactic expansion / Mood > declarative: past / Transitivity > material: action.

עַד־חָרָן	וַיָּבֹאוּ	**Constituents**
to Charan	*and they came*	**Translation**
	Theme	**Textuality**
	Finite	**Mood**
Circumstance	Process	**Transitivity**

וַיָּבֹאוּ. Theme: textual / clause conj + Theme: experiential / Finite > wayyiqtol 3mp / Process > qal בוא.

עַד־חָרָן. Circumstance > location: prep phrase: prep - noun proper.

וַיֵּשְׁבוּ שָׁם. (d) Textuality > conj paratactic expansion / Mood > declarative: past / Transitivity > material: action.

שָׁם	וַיֵּשְׁבוּ	**Constituents**
there	*and they dwelled*	**Translation**
	Theme	**Textuality**
	Finite	**Mood**
Circumstance	Process	**Transitivity**

וַיֵּשְׁבוּ. Theme: textual / clause conj + Theme: experiential / Finite > wayyiqtol 3mp / Process > qal ישׁב.

שָׁם. Circumstance: location, place > pronoun textual, antecedent is חָרָן *Charan* in the preceding clause.

11:32 /// וַיִּהְיוּ יְמֵי־תֶרַח חָמֵשׁ שָׁנִים וּמָאתַיִם שָׁנָה //
וַיָּמָת תֶּרַח בְּחָרָן׃ ס

וַיִּהְיוּ יְמֵי־תֶרַח חָמֵשׁ שָׁנִים וּמָאתַיִם שָׁנָה. (a) Textuality > conj paratactic expansion / Mood > declarative: past / Transitivity > relational: attribution.

חָמֵשׁ שָׁנִים וּמָאתַיִם שָׁנָה	יְמֵי־תֶרַח	וַיִּהְיוּ	**Constituents**
five years and two hundred years	*the days of Terach*	*and they were*	**Translation**
		Theme	**Textuality**
	Subject	Finite	**Mood**
Attribute	Carrier	Process	**Transitivity**

וַיִּהְיוּ. Theme: textual / clause conj + Theme: experiential / Finite > wayyiqtol 3mp / Process > qal היה.

יְמֵי־תֶרַח. Subject > mp (יְמֵי) / Carrier > nominal group: noun common mp const - noun proper. The first word of the group is the Subject.

חָמֵשׁ שָׁנִים וּמָאתַיִם שָׁנָה. Attribute > nominal group complex: numeral fs | noun common fp | group conj + numeral fd | noun common fs.

וַיָּמָת תֶּרַח בְּחָרָן. (b) Textuality > conj paratactic expansion / Mood > declarative: past / Transitivity > material: event.

בְּחָרָן	תֶּרַח	וַיָּמָת	**Constituents**
in Charan	*Terach*	*and he died*	**Translation**
		Theme	**Textuality**
	Subject	Finite	**Mood**
Circumstance	Actor	Process	**Transitivity**

וַיָּמָת. Theme: textual / clause conj + Theme: experiential / Finite > wayyiqtol 3ms / Process > qal **מות**.

תֶּרַח. Subject > ms / Actor > noun proper.

בְּחָרָן. Circumstance: location, place > prep phrase: prep + noun proper.

GLOSSARY

Each term is identified in relation to the metafunctional system within which it operates. This is indicated by the category in parentheses after the definition of the head term. In the definitions, words that designate functions are capitalized.

action—The type of material process in which the doing of the Process acts upon a Goal. (Transitivity)

actor—The doer of the action in a clause; the action is represented by the clause Process. (Transitivity)

adjunct—A word that is not a core component of a metafunctional system but is an optional enhancement; for example, a modal adjunct is not a component of the Mood structure of a clause (meaning it is not a Subject or Finite); likewise for textual and experiential adjuncts. (All metafunctions)

anaphora, anaphoric—An element that refers to an earlier element in the text. (Textuality)

antecedent—Regarding pronouns, the earlier element in the text to which the pronoun refers. (Textuality)

apposition, appositive—Placing one element next to another element without the benefit of a formal connective word; this is realized by conjunction-less juxtaposition rather than by conjunction. (Textuality)

aside—A clause or clause complex this is enclosed within another clause, but which is not part of the structure of the enclosing clause; it is linked to the enclosing clause only by a nonstructural cohesive reference. (Textuality) See Gen 6:4(a).

aspect—Viewing the form of Finite verbs as indicating the completeness or incompleteness of the action indicated by the verb, in distinction from viewing the form of finite verbs as indicating tense. (Mood)

attribute, attribution—Used with relational processes, an Attribute describes or characterizes the Carrier in some way; typically realized by an indefinite nominal group or a prepositional phrase. (Transitivity)

behaver—Found in behavioral processes, the Behaver is the participant who exhibits the Behavior encoded in the verb process. (Transitivity)

behavior—Found in behavioral processes, the Behavior is what the Behaver does. (Transitivity)

behavioral process—A verb process in the middle voice that characterizes the behavior of the Behaver, who is also the Subject of the Finite verb. (Transitivity)

beneficiary—The Participant that benefits from the performance of a material process; in traditional grammar it is called the indirect object. (Transitivity)

carrier—Found in relational processes of attribution, the Carrier is the entity described by the Attribute. (Transitivity)

cataphora, cataphoric—An element that refers to a later element in the text; the opposite of anaphora. (Textuality)

circumstance—One of the three main components of the transitivity system, along with Process and Participant; it specifies the location or conditions of the Process. (Transitivity)

clause—The basic unit of textual meaning, minimally constituted by a Process with at least one Participant; also called a major clause; a minor clause is one which lacks a process, such as an exclamation. (All metafunctions)

clause complex—A collection of clauses that forms a cohesive text unit; the beginning of a clause complex is indicated by three slashes, ///. (Textuality)

cognate—Having the same linguistic derivation or root as another word. (Textuality)

cohortative—A first person finite verb form in the class of directives; the first person "command" form of the verb. (Mood)

complement—A nominal group found outside the mood structure (i.e., the Subject plus Finite structure of the clause) but which could have been chosen as the Subject. (Mood)

complex—A complex is two or more of the same class of constituent which together function as one constituent at the clause level; clause complexes, verbal group complexes, nominal group complexes, and prepositional phrase complexes all exist in BH. (Textuality)

conjunction, conjunctive—A clause conjunction joins clauses into a clause complex, primarily וְ and כִּי; the group conjunction וְ joins words, phrases, or groups of the same rank into a single clause constituent; when present, a clause conjunction is obligatorily a component of the clause theme. (Textuality)

conjunctive adjunct—Constituent that links a clause to a prior clause complex, such as עַל־כֵּן. (Textuality)

constituent—A component of a clause, a group, or a phrase; in clause analysis tables, a constituent is a functional component of the clause, depending on which function is under analysis; it may be a word, a component of a word, a phrase, a group, or an embedded clause. (All metafunctions)

declarative—A clause that makes a statement. (Mood)

dependent clause—In reference to logical dependency relationships, a dependent clause is subordinate to a dominant clause; see also parataxis and hypotaxis. (Textuality)

directive—A clause that issues a command; realized as cohortative, imperative, or jussive. (Mood)

ellipsis—The intentional omission of an element from a clause to avoid needless repetition, because the speaker knows the hearer will insert it from a previous clause or the context. (Textuality)

embedding, embedded clause—A clause that has been transformed and rank-shifted from independent to dependent so that it can be included within another clause; indicated by [[double square brackets]]. (Textuality)

event—The type of material process in which the happening of the Process acts upon the Actor itself rather than upon a Goal; in traditional grammar, an intransitive verb. (Transitivity)

existent—Found in existential process clauses, the Participant whose existence or non-existence is posited. (Transitivity)

existential process—The process type which affirms the existence or non-existence of the Existent. (Transitivity)

expansion—Used in reference to logical semantic relations; it labels a clause that expands in some way upon the meaning of the prior clause. (Textuality)

finite—A verb form that defines the person, gender, and number of its Subject, or in the case of a participle, the gender and number. (Mood)

goal marker—The function word אֶת־, אֵת used primarily in a material process of action to identify the Goal of the Process. (Transitivity)

goal—The doing of a material process is directed at the Goal; in traditional grammar this is called the direct object. (Transitivity)

group—One or more words that function together as a unit in the structure of the clause; nominal, adjectival, and verbal groups exist. (Textuality)

hapax legomenon—A word that occurs only once in a text corpus, which in our case is the Masoretic Text of the Hebrew Bible. (General)

head—The core element in a nominal or verbal group, which may be expanded by a second element that classifies or specifies it, typically a Post-modifier. (Textuality)

hendiadys—Literally, one through two; a special type of group in which two elements combine to communicate what is essentially one notion, which then functions as a single constituent within the structure of the clause; occurs with nouns, adjectives, and absolute infinitives. (Textuality)

hypotaxis, hypotactic relationship—A pair of clauses in which one clause is dependent upon the other; indicated by a single slash, /. (Textuality)

identified—Used in relational processes of identification to designate the known Participant which will be tagged by the Identifier. (Transitivity)

identifier—Used in relational processes of identification to label the nominal group that provides specific identification of the Participant that is the Identified. (Transitivity)

imperative—A second person finite verb form in the class of directives; the second person "command" form of the verb. (Mood)

included clause—A clause that interrupts the clause in which it is inserted, without being embedded in it; indicated by double wedge brackets, << >>; see 3:3(a). (Textuality)

indicative—An independent clause that either makes an offer (declarative) or issues a request (interrogative). (Mood)

jussive—A third person finite verb form in the class of directives; the third person "command" form of the verb. (Mood)

juxtaposition—Placement of one element directly next to another element without conjunction; also see apposition. (Textuality)

major clause—A clause that consists minimally of a Process and one Participant, in distinction from a minor clause. (Transitivity)

marked, unmarked—Used in reference to a variety of clause structures, whereby a structure is considered statistically normal (unmarked or default) or rare (marked), meaning infrequent or otherwise unusual. (Textuality)

material process—In reference to basic transitivity types, a material process is a Process of doing or happening involving an Actor and optionally a Goal, Beneficiary, and Circumstances; two sub-types are identified, action (in traditional grammar, a transitive verb) and event (in traditional grammar, an intransitive verb). (Transitivity)

mental process—A basic transitivity process type that involves a Senser and a Phenomenon, and can be realized in the sub-types perception, emotion, and cognition. (Transitivity)

minor clause—A clause that lacks a fully formed transitivity structure and consists only of a Participant or other non-process element. (Transitivity)

modal, modality—Modal constituents of a clause express the speaker's attitude or something about the Finite. (Mood)

mood—In reference to the interpersonal view of the clause, this metafunction has to do with how the clause is structured as the interaction between two parties; the Mood structure proper is the Subject and the Finite constituents of the clause, all else being the Residue. (Metafunction)

nominal group—A noun that functions as a constituent in a clause, along with any other words and phrases that modify that noun; somewhat counterintuitively then, a nominal group can be a single word or a head noun along with the words and phrases that qualify it; a nominal group complex is constituted by two or more nominal groups. (Textuality)

non-finite—A verb form that does not specify person, gender, and number; an infinitive. (Mood)

parataxis, paratactic relationship—A relationship between two clauses characterized by equality rather than dependency; indicated by double slashes, //. (Textuality)

participant—In reference to transitivity structures, Participant is one of the core components, along with the Process; participants are labeled differently depending on the particular process type. (Transitivity)

past, non-past—In the interpersonal view of clauses, the event time of the Finite is identified as past or non-past; the finite verbal system is binary in the sense that qatal and wayyiqtol both reference past time (yet differing in their textuality), while yiqtol and weqatal both reference non-past time, either present or future; relational clauses do not select for tense unless היה is used; also see tense. (Mood)

phenomenon—A participant in mental processes, the Phenomenon is the thought, perception, or feeling apprehended by the Senser of the Process. (Transitivity)

polarity—Positive or negative polarity define the validity of a proposition; positive is the default polarity. (Mood)

post-modifier—The second element of a nominal group complex that expands the head; it can be realized by an adjective, a nominal group in apposition, a pronoun suffix, a noun in construct relationship, or an embedded relative clause; it can also be the second element of a verbal group complex, typically realized as an infinitive construct. (Textuality)

preposed theme—The device of fronting a clause constituent for textuality reasons, then substituting this constituent later in the clause with a pronoun. (Textuality)

process—In reference to transitivity structure, the Process is the doing or happening encoded in the clause; the Process is performed by a Participant under certain Circumstances. (Transitivity)

projection—One of two basic logical semantic relations between clauses, the other being expansion; in projection, an original language event in the outside world is incorporated into the message of a text, either as a quote or as the report of a quote. (Textuality)

quote—In reference to logical semantic relations between clauses, a report is one type of projection clause; it records more or less accurately the original wording of a prior language event external to the text and brings it into the text. (Textuality)

range—Specifies the range or domain of the Process, often realized by a prepositional phrase; distinguishable from Circumstance and Scope. (Transitivity)

receiver—Used in connection with verbal processes, the Receiver is the one to whom the statement is made. (Transitivity)

relational process—One of the six general types of processes, a relational process establishes a relationship between two clause constituents; in attributive relational processes the relationship is between the Carrier and the Attribute, and in identifying relational processes it is between the Identified and the Identifier. (Transitivity)

relative clause—An embedded clause that post-modifies its antecedent in the enclosing clause; the relative pronoun אֲשֶׁר is the first constituent of a relative clause, except for asyndetic relative clauses, and it functions as the textual Theme of its clause. (Textuality)

report—In reference to logical semantic relations between clauses, a report is one type of projection clause; in distinction from a quote, a report does not duplicate the original message but rewords the quote to fit the wording of the text. (Textuality)

residue—In the interpersonal view, the constituents of a clause minus the Mood structure of Subject and Finite. (Mood)

rheme—In the textuality view, all the constituents of a clause minus the Theme. (Textuality)

sayer—Used in reference to verbal processes, the Sayer is the one making the verbal statement. (Transitivity)

scope—Used with material processes, a nominal group that works together with a verbal group to express the process of the clause, for example, sing a song; Scope may look like a Goal because it is a nominal group and not a prepositional phrase, but it is not a genuine Participant; rather, it is more like a circumstantial element because it specifies something about the Process. (Transitivity)

subject—Used in reference to the Mood structure of clauses, the Subject is the constituent in a clause about which the speaker makes a claim to the hearer, and the item upon which the validity of the clause hangs. (Mood)

substitution—A word which substitutes for a prior constituent or clause, for example, כֵּן. (Textuality)

target—Used in reference to verbal processes, the Target is the Participant about which the statement is made; to be distinguished from the Receiver, which is the Participant to whom the statement is delivered. (Transitivity)

taxis—General category of logical dependency, realized as parataxis or hypotaxis. (Textuality)

tense—Declarative clauses evidence either past tense or non-past tense; past tense is realized by wayyiqtol or qatal; non-past is realized by yiqtol, weqatal, or participle, and in verbless relational clauses by juxtaposition. (Mood)

textuality—In reference to the structure of clauses and texts, this has to do with how messages are worded in order to constitute cohesive units. (Metafunction)

theme—Used in reference to the textual structure of clauses, the Theme is the first experiential constituent of the clause and anything that might come before that constituent, such as a conjunction or a textual adjunct. (Textuality)

transitivity—In reference to the experiential view of the clause, the Transitivity structure refers to the Process, Participants and Circumstances. (Metafunction)

verbal group complex—Two verbs in one clause: a finite followed by an infinite; the second verb expresses the main clause process, not the first; typically, it is the job of the first of the two verbs to indicate how the process unfolds, whether starting, continuing, or concluding. (Textuality)

verbal process—A process of saying, and can be followed by a quote or a report of a quote. (Transitivity)

verbiage—A nominal group that is the message of a verbal process; it functions as a Participant in the Process. (Transitivity)

BIBLIOGRAPHY

Bandstra, Barry L. *The Syntax of Particle KY in Biblical Hebrew and Ugaritic.* Ph.D. diss., Yale University, 1982.

Botterweck, G. Johannes. *Theological Dictionary of the Old Testament.* Edited by G. Johannes Botterweck and Helmer Ringgren. Translator: John T. Willis. Grand Rapids: Eerdmans, 1974–.

Brown, Francis, with S. R. Driver and Charles A. Briggs. *A Hebrew and English Lexicon of the Old Testament.* Oxford: Clarendon Press, 1907.

Butler, Christopher S. *Structure and Function: A Guide to Three Major Structural-Functional Theories.* Studies in Language Companion Series 63–64. Amsterdam; Philadelphia: J. Benjamins, 2003.

Friedman, Richard Elliott. *Commentary on the Torah.* New York: HarperCollins, 2001.

Halliday, M. A. K. *An Introduction to Functional Grammar.* London: Arnold. First ed., 1985; Second ed., 1994; Third ed., rev. by M. I. M. Matthiessen, 2004.

Joosten, Jan. "The Predicative Participle in Biblical Hebrew." *Zeitschrift für Althebräistik* 2 (1989), 128–59.

———. "The Indicative System of the Biblical Hebrew Verb and Its Literary Exploitation," in *Narrative Syntax and the Hebrew Bible: Papers of the Tilburg Conference 1996.* Edited by Ellen van Wolde; Biblical Interpretation Series 29. Leiden: Brill, 1997, 51–71.

Koehler, Ludwig and Walter Baumgartner. *The Hebrew and Aramaic Lexicon of the Old Testament.* Leiden: E. J. Brill, 1994–2000.

Merwe, C. H. J. van der, Jackie A. Naude, and Jan H. Kroeze. *Biblical Hebrew Reference Grammar.* Sheffield: Sheffield Academic Press, 1999.

Miller, Cynthia L. *The Representation of Speech in Biblical Hebrew Narrative: A Linguistic Approach.* Harvard Semitic Museum Monographs 55. Atlanta: Scholars Press, 1996.

New Jewish Publication Society Tanakh. New York: Jewish Publication Society, 1984, 1999.

New Revised Standard Version Bible. New York: National Council of the Churches of Christ, 1989.

Scott, William R., and Hans Peter Rüger. *A Simplified Guide to BHS. Critical Apparatus, Masora, Accents, Unusual Letters and Other Markings.* 3rd ed.. N. Richland Hills, TX: Bibal Press, 1995.

Smith, Mark S. "Grammatically Speaking: The Participle as a Main Verb of Clauses (Predicative Participle) in Direct Discourse and Narrative in Pre-Mishnaic Hebrew," in *Sirach, Scrolls, and Sages: Proceedings of a Second International Symposium on the Hebrew of the Dead Sea Scrolls, Ben Sira, and the Mishna*, held at Leiden University, 15–17 December 1997. Edited by T. Muraoka and J. F. Elwolde. Leiden: Brill, 1999, 278–332.

Thompson, Geoff. *Introducing Functional Grammar.* London: Arnold. First ed., 1996; Second ed., 2004.

Waltke, Bruce K., and M. O'Connor. *An Introduction to Biblical Hebrew Syntax.* Winona Lake, Ind.: Eisenbrauns, 1990.

Wenham, Gordon J. *Word Biblical Commentary Volume 1. Genesis 1–15.* Waco, Tex.: Word, 1987.

Westermann, Claus. *Genesis 1–11: A Commentary.* Translated by John J. Scullion. Minneapolis: Augsburg, 1984.

Yeivin, Israel. *Introduction to the Tiberian Masorah.* Edited ranslated and edited by E. J. Revell. Missoula, Mont.: published by Scholars Press for the Society of Biblical Literature and the International Organization for Masoretic Studies, 1980.

AUTHOR AND SUBJECT INDEX

Milton Keynes UK
Ingram Content Group UK Ltd.
UKHW011302030624
443658UK00023B/116